Entrepreneurship: Owning Your Future

Network for Teaching Entrepreneurship

Twelfth Edition

PEARSON

Boston   Columbus   Indianapolis   New York   San Francisco

Amsterdam   Cape Town   Dubai   London   Madrid   Milan   Munich   Paris   Montreal   Toronto

Delhi   Mexico City   Sao Paulo   Sydney   Hong Kong   Seoul   Singapore   Taipei   Tokyo

Vice President, Business Publishing: Donna Battista
Editor-in-Chief: Stephanie Wall
Editorial Assistant: Linda Abelli
Vice President, Product Marketing: Maggie Moylan
Director of Marketing, Digital Services and Products: Jeanette Koskinas
Field Marketing Manager: Lenny Ann Raper
Product Marketing Assistant: Jessica Quazza
Team Lead, Program Management: Ashley Santora
Team Lead, Project Management: Jeff Holcomb
Project Manager: Alison Kalil
Operations Specialist: Carol Melville
Creative Director: Blair Brown
Art Director: Janet Slowik
Vice President, Director of Digital Strategy and Assessment: Paul Gentile
Manager of Learning Applications: Paul DeLuca

Digital Editor: Brian Surette
Director, Digital Studio: Sacha Laustsen
Digital Studio Manager: Diane Lombardo
Digital Studio Project Manager: Monique Lawrence
Digital Studio Project Manager: Alana Coles
Digital Studio Project Manager: Robin Lazrus
Full-Service Project Management: Emergent Learning LLC
Composition: Moore Media, Inc.
Interior Designer: Moore Media, Inc.
Cover Designers: Keithley & Associates, Inc., Monroe Blakes, and Janet Romero
Cover Art: JGI
Printer/Binder: RR Donnelley/Kendallville
Cover Printer: Lehigh Phoenix/Hagerstown
Text Font: ITC Gallard Std

NFTE would like to recognize Diana Davis Spencer and her daughters Abby S. Moffat and Kimberly F. LaManna for their years of commitment to our mission and specifically for their support of this project.

The Diana Davis Spencer Foundation

Entrepreneurship: Owning Your Future is the 12th edition of this textbook. The 10th edition was titled *How to Start & Operate a Small Business*. The Network for Teaching Entrepreneurship was previously named the National Foundation for Teaching Entrepreneurship.

11 10 9 8 7 6 5 4 3 2 1

V011

ISBN 10: 0-13-432482-X
ISBN 13: 978-0-13-432482-1

AUTHORS & REVIEWERS

Authors

Steve Mariotti

Tony Towle

Jason Delgatto

Reviewers

Dee Coyle
Harold Wendell Lang Middle School
Dallas, TX

Thomas Gold
VP, Research & Evaluation
NFTE

John Griffin
Pathways To Technology High School
East Hartford, CT

Raghib Muhammad
McCluer South-Berkeley High School
Ferguson, Missouri

Lucinda Oates-Wiley
Newark High School
Newark, DE

Robert Pauls
Senior Manager, Alumni Programs
NFTE

Troy Pressens
Director, Digital Initiatives
NFTE

Jordan Runge
Director, Career Programs
NFTE

Kimberly Smith
Senior VP, Programs & Research
NFTE

Zachary Tausanovitch
Lead Research Associate
NFTE

Stephen Thomas
W.E. Greiner Middle School
Dallas, TX

THE NFTE STORY

"I want others to learn the lesson I learned from entrepreneurship: that no dream, goal, or idea is impossible. All it takes is a little confidence in one's self and a determination to succeed."

— *Richard Tan, NFTE class of 2013*

"The NFTE program provided me with an opportunity to re-engage my students in a fun and exciting way."

— *Lucinda Oates-Wiley, Newark High School*

The NFTE Vision

Network for Teaching Entrepreneurship (NFTE)'s goal is to provide programs that inspire young people to stay in school, to recognize business opportunities, and to plan for successful futures. From its roots in the Bronx, NFTE's mission has expanded into an international movement for teaching entrepreneurial skills to young people worldwide.

NFTE's work focuses on activating the entrepreneurial mindset in youth and building their knowledge about business startup. As a result of participating in NFTE, students approach learning with a new vigor and a focus on their futures.

NFTE's Content and Pedagogy

NFTE programs are known for their project-based learning methodology that allows students to learn by doing in the context of creating something deeply personal—their own business concept. As students work through lessons covering various business principles such as market research, managing spending, return on investment (ROI), and communications, they build and refine their business concept with new knowledge gained.

As society faces the challenges of record-high-and-rising youth unemployment rates and engaging students in active, relevant learning, NFTE feels a moral imperative to share with our students not only the cognitive but also the non-cognitive skills necessary to succeed in the 21st Century's innovation economy.

While all NFTE curriculum leads up to the creation of an original business idea and pitch, every student who undergoes a NFTE program is also introduced to the entrepreneurial mindset, the life-changing set of skills and behaviors that equip youth to recognize opportunity, take initiative, and innovate in the face of challenges—whether they go on to become entrepreneurs or entrepreneurial employees and citizens.

NFTE has identified the following skills as critical to an entrepreneurial mindset:

- Opportunity Recognition
- Comfort with Risk
- Creativity & Innovation
- Future Orientation
- Flexibility & Adaptability
- Initiative & Self-Reliance
- Critical Thinking & Problem Solving
- Communication & Collaboration

In addition to imparting hard skills, NFTE curriculum helps to activate and develop the entrepreneurial mindset in youth, with pedagogical features that allow students to progressively exercise their entrepreneurial muscles for each of the eight factors listed above.

Awards and Affiliations

NFTE's *Owning Your Future* curriculum is Winner of the 2011 Distinguished Achievement Award for Math Grades 9–12 and the 2002 Golden Lamp Award, both awarded by the Association of Education Publishers.

NFTE is a partner in many thought leadership and field building activities, including the World Economic Forum. In 2015 NFTE launched the Entrepreneurial Mindset Summit—with signature support from EY and *Harvard Business Review* as a media partner—gathering thought leaders from the private and public sectors to address how to best equip youth with the entrepreneurial skills required in the innovation economy. NFTE is regularly featured in leading media outlets such as *Entrepreneur*, CNBC, *The Huffington Post*, and more.

The NFTE Community

Volunteers and mentors play an integral role in NFTE programming, bringing the real world into the classroom and connecting concepts to real life situations and opportunities.

Each year NFTE teaches the skills and mindset of entrepreneurship to 60,000 middle- and high-school students, through in-school, online, and community programming. Since our founding in 1987, NFTE has reached over 600,000 young people. NFTE has programs in 23 locations and 10 countries.

Other NFTE Programs

Introduction to Entrepreneurship

World Series of Innovation (innovation.nfte.com) is a global educational experience that inspires students to think big about new businesses, products, or services. Real companies pose real problems, and young thinkers propose innovative solutions.

Middle-school and high-school level

A Deeper Dive

Exploring Careers focuses on academic, career, and life planning through entrepreneurship and personal skills reflection.

Middle-school level

BizCamps offer a short-form version of NFTE's year-long Owning Your Future course. The camp experience includes student assessment and the creation and pitch of a business concept.

Middle-school and high-school levels available

Industry Expertise and Career Launch

Startup Tech is a tech-entrepreneurship program that provides hands-on learning experiences and mentorship opportunities for students interested in transforming the world through tech-based innovations.

Middle-school and high-school levels available

Startup Summer helps graduates of Owning Your Future or a NFTE BizCamp to make their businesses operational.

To learn more, visit www.nfte.com, like NFTE on Facebook at www.Facebook.com/NFTE, or follow us on Twitter @NFTE, or write to us at NFTE@NFTE.com.

ACKNOWLEDGMENTS

First, NFTE would like to acknowledge the following NFTE staff and teachers for their efforts in supporting the release of this 12th edition: Dee Coyle, Thomas Gold, John Griffin, Raghib Muhammad, Lucinda Oates-Wiley, Robert Pauls, Troy Pressens, Jordan Runge, Kim Smith, Zachary Tausanovitch, and Stephen Thomas. A special thank you to Jason Delgatto for his leadership of the authoring and publication that made this edition possible.

Thanks to all the NFTE staff, teachers, and consultants who worked on previous editions of this book: Steve Mariotti, Richard Adamo, Darlene Ajayi, Stacey Alderman, Luke Anderson, Cathy Blanchard, Ann Carranza, Del Daniels, Gary Giscomb, James G. Hawkins, Michae Iacarella, Julie Kantor, Erin Koblitz, Gwen Kassep, Deidre Lee, Clare McCully, Rupa Mohan, Deb Moore, Connie Moran, Neelam Patel, Angela Powell, Susi Price, Daniel Rabuzzi, Estelle Reyes, Nicole Rottino, Victor Salama, Blair Sawyers, Laura Scarlett, Monica Smalls, Scott Steward, Keri Teplitzky, Tony Towle, Kene Turner, Edward Youngblood, and Katerina Zacharia.

In addition, we recognize the efforts and contributions of NFTE's Board of Directors: Patricia Alper, Matthew J. Audette, Peter J. Boni, Kyle Garman, Ronald E. Garrow, Noah Hanft, Gus Harris, Sanford Krieger, Shawn Osborne, Victor Oviedo, Maria Pinelli, Jason Port, Anthony Salcito, Diana Davis Spencer, David Spreng, Deryck van Rensburg, Peter B. Walker, and Tucker York. We acknowledge the guidance provided by our Board of Overseers Stephen Brenninkmeijer, Eddie Brown, Dr. Thomas Byers, Russ Carson, James I. Cash, Ray Chambers, Sean Combs, Mark Ein, Vince Gioe, Stedman Graham, Reid Hoffman, Daymond John, Moushumi Khan, Elizabeth Koch, Loida Nicolas Lewis, James Lyle, Dr. Richard K. Miller, Wes Moore, Alan Patricof, Jeffrey S. Raikes, Anthony Scaramucci, Jane Siebels, John P. Stack, and Prof. Howard Stevenson.

We appreciate the valuable support of NFTE's equity investors: The Citi Foundation, MasterCard, Verizon, EY and the Karen Pritzker & Michael Vlock Seedlings Foundation.

NFTE would like to recognize Diana Davis Spencer and her daughters Abby S. Moffat and Kimberly F. LaManna for their years of commitment to our mission and specifically for their support of this project.

The Diana Davis Spencer Foundation

TO THE STUDENT

This course has been designed to teach you everything you will need to know to start and maintain your own small business. We hope that what you learn here will help you achieve financial independence and personal satisfaction. Knowing how business works will be of great value in any future career path you may take.

Learning the principles of entrepreneurship will teach you about more than just business and money, however. In this textbook, you will learn, among other things, how to negotiate, calculate return on investment, perform cost/benefit analysis, and keep track of your income and expenses. These skills will apply to your personal as well as your business life. Even if you don't become a lifelong entrepreneur, learning how to start and operate a small business will give you an understanding of the business world that will make it much easier for you to get jobs and create a fulfilling career for yourself, and thus "own your future."

The characteristics of the successful entrepreneur—a positive mental attitude, the ability to recognize opportunities where others only see problems, and openness to creative solutions—are qualities worth developing. They will help you perform better in any situation life throws at you.

Owning your future will be the key to happiness. You can do so much good for your family, friends, and community by being aware of the opportunities and resources around you. Entrepreneurship is a way to do that—to make your dreams come true and help support the goals of those you care about.

What you learn from this course can help you make good personal decisions for the future. NFTE is here to support you. I hope you will visit our website for NFTE graduates—https://www.nfte.com/resources/alumni. Good luck!

Sincerely yours,

Steve Mariotti

Steve Mariotti,
Founder, NFTE

Before You Begin

Here are some thoughts for you to consider. Thoughts are the foundation for everything you create—your education, your business, and, ultimately, your life.

The secret of success in life is for a man to be ready for his opportunity when it comes.

— Benjamin Disraeli (b. 12/12/1804, d. 4/19/1881)

If I had eight hours to chop down a tree, I'd spend six sharpening by ax.

— Abraham Lincoln (b. 2/12/1809, d. 4/15/1865)

When there's nothing to lose and much to gain by trying, try.

— W. Clement Stone (b. 5/4/1902, d. 9/3/2002)

You must do the thing you think you cannot do.

— Eleanor Roosevelt (b. 10/11/1884, d. 11/7/1962)

You are equal to anyone, but if you think you're not, you're not.

— Jake Simmons, Jr. (b. 1/17/1901, d. 3/24/1981)

Everyone lives by selling something.

— Robert Louis Stevenson (b. 11/13/1850, d. 12/3/1894)

Many a small thing has been made large by the right kind of advertising.

— Mark Twain (b. 11/30/1835, d. 4/21/1910)

In the midst of difficulty lies opportunity.

— Albert Einstein (b. 3/14/1879, d. 4/18/1955)

CONTENTS

UNIT 2
Big Idea: Opportunity Recognition & Market Analysis

Chapter 6
Idea Generation 118

Chapter 7
Turning Ideas into Opportunities 132

UNIT 6
Big Idea: Financial & Expense Management

Chapter 26
The Cost of Doing Business   482

BIG IDEA: DEVELOPING AN ENTREPRENEURIAL MINDSET

IMPORTANCE OF ENTREPRENEURSHIP

OBJECTIVES

- Compare and contrast the functions of an entrepreneur and an employee.
- Analyze the pros and cons of being an entrepreneur.
- Describe how entrepreneurs solve problems through products or services.

NFTE Entrepreneurial Mindset Characteristic Focus

☑ Opportunity Recognition

National Entrepreneurship Standards

- **A.09** Describe entrepreneurial planning considerations
- **A.12** Assess risks associated with venture
- **C.01** Explain the role of business in society
- **C.02** Describe types of business activities
- **F.01** Distinguish between economic goods and services
- **F.12** Explain the concept of organized labor and business
- **F.24** Determine factors affecting business risk

Common Career Technical Core Standards

- **BM.3** Explore, develop and apply strategies for ensuring a successful business career.
- **BM-HR.1** Describe and follow laws and regulations affecting human resource operations.
- **CRP.1** Act as a responsible and contributing citizen and employee.
- **CRP.3** Attend to personal health and financial well-being.

National Entrepreneurship Standards: Career Competencies

☑ **H.02** Analyze employer expectations in the business environment

LESSON VOCABULARY

- business
- dot-com company
- employee
- entrepreneur
- entrepreneurial
- entrepreneurship
- product
- reward
- risk
- serial entrepreneur
- service

1.1 Entrepre-What?

Have you ever thought about starting your own **business**? A business is an organization that provides **products** or **services**, usually in order to make money. An **entrepreneur** (on-tra-prah-NEWR) is someone who creates and runs a business. If you have a business idea, you could become an entrepreneur and create a business. However, entrepreneurship isn't for everybody. Many chose to be an **employee**, a person who works for a business owned by someone else. Even if you have never thought about starting your own business, learning about how to think and act like an entrepreneur, or thinking and acting **entrepreneurial**, can be helpful for the future. This unit will show you how thinking and acting like an entrepreneur can help you develop a plan for your own future.

How Employees and Entrepreneurs Differ

When an entrepreneur starts a new business, it involves risk. **Risk** is the chance of losing something. An entrepreneur makes an investment of money, time, and energy in the hope of getting greater rewards, or benefits. The saying, "No risk, no reward," relates to this concept.

Because employees work for someone else, but entrepreneurs work for themselves, entrepreneurs risk more than employees. Employees may risk losing a job if they do not perform the job well, but they are paid for their work. Entrepreneurs risk not being able to pay themselves if business is "slow." A failed business might also mean losing the money the entrepreneur invested into it.

The rewards that employees and entrepreneurs get from their work can also be different. A **reward** can involve money, but it can also be something such as personal satisfaction or independence. As a business owner, an entrepreneur is in control of the money made by his or her business. He or she also has the "final say" in all business decisions. As a result, entrepreneurs are ultimately responsible for the success or failure of their businesses.

Consider this example to understand the risks and rewards for an entrepreneur vs. her employee. Carla Hernandez decides to start a fruit "smoothie" drink shop in her neighborhood. Carla invests a lot of money, time, and effort to get the business started. Tony Bertelli, one of her employees, creates a new juice combination that Carla decides to put on the menu. By doing so, she risks the money spent on ingredients. She also risks a drop in sales if customers don't like the drink. As it turns out, the new drink is a great hit with customers and sales dramatically increase. Tony receives a small raise as a reward. Carla will benefit the most because she owns the business and took the bigger overall risk. Risks involve making choices and entrepreneurs need to weigh their choices carefully to achieve their goals for their businesses.

◀ **Figure 1-1**
Small Business Owners.
When you own a business, you are your own boss.

Applying Concepts.
Do you know someone who owns a "small business" in your town? Is there a "big business" that is in competition with them?

Big Business versus Small Business

When most people think about businesses, they tend to think of big businesses, like Walmart, Microsoft, or Nike. In reality, more businesses are considered "small" than "big." Small firms are the engine to our economy. They employ about half of the U.S. private work force, and they create around 64 percent of all new jobs. A commonly used size standard created by the Small Business Administration (SBA) defines a small business as having less than 100 employees (less than 500 employees in the case of companies that build things from scratch). The SBA is an agency of the U.S. government that provides aid and advice to small businesses.

According to the SBA, 800,000 new businesses were started in the United States in 2011—and about 750,000 close. This means that many new small businesses close right away, while others close after a short period of success. Even though most businesses begin small, they obviously don't all stay that way. An entrepreneur's goals will affect how large a business becomes. For example, suppose someone starts a neighborhood restaurant. He or she may not want to expand the business to include more than one restaurant if personal and financial needs are being met.

Figure 1-2 ▶

Life Cycle of the Business.

Many business start, and just as many fail each year.

Applying Concepts.

Why do you think so many businesses close?

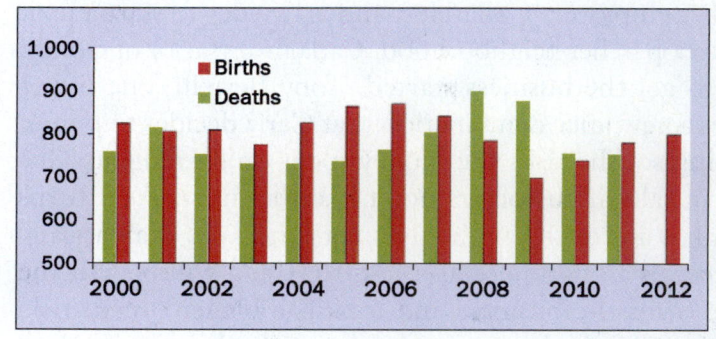

In other cases, a business may become so successful that it grows beyond the wildest expectations of its owners. That is exactly what happened to Whole Foods Market, Inc. It started in 1980 as one small store in Austin, Texas. Four businesspeople decided the natural food industry was ready for a supermarket format. And they were right! Beginning with a staff of 19, Whole Foods Market was an immediate success. Now Whole Foods Market is the world's leader in natural and organic foods, with more than 385 stores and over 58,000 employees worldwide.

There may be many reasons why you might want to start your own business. Before doing so, however, it's a good idea to consider the pros and cons of being an entrepreneur. The key is evaluating whether the potential rewards are worth more to you than the risks you will take.

Apply Your Knowledge What is an entrepreneur? Think back to your LifeProof investigation. Why was Gary Rayner an entrepreneur and not an employee? Explain your answer.

ENTREPRENEURIAL CASE STUDY: OPPORTUNITY RECOGNITION

Vincent Quigg— TechWorld

Finding Ways to Be Entrepreneurial

At 18 years old, Vincent Quigg became the CEO and founder of TechWorld (www.techworldfix.com), a business he launched while taking his entrepreneurship course at Downey High School in California. His business specializes in customizing and repairing iPhones. The business was so successful that he kept operating it beyond high school when he got to college, earning over $1,500 a month. For his business, Vincent was the 2012 winner of the Network for Teaching Entrepreneurship (NFTE)'s Youth Entrepreneurship Challenge, besting more than 15,000 students nationwide.

Vincent Quigg.

Vincent always had a mind for business, even at a young age. He was always finding interesting ways to make extra dollars. However, it was a sudden event in his family that required him to re-visit alternate ways of making money. "My mom became single a couple of years ago and I had to grow up. And in order to keep my lifestyle, I had to find different ways to stay financially ahead of the game, to keep my phone, keep a car, transportation, and all that stuff. So I had to find ways to be entrepreneurial," he said.

Solution to a Common Problem

While Vincent has always demonstrated an entrepreneurial spirit, he almost missed out on this opportunity in his entrepreneurship class. "It was extremely hard for myself to find a business to start and run with it. But once I had that 'a-ha moment' and knew what I wanted to go with, it was really easy and extremely fun."

His "a-ha moment" came when he identified a problem that he wanted solved. Vincent always had an interest in technology, and even had a job working with iPhones at Best Buy while he was in high school. Since he was interested in the newest gadgets, he would try to get his hands on the newest iPhones, which would then soon break unexpectedly. He was tired of driving far away any time he needed any phone maintenance, so he taught himself how to repair iPhones and cracked screens. Soon, he was advertising his services on Craigslist, at a cheaper rate and faster than Apple!

1.2 To Be or Not To Be an Entrepreneur: The Risks and Rewards

Rewards of Being an Entrepreneur

Why do you think most people become entrepreneurs? Money, fame, and power? More often, the biggest reward that most entrepreneurs cite is having ownership of their choices and decisions. Entrepreneurs gain personal satisfaction from having the freedom to make their own business decisions, and then act on them. Here are some additional rewards of being an entrepreneur:

- **Making Your Own Rules.** When you own a business, you get to be your own boss. You decide what type of schedule you work, where you work, and how and when you get paid. You also have the final word on what products or services the business provides, and how they are provided. For example, when you get a creative idea, you have the power to put that idea into action.

- **Doing Work You Enjoy.** The majority of most peoples' lives are spent working. Why not spend that time doing something you enjoy? People tend to stay more focused and motivated when they are passionate about their work. This makes a business more likely to succeed.

◀ **Figure 1-3**
Making Your Own Rules.
When you own a business, you are your own boss.

Applying Concepts.
What do you think the advantages of being your own boss would be? The disadvantages?

- **Creating Greater Wealth.** Typically, an employee can only make the salary a company is willing to pay. However, there's no limit on what an entrepreneur can make. Entrepreneurs can also do more than just make a living from their yearly business earnings. A successful business, particularly one that keeps growing, can often be sold for much more than the amount that was invested in it.

- **Helping Your Community.** Being an entrepreneur opens up opportunities to help make your community and world a better place to live. For example, entrepreneurs help others by providing products or services needed by the community. They also create jobs for people. Entrepreneurs often gain personal satisfaction and community recognition from the time and money they donate to worthy causes.

Risk of Being an Entrepreneur

But as we saw earlier in the smoothie example, business ownership is not without risks. Entrepreneurs need to be able to quickly assess their risks to decide if they should pursue their business idea. Here are some potential risks that every entrepreneur needs to consider:

- **Potential Business Failure.** The "flip side" of getting to make all the business decisions is the possibility of making the wrong ones. Being fully responsible means that the success or failure of your business rests on you. The time and money you invest in starting and running a business just might not pay off.

- **Unexpected Obstacles.** Many times, problems will happen that you won't expect. This can be discouraging and frustrating unless you choose to keep a positive attitude. It can get scary and lonely when facing these challenges, especially if you don't have the emotional support of family and friends.

Figure 1-4 ▶

Business Ownership and Risk.

There is a great deal of risk that comes with being your own boss.

Applying Concepts.

What types of risks does a new business owner face? What might happen if the owner hired more employees than they actually needed?

- **Financial Insecurity.** The amount of money you can pay yourself may go up and down depending on how well your business is performing. Many new businesses don't make much money in the beginning, so there may even be times when you can't pay yourself. During rough times, you may even have to pour more money into the business in order to pay your employees.

- **Long Hours and Hard Work.** It's not unusual for entrepreneurs to work a lot of extra time in order to make their businesses successful. This is especially true during the initial start-up process. Until you can afford to hire other people to help, you may have to perform many types of tasks. This requires discipline and a willingness to do whatever needs to be done.

 **Apply Your Knowledge** Consider your investigation of Gary Rayner and LifeProof. What do you think were two potential rewards Gary was motivated by? What were two potential risks you think he faced?

CAREER COMPETENCIES

☑ **Analyze Employer Expectations in the Business Environment**

All people have expectations of one another. At home, your parents may expect you to listen to their rules and do certain chores. At school, your teacher may expect you to respect your classmates and do your homework. Your friends may expect you to offer support and advice. Many times these types of expectations are understood and unspoken.

When an employer hires you, he or she will also have expectations, like being on time and being honest. Every employer has different expectations based on management and personality style. As an employee, it's helpful to know exactly what an employer expects. It's always good to ask and clarify expectations so that you can do the best job possible. Here are some standard expectations most employers have for their employees:

1. Be on time.

2. Follow your directions.

3. Don't talk on your cell phone when you're working.

4. Maintain a positive attitude.

5. Treat your team members with respect.

As we've learned, entrepreneurs are often employers as well and have similar expectations of their employees. As an entrepreneur, you want to build a team that supports and complements the skills you have. Being clear and communicating expectations can help support the growth of your employees and your business.

Career Skills in Action

Now imagine you had your own business. As an entrepreneur, what do you think would be your expectations of those who work for you?

- Make a list of 5–10 expectations you have of your employees.
- Make a list of 5–10 expectations your employees may have of you as an employer.

Share your lists with your peers and teacher for feedback.

1.3 Entrepreneurship Through the Years

As we've learned, **entrepreneurship** (on-trah-prah-NEWR-ship), the process of being an entrepreneur, is more than just learning how to run a business. It can affect business, the economy, your community, and ultimately the world in which we live. Here is a list of some entrepreneurs who have changed the world by solving a problem with a business idea.

The 1800s

- At age 12, Thomas Edison already showed signs of being an entrepreneur. He was selling newspapers, candy, and snacks at the local railroad station. By 14, he had his own newspaper business. Gathering the daily news releases teletyped into the station, he pulled out the "scoops" and convinced over 300 commuters to subscribe to his paper, which he called the *Weekly Herald*. One of the most prolific inventors in history and holding over 1,000 patents, Edison is credited with numerous inventions that contributed to mass communication. One of his inventions was the phonograph. Edison's greatest achievement, however, was creating a practical and economical system to distribute electricity, light, heat, and power. That, and the light bulb, changed the world forever.

- P.T. Barnum was 60 years old when his circus staged its first show. The circus generated $400,000 in sales in the first year. Later, it became known as the "Greatest Show on Earth," and still tours all over the United States today.

Figure 1-5 ▶

Early Edison Phonograph.

A phonograph was one of the many products that Thomas Edison created.

Applying Concepts.

Which of Thomas Edison's other inventions do we still use today?

Early 1900s

- In 1903, two friends—William Harley and Arthur Davidson—wanted to improve on the two-wheeled bicycle, and the motorcycle was born. Harley-Davidson was one of only two motorcyle producers to stay afloat during the Depression of the 1930s. Now it has outridden its competition to become the world's largest producer of motorcycles, with revenues of over $41 million annually.

- Maggie Lena Walker was a staunch advocate of human rights, humanitarian causes, self-sufficiency, and race relations. With the philosophy of turning "nickels into dollars," she became the first woman to charter a bank in the United States. Her bank, the St. Luke Penny Savings Bank, opened in 1903 with receipts totaling $9,430.44. Today it has assets of over $116 million. Now known as the Consolidated Bank and Trust Company, Walker's bank is the oldest continuously operating minority-owned bank in the United States. Actively committed to its philosophy, Walker remained its chairperson until her death. Among her many honors, she was inducted into the U.S. Business Hall of Fame, a school was built in her honor, and her home is designated as a historic site.

Mid-to-Late 1900s

- Ingvar Kamprad learned at an early age how to make money from available resources. By buying matches in bulk at a low price, he could sell them in smaller quantities at a higher price. He invested the money he made in buying and selling matches into other small business ventures. When he was 17, he used his investment earnings to found IKEA, a furniture business. Today, IKEA has expanded from Sweden to more than 300 stores in over 35 countries.

- Who can imagine a world without computers? In 1976, Steve Wozniak and Steve Jobs started a company in Job's garage with the goal of bringing computer technology to everyone. To help pay for their venture, they sold some of their personal possessions for a total of $1,300. Weeks later, the first Apple computer was sold. Today, Apple sells popular devices such as the iPhone, iPad (pictured), and the Apple Watch.

◀ **Figure 1-6**
Apple's iPad.
The iPad revolutionized how people used portable computers by introducing a tablet format.

Applying Concepts.
How many of Apple's inventions have you used?

- When Russell Simmons was a young man, he turned his passion for hip-hop into a venture that today is worth millions. Since the mid-1980s, Simmons has created a record label (Def Jam Records), a management company, a clothing company (Phat Farm), a movie production house, a magazine, an advertising agency, two television shows, and co-founded the Rush Philanthropic Arts Foundation.

- In 1995, Dineh Mohajer really wanted some light blue nail polish to match her sandals. So, she decided to combine different polishes in her bathroom to get the color she wanted. When she wore her custom nail polish, lots of people noticed. As a result, she began taking orders. Now she runs a million dollar company called Hard Candy that produces dozens of fancy colors.

Today's Entrepreneurs

As in the past, present-day entrepreneurs pay attention to social trends to attract customers. To be successful in today's business world, most entrepreneurs use the Internet in some way. In fact, more and more companies are making the Internet their primary business resource. Amazon.com is a good example, doing its business entirely on the Internet. Typically, these companies use an electronic address that ends in "com" and are sometimes referred to as **dot-com companies**.

Another more recent trend is that a growing percentage of people who start businesses do it again. And again. This is called **serial entrepreneurship**. These serial entrepreneurs take the lessons learned from their first businesses and apply them to new businesses. An example of a serial entrepreneur would be Peter Thiel, one of the co-founders of PayPal®. He used his experience to start other successful ventures, such as Clarium Capital. He also used his earnings to invest in other startups that he believed in, including being the first outside investor in Facebook.

For several reasons, serial entrepreneurship is more common now than in the past. First, companies—particularly technology companies—develop and mature more quickly now and can be sold while the founders are still young. Second, resources for growing a company are more easily available because of the Internet and the concentration of new businesses in certain geographic areas, such as Silicon Valley in California. With customers only a click away, many new businesses can become wildly profitable in just a few years.

Serial entrepreneurs report that they are not driven by the desire for money so much as the impulse to innovate and to challenge themselves. There are resources specifically designed to help entrepreneurs who want to start not one, not two, but several successful businesses.

Entrepreneurs come from all different backgrounds with different experiences. What they have in common, though, is that they identify problems that everyday people have and find solutions to help solve these problems.

 **Apply Your Knowledge** Think back to your investigation of LifeProof. Would you consider Gary Rayner a serial entrepreneur? If so, do you believe that being a serial entrepreneur helped his success with LifeProof?

✔ APPLICATION TO BUSINESS PLANNING

Problem Identification

Use what you learned in this chapter on entrepreneurship to practice recognizing problems:

- Make a list of everyday problems that you face at school, home, and extracurricular activities. List as many problems as possible.
- Share your list of problems with a peer or your teacher.
- Compare and contrast your lists.
- Discuss some potential solutions for each of these problems.

ASSESSMENT

REVIEWING OBJECTIVES

1. Compare and contrast the functions of an entrepreneur and those of an employee.
2. What are the pros and cons of being an entrepreneur?
3. Describe how entrepreneurs solve problems through products or services.

CRITICAL THINKING

1. What's the difference between "entrepreneur" and "entrepreneurship"?
2. Why do you think an entrepreneur might choose to keep a business small rather than expand it?

ENTREPRENEURIAL THINKING EXERCISE: OPPORTUNITY RECOGNITION

Think back to your investigation of LifeProof and founder Gary Rayner. As a serial entrepreneur in the technology industry, he's always coming up with new problems to solve. Suppose Gary asks you for problems he could solve, what problems would you share with him? Why?

EXTENSION ACTIVITIES

Entrepreneurship & Literacy Skills

Complete the following task to demonstrate your understanding of entrepreneurship:

1. Grades 9–10: Choose an entrepreneur from the past who is not discussed in this chapter, and write a report that describes the risks and rewards involved in starting his or her business. Discuss whether the entrepreneur made life better in some way with a product or service. Support your findings with well-chosen, relevant, and sufficient facts, extended definitions, concrete details, quotations, or other information and examples.

2. Grades 11–12: Choose an entrepreneur from the past who is not discussed in this chapter, and write a report that describes the risks and rewards involved in starting his or her business. Discuss whether the entrepreneur made life better in some way with a product or service. Support your findings with the most significant and relevant facts, extended definitions, concrete details, quotations, or other information and examples.

2 CHARACTERISTICS OF AN ENTREPRENEUR

APPLICATION TO BUSINESS PLANNING:

☑ Personal Skills/Characteristics

OBJECTIVES

- Learn about different types of entrepreneurs and determine their unique skills and characteristics.
- Evaluate one's own strengths, weaknesses, and opportunities for growth to measure entrepreneurial potential.
- Identify skills and characteristics demonstrated by an entrepreneurial mindset.

NFTE Entrepreneurial Mindset Characteristic Focus

☑ Initiative & Self-Reliance

National Entrepreneurship Standards

- **A.01** Explain the need for entrepreneurial discovery
- **B.12** Describe desirable entrepreneurial personality traits
- **B.15** Evaluate personal capabilities
- **B.16** Conduct self-assessment to determine entrepreneurial potential

Common Career Technical Core Standards

- **BM.3** Explore, develop and apply strategies for ensuring a successful business career.
- **CRP.2** Apply appropriate academic and technical skills.
- **CRP.10** Plan education and career path aligned to personal goals.

National Entrepreneurship Standards: Career Competencies

☑ **H.12** Prepare a resume
☑ **H.16** Determine skills needed to enhance career progression

LESSON VOCABULARY

- attitude
- characteristic
- mentor
- NFTE entrepreneurial mindset
- professionalism
- self-assessment
- skill

2.1 Who Are Entrepreneurs?

Background of Entrepreneurs

As you learned in the previous chapter, entrepreneurs come from various backgrounds and places. They all share a common purpose, to identify problems and solve them. Who these entrepreneurs are and where they come from can help us understand the types of people that become entrepreneurs. The United States Census Bureau conducts a survey of business owners periodically. A recent survey received feedback from an estimated 16.7 million businesses from all over the country. Here are some highlights from the survey:

- Sixty-seven percent of the business owners had some college education when they started the business. Another twenty percent started a business with just a high school diploma.

- More than 60 percent of the business owners used money of their own, or from their families, to start or buy their business. Around 40 percent were able to start their business with outside funding.

- Slightly more than half of business owners who had employees worked overtime (more than 40 hours per week total). Twenty-six percent of the business owners with no employees worked overtime. About half the businesses were home-based.

- Over a third of the business owners were over 55 years old; 30 percent were between 45 and 54; 21 percent were between 35 and 44; 10 percent were between 25 and 34; and over 2 percent were under 25.

According to research by the Small Business Administration, the number of women and minority entrepreneurs in the U.S. has steadily increased in recent years. Studies show that minority-owned businesses went from 7 percent of all businesses to 21 percent between the years of 1982 and 2007. Businesses owned by women have also increased from 1.76 million to 7.79 million between 1976 and 2007.

21% Minority Owned

2007

Based on these surveys, you can say this about entrepreneurs: many work from home, invest their own money, are educated, and are men and women of all ages and nationalities—and they work hard. It is also important to note the historically low number of young entrepreneurs. While it is impossible to know the exact reason, one hypothesis could be that high school students are not usually taught entrepreneurship in school. By taking this course, you will be getting an edge over other high school students, and help make that number grow!

Apply Your Knowledge Is it necessary to have a college degree before starting a business? Consider your investigation of the top entrepreneurs for 2012. Did the four entrepreneurs all have college educations? What level of education did each entrepreneur achieve?

◀ **Figure 2-1**
Diverse Entrepreneurs.
Entrepreneurs come in all different ages and from all different backgrounds.

Applying Concepts.
Would you agree with the argument that anyone can be an entrepreneur?

ENTREPRENEURIAL CASE STUDY: INITIATIVE & SELF-RELIANCE

 ## Mike McGee & Neal Sales-Griffin —The Starter League

Turning Personal Skills into Opportunity

Mike McGee and Neal Sales-Griffin created their business, The Starter League (www.starterleague.com), out of a personal frustration. Wanting to teach themselves computer programming, they spent a year trying to

Mike McGee (top) and
Neal Sales-Griffin (bottom).

learn how to code by reading books and watching online tutorials. However, Neal and Mike had a difficult time getting the results they needed. They believed they could build a better experience for other people trying to learn how to build web applications. Mike and Neal saw Chicago as the perfect place to build this school. There were a lot of people who wanted to build online startup businesses, but didn't have the coding skills to make them real. If people came to The Starter League, they could learn how to do this!

Getting the Word Out

Once they came up with the idea, Mike and Neal went around Chicago telling the local community about the idea. People loved the idea and decided to help them make it happen. Through these efforts, the two were able to find an instructor and space for the school. The original idea for the school was that it would be taught at a local university. After doing more brainstorming and calculating costs, they decided to shorten the length of the program from nine to three months, and focus on teaching students how to code.

Because Neal and Mike were just starting out, they didn't have any money to pay for advertising. Instead, they decided to do a "word-of-mouth" campaign. This meant that they relied on free social media and writing blog posts about their efforts. They also made connections with local programmers and entrepreneurs to help the spread the word.

Following Passion

Mike and Neal were so passionate about this idea that they turned down an opportunity to work on President Obama's re-election campaign to focus on growing The Starter League. Their risk paid off, though, as they ended up with 88 applications for 12 spots after only a month of advertising their school. Their efforts have also continued to gain media buzz, providing them with more and more growth opportunities for the future.

When asked about what keeps them invested in The Starter League, it's their interest in helping others. "My sworn purpose is to solve meaningful problems through technology, and empower everyone I can," said Neal of his future goals. Mike agrees that he "likes to motivate others to exceed their potential." Both truly believe that anyone has the ability to build ideas using technology. You don't have to be an A+ student or go to Harvard, if you are passionate about solving a problem and willing to work hard, you can learn, too. With this school, they are hoping to create a world of entrepreneurial problem-solvers.

Thinking and Acting Like an Entrepreneur

- What personal skills and characteristics did Neal and Mike possess that helped them start their business?
- How do Mike and Neal demonstrate the entrepreneurial mindset behavior of initiative and self-reliance?
- What other entrepreneurial mindset characteristics did you observe?

2.2 Assessing Characteristics and Skills

Characteristics of Successful Entrepreneurs

Research shows extensive growth in new business and entrepreneurship around the world. But what this data doesn't explain is what makes entrepreneurs successful or unsuccessful. For an entrepreneur, **self-assessment** is key to evaluating strengths and weaknesses. Self-assessment helps an entrepreneur determine what unique knowledge they have. This might be a better way of making a certain type of food, a knowledge of trends in fashion, or having computer programming skills that not many other people have. Identifying this unique knowledge can be used to make a profit. Doing a self-assessment also helps maximize strong points and strengthen weaker ones. It's important to remember that everybody has strengths and weaknesses. It's what you do with what you have that counts.

Attitude

An **attitude** is a way of viewing or thinking about something that can affect how you feel about it. Entrepreneurs tend to be people with positive attitudes and work ethics. Instead of seeing something as a problem, they look at it as an opportunity. This helps them find solutions more easily than people who think negatively. In turn, they are more productive in their work and tend to perform their tasks and duties at a higher level.

Think about your own experience. Positive thinking and talking tends to make you feel happier and have more energy. You feel motivated to take steps towards accomplishing your goals. In contrast to that, negative thinking and talking tends to make you feel helpless and depressed. You are much less likely to take action toward solving a problem.

A positive attitude can make the difference between failure and success. Someone with a negative attitude will probably achieve less than someone who has less natural ability, but who keeps a positive attitude.

Professionalism

Professionalism is the ability to show respect to everyone around you while you perform your responsibilities as best as you can. It includes a basic set of personal qualities that make an individual successful—no matter what type of business he or she owns or what profession he or she is in. The personal qualities that combine to create professionalism include integrity, courtesy, honesty, dependability, and responsibility. For example, you are punctual and considerate of others. You state your opinions confidently and actively listen to others. You dress and speak in a professional manner. You follow through on your commitments. When you show professionalism, you earn the trust and respect of your employees, your customers, your suppliers, and your community.

Personal Characteristics

Think about if you were asked to describe your friends, family, co-workers, or teachers. You would probably explain how the person behaves. For example, your favorite relative might be very considerate, while your best friend might be a good listener. These behaviors usually are a result of the person's personality dimensions. Where people fall on these dimensions determine how they they appear to others. In psychology, the five dimensions of human personality include:

Watch your thoughts — they become words.

Watch your words — they become actions.

Watch your actions — they become habits.

Watch your habits — they become character.

Watch your character — it becomes your destiny.

▲ **Figure 2-2**
Defining Your Character.
Based on a Chinese proverb.

Applying Concepts.
How does this relate to doing an assessment on one's own characteristics?

- **Openness to experience:** Is the person inventive? Curious or cautious? Do they enjoy new things or do they like routine?

- **Conscientiousness:** Are they organized and dependable? Easy-going and careless? Do they plan for everything or prefer spontaneous behavior instead?

- **Extraversion:** Are they outgoing and energetic, or are they solitary and reserved?

Enthusiasm.
Being enthusiastic can be helpful in business.

Drawing Conclusions.
How can a positive, productive work ethic help you achieve your goals?

- **Agreeableness:** Are they friendly and compassionate, or analytical and detached? Do they cooperate with others, or are they suspicious of others?

- **Neuroticism:** Are they sensitive and nervous, or secure and confident?

Many of these descriptions in these dimensions are **characteristics**, which can be used to describe a quality or behavior of a person.

There are certain characteristics shared by successful entrepreneurs. No one is born with all the characteristics needed to be a successful entrepreneur. But, if you keep a positive attitude and believe in yourself, you can develop many of them. In the following list, notice the characteristics you already possess, then focus on the ones you think you need to develop:

- **Courage.** A willingness to take risks in spite of possible losses
- **Creativity.** Inventing new ways of doing things; thinking "outside the box"
- **Curiosity.** The desire to learn and ask questions
- **Determination.** Refusing to quit in spite of obstacles
- **Discipline.** The ability to stay focused and follow a schedule in order to meet deadlines
- **Empathy.** Being sensitive to the thoughts and feelings of others
- **Enthusiasm.** Being passionate about something; the ability to see problems as opportunities
- **Flexibility.** The ability to adapt to new situations; a willingness to change
- **Honesty.** A commitment to being truthful and sincere with others
- **Patience.** Recognizing that most goals are not reached overnight
- **Professionalism.** The ability to treat others with respect while performing your job responsibilities as best as you can
- **Responsibility.** Being accountable for your decisions and actions; not "passing the buck"

Skills

In addition to characteristics, entrepreneurs need to assess their skills. A <mark>skill</mark> is an ability that's learned through training and practice. For example, you didn't know how to tie a shoe when you were born. You learned this skill through practice and the help of adults. Some of the skills that entrepreneurs need to be successful include:

- **Business Skills.** Understanding how to create and manage a business
- **Communication Skills.** The ability to listen well, write well, and speak well
- **Computer Skills.** The ability to use technological tools effectively
- **Decision-Making and Problem-Solving Skills.** Knowing how to apply logic, information, and past experiences to new decisions and problems
- **Mathematical Skills.** Using math to create budgets, keep accurate records, and analyze financial statements
- **Organizational Skills.** The knack of keeping tasks and information in order; the ability to plan well and manage your time
- **People Skills.** The ability to persuade and motivate people; knowing both how to be a leader and work in a team

Don't be discouraged from becoming an entrepreneur just because you don't yet have all the traits and skills you will need. You can increase your business and entrepreneurial potential by focusing on six specific areas. These six specific skill areas can be referred to as Business and Entrepreneurship Core Skills. Even if you never become an entrepreneur, paying attention to these areas will help you be more successful in life.

Business Knowledge

Make a habit of reading magazine and newspaper articles on business topics. Use the Internet to research business subjects. Watch films or television programs about successful entrepreneurs. This can help you learn more about business. If you know someone who owns their own business, discuss the business with him or her.

Financial Skills

Strengthen your math skills by taking a course in accounting, personal finance, or investing. If math is a difficult subject for you, ask a teacher to spend a little extra time with you before or after school. Team up with a friend who is good at math. Play math games or do math homework with them.

Career Exploration

First, evaluate your strengths and weaknesses. Be as honest as you can about your characteristics without being too easy or too hard on yourself.

◀ **Figure 2-4**

Business and Entrepreneurship Core Skills.
Grades 7 through 12 are an excellent time to work on developing these skills.

Applying Concepts.
Why is it important to have experience with practicing many of these skills before post-secondary college or a career?

Remember, nobody is perfect, but everyone has something they can contribute to the world. Practice thinking and acting as if you already have the characteristics you want to develop. A positive attitude will keep you on the right track.

Next, explore different career areas that interest you. Include careers that match up with interests and skills you have or are developing. There are many books, magazines, and Internet sites on careers. Ask a career or guidance counselor at your school for research suggestions.

Finally, talk with people who have a career you think you'd like. Some companies have programs that allow their employees to bring someone to work with them for a day. During that day, you get to observe what it's like to work in a particular job.

Community Awareness

Look for opportunities in your local community to volunteer. Also, find out if any companies in your local area provide internships where you can get some practical, on-the-job experience. If you know of a particular problem in your community, consider ways that you can help improve the situation.

Education

Learning is a lifetime occupation, no matter what career you choose. Take advantage of changes to learn new things, ask lots of questions, and strive to do your best in whatever you do. Obtaining an educational certificate, diploma, or degree not only benefits you personally, it can help "open doors" to more career opportunities. Whether in school or working in a job, remember that you are responsible for what you learn—and no one else.

Relationships

Spend time with people who believe in you and inspire you. Being around positive people will help you stay positive and accomplish more. People who are negative and complain all the time will influence you to be the same way. Some organizations have programs in which experienced people volunteer to share their knowledge. These <mark>mentors</mark>, as they are called, provide free guidance, tutoring, and suggestions for achieving your goals.

You'll notice that many of these skills and areas of focus can be helpful to you even if you choose not to be an entrepreneur, they can help you be a more successful person. In the next section, you will learn about how you can apply these entrepreneurial skills to a toolkit that will allow for entrepreneurial success.

 **Apply Your Knowledge**   What are some skills and characteristics you can develop to increase your entrepreneurial potential? How can a positive attitude affect your work ethic and on-the-job performance? Think back to your investigation of the top entrepreneurs. What personal characteristics and skills do each share? Are there any missing from this list that you would add based on your investigation?

CAREER COMPETENCIES

 **Determine Skills Needed to Enhance Career Progression; Prepare a Resume**

A resume is a document that provides a snapshot of your qualifications for a job opportunity. It summarizes your skills and abilities and also serves as a personal statement of who you are, what you've done, and what you want to do next. Your resume is usually your first communication to a potential employer. You want to make sure your resume describes you and your work in a way that will make an employer want to meet you.

There are many ways to format a resume. Most word processing programs have resume templates and samples. Choose a format that highlights your experiences, as well as your entrepreneurial characteristics and skills so they stand out to someone who might just glance at your resume quickly. Consider the following tips:

- Make it easy to read. Don't overcrowd the page.
- Use one font and bold to emphasize key abilities.
- Bullet your lists.
- Check your spelling and punctuation.
- Use action verbs (e.g., managed, created).
- Keep it short and simple and limit to one page.

Today many job seekers and entrepreneurs use LinkedIn, an online resume profile where employers can check. Since it's online, it's important to keep this current and up-to-date. Resumes can help you identify areas for skill development to advance your career. For example, if you want to be a programmer, you may need to get your C++ certification.

Career Skills in Action

Now, you practice using putting together a resume and LinkedIn profile as an entrepreneur. Be sure to:

- List relevant work history.
- Identify specific entrepreneurial skills and characteristics that make you qualified for this business.
- Use the tips above to develop a well-formatted resume and profile.
- Identify additional skills you need to develop to run your business.

Share your resume with your peers and teacher for feedback.

2.3 NFTE Entrepreneurial Mindset

NFTE Entrepreneurial Mindset in Action

From the previous section, you learned about many different characteristics and skills that an entrepreneur might possess. However, it is how the entrepreneur uses all of those characteristics and skills together that can make them successful. In fact, successful entrepreneurs share a blend of characteristics, attitudes, and skills called the **NFTE entrepreneurial mindset**.

◀ **Figure 2-5**
NFTE Entrepreneurial Mindset.

Successful entrepreneurs all demonstrate an entrepreneurial mindset.

Applying Concepts.
What does it mean to demonstrate an entrepreneurial mindset? How do you know if someone is acting or thinking like an entrepreneur?

The NFTE entrepreneurial mindset includes important skills like flexibility, critical thinking, and communication skills but also includes important behaviors or attitudes like persistence and looking at problems as opportunities. In many ways the mindset is a set of tools that entrepreneurs can develop, and use when needed. Although no one entrepreneur can claim mastery over all of the mindset areas, they can demonstrate some level of competency in each of the areas. The NFTE Entrepreneurial Mindset Characteristics, specific areas of activity or knowledge, are listed with descriptions in Table 2.1.

Table 2.1   NFTE Entrepreneurial Mindset Characteristics

Mindset Domain	Description
Initiative & Self-Reliance	• Set goals and establish action plans to accomplish them. • Manage time effectively. • Face challenges with an optimistic attitude. • Adjust plans to move forward and meet goals.
Flexibility & Adaptability	• Adapt to different roles. • Understand how to incorporate feedback effectively. • Learn from and how to act with setbacks. • Reflect critically on learning experiences and processes.
Communication & Collaboration	• Articulate thoughts and ideas effectively to individuals and groups. • Work effectively in groups. • Respect team members and alternative points of view.
Critical Thinking & Problem Solving	• Analyze and evaluate different points of view. • Synthesize information and arguments from a variety of sources. • Interpret information and draw conclusions.
Future Orientation	• Prioritize long-term success in the face of short-term sacrifice/work. • See beyond and plan for a time horizon greater than one year.
Opportunity Recognition	• Identify problems as opportunities. • Understand when there is a "window of opportunity." • Assess business ideas to identify opportunities.
Comfort with Risk	• Understand the difference between risk and reward. • Learn how to calculate risk. • Differentiate between short-term and long-term risks.
Creativity & Innovation	• Brainstorm and use other creative-thinking exercises. • Find creative solutions, evaluate and refine ideas. • View failure as an opportunity to learn.

You will have the chance to discuss and practice your entrepreneurial mindset in the class. In fact, you have already started! Throughout this textbook, you'll have the opportunity to see various entrepreneurial mindset areas in action through entrepreneurial case studies. You will also practice and apply entrepreneurial thinking through various exercises. Finally, an entrepreneurial mindset is critical in your development as an entrepreneur—planning for and starting your own business. Keep these entrepreneurial mindset domains in mind as you progress through the textbook, and redo your self-assessment as time goes on to see how your entrepreneurial mindset is coming along.

Apply Your Knowledge   Now that you have learned about the mindset of successful entrepreneurs, let's return to our investigation of *Essence*'s top entrepreneurs of 2012 that you read about earlier. Consider the list of characteristics and behaviors in the NFTE entrepreneurial mindset and answer the following questions:

1. For each entrepreneur, identify which 2–3 NFTE entrepreneurial mindset characteristics are most developed. Provide examples from your research.

2. What entrepreneurial characteristics do they have that are not included in the mindset (if any)?

3. Compare and contrast two of the entrepreneurs' NFTE entrepreneurial mindsets? Do your findings suggest that one entrepreneur is more successful than another?

Write down your responses and be prepared to share your responses with your teacher or class.

APPLICATION TO BUSINESS PLANNING

Personal Skills/Characteristics

Use what you learned from this chapter on the NFTE entrepreneurial mindset to identify specific skills, characteristics, and NFTE entrepreneurial mindset domains you have. You can also identify the ones you need to develop. Use the lists from the chapters to create a comprehensive list and chart like the one below. Consider the six areas of focus to develop your entrepreneurial potential. Remember everyone needs practice to develop these skills and creating a plan can help you achieve your goal faster!

NFTE Entrepreneurial Mindset Characteristic	Skill/Characteristic	I have/I need to develop	I will develop through...
Communication & Collaboration	Articulate thoughts and ideas effectively to individuals and groups	I need to develop	Presentations in my entrepreneurship class and Debate team.

REVIEWING OBJECTIVES

1. What are the different types of entrepreneurs and their unique skills and characteristics?

2. How can one evaluate their own strengths, weaknesses, and opportunities for growth to measure entrepreneurial potential?

3. What are the skills and characteristics demonstrated by an entrepreneurial mindset?

CRITICAL THINKING

1. What is professionalism? What actions and qualities demonstrate your professionalism in the workplace?

2. List several personal characteristics that might hinder someone from becoming an entrepreneur. In what ways could these characteristics also prevent someone from becoming a valued employee?

3. Time management skills fall within the Initiative & Self-Reliance entrepreneurial mindset domain. Being able to prioritize tasks, follow schedules, and complete activities to meet goals are important skills in anything you do. What techniques and tips might entrepreneurs use to efficiently manage their time?

ENTREPRENEURIAL THINKING EXERCISE: INITIATIVE & SELF-RELIANCE

Think back to your investigation of *Essence*'s most successful African-American female entrepreneurs of 2012. Suppose one of the top entrepreneurs asked you for help to develop a personal skill or characteristic. How would you help them create a plan to develop and practice this skill or characteristic?

EXTENSION ACTIVITIES

Entrepreneurship & Literacy Skills

Complete the following task to demonstrate your understanding of entrepreneurship:

1. Grades 9–10: Using the NFTE entrepreneurial mindset characteristics, create a word poster to describe one of the characteristics in your own words. Select entrepreneurs who you believe possess this characteristic, skill or attitude and post on the wall. Present to the class.

2. Grades 11–12: Using the NFTE entrepreneurial mindset characteristics, create a word poster to describe one of the characteristics in your own words. Select entrepreneurs who you believe possess this characteristic, skill or attitude and post on the wall. Provide a process for updating definitions as the class learns more about each domain. Present to the class.

3 BEING AN INTRAPRENEUR

OBJECTIVES

- Explain the value of learning entrepreneurship in relation to one's own career path.
- Identify ways to utilize the entrepreneurial mindset while acting as an intrapreneur.
- List the 16 career clusters and entrepreneurial pathways within each.

LESSON VOCABULARY

- apprenticeship
- career cluster
- internship
- intrapreneurship
- pathways
- vision

NFTE Entrepreneurial Mindset Characteristic Focus

☑ Future Orientation

National Entrepreneurship Standards

- **A.01** Explain the need for entrepreneurial discovery
- **A.02** Discuss entrepreneurial discovery processes
- **B.12** Describe desirable entrepreneurial personality traits
- **B.14** Determine interests
- **F.12** Explain the concept of organized labor and business
- **H.01** Evaluate career opportunities based on current/future economy
- **H.04** Select and use sources of career information
- **H.05** Determine tentative occupational interest
- **H.13** Describe techniques for obtaining work experience (e.g., volunteer activities, internships)

Common Career Technical Core Standards

- **BM.3** Explore, develop and apply strategies for ensuring a successful business career.
- **CRP.1** Act as a responsible and contributing citizen and employee.
- **CRP.3** Attend to personal health and financial well-being.
- **CRP.10** Plan education and career path aligned to personal goals.

National Entrepreneurship Standards: Career Competencies

☑ **H.17** Utilize resources that can contribute to professional development

ENTREPRENEURIAL INVESTIGATION
An Idea That Sticks

In 1968, a 3M scientist Spencer Silver developed a lightweight adhesive that could be take apart and re-stuck. He came up with this idea at 3M due to their policy called "bootlegging." This allows the employees to spend up to 15 percent of their time working on developing their own ideas. Silver was unsure how to use this adhesive, but still conducted a lot of seminars to try to explain how great the adhesive was. Five years later, one of his colleagues, Art Frey, noticed his bookmarks kept falling out of his choir hymnbook. He contacted Silver to get his adhesive and the Post-It was born. It wasn't until 1980 that it went to market. Today, Post-It Brand is one of 3M's biggest earners and is now comes in multiple colors and sizes.

Based on the case, answer the following questions:

1. Is Spencer Silver an entrepreneur? Explain your answer
2. Who was more entrepreneurial: Spencer Silver or Art Frey? Why?
3. Describe 2–3 characteristics you believe Spencer Silver shares with successful entrepreneurs.

Be prepared to share your responses with your teacher and class.

3.1 Why Study Entrepreneurship?

So far in this unit, we have learned about who becomes entrepreneurs, and their reasons for doing so. We also learned about the entrepreneurial mindset and its importance to entrepreneurs. In this chapter, we will explore how learning entrepreneurship, and developing an entrepreneurial mindset, can help in any career path that you choose.

Owning a business isn't for everyone. But that's okay because both employees and entrepreneurs are needed in the world of work. Whether or not you choose to become an entrepreneur, the things you will learn in this book can benefit you in many ways. There are two primary reasons why studying entrepreneurship makes sense, even if you don't plan to be an entrepreneur: you can learn to think like an entrepreneur and you develop a vision for your life.

Thinking Like an Entrepreneur, Being an Intrapreneur

Even if you don't want to be an entrepreneur you can still develop a lot of the entrepreneurial mindset characteristics to think and approach life in a more positive and opportunity-focused way. For example, having a future orientation and being able to set goals is important for anyone to be successful in career or otherwise. Thinking like an entrepreneur and being conscious of how to make a business run more successfully can help you be a better employee. Acting like an entrepreneur means pursuing opportunities that one is passionate about. Having **passion** means to have a very strong positive interest in something. If you have a passion for fashion and get a job working in a clothing store, you should find opportunities on the job to pursue your passion. Start conversations with customers about the latest fashions and your recommendations. Offer your services to customers to act as a personal stylist and help them pick out an outfit. Give your thoughts to the owner about what new fashions the business should be carrying based on your experience. Provide suggestions that will make the store run better. In effect, you can treat someone else's business as if it were yours. Employers often promote these kinds of employees, the ones who think entrepreneurially. And the upside is that you get to pursue your passion while earning a paycheck!

Here are three easy ways to practice thinking like an entrepreneur when you are working as an employee:

1. **Observe.** Keep on the lookout for chances to learn new skills and accept new responsibilities. Staying aware of what goes on around you can help generate new ideas for business growth. This includes ideas for new products or services that customers may need or want.

2. **Listen.** Pay attention to what others have to say. Challenges that other employees are facing may give you ideas for making business improvements.

3. **Think.** Instead of complaining about a problem, analyze it. Then suggest possible solutions.

◀ **Figure 3-1**
Vision.
Entrepreneurship can help you form and fulfill your life's vision.

Applying Concepts.
After reading this chapter, what type of vision do you see for your life?

More and more businesses today encourage the practice of **intrapreneurship** (in-tra-prih-NER-ship). That is, they give employees opportunities to be creative and try out new ideas, almost like being an entrepreneur within the company.

Thinking like an entrepreneur can also help you make smarter decisions about managing the money you earn. This includes how to keep good personal records, make wise purchases, invest personal funds to earn more money, and plan for retirement.

Learning about entrepreneurship often inspires people to develop a **vision** for their life. A vision is a 'picture' of what you want the future to be. Your vision should include you pursuing opportunities that you are passionate about. In the next section, you will learn more about various career paths, and how developing an entrepreneurial mindset can be beneficial for each.

 **Apply Your Knowledge**   How can learning about entrepreneurship help an employee be intrapreneurial? Think back to your investigation of the 3M "bootlegging" policy and consider Spencer Silver. Was he an intrapreneur? What else could Spencer Silver have done to pursue his entrepreneurial passion if 3M didn't have the bootlegging policy?

ENTREPRENEURIAL CASE STUDY: FUTURE ORIENTATION

 # Sofia Contreras—Las 5 Americas Restaurant Corp.

Developing a Vision for Her Life

Sofia Contreras is Founder and CEO of Las 5 Americas Restaurant. Sofia first got her idea for her restaurant while taking an entrepreneurship course sponsored by the Network for Teaching Entrepreneurship (NFTE) at her high school in Brooklyn, New York. Since becoming involved with NFTE and inspired by her mother's dream of owning a restaurant, Sofia became determined to share her family's passion for delicious food. Using what she learned from her NFTE class and NFTE Startup Summer camp, she generated over $12,000 in revenue. Her business went from selling food at school and to friends, to laying the groundwork for opening a restaurant.

Sofia Contreras.

Thinking Like an Entrepreneur as an Employee

All her young life, Sofia has had to work hard and think entrepreneurially. As a small child, she learned that there was nothing to be ashamed of from selling things to people to make money. A woman that she loved like a grandmother, her "Mamá Rosa," acted as a mentor. Sofia helped Mamá Rosa make and sell sweet apples, fried plantain chips and other homemade foods, to earn some pocket money.

She came to the United States from El Salvador at the age of thirteen and has been cooking alongside her mother ever since she can remember. When her family immigrated to the United States, her mother got a job as the manager of a Salvadorian restaurant. Sofia began to help out in the restaurant. As a result, her real love of business grew stronger and stronger. She learned the ins and outs of the restaurant industry from her mother. This included everything from negotiating deals, to figuring out which supermarkets offered the best quality and most affordable products.

In her entrepreneurship class, she developed a business plan for a restaurant. The plan was to provide busy clients with healthy, delicious, and homemade authentic Salvadorian and Latin American cuisine, while providing unmatched quality and service to customers. Her plan was so well-done, that she was able to showcase her idea at the 2014 Global Young Entrepreneur marketplace alongside the other top 55 young entrepreneurs' businesses and products. As a result of these experiences, Sofia was inspired to actually go ahead and start her own restaurant, but she did not think it could be a reality until she took the NFTE class. "I always wanted to start a restaurant," Sofia said, "but until I took the NFTE class I didn't believe it was truly possible."

Looking to the Future

Now she is looking to the future. Sofia recently graduated from Brooklyn International HS. She is currently attending the Borough of Manhattan Community College with plans to major in accounting to open additional opportunities. In 2014, Sofia opened Las 5 Americas Restaurant, a Latin American and Salvadorian restaurant in Brooklyn.

Thinking and Acting Like an Entrepreneur

- What career pathway did Sofia show an interest in?
- How did Sofia gain experience and skills as an employee that helped her become an entrepreneur?
- In what ways does Sofia demonstrate the entrepreneurial mindset behavior of future orientation?

3.2 Career Clusters

Whether you decide to be an entrepreneur or an intrapreneur, understanding what jobs exist can be helpful to determine what you want to do. Matching your interests, skills, and aptitude to career requirements can help you identify opportunities for work that you will love. Many entrepreneurs start off in a career that they love and then innovate within their career field. This creates a lasting impact on a field that's important to them. Many people in careers like plumbing and architecture start their own businesses after working for larger companies as independent contractors. They have more ownership of their time, assume additional risk, and potentially greater rewards.

Analyzing the Career Clusters

To organize the various and overwhelming career options, the National Association of State Directors of Career Technical Education Consortium (NASDCTEc) identifies 16 career clusters by classifying specific jobs and industries into similar categories. You can use the information on career clusters to learn about careers while you are in school or any time you are doing career research.

Within each of the 16 career clusters are related job, industry, and occupation types known as pathways. For example, the Architecture & Construction cluster has three pathways: Construction, Design/Pre-Construction, and Maintenance/Operations. The pathways are the building blocks of the 16 career clusters. Each pathway offers a variety of careers you might choose. There are also relationships between occupations in different clusters. For example, an information technology manager (Information Technology cluster) may work in almost any industry, including health care (Health Sciences cluster), legal services (Law, Public Safety, Corrections & Security cluster), and airline reservation systems (Hospitality & Tourism cluster).

The clusters and their pathways help job seekers and individuals interested in specific careers to identify professions that best suit their interests and abilities. Through the clusters and pathways, you can learn about the education and skills you will need to be effective in a specific job and career. They provide you with clear-cut choices and options as you begin your career exploration. In this section of the chapter, you will learn about each cluster, pathway and job opportunities. Think like an entrepreneur and consider how you might identify entrepreneurial opportunities in each cluster. Consider the benefits and drawbacks.

Exploring the Career Clusters

1. Agriculture, Food & Natural Resources

The Agriculture, Food & Natural Resources career cluster is for people interested in the production, processing, marketing, distribution, financing, and development of agricultural commodities—economic goods—and resources. Their interests in the field might include food, fuel, fiber, wood products, natural resources, horticulture, and other plant and animal products and resources. People in this field select jobs as diverse as farmer, food scientist, and meat inspector.

Pathways include the following:

- Agribusiness Systems
- Animal Systems
- Environmental Service Systems
- Food Products and Processing Systems
- Natural Resources Systems
- Plant Systems
- Power, Structural, and Technical Systems

Sample occupations include the following:

- Agricultural Communications Specialist
- Animal Scientist
- Embryo Technologist
- Feed Sales Representative
- Fish and Game Warden
- Food Scientist
- Greenhouse Manager
- Livestock Buyer
- Microbiologist
- Tree Trimmer and Pruner

◀ **Figure 3-2**
Fish and Game Warden.

A fish and game warden is responsible for enforcing laws relating to the hunting, fishing, and trapping of wild animals.

Applying Concepts.

What skills and interests do you think might be necessary to become a fish and game warden?

2. Architecture & Construction

People in the Architecture & Construction career cluster design, plan, manage, build, and maintain the built environment. Take a look around you. The houses across the street, the roads that cars drive on, and the parks that you walk through every day were created or maintained by the people performing jobs in this cluster and its pathways.

Pathways include the following:

- Construction
- Design/Pre-Construction
- Maintenance/Operations

Sample occupations include the following:

- Architect
- Architectural and Civil Drafter
- Carpenter
- Civil Engineer
- Civil Engineering Technician
- Code Official
- Computer Aided Drafter (CAD)
- Concrete Finisher
- Construction Worker
- Cost Estimator
- Drywall and Ceiling Tile Installer
- Pipelayer

Figure 3-3 ▶

Construction Worker.

A construction worker builds houses and buildings.

Applying Concepts.

What skills and interests do you think might be necessary to become a construction worker?

3. Arts, Audio/Video Technology & Communications

Have you ever wanted to design, produce, exhibit, perform, write, and publish anything by making music or creating multimedia visual content? Do you love the performing arts? You could be dreaming of becoming an actress on the stage or television. Or perhaps you would rather be a world-renowned painter. Then again, your interests might direct you to journalism as the next star anchor of the evening news or as a respected blogger. You might want to be a public-relations specialist working behind the scenes to guide the careers of the rich and famous. If so, this cluster is for you.

Pathways include the following:

- Audio and Video Technology and Film
- Journalism and Broadcasting
- Performing Arts
- Printing Technology
- Telecommunications
- Visual Arts

Sample occupations include the following:

- Animation Technician
- Broadcast Technician
- Cinematographer Editor
- Graphics and Printing Equipment Operator
- Journalist
- Publisher
- Reporter
- Special Effects Technician
- Video Graphics Engineer
- Video Systems Technician

◀ **Figure 3-4**
Journalist.
Journalists report the news in newspapers and on television and radio stations.

Applying Concepts.
What skills and interests do you think might be necessary to become a journalist?

4. Business Management & Administration

Every business hires individuals to manage its operations. Businesses need office managers and accountants to ensure that the calls are answered and that the books are in order. These businesses can range in size from small convenience stores to large hospitals. They all need employees who ensure that operations run smoothly within the organization. The employees who choose careers in the Business Management & Administration cluster play this role.

Pathways include the following:

- Administrative Support
- Business Information Management
- General Management
- Human Resources Management
- Operations Management

Sample occupations include the following:

- Accountant
- Accounting Manager
- Accounts Payable Manager
- Assistant Credit Manager
- Billing Manager
- Business and Development Manager
- Chief Executive Officer
- Compensation and Benefits Manager
- Credit and Collections Manager
- Entrepreneur
- General Manager
- Payroll Manager
- Risk Manager

Figure 3-5 ▶
Payroll Manager.

A payroll manager ensures that all employees in a company receive accurate paychecks on time.

Applying Concepts.
What skills and interests do you think might be necessary to become a payroll manager?

5. Education & Training

Much thought and care go into planning, managing, and providing education as well as training and related learning-support services. People employed in this field educate children and adults. Workers in this cluster need patience and good customer service skills to be effective in their jobs.

Pathways include the following:

- Administration and Administrative Support Professional
- Support Services
- Teaching/Training

Sample occupations include the following:

- College President, Dean, Department Chair, Program Coordinator
- Corporate Trainer
- Curriculum Specialist
- Education Researcher, Test Measurement Specialist/Assessment Specialist
- Elementary and Secondary Superintendent, Principal, Administrator
- Museum Coordinator
- Post-Secondary Administrator
- Supervisor and Instructional Coordinator
- Teacher

◀ **Figure 3-6**
Corporate Trainer.

A corporate trainer provides short, specialized courses to employees of large and small firms.

Applying Concepts.

What skills and interests does a corporate trainer need?

6. Finance

Finance is often linked to banking, but the industry has many facets because there are so many different types of financial institutions. Employees in this field provide services for financial and investment planning, banking, insurance products, business/financial management, and more. This field is directly connected to the stock market, which monitors the economic stability of the world's financial markets.

Pathways include the following:

- Banking Services
- Business Finance
- Insurance
- Securities and Investments

Sample occupations include the following:

- Brokerage Representative
- Development Officer
- Insurance Agent
- Investment Advisor
- Personal Financial Advisor
- Sales Agent, Securities and Commodities
- Securities/Investments Analyst
- Stock Broker
- Tax Preparation Specialist

Figure 3-7 ▶
Insurance Agent.

An insurance agent sells insurance to people who need it.

Applying Concepts.
What skills and interests do you think might be necessary to become an insurance agent?

7. Government & Public Administration

Local, state, and federal governments need employees to perform functions that include governance—or making decisions about how government will act—national security, foreign service, planning, revenue flows and taxation, regulation, and management and administration. For example, the Secretary of State is the chief diplomat for the United States. As chief diplomat, the Secretary of State represents the United

States at important meetings on the world stage. People employed in this field typically develop strong communication, problem-solving skills, and critical-thinking skills.

Pathways include the following:

- Foreign Service
- Governance
- National Security
- Planning
- Public Management and Administration
- Regulation
- Revenue and Taxation

Sample occupations include the following:

- Ambassador
- Airborne Warning/Control Specialist
- Assessor
- Congressional Aide
- Diplomatic Courier
- Equal Opportunity Representative
- Legislative Aide
- National Security Advisor
- President
- Senator
- Special Forces Officer
- Tax Attorney
- Vice President

◄ **Figure 3-8**
Ambassador.

Ambassadors represent their governments in foreign countries.

Applying Concepts.

What skills and interests do you think might be necessary to become an ambassador?

8. Health Science

Health Science cluster employees plan, manage, and deliver therapeutic services, diagnostic services, health informatics, support services, and biotechnology research and development to individuals throughout the United States. They work in cities, suburbs, rural areas, and other communities to provide crucial services to a diverse client base. Individuals employed in these fields take on legal responsibilities, must have strong ethics, and often use their technical skills.

Pathways include the following:

- Biotechnology Research and Development
- Diagnostic Services
- Health Informatics
- Support Services
- Therapeutic Services

Sample occupations include the following:

- Acupuncturist
- Anesthesia Technologist/Technician
- Anesthesiologist/Assistant
- Art/Music/Dance Therapist
- Athletic Trainer
- Audiologist
- Certified Nursing Assistant
- Chiropractic Assistant
- Chiropractor
- Dental Assistant/Hygienist
- Dental Lab Technician
- Dietitian/Nutritionist
- Doctor
- Nurse

Figure 3-9 ▶
Doctor.

Doctors consult with their patients about their ailments and recommend treatments they need to recover from illnesses.

Applying Concepts.

What skills and interests do you think might be necessary to become a doctor?

9. Hospitality & Tourism

Hospitality and tourism careers comprise the world's largest industry. Its workers manage, market, and operate restaurants and other food services, lodging, attractions, recreation events, and travel-related services. They are very busy people who cater to the needs of individuals that visit your town, city, state, and other countries of the world as tourists. If you enjoy a vacation, a large part of the reason why is the services these employees perform.

Pathways include the following:

- Lodging
- Recreation, Amusements and Attractions
- Restaurants and Food/Beverage Services
- Travel and Tourism

Sample occupations include the following:

- Bell Captain
- Catering and Banquet Manager
- Chef
- Concierge
- Convention Planner
- Gaming and Casino Manager
- Hotel Manager
- Kitchen Manager
- Restaurant Owner
- Service Manager
- Tour Guide
- Travel Agent

◀ **Figure 3-10**
Hotel Manager.

Hotel managers are responsible for making sure guests are happy and satisfied.

Applying Concepts.

What skills and interests do you think might be necessary to become a hotel manager?

10. Human Services

Human services careers prepare individuals for employment in pathways that relate to families and human needs. They work in day-care centers, drive the elderly and disabled to their appointments, provide massages in spas, and counsel those in need of emotional support. Their clients include students having problems in school, brides needing beautiful hairstyles for a wedding, congregants looking for guidance from their clergy, and homeless families trying to find housing. Working in this field can be very rewarding if you like to interact with people. The work that you do will help children and adults, but you must have a lot of compassion and patience to be effective in this field.

Pathways include the following:

- Consumer Services
- Counseling and Mental Health Services
- Early Childhood Development and Services
- Family and Community Services
- Personal Care Services

Sample occupations include the following:

- Barber
- Clergy
- Embalmer
- Guidance Counselor
- Hairdresser/Cosmetologist
- Manicurist and Pedicurist
- Nanny
- Social Worker

Figure 3-11 ▶
Social Worker.
Social workers help people focus on improving their lives.

Applying Concepts.
What skills and interests do you think might be necessary to become a social worker?

11. Information Technology

Individuals employed in this cluster build the bridges between people and technology. They design, develop, support, and manage hardware, software, multimedia, and systems integration services that allow you to have access to the Internet, operate your remote control device, and use your mobile devices Most people in this field have a strong mathematical and scientific academic foundation and are willing to learn information technology applications and systems. Its employees are constantly working on cutting-edge technology aimed at making life easier for everyone.

Pathways include the following:

- Information Support and Services
- Network Systems
- Programming and Software Development
- Web and Digital Communications

Sample occupations include the following:

- Analyst
- Computer Programmer
- Computer Security Specialist
- Computer Technician
- Database Developer
- Modeler
- Network Designer
- Network Developer
- Web Administrator

◀ **Figure 3-12**
Computer Technician.
Computer technicians work to build or repair computer systems.

Applying Concepts.
What skills and interests do you think might be necessary to become a computer technician?

12. Law, Public Safety, Corrections & Security

Individuals who plan, manage, and provide legal, public safety, protective services, and homeland security, including professional and technical support services, play important roles in your community. They are police officers, lawyers, security guards, and firefighters, and they deliver the services that make you feel safer in times of crisis.

Pathways include the following:

- Correction Services
- Emergency and Fire Management Services
- Law Enforcement Services
- Legal Services
- Security and Protective Services

Sample occupations include the following:

- Arbitrator, Mediator and Conciliator
- Correctional Officer and Jailer
- Detective and Investigator
- Dispatcher
- Firefighter
- Immigration and Custom Inspector
- Judge
- Lawyer
- Paramedic
- Police Officer

Figure 3-13 ▶
Police Officer.

Police officers keep you safe, respond to emergencies, and issue citations to people who break the law.

Applying Concepts.

What skills and interests do you think might be necessary to become a police officer?

13. Manufacturing

Products ranging from plastic bottles to cars are built in factories and developed in manufacturing plants all over the world through specific processes. Those employed in the Manufacturing cluster perform the steps that go into intermediate or final products and related professional and technical support activities such as production planning and control, maintenance, and manufacturing/process engineering. They are in a field for individuals who love to use their hands to make things that are important to daily living such as cars, cabinets, or books.

Pathways include the following:

- Health, Safety and Environmental Assurance
- Logistics and Inventory Control
- Maintenance, Installation and Repair
- Manufacturing
- Production
- Production Process Development
- Quality Assurance

Sample occupations include the following:

- Assembler
- Automated Manufacturing Technician
- Bookbinder
- Calibration Technician
- Electrical Installer and Repairer
- Electromechanical Equipment Assembler
- Logistical Engineer
- Machinist

◀ **Figure 3-14**
Factory Worker.

Factory workers assemble a wide variety of products.

Applying Concepts.

What skills and interests do you think might be necessary to become a factory worker?

14. Marketing

Marketing professionals plan, manage, and perform activities to reach organizational objectives. Their work can range from handing out flyers to publicizing an event or working in an office to researching consumers' spending habits. They work for small or large firms or independently as contractors in a number of roles where they develop their leadership and teamwork abilities as well as their analytical skills.

Pathways include the following:

- Marketing Communications
- Marketing Management
- Marketing Research
- Merchandising
- Professional Sales

Sample occupations include the following:

- Account Executive
- Creative Director
- Key Account Manager
- Market Research Analyst
- Merchandise Displayer and Window Trimmer
- Real Estate Agent
- Sales Representative
- Store Manager
- Telemarketer
- Wholesale and Retail Buyer

Figure 3-15 ▶
Store Manager.

Store managers oversee the day-to-day operations of the stores, shops, and retail outlets in which you buy things.

Applying Concepts.

What skills and interests do you think might be necessary to become a store manager?

15. Science, Technology, Engineering & Mathematics

Can you see yourself planning, managing, and providing scientific research as a career? Are you interested in laboratory and testing services or in research and development? If you answer yes to any of these questions, then take a closer look at these pathways and occupations.

Pathways include the following:

- Engineering and Technology
- Science and Math

Sample occupations include the following:

- Anthropologist
- Biologist
- Geneticist
- Mathematician
- Nuclear Chemist
- Paleontologist
- Physicist
- Statistician
- Technical Writer

◄ **Figure 3-16**
Physicist.
Academic institutions, government laboratories, and private industry hire physicists to study matter or energy within the universe.

Applying Concepts.
What skills and interests do you think might be necessary to become a physicist?

16. Transportation, Distribution & Logistics

How does food get to your supermarket shelves or fuel to your local gas station? A lot of planning goes into the transportation and shipping of products around the globe. Many people work behind the scenes to coordinate, manage, and move these goods to their final destinations by arranging for their transportation by road, pipeline, air, rail, and water. They also oversee the related professional and technical support services that are a part of the process. Beyond planning for the transportation of goods, there is another related sector in this field: urban planning. Planners decide where houses, parks, and stores should be built so that neighborhoods are organized in a way that is convenient for everyone living in them. Here are the pathways and some of the occupations that make up this cluster.

Pathways include the following:

- Facility and Mobile Equipment Maintenance
- Health, Safety and Environmental Management
- Logistics Planning and Management Services
- Sales and Services
- Transportation Operations
- Transportation Systems/Infrastructure Planning, Management and Regulation
- Warehousing and Distribution Center Operations

Sample occupations include the following:

- Air Traffic Controller
- Driver
- Industrial and Packaging Engineer
- Logistician
- Storage and Distribution Manager
- Surveying and Mapping Technician
- Traffic Manager
- Traffic, Shipping, and Receiving Clerk
- Urban and Regional Planner
- Warehouse Manager

Figure 3-17 ▶
Urban Planner.

Urban planners oversee how land is used by and in communities.

Applying Concepts.

What skills and interests do you think might be necessary to become an urban planner?

 **Apply Your Knowledge** Think back to your investigation of 3M and the Post-It Note. Which career cluster do you think Spencer Silver was originally interested in? What makes you think he made an impact on the field and his company?

CAREER COMPETENCIES

Utilize Resources That Can Contribute to Professional Development

You can use career search resources to learn about the types of work that match your interest, skills and abilities.

Resources at School

Some of the best resources for learning about career opportunities are available at school. Your guidance and career counselors have books, computer programs, videos, and lists of useful websites that provide information about types of careers. Your teachers can help you identify your strengths and abilities and match them with career requirements.

School clubs and career and technical organizations may also have information about types of careers. A business club might invite a representative from the community to speak about his or her occupation. An organization such as Family, Career and Community Leaders of America (FCCLA) or Health Occupations Students of America (HOSA) has career-related projects and activities. These organizations also provide members with opportunities to develop their leadership, teamwork, management, and citizenship skills.

The Bureau of Labor Statistics

The U.S. Bureau of Labor Statistics (BLS) is a government agency responsible for tracking information about jobs and workers. Its website has a section specifically for students (www.bls.gov/audience/students.htm). It includes information on more than 60 occupations, including descriptions of responsibilities, education requirements, salary ranges, and job outlook. A job outlook includes statistics and trends about whether the job is in an industry that is growing or shrinking.

The BLS also publishes the *Occupational Outlook Handbook* (OOH) in printed and online editions. The OOH describes more than 200 occupations, including responsibilities, working conditions, education requirements, salary ranges, and job outlook. You may find it easier to use the online version at www.bls.gov/ooh. Online, you can search for specific careers, use the alphabetical listing to locate a career that interests you, or browse through the career clusters. As you look through the OOH, you might want to take notes on the information you find, and record the source—including the page number in the printed copy or the web page address online.

Resources in Your Community

One of the best ways to learn about different careers is from someone who is employed. For example, you can job-shadow someone who has a job you find interesting. Job shadowing means to follow someone around at work for a day or part of a day. By job shadowing, you can see exactly what the responsibilities, tasks, and rewards are for a particular job.

Informational interviews are also a good way to explore careers. An informational interview gives you the opportunity to sit down with someone who is employed in a career or industry that interests you. You can ask specific questions about the job responsibilities, see the work environment, and maybe even meet other people in the industry.

Talking directly to someone in the job can teach you a lot more than you can learn from a book or online. For example, a roofer can tell you what it feels like to work on top of a house, 30 feet above the ground. Your career counselor may be able to help you arrange an informational interview.

Here are some steps for managing an informational interview:

- Call and make an appointment.
- Create and write down the questions before your interview.
- Arrive on time for the interview.
- Write down answers to your questions.
- Thank the person and send a follow-up thank-you note.

Career Skills in Action

Explore the resources discussed above to learn more about careers that interest you.

- Identify two to three career and technical student organizations that interest you. Write a summary paragraph about each that explains its mission or purpose, the skills it can help a member develop, and how participating in it can help you in your career pursuits.

- Select a career that interests you and gather information from the BLS website on responsibilities, education requirements, salary range, and the job outlook.

- Identify an entrepreneur in your career area of interest and set up an informational interview. Develop a list of at least 10 questions to ask the interviewee.

Share your findings with your peers and teacher.

3.3 Using an Entrepreneurial Mindset in Career Exploration

After seeing that list of career clusters, you may be even more confused on what career path to follow. Trying things out first can help you understand the requirements of a career, determine your interest level, and develop the skills you need to do a job.

As a student, one way to test a career track out is to take an internship. **Internships** are work programs that provide practical, on-the-job training in a business setting and are available to high school and college students. Another word for internships is **apprenticeships**. In some apprenticeships, a technical or trade skill is taught, such as carpentry or plumbing. Internships and apprenticeships are usually short-term programs that can last from a few weeks to a year. During this time, you may or may not be paid for your time. Even so, the experience and skills you gain will help you later on to select your career, either as an employee or an entrepreneur.

◀ **Figure 3-18**
Internship.

Working as an intern or apprentice provides practical experience for students.

Predicting.

What kinds of useful business knowledge might you learn through an internship?

In addition to internships and apprenticeship there are lots of ways to gain career-related and skills-related experience.

- **Volunteers** are unpaid workers. Many volunteer positions are in service organizations, such as homeless shelters, health clinics, or animal shelters. Generally organizations that rely on volunteer support are nonprofits or have little additional money. You can do direct service or help develop mailings or make phone calls. If you're interested in a career area, you can find an organization in the field to gain experience.

- **Mentoring programs** pair experienced workers with students. The mentor acts as an advisor, providing advice, job contacts, and support in skill building.

- **Job shadowing** allows you to follow an experienced worker through his or her workday to see the specific responsibilities and tasks required on the job.

- **School clubs and organizations** offer opportunities to develop leadership and management skills.

- **Entrepreneurial thinking** can help you develop your own job in a select career area and gain valuable experience.

While participating in any of these career exploration activities, it is also always important to keep applying your entrepreneurial mindset for potential intrapreneurial opportunities. For example, let's say you are interested in food, and might want a career in the Hospitality & Tourism career cluster. Traditional career pathways might include training to be a chef, or owning your own restaurant. However, you could also act as an intrapreneur and invent the following:

- Chef hat and clothes that keep the wearer cool in the hot temperatures in the kitchen
- A kitchen tool that better helps with food preparation or storage
- An app that automates the seating and reservation process for a restaurant

All of these ideas are items that you could invent without having to start your own restaurant. Utilize your time during internships to find out what problems exist for employees in this career cluster. As you develop your entrepreneurial mindset, you will learn to look for problems and potential solutions wherever you go!

 **Apply Your Knowledge**   Think back to your investigation of 3M and the Post-It Note. How do you think it helped Spencer to work for 3M before coming up with his idea? What other work experiences do you think he had before his big idea? Explain your answers.

APPLICATION TO BUSINESS PLANNING

Career Cluster Identification

Problem-solving is an important part of being an entrepreneur. All careers and businesses face problems and challenges every day.

- Review the career clusters and select one that you have a passion for or at least are interested in.
- Brainstorm problems or challenges you might face in a career within the cluster and write them down in your notebook. For example, in tourism, a reservations associate may struggle with a system that crashes all the time.
- Start to think of ideas that could solve these common problems for when you start coming up with a business idea in the next unit.

3 ASSESSMENT

REVIEWING OBJECTIVES

1. Explain the value of learning entrepreneurship in relation to one's own career path.
2. List the 16 career clusters and entrepreneurial pathways within each.
3. Identify ways to utilize the entrepreneurial mindset while acting as an intrapreneur.

CRITICAL THINKING

Develop a vision and mission for your life now as a student. Based on that, develop a vision and mission for your future life.

ENTREPRENEURIAL THINKING EXERCISE: FUTURE ORIENTATION

Think back to your investigation of the Post-It Note. Imagine that you have the opportunity to learn about the experience by interviewing Spencer Silver and Art Shay. You plan to interview them to learn about their advice on career pathways, required skills, as well as their entrepreneurial journey. Develop 6–8 interview questions you would ask them and write a paragraph describing why you selected the questions.

EXTENSION ACTIVITIES

Entrepreneurship & Literacy Skills

Complete the following task to demonstrate your understanding of entrepreneurship:

Grades 9–12: Select a problem to solve that a person may face in a career cluster. Identify and write down as many solutions as possible. Develop a short report that describes why you believe your solution solves the problem and how this can benefit the entire career cluster. Finally, explain whether you would solve this problem as an entrepreneur or an intrapreneur. Be prepared to share your findings with your peers.

4 SOCIAL ENTREPRENEURSHIP

OBJECTIVES

- Identify social problems solved by entrepreneurs.
- Explain the purpose of having a mission statement for a business.
- List examples of socially responsible business practices.

NFTE Entrepreneurial Mindset Characteristic Focus

☑ Critical Thinking & Problem Solving

National Entrepreneurship Standards

- **A.01** Explain the need for entrepreneurial discovery
- **A.02** Discuss entrepreneurial discovery processes
- **B.12** Describe desirable entrepreneurial personality traits
- **C.01** Explain the role of business in society
- **C.05** Determine issues and trends in business
- **C.09** Describe the need for and impact of ethical business practices
- **H.01** Evaluate career opportunities based on current/future economy
- **O.05** Develop business mission

Common Career Technical Core Standards

- **BM-MGT.2** Access, evaluate and disseminate information for business decision making.
- **CRP.5** Consider the environmental, social and economic impacts of decisions.
- **CRP.9** Model integrity, ethical leadership and effective management.

National Entrepreneurship Standards: Career Competencies

☑ **H7** Utilize job-search strategies

LESSON VOCABULARY

- carbon footprint
- carbon offset
- cause-related marketing
- corporate social responsibility
- ethical sourcing
- green company
- greenwashing
- mission statement
- nonprofit organization
- philanthropy
- sponsorship
- sustainable
- sustainable economic development
- sustainability
- vision statement

ENTREPRENEURIAL INVESTIGATION

Earlier in this unit, you were introduced to Whole Foods Market, a supermarket that specializes in providing natural and organic foods. Part of what made Whole Foods so successful was their attempt to run their business differently. Instead of running their business just to make money, their founder, John Mackey, also wanted to make a positive difference. John truly believed that a business should not just be about making as much money as possible, but also making sure everyone involved—from customers to employees to the community—benefits as well.

Do some research on John Mackey and the core values of Whole Foods to answer the following questions:

- What are some of the core values that Whole Foods believes in?
- How does Whole Foods help other people or the community?
- Do you agree or disagree with John's beliefs that entrepreneurs should "give back"? Explain your answer.

Be prepared to share your responses with your teacher and class.

4.1 Doing Well by Doing Good

Corporate Social Responsibility

As you have seen so far, one of the key behaviors of having an entrepreneurial mindset is being able to solve problems. However, there has been a shift in the types of problems that entrepreneurs try to solve. Many have started to go a step further to help solve larger societal problems, such as: hunger, poverty, and education. As you look to develop your entrepreneurial mindset, you should begin to look at ways to solve societal problems as well.

Let's look at a couple of examples. Barny Haughton is owner and executive chef at the upscale Bordeaux Quay Restaurant in Bristol, England. Katie VandenBerg owns Eli's Coffee Shop in the small town of Morton, Illinois. What do these two people, in very different circumstances and half a world apart, have in common? They both are entrepreneurs. And they both demonstrate **corporate social responsibility**—their respective businesses act in ways that balance profit and growth with the good of society. Corporate social responsibility is based on the concept that the relationship between business and society ought to go deeper than economics. Barny designed Bordeaux Quay as a model of resource conservation, from its recycling program to its low-flush toilets (which are refilled by captured rainwater). At Eli's Coffee Shop, Katie serves only ethically sourced coffee. **Ethical sourcing** means buying from suppliers who provide safe working conditions and respect workers' rights.

The examples of Barny Haughton and Katie VandenBerg demonstrate that corporate social responsibility is an opportunity for entrepreneurs at every level. What's more, it's not just an afterthought, separate from daily operations. Increasingly, behaving in a way that is socially responsible is part of how a company does business. In some cases, it is a company's business.

Corporate social responsibility also makes good business sense. Whether it's a large corporation sponsoring a charity telethon or a local supermarket offering a refund for using canvas shopping bags, corporate social responsibility often translates into profits. This advantage for business is sometimes described as "doing well by doing good."

The good a socially responsible company does can impact people, the community, and the environment. What's important to note is that one company does not need to do everything to be considered socially responsible. In fact, many businesses can be socially responsible just by running their business every day. We will look at examples of this in this chapter.

Corporate Social Responsibility	=	Doing Well by Doing Good
Burt's Bees	=	Sustainable Packaging
Method Cleaning Supplies	=	Non-Hazardous Chemicals
TOMS Shoes	=	Donation for each Pair Sold

◀ **Figure 4-1**
Corporate Social Responsibility.
Social responsibility should be the foundation of every business.

Applying Concepts.
What are small ways that new businesses can do good while doing well?

Mission and Vision Statement

Regardless of how an entrepreneur is socially responsible, he or she must consider their social responsibility plan and how to communicate this to their customers. Often companies communicate their social responsibility vision in a company mission statement.

The mission statement describes why a company exists and guides a company's work and actions. By connecting the mission statement and social responsibility, the company ensures it is true to its central purpose of solving both a societal and a business problem.

Here is the mission statement for the social business TOMS® Shoes: "To make life more comfortable. Towards that end, TOMS not only ensures that every pair of its slip-ons are soft, breathable, and lightweight for an optimal fit—the company has also charged itself with the responsibility of providing for the comfort of children in impoverished regions worldwide. For every pair of TOMS shoes purchased online or at retail, the company will provide a pair to a child in need." In this mission TOMS shoes describes the three key components of the mission statement:

1. **The company goal**—To create comfortable shoes and comfort to impoverished children.

2. **How the company will achieve this goal**—Donate a pair of soft, breathable, and lightweight shoes to disadvantaged youth.

3. **How this appeals to customers**—Describing a quality product that makes a customer feel good for buying the product.

A good mission statement should also support a larger <mark>vision statement</mark>, or the ultimate goal of the business. While the mission statement lays out the specifics of how the business will operate, the vision can be an overarching goal to reach. Sometimes the vision statement might even seem impossible, but provides a driving reason for the business to stay in business. In the case of TOMS Shoes, it would be to ensure that everyone in the world has access to comfortable footware.

Responsibility to Individuals

Corporate social responsibility builds from the ground up. It can affect all the individuals who are connected in some way to the business: the employees, customers and suppliers.

In a way, your first responsibility to all these individuals, as well as to yourself, is to run the business to the best of your abilities. All of these people rely on your company for something. Your employees count on you for their incomes. Your customers trust you to supply a quality product or service. Your investors and creditors have trusted your business judgment and rely on you to fulfill your financial obligations. Treating a business seriously and making well-thought-out decisions shows that you take your responsibilities to heart.

Employees

Entrepreneurs have legal obligations to provide a safe workplace and fair employment policies. (You'll read more about these in later chapters.) If you've ever held a job yourself, however, you know that these conditions are only part of what employees need and want.

Figure 4-2 ▶

Employers Value Employees.

Employees would rather work for an employer who trusts and respects them.

Applying Concepts.

If you were an employer, how would you show that you respected and trusted your employees?

On a practical level, employees need the tools to do the jobs expected of them. Imagine the director of a preschool asking a teacher's aide to lead a class in an art activity without supplying the paper, crayons, paints, glue, or other necessary materials. Or suppose the director of the preschool asked the aide to plan a menu for a child with diabetes, without knowing whether the aide had any knowledge of nutrition or special diets. The results could be frustrating and even dangerous.

On the other hand, employees also need trust. They need respect for their skills and the freedom to use them. Trust may come easily when you have only a few employees and work with them closely. The test comes in giving them responsibilities without supervision. Yet that's a necessary step if a business is to grow.

Some employers are cautious about trusting workers, especially with jobs that encourage them to learn new skills. They don't want employees to outgrow the job and move on to another competing business. In contrast, other entrepreneurs feel a responsibility for helping employees grow personally and professionally. They might practice job rotation, for instance, training workers for different jobs in the company. These business owners value employees' personal satisfaction—and enjoy the advantage of having a backup to fill a position in an emergency.

Employees also deserve consideration for personal needs. If you're needed at home to care for a sick child, or if your car is in the shop, or if the bus was late, you can appreciate an understanding and considerate boss. Employers must recognize that an employee may have a spouse, children, and day-to-day responsibilities. Employers must respect and understand their employees' needs to meet these commitments. In fact, companies that are rated by employees as the best places to work usually help employees balance work and personal needs.

Customers

As with employees, business owners are bound by law to treat customers fairly. A wise entrepreneur, however, understands that the ethical obligation goes beyond these legal minimums. As a practical consideration, attracting new customers also costs more than maintaining existing ones. The following four qualities, which cost nothing to put into practice, mark a responsible relationship with customers:

- **Honesty.** Be honest and transparent in all areas. Inform customers about your products, both the advantages and drawbacks. If you offer a service, describe your qualifications and abilities accurately. Carefully estimate the time and cost of completing a project. Admit to mistakes without offering excuses.

- **Respect.** Customers come to you hoping you can meet their needs or solve their problems. Their needs and problems are important to them, and they should be to you, as well. Take customer complaints seriously. These are opportunities to improve your business. Research suggests that only one of every fifty dissatisfied customers complains to the merchant. When you fix a situation that made one customer unhappy, you may be saving forty-nine other customers from the same frustration—and keeping them as customers.

- **Accessibility.** Be available when you promise to be. Keep to the business hours you advertise. Honor your appointments with clients and don't be late. Give customers contact information where they can reach you with questions. Take the initiative on keeping them updated about the status of an order or work in progress.

- **Attention.** Whether you're selling a single light bulb to a walk-in customer or installing solar panels on a university library, focus your attention on the customer with whom you are working at the moment. Be present for that customer. Don't be distracted by your cell phone or other obligations.

Suppliers

Acting responsibly toward suppliers or vendors carries its own reward. The people who sell the materials your business needs are also those who can advise you on making the best choices and using the materials wisely.

It should go without saying that you owe suppliers timely payment in the amount and method on which you agreed. You also need to respect their decisions on pricing. Although it is acceptable to attempt to negotiate with suppliers, you have the option of going elsewhere if you're not satisfied. Complaining or suggesting that the supplier is being unfair or dishonest is not appropriate.

If you mislead suppliers into thinking you might do business with them when you are really using them as "bargaining chips" to get another supplier to lower a price, you are not bargaining in good faith.

Figure 4-3 ▶
Supplier.
Acting responsibly toward suppliers or vendors carries its own reward.

Applying Concepts.
How can suppliers and vendors help a business owner?

Suppliers appreciate cooperation in making a transaction as efficient as possible. Have a clear idea of what you want so you can help the supplier sell it to you. Have realistic expectations for the supplier's policies when it affects your satisfaction as a customer. For example, if you order a product, expect a reasonable amount of added time and money for shipping and handling. Suppliers deserve to hear that you're a satisfied customer—or that you are not. They benefit from knowing when a product or service could be improved. Give a supplier the chance to keep you as a customer before you switch to another. Staying with the same suppliers builds helpful relationships that will serve you well over time.

Investors and Creditors

Investors and creditors provide the money to start and run a business and, along with it, an emotional boost. After all, people don't invest or loan money unless they believe in both the idea behind the business and the entrepreneur whose work will make it a success. Likewise, vendors who extend credit are showing faith that you'll be able to pay for your purchase.

Investors are not guaranteed a financial return, but they have a right to regular, and timely, communication. Understandably, they will want to know the status of their investments. Investors with experience in your field of business may be equally ready to offer advice and help. They might put you in touch with other contacts or suggest other resources. Often investors actually assume some control of the business in exchange for their financial support. (You'll read more about different types of investors in a later unit.)

Whatever the relationship, you need to give an investor's input the weight it deserves. A friend with little understanding of your business (but a lot of faith in you) who has made a modest investment and the professional investor who has bankrolled half of your business have both contributed to your potential success. Both deserve respect.

Unlike investors, creditors are owed a return on their money, usually with interest. They too need ongoing updates, especially if the business is struggling. Again, this is to your benefit. Creditors are as eager to be paid back as you are to get out of debt. If they see that you're working hard but still having trouble, they're sometimes willing to rework the terms to make repayment more manageable. Communication with investors and creditors alike must be based on honesty and transparency. Taking money based on false expectations may be illegal and, in any case, can hurt you and your business.

Apply Your Knowledge   What are the four groups of individuals that entrepreneurs should build a responsible relationship with? Think back to your investigation of Whole Foods. How do they build relationships with these individuals?

ENTREPRENEURIAL CASE STUDY: CRITICAL THINKING & PROBLEM SOLVING

 ## Michael K. Pearson— Union Packaging

Creating a Triple Bottom Line

Originally from West Philadelphia, Michael (Mike) K. Pearson created a plan for a business while living in Philadelphia's Fairmount neighborhood in 1996. By 1999, Mike had started this business and became the CEO and President of Union Packaging, LLC (www. unionpkg.com). Initially, the plan was to manufacture FDA-compliant paperboard food packaging. Food around the nation started being packaged, shipped, and served in cartons made by Union

Michael K. Pearson.

Packaging. Soon, the business found even more success when operations shifted to focus on socially responsible practices. Now, Union Packaging continues to grow its expertise in eco-friendly biodegradable food paperboard packaging. Mike also now gauges the success of his business with a triple bottom line. This measures sustainability through financial, social, and environmental performance measures.

Responsibility to the Environment

While trying to grow his business, Mike found a way to make his packaging company unique. Many packaging companies were wasteful in how they made their packaging, using many non-recyclable materials. He decided to dedicate his company to manufacturing earth-friendly paper packaging for the fast-food and foodservice industries. This was done by utilizing water-based printing technologies. Union Packaging also uses paperboards sourced from environmentally responsible paper mills and frequently utilizes stock made from recycled fibers.

Today, Union Packaging utilizes this earth-friendly converting technology to provide competitively priced paperboard cartons. Their clients have grown to include quick service restaurants, supermarkets, convenience stores, and food service companies. Mike's business has grown from his initial plan to supplying some of the largest companies in North America, along with nine Caribbean and six Latin America countries. His efforts paid off, as Union Packaging was ranked as one of the fastest-growing, privately-held businesses in the Philadelphia region. Mike's business also made it onto Black Enterprise's 100 Largest Black Business in the United States in 2013.

Giving Back to the Community

Mike's commitment to socially responsible business practices goes beyond using earth-friendly materials. As both a minority- and veteran-owned business, Mike has dedicated himself to acting as a consultant to other minority-owned businesses. Mike employees of around 100 people who have been actively brought on from non-traditional sources. The company's workforce is extremely diverse at 60 percent African-American, 20 percent White, 15 percent Asian and 5 percent Latino. He also established partnerships with nonprofits so that his business could hire Philadelphia Public Schools graduates with learning differences, job-ready participants from the Philadelphia Prison System, and documented new arrivals from sixteen nations around the world. His commitment to customers, employees, and the community has been rewarded by his business's success, and the numerous awards and honors he has received.

Thinking and Acting Like an Entrepreneur

- How is Mike's business an example of socially responsible business practices, or, "doing well while doing good"?

- In what ways does Mike demonstrate a responsibility to employees/customers? The environment? The community?

- How does Mike demonstrate the entrepreneurial mindset skill of critical thinking and problem solving?

4.2 Taking Responsibility for the Environment

Another contemporary trend is running a business in ways that are friendly to the environment. A **green company** is one that adopts business practices aimed at protecting or improving the environment. For instance, Excellent Packaging & Supply distributes products made from green resources. One of these products is SpudWare, utensils made from corn and potato starch that can withstand boiling water. Another example of a green company is SELCO-India. It provides solar-powered lighting to mostly rural areas in India and other developing countries.

Entrepreneurs, like the rest of us, want to preserve our environment for the future. Many businesses go green to support our environment, and for entrepreneurs being environmentally green can be profitable. Surveys and sales figures show that consumers look favorably on businesses that show a commitment to protecting the environment.

Figure 4-4 ▶
Green Business Practices.

Green businesses are friendly to the environment.

Applying Concepts.

Do you know of any green businesses? What makes them environmentally friendly?

Environmentally Friendly Enterprises

Like other societal trends, concern for the environment is creating new industries and expanding older ones. Opportunities for the individual with imagination and initiative—in other words, the entrepreneur— seem to arise almost daily.

For example, it is important that economic development does not harm society or the environment but ensures that human and natural resources are maintained for future generations. This is referred to as **sustainable economic development**, or **sustainability**. The goal of sustainability is to maintain and perhaps even to improve the quality of human life and the quality of the environment. By using recyclable packaging in their business practices, entrepreneurs support sustainability by considering the welfare of people and the environment.

What entrepreneurial ventures can you see in the following four fields?

- **Sustainable Design.** Traditionally, products were made and used without much thought for their long-term impact on people or the planet. In contrast, design that is **sustainable** meets the planet's current needs while preserving resources for future generations. Sustainable design ranges from planned, "walkable" cities that reduce the need for automobiles, to fashions made from natural fabrics and dyes.

- **Alternative Energy.** Researchers are working to make alternatives to oil and coal—such as solar, wind, and hydrogen power—more efficient. They're testing newer forms of biofuels extracted from corn, sugar cane, and even vegetable oil left over from frying foods. Investors are particularly excited about the potential of these clean technologies and have sunk hundreds of millions of dollars into their development.

◀ **Figure 4-5**

Sustainable Business Practices.

Sustainable businesses improve the quality of human life and the environment.

Applying Concepts.

Why is it important for all businesses to try to be sustainable?

- **Organics.** Concerns about personal health, as well as the environment, have increased interest in organic products, those made from crops and animals that are raised without manufactured chemicals. Organic produce, grains, and meats make up a small but steadily growing segment of the food market. Independently-owned producers and natural food stores generate a large percentage of those sales. Organic personal care items are also gaining popularity.

- **Fair Trade.** Fair trade is a way of doing business that is based on principles of social and environmental responsibility and promoting sustainable growth. Most producers involved in fair trade are small farmers and skilled crafters in developing countries. These micro-entrepreneurs form cooperatives to set prices and product standards. Most fair trade items are then sold through a network of independent wholesalers and retailers. Sales of fair trade goods have risen worldwide by double digits in the last twenty years as consumers grow more aware of the impact of their spending decisions.

◀ **Figure 4-6**

Fair Trade Products.

Through fair trade, entrepreneurs help each other succeed.

Applying Concepts.

Why do you think entrepreneurs are especially important to the economies of small, developing nations?

Energy-Efficient Workplaces

It's not feasible for all companies to be green. However, many businesses and entrepreneurs utilize green practices to save our environment and money while attracting socially conscious customers. The most efficient, money-saving appliances, equipment, and electrical-system components bear the Energy Star® label. To earn this designation, an item must meet strict specifications. For example, suppose you own a copying service. Using Energy Star®-designated copiers can cut electrical costs by 25 percent. They also power down when not in use, saving even more money over standard models. You could post signs advertising these facts to customers, along with the hint that they could save money and reduce waste by printing on both sides of the paper. To add appeal, you might offer a low-cost or no-cost, environmentally helpful service—such as placing containers for customers to drop off ink cartridges for recycling.

Figure 4-7 ▶

Energy-Efficient Designations.

The Energy Star label (left) and Recycling Symbol (right). Many companies advertise that their products or services are energy-efficient.

Applying Concepts.

In what ways is it beneficial to communicate that a business is energy-efficient to others?

Here are some additional ways that a business can lower its expenses, while also helping the environment:

- **Get into the recycling loop.** First, recycle everything your community has facilities for. Most localities have paper and plastic recycling programs. Your community also might have businesses that recondition older computers and other office equipment. Then use recycled and recyclable products when available. Look for the triangular arrow-chasing-arrow symbol on containers. Read product packaging, being alert for any indication that it is recyclable. Tell suppliers that you prefer these items.

- **Do business electronically.** Reduce paper as much as possible. Take advantage of vendors' toll-free telephone numbers and websites to place orders. If you send out newsletters to regular customers, encourage them to take an e-mail version instead of paper.

- **Buy supplies in bulk.** Items sold in large quantities usually cost less per piece and may use less packaging.

- **Replace incandescent light bulbs with fluorescent ones.** Compact fluorescent light bulbs have a longer life and greater efficiency and will save money in the long run.

- **Use environmentally friendly transportation.** You might adjust schedules or business hours to take advantage of carpooling or public transportation. Offer employees low-cost incentives, such as a gift card from a bicycle shop for those who ride to work. Encourage the use of hybrids or other energy-efficient cars.

You may have heard of the **carbon footprint**, which measures the amount of carbon you use and thus release into the atmosphere. Carbon is a byproduct of burning coal and oil-based fuels. A combination of factors—such as the type of car you drive, how much you drive, the method of heating your home—determine your personal carbon footprint. One recent development in environmental responsibility is the practice of buying carbon offsets. Through a **carbon offset** you "buy" a certain amount of carbon, usually at a per-ton price, to help offset your carbon footprint. Both nonprofit groups and for-profit traders, who invest the money in renewable energy producers or resource-conservation projects, sell offsets.

◀ **Figure 4-8**

Compact Fluorescent Light Bulb.

CFL bulbs can make a big impact on the environment.

Applying Concepts.

Businesses can find small ways to do good, even if they when they are just starting off.

Following the guidelines above for energy efficiency is the surest way to lighten a business's carbon footprint. If your company leaves a heavy footprint because you do a lot of automobile travel, for instance, you might want to look at carbon offsets as an option. You might find that a company you do business with has an innovative carbon offset program.

As you learned in the prior section, it's important for an entrepreneur to be honest about his or her business's environmental impact. Some businesses try to appear environmentally responsible by overstating their commitment; this is called **greenwashing**. Such businesses take small steps, more for appearance than for impact, or advertise a practice that's required by law anyway. For example, a lawn and garden shop may claim, "All our pesticides meet federal guidelines for environmental protection." In reality, it would be illegal to sell products that did *not* meet these standards. Greenwashing is unethical at the very least and can hurt a business's reputation.

Apply Your Knowledge   What are at least five things a business can do to help the environment? Think back to your investigation of Whole Foods. Did they do any of these in their core values?

CAREER COMPETENCIES:

 ## Utilize Job-Search Strategies

Searching for a job is hard work! When you start looking for a job in any career, you will need to use many of your entrepreneurial mindset skills. For example:

- Communication skills to write job search materials, describe your strengths, and convey your interests nonverbally.
- Critical thinking skills to identify job opportunities and to accept or turn down a job offer.
- Problem-solving skills to negotiate employment needs and improve your search materials or interviewing technique.

A successful job search depends on being organized and thorough, as well as knowing how to use all available resources—in other words, it depends on being an effective manager.

Keeping your job search materials organized in a folder or binder will help you follow up on every possibility. When you are actively looking for work at many companies, it is easy to forget who you spoke to and even what you spoke about. An employer might not look favorably on someone who repeats the same conversation or cannot remember who referred her in the first place.

- Keep a to-do list of tasks you want to accomplish each day, such as people you want to contact, resumes you have to send out, and thank you notes to write. Cross-off each item you complete, and add new items as they come up.
- Contact some people in your network every day. Make brief phone calls, or send brief e-mail messages to let them know you are looking for work, and to ask for assistance finding job opportunities.
- Follow up on all leads. Keep a record of the people you contact, including phone numbers, e-mail addresses, and mailing addresses. Include the dates and times, the method of communication, and the result. Did they invite you in for an interview? Did they refer you to someone else?
- Set up folders for storing documents that relate to your job search. Use the folders to keep track of information you send to each contact or potential employer and the response you get back. The folder might include copies of the cover letter and samples of your work that you sent. It might also include notes you took during a phone call or interview, a brochure about the company, and a printout of an e-mail message you received.

4.3 Supporting the Community

Serving the Community

All entrepreneurs interact with the communities that their businesses serve. Building and developing these communities through investment is one way that many businesses give back. For example, an entrepreneur in a town may support local student activities or sponsor an event. This type of giving can be volunteer time or money, but shows potential customers that the entrepreneur wants to create positive change.

Other people prefer to use their entrepreneurial skills to start a nonprofit rather than a for-profit business. A **nonprofit organization** (often called a not-for-profit) operates solely to serve the good of society. Nonprofits are not governmental organizations. They operate much like for-profit businesses. Money comes into the nonprofit from personal

◀ **Figure 4-9**
Nonprofit Business.

Entrepreneurs who start nonprofits sacrifice profit for furthering a cause.

Applying Concepts.

What are the pros and cons of starting a nonprofit versus a traditional business?

donations; corporate, foundation, or government grants; or the sale of goods or services to consumers. Nonprofit companies also have expenses. If the money coming in is greater than the money going out, a nonprofit company will have money left over. However, any extra money a nonprofit earns must, by law, be used to support the organization's social mission. It cannot be used for the financial gain of the people running the nonprofit. These entrepreneurs sacrifice the chance to build personal wealth and financial independence for the personal satisfaction they obtain through nonprofit work.

Community Outreach

Whether they are a for-profit or nonprofit, every business should find ways to interact with their community. Here are some ways entrepreneurs can help their businesses while helping their communities:

Cause-related marketing is a partnership between a business and a nonprofit group for the benefit of both. At its best, cause-related marketing accomplishes two goals: it increases sales for the business and raises money and awareness for the nonprofit group.

One form of cause-related marketing that you're probably familiar with is sponsorship, in which a business sponsors a community event or service in exchange for advertising. For example, a travel agency might want to sponsor the local Little League baseball team. The agency's financial support makes participating in Little League affordable for more children. In exchange, the business's name and logo appear on the ball-field fences and the back of team shirts. The travel agency contributes to the community's quality of life while advertising to the community. The community and the business both benefit.

Figure 4-10 ▶
Sponsorship.

Many local companies sponsor Little League teams.

Applying Concepts.

How does this type of sponsorship help a business?

Philanthropy

The energy and initiative that make entrepreneurs leaders in business can also make them leaders in **philanthropy** when they donate money and other resources for socially beneficial causes. Although philanthropy is often associated with large corporations, owners of much smaller businesses are often actively involved in giving back to their communities. In fact, many local service groups couldn't survive without the contributions of local entrepreneurs and small businesses.

Money is the chief way of being philanthropic. Besides writing a check to support a nonprofit group's immediate needs, entrepreneurs can invest by creating or contributing to an endowment fund. The nonprofit group uses the income from the endowment for ongoing needs or for a specific project. Other business owners have established matching gift programs in which they match contributions made by employees or clients.

Some businesses find themselves in a position to donate property. A restaurant that's changing its decor could give its curtains, wall hangings, or dinnerware to a social service agency that helps clients transition from homelessness. A business that's switching to a new computer network might have old hardware and software that would be an upgrade for a nonprofit group. Charitable organizations need donations of products and services to make silent auctions a success, as well as snacks for volunteers who work at nonprofit-sponsored events.

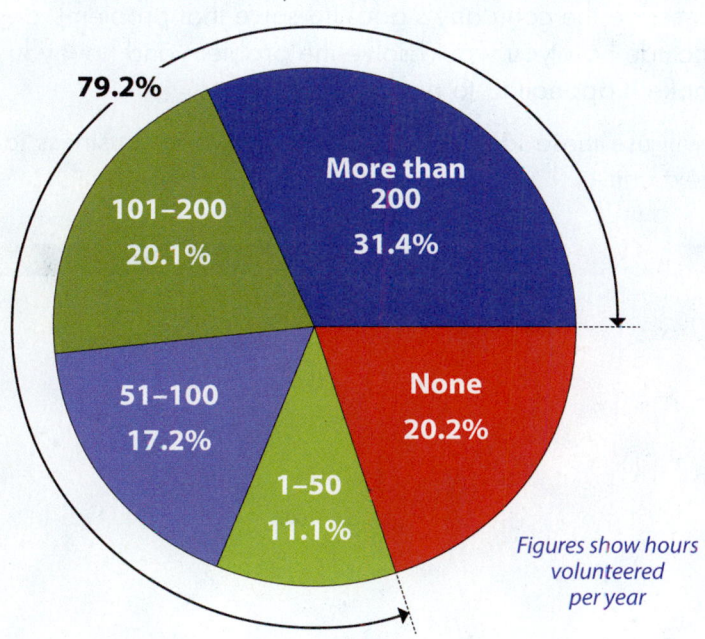

Figures show hours volunteered per year

◀ **Figure 4-11**

Percentage of Entrepreneurs That Volunteer.

Of the entrepreneurs surveyed, almost 80 percent said they and their families did volunteer work. This chart breaks down that figure by the number of hours volunteered annually.

Analyzing Data.

In which hour range did the largest percentage of entrepreneurs and their families fall? How do you explain this finding?

A business's workforce can be an asset to a service group, as well. Volunteers from a local business who help with a community project are making a visible statement about that business's commitment. This sort of volunteering also helps the business. Experts on workplace relations recognize volunteer projects as an effective, low-cost way to foster unity and teamwork among employees.

 **Apply Your Knowledge** What are at least three ways entrepreneurs can support the community? Think back to your investigation of Whole Foods. How do they support the communities they are in?

APPLICATION TO BUSINESS PLANNING

Mission Statement

In the previous chapters, you identified problems that you face every day, along with problems in a career cluster that interests you. Use those lists to complete the following:

1. Select 2–3 problems from your lists and identify potential solutions for each of those problems.

2. Imagine you had a business that provided a solution for each of the problems. Write a different mission statement that would describe the company's goal (to solve that problem). Be sure to include how you would solve the problem and how you would make it appealing to potential customers.

You will use these ideas as the start of potential business ideas in the next unit.

4 ASSESSMENT

REVIEWING OBJECTIVES

1. Identify at least three social problems solved by entrepreneurs.
2. List examples of socially responsible business practices.
3. Explain the purpose of having a mission statement for a business.

CRITICAL THINKING

Meredith owns an orchard. She is alarmed by the mysterious loss of honeybees that pollinate her fruit trees. She wants to use facilitated giving to support a nonprofit group investigating the situation. However, she's worried that very few people have heard of the problem so she won't be successful raising money. What should she do?

ENTREPRENEURIAL THINKING EXERCISE: CRITICAL THINKING & PROBLEM SOLVING

Think back to your investigation of John Mackey and Whole Foods Market. Imagine that you were just hired to be part of the team that plans the business's social responsibility plans. How would you go about deciding what new ways the business could give back to individuals, the environment, or the community? Provide a clear process on how you would determine what additional problems Whole Foods could solve.

4 ASSESSMENT

EXTENSION ACTIVITIES

Entrepreneurship & Literacy Skills

Complete the following task to demonstrate your understanding of entrepreneurship:

1. Grades 9–10: Work in groups of three or four. Have each member assume the role of an entrepreneur for a specific business. Then choose a cause that all members can support. Assign each member to use one form of cause-related marketing or philanthropy to raise money or awareness for the cause. Be sure to include charts and research data that supports why this is a problem that needs to be solved. Present your plans to the class.

4 ASSESSMENT

2. Grades 11–12: Work in groups of three or four. Have each member assume the role of an entrepreneur for a specific business. Then choose a cause that all members can support. Assign each member to use one form of cause-related marketing or philanthropy to raise money or awareness for the cause. Create a live presentation, or recorded commercial, that includes relevant data from multiple sources to support why this is a problem that needs to be solved. Be prepared to present to the class.

MANAGING RISK

OBJECTIVES

- Explain ways that entrepreneurs can promote ethical behavior in the workplace.
- List potential challenges that entrepreneurs might face while starting or operating a business.
- Describe how a business plan helps entrepreneurs manage entrepreneurial risk.

NFTE Entrepreneurial Mindset Characteristic Focus

☑ Comfort with Risk

National Entrepreneurship Standards

- **A.09** Describe entrepreneurial planning considerations
- **A.10** Explain tools used by entrepreneurs for venture planning
- **A.12** Assess risks associated with venture
- **B.12** Describe desirable entrepreneurial personality traits
- **B.15** Evaluate personal capabilities
- **C.08** Explain the nature of managerial ethics
- **C.16** Explain the concept of risk management
- **N.01** Describe types of business risk

Common Career Technical Core Standards

- **BM.3** Explore, develop and apply strategies for ensuring a successful business career.
- **BM.5** Implement systems, strategies and techniques used to manage information in a business.
- **CRP.3** Attend to personal health and financial well-being.
- **CRP.9** Model integrity, ethical leadership and effective management.

National Entrepreneurship Standards: Career Competencies

☑ **H.11** Write a letter of application

LESSON VOCABULARY

- business ethics
- business plan
- business risk
- conflict of interest
- copyright
- ethics
- executive summary
- fair use
- infringement
- integrity
- intellectual property
- patent
- public domain
- trademark
- transparency
- universal values

5.1 Managing Entrepreneurial Risks

In this unit, you have learned what it means to think and act like an entrepreneur. As you continue down the process of entrepreneurial discovery, one of the key things to learn is how to become comfortable with risk. As you learned in previous chapters, entrepreneurs assume a lot of risks that include unreliable income, unanticipated challenges, and loneliness. Entrepreneurs have to work a lot of extra hours to ensure their businesses are successful. They are willing to take these risks for the potential rewards of ownership, income, and work satisfaction. But as the saying goes, sometimes the best laid plans do not work out. Successful entrepreneurs understand the uncertainty of the future but strive to look forward and are flexible and adaptable.

In this chapter, you will look at some of the ways that entrepreneurs navigate **business risk**, or the possibility of loss that comes with operating the business. Some of these approaches are ways to run their business that try to prevent any challenges from even arising. You will also have your first look at a business plan, which is the entrepreneur's ultimate road map for navigating risk.

Business Ethics

The best way to navigate business risk is try to structure the business so that risky situations are avoided before they arise. Entrepreneurs should envision the type of well-run business they hope to own. One thing for entrepreneurs to identify are their values, which are intangible things that are important. Values for entrepreneurs might include: hard work, helping others, and showing **integrity**, which means you are honest and have strong moral principals. Values are influenced by one's cultural background and personal experiences. Values are fundamental to form the basis of **ethics**, a set of moral principles that govern decisions and actions. To act ethically is to act in ways that are in keeping with certain values. Setting these values and practicing business ethics can help entrepreneurs navigate business risk by avoiding risky behavior.

Suppose you ask three people if friendships are important. All three will probably say yes. You then ask if succeeding in school and volunteering for a good cause are important. Again, everyone will likely agree. Now suppose you ask: Which is more important: spending time with friends, studying, or volunteering? Here, disagreement may arise, with such answers as "Volunteering is always more important than just hanging out with friends" or "Spending time with friends is fine—unless you need to study to bring up your grades." People tend to agree on values but have different ideas about how to apply them. That pattern is repeated throughout society. You could study cultures with vastly different foods, languages, and governments. Yet you'll find that they all value friendship, success, and helping others. They all nurture the young and care for the old or sick.

These are examples of **universal values**, values shared by all cultures throughout history.

◀ **Figure 5-1
Universal Values.**
Nurturing the young is a universal value.

Applying Concepts.
What would happen to a society that didn't nurture its young?

Universal values are recognized because they promote the conditions needed for individuals to survive, enjoy life, and get along with others. They start with the basics of life: food, water, shelter, and physical safety. Actions that further the common good are universally accepted as right: obeying the law, for example, and caring for the young and the old. Likewise, certain acts are seen as wrong: killing, stealing, and irresponsible behavior. Positive qualities such as generosity and fairness are encouraged everywhere, while greed and dishonesty are universally discouraged.

This agreement on values creates a similarity in ethics as well. However, just as individuals differ in their opinions on values, cultures differ in how they express and enforce ethical standards. For instance, all cultures have laws, written or unwritten, to punish dishonest actions. But what actions are considered dishonest and how they are punished varies with different cultures

Although we have universal values, not all businesses do good. If you follow the news, you may have learned of illegal deals involving large corporations. One company lied to employees about its financial health, encouraging workers to invest millions of dollars in company stock. Then the business declared bankruptcy, wiping out the savings the workers had counted on for retirement. Another company knowingly sold toys containing lead-based paint, which was banned years ago as a health hazard to children.

Stories like these, along with common complaints such as hidden fees and poor customer service, have tarnished the image of business. They've also brought attention to the topic of **business ethics**, moral principles applied to business issues and actions. Many people now wonder if such a thing as business ethics exists at all. Entrepreneurs have considerable influence on their company's business ethics. Like operating a business itself, this is both an opportunity and a responsibility.

Why Practice Business Ethics?

So if some businesses get away with bad ethics why should entrepreneurs strive to practice business ethics? The main reason for behaving ethically, in business or in any area of life, seems obvious. It shows your integrity and that you understand the importance of treating others as you would like them to treat you.

However, there are three practical reasons why you should practice business ethics:

- Customers are more confident when buying goods and services from an ethical company. As a consumer yourself, you may prefer buying from companies with a history of acting ethically. Consumer surveys show you're not alone. This makes sense—people don't trust a company to offer high-quality goods and services if it has a reputation for acting unethically.

- An ethical workplace motivates employees. Have you ever seen other students copy a paper or cheat on a test and not get caught? You may have wondered why you should play by the rules when people who break them seem to succeed just as well. Employees also feel discouraged and frustrated when that happens in the workplace. In contrast, people are proud to work for someone with high ethical standards. They feel more confident about their work and more loyal to a fair and ethical employer.

- Ethical behavior also prevents legal problems. Defending yourself in court can be expensive. Lawsuits obviously cost a company money for lawyers' fees, judgments, and penalties. They also damage your reputation, which can lead to lost customers for years to come. It may even be enough to cause your business to fail and ruin your career.

◀ **Figure 5-2**
Avoiding Risky Behavior.
All risky behavior can lead to negative consequences.

Applying Concepts.

Why is it even more important for entrepreneurs to avoid risky behavior by acting ethically?

Establishing an Ethical Workplace

By clarifying guidelines for a business, an entrepreneur avoids risks with employees and customers. Universal values establish a strong foundation for society. Universal values are also a good basis for running your business. Deciding how to apply these values will be as important as any other planning you do. This section describes issues and ideas that will help you foster an ethical atmosphere in your workplace. It points out opportunities to show that you take ethics seriously and expect others to do the same.

Creating Transparency

Have you heard the expression "The buck stops here"? It describes a management style that assumes someone has the authority to make decisions and takes responsibility for those decisions. That's the idea behind **transparency**, or openness and accountability in business decisions and actions. Letting people see what a company is doing, and why, is a strong deterrent to unethical behavior. For example, when transparency is practiced, employees know how their retirement fund is being invested. Consumers know that wrongdoers are punished.

Figure 5-3 ▶
Harry Truman.

Harry Truman is famous for the sign on his desk saying "The buck stops here."

Communicating.

What was Harry Truman saying to the American people through that sign?

Communication is essential to transparency. Companies have traditionally communicated through memos to employees and press releases and press conferences for the public. Of course, not everyone has a need or even a right to know everything a company does. A business is justified in concealing a "trade secret" that is crucial to its success, such as a recipe for a food it sells or plans for a new product. Revealing personal information, even voluntarily, should be done with care. You need to ask whether the value of transparency outweighs the invasion of privacy and the possible harm that may result.

Writing a Code of Ethics

A code of ethics describes a business's moral philosophy and gives concrete guidelines for carrying it out. Writing a code and distributing a copy to every employee is a wise move for several reasons. First, writing a code of ethics forces you to clarify your own values and principles. Before you can write such a code, you will have to ask yourself what you believe is important. Answering those questions helps you understand the concepts in more concrete terms. Everyone says they value honesty, for instance, but what does that word mean to you exactly? Having a code will also help prevent and resolve problems. When a question arises about whether an action is ethical, you and others can see how it compares to the code.

Our Code of Ethics

I. **We value learning and will dedicate ourselves to giving each child the best education possible.**

We believe that education must encompass the whole child, both the body and the mind. We bring all of our skills and knowledge to promoting good physical health, fostering a full range of healthy emotions as well as social and relationship skills, and developing the mind to the fullest.

II. **We value equality and will attack barriers of prejudice and injustice.**

We believe that each child has untold potential that must not be hindered by unfair limitations of stereotypes or bias. Rather, each child deserves the opportunity to identify and develop all the talents and skills that he or she is interested in.

III. **We value human dignity and will treat each child as a worthy, unique, and valued individual.**

We believe that dignity and worth are inborn qualities in every human being. Each child must be made to feel valued and loved unconditionally, regardless of abilities, social circumstance, behavior, personality traits, or any other interior or exterior condition.

◀ **Figure 5-4**
Code of Ethics.
This code of ethics would be used by the owner of a childcare center.

Relating Concepts.
Suggest a practical rule or guideline that could be based on these values and beliefs.

Finally, a written code provides some protection against claims of unfairness. Employees know from their first day what behavior is encouraged and what could result in dismissal. Suppliers can see your reasons for choosing another business over their own. The code shows that you don't knowingly tolerate unethical behavior.

Because business ethics can be so complex, professional advice on writing and maintaining a code of ethics is a worthwhile investment. Many large companies hire a compliance officer to ensure that their practices comply with their written code and that the code follows state and federal law. Compliance officers also answer employees' questions about how the code is applied and investigate reports of possible unethical behavior.

Developing a useful code of ethics can be difficult. The challenge can be summed up in one word: balance. The code must balance contrasting qualities in an effective way. For example:

- The code must be general enough to apply to many situations, yet specific enough to offer practical help. Likewise, it should hold true to moral principles, yet be flexible enough to make allowances for the circumstances of the individual case. To strike this balance, codes are often divided into several parts: the first lays out the general values and ethical goals. Next are rules for behavior in particular situations.

- The code should reflect your values but also respect the beliefs of those who will be affected. Recall that people can hold the same values but act on them differently. Suppose one point in a code concerns the importance of giving back to the community. One employee might carry out this value by volunteering with a wildlife preservation group. Another might join the Chamber of Commerce, which promotes economic development. To bring in a range of opinions, you may want to involve employees, trusted advisors, and experienced businesspeople in your efforts.

- The values can be idealistic, but the guidelines must be realistic. A code needs achievable language, such as "encourage" and "promote." Reserve absolutes and terms such as "always" and "never" for clear issues of right and wrong. Compare these two statements: "We prefer environmentally friendly products when available" and "We will use only recyclable products." Which statement is practical?

A code of ethics should be continually evolving without drifting from its core beliefs. Universal values may stay the same over time, but your views on how to carry them out may change. You may need to adapt and revise your rules to meet new situations and developments in technology.

Establishing and practicing business ethics can save entrepreneurs a lot of unnecessary risk and support more rewards in the long run.

 **Apply Your Knowledge** Why do entrepreneurs need to practice business ethics to help manage the risks they face? How does this demonstrate an entrepreneur's integrity? Think back to your investigation of the social media websites. Did you find a code of conduct for the business? Do you see it reflected in their customer experiences? Explain your answer.

ENTREPRENEURIAL CASE STUDY: COMFORT WITH RISK

 ## Cheri Garcia— Luminous Envy

Inspiration Strikes

At 21, Cheri Garcia was originally planning to pursue a career in news broadcasting, but her entrepreneurial spirit pulled her to become an Inventor. She first drew inspiration while swimming with her family. While hoping to get a suntan that day, she wished there was a way she could accelerate the tanning process, without having to use suntan oil. This lead Cheri to her invention: the first-ever tanning bed you can inflate, deflate, and take with you. By 23, Cheri had started, and was operating her business, Luminous Envy (www.luminousenvy.com). Luminous Envy has since been picked up by "As Seen On TV", Leslie's Pool, and many other pool supply retailers. However, her quick path to success was not free of challenges.

Cheri Garcia.

After inspiration for her portable tanning bed struck, Cheri started sketching the vision for her product. From these sketches, she came up with the design for the Luminous Envy tanning bed, making it inflatable, and with a reflective material on the bottom and angled side panels to maximize results. She was extremely excited about her idea and was ready to market it to developers who would make it for her. However, there was one problem, "I called every factory in America," Cheri said. "Nobody would touch it without $100,000 up front."

Risky Venture

Cheri did not give up. She eventually found a developer who would help get her business off the ground if she was able to raise $38,000. But as a 23-year-old, it wasn't easy coming up with $38,000 for inventory. She was able to borrow money from family investors to help start her business, but borrowing money for a new idea can be super risky. Cheri remembers, "I had to take the risk of borrowing $20,000 from two different people, when I didn't even make that much in a year." However, the extra pressure to succeed made sure that she that took that risk head on. "Some people say, 'the greater the risk, the greater the return'. I don't believe that. I say, 'the greater the risk, the harder you should work.'"

Cheri's risk paid off. After making a first batch of 1,000 beds, she quickly gained national attention and media buzz for her invention. With the exposure to a larger customer and investor base, her business took off. She continued to grow her business and obtained the patent rights in 2013. Her $38,000 risk paid off, allowing her to make ten times what she did as an employee of a business.

Risk with Unexpected Rewards

Cheri's experience with Luminous Envy has given her credability to pursue numerous other opportunities. Since then, she has started several other businesses. This has included inventing an apartment evaluation app called RentEval (http://www.renteval.com/). Her new inventions have given her media buzz, including a segment on the Steve Harvey show. She has also used her new ventures to help her on the path to her ultimate goal of becoming a motivational speaker and invention consultant. Cheri said of her goals, "I not only want to motivate, but INSPIRE others to realize their passion and take risks to achieve their goals. It is my personal challenge to be a part of helping others make their wildest entrepreneur dreams come true!"

Thinking and Acting Like an Entrepreneur

- What was risky for Cheri in borrowing money for her business? What other outcomes could have happened?
- How did Cheri demonstrate the entrepreneurial mindset behavior of being comfortable with taking on business risk?
- What would you have done in her scenario? Would you have taken the same risk with your idea?

5.2 Navigating Ethical Scenarios

Generally running a business ethically and with integrity can help an entrepreneur from losing the business that she or he worked hard to create. However, there are also ethical decisions that can pose a risk if entrepreneurs choose to not act ethically. In this section, you will look at the risk involved with stealing ideas from other businesses, engaging the business in a conflict of interest, or breaking confidentially agreements. Knowing how to navigate these risky scenarios and comply with applicable rules, laws, and regulations can help keep a business on track.

Intellectual Property

In the early 2000s, a company named Napster was at the forefront of providing customers with the ability to download free MP3s. Their success was short-lived when artists and record labels sued the company, saying that they owned the songs being downloaded. The lawsuit bankrupted the young company by 2002. Can music be stolen? Yes. Music, paintings, literature, inventions, and architectural designs are types of

Figure 5-5

Protecting Intellectual Property.

A song you write is something you own.

Relating Concepts.

What would you do if someone claimed that they created a song that you wrote?

intellectual property. **Intellectual property** is artistic and industrial creations of the mind. "Possession" of these creations is protected by law. The owners are entitled to credit and usually some form of payment when their works are used, especially when used for commercial gain. Artistic creations are protected by copyright. Copyright is the exclusive right to perform, display, copy, or distribute an artistic work. **Copyright** applies automatically as soon as a work is created. It covers all forms of expression, whether words, music, images, or concrete objects. It includes works published on the Internet. Another type of intellectual property—industrial invention—is protected by patent. A **patent** is the exclusive right to make, use, or sell a device or process.

Many types of creations can be patented, from an improved design for a ketchup bottle, to a variety of tomato used to make the ketchup, to a process for bottling the ketchup.

A **trademark** is a symbol that indicates that the use of a brand or brand name is legally protected and cannot be used by other businesses. A trademarked brand or brand name is a type of intellectual property. Two symbols are associated with U.S. trademarks. The trademark symbol ™ is used to indicate that the brand is protected in a general way, but does not have formal legal protection.

The registered trademark symbol ® can only be used if the owner of the brand or brand name has registered it with the U.S. Patent and Trademark Office. Violating a copyright, trademark, or patent holder's rights is called **infringement**. A shop owner who plays music for customers' enjoyment commits copyright infringement. A fashion designer who copies software that creates dress patterns commits patent infringement. There are ways to avoid infringement. A doctrine called **fair use** provides for the limited quotation of a copyrighted work without permission from or payment to the copyright holder. Also, some creative works or inventions have the status of **public domain**, meaning that their copyright or patent has expired. Works produced by the United States government are included in the public domain.

With every image, video, song, and writing excerpt an Internet search away, it is becoming increasingly difficult to know what is okay to use and what is not. Organizations such as Creative Commons work with artists and entrepreneurs to explain some details regarding what works are okay for others to use. Always be sure to find out if anything you pull from the Internet is safe to use.

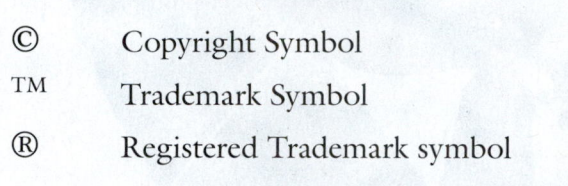

©	Copyright Symbol
TM	Trademark Symbol
®	Registered Trademark symbol

Patent infringement isn't an issue for most entrepreneurs. Almost every item you use, buy, or sell is patented, so the inventor has been compensated.

However, imagine that you invented a new knee pad for athletes and that Velcro® fasteners were essential to the design. To sell the pads without patent infringement, you would have to compensate Velcro Industries B.V., which holds the patent for Velcro® products. Otherwise, you would have to redesign the new pad to close in some other way, using an unpatented method—perhaps laces (which would be a device in the public domain).

Making sure that your business is not copying someone else's is extremely important. In addition to looking to see if someone already owns the intellectual property, you'll want to do some basic searches to see if anyone else is doing business in your market with the same name/slogan. A general rule of thumb is that if the business sells something completely different and/or is located very far away, you might be able to operate with the same name. But it's safer to try to revisit the name to avoid the trouble of having to stop your business after opening. In a later chapter, we will look at protecting your own works against others.

Conflict of Interest

Another ethical decision that entrepreneurs often face is related to conflicts of interest. A **conflict of interest** exists when personal considerations and professional obligations interfere with each other. It's wise to avoid such situations—or even the appearance of such situations—even if you think you can act fairly and objectively. For example, Dan has a lawn care business, specializing in commercial lawn maintenance. Often customers ask Dan to recommend full-year programs using lawn treatment products. Dan has been approached by sales people representing these products. They have offered to pay Dan a percentage of the cost of any products purchased by his customers. Recently, a customer asked Dan for a recommendation and he had to choose between a product for which he receives a percentage and a similar product for which he doesn't receive a percentage. If the two products were equally useful, and cost the same, Dan could be accused of having a conflict interest in recommending the product for which he receives a percentage.

A well-thought-out code of ethics can help identify and prevent such problems. Besides addressing specific scenarios, the code should also call for employees to report questionable situations so you can decide on the best way to handle them.

Confidentiality

As an entrepreneur, you will be gathering a good deal of information. You may run a background check and find that a job applicant has a criminal record, or discover sensitive financial data through a credit check on potential investors or partners.

How you and others in your company use this information can be an ethical matter, and the decision isn't always clear-cut. On one hand, you have a duty to respect the confidentiality (privacy) of others. On the other hand, keeping silent could expose some people to harm. Someone may have a criminal conviction on record, for example, but you should ask yourself whether you have a reason, or a right, to make it known. Confidentiality can also create conflict of interest. As an accountant with a large company, Angela knew the financial details of many clients businesses. When she left to start working for herself, she could have used this knowledge and asked the clients if they would like to work with her. Instead, she chose to build up her own clientele through her talent and hard work and not to steal her old company's customers. Confidentiality also has legal aspects. An employee who signs a nondisclosure agreement is legally barred from sharing some types of information with others, even after leaving the company. Health care professionals can lose their license for revealing facts about a patient's condition without permission. In some professions, taking advantage of insider information—facts about a business's dealings that aren't made public—can lead to a prison sentence!

◀ **Figure 5-7**
Secret Recipe.

If you were a business owner with a recipe for fried chicken, you would probably ask your employees to sign a confidentiality agreement.

Predicting.

How would you feel if one of your employees violated the confidentiality agreement and started a restaurant that served chicken made from your recipe?

 **Apply Your Knowledge** How can complying with rules, laws, and regulations help entrepreneurs avoid business risk and demonstrate their integrity and commitment to ethical practices? Think back to your investigation of the social media websites. Would you use any of these sites if you found out they were not complying with applicable laws and regulations, like not following confidentiality rules? Why or why not? Explain your answer.

CAREER COMPETENCIES

 ### Write a Letter of Application/ Cover Letter

When you include a cover letter with your resume, you make a better impression on the employer than if you send the resume alone. Including a cover letter shows that you have taken the time to match your qualifications with a specific job. A cover letter should be short and to the point. Direct it to the person who is responsible for hiring. If you do not know the person's name, title, and address, call the company and ask.

You can customize the cover letter to the job opening you are applying for. Use it to tell the employer why you are interested in that job and why you are qualified to do the work.

When writing your cover letter, it might be tempting to exaggerate or be misleading if you are concerned about your lack of work experience. As you have learned in this chapter, businesses respect honesty and transparency. You can still write a very impressive cover letter detailing the experience you do have and why they should take a chance based on your personal characteristics. Remember, you want to avoid getting into a risky scenario of being hired for qualifications you do not have.

When you write a cover letter, ask yourself these questions:

- Have I identified the job title for the job I want? Have I stated where I learned about the position?
- Have I listed the skills I have that qualify me for the position?
- Have I thanked the reader for his or her time and consideration?
- Have I corrected all spelling and grammatical errors?

Career Skills in Action

Now, you practice writing a cover letter as an entrepreneur. You will describe why you are distinctly qualified to run a business of your choice. Remember to ask yourself the questions above. Type your cover letter and share with your peers and teacher for feedback.

5.3 Here's the Plan: Managing Predictable Risks

Successful entrepreneurs recognize risk and can quickly assess if the reward is high enough. Imagine a scale with risk on one side and rewards on another. Successful entrepreneurs can utilize entrepreneurial mindset skills to visualize this scale. They can then identify ways to mitigate or reduce the risk by identifying risks they can control, which are generally those that arise internally and which the business has direct control over. There are also uncontrollable risks related to things such as the economy, the political climate, and technology.

In addition to establishing their ethical practices and company values, entrepreneurs can also control risk through careful planning. As you read earlier in the chapter, successful entrepreneurs can do their best to plan to avoid risks they can predict. However, these plans are not cast in stone. Entrepreneurs and businesses use a plan, called a business plan, as a road map for identifying potential challenges and navigating risk.

Purpose of a Business Plan

Creating a business could be one of the most important things you do in your life. So it would only make sense to spend time planning it. Most entrepreneurs initially develop a business plan as a way of describing their business precisely. A **business plan** is a statement of your business goals, the reasons you think these goals can be met, and how you are going to achieve them. An important element of the business plan is the company description, which describes the nature of the business, the marketplace needs it will satisfy, the market(s) it will serve, and its advantage over the competition.

If you start your business without a plan, you will soon be overwhelmed by questions you haven't answered. A business plan forces you to figure out how to make your business work. A well-written business plan will show investors that you have carefully thought through what you intend to do to make the business profitable. It will also show investors that you are more than qualified to navigate the risk associated with starting and running the business. The more explanation you offer investors about how their money will be used, the more willing they will be to invest. Your plan should be so thoughtful and well written that the only question it raises in an investor's mind is "How much can I invest?"

A well-written plan will also guide you every step of the way as you develop your business. It becomes a decision-making tool. An entrepreneur uses the business plan to track whether the company is meeting its goals. From time-to-time, the business plan needs to be revised to keep up with the changing nature of the business. Some business owners might do this on an annual basis; others, in well-established industries, might do it every three years. Still others, in newly developed or high-tech areas, may need to do it monthly or even weekly.

If your company is for-profit, your business plan will typically focus on your financial goals. If you are a nonprofit, your plan will typically focus on your mission and services in support of that mission. (As you know from previous chapters, a nonprofit company can make a profit, but the profit must remain in the company and be used in pursuing its mission.)

Types of Business Plans

Business plans have no set format. A plan is developed based on the type of business that is intended. However, it is also based on the audience. Businesses need different types of plans for different audiences. There are four main types of plans for a startup business:

- **Quick Summary.** This is a brief synopsis lasting no more than thirty seconds to three minutes. It's used to interest potential investors, customers, or strategic partners. It may seem strange to consider this a type of business plan, but it is. In some cases, the quick summary may be a necessary step toward presenting a more fully developed plan.

- **Oral Presentation.** This is a relatively short, colorful, and entertaining slide show with a running narrative. It is meant to interest potential investors in reading the detailed business plan.

- **Investor's Business Plan.** Anyone who plans to invest in your startup business (banks investors, and others) needs to know exactly what you are planning. They need a detailed business plan that is well-written and formatted so all the information can be easily understood. When entrepreneurs talk about a business plan, this is typically the type of plan they mean. To ensure that investors understand the key points of your idea, the plan should include an executive summary, a one- or two-page summary of highlights, including the key selling points of the investment opportunity.

- **Operational Business Plan.** Often a startup business will develop an *operational* plan that is meant for use within the business only. This plan describes in greater detail than the investor's business plan how the company will meet its goals. It is also often less formal than an investor's business plan.

Although there is no set format for a business plan, each type of plan will address The Three C's:

- **Concept.** What is your product or service and how is it different from similar products or services?

- **Customer.** Who will be buying your product or service and why?

- **Capital.** How will you locate the initial money your business will need? What will be your costs and what kind of profit can you expect?

The Internet offers many sources of information about business plans. One of the best is the Small Business Administration's website (www.sba.gov), which has links to other organizations that provide

Figure 5-8 ▲
Oral Presentation.

Be sure to maintain your audience's interest when making an oral presentation.

Communicating.

What are some of the ways you could maintain an investor's interest when presenting a business plan?

business planning templates, outlines, and other resources. Another good source for help with business plans is www.entrepreneur.com.

Entrepreneurial Discovery

In this course, you will go through the entrepreneurial discovery process to create a business plan for a unique business idea. Before even touching your plan, you will learn how to use a canvas tool for validating your business idea. Your business plan will be a living and breathing document that will change as you learn more about entrepreneurship, and do more research on your business idea. When you eventually put your plan into action, you will also continue to revisit your plan once you get more information from customers and/or face new challenges.

On the following pages are a snapshot of the entrepreneurial discovery process outlined in this textbook, and where you learn about new topics that will be represented in your final business plan. You will also find a sample business plan in the Appendix of this textbook. Be sure to revisit the appropriate application to your business planning after each chapter in this textbook.

The good news is this text is designed to guide you through the entire process in how we structure our units. In the next unit of learning, you will learn how to solidify your idea and use ongoing research to shape your business plan over this course. Like other successful entrepreneurs, you can plan and test your theories first before starting your business.

Apply Your Knowledge   Why is going through business planning important? Visit the www.sba.gov and www.entrepreneur.com websites to research outlines, templates, and other resources you could use to develop a business plan and create a table that lists and describes each of the resources. Think back to your investigation of the social media companies. Do you think the teams in your entrepreneurial investigation had business plans? Does their business look like their original plans? Explain your rationale.

APPLICATION TO BUSINESS PLANNING

Qualifications

Using what you learned about managing risks in this chapter, describe why you believe you are qualified to assume the risks of creating and running a business. Remember, you should focus on distinct skills and characteristics you possess that make you the best candidate to start this business. You should also include the entrepreneurial mindset skills you have started developing.

Unit	Chapter	Business Plan Section & Key Questions
Business Plan Phase: Ideation		
Developing an Entrepreneurial Mindset	1	1.1 Problem Identification: What problem is my business solving?
	2	1.2 Personal Characteristics/Skills: What personal characteristics do I have that will be helpful in running my business?
	3	1.3 Career Cluster: What career cluster does my business fit within?
	4	1.4 Mission Statement: What is the mission statement for my business? How does it describe my socially responsible practices?
	5	1.5 Qualifications: Why am I qualified to take on the business risk?
Business Plan Phase: Ideation		
Opportunity & Market Analysis	6	2.1 Idea Generation: What is my business idea?
	7	2.2 Business Opportunity: Why is my business idea a real business opportunity?
	8	2.3 Opportunity Screening: How do I know that my business opportunity is the best opportunity to pursue?
	9	2.4 Market Research Questions: What information will I need to gather to validate my business opportunity?
	10	2.5 Market Research Tools: What tools will I use to gather, organize, and interpret ongoing market research data on my business?
Business Plan Phase: Business Model Validation		
Competition	11	3.1 Industry & Industry Statistics: What industry does my business belong to? What are the statistics about the competitors in my industry?
	12	3.2 Availability of Product/Service: How do supply and demand principles influence the availability of my product or services?
	13	3.3 Direct and Indirect Competition: Who are my direct and indirect competitors?
	14	3.4 Competitive Pricing: What price can I sell my product or service for to be competitive, and still make a profit?
	15	3.5 Competitive Advantage: What are my business's competitive advantages?

Unit	Chapter	Business Plan Section & Key Questions
Business Plan Phase: Business Model Validation		
Delivering Value to Customers	16	4.1 Target Market Segment: Who are potential customers for my business? What characteristics do they share?
	17	4.2 Value Proposition: What key benefits does my business offer to my potential customers?
	18	4.3 Marketing Mix: What is my plan for communicating the value of my business to customers? Does it include the 5P's of Marketing?
	19	4.4 Business Pitch: How will I sell the value of my product or service to potential customers and investors?
	20	4.5 Promotional Plan: How will I promote my business to attract and keep customers?
Business Plan Phase: Business Model Validation		
Business Model	21	5.1 Distribution Channel: What are the steps to getting my product or service to my potential customers?
	22	5.2 Internal Resources: What internal resources (human, physical, financial, intellectual) will I need to run my business?
	23	5.3 Operating Policies: What operating policies will need to be put in place to make my business run?
	24	5.4 External Partnerships: What external partnerships will I need to build to operate, protect, and grow my business?
	25	5.5 Legal Structure: What legal structure should I choose for my business and why?
Business Plan Phase: Business Model Validation		
Financial and Expense Management	26	6.1 EOU & Variable Expenses: What does it cost to make my product or deliver my service? What will I charge for each unit sold to ensure a profit?
	27	6.2 Fixed Expenses & Break-Even Units: What are my business's ongoing fixed expenses? How many units will I have to sell to stay in business?
	28	6.3 Projected Income Statement: What is all of the income I plan to generate for the business through revenue streams? How much profit will my business generate after accounting for expenses?
	29	6.4 Start Up Investment: What will my start-up expenses be? How will I raise money to finance my startup?
	30	6.5 Financial Ratios: What financial ratios do I need to calculate to determine the financial health of my business?

Unit	Chapter	Business Plan Section & Key Questions
Business Plan Phase: Creation		
	N/A	Assemble your final business plan and/or build your final prototype based off of your research to launch your business!
Business Plan Phase: Implementation Plan		
Operating the Business	31	7.1 Organizational Structure: What organizational structure is appropriate for my business?
	32	7.2 Business Compliance Plan: What government regulations does my business need to consider?
	33	7.3 Financial Records: What financial records will my business generate? What recordkeeping systems will my business use?
	34	7.4 Accounting System: What recordkeeping and account systems will my business use?
	35	7.5 Plan for Filing Taxes: What is my plan for paying and filing taxes?
Business Plan Phase: Growth Plan		
Growing the Business	36	8.1 Growth Plan: What can I do to make my business grow?
	37	8.2 Plan for Scaling: What steps will I take to help my business scale?
	38	8.3 Hiring Needs: How will I hire additional staff to support my business growth?
	39	8.4 Franchising & Licensing: What are my franchising or licensing opportunities?
	40	8.5 Exit Strategy: When and how should I exit my business?

ASSESSMENT

REVIEWING OBJECTIVES

1. What are ways that entrepreneurs can promote ethical behavior in the workplace?
2. List potential challenges that entrepreneurs might face while starting or operating a business.
3. How does a business plan help entrepreneurs manage entrepreneurial risk?

CRITICAL THINKING

1. Distinguish between business risks that are controllable vs. uncontrollable. Provide an example of each.
2. In a business plan, what should be included in the company description? Create one for a business that you would like to start.
3. Some of the information you obtain from clients and employees can be sensitive and should be treated with confidentiality. How would you address this in a code of ethics?

ENTREPRENEURIAL THINKING EXERCISE: COMFORT WITH RISK

Select one business from your entrepreneurial investigation. Based on your research, list the risks the company took by changing directions with the product. Do you believe the risk was worth the reward? Explain your answer.

EXTENSION ACTIVITIES

Entrepreneurship & Literacy Skills

Complete the following task to demonstrate your understanding of entrepreneurship:

1. Grades 9–10: Choose a side in the following argument: "Using social media can help a business's image" OR "Using social media can hurt a business's image." Write an argument that you will present as a debate in class. Be sure to cite information in this text as evidence to support your claims.

2. Grades 11–12: Choose a side in the following argument: "Using social media can help a business's image" OR "Using social media can hurt a business's image." Write an argument that you will present as a debate in class. Be sure to cite information in this text as evidence to support your claims. Be prepared with counterarguments as well.

Unit 1: Developing an Entrepreneurial Mindset

1. Importance of Entrepreneurship
2. Characteristics of an Entrepreneur
3. Being an Intrapreneur
4. Social Entrepreneurship
5. Managing Risk

CHAPTER SUMMARY

1. Importance of Entrepreneurship

An entrepreneur is someone who creates and runs his or her own business. In contrast, an employee is a person who works in a business owned by someone else. When an entrepreneur starts a new business, risk is involved. An entrepreneur is willing to risk an investment of money, time, and energy in the hope of gaining greater rewards, or benefits. Perhaps the biggest reward for an entrepreneur is empowerment. Other rewards are making your own rules, doing work you enjoy, helping your community, and creating wealth. Some of the risks of being an entrepreneur are potential business failure, unexpected obstacles, financial insecurity, and long hours and hard work. Entrepreneurs throughout history have demonstrated that entrepreneurship involves more than just learning how to run a business. It can affect the economy, the community, and ultimately the world. As a result, entrepreneurs help to improve life not only for themselves, but also for many others by providing products, services, and jobs.

2. Characteristics of an Entrepreneur

Entrepreneurs include people of all ages from all over the world. In the United States, more than half of the entrepreneurs have some college education, invest their own money in their businesses, and work over 40 hours per week. Before becoming an entrepreneur, self-assessment is important. Evaluating your attitudes, personal characteristics, and skills will help determine what unique knowledge you have, and what areas you need to strengthen. Entrepreneurs tend to be people with positive attitudes. Instead of seeing problems, they see opportunities. Practicing to think and act like an entrepreneur means to develop an entrepreneurial mindset. Engaging in entrepreneurship exercises can help develop an entrepreneurial mindset that can be applied to careers and life.

3. Being an Intrapreneur

Even if you choose not to become an entrepreneur, here are two good reasons for studying entrepreneurship: thinking and acting like an entrepreneur will help you become a more valued employee, and it can lead you to develop a vision for your life. More and more businesses today encourage the practice of intrapreneurship. This is the opportunity to pursue opportunities that you are passionate about while at your job, almost like being an entrepreneur within the company. There are 16 different career clusters defined by the National Association of State Directors of Career Technical Education Consortium. It is possible to identify entrepreneurial opportunities within any career path. Participating in activities like internships and apprenticeships can provide you with skills and experience that will be beneficial in achieving your vision of the future.

4. Social Entrepreneurship

Businesses demonstrate corporate social responsibility when they act in ways that balance profit and growth with the good of society. Businesses have a responsibility to treat employees, customers, suppliers, investors, and creditors ethically. Four qualities mark a responsible relationship with customers: honesty, respect, accessibility, and attention. Increasingly, companies are becoming concerned with sustainable economic development that does not harm society or the environment, but ensures that human and natural resources are maintained for future generations. Socially responsible entrepreneurs also try to preserve and protect the environment. Businesses and entrepreneurs give back to the community through cause-related marketing, which can include sponsorships, facilitated giving, and purchase-triggered donations. They also start nonprofit organizations to help solve societal problems facing their community or the world. Entrepreneurs explain what problem their business is trying to solve through their mission statement.

5. Managing Risk

Entrepreneurs manage risk by implementing ethical business practices to avoid ethical pitfalls. Ethics are moral principles that govern decisions and actions. They are based on universal values that have been shared by all cultures throughout history. Cultures differ in how they express and enforce ethical values. Business ethics are moral principles applied to business issues and actions. Practicing business ethics benefits entrepreneurs. Businesses demonstrate ethics by practicing transparency, encouraging whistle-blowers, and writing a code of ethics. Transparency is openness and accountability in business decisions and actions. An important ethical concern for entrepreneurs is intellectual property, which is an artistic or industrial creation or invention. The protections for intellectual property are copyrights for artistic work, trademarks for brands and brand names, and patents for inventions. Other ethical concerns for entrepreneurs are conflicts of interest and confidentiality. Another way that entrepreneurs navigate risk is through creating a business plan. A business plan is a statement of your business goals, the reasons you think these goals can be met, and how you are going to achieve those goals. Business planning is an ongoing process as you work to validate the business model of your proposed business model.

UNIT 1 VOCABULARY

apprenticeship	entrepreneurship	product
attitude	ethical sourcing	professionalism
business	ethics	public domain
business ethics	executive summary	reward
business plan	fair use	risk
business risk	green company	self-assessment
carbon footprint	greenwashing	serial entrepreneur
carbon offset	infringement	service
career cluster	integrity	skill
cause-related marketing	intellectual property	sponsorship
characteristic	internship	sustainability
conflict of interest	intrapreneurship	sustainable
copyright	mentor	sustainable economic development
corporate social responsibility	mission statement	
dot-com company	nonprofit organization	trademark
employee	passion	transparency
entrepreneur	patent	universal values
entrepreneurial	pathway	vision
entrepreneurial mindset	philanthropy	

CHECK YOUR UNDERSTANDING

Choose the letter that best answers the question or completes the statement.

1. An entrepreneur
   a. does not have the final say in business decisions
   b. may not employ anyone else
   c. is responsible for the success or failure of his or her business
   d. all of the above

2. Which of the following is not a risk for an entrepreneur?
   a. potential business failure
   b. financial stability
   c. financial insecurity
   d. long hours and hard work

3. When a business encourages employees to be creative within the company, the practice is called
   a. entrepreneurship
   b. creating a vision
   c. implementing a mission
   d. intrapreneurship

4. The company description part of a business plan should include which of the following?
   a. a complete list of all competitors
   b. the markets the business will serve
   c. the names and titles of key employees
   d. a code of ethics

5. How does the SBA define "small business"?
   a. one with 1,000–1,250 employees
   b. one with 750–1,000 employees
   c. one with 500–750 employees
   d. one with fewer than 100 employees

6. As an entrepreneur, the amount of money you receive from your company
   a. is constant, like a paycheck for any other employee
   b. is typically less than for an employee
   c. is typically more than for an employee
   d. may go up or down, depending on the business

7. As an entrepreneur, the amount of time you spend working is typically

a. constant—35 to 40 hours a week, just like an employee

b. a little less than for an employee

c. more than for an employee, particularly during initial start-up

d. signifiantly less than for an employee—around 20 hours a week

8. An experienced person who volunteers to provide free guidance, tutoring, and suggestions to younger individuals is called a(n)

a. mentor

b. intrapreneur

c. entrepreneur

d. employee

9. Greenwashing is unethical because it

a. infringes on copyright

b. misleads consumers

c. creates conflict of interest

d. all of the above

10. Pauline's Pooch Palace gives $1 from every dog grooming to the local animal shelter. This is an example of

a. sustainable design

b. fair trade

c. business ethics

d. philanthropy

11. A well-written code of ethics

a. enhances a business's reputation

b. helps attract quality employees

c. helps prevent legal problems

d. all of the above

12. The owner of a children's clothing store uses popular cartoon characters in her ads. This might be an example of

a. copyright infringement

b. social media

c. cause-related marketing

d. conflict of interest

13. By donating much of his fortune to building libraries, the American industrialist Andrew Carnegie demonstrated his belief in

a. sponsorship

b. philanthropy

c. sustainability

d. ethical sourcing

14. One way to reduce a business's carbon footprint is through

a. greenwashing

b. sponsorship

c. communicating with investors

d. sustainable design

15. Lila, a kitchen designer, helps clients choose appliances. An appliance dealer gives her gifts and tickets to shows. This situation has the potential for

   a. cause-related marketing

   b. patent infringement

   c. conflict of interest

   d. fair use

16. Which of the following is true about a business plan?

   a. developing it is simple and straightforward

   b. once developed, it doesn't change

   c. it has a set format

   d. it will need to be changed from time to time

BUSINESS COMMUNICATION

1. Make a list of activities or tasks you've done in the past (hobbies, part-time jobs, Boy Scouts or Girl Scouts, science fairs, school activities, classes, and so on). Then create another list that identifies the kind of personal characteristics and skills needed to perform those activities. Based on the two lists, write an essay that describes how past experiences could help you as an entrepreneur.

2. Using a library and/or the Internet, research information about the use of the Internet by small businesses. Consider these questions:

   a. Do small businesses use the Internet more than large ones?

   b. How important is the Internet for a small business compared to a big business? Write a report on your findings.

3. Create a poster with a collage that illustrates the vision you currently have for your life.

4. Working in small groups, choose a specific type of business. Write three items of a code of ethics that apply to that business. With each, explain how it relates to universal values.

5. Imagine that you made a mistake that inconvenienced and angered customers. Write a paragraph that will be posted on your company's website. Keep in mind the importance of both transparency and confidentiality.

6. In small groups, write and perform a scene in which you give a financial report for your business at a meeting with investors. The business hasn't done well, and you need money. How will you answer investors' questions, accepting responsibility without causing them to lose confidence?

UNIT 1 REVIEW & ASSESSMENT

BUSINESS MATH

1. Studies show that about 18 percent of all businesses in the United States are minority-owned. Brian lives in Centerville, a town with a population of 25,000 and 200 businesses. Assuming that the national percentage holds true for the businesses in Centerville, how many of these are minority-owned?

2. Businesses owned by women increased from 1.76 million to 3.75 million between the years of 1976 and 2000. Calculate the percentage that women-owned businesses increased during this time period.

3. See the table below. For each unit, what percentage of the operating cost goes to electricity? How much money in water costs could be saved by replacing three conventional dishwashers with three Energy Star® models?

Operating Costs	Energy Star® Unit	Conventional Unit
Electrcity	$890	$15,556
Water	$112	$222
Total	$1,002	$1,1778

4. In a survey of 809 small-business owners, 85 percent said they donated money to a charity the year before. Specifically, how many made charitable contributions?

BUSINESS ETHICS

1. You are walking to work with one of your employees. On the way, you stop to get a newspaper at a self-pay newspaper box. You insert the required number of coins, open the door, and pick up a newspaper. Before closing the door, you ask your employee if he would like a newspaper too. "Two for the price of one," you say. First, resolve whether this is an ethical action. Then describe the impact it could have on your employee. Finally, consider whether this action could have a larger impact on your company.

2. Your business went through a slump last month, and you weren't sure you could pay your employees. You decided that, if needed, you would take the money from your own savings. Fortunately you didn't have to, but one employee found out and told the others. She said she thought they had the right to know when their jobs were in danger and that you had acted dishonestly in not telling them. She also said she would do the same thing in the future. How would you handle this situation?

BUSINESS IN YOUR COMMUNITY

1. Working with another student, research businesses in your community that welcome volunteers. What kind of experience or training, if any, is needed by a volunteer? What type of entrepreneurial skills could you strengthen if you became a volunteer?

2. Interview an entrepreneur or small business owner in your community. Ask this individual to share stories of successes and failures. Ask which personal characteristics or skills have contributed most to their business success. Then ask what the owner would do differently if starting the business today.

3. Contact your local Better Business Bureau. Ask what ethical standards a company must uphold to be accredited by the Better Business Bureau. Does the Better Business Bureau feel that membership in the Bureau has an effect on profits, employees, or other aspects of business?

4. Working in a group, conduct a telephone or walking survey of area businesses to learn what steps they are taking to improve energy efficiency. Which steps do the people you talk to think are most useful? Why? Present your findings in a presentation to the class.

INFORMATION TECHNOLOGY

When you combine computers with communications technology, you get information technology. Broadly defined, **information technology (IT)** is the study, design, development, implementation, support, and management of computer-based information systems. It is particularly focused on software applications and computer hardware.

Whenever you use a computer or computer software to convert, store, process, transmit, or retrieve information, you are using information technology. Think about it. A video game is an example of information technology. So is word processing software, such as Microsoft Office Word®. So is a spreadsheet program, such as Microsoft Office Excel®. So is a search engine, such as Google®. A program for manipulating any type of data is an example of information technology.

Data Storage

Data storage is one of the most important aspects of information technology. It's also an area in which vast improvements have been made over the last decade. There are two basic types of storage: primary storage and secondary storage. **Primary storage** is contained in the computer and is directly accessed by the **central processing unit (CPU)**. The CPU does all the actual computing. Primary storage is also referred to as **random access memory (RAM)**. When you turn off your computer, all the data stored in its primary storage, in RAM, is wiped clean.

Secondary storage isn't directly accessed by the CPU. It's a more permanent type of storage and doesn't lose data when the computer is turned off. The most common type of secondary storage is a computer's hard drive. Other common types of secondary storage are CDs, DVDs, USB sticks, floppy disks, and tape drives. Because these drives aren't directly accessed by the CPU, it takes more time for the CPU to access them. For example, the time it takes to access data in primary storage is measured in billionths of a second (**nanoseconds**), while the time it takes to access information on a hard drive is measured in thousandths of a second (**milliseconds**).

IT Professionals

Most businesses require the assistance of information technology professionals to install applications, design networks and information databases, and manage data and all aspects of that business's information technology. Large companies tend to have IT groups—employees within the company—who provide these services. Smaller companies often hire independent IT specialists. A small company may pay IT specialists by the hour or, as a way to budget for their IT needs, pay a set amount each month for the assistance of an independent IT group who then is on call.

As information systems become more complex and businesses require websites and sell their products on the Internet, the day when business owners could take care of their own IT needs is fast disappearing.

Tech Vocabulary

central processing unit (CPU)

information technology (IT)

milliseconds

nanoseconds

primary storage

random access memory (RAM)

secondary storage

Check Yourself

1. What is information technology?

2. What are the two types of storage?

3. What are some types of secondary storage?

4. What does an IT professional do?

What Do You Think?

Solving Problems. If you were a business owner who was experienced with information technology, would you choose to manage your company's IT? Explain your answer.

CASE STUDY

Developing an Entrepreneurial Mindset

BECOMING AN ENTREPRENEUR

Although she didn't realize it at the time, Eva Tan became an entrepreneur when she was a high school student in Westerville, Ohio. Follow her story, beginning here and continuing at the end of each unit of the book.

Planning for Success

One summer, when Eva was in high school, she helped plan her older sister's wedding. There were so many issues! Invitations, flowers, clothing, and music were just a few of the things that had to be arranged.

Helping the entire process go smoothly was a big challenge, but one that Eva really liked. The reception menu planning was particularly interesting, because Eva's parents came from two very different backgrounds: Irish and Filipino.

The event was a success. After it was over, Eva said, "As my sister's wedding planner, I had to wear many hats. The whole experience helped me realize the importance of problem-solving, paying attention to details, being organized but flexible, and remaining cool under pressure. The wedding took a lot of time and effort, but the results were worth it. My sister was pleased, and I discovered I could do things I didn't know I could."

That fall, back in high school, Eva took an "Introduction to Business" class as one of her electives. The class, and her experience with her sister's wedding, made her think of creating an event-planning business. She wondered what she could do to develop her skills and gain experience.

Eva began looking for opportunities to volunteer for more event-planning. She helped plan her Junior Prom and organized fund-raising events to nance a senior class trip to Florida.

Her mother, a high school teacher who earned her degree at Ohio State University (OSU), introduced Eva to friends from the university who needed event planning. They began asking Eva to plan small events like birthday parties and baby showers.

Eva's grandmother was a widow who lived with Eva's family. Although Eva's grandmother had never done event planning, she had run a small restaurant with her husband. Eva had always found her grandmother's stories about the restaurant entertaining, but now Eva began asking her for advice about upcoming events.

A Business Is Born!

During her senior year, Eva had difficulty deciding what career route to take after graduation. At the time, event planning seemed more like a hobby than a long-term career goal.

Eva decided to enroll in the two-year Business Management program at Columbus State Community College. She said, "I think the general business courses will be useful, no matter what career path I eventually decide to take." An agreement between Columbus State and OSU would also allow her to transfer her associate degree credits to OSU if she wanted to complete a four-year degree.

Eva continued to work part-time, planning events to help pay for college. Charging for her services by the hour, Eva researched vendor options, placed orders for goods and services, and coordinated their delivery. She began to wonder if she could increase her profits by making some of the food and party decorations herself.

To test this, Eva created samples of her food for customers. They loved it! As a result, she landed her first order that included her handmade food items. With her grandmother's help, she filled the order on time and to the customer's satisfaction. Eva's Entertainment Services was off and running!

An Ethical Problem

The start of the business was not without challenges. Eva had a customer named Tom who hired her to plan personal parties. One day, Tom asked Eva to plan a big event for the corporation where he worked. He asked her to order more supplies for the event than were actually needed. With a grin, he said, "I'm going to use the extra supplies for a party at my house. I'll ask you to handle it."

Eva was stunned. This was a real ethical problem! Eva thought about it. She decided she would rather risk losing Tom and his company as customers than be dishonest. Not only would Eva's conscience bother her, but also her reputation as a business person could be ruined if the fraudulent transaction was discovered.

Eva's experience led her to consider what types of ethical and social standards she would like her business to have. She wrote a code of ethics that reflected her values and made sure to mention the respect she had for her customers and vendors.

One item in her code of ethics almost always drew comments. It stated that Eva's company would be as "green" as possible. In keeping with her own code of ethics, Eva worked on making her home office energy-efficient. She also made an effort to choose vendors who were environmentally and socially responsible.

She gave her code of ethics to potential customers and vendors as a way of informing them what kinds of standards her company had—and hoping never to have another experience like the one with Tom again!

What Would You Have Done?

1. **Applying Concepts.** How would you have increased your knowledge about event planning if you were in high school, like Eva?

2. **Communicating.** If you had been in Eva's shoes, what would you have said to Tom? Do you think Eva had a responsibility to report Tom's conduct to someone else at his corporation?

3. **Drawing Conclusions.** What entrepreneurial mindset behaviors do you observe being demonstrated by Eva?

BIG IDEA: OPPORTUNITY RECOGNITION & MARKET ANALYSIS

CHAPTER 6

IDEA GENERATION

OBJECTIVES

- Explain how thinking of a new business idea is part of the entrepreneurial process.
- Identify the importance of creative thinking in generating business ideas.
- List various creative thinking activities for idea generation.

LESSON VOCABULARY

- brainstorm
- creative thinking
- creativity
- idea generation
- idea map
- ideation
- innovation
- lateral thinking

NFTE Entrepreneurial Mindset Characteristic Focus

☑ Creativity & Innovation

National Entrepreneurship Standards

- **A.01** Explain the need for entrepreneurial discovery
- **A.02** Discuss entrepreneurial discovery processes
- **A.03** Assess global trends and opportunities
- **A.04** Determine opportunities for venture creation
- **A.05** Assess opportunities for venture creation
- **A.06** Describe idea-generation methods
- **A.07** Generate venture ideas
- **A.31** Use creativity in business activities/decisions
- **B.14** Determine interests
- **B.27** Demonstrate creativity
- **L.01** Explain methods to generate a product/service idea
- **L.02** Generate product/service ideas

Common Career Technical Core Standards

- **BM.3** Explore, develop, and apply strategies for ensuring a successful business career.
- **CRP.6** Demonstrate creativity and innovation.
- **CRP.11** Use technology to enhance productivity.

National Entrepreneurship Standards: Career Competencies

☑ **K.09** Demonstrate writing/publishing applications

6.1 Creativity and the Entrepreneurial Process

Thinking Creatively

At this point, you may be excited about starting the entrepreneurial process. However, one thought that has probably crossed your mind: what will your business actually sell? Some entrepreneurs start with a very clear idea for a business. Others might start with a basic idea, but no clue on what to do to start their business. And others might be interested in entrepreneurship, but not have any idea at all. Therefore, if you are still trying to finalize your business idea, you are in good company!

The first step in the entrepreneurial process is the **ideation** phase. Ideation is the process of forming ideas. For entrepreneurs, this includes coming up with many different ideas for potential businesses. You already started the ideation phase in the first chapter while identifying problems

Thinking Creatively.
Being able to think of new innovations or new solutions to problems.

Applying Concepts.
Why is thinking creatively a foundational part of entrepreneurship?

and solutions. Entrepreneurs are constantly coming up with business ideas by using an entrepreneurial mindset skill called <mark>creativity</mark>, which is the process of developing original ideas. You may have heard this word used before in your other classes. Artists, writers, and musicians are usually described as creative because they are able to make new things of value (art, written text, and music).

Entrepreneurs also demonstrate a high level of creativity by training themselves to use creative thinking. <mark>Creative thinking</mark>, or <mark>lateral thinking</mark>, is a thought process that involves looking at a situation or object in new ways. This can include putting your imagination to work to make something new, to come up with new solutions to problems, even to think of new problems or questions. The phrases "thinking outside the box" and "using your imagination" refer to creative thinking. You may have also heard the new solutions that entrepreneurs create referred to as <mark>innovations</mark>, which are new ideas, devices, or methods introduced by entrepreneurs.

Barriers to Creative Thinking

While it may seem that only certain people can think of revolutionary ideas, that is not necessarily the case. Anyone can train themselves to think like an entrepreneur with some practice. There are also sometimes unseen barriers that can block creativity. The following internal barriers are road blocks to creativity:

- Thinking you need to know the "right" answer to create a great idea
- Concerned with looking silly in front of peers or investors
- Fear of failure when trying to pursue the business idea

Figure 6-2 ▶

Barriers to Creative Thinking.
You may face barriers while trying to think creatively.

Applying Concepts.
Why do these barriers to creative thinking exist?

In order to train yourself to think creatively, you have to face these barriers head on. Many new innovative ideas are met with resistance at first. Part of the ideation process is to know how to keep developing creative ideas despite resistance. Consider if the entrepreneurs who created some of the most influential inventions gave up after hearing these initial reactions.

"There is no reason anyone would want a computer in their home."
— Ken Olson (1926–2011), Founder of Digital Equipment Corp., 1977.

"This 'telephone' has too many shortcomings to be seriously considered as a means of communication. The device is inherently of no value to us."
— Western Union internal memo, 1876.

"Everyone acquainted with the subject will recognize it as a conspicuous failure."
— Henry Morton (1841–1904), President of the Stevens Institute of Technology, on Edison's light bulb, 1880.

"The horse is here to stay but the automobile is only a novelty, a fad."
— The President of the Michigan Savings Bank advising Henry Ford's lawyer not to invest in the Ford Motor Co., 1903.

"Flight by machines heavier than air is unpractical and insignificant, if not utterly impossible."
— Simon Newcomb (1835–1909); The Wright Brothers flew at Kittyhawk 18 months later.

"Television won't last. It's a flash in the pan."
— Mary Somerville (1897–1963), pioneer of radio educational broadcasts, 1948.

◀ **Figure 6-3**

Crazy Ideas That Worked.

Not all amazing new ideas are recognized as useful at first.

Applying Concepts.

How would the world be different if these entrepreneurs did not have the courage to think creatively?

Apply Your Knowledge   Why is creative thinking important for entrepreneurship? From your investigation, how did the team at Apple overcome resistance to new ideas?

ENTREPRENEURIAL CASE STUDY: CREATIVITY & INNOVATION

 ## Melverton Hunter, Jayson Isaac, Karishma Maraj, Jin Ruan, and Alan Tenemaza—SproutEd

Bringing the Classroom to the Phone

SproutEd is an education-based mobile application that can be downloaded through online stores such as Google Play. Its mission is to bring the classroom experience to mobile devices. SproutEd was created and built by five high school students: Karishma Maraj, Melverton Hunter, Jayson Isaac, Alan Tenemaza, and Jin Yan Ruan. These five young entrepreneurs have already accomplished more than many of their adult counterparts, including earning large amounts of educational and venture grants, as well as meetings with some of the biggest names in venture capital.

Finding an Idea

So, how did these five entrepreneurs come together? They met while attending NYC Generation Tech (GenTech), a summer camp held over 11 weeks, sponsored by the Network for Teaching Entrepreneurship (NFTE). The program's participants learned the principles of entrepreneurship, and received advanced training on how to write code and create mobile apps. Over the course of the GenTech camp, teams learned to code in HTML, CSS, and JavaScript, and created a mobile app prototype, business plan, and pitch presentation with the help of volunteer tech mentors.

While going through creative thinking exercises to come up with their business idea, they locked on to problems faced by anyone who has ever attended school. They thought about the frustration that comes with trying to ask teachers or peers questions about assignments outside of school hours. They recognized that while social media sites and e-mail make it somewhat possible to ask questions and discussion, it becomes distracting when the main focus is not on education.

Finding New Opportunities

The SproutEd team ran with their idea and built their app as an education network that creates an online environment for students and their peers to collaborate, get organized, and discuss school-related topics and events. SproutEd's message board encourages students to ask questions they might have when trying to complete a homework assignment or study for a test. Pursuing their idea paid off. The team took home first place honors at the GenTech's second annual Demo Night. In addition to a cash prize of $5,000, the five teen co-founders earned the opportunity to pitch SproutEd to partners at Union Square Ventures.

The SproutEd team have begun to use their experience at NFTE's GenTech to jump on more opportunities that have come their way. While all of them are still invested in SproutEd, they have used their new-found skills to create side projects, such as Ducky, a website that will serve as a hub for teenagers seeking extracurricular opportunities and programs. Each are also planning on finishing high school, and they will then pursue business and/or computer science in college. Of his experience in GenTech, SproutEd's Operation Officer, Melverton Hunter writes: "GenTech changed the way I think in many ways . . . I actually have the chance to create my own business. When I was younger, I never thought I would have the skills to create a business, but with the skills GenTech gave me I believe that I can be a technological mogul. Generation Tech opened many doors for me and I can't wait to see what's next."

Thinking and Acting Like an Entrepreneur

- How did the team at SproutEd use creative thinking to come up with their business idea?

- What skills did these students learn that helped them launch their business?

- In what ways did these five demonstrate the entrepreneurial mindset behavior of creativity and innovation?

6.2 Creative Thinking Exercises

Creative Thinking Techniques

Creative thinking is a muscle that needs exercise, just as any other. There are many ways you can help yourself think more creatively in entrepreneurship and other areas of your life. Here are a few techniques that you can use:

- **Challenge the Usual.** Ask lots of "Why?" and "What if?" questions. Challenge what you believe about how products should work or how things are done.

◀ **Figure 6-4**
Creative Thinking Techniques.
Many successful entrepreneurs engage in these approaches regularly.

Applying Concepts.
Why is it important to practice thinking creatively as you would any other skill?

- **Think Backwards.** Sometimes it's easier to solve a problem when you start by imagining the end result you want. Then mentally trace your imaginary steps backward to see how you would get there.

- **Be Flexible.** There is almost always more than one way to solve a problem. Force yourself to examine things from many different kinds of angles. Problems can even become solutions. Take, for example, Post-It® Notes. A glue created by 3M chemists was originally considered a failure because it was too weak for its intended purpose. But, using it in a different way produced a very successful product.

- **Judge Later.** When brainstorming ideas, don't worry about being practical. Also, try not to be negative or prejudiced. Those attitudes lower creativity. Not all ideas have to make sense in the beginning. You'll have time later to decide which ones are not useful. Sometimes ideas that seem silly at first, inspire other, more useful solutions later.

- **Draw Idea Maps.** Use whiteboards, chalkboards, and poster boards to sketch out ideas. For example, one idea might branch out into six other different directions, and some of those branches might generate additional items. Drawing your ideas in this way often helps you to see a bigger picture, with new possibilities that you might otherwise miss. You might also try using sticky notes on a wall or poster board. This method allows you to move ideas around.

- **Brainstorm in a Group.** Ask your friends, family, and classmates to help you generate ideas. The old saying, "two heads are better than one," is often true. All of these creative thinking techniques can also be used when working in a group.

Figure 6-5 ▶
Brainstorming.

Brainstorming can help you generate ideas.

Applying Concepts.

Why is it good to brainstorm alone and in a group?

- **Daydream.** It's okay to let your mind wander, just make sure you pick an appropriate time. With your eyes closed, practice visualizing what your new product or service would be. What would it look like, smell like, taste like, feel like, and sound like.

- **Pain Points.** Ask people to tell you their biggest problems or pain points. Something that might not bother you might be a huge problem for somebody else. Ask others to finish the sentence: "Wouldn't it be nice if . . ." and use their responses as potential business ideas.

- **Career Clusters Analysis.** Look at the career clusters that interested you from Unit 1. Think of ideas related to each career cluster.

Whether thinking creatively on your own or in a group, keeping a positive attitude helps build creativity. Eleanor Roosevelt, wife of U.S. President Franklin D. Roosevelt, wrote: "The future belongs to those who believe in the beauty of their dreams." In the next section, we will look at applying these creative thinking techniques specifically to coming up with business ideas.

Apply Your Knowledge Why is it important to practice creative thinking techniques? Think back to your investigation. Which of these creative thinking exercises do you think the team at Apple used when creating their products?

CAREER COMPETENCIES

Demonstrate Writing/ Publishing Applications

Technology has many functions for entrepreneurs. Among other things, it can be used to help with the idea generation process. Entrepreneurs can use technology as a tool to visualize new ideas. A computer application, or program, is a tool you use to perform specific tasks on a computer or smartphone. Employers look for employees who have experience using computers or applications. You may have already have some experience with applications in school or at home.

There are a few applications to familiarize yourself with when you're trying to create and publish documents for others to view:

- A word processor is probably the one with which you are most familiar. Modern word processors allow you to quickly edit and rearrange your written thoughts. If you are unhappy about a certain paragraph, you can move it somewhere else in the document or delete it entirely. Word processors also automatically check your spelling, so there are fewer mistakes in your work.

- A graphic design program lets you create sophisticated graphics or repair or manipulate photographs.

- A page layout program lets you place type and graphics on pages for publications.

Understanding how to use word processors and publishing applications are critical for success in school and almost any career. Mastering publishing programs, in addition to simple word processing, can allow you to enhance your writing with images and advanced features.

Word processors and publishing applications are also great tools during the idea generation phase of the entrepreneurial process. Here are just some of the ways you can use these tools while engaging in idea generation exercises:

- Perform free-writing or quick brainstorming for business ideas.
- Keep a "business idea" journal that can updated whenever inspiration strikes!
- Publish an idea map with images.
- Create a design for a new invention that can be shared more easily than it can be described with words.

Career Skills in Action

Now, you practice using writing and publishing applications for one of your business ideas that doesn't exist yet. Follow these steps:

- Utilize a word processor to explain how your invention works.
- Utilize a graphic design program to create an image of what it would look like.
- Publish a final document that puts the text and image on the same page.

Share your new invention with your peers and teacher for feedback.

6.3 Creative Thinking for Idea Generation

As stated previously, an important part of the entrepreneurial process is **idea generation**, or coming up with many business ideas. It is important to remember that many of these ideas might not actually work—but that's okay! The first stage is all about thinking of as many ideas as possible. You will learn how to trim down your idea list in future chapters.

Here are some examples of using creative thinking techniques to generate business ideas.

Brainstorm Potential Ideas

As mentioned before, one of the most effective ways to come up with many new ideas at once is to **brainstorm**. To brainstorm is to think about as many possible answers to a question, no matter how ridiculous,

◀ **Figure 6-6**
Brainstorming Practice.
Focusing on answering one question can sometimes help focus the brainstorming session.

Applying Concepts.
How many different businesses can you think of that you could start with this pushcart?

as quickly as possible. Let's try it on your own. Take a look at this ordinary pushcart. How many different business ideas can you think of that would use this cart? Give yourself a minute to think of potential ideas.

How many ideas were you able to think of? Did most of your businesses use the pushcart in traditional ways (such as lemonade or hot dog stand), or did you think of new uses (mobile dog wash; solar-powered mobile phone charging station)? Practice these exercises to start looking at existing things in new ways.

Challenge the Usual

Use "why" and "what if" questions to help you think of new ways to change an existing business. Start with the assumptions for business as usual and try to figure out what would break the rules. For each new proposal, try to ask yourself how you could make it work. Here is an example of challenging the usual with a restaurant idea:

- **Step 1:** State your challenge ("I want to create a different restaurant experience.")
- **Step 2:** State your assumptions ("Restaurants all have menus.")
- **Step 3:** Challenge the usual ("Restaurants don't HAVE to have menus.")
- **Step 4:** Ask "what if" questions ("What if my restaurant did NOT have menus? How could I make that work?")

Draw Idea Maps

Drawing **idea maps** can help you come up with numerous potential business ideas all at once. The central idea should always be an interest or problem from your identified career cluster. From there, let yourself freely think of ideas and additional problems that have to do with the central idea. You should list these as branches to your central idea. Keep expanding on each branch until you have numerous potential ideas related to your central idea.

For example, here could be the potential start to an idea map if you were a drummer:

Figure 6-7 ▶
Idea Map.

A simple idea map can help tease out business ideas.

Applying Concepts.

How many other categories can you think of involving a new drum set?

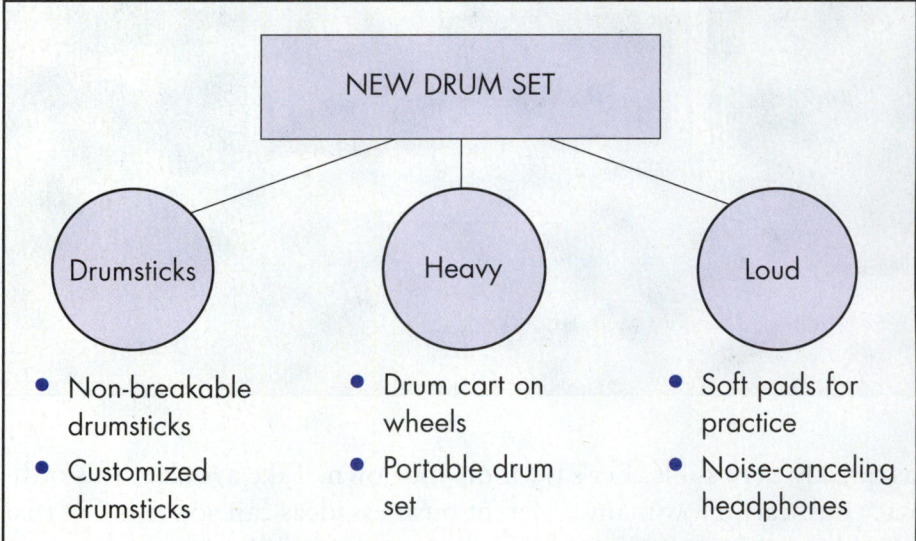

In this chapter, we looked at creative thinking techniques for coming up with a wide variety of new innovations and business ideas. In the next chapter, we will continue down the ideation process by looking at where to find inspiration for more targeted business ideas.

 **Apply Your Knowledge** Why is going through idea generation important, even if you think you have an idea for a business? Do you think the team at Apple did idea generation once or many times over the years? Explain your answer.

APPLICATION TO BUSINESS PLANNING

Idea Generation

Use the creative thinking techniques you learned about in this chapter to come up with as many business ideas as possible. Remember, there is no bad idea at this stage, so generate as many as possible (at least ten)! Include some of your great ideas from the first unit as well. You can use any of the following approaches:

- Challenge the usual
- Think backwards
- Draw idea maps
- Brainstorm in a group
- Daydream
- Pain points
- Career clusters analysis

6 ASSESSMENT

REVIEWING OBJECTIVES

1. How is thinking of a new business idea an important part of the entrepreneurial process?

2. Why is creative thinking important for generating business ideas?

3. List various creative thinking activities for idea generation.

CRITICAL THINKING

Compare and contrast the various approaches to idea generation. Which one do you think would be the most effective for you? Why do you think that is?

ENTREPRENEURIAL THINKING EXERCISE: CREATIVITY & INNOVATION

Think back to your investigation. Imagine you are a new employee at Apple! You have been charged with conceiving of a new tech device that will revolutionize the industry. Explain how you would use creative thinking techniques to come up with new ideas. Use those techniques to come with ideas that you could pitch to the development team at Apple.

EXTENSION ACTIVITIES

Entrepreneurship & Literacy Skills

Complete the following task to demonstrate your understanding of entrepreneurship:

Grades 9–12: In this chapter, you read about people who criticized new innovations that eventually went on to become extremely important inventions that impacted society in many ways. Choose one of the inventions listed in the chapter, or one of your own favorite modern innovations. Write a response letter to one of the critics who did not initially understand the idea. What would you tell them about the importance of this invention? How would you help them understand the features and benefits of the invention? Be sure to back up your claims with accurate statements about the invention, using a tone appropriate for a business letter.

OBJECTIVES

- Explain the difference between a business idea and a business opportunity.
- Identify external sources of business opportunities.
- List approaches for turning good ideas into business opportunities.

NFTE Entrepreneurial Mindset Characteristic Focus

☑ Opportunity Recognition

National Entrepreneurship Standards

- **A.01** Explain the need for entrepreneurial discovery
- **A.02** Discuss entrepreneurial discovery processes
- **A.03** Assess global trends and opportunities
- **A.04** Determine opportunities for venture creation
- **A.05** Assess opportunities for venture creation
- **A.06** Describe idea-generation methods
- **A.07** Generate venture ideas
- **A.31** Use creativity in business activities/decisions
- **L.01** Explain methods to generate a product/service idea
- **L.02** Generate product/service ideas

Common Career Technical Core Standards

- **BM.1** Utilize mathematical concepts, skills, and problem solving to obtain necessary information for decision-making in business.
- **BM.3** Explore, develop, and apply strategies for ensuring a successful business career.
- **CRP.6** Demonstrate creativity and innovation.
- **CRP.11** Use technology to enhance productivity.

National Entrepreneurship Standards: Career Competencies

☑ **E.11** Demonstrate basic search skills on the Web

LESSON VOCABULARY

- business broker
- business opportunity
- franchise
- franchisee
- franchisor
- need
- nondisclosure agreement
- pivot
- prototype
- royalty fee
- trade show
- want
- window of opportunity

Turning Ideas into Opportunities ● **133**

ENTREPRENEURIAL INVESTIGATION
Solve a Problem, Make a Million

Madame C.J. Walker was born to a family of poor farmers and ex-slaves in Louisiana in 1867. By the time of her death, she had become the first American self-made woman millionaire by creating hair and skin care products for African-American women. Recognizing that women with dark skinned complexions had different needs than skin of lighter complexion, she experimented until she found a formula that would address those needs. After some experiments on herself and her family, she became convinced that her business would be successful.

Do some research on Madame C.J. Walker and her business operations, specifically:

- Hair and skin care products that existed before her business
- "The Walker Method" that she sold as part of her products
- "Walker Clubs" or the way her sales agents sold her product

After you research, respond to the following questions:

- Why did Madame C.J. Walker believe her idea would be successful?
- What did she do to make sure it was successful?
- Why do you think she was such a success?

Be prepared to share your responses with your teacher or class.

7.1 Recognizing Business Opportunities

Ideas vs. Opportunities

In the previous chapter, you learned how entrepreneurs generate numerous business ideas. In this chapter, you will learn how to use another entrepreneurial mindset skill, which is to recognize which of those ideas are actual business opportunities. A **business opportunity** is a consumer need or want that can potentially be met by a new business. In economics, a **need** is defined as something that people must have to survive, such as water, food, clothing, and shelter, whereas a **want** is a product or service that people strongly desire. Usually you start a business because you see a business opportunity. People who think entrepreneurially are skilled at opportunity recognition, which is the process of recognizing opportunities in business and their lives.

Not every business idea is a good business opportunity. For example, you might have an interesting idea for a neighborhood restaurant. But if that idea has no real commercial potential, if it can't make a profit, then it isn't an opportunity. If no one likes the type of food you plan to serve, the business would be doomed to fail.

Your idea could be an opportunity in a different location, however. Let's say that the people in another town really desire your potential restaurant's kind of food. In addition, no similar restaurant currently exists nearby. In this case, your idea *could* be a real opportunity.

You may wonder why the ideation phase of the entrepreneurial process starts with idea generation, when many of those ideas might not actually be good business opportunities. The answer is that both—generating new ideas and recognizing business opportunities—are important and related. By starting with idea generation, you are more likely to identify ideas that you are passionate about. This will ensure that the business opportunity you select will be aligned to something you will be driven towards.

Recognizing business opportunities builds on the initial brainstorming in a more targeted approach. Let's say your brainstorming led you to wanting to knit homemade wool socks. This is a great business idea . . . unless you are trying to sell in a beach town during the summer, because no one needs or wants those socks. Recognizing that this might not be the best opportunity lets you return to your idea list and select a potentially better opportunity (i.e., customized sunglasses). It also allows you to **pivot**, or change and revise, your initial idea until you get a better opportunity (i.e., sell wool socks during holiday season online).

You can ask yourself five questions to begin the process of determining if a business idea might be a real business opportunity. As you read this book, you'll discover practical ways of answering the questions.

- Does the idea fill a need or want that's not currently being met?
- Will the idea work in your chosen location or in the way that you plan to sell it?
- Can you put the idea into action within a reasonable amount of time? That is, before someone else does, or while resources are still available? This concept is called the **window of opportunity**—the period of time you have to act on a business opportunity before it disappears.
- Do you have the resources and skills to create the business (or know someone else who could help you do it)?
- Can you provide the product or service at a price that will attract customers, but still earn a reasonable profit?

Apply Your Knowledge   When is a business idea a business opportunity? Why was Madame C.J. Walker's business a good opportunity?

ENTREPRENEURIAL CASE STUDY: OPPORTUNITY RECOGNITION

 ## Melissa Ruiz-Vera— Vera Natural

Best of the Best Business Ideas

Vera Natural is an all-natural skin cream based on a family recipe handed down through generations. This business is the creation of CEO and Founder, Melissa Ruiz-Vera. She started this business in her entrepreneurship class while she was a high school junior at the Academy of Finance and Enterprise in New York City. Melissa's class was sponsored by the Network for Teaching Entrepreneurship (NFTE), which holds an annual business plan competition for young entrepreneurs. Entering the competition, Melissa was the first place winner of the NFTE 2013 New York Metro Youth Entrepreneurship Challenge (YEC).

Identifying a Business Opportunity

Melissa and her family immigrated to the United States thirteen years ago from Colombia. Melissa's family, while happy to have settled in the U.S., struggled with leaving everything they had in Colombia. Moving meant that they had to recreate their lives here, including having to go

Melissa Ruiz-Vera.

back to school. "My parents came here with nothing," Melissa remembers. "We lived in this small apartment. And now we have a house. They were able to turn a small thing into something big. My parents taught me that organization is key."

While in her entrepreneurship class, Melissa was tasked with finding an idea for a business opportunity. At first, she wasn't sure what she was going to do for her business. But then she came across an old recipe for skin cream made by her grandmother. Melissa remembers of her experience, "There was a competition in school, and I presented it, and I came in third." After that, her teacher suggested that she compete in the NFTE YEC competition. Melissa explains, "That's when I noticed that Vera Natural could really be a business, that this was no joke."

From this idea, Melissa decided that the best route to turn her idea into an opportunity was to create a business that sold an updated version of her grandmother's recipe. And from that Vera Natural was born. Vera Natural now creates all-natural, homemade body creams for both men and women. Vera Natural offers these nourishing creams at an affordable price using a unique formula of ingredients first developed by Melissa's grandmother in Columbia and shared with her by her father. Melissa has since perfected this family recipe to give her customers the optimal outcome they desire.

Putting the Idea into Action

Melissa entered the NFTE Youth Entrepreneurship Challenge with her business plan for Vera Natural and won first place. Since then, it has been a whirlwind. "My biggest surprise is just how far and how fast we've gotten. We've gone from selling, like, ten in a month, if anything, to seventy per week in a matter of five months," said Melissa of her experience after the competition. In addition to the $1,500 she won from NFTE, she also received $5,000 grant from E*Trade, thanks to her mentor, Mathew Audette the E*Trade Chief Financial Officer. She was also awarded a $1,000 scholarship as one of the Ernst & Young Entrepreneurs of the Year.

Melissa is now working on expanding her business by building a reputable brand and expansive product line that will attract more customers. In January 2015, she began attending Babson College to gain more skills in running a business.

Thinking and Acting Like an Entrepreneur

- What source of external opportunity did Melissa use to find her business idea?
- How did Melissa turn her idea into an actual opportunity?
- In what ways does Melissa demonstrate the entrepreneurial mindset behavior of opportunity recognition?

7.2 Sources of Opportunity

Internal Sources of Opportunity

In addition to the initial idea generation you did previously, you should look internally for potential business opportunities. Ask yourself the following questions:

- **Hobbies.** What are some things I love to do? What would I do every day, even if I was not getting paid to do it? Is there any way I could get anyone to pay me to do that hobby?
- **Interests.** What are some things I am interested in? Do I know a lot about a specific topic that others do not? Would others pay me for the knowledge that I have?
- **Talents.** What are things that I'm naturally gifted at? What are things that people compliment me on? What awards have I won for performing, academics, or athletics?

- **Skills.** What entrepreneurial mindset skills do I have? Do I have a skillset that many others do not? Would others pay me if I applied my skill to a task to a job in a specific career cluster?

External Sources of Opportunity

Staying aware of certain things going on around you can help you recognize potential business opportunities. Here are just a few sources of ideas for potential business opportunities:

- **Problems.** Many well-known companies got started because an entrepreneur wanted to solve a problem. A problem could be something you are experiencing personally. Or it could be a problem you observe others experiencing. What product or service would improve your life or the lives of others? What would you like to buy, but it is not available for purchase in your area? In the previous unit you learned that many businesses also try to solve societal problems. Try to find societal problems that could be solved while making a profit.

- **Changes.** Our world is continually changing—changes in laws and regulations, social customs, local and national trends, even the weather. Change often produces needs or wants that no one is currently meeting. Consider global warming and the trend toward taking better care of the environment. Many new business opportunities have occurred because people are more interested in purchasing "green" products and services. Trends in population changes can also lead to business opportunities. Shifts in population numbers or breakdowns can be obtained to find new customers with unique needs.

Figure 7-1 ▶
Trends.

This graph projects U.S. population growth from 2000 to 2050 based on U.S. Census Bureau estimates.

Applying Concepts.

What area suggests the greatest increase in business opportunity?

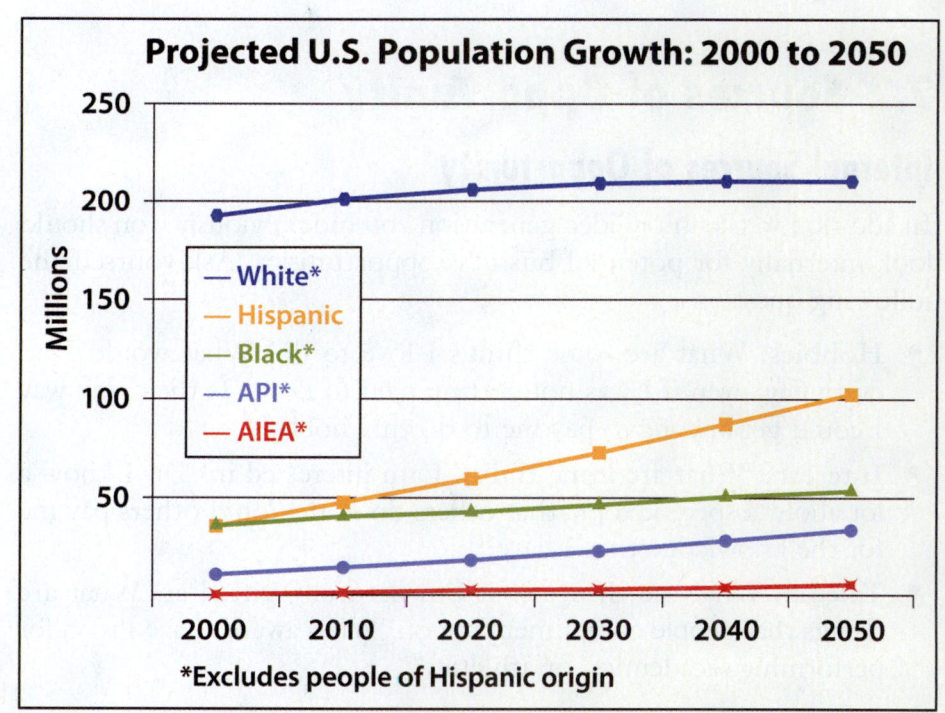

Projected U.S. Population Growth: 2000 to 2050

— White*
— Hispanic
— Black*
— API*
— AIEA*

*Excludes people of Hispanic origin

- **New Discoveries.** The creation of totally new products and services can happen by accident. For example, someone participating in a hobby they enjoy can discover something new that they recognize as a business opportunity. Inventions also come about because someone wanted to find a way to solve a problem. Other examples include medical and technological discoveries that entrepreneurs find ways to convert into products and services.

- **Existing Products and Services.** You can get ideas for business opportunities from things that already exist. This is not the same thing as copying a product or service, and then calling it by another name (which can be illegal). Instead, it means looking for ways to significantly improve a product, perhaps at a lower price. It could also involve improving the quality and manner in which customers are served—including such things as better locations, longer hours, or quicker service.

- **Unique Knowledge.** Entrepreneurs sometimes turn one-of-a-kind experiences or uncommon knowledge into a product or service that benefits others. Think about your own knowledge and experiences. Is there anything unique or unusual that you could use to create something new, or to help someone?

Where to Look for Opportunities

There are many ways to locate business opportunities. Your own community is a good place to begin looking. Here are some information resources you might find useful:

- **Newspapers and Magazines.** Examine not only your local newspapers, but ones from metropolitan areas such as New York City, Miami, Chicago, Dallas/Fort Worth, and Los Angeles. Sampling the news from across the country may help you see a developing national trend. News magazines such as *Time* and *Newsweek* are other news resources, as are magazines published about your particular city. In addition, take a look at specialized magazines that focus on a hobby or subject you enjoy.

- **Business and Governmental Agencies.** Some good examples of government agencies that provide useful statistical data and other information are: U.S. Census Bureau, U.S. Department of Labor, and U.S. Small Business Administration. You can also contact your local Better Business Bureau® or chamber of commerce for information on businesses in your area.

- **Trade Resources.** Various types of trade resources can help you get ideas for new businesses. A <mark>trade show</mark> is a convention where related businesses come to promote their products or services. Similarly, trade magazines are published for specific types of businesses. Trade associations exist for nearly every industry. A few examples of trade associations include the American Booksellers Association, Pet Sitters International, Soap and Detergent Association, and the National Roofing Contractors Association.

Figure 7-2 ▶
Trade Show.
Trade shows can help give you ideas for new businesses.

Applying Concepts.
How might going to trade shows outside of your industry help you find new opportunities?

- **World Wide Web.** Surfing the Web is a great way to explore just about any topic. By surfing you might discover important sites that otherwise would not have known.

 **Apply Your Knowledge** Think back to your investigation. What internal sources of opportunity did Madame C.J. Walker identify to create her business opportunity? What external sources of opportunity did she identify?

CAREER COMPETENCIES

✔ Demonstrate Basic Search Skills on the Web

Have you ever used the Internet to search for information? If so, then you already possess several basic, transferrable skills that you will need to interact with technology in your career. And the best part is, since technology is everywhere in the world of work, if you have one or more of these basic skills, you can take them wherever you go:

- Turn a computer on and start a program.
- Type on a computer keyboard without making any mistakes.
- Access the Internet and move from one website to another.
- Use a search engine to do basic Internet research.
- Write and send e-mail.

Some of these skills might seem easy to you. Others might sound difficult or new. Either way, these are skills worth having. The important thing to know is that you might be asked to use these or other basic, transferrable skills at some point in your career. Even if you do not know how to do some of these things, you can learn.

All of these skills are absolutely necessary for being an entrepreneur. One very important skill that can be overlooked is being able to use a search engine, such as Google, to do a basic Internet search. As more and more information is moved from being paper- and book-based to digital, being able to find information online is critical for finding out about business opportunities.

Let's say you wanted to research opportunities around fixing "food deserts," a term for when a community does not have easy access to healthy food. If you do a search for food deserts, you will get a lot of information about food, and a lot of information about deserts separately.

That is because to make this search more powerful, you should use what is called a Boolean operator. These are special words or quotes around a phrase to search a phrase exactly. So if you search for "food desert" instead, you will find what you are looking for.

Also, being able to use search engines appropriately can help with identifying new business opportunities. Take time every morning and practice searching for a new topic that you know nothing about. Open up some links in new tabs or windows to read later. This new information could lead you to an awesome new business opportunity that you previously knew nothing about!

Career Skills in Action

Now, you practice doing some basic searches to identify some business opportunities. Try the following:

- Do a search on one of your potential ideas to get more information
- Do a search on a topic that you want to know more about that could be an opportunity
- Do a search on a new topic that you know nothing about

Share what you found during your searches with your teacher and peers.

7.3 Turning Ideas into Opportunities

After you've generated a number of business ideas, the next step is to compare options for applying those ideas. Should you start a new business, or buy one that already exists? Does the problem you've identified call for a new invention, or the modification of an old product?

There are four common ways to turn ideas into opportunities:

- Start a new business
- Buy an independent business
- Buy a franchise
- Become an inventor

Starting a New Business

The beauty of starting a new business lies in the fact that you can build it your own way. However, this also means that many decisions and tasks have to be completed before a new business can run effectively. This could initially turn out to be a real challenge if you don't have the necessary resources or skills. How much time and effort are you willing to invest? How will you obtain the knowledge and skills needed to start and operate a new business?

A potential disadvantage of starting a new business is the amount of risk or uncertainty involved. If your product or service is new, it may be harder to predict how well it will sell. There typically will be less information available on which you can base your decisions. How much are you willing to risk?

Although starting a new business may seem overwhelming, everything doesn't have to happen at once. As the saying goes, "Rome wasn't built in a day." With proper planning and strong motivation, you can succeed in building a new business, one step at a time.

Buying an Independent Business

When you start a business from the ground up, it can take a long time before it becomes successful. That's one reason why some entrepreneurs prefer to purchase or expand a business that already exists. Finding a business for sale is similar to looking for a house to buy. You can start by reading advertisements in local newspapers and real estate magazines. You may also want to hire a **business broker**, someone who is licensed to sell businesses.

An existing business normally has much already in place: trained employees, operating equipment, merchandise and supplies on hand, established credit for making new purchases, and established procedures for running the business. Most important of all, an existing business already has customers. If current customers are happy with the products or services, their repeat purchases will help to ensure your success.

Sometimes, the previous owner of an independent business is willing to provide a period of training for the new owner. The business seller may also allow for a down payment, followed by monthly installments. This can reduce the amount of money you need to borrow from a bank, family, or friends.

Buying an independent business is still very much an entrepreneurial activity. You may not have initially created the business, but you are responsible for its continued growth and success. For example, you can use your business skills and creativity to attract additional customers. You might also find new ways to improve the current processes and procedures of the business. You may even decide to add new products or services at some point.

Buying a business usually requires a large amount of money initially. In comparison, when starting a new business, you may not have to invest much money at the beginning. When buying a business you also risk inheriting problems—both visible ones and hidden ones.

Buying a Franchise

Some entrepreneurs might find that they would rather own and manage a business that is already implementing an opportunity. For example, if an entrepreneurs notices the need for a lunch place near an office building, she or he might pay for the rights to open a Subway in that location, instead of starting a restaurant from scratch. This process is referred to as buying a **franchise**. This legal agreement gives the **franchisee**, or franchise buyer, the right to sell the company's products or services in a particular location, and for a specified amount of time. The franchise seller is called a **franchisor**. Many fast food businesses are franchises, for example.

◀ **Figure 7-3**
Franchises.
Many fast-food restaurants are franchises.

Recognizing Patterns.
What are the names of some fast food franchise businesses located in your community?

As you've already learned, buying a business has less risk than starting a new one. This is particularly true of franchises. Some sources estimate that franchises have a 90% or better chance of success. Some of the reasons for this include the following:

- **Proven System.** Most franchises have an established system in place that's already been tested. Following the proven processes and procedures created by the franchisor help ensure the success of your business as well.

- **Customer Awareness.** People tend to buy from businesses they recognize and trust. When you buy a franchise that is well-known and well-liked, you benefit from the name and reputation already established.

- **Multiple Benefits Provided by the Franchisor.** A franchisor provides initial training on how to operate the business. In addition, the franchisor provides on-going support when you have questions. An individual franchise also benefits from national advertising done by the franchisor.

- **Exclusive Geographical Area.** A franchisor only allows a certain number of franchises to operate within a particular region. This keeps competition down.

- **Easier Financing.** Bankers are often more likely to loan money to a person buying a franchise because historically franchises have a high rate of success. From the bankers' point of view, a franchisee is less likely to default on a loan than owners of other types of businesses.

Owning a franchise may also give you additional opportunities to grow as an entrepreneur. Once you're a successful franchise owner, you may want to buy additional units of the same franchise in other locations. As the owner, you manage all the teams who work at the various sites.

There are also some downsides to consider before buying a franchise:

- **Initial and Ongoing Fees.** When you first buy a franchise, you pay a fairly high fee for the right to operate it. This cost can range from $5,000 to $100,000 and can go much higher. Additional money is needed to set up and operate a franchise. For example, equipment has to be purchased. Extra money has to be set aside to pay bills and employees until the business is making enough profit. A franchise owner also pays a royalty fee to the franchisor. This is a regular, ongoing payment that's based on a percentage of the sales a franchise earns.

- **Less Entrepreneurial Freedom.** Starting a new business, as well as buying an independent business, provides plenty of decision-making freedom. When you own a franchise, however, you must abide by the rules in the agreement. If you fail to meet the conditions of the franchise, the franchisor can cancel your agreement and put you out of business. There is also no guarantee that the franchisor will renew your agreement when it expires.

Becoming an Inventor

Some entrepreneurs invent new products, designs, or processes. They may choose to sell or license their inventions to someone else. Or, they may create a business of their own that uses or manufactures the invention. Often inventors significantly change an existing product or process, rather than create a totally new one, just as the following two companies did:

- **HurriQuake Nail.** The HurriQuake nail is designed to resist being pulled out of wood during hurricanes and earthquakes. Because it only costs about $15 more to build a house with HurriQuake nails, a lot of builders are likely to purchase HurriQuake instead of regular nails.

- **XO Laptop.** One Laptop Per Child (OLPC) is a nonprofit organization with the goal of providing a laptop for children worldwide. OLPC found a way to create a low-cost laptop called the XO. They also reduced the laptop's energy use by 90 percent. This was achieved by inventing a new kind of screen display.

Whether you want to create a new invention or improve an existing one, here are some of the things you will need to do:

- **Keep a Logbook.** Keep a detailed record, with dates, of everything related to your potential invention. Start with the date when you first thought of the idea. Use a type of notebook that is hardbound, not a loose-leaf binder. Your logbook can be used in the future to help prove the beginning of an invention. In addition, a logbook is a good way to keep track of all your sketches, notes, and research information.

◀ **Figure 7-4**
Logbook.

Inventors should keep a detailed logbook.

Applying Concepts.

Why would it be important to keep a logbook with you at all times?

- **Conduct a Search.** Find out whether somebody else has already patented an invention that's the same or similar to your idea. A patent provides a legal means for protecting an invention. A patent gives the inventor the exclusive right to make, use, and sell the invention for a certain period of time. Patents are issued by the U.S. government's Patent and Trademark Office (www.uspto.gov). If no one has patented an invention like yours, you may want to consider getting your own patent.

- **Create a Prototype.** A <mark>prototype</mark> is a model on which future reproductions of an invention are based. Start by building a non-working model out of materials such as foam, wood, or cardboard. This step helps you determine the correct form and shape of the product. With CAD (computer aided design) software, you can also make an electronic drawing of your invention. Later, you will also need to create a working prototype. This is an exact sample of how the final product will look, move, and operate. Any manufacturer or designer with whom you discuss your product should be asked to sign a <mark>nondisclosure agreement</mark>. This is a legal document in which the person or group agrees to keep certain information confidential.

You should apply your initial list of potential ideas to these steps to see which would be the most realistic for each. Once you have a clear idea of how you could turn your idea into a business, you have a potential business opportunity. In the following chapter, we will look at ways of evaluating business opportunities for the best one!

 **Apply Your Knowledge** What are four common ways you can turn an idea into a business opportunity? From your investigation, how did Madame C.J. Walker turn her business idea into an opportunity?

APPLICATION TO BUSINESS PLANNING

Business Opportunities

Use what you learned in this chapter on ideas versus opportunities to narrow down your list of business ideas to actual business opportunities. Be sure you can do the following for each:

- Explain why it could be a business opportunity.
- Explain how it meets the needs of the market.
- What source of opportunity does it match? (external or internal)
- How would you turn your idea into an opportunity if implemented?
- What issues are involved with starting a business or taking over or expanding an existing business?

ASSESSMENT

REVIEWING OBJECTIVES

1. What is the main difference between a business idea and a business opportunity?

2. What are external sources of business opportunities?

3. List approaches for turning good ideas into business opportunities.

CRITICAL THINKING

List ten major issues that have appeared in the local news over the past few months. Which of these could be solved reduced by creating a business that doesn't exist yet in your community?

ENTREPRENEURIAL THINKING EXERCISE: OPPORTUNITY RECOGNITION

Think back to your investigation of Madame C.J. Walker. Her business was a success because she identified a problem and created a business that solved that problem. Imagine that she were alive today. If you were to team up with her to start a new business, what problems do you think she would be able to solve with her experience? Can you think of possible business solutions to that problem?

ASSESSMENT

EXTENSION ACTIVITIES

Entrepreneurship & Literacy Skills

Complete the following task to demonstrate your understanding of entrepreneurship:

1. Grades 9–10: Read a variety of local media sources (i.e., newspaper articles, blog entries, etc.) that each discuss the same local problem in your town or community. Read each to pull out the key ideas of what the problem is, and what they each feel is the root of the problem. Find where each state similar ideas, and where their opinions differ. Identify a business opportunity that would solve the common problem that's been identified. Be prepared to share with your teacher and your peers.

2. Grades 11–12: Read a variety of local media sources (i.e., newspaper articles, blog entries, etc.) that each discuss the same local problem in your town or community. Read each to pull out the key ideas of what the problem is, and what they each feel is the root of the problem. Note if any of the writings contradict or oppose each other. Come up with a business opportunity that would most closely fix the root of the problem that's been identified by each. Be prepared to share with your teacher and your peers.

"How do I know which of my ideas is the best business opportunity?"

APPLICATION TO BUSINESS PLANNING:

☑ Screened Business Opportunity

OBJECTIVES

- Explain how creative and critical thinking are both needed in entrepreneurship.
- Describe techniques to use for determining the most feasible business opportunities.
- Identify questions entrepreneurs must answer for ongoing evaluation of a business opportunity.

NFTE Entrepreneurial Mindset Characteristic Focus

☑ Critical Thinking & Problem Solving

National Entrepreneurship Standards

- **A.02** Discuss entrepreneurial discovery processes
- **A.04** Determine opportunities for venture creation
- **A.05** Assess opportunities for venture creation
- **A.08** Determine feasibility of ideas
- **A.26** Evaluate risk-taking opportunities
- **F.04** Explain the concept of opportunity costs
- **F.10** Describe cost/benefit analysis
- **F.24** Determine factors affecting business risk
- **O.01** Conduct SWOT analysis

Common Career Technical Core Standards

- **BM.5** Implement systems, strategies and techniques used to manage information in a business.
- **BM-MGT.2** Access, evaluate and disseminate information for business decision making.
- **CRP.2** Apply appropriate academic and technical skills.
- **CRP.8** Utilize critical thinking to make sense of problems and persevere in solving them.

National Entrepreneurship Standards: Career Competencies

☑ **K.10** Demonstrate presentation applications

LESSON VOCABULARY

- business canvas
- calculated risks
- cost/benefit analysis
- critical thinking
- feasibility
- intangible
- objective
- opportunity cost
- subjective
- SWOT analysis
- vertical thinking

One Man's "C" is Another Man's "Billion Dollar Idea"

Fred Smith, the founder of Federal Express, or FedEx, first came up with his idea while in business school at Yale University. Fred's idea was a shipping system using airplanes for time-sensitive shipments such as medicines and electronics. Legend has it that his professor was not impressed with his idea. Fred got a "C" for his overnight shipping idea, but he knew that he had a great idea.

Fred kept working on his idea. He eventually started his overnight delivery service with seven packages on the first try. While it was an uphill process, his persistence eventually paid off. Now FedEx is one of the largest global delivery services. It brought in over $45 billion in revenue during 2013.

Do some research on FedEx and Fred Smith's attempts to start his business. After you research, respond to the following questions:

• Why did his professor not think his idea would work?

• What made him confident in his idea?

• Do you think he had a good idea or an actual business opportunity? How do you know?

Be prepared to share your responses with your teacher or class.

8.1 Critical Thinking and the Entrepreneurial Process

Using Critical Thinking

In previous chapters, you used creative thinking techniques to identify potential business ideas, and then did some initial screening to see which could be potential business opportunities. Now, you will learn some techniques to identify which of those identified business opportunities might be the best to pursue.

The best way for entrepreneurs to evaluate business opportunities is to use the entrepreneurial mindset skill of critical thinking. **Critical thinking**, or **vertical thinking**, refers to a logical thought process that involves analyzing and evaluating a situation or object. Perhaps you've asked someone to help critique an essay or project on which you were working. They read or analyze what you've done. Then, they usually evaluate the essay, creating a list of errors or suggestions of things you should change. Critical thinking doesn't mean you are being negative; it means you are examining something while being honest, rational, and open-minded.

Critical thinking can be used for making decisions, setting goals, and solving problems. When you think critically, you try not to let how you feel or what you believe get in the way of choosing the best course of action. Using critical thinking in situations requires:

- Acknowledging personal feelings and preexisting opinions
- Relying on reason and thought instead of on emotion or impulse
- Evaluating all possible options—even those that are unpopular

Thinking critically doesn't mean you should ignore emotions or any other influence factors; it just means you should consider all possibilities before rushing to judgment. You should look objectively at information. **Objective** means fair, without emotion or prejudice. Not being objective would be looking at information subjectively. **Subjective** means affected by existing opinions, feelings and beliefs. Having a critical thinking perspective is important for entrepreneurs to honestly assess a potential business opportunity. You may really love the recipe for your grandmother's brownies, but if no one is willing to buy them, then selling those brownies is not a smart business opportunity.

In entrepreneurship, creative and critical thinking are both important, but they tend to produce different results. So it is wise to learn when and how to apply them. For example, we already learned that creative thinking works well for generating ideas and recognizing opportunities. In this chapter, you'll learn more about how to apply critical thinking when evaluating business opportunities.

Apply Your Knowledge   What is the difference between critical thinking and creative thinking? Think back to your investigation. How did Fred Smith have to use both?

ENTREPRENEURIAL CASE STUDY: CRITICAL THINKING & PROBLEM SOLVING

 ## Gregg Kaplan—redbox

Billion Dollar Idea

Many people know redbox Automated Retail (www.redbox.com) from the red kiosks that rent new release DVDs to consumers for the low price of $1

per day. If you have not used this service, you have most likely seen these red boxes popping up everywhere. This business is the brainchild of founder and CEO, Gregg Kaplan. Over Gregg's 11 years either running or overseeing redbox, it went from a small startup to a nationally-recognized brand. Redbox has now become the leading renter of DVDs in the US, passing competitors such as Movie Gallery, Hollywood Video, Blockbuster and Netflix. As of 2014, redbox has 44,000 kiosks in every state,

Gregg Kaplan.

Canada and Puerto Rico and is one of the fastest growing companies ever, taking only seven years to reach $1B in revenue.

Providing Convenience to Customers

Prior to redbox, Gregg was an early employee at another entrepreneurial venture, Streamline. Streamline set out to simplify the lives of busy suburban families by providing them with Internet-based ordering of a wide range of goods and services, such as groceries, dry cleaning, video rentals, prepared meals, film processing, UPS package pickup and shoe repair. Streamline delivered these goods and services to families' homes on a weekly, scheduled unattended basis.

Gregg founded redbox in 2002 while serving as senior director of strategy for McDonald's Corporation. McDonald's was initially interested in starting lots of new consumer-focused businesses, but eventually asked Gregg to use redbox to help McDonald's drive more people into their restaurants. The redbox idea originally started with a variety of automated convenience options, including fully automated "convenience store" kiosks. While customers liked the convenience, the concept of getting new release DVD rentals emerged as the most appealing to consumers. Based on customer feedback, that was the opportunity Gregg decided to pursue.

Growing and Improving the Business

Under McDonald's ownership, Gregg spent several years refining the redbox concept with a series of market tests, starting with a handful of kiosks in Washington DC. Redbox's first full market test launched in 2004 in Denver, Colorado-area McDonald's restaurants. Following more positive customer feedback, in 2005, McDonald's expanded the test to more than 800 restaurants across five additional markets. Soon, it was apparent to Gregg that redbox was enough of an opportunity to take on the risk of starting it up as its own business. The risk paid off. Gregg ran or oversaw redbox for 11 years. During that time, he brought redbox from incubation with just a few DVD kiosks in one market to over 44,000 kiosks across USA and Canada and from $0 in revenue to over $2 billion. Redbox's success comes from their focus on the original problem: constantly finding ways to bring convenience to customers.

In 2009, McDonald's sold redbox to a public company called Coinstar, where Gregg became president and COO. He has also received numerous awards for his effort. In 2009, Mr. Kaplan was a finalist for Ernst & Young's "Entrepreneur of the Year" and a finalist for Illinois Technology Association's "CEO of the Year" award. Mr. Kaplan was also named by Crain's Chicago Business as one of the "40 under 40"—40 top businesspeople in Chicago under age 40.

Thinking and Acting Like an Entrepreneur

- How did Gregg's initial idea change from its initial form? Did the problem they were solving change or stay the same?
- What approaches did Gregg take to evaluate the opportunity over time?
- In what ways does Gregg demonstrate the entrepreneurial mindset behaviors of critical thinking and problem solving?

8.2 Tools for Evaluating Opportunities

Evaluating an Opportunity

Once you've gathered your ideas and compared different ways of activating them, you need to do a more detailed evaluation. Start with the business ideas you like best. Then use critical thinking to logically evaluate the **feasibility** of each idea. Feasibility refers to how possible or worthwhile it is to pursue your idea, to see if it is actually an opportunity. You can use three practical methods for analyzing the feasibility of your business ideas:

- Cost/benefit analysis
- Opportunity cost analysis
- SWOT analysis

Cost/Benefit Analysis

Even though it is necessary to take risks as an entrepreneur, successful people take **calculated risks**. This means that the potential costs and benefits are carefully considered before starting a business. One method used to determine a calculated risk is called a **cost/benefit analysis**. It is the process of adding up all the expected benefits of an opportunity, and subtracting all the expected costs. If the benefits outweigh the costs, then the opportunity may be worthwhile.

Costs can be one-time payments or ongoing costs. Benefits are most often received over a period of time. For example, let's say you want to buy a computer, but you don't have the money to pay for it. The purchase price could be a one-time cost if you save up and pay cash for it in six months. But, if you use a credit card to buy the computer today, you should calculate how much extra you will pay in interest charges over the next six months. If buying the computer now enables you to earn more money than the total interest, the benefit may outweigh the cost.

A difficult part of doing a cost/benefit analysis is assigning a monetary value to **intangible** (non-material) things. For example, what is the value of your time? In what ways can you use your time most profitably? Obviously, some costs and benefits have to be based on personal values and priorities. What is important to you, may not be the same as for someone else.

Another difficult part of doing a cost/benefit analysis is that you can't really assign numbers to the costs or the benefits at the beginning of your evaluation. You may only be able to think in general terms. Eventually, as you continue with the business planning process, you will need to calculate the actual costs and benefits as carefully as you can.

Figure 8-1 ▶
Cost/Benefit Analysis.
The ends need to justify the means.

Applying Concepts.
Why is it important to make sure that the end benefit or opportunities outweigh the financial cost? Is it important to weigh time cost as well?

Opportunity Cost Analysis

An important factor often overlooked when evaluating ideas is the **opportunity cost**. This is the value of something you get in exchange for something you give up. An opportunity cost analysis examines the potential benefits that you forfeit when you choose one course of action over others.

Suppose you are offered a one-year internship at a company where you can gain valuable work experience, but you will not receive wages. To make the best decision, you should compare the benefits the internship offers against the benefits of opportunities you will be losing or postponing. These might include the chance to go to college immediately, earn money at a different job, or start a business.

Money can be invested to earn more money over a period of time. An opportunity cost is the benefit you don't receive by investing the money in one way versus another. For example, if you spend $500 instead of depositing it in a savings account, you won't get the interest you would have earned on the money. Your calculated risk would be that you would earn more on the thing you spent $500 for, than you would have earned in interest on the money.

SWOT Analysis

Another way to determine an idea's feasibility is to perform a **SWOT analysis**. This business evaluation method focuses on four categories:

- **Strengths.** What skills do you have that would enable you to do well in this specific opportunity? What resources do you have available (time, money, and people who can help you)? Do you have any unique knowledge or experiences that could give you an edge?

- **Weaknesses.** In what skill or knowledge areas do you need to improve? What resources are you lacking? What might potential customers see as a weakness in your product or service?

- **Opportunities.** Does this business idea fill an unmet need or want? Are there any trends or changes happening in your community that you could use as an advantage? What could you do better than other companies already in the same type of business? Does the proposed business location give you any advantages?

- **Threats.** What obstacles stand in the way of you pursuing this opportunity? What current trends could potentially harm your business? How fierce is the competition in this business area? Does this business idea have a small window of opportunity?

Figure 8-2 ▶

SWOT Analysis.

A SWOT Analysis can help evaluate the business opportunity.

Applying Concepts.

Why is it important to identify your Weaknesses and Threats in addition to your Strengths and Opportunities?

Table 8.1 shows an example of a simple SWOT analysis for starting a DJ business. Notice that strengths and opportunities are placed side-by-side in the chart. This helps you to see if you currently have the strengths needed to take advantage of existing opportunities. Ask yourself, "What can I do to build my strengths in order to make the most of my opportunities?"

Figure 8-3 ▶

Starting a DJ Business.

A SWOT Analysis can help determine if a DJ business is a good opportunity.

Applying Concepts.

What would you do if your SWOT Analysis said that your DJ business was not a good opportunity?

Table 8.1   SWOT Analysis: Starting a DJ Business

Strengths	Opportunities
I have experience working in a music store, and know what type of music is bought most often.	Some friends have already asked me to DJ at upcoming parties.
Together, my potential partner and I both have the necessary equipment and music resources.	My potential partner knows another DJ who says we can sub for him.
I have an older brother who was a DJ when he was younger. He can answer questions and provide helpful tips.	There's a real desire for salsa music in the area. Maybe we could add that to our play list.
Weaknesses	**Threats**
I'm not sure how dependable my potential partner will be. He is often late.	There are several good DJs already in the neighborhood.
We need money to continue building our music library and keep it current.	People planning parties don't know us and already know the established DJs.
We need a way to transport our equipment from place to place.	If times are hard economically, people won't pay for expensive parties with DJs.

Likewise, weaknesses and threats are placed side-by-side in a SWOT analysis. This allows you to evaluate if your weaknesses may make existing threats more harmful. Ask yourself, "What can I do to address my weaknesses so that I can minimize potential threats?"

Keep in mind that a SWOT analysis can also be used to evaluate a business after it is up and running. Many companies perform a SWOT analysis periodically to stay aware of changes that could help or harm their businesses.

By using your critical thinking skills and one of these tools to evaluate your business opportunities from Chapter 7, you should be able to find the one that seems the most feasible. However, this does not mean that your opportunity is completely validated—just that you have done some screening to support your thinking. In the next section, we will look at how to continue the opportunity evaluation process while continuing to revise your idea.

Apply Your Knowledge   What do we call the value of something given up to get something else? From your investigation, do you think that the professor who gave Fred Smith a "C" thought the opportunity outweighed the cost? Explain your answer.

CAREER COMPETENCIES

 ## Demonstrate Presentation Applications

Understanding how to create an effective presentation slide show is an important tool to use in both a classroom and work setting. People use presentation slides to highlight key ideas, show images/videos as examples, and engage their audience in the presentation. Entrepreneurs often use presentation slides when presenting their business opportunities to potential customers and investors. Being able to effectively communicate using presentation slides can mean the difference between getting a sale and not.

A computer application, or program, is a tool you use to perform specific tasks on a computer or smartphone. Employers look for employees who have experience using computers or applications. You may have already have some experience with applications in school or at home.

Presentation software can produce slide shows that are very helpful for presenting certain types of information.

Here are some helpful tips when creating and presenting with presentation slides:

- Express points clearly and concisely; too much text can be overwhelming
- Watch for grammar errors and incorrect verb tense
- Demonstrate numbers with visuals
- Avoid wild colors and overuse of animation
- Use your slides as a guide; you should not read off of slides while presenting

Career Skills in Action

Now practice putting together a brief presentation on your business opportunity. Be sure to include:

- What your business opportunity is
- Why it's a business opportunity (what need or want it solves)
- The method you used to evaluate your opportunity

Share your presentation with your peers and teacher for feedback.

8.3 Ongoing Opportunity Evaluation

Using one of the opportunity evaluation tools from Section 8.2 is a great way to determine which of your potential opportunities is the best to start pursuing. However, you may already be having second guesses about your business opportunity. How do you know if this is the one you want to stick with? What happens if you find out more information that makes it not as feasible as you thought? Again, as you read in Chapter 5, this uncertainty is a completely normal part of the entrepreneurial process.

You may have your initial business opportunity identified, but this does not mean that you have reached the end of the planning process. In fact, there are numerous questions that an entrepreneur needs to be able to answer before the idea is truly a validated opportunity. The next phase of the entrepreneurial discovery process is the business model validation phase. As you saw in Chapter 5, this textbook will allow you to continue to evaluate and revise your opportunity as you learn how to answer many additional questions about your business, including the following:

- **Competition:** Is there someone else providing my product or service better than I can? (Unit 3)
- **Value Proposition:** Will customers value my product or service enough to buy it? (Unit 4)
- **Business Model:** Can I actually put my business into operation given the appropriate resources? (Unit 5)
- **Cost Structure:** Does each sale make enough money to generate a profit? (Unit 6)

Since your business opportunity will change over time, it is recommended to use a business canvas tool as part of your ongoing opportunity evaluation. A **business canvas** tool is an alternative to traditional business planning that allows you to make changes to your opportunity as more information is gathered. Business canvases can be detailed or simple based on your planning needs. To set up a shortened version of a canvas tool, divide up a piece of paper with a section for each of the outstanding questions you have about your business opportunity. An example using these basic four questions is included:

Competition	Value Proposition
Is there someone else providing my product or service better than I can?	Will customers value my product or service enough to buy it?
Business Model	**Cost Structure**
Can I actually put my business into operation given the appropriate resources?	Does each sale make enough money to generate a profit?

As you gather additional information towards answering these and other questions, you should include that data directly on your canvas. Setting up your canvas with chart paper and sticky notes will allow you to make easy changes and work in groups. When you have a final answer for each box of your canvas, you have a fully validated business opportunity. You can then move on to the next phases of the entrepreneurial process. You will learn specifics about gathering information to complete each of the canvas sections in later chapters. You can also look at the appendix of this book to see the canvas that Eva put together before assembling her business plan for Eva's Edibles.

 **Apply Your Knowledge** Think back to your investigation of FedEx and Fred Smith. Why do you think Fred Smith continued to evaluate his business opportunity after his business class? Explain your answer.

APPLICATION TO BUSINESS PLANNING

Screened Business Opportunity

Use what you learned in this chapter on evaluating business opportunities to narrow down your list of business opportunities to the most feasible. Be sure you can answer the following:

- Explain why it could be a business opportunity. (what need or want does it solve)
- What tool did you use to validate the opportunity? (external or internal)
- What questions about your opportunity do you still have?

ASSESSMENT

REVIEWING OBJECTIVES

1. How are creative and critical thinking both needed in entrepreneurship?
2. Describes techniques to use for determining the most feasible business opportunities.
3. What are questions entrepreneurs must answer for ongoing evaluation of a business opportunity?

CRITICAL THINKING

Compare the advantages and disadvantages of buying an independent business versus buying a franchise. How are these business opportunities alike? How are they different?

ENTREPRENEURIAL THINKING EXERCISE: CRITICAL THINKING & PROBLEM SOLVING

Think back to your investigation of Fred Smith and FedEx. Imagine that you are helping him start his overnight shipping service. After doing a cost/benefit analysis, you find that using airplanes would be too expensive. How else could FedEx have started while solving the same problem of shipping things quickly? How else could Fred have structured the business? Explain your rationale.

EXTENSION ACTIVITIES

Entrepreneurship & Literacy Skills

Complete the following task to demonstrate your understanding of entrepreneurship:

Grades 9–12: Working in teams, do research on the opportunity cost of a high school diploma, an associate degree, and a bachelor's degree. Assume that college tuition is $15,000 for an associate's degree, and $30,000 for a bachelor's degree. Select a specific career from your career cluster and find the annual salary each type of degree would earn within that career. Present all of your data in a report, and write a paragraph summarizing your findings while answering the following question: Does the cost of education outweigh the long-term earning potential?

OBJECTIVES

- Explain the importance of market research in entrepreneurship.
- Compare and contrast primary and secondary data and their functions.
- Conduct market research by gathering information from both primary and secondary resources.

NFTE Entrepreneurial Mindset Characteristic Focus

☑ Future Orientation

National Entrepreneurship Standards

- **A.10** Explain tools used by entrepreneurs for venture planning
- **B.13** Determine personal biases and stereotypes
- **K.15** Select sources of business start-up information
- **K.16** Conduct an environmental scan to obtain marketing information
- **L.12** Explain the concept of market and market identification
- **L.16** Conduct market analysis

Common Career Technical Core Standards

- **BM-MGT.2** Access, evaluate and disseminate information for business decision making.
- **BM-MGT.8** Create strategic plans used to manage business growth, profit and goals.
- **CRP.7** Employ valid and reliable research strategies.
- **CRP.8** Utilize critical thinking to make sense of problems and persevere in solving them.

National Entrepreneurship Standards: Career Competencies

☑ **K.11** Demonstrate database applications

LESSON VOCABULARY

- business environment
- carrying capacity
- focus group
- future orientation
- list-rental companies
- market
- market research
- primary data
- product management
- product planning
- secondary data
- UE testing

9.1 Why Is Market Research Important?

Product Planning and Management

In the previous chapter, you were able to identify a business opportunity. In this chapter, you will look at how to gather ongoing data to make informed decisions that turn the opportunity into reality. This is a vital step in product planning and product management. **Product planning** is the process of guiding your business idea from inception through development and introduction to the market. **Product management** is a broad set of activities and functions that support the development, marketing, and sale of your product or service. You will learn about product planning and product development throughout this text.

As with many steps within the entrepreneurial process, gathering data to validate your business opportunity is just the first step toward a much larger goal of refining your business opportunity. Going through this process requires entrepreneurs to demonstrate the entrepreneurial mindset characteristic of having a **future orientation**. This is because you will need to be able to plan for a long-term strategy for your business beyond these initial stages.

Understanding Your Market

As you refine your business opportunity, it is important that you stay informed about its market. A **market** is simply a group of potential customers—people or businesses—for a particular product or service. **Market research** is an organized way to gather and analyze information needed to make business decisions. For example, market research can help you decide to start a new business. But market research isn't just something you do when starting a business. In order to ensure a company's continued success, market research needs to be an ongoing activity.

Market research tends to focus on three main areas. Just as each piece of a jigsaw puzzle is important for seeing the whole picture, researching each of these areas is key to understanding your market. Let's look at each of these three main areas through the lens of a dry cleaning business as an example.

- **Customers.** Customers can be individual consumers or businesses. To be successful, businesses need to satisfy their customers while making a profit. You can't do this without knowing who your customers are and what they need or want. Market research helps you determine very specific information about potential customers. It will also help you precisely define their needs and wants. In the case of the dry cleaning business, you would want to know the type of customer that will use your business. If you realize that most of your customers are busy professionals that work late, you might consider staying open late to serve them. You will learn more about researching your customers in Unit 4.

- **Competition.** Running a business would be a lot easier if it was the only one of its kind. However, this doesn't happen very often. Usually, there are already a number of competitors in the marketplace. They may offer a similar product or service as your business, or one that fills the same customer need or want. Market research helps you identify who your competitors are and how they operate. This information is helpful in planning successful marketing tactics, or strategic actions related to your market. Going back to our dry cleaner example, you might want to make sure that there aren't already other dry cleaners on the street you were planning on opening. You will learn more about researching your competition in Unit 3.

▼ **Figure 9-1**
Market Awareness.

Rising gasoline prices is a market trend that affects various businesses in different ways.

Inferring.

What negative and positive effects could rising gasoline prices potentially have on a travel agency?

- **Business Environment.** In its broadest sense, the **business environment** refers to any social, economic, or political factors and trends that could impact your business. This includes global and national factors related to the type of business. Gathering data related to the business environment helps you stay aware of trends or important events. In turn, this information may reveal new business opportunities or threats. Once again, if you were opening a dry cleaning business, you would want to know recent trends in the business. Once done doing research, you may find out that many dry cleaners are using new eco-friendly methods of cleaning. You would absolutely want to do the same so that you do not miss out on the opportunity to be ahead of the curve.

Avoiding Costly Mistakes

Making incorrect guesses about your market can lead to wrong decisions. If an incorrect decision has a major impact on your business, your business could fail. Market research helps you test **assumptions**, which is something that you assume is true about your business and what the customer wants. You might be considering offering tutoring services online, but if you asked a potential student, they might prefer meeting their tutor face-to-face. Doing market research to test your assumption first would ensure that you don't misjudge what your potential customers need or want. It helps you to avoid spending time and money developing a product or service that won't sell.

For example, you may want to use market research to test a prototype so you can evaluate your potential customer reactions to a new product. Or, you may want to find out the carrying capacity of the industry you want to enter. In the business world, **carrying capacity** refers to the maximum number of companies an industry can support based on its customers. If there is little room for growth in a particular industry, there may not be room enough for your business to prosper.

Sometimes what you don't know can hurt you. Ignorance of your market or failure to react to your market can mean lost customers and lost opportunities. This means lost income and lost profit. While it is true that everyone makes mistakes, an entrepreneur can avoid costly ones by doing his or her homework.

Obtaining Finances

It is much easier to attract people, banks, or companies to invest in your business or loan you money, if you've done thorough market research. Most potential investors and business partners aren't willing to risk their time or money without evidence that backs up your business concept. Market research may also provide you with information about people or companies who have invested in competing businesses. If you can learn more about the investors who already have a stake in the market, then you can better understand the expectations of your potential investors.

Applying Concepts.

What types of questions would you want answered if you were an investor?

Apply Your Knowledge Explain product planning and product management. What is market research and what is its role in product planning and management? From your investigation, what information are the Nielsen ratings trying to gather?

ENTREPRENEURIAL CASE STUDY: FUTURE ORIENTATION

 ## Tina VonderHaar— Brighton Agency

Transitioning from Being an Intrapreneur to an Entrepreneur

Tina VonderHaar is the President, CEO, and owner of the St. Louis-based Brighton Agency (www.brightonagency.com), whose service is to help entrepreneurs promote their business to other people. Founded in 1989 as a traditional advertising agency, Brighton now offers a wide range of services for businesses and entrepreneurs. Their services now include overall strategic consultation, interactive solutions and services, public relations, media buying, traditional advertising, online marketing, and video

Tina VonderHaar.

and audio production. Tina is responsible for directing all aspects of processes and operating functions, personnel management and strategic and tactical leadership.

Tina took a roundabout path to owning Brighton Agency. She graduated of Florida State University with a Bachelor of Science degree in

Computer Science and Mathematics. After college, Tina began her career with Accenture, a global consulting company with 75,000 people. Starting as systems/business consultant and progressing to Global HR Business Process Director, she worked with clients such as Boeing, Eveready Battery, and the State of Kansas to provide business, systems, and process consulting. After leaving Accenture, Tina founded a small business consulting firm called HRCounts, and Brighton was one of her clients. Brighton's owner convinced Tina to join the company in 2005, and she served as the company's Chief Operating Officer until she bought the company in 2009. Tina is now Brighton's sole owner.

Think-Create-Engage

One of Brighton's most important functions is consulting with entrepreneurs and businesses on how to grow their business through marketing. The agency starts by asking their client about their goals and vision for the business in the future. The team at Brighton then sets research objectives based on those goals. They then collect market research for the client, finding information on the customer, competition and business environment. Then the experienced and inspired marketers, strategists, and creatives integrate this information into the advertisements and promotional strategies they create for the business. This process, which Brighton calls, "Think-Create-Engage," is designed to help entrepreneurs and businesses accomplish their long-term goals.

Tina's innovative approach to marketing and market research has paid off. Under Tina's leadership, Brighton's business has grown exponentially. With approximately 70 employees, Brighton had 2013 revenues of $11.1 million, ranking eighth in the *St. Louis Business Journal*'s 2014 list of largest advertising, marketing, and PR firms; and 24th in the *St. Louis Business Journal*'s 2014 list of largest women-owned businesses. Tina was named by the *St. Louis Business Journal* as one of St. Louis' Most Influential Business Women in 2010.

Giving Back to the Community

A strong believer in giving back to the community, Tina has also been responsible for Brighton contributing to and sponsoring numerous nonprofit organizations dedicated to the advancement of the St. Louis region, where the company is based. She also hopes to inspire a younger generation of entrepreneurs by serving as a member of the Board of Directors for the Network for Teaching Entrepreneurship (NFTE) in the St. Louis area.

Thinking and Acting Like an Entrepreneur

- How do Tina and her team help entrepreneurs make business decisions from market research?
- What process does Tina's business follow to ensure data collected is based on business goals?
- In what ways does Tina demonstrate a future orientation, specifically, being able to set goals beyond the short term?

9.2 Sources of Research Data

Market Research Methods

The methods and data sources you choose for your market research largely depends on what type of information you need. The common types of information you will need in starting up a business include potential markets, demand, existing competition, comparable sales, and industry trends. If you have your market research goals identified, you can then access the appropriate data to answer those types of questions.

There are two basic types of market research: primary and secondary. For a reason you will soon read about, we will talk about secondary research before primary research.

- **Secondary Data.** Existing information that was previously gathered for a purpose other than the study at hand is **secondary data**. Examples of secondary data are economic forecasts issued by financial organizations and demographic data collected by the U.S. government. Secondary data is relatively cheap and easy to obtain. However, it may not be specific enough to answer all your questions.

- **Primary Data.** New information that is collected for a particular purpose is **primary data**. It is obtained directly from potential customers. Primary data can be very useful because it is up-to-date and aimed at your target market. But, gathering primary data is more time consuming and expensive to collect than obtaining secondary data.

While it may be confusing to think about, secondary data is usually accessed before primary data. This is because it is easier and less expensive to access data that already exists.

Secondary Data Sources

When you first begin your market research, and don't know much about your area of interest, it's a good idea to do some general, exploratory research. Examining existing secondary data is very useful for this purpose. Some resources that provide a wide range of market information are:

- **Government.** Divisions in the U.S. federal government, as well as state governments, collect a great deal of data that can be used to generate a demographic profile of a particular location or tell you the types of businesses located in a specific neighborhood. There are also government databases where you can find data on economic activity and customer spending (The Bureau of Economic Analysis; www.bea.gov), data on trends in jobs (the Bureau of Labor Statistics; www.bls.gov), and data about the population and communities (Census Bureau; www.census.gov). Another excellent online resource is FedStats (www.fedstats.gov). It provides information on over a hundred agencies. It also allows you to search by state, by subject, and alphabetically.

Figure 9-3 ▶
**Researching
Opportunities.**

Local bakeries would want to
do research on other bakeries
in their area.

Applying Concepts.

Where could a local bakery
find secondary research?

- **Trade Groups and Journals.** Trade associations often conduct market research related to their particular industry. You may find some of this information on the website for a particular association or by reading trade journals that associations publish. A good place to learn about associations for your industry is in the Encyclopedia of Associations (which many libraries will have). The American Society of Association Executives has a database that you can use to search for associations by name, industry area, or geographic location (www.asaecenter.org/directories/associationsearch.cfm). While many of these resources cost money, with the right targeted searching, you may be able to find free articles online from these sources as well.

- **Business Magazines and Reports.** Examples of companies that publish business data or business news include Forbes (www.forbes.com), American City Business Journals (www.bizjournals.com), and Dun and Bradstreet (www.dnb.com/us). BizStats, owned by the Brandow Company, is a free online source of business data (www.bizstats.com). MarketResearch.com (www.marketresearch.com) is a huge collection of market research that is continuously updated. However, they do charge a fee that varies in price depending on the specific report. Another source is the *Thomas Global Register*®, a directory of worldwide industrial suppliers and product information (www.thomasglobal.com).

- **Local Community Resources.** Most communities have a chamber of commerce or other business development agency. For example, if you lived in the borough of Manhattan in New York City, you could find information on local businesses through their website (www.manhattancc.org/). Doing a targeted search online with your city/neighborhood name and "Chamber of Commerce" usually results in success. Examples of information and services provided by these organizations include demographic reports, business directories, and market-related seminars. A simple but effective print resource is your local *Yellow Pages* phone book. It provides a brief overview of potential local competitors. Don't overlook local business schools or colleges. They have libraries and career centers that you may find helpful. Again, doing a targeted search for a university or college near you and "Career Center" will help you find local resources. If you attended Temple University in Philadelphia, doing a search as described would take you to their website (www.temple.edu/provost/careercenter).

- **Social Media.** Many times you can find information that people posted online for other various purposes. Various media outlets usually have Facebook and Twitter accounts that post relevant articles and statistics. Blogs written by others might can often contain data that would be useful for research purposes. Sites that offer customer reviews, such as Yelp (www.yelp.com), can help your find information on competition.

Figure 9-4
Census Bureau Home Page.

The Census Bureau is a very good source of demographic and geographic information.

Analyzing Information.

Why might information such as income, housing, or health insurance be important for a B2C company?

Primary Research Techniques

Once you have a sense of who your potential customers may be, you can begin to gather data directly from that potential group of customers. Some common ways to obtain primary data are:

Figure 9-5
Effective Questioning.
Before you do research, be sure you know what you want to ask first.

Applying Concepts.
What can be gained from effective questioning of customers?

- **Interviews/Surveys.** This technique uses a one-to-one approach. A questionnaire is developed that can be used in person, by telephone, by regular mail, or by e-mail. Names and contact information for specific groups of consumers or businesses can be obtained through trade associations or from list-rental companies. These companies provide lists of names and addresses for targeted markets, typically allowing you to use the list for a single mailing. Both trade associations and list-rental companies will typically charge for their services. There are also free online survey tools such as Survey Monkey (www.surveymonkey.com), that will allow you to send surveys and collect data online for no charge. E-mail distribution services like Mail Chimp (www.mailchimp.com) allow you to effectively send and track surveys electronically.

- **Focus Groups.** A focus group is a small number of people who are brought together to discuss a particular problem, product, or service. A focus group discussion is typically led by a moderator, who asks questions, directs the discussion, and makes sure the meeting agenda is covered in a specified amount of time. A focus group is usually recorded so that the feedback can be studied in detail later.

- **Observations.** You can learn a lot about potential customers' reactions and behaviors without talking with them. Observation can sometimes be an advantage because people may act differently when they are not being formally asked to participate in a study. For example, you can observe which stores attract the most customers in a shopping mall. Or, you could offer a complimentary product sample such as food or perfume and watch how people react to it. Many times in the tech space, researchers will turn to UE testing (user experience testing). Instead of asking questions, they will provide customers with the product and observe how they use it.

- **Social Media.** Use social media sites such as Twitter, Facebook, and Pinterest to find out information about your potential customers. You can also learn a great deal of information on your competition and business environment from websites that offer customer reviews, such as Yelp. You can also use question sourcing sites such as Quora (www.quora.com) to post questions and have them answered by a community of users. In addition to getting information directly from customer opinions, social media is a great tool to measure customer engagement through participation. For example, if you post something on Twitter, you can gauge interest by how many retweets or followers you get after the posting.

Understanding the Limitations of Market Research

While market research and the data gathered can be invaluable to the business owner, it is equally important to understand the limitations of that research. As you have learned, many research techniques are conducted on people whose opinions and answers can be influenced by a broad range of variables. For example, if they know they are being observed or formally questioned, their responses and reactions may be artificial or biased. Their moods can affect their responses; even the weather can have an impact!

Marketing research can also be limited by time and budget constraints. In addition, those conducting and analyzing the research may not be trained properly or may not have a good understanding of the research goals. While market research can help you avoid costly mistakes in product planning and development, it's important to understand that it is not an exact science.

Apply Your Knowledge What is the difference between primary and secondary data? Think back to your investigation. What kind of data does the Nielsen ratings represent?

CAREER COMPETENCIES

Demonstrate Database Applications

A computer application, or program, is a tool you use to perform specific tasks on a computer or smartphone. Employers look for employees who have experience using computers or applications. You may have already have some experience with applications in school or at home.

Database management programs help you organize and manipulate data. You might use data analysis at work in marketing, pharmaceutical research, or retail sales. A politician might use it to decide whether or not to run for office. Schools and colleges use database systems to track student information.

Entrepreneurs can use database applications to organize and analyze market research data. Once you collect market research data, you analyze it and turn it into statistics. For example, an entrepreneur who wants to open up a restaurant might want to survey people on how often they eat out a week. From this data, the database can be used to find:

- How often people eat out on each day of the week
- The total number of times people eat out every week

9.3 Determining Market Research Questions

Primary or Secondary Research

Being able to clearly identify questions that you need answered will help you focus your research efforts. If you know what type of research will answer each of your questions, it will also save you time in making sure you are gathering information in the most effective manner.

For example, imagine that you want to start a business hosting children's birthday parties. When starting out researching children's birthday parties, it would not be helpful to ask the following types of questions:

- "How many people live in my state?"
- "What is the most popular gift for children right now?

These questions do not find information that is specific to your business. Instead, good questions that you could ask might be:

- "How many families with young children are there in my town?"
- "What is the average household income for families in my town?
- "Do I need to have a special license to work with young children?"

These are good questions because they all get you specific data that can be used for your business. All of these questions can be answered by secondary research, because the data already exists from other research efforts. Government census websites can tell you the answers to the first two questions, and a local chamber of commerce website might be able to tell you the third one. This saves you time of having to find out the answers to these questions by yourself.

Once you get in front of potential customers, you will want to make sure you ask good questions as well. Again, these would not be helpful in your research:

- "Do you like parties?"
- "Did you celebrate your birthday last year?"

These questions are too narrow, and do not give the researcher specific information to use for the business. Examples of good questions for primary research include:

- "What type of entertainment do kids in my town enjoy at birthday parties?"
- "How much are families in my town willing to spend on birthday parties?"
- "Are there any other businesses hosting children's birthday parties in my town?"

All of these questions need primary research data to answer because you have to go find out the answer by asking people yourself. You would then choose the best way to find the answer to these questions. For example, you might be able to get families to fill out a survey through social media to find out how much they would spend. But asking kids what they would enjoy might be better to do in-person.

Creating Survey Questions

When setting out to do primary research, it is important to use effective survey questions. You want to make sure that you getting the appropriate response you want for your research purposes. For the birthday party example, it might not be effective to directly ask families, "How much are you willing to spend on your child's birthday party?" Even though that is what you are trying to find out, phrasing a question differently might get different results. Just because a parent MIGHT spend $200 on the party, does not mean they always will. A better question to ask is: "What did you spend on your child's last birthday party?"

◀ **Figure 9-6**
Market Research Survey.
You can develop your own market research survey.

Applying Concepts.
Why is it important to know how to write questions effectively?

Here are some tips when crafting survey questions of your own:

- Keep the questions simple and clear so that respondents know what is being asked
- Use warm-up questions that are easy to make the respondent feel comfortable
- Be sure that there aren't words that the respondent wouldn't know (for example, if you are asking about a new technology, be sure they know what it is)
- Consider the order of questions; you wouldn't want a question about your business to follow questions about a frustrating experience at another business
- Make the answer responses easy to choose

 Apply Your Knowledge From your investigation, what questions do you think Nielsen families were asked to answer for their journals?

APPLICATION TO BUSINESS PLANNING

Market Research Questions

Use what you learned in this chapter on market research to determine questions that you need answered about your opportunity. Be sure you can answer the following:

- What types of information do you need to gather about your opportunity (target markets, demand, competition and comparable sales, industry trends, etc.)?
- What type of research would answer each question (primary or secondary)?
- Where will you go to find potential answers for each question?
- What types of questions will you have to ask potential customers?

9 ASSESSMENT

REVIEWING OBJECTIVES

1. What is the importance of market research in entrepreneurship?
2. Compare and contrast primary and secondary data and their functions.
3. Describe how to conduct market research by gathering information from both primary and secondary resources.

CRITICAL THINKING

1. Technology in the form of Internet search engines and computer programs, such as database applications, is an indispensable market research tool. For your business opportunity, what technology tools would you use to obtain information about customers, competitors, and the industry in general?
2. Imagine you are doing research on a new movie that is out. What questions would you ask to find out how the audience thought of the movie? List as many questions as you can identify. What are the limitations of this type of market research?

ENTREPRENEURIAL THINKING EXERCISE: FUTURE ORIENTATION

Imagine that you just received a job working for the Nielsen company. One of the challenges that they are facing is that families are no longer watching television on TV anymore! Being able to stream TV shows online means that people are watching shows on their computers and phones, and using video services like Netflix and Hulu as part of their video habits. How would you help the company adjust their data collection efforts? How could you put in steps now to anticipate a change in technology down the road?

EXTENSION ACTIVITIES

Entrepreneurship & Literacy Skills

Complete the following task to demonstrate your understanding of entrepreneurship:

Grades 9–12: Imagine that you are planning to survey students at your school about a potential bookstore to be located on school grounds. The proposed store will be run by students with teachers' guidance. Profits will go to a charitable group chosen by students. Working in a small group, develop a questionnaire for the survey with no more than twenty questions. Make sure the questions are clear, simple to understand, and appropriate for a professional correspondence with peers. Be sure that the questions ask about the most important issues involved in this startup.

10 USING DATA TO MAKE BUSINESS DECISIONS

OBJECTIVES

- Describe how ideas are refined through ongoing evaluation of research data.
- List the six cyclical steps of ongoing research.
- Identify how business plans develop over time and change as new research is found.

NFTE Entrepreneurial Mindset Characteristic Focus

☑ Flexibility & Adaptability

National Entrepreneurship Standards

- **A.10** Explain tools used by entrepreneurs for venture planning
- **A.16** Use components of a business plan to define venture idea
- **A.33** Create processes for ongoing opportunity recognition
- **A.34** Adapt to changes in business environment
- **L.04** Determine product/service to fill customer need

Common Career Technical Core Standards

- **BM.6** Implement, monitor and evaluate business processes to ensure efficiency and quality results.
- **BM-MGT.2** Access, evaluate and disseminate information for business decision making.
- **BM-MGT.8** Create strategic plans used to manage business growth, profit and goals.
- **CRP.7** Employ valid and reliable research strategies.

National Entrepreneurship Standards: Career Competencies

☑ **E.12** Evaluate credibility of Internet resources

LESSON VOCABULARY

- business model validation
- lean startup methodologies
- minimum viable product
- research cycle
- research objective

ENTREPRENEURIAL INVESTIGATION
Coca-Cola's Evil Twin: New Coke

Almost everyone has tried a Coca-Cola, or a Coke, at some point in their lives. As of 2013, more than 1.8 billion Coke products are consumed worldwide daily. However, not every idea Coke has had was as successful. In 1985, Coke announced that it was going to change its extremely well-known formula for a "New Coke" taste. The executives did market research through surveys and focus groups. The surveys were generally positive. However, focus groups were much more negative, with a number of participants convincing other participants that it was a bad idea. While interpreting the results, they decided to put more focus on the surveys and move ahead. After a nation-wide backlash and decline in sales, the company re-introduced the old formula as Coca-Cola Classic three months later. Sales of Coca-Cola surged once the old formula returned to the market, and the New Coke has since been phased out.

Do some research on this launch of New Coke. After you do research, respond to the following questions:

- Where do you think the market researchers went wrong in interpreting the data?
- What would you have done if you got negative results in the focus group?
- Do you think the company did the right thing listening to customer feedback and switching back?

Be prepared to share your responses with your teacher or class.

10.1 Evaluating Research Data

Business Model Validation

In the previous chapter, you learned about the function of market research. You also looked at some potential ways of gathering market research data based on the research questions you have. In this chapter, you will be introduced the second part of the entrepreneurial process, which is business model validation. **Business model validation** means to prove through ongoing market research and data analysis that your business idea is truly a business opportunity.

Let's look at another example of why this is important. Let's imagine that you have an idea for a daycare service that also picks up and drops off kids at their homes to help out busy parents. You did some initial screening, talked to some potential customers, and determined that your idea is indeed a business opportunity.

◀ **Figure 10-1**

Pickup/Dropoff Daycare Service.
Not all opportunities that sound great will actually work.

Applying Concepts.
Finding out if parents will actually use the daycare service is important in determining the opportunity.

You move forward with starting your business. However, as soon as you open, you are faced with these challenges:

- You find out that many parents do not feel comfortable having strangers drive their kids in cars
- The cost to pay for gas and the driver is extremely expensive
- Running the daycare requires special certifications and trainings that you did not get

One or all of these would be a disaster for your new business. But, it could have been avoided by doing ongoing market research to test assumptions about your product or service. This process allows you to validate the business model first.

Think of market research as a process. The market data you collect may support your idea for a business. Or, it may not. It is most likely that it will make you change your business idea in some way. Don't be discouraged if the data suggest that you change your direction or even start over with another idea. One of the purposes of market research is to help you avoid costly mistakes. Everything you learn from market research is valuable and will help you in the future. Undergoing this process will also help you develop the entrepreneurial mindset behavior of **Flexibility & Adaptability**.

You can use the canvas approach you learned about in Chapter 8 to help with the market research process. If you are able to answer all of the research questions in the canvas about your opportunity, you will be less likely to run into problems like the ones in the example. Using this approach allows you to make changes to the business *before* it gets costly. The next four units in this book will help you identify research questions that will help with the business model validation process.

Apply Your Knowledge What does the business model validation process do? Think back to your investigation. How could have the team introducing New Coke have been used the business model validation process?

ENTREPRENEURIAL CASE STUDY: FLEXIBILITY & ADAPTABILITY

 ## Seth Goldman— Honest Tea

Solving Social Challenges with a Business Opportunity

Seth Goldman is co-founder & "Tea"EO of Honest Tea, the company he created out of his kitchen in 1998 with his Yale School of Management professor, Barry Nalebuff. Honest Tea (www.honesttea.com) was founded with a mission to bring a low-calorie drink to market and make it widely

Seth Goldman.

available, while supporting ecosystems and communities from where its ingredients are sourced. Honest Tea is now the nation's top selling ready-to-drink organic bottled tea, and is carried in more than 100,000 outlets. Through an acquisition by Coca-Cola in March 2011, Honest Tea has furthered its reach and impact by becoming the first organic and Fair Trade Certified™ brand in the world's largest beverage distribution system.

Even though Honest Tea has been around 1998, Seth's entrepreneurial career started decades ago. At the age of six, he retrieved golf balls from the woods of a golf course near his home in Wellesley, Massachusetts and would then sell them, along with lemonade, back to the golfers for a tidy profit. Before launching Honest Tea, Seth directed a demonstration project for AmeriCorps and oversaw marketing and sales for Calvert, the nation's largest family of socially responsible mutual funds.

Making Tough Business Decisions

Seth's passion for Honest Tea's mission has kept him working closely with the company's day-to-day operations out of its Bethesda, Maryland headquarters. One of the things that Seth oversees is the product development cycles, which includes creating new products. Seth compares the development of a new product to that of planting and growing a tree. Before planting any ideas as seeds, Seth and his team make sure the drink can be made with organic and fair trade products. If the ideas take root, they move to a growth and greenhouse phase, where they let the idea further develop. They also ask customers to provide feedback on everything from the taste to the design to see if they are on the right track. "Over the course of our product development process, which can run anywhere from three to nine months, we fall in love with the end result," says Seth

But as the TeaEO, Seth has to make the tough decisions about which products are not going to make it. "It's tempting to want to blame the retailers or the consumers for a failed product, but ultimately it's our fault." To help with the decision, Seth gathers customer feedback and sales data. "Aside from firing an employee, firing a product is the worst part of my job," Seth explains, "We inevitably receive impassioned calls and e-mails from frustrated consumers who can't find their favorite drink. They ask why we can't just keep selling the drink even though it's not selling as well as our other drinks. In an ideal world, we'd never discontinue anything, but a slow-moving item takes away shelf-space from a fast-moving item. And since we only have limited shelf-space, just as in the plant and animal world, it really is a case of survival of the fittest."

Bettering the Body and the Planet

Seth's passionate efforts to create a socially-minded lower-calorie drink option have resulted in him receiving numerous awards and honors. He received the REAL Food Innovator Award by The United States Healthful Food Council for providing options that are healthier for the body and planet. Along with Barry Nalebuff, Seth co-authored *Mission in a Bottle —The Honest Guide to Doing Business Differently—and Succeeding*, a business book told in comic book form that shares the successes and challenges behind launching Honest Tea.

Thinking and Acting Like an Entrepreneur

- In what ways does Seth and his team use market research data to make decisions?
- How does Seth demonstrate the entrepreneurial mindset skill of flexibility and adaptability?
- In what ways does Seth involve socially responsible practices as part of the business opportunity?

10.2 Market Research Cycle

Steps in Researching a Market

Now you've learned the basics of market research. Here's a quick review of the six basic steps in market research. These are the steps an entrepreneur would follow to answer a **research objective**, which is a question about a prospective business opportunity. Let's look at the example of the day care service from the previous section to see how the entrepreneur should have proceeded.

1. Identify Research Objectives

Before you actually start gathering data, make a general list of the research objectives that you want your research to accomplish. Determine the information you need. What problems are you trying to solve? What questions do you have? Make a specific checklist of all the information you need in order to resolve the problems and questions you've identified. From our example, research objectives that should have been defined might have included:

- What type of certification do I need?
- How much does it cost to transport kids?
- Do parents feel comfortable with their kids riding in cars with an employee of this business?

2. Determine Methods and Sources

Based on your objectives, decide which research methods will best help you achieve your goals. For each of your questions, you might list if primary or secondary research would be helpful to answer the question. You might also include where you might find this information. For our day care service, this might look like this:

Research Objective	Primary or Secondary	Source
What type of certification do I need?	Secondary	Local chamber of commerce
How much does it cost to transport kids?	Secondary/Primary	Government sites on gas prices
Do parents feel comfortable with their kids riding in cars with an employee of this business?	Primary	Focus groups and interviews

3. Gather the Data

You would then act on the plan you put together in Step 2. For our day care service example, you would then find information from the local chamber of commerce and government sites to answer those research objectives. You would also hold focus groups and interviews to ask parents how they would feel about the service. As you collect the data, you may discover additional things you need to find out. Market research is usually a process of discovery. You typically will have to make adjustments to your course of action depending on what you learn.

Make sure the secondary data you collect is relevant to your industry and target market. Also, don't forget to confirm research results with more than one secondary source, if possible. Use an adequate number of customers when doing primary research.

◄ **Figure 10-2**
Focus Groups.

Focus groups can be used to discover what customers think about your competitors and your business ideas.

Drawing Conclusions.

What advantage might a focus group have over mailed surveys?

4. Organize the Data

As you gather information, begin to organize it. Putting responses in charts or data tables can help you quickly identify trends. For our example, making a pie graph of the parent responses would help you see at a glance if parents are ok with the service. Look for areas where important data may be missing. Go back and collect more information if necessary.

5. Analyze the Data

Use critical thinking skills to look at the data you organized. Make comparisons between categories. Pay attention to patterns or trends in the data. Be sure that you are objective when looking at the data. That is, try not to be overly positive or negative. Let's assume that 80 percent of parents did not feel comfortable with strangers driving their kids to the day care. While you might want to side with the 20 percent that liked your idea, you need to be able to tell if the data backs your idea or not.

◄ **Figure 10-3**
Stop or Go?

Based on market research you decide whether to proceed with your business idea or stop.

Applying Concepts.

What would be a "red light" for the daycare service example?

6. Draw Conclusions

Using the information in Step 5, decide whether to proceed with your business idea as is, or to stop and revise. For our day care service, finding out that 80 percent of parents would not be comfortable should be a red flag to revise. You might consider removing the driving service from the model. Or, even better, ask parents what they *would* prefer instead. Again, when making your decision, attempt to be as objective as you can. The following focus areas may help you draw realistic conclusions:

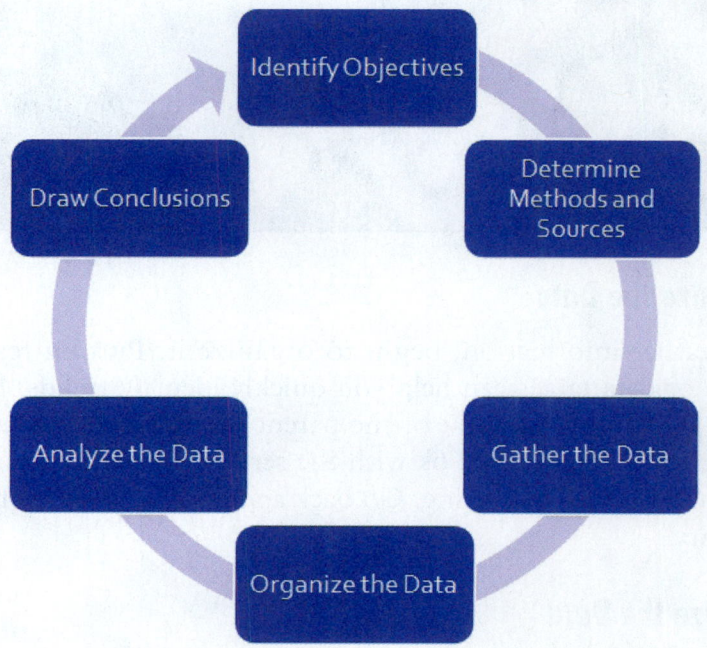

 **Apply Your Knowledge**   What six steps are involved in researching a market and making a preliminary go/no-go decision about pursuing a prospective business opportunity? From your investigation about New Coke, which steps were done incorrectly?

CAREER COMPETENCIES

 ### Evaluate Credibility of Internet Resources

The Internet provides a wide wealth of information that anyone can access at any time, which has made getting accurate information faster and easier than ever before in human history. Entrepreneurs have benefited greatly as they have been able to access information that is relevant to their businesses in a blink of an eye.

However, one thing to keep in mind is that due to the open-source nature of the Internet, it is can sometimes be difficult to know if information that you find online during market research is correct or not. For example, online wikis, such as Wikipedia, have gained popularity because anyone is able to edit the entries with their expertise, removing any editorial bottleneck. While there are processes in place to make sure that the information is as accurate as possible, that doesn't stop people from posting false information on sites that look very reputable. Be sure to follow the sources linked in online blogs and wiki entries to confirm that they are using correct information. You should also see if you can confirm this data from a second source before using.

Also as you conduct market research online, try to stay alert for potential biases in data as well. For example, a source might tend to emphasize negative results over positive ones, or vice versa. When evaluating any data found online, ask yourself these questions:

- Is the source well-known and reliable?
- Is this set of data collected and updated on a regular basis?
- Have I confirmed research results with more than one source or method?

Career Skills in Action

Now, you practice evaluating the credibility of Internet resources. Find an article that relates to your business or career cluster you identified. Look carefully at the source of the article and answer the following questions:

- Is the source of the article well-known and reliable?
- Does the source seemed biased in any way?
- Can I confirm the research results with another source or method?

Share your findings with your teacher or peers.

10.3 Acting on a Business Plan

Putting Your Plan Together

At some point during the entrepreneurial process, you will need to put together your own business plan for investors and other stakeholders. As was discussed previously, if this is started too early, you may discover that what you thought was a business opportunity, is not quite the opportunity you thought. You might need to abandon the idea or discover some tweak that changes the nature of your business. No matter what, it is much better to discover that your business doesn't work on paper before you invest significant time and money in it.

It's important to realize that developing a business plan is not a simple, straightforward process. You don't start at the beginning and move to the end. Each new piece of information or financial calculation could cause you to re-examine, and possibly change, everything that you have done up to that point.

That is why it is encouraged to complete a business model validation with the canvas approach before finalizing any pieces of your business plan. Your business plan will come across as more informed to investors and other stakeholders if you are able to demonstrate your validated opportunity through ongoing market research. The remainder of this book will help you answer the important questions you need to know in order to complete a business canvas, and ultimately, put together your business plan for others to see.

Acting Before/While You Plan

In this textbook, you will mainly learn how to approach business planning by doing ongoing research to validate your business opportunity, and then moving to the creation phase. In reality, many entrepreneurs choose to move to the creation phase before doing formal planning. Reasons for this might include a short window of opportunity for the business, or a relatively low risk of failure. This approach is just as valid as well!

Entrepreneurs that launch their businesses by first building a product before conducting extensive market research usually use ==lean startup methodologies==. In this approach, entrepreneurs create a working prototype of their product, called a ==minimum viable product (MVP)==, and try to sell this version of the product. An MVP is a prototype example of the product or service that the entrepreneur uses with potential customers to gather feedback. Although the product might not be close to the final version, testing with a prototype is a way to see how customers interact with your product.

Figure 10-4 ▶

Testing a Prototype.

Getting a Minimum Viable Product into the market can help accelerate the research process.

Applying Concepts.

What are the pros and cons of starting out with a minimum viable product? Can any business do so?

By doing this, they will receive valuable feedback from potential customers, and they will quickly determine whether or not there is a demand for their product. Entrepreneurs then take the feedback they received from potential customers to create a newer, better version of their product. This process of creating a prototype, getting feedback from the market, and improving on the design is a form of extended market research.

For example, an entrepreneur who wants to create a web site to help teens find jobs might want to create a test MVP, minus building out the actual website, to see if anyone would be interested in the idea.

While you are working through your business model validation in this textbook, you are encouraged to apply lean startup principles to your business planning in the following ways:

- Putting together a prototype that can be tested as your ongoing research
- Trying to sell an MVP of your product or service to see if anyone would buy it
- Testing out revisions to your business based on research data

The important thing to remember is that approaching business planning through a lean startup approach does not mean to skip the market research and business model validation phase. In fact, it allows the entrepreneur to do more with the ==research cycle==. However you decide to approach your business planning, ongoing market research will be the driving force through creating your business plan and into running your business.

Apply Your Knowledge Think back to your investigation. What could the Coca-Cola company have done to introduce an MVP version of New Coke? Could they have adjusted their approach?

 **APPLICATION TO BUSINESS PLANNING**

Market Research Tools

Use what you learned in this chapter on the market research cycle and business planning to put together a plan for your business planning. Be sure you can answer the following:

- What are your main research objectives?
- What tools will you use for data collection, organization, and analysis?
- Will you be able to create a prototype or MVP to help your research?

10 ASSESSMENT

REVIEWING OBJECTIVES

1. How are ideas refined through ongoing evaluation of research data?

2. List the six cyclical steps of ongoing research.

3. How do business plans develop over time and change as new research is found?

CRITICAL THINKING

Suppose you've recently built a prototype for a new video game. What would be the best way to test it in the marketplace? Why?

ENTREPRENEURIAL THINKING EXERCISE: FLEXIBILITY & ADAPTABILITY

Think back to your investigation. Imagine you were a consultant for the Coca-Cola company during the launch of New Coke. What market research objectives would you have set to learn about the new product? How would you have gotten information from potential customers? What differences in the product would you have suggested based on the data? Be prepared to share your responses.

10 ASSESSMENT

EXTENSION ACTIVITIES

Entrepreneurship & Mathematics Skills

Complete the following task to demonstrate your understanding of entrepreneurship:

Grades 9–12: Suppose there are 400 homes in your housing community. You survey 40 to help determine the feasibility of opening a daycare center in the neighborhood. Following are the results. Each number (separated by a comma) represents the number of children who live in one of the houses:

1, 0, 0, 3, 0, 0, 0, 3, 0, 0,
0, 2, 0, 0, 3, 0, 0, 2, 3, 0,
0, 4, 0, 0, 3, 0, 3, 0, 1, 0,
0, 3, 0, 0, 0, 2, 0, 0, 1, 2

Use the survey results to answer the following questions:

1. What is the average number of children per home in your community?

2. What is the average number of children per home, in houses that have children?

   Find the margin of error for each sample mean using the equation:

   $$\left(z * \frac{\sigma}{\sqrt{n}} \right)$$

   where σ is the population standard deviation, n is the sample size. Assume the confidence level of 95 percent ($z = 1.96$).

3. Which of these two averages would be the best statistic to use when deciding whether or not to open a daycare?

Unit 2: Opportunity Recognition & Market Analysis

CHAPTER SUMMARY

6. Idea Generation

Coming up with a new business idea is an important part of the entrepreneurial process. Creative thinking is an important entrepreneurial mindset skill for generating business ideas. There are numerous creative thinking activities to use to generate business ideas. Some of the more common exercises for idea generation include brainstorming, challenging the usual, and idea maps. Entrepreneurs should also look to their passions and personal interests for ideas as well. Entrepreneurs should start by trying to identify as many potential ideas as possible, regardless of initial reaction from others. It is important to overcome barriers to creative thinking. Many ideas seem strange at first, but can lead to even better ideas.

7. Turning Ideas into Opportunities

A business opportunity is a consumer need or want that can be met by a new business venture. However, not every idea is an opportunity. An idea with no commercial potential isn't an opportunity. Ideas for business opportunities can arise from problems, changes/trends, new discoveries and inventions, existing products and services that need improvement, and unique knowledge or experiences. Places to look for opportunities include newspapers, magazines, business and governmental agencies, trade resources, and the Internet. Once you've generated an idea, the next step is to compare options for applying it. Major choices include starting a new business, buying an independent business, buying a franchise, and becoming an inventor.

8. Evaluating Opportunities

Critical thinking is an important entrepreneurial mindset skill for evaluating business ideas. You need to evaluate the feasibility of your ideas by staying objective. Practical ways to do this include performing a cost/benefit analysis, an opportunity-cost analysis, and a SWOT analysis. It is also smart to do ongoing evaluation of business opportunities. This can be done by using a canvas planning tool to update information after testing and gathering data on the opportunity. Business ideas are not fully thought out opportunities until they have clearly identified a value delivered to a customer segment, a competitive edge, a feasible business model and a profitable cost structure. Perfecting the opportunity will lead to a more effective business plan to present to external audiences.

9. Market Research Methods

Market research is an organized way to gather and analyze information needed to make business decisions. It helps you avoid costly mistakes as well as obtain financial support for a new business. Market research tends to focus on three areas: the business environment, potential customers, and the competition. Secondary data sources—existing information that was gathered previously—can be valuable and relatively easy to find. Primary data is new information that is collected for a particular purpose. It is obtained directly from consumers. When asking questions during market research, it is important to ask questions that will provide information that is relevant your business. Questions that are open-ended and specific are more effective when doing your market research.

10. Using Data to Make Business Decisions

For any new business idea, it is important to test parts of it out and make decisions off of the results. This is called testing assumptions. Business opportunities should change as new customer feedback is provided. The general steps taken during this ongoing market research are (1) identify research objectives, (2) determine methods and sources, (3) gather data, (4) organize data, (5) evaluate data, and (6) draw conclusions. This cycle can be used with the business canvas tool to engage in ongoing market research. Following lean startup methodologies and creating a minimum viable product to test during the process will allow for more effective data.

UNIT 2 REVIEW & ASSESSMENT

UNIT 2 VOCABULARY

assumption

brainstorm

business broker

business canvas

business environment

business model validation

business opportunity

calculated risks

carrying capacity

cost/benefit analysis

creative thinking

creativity

critical thinking

feasibility

focus group

franchise

franchisee

franchisor

idea generation

idea map

ideation

innovation

intangible

lateral thinking

lean startup methodologies

list-rental companies

market

market research

minimum viable product

need

nondisclosure agreement

objective

opportunity cost

pivot

primary data

product management

product planning

prototype

research cycle

research objective

royalty fee

secondary data

subjective

SWOT analysis

trade show

UE testing

vertical thinking

want

window of opportunity

CHECK YOUR UNDERSTANDING

Choose the letter that best answers the question or completes the statement.

1. Carrying capacity refers to

   a. the number of differentiators a business can have

   b. how current your secondary data is

   c. the maximum number of companies an industry can support based on its potential customer base

   d. all of the above

2. Companies that sell to other companies are called

   a. C2C

   b. B2C

   c. B2B

   d. none of the above

3. Market research

   a. does not include global factors

   b. is used to help sales efforts

   c. is only needed when planning a new business venture

   d. all of the above

4. The process of guiding your business idea from inception through development and introduction to the market is called

   a. product planning

   b. SWOT analysis

   c. business model validation

   d. ideation

5. Which of the following is not a source for obtaining secondary data?

   a. interviews about your product

   b. government statistics

   c. annual business reports from other companies

   d. chamber of commerce

6. Social, economic, and political factors that could impact your business are called

   a. industry dynamics

   b. carrying capacity

   c. mass market

   d. business environment

7. All primary research

   a. involves talking directly to people

   b. requires a questionnaire

   c. involves a focus group

   d. is collected for a specific purpose

8. Which of the following is least important when collecting and evaluating data?

   a. finding data that supports your idea

   b. confiming research results with more than one source or method

   c. making sure data is relevant to the target market

   d. staying alert to biased sources

9. The period of time you have to act on a business opportunity before it disappears is called the

   a. opportunity time limit

   b. window of opportunity

   c. reasonable time frame

   d. none of the above

10. The type of business that provides the greatest amount of entrepreneurial freedom is a(n)

    a. business you start from scratch

    b. independent business you purchase

    c. franchise

    d. family business

11. Which of the following is not used to evaluate the feasibility of a business opportunity?

    a. invention analysis

    b. cost/benefit analysis

    c. opportunity-cost analysis

    d. SWOT analysis

12. Which of the following is not a characteristic of creative thinking?

    a. using your imagination

    b. lateral thinking

    c. looking at a situation in new ways

    d. vertical thinking

13. A royalty fee is a(n)

    a. single fee paid when a franchise agreement expires

    b. ongoing payment based on a percentage of sales

    c. single fee paid when the franchise agreement is signed

    d. ongoing payment based on the value of the business

BUSINESS COMMUNICATION

1. Research real-life stories of how entrepreneurs recognized the business opportunity that made them successful. Find an example for each of the following sources of business opportunities: problems, changes, new discoveries, existing products and services, and unique knowledge. Create a presentation about your findings (include pictures).

2. Working with a partner, select a local business with which you are both familiar. Construct a SWOT analysis of the business.

3. Identify a local business with which you are familiar. Write a 30-second brief summary describing the concept and customer to an investor. Present your summary to the class and ask them whether they would invest in the business.

4. Choose a business opportunity and do market research to identify potential customers, competitors, investors, and industry factors and trends affecting it. Then create a poster of how you see the marketplace. For example, use shapes (such as circles or boxes) to represent the different factors that affect and help define the opportunity. Use lines and arrows to show relationships between shapes. Be creative.

BUSINESS MATH

1. You've been told that a potential investor wants at least 22% of the business plan to focus on market analysis. If your business plan is 18 pages, about how many pages should be devoted to market analysis?

2. You own a franchise and need to pay an 11.25% monthly royalty fee to the franchisor. Your franchise had sales of $36,780 in August. What is your August royalty fee?

3. You live in a town with four bookstores and a population of 10,000 people. A recent survey showed that 50% of the population shops at bookstores. Assume that all factors (such as products, customer service, convenience of location, number of hours open) are the same for all four of the stores. What is the number of potential customers for each?

4. You are opening a dry-cleaning business in a town of 20,000 adults. There are two dry cleaners in town. The ABC bank is your source of funding. ABC considers the town's carrying capacity to be a minimum of 7,500 potential adult customers per dry cleaner. If every adult in town is a potential customer, what would the average number of potential customers be per dry-cleaning business if you started your business? Is this figure within the bank's requirement?

BUSINESS ETHICS

1. When choosing a business to start or to buy, evaluating and planning is important. One way of evaluating a business opportunity is to ask whether it agrees with your ethical values. Think of a service or product that is legal according to the law but may conflict with your beliefs. Write one or more paragraphs explaining your position. Then write at least one paragraph suggesting why others may view the service or product differently from the way you do.

2. Market research professionals operate by a code of ethics. Use the Internet to find several sets of rules. Print out at least two of these. Working in groups of three, analyze the rules you printed. What do they have in common? In what ways do they differ? Write a code of ethics to use when conducting research of your own. Exchange your set of rules with another group's. Analyze their rules compared to yours. As a way of determining how good their rules are, try to imagine scenarios that would present problems for them. After your analysis, return the rules to the group that wrote them, along with your suggestions for making them better. Each group should then revise its own set of rules based on the other group's suggestions.

BUSINESS IN YOUR COMMUNITY

1. Imagine that you've been asked to help plan a mall to be built near your school. Working in a small group, brainstorm ideas for businesses. What types of businesses would do well in this location? Have each person pick a potential business and do a SWOT analysis, pretending to be the business owner. Share your results. Which ideas have the most potential? The least?

2. Interview a small-business owner, a franchisee, or an inventor in your community. Ask what types of planning he or she did before starting/buying the business or before marketing the invention. How did he or she determine whether the business/invention had a good chance of succeeding? What were the advantages and disadvantages of this type of entrepreneurship? Share your research results with the class.

3. Contact a local market research firm in your area. Ask if you may have a few samples of old survey questionnaires. Or ask if you may observe a survey or focus group in progress. Later, make a list of ways you might adapt what you saw to research projects of your own.

4. Interview an officer at your local bank who lends money to new businesses. Ask what type and amount of market research the bank likes to see before considering a loan. Also, what advice would he or she give to someone who wants to attract financial investors?

INFORMATION TECHNOLOGY

Web Design

Web design is the process of manipulating graphics and text to create a unique and eye-catching website. In an increasingly crowded Internet, Web owners hire independent **Web designers**—professionals who will design a website that will stand out from others. Web design can be a big project, because a website can have hundreds of individual pages.

HTML Language

As you learned in earlier chapters, Web pages are designed in HTML (Hypertext Markup Language), a unique type of computer language that uses a series of brackets and other commands that determine how the site is displayed online. For example, here's HTML code for creating color on a website's background:

```
<body style="background:#0404B4">
```

The numbers and letters after "#" stand for a particular color. Changing #0404B4 to #FF0000 would change the background from blue to red. Each color has a unique number and letter combination. In fact, every font, border, and graphic has a unique HTML code. As you can imagine, HTML is a complicated language that can take a long time to master. Beginners can bypass this code by using a pre-made **Web template**. This is a website that includes already-created graphics and an established layout. Web templates make quality Web design available to people who are new

to it. Web design software is also available for both professional Web designers and beginning users.

Website Components

Web designers use a number of components to design a high-quality site. (These also are included on Web templates.) **Drop-down menus** are at the top of the page and allow users to navigate through the site. Websites are often broken up by adding a **sidebar** on the left or right of the page, where there are links to pages within the site or to other websites. Some sites use **flash animation**. This is a software program used to create animated graphics. The goal in using these features is to make the site both interesting and easy to navigate.

Website Navigation

Creating a user-friendly site is an important component of Web design. Some websites may work well with certain Web browsers (Firefox, Safari, or Internet Explorer) but not with others. A website may have several sections.

For instance, there may be individual pages within the site for a variety of products. A drop-down menu may include choices for different products, such as books, music, apparel, or whatever the website sells. Because many websites are designed to sell products, a Web designer needs to make it easy for visitors to the site to find and buy products.

Tech Vocabulary

drop-down menu

flash animation

sidebar

Web designer

Web template

Check Yourself

1. What does HTML do?

2. What is a Web template and why would you use one?

3. What are some of the main components of Web design?

4. What is a drop-down menu?

What Do You Think?

Applying Concepts. What are the most effective forms of Web design and why?

CASE STUDY

Opportunity Recognition & Market Analysis

STARTING A NEW BUSINESS

Eva graduated from Columbus State Community College with an associate's degree in Business Management. She then worked full-time so she could pay back her college loans. But she kept on the lookout for an opportunity to start her own full-time business. Join Eva as she adds to her work experience and considers a new business opportunity.

Something's Cooking!

After graduating, Eva decided to work full-time. Her mother told her about an opening at Ohio State University. "It's an administrative assistant job with the Campus Dining Services," she said. "They manage ten restaurants and a catering service on campus. With your business degree and experience in event planning, it could be a good match."

Eva got the job. She worked for the Director of the Campus Dining Services. Eva's job allowed her to apply her business skills, while learning how various types of food service are managed.

Although she enjoyed her work, Eva missed running her own business. She realized that, of all the event-planning tasks, she had most of all enjoyed cooking.

One day Eva was talking with a friend who said, "After working all day, I wish I had someone to cook dinner for me!" "Wow," Eva thought, "what a great idea! People who work all day might appreciate having someone prepare their meals. That's an idea for a business. I could become a personal chef for working people." It seemed like a great way for Eva to combine her passion for cooking and her desire to start a full-time business.

Eva knew that some of her cooking skills were weak. She needed improvement in knife technique, cost-cutting, and efficiency. Eva also figured that people might be reluctant to hire a personal chef who had no formal culinary training. She decided to do some market research to help her decide if her idea was a viable business opportunity.

Making It Personal

Here's what Eva discovered through her market research:

- **Description of Service.** Eva would be responsible for planning, buying, and preparing five dinners for a household. Food is often prepared at customers' homes. The chef packages dinners family-style with heating instructions and stores them in the customer's refrigerator or freezer. Kitchen clean-up is the personal chef's responsibility.

- **Start-Up Expenditures.** A low financial investment is needed to start a personal chef business. Eva would have to purchase her own set of professional knives, and possibly some cooking utensils.

- **Training and Certification.** Both homestudy and on-site training courses were available through associations such as the American Personal and Private Chef Association (APPCA) and the U.S.

Personal Chef Association (USPCA). A personal chef could become certified after meeting educational and work-experience guidelines. Eva figured that certification would help potential customers have more confidence in her.

- **Competition.** In the greater Columbus area, there were currently 15 personal chefs.

- **Market.** Columbus had a growing market segment of professionals. Eva thought households of professionals making a combined income of over $50,000 would be her most likely market. In the greater Columbus area this market was growing steadily. Like her friend, these professionals were often too busy to cook dinner.

- **Growth Potential.** Personal chef businesses made up one of the fastest growing segments in the food-service industry. According to the APPCA, about 9,000 personal chefs were currently serving about 72,000 clients nationwide. Those numbers were expected to double over the next five years.

Eva created a customer survey, which she conducted at a local mall. She discovered that people didn't use personal chefs because they weren't aware they existed. They also assumed that the cost of a professional chef would be out of their price range.

Based on her love of cooking and market research, Eva decided to switch from being a part-time event-planner to a full-time personal chef. She created a new name for her company, Eva's Edibles. On a vacation from her job at the Campus Dining Services, Eva took a five-day personal-chef training course to prepare for certification tests.

When Eva returned from vacation, she did ongoing market research and prepared a business plan on evenings and weekends. When she was satisfied with it, she did something everyone had advised her not to do: she quit her day job (but with appropriate notice).

She was going to be a personal chef. She was about to start Eva's Edibles!

Eva Tan's business plan for Eva's Edibles can be found in an Appendix of this textbook.

What Would You Have Done?

1. **Applying Concepts.** After Eva's graduation from community college, she took a full-time job to pay for her college loans. What did Eva give up by beginning to work full-time? Would you have made the same choice?

2. **Analyzing Information.** Based on Eva's background, her personal skills, and her market research results, draw up a SWOT chart for Eva's Edibles. Do you think her business idea is a good opportunity?

UNIT 3

BIG IDEA: COMPETITION

11

ENTREPRENEURSHIP AND THE ECONOMY

OBJECTIVES

- List the factors that affect the development of economic systems.
- Compare and contrast the various types of economic systems.
- Evaluate the role of entrepreneurs within an economic system.

NFTE Entrepreneurial Mindset Characteristic Focus

☑ Communication & Collaboration

National Entrepreneurship Standards

- **F.03** Explain the concept of scarcity
- **F.05** Describe the nature of economics and economic activities
- **F.19** Explain the types of economic systems
- **F.20** Describe the relationship between government and business
- **F.21** Assess impact of government actions on business ventures
- **F.22** Explain the concept of private enterprise
- **F.27** Determine the impact of small business/ entrepreneurship on market economies

Common Career Technical Core Standards

- **BM-MGT.3** Apply economic concepts fundamental to global business operations.
- **CRP.1** Act as a responsible and contributing citizen and employee.

National Entrepreneurship Standards: Career Competencies

☑ **D.16** Use communications technologies/systems (e.g., e-mail, faxes, voice mail, cell phones, etc.)

LESSON VOCABULARY

- capital
- capitalism
- command economy
- economic system
- economics
- economy
- enterprise
- free enterprise system
- industry
- local economy
- market economy
- mixed economy
- North American Industry Classification System (NAICS)
- scarcity
- voluntary exchange

11.1 Economics and Economic Systems

In the previous unit, you learned about identifying a business opportunity. You also learned about going through a process of business model validation to refine your idea through research until you reach a true business opportunity. In this unit, you will find information to answer the canvas question on competition: "Is there someone else providing my product or service better than I can?" To be able to answer this question, one of the first questions an entrepreneur needs to be able to answer is if there a demand for a good or service. They also need to know if there are other businesses, or competitors, fulfilling those demands. All of this requires an understanding of economics.

What Is an Economic System?

Economics is a social science concerned with how people satisfy their demands for goods (things you can buy) and services (things that people do for you for a fee) when the supply of those goods and services are limited. This is a somewhat technical definition, but what does it really mean?

Economics is all about the flow of goods and services between people. This is measured with numbers, so economics will always involve mathematics. However, economics is called a social science because *people* play the central role in it. It is people who decide which goods and services have value and what that value is. It is people who decide how goods and services should be used and how they should be distributed within a society. It is people who decide whether to buy or to sell goods and services. Ultimately, math may be the language of economics, but people are its soul.

Earth's population grows larger every day. More people means there is a greater demand for food, clothing, housing, and all the other essentials of life. These essentials are what we *need*. But we also want other things that are not necessary to survive. These are our *wants*. People try to satisfy their needs and wants by buying goods and services that have value to them. The demand for goods and services is often larger than the supply that can be provided. When there are not enough goods or services to meet the demand, then there is a **scarcity** of those goods and services.

Scarcity is one of the most important principles of economics. It means that there is never enough of everything to satisfy everyone completely. Money doesn't grow on trees, and there's never enough time in the day. Every day, you are faced with economic principle of scarcity. Have you ever stood in front of a vending machine with only a dollar bill to spend and debated between two equally desirable options? Because your resources were limited (scarce) you were forced to make a choice. Scarcity isn't limited to the amount of money you have to buy things. All resources, including time, are limited to some degree.

An **economic system** (or **economy**) is a system used by a society to allocate goods and services among its people and to cope with scarcity. Political, moral, and cultural factors affect what kinds of economic systems develop and thrive in different societies.

Every economic system answers four basic questions. They are called the fundamental questions of economics.

Fundamental Questions of Economics

- What goods and services are produced?
- What quantity of goods and services are produced?
- How are goods and services produced?
- For whom are goods and services produced?

Apply Your Knowledge   What factors make up an economic system? How do you participate in the economic system of your own country?

ENTREPRENEURIAL CASE STUDY: COMMUNICATION & COLLABORATION

Koran Bolden— Street Dreamz

Creating Young Entrepreneurs

Koran Bolden is the founder and CEO of Street Dreamz in St. Louis, Missouri. Street Dreamz hopes to bring social change and increase graduation rates through mentoring, entrepreneurship, and creating more positive media messages for youth. Through his work with his business, Koran has become nationally recognized as a national youth motivational speaker, entrepreneur, and youth empowerment and outreach consultant who advocates for students to graduate from school by educating them to make healthy life choices. His efforts are summarized through his ultimate vision statement for his business: "I am a young entrepreneur, who creates other young entrepreneurs."

Koran Bolden.

Finding a New Dream

At first, Koran's ultimate goal wasn't to own a recording studio, but rather be a recording artist himself. He had originally received a $150,000 contract with Def Jam Records when he was met with ultimate disappointment. "The record deal was a really good moment in my life. I got a deal with Def Jam. The leadership changed at Def Jam and I was forced out," Koran remembers. "After I lost my record deal with Def Jam, I went on this faith journey. I wanted to discover who I really was."

After missing out on this opportunity, Koran looked for his next career move. Soon he was inspired by his passion for music and social change to leave corporate America to open a leadership-focused recording studio called Street Dreamz in 2010 with his wife LaPortcia. Instead of opening a standard recording studio, Koran wanted to create a safe, positive, and supportive experience for young emerging artists. Street Dreamz Recording Studio and Party Center has now become a safe house and exciting alternative for young, aspiring musicians to build their self-esteem through writing positive lyrics, challenging and restricting kids from recording songs containing profanity. This strict "No Profanity" pledge soon gained attention from parents, schools boards, government officials, corporations, and local news media outlets, which did several feature stories on Koran's mission. This media attention has led to new growth opportunities. As of 2014, Street Dreamz opened two new satellite locations that also focus on entrepreneurship, mentoring, and the arts.

Koran's vision for social change has been validated by the impact he's had on over 30,000 students. They inspired the creation of an award-winning Dream Success curriculum that led him to being the recent recipient of the Verizon Wireless Everyday Hero Award, the Cadillac City Shapers Salute, and then being tapped by Walgreens as the spokesperson for their regional Walgreens Expressions Challenge. His most recent honor was being featured on the Gap Inc. website for his impact on youth leadership and entrepreneurship. He was later asked to deliver a keynote speech on stage for the Banana Republic Conference at the Bellagio Hotel in Las Vegas. After the County Executive's office heard of Koran's Gap Inc. story, they officially declared March 21, 2014 as Koran Bolden Day in Saint Louis County. He released his most recent guide for young entrepreneurs, "Rock, Paper, Scissors," in 2014.

Thinking and Acting Like an Entrepreneur

- How does Koran use his passion, interests, and skills to impact the local economy?

- Explain the ways that Koran's business is socially responsible.

- In what ways does Koran demonstrate entrepreneurial mindset behaviors of communication and collaboration?

11.2 Types of Economic Systems

What Are the Types of Economic Systems?

Two very different types of economic systems are often used to compare how societies deal with the fundamental questions of economics. These two types of economic systems are the command economy and the market economy. In a **command economy,** the government controls the production, allocation, and prices of goods and services. In a **market economy**, suppliers and consumers control the production, allocation, and prices of goods and services.

In reality, no country has a pure command system or a pure market system. This leads to a third type of economic system, a **mixed economy**. This is an economic system that blends elements of the command system and the market system. All modern economies are actually mixed economies; however, most countries lean so strongly toward one model or the other that their economic systems are called command systems or market systems.

The Command Economy

In a command economy, the government owns or manages the nation's resources and businesses. The government controls what suppliers produce, how much is produced, and how it is produced. The government also controls how goods and services are distributed throughout the country to its citizens and the prices that people pay for them. Ultimately, the government decides the answers to the fundamental questions of economics.

Command economies are associated with political systems in which the government has strict control over social and economic affairs. Socialism and communism are two political systems that are strongly associated with command systems. The former Soviet Union featured many elements of a pure command system. Governments run by dictators or controlled by one political party or one ruling family also lean toward the command system.

Although no modern country has a pure command system, some nations come close to it. Syria, Iran, Cuba, and North Korea are said to have command systems. In these countries, central government planners usually make economic decisions and long-term economic plans for the nation. The government controls most resources and businesses. Entrepreneurship may be allowed to a small degree so long as it does not interfere with the overall government control of the economy.

The Market Economy

In a market economy, suppliers produce whatever goods and services they wish and set prices based on what consumers are willing to pay. Prices are responsive to consumer demand. The government does not tell businesses what to produce nor does it tell consumers what to buy. This system is characterized by individual freedom of choice and voluntary exchange. **Voluntary exchange** is transaction in which both suppliers and the consumers believe they benefit.

Figure 11-1 ▶

Voluntary Exchange.

Voluntary exchange is a transaction in which both suppliers and consumers believe they benefit.

Drawing Conclusions.

How does the consumer benefit in this transaction?

Another name for the market system is the **free enterprise system**. This is because people are free to become entrepreneurs and own and operate an **enterprise** (business). There are also many investment opportunities in a market economy. Individuals can invest money in their own businesses or others' businesses. Another name for the cash and goods that a business owns is **capital**. That's why the market system or free enterprise system is also referred to as **capitalism**. Individuals and businesses are free to own and trade goods and invest cash in businesses.

The democratic political system is strongly associated with the market economy. Democracies typically favor personal choice, voluntary exchange, and the right of individuals to own property, businesses, and capital. Although no country has a pure market system, the United States, Canada, Australia, Hong Kong, Singapore, and many Western European nations are said to have market systems, because they allow much economic freedom for individuals. This does not mean that their governments exert no control over economic decisions. The level of government intervention varies by country, so some free enterprise systems are actually "freer" than others.

The United States has one of the freest market systems in the world. In the United States, people are free to become entrepreneurs and engage in whatever legal enterprise they choose. Suppliers and consumers largely determine what goods and services are offered for sale and at what prices. However, the U.S. government does exert some economic control. It regulates businesses, enforces labor and product safety laws, imposes taxes, and takes other actions that affect economic flow.

Apply Your Knowledge   What is the main difference between the command and market economy? Based on your investigation of different economies at the start of the chapter, what economic system do you believe China is moving toward today?

CAREER COMPETENCIES

Use Communications Technologies and Systems

Do you text? Can you send an e-mail or a fax? Can you use a smartphone? If yes, you are like millions of Americans who carry out these tasks every day. These skills are not just important to keep in touch with friends and family. Excellent communication skills have become a fundamental entrepreneurial mindset behavior for entrepreneurs to demonstrate.

Advancements in shipping, travel, and telecommunications permit much more entrepreneurial activity around the world than in the past. Goods ship over water, land, and air routes, and can circle the world in a matter of days or weeks. Passenger and freight airlines add more foreign destinations to their routes, allowing goods and business people greater access to international trading. Modern means of telecommunications—phone, fax, e-mail, and Internet—connect suppliers and consumers around the world. The Internet, in particular, has made international trade easier, faster, and more convenient than ever before.

All of these tools have numerous benefits in running a business, but below are some ways that communications technologies help entrepreneurs do business locally and globally:

- E-mail, the communications medium of choice, can be used at any time of day. This allows entrepreneurs to communicate with customers and employees without everyone having to be available at the same time.

- Smartphones can be used to make/receive phone calls and to check e-mail. They can also be useful in sending text messages. Texting involves sending small written messages from one cell phone to another. This approach can save time over placing calls.

- Fax machines send an exact copy of a document to someone electronically. This can be very important when sending order forms or receipts to customers. The fax is slowly being replaced by other similar communication technologies, such as being able to send a fax to a smartphone. It is also possible to scan documents using a copy machine or smartphone and send them electronically.

- Instant messaging allows entrepreneurs to communicate with staff, customers, and vendors via computer or smartphone in real-time. This is a great tool for businesses looking to increase their efficiency.

Career Skills in Action

Now, think about your own business. Think about how you would operate your business and answer the following questions:

- What communications tools would you use to run your business?
- What communications tools would you use tell people about your business?
- What communications tools would you use to sell your product?

11.3 The Role of Entrepreneurs in the Economy

Role of Entrepreneurs in Industry

So, what roles do entrepreneurs play in these economic systems? Regardless of the economic system, all entrepreneurs contribute to an industry. **Industry** refers to the production of goods or services within an economy. Industries can include anything from farming, to furniture making, to healthcare services. There are many ways to categorize industries, either by similar processes (such as all businesses doing software development) or by financial behavior.

The **North American Industry Classification System (NAICS)** assigns a numerical code to every industry in North America based on the primary business function of the industry (see Table 11.1). You can access these codes on their website: https://www.census.gov/eos/www/naics/. NAICS codes are useful for classifying particular types of businesses, and are a great resource to determine what industry your business is in. It also has industry statistics and other information about the role your business plays in that industry. The U.S. Department of Labor makes predictions about which industries will likely experience the largest growth in number of employees over the coming decade. There is one thing all of the top ten industries have in common—they provide some type of service. This is just one indication that service businesses are expected to dominate the U.S. economy, at least through the next decade.

Table 11.1 Fastest Growing Industries

Rank	Industry	NAICS #
1	Management, scientific, and technical consulting services	5416
2	Individual and family services	6241
3	Home health-care services	6216
4	Financial investments and related services	523
5	Facilities support services	5612
6	Residential care facilities and related services	6232, 6233, 6239
7	Independent artists, writers, and performers	7115
8	Computer-systems design and related services	5415
9	Museums, historical sites, and similar institutions	712
10	Child daycare services	6244

Role of Entrepreneurs in the Local Economy

Entrepreneurs also have a large impact on their local economies. A **local economy** is the economy of a local area, such as a community or town. Because many entrepreneurs operate small businesses that sell primarily to local consumers, entrepreneurship has a profound effect on local economies.

◀ **Figure 11-2**
Local Entrepreneurs.
Entrepreneurs play a huge role in the local economy.

Applying Concepts.
How can entrepreneurs who own small businesses play a larger role in the local economy that large businesses?

Entrepreneurs can benefit their local economies in the following ways:

- Purchasing materials and supplies from local merchants
- Opening an account at a local bank, credit union, or other financial institution
- Joining a local business association, trade group, or civic organization that supports local economic development
- Paying local taxes that benefit schools and other public services
- Investing money in local businesses
- Donating money, time, or goods to local charities and organizations
- Hiring local employees (this produces multiple benefits for the local economy, because the employees will likely spend their wages in the area)
- Supplying goods and services to local consumers

 Apply Your Knowledge Think back to your investigation of China's economy. How are Chinese citizens having a greater contribution to the local economy by starting more businesses? Did the Chinese economy grow or shrink during that time period? What makes you think that?

APPLICATION TO BUSINESS PLANNING

Industry and Industry Statistics

Use what you learned from in chapter to identify what industry your business is in. You can use the North American Industry Classification System or any other available classification resources. In your business planning, be sure to include:

- Name and size of the industry
- Statistics about trends in the industry
- Description of the impact your business will have on the local economy

11 ASSESSMENT

REVIEWING OBJECTIVES

1. What are the factors that affect the development of economic systems?

2. List the various types of economic systems and the characteristics of each.

3. Explain the role of entrepreneurs within an economic system.

CRITICAL THINKING

The United States is a large and wealthy nation with many natural and human resources within its own borders. So why does the United States import goods and services?

ENTREPRENEURIAL THINKING EXERCISE: COMMUNICATION AND COLLABORATION

Consider your investigation of entrepreneurship in China. Imagine you were going to open a small business selling screen-printed t-shirts through a distribution company based in China. Write a paragraph that outlines explicitly how you would initiate communication with the company. What communication technologies would you use? How would you address the team? What would you need to find out about the business operations?

EXTENSION ACTIVITIES

Entrepreneurship & Literacy Skills

Complete the following task to demonstrate your understanding of entrepreneurship:

Grades 9–12: Working in a team, pick two countries with different economic systems. Using the Internet and library resources, study the economies of these two countries and learn about the role of played by entrepreneurs in each. Prepare a short presentation that describes the economic systems of each country and the role of entrepreneurship in each economic system.

12 SUPPLY AND DEMAND

GUIDING QUESTION:

"How do supply and demand principles influence the availability of my product or service?"

APPLICATION TO BUSINESS PLANNING:

☑ Availability of Product/Service

OBJECTIVES

- Examine the relationship between suppliers and buyers as opposing forces.
- Explain how supply and demand relationships impact the availability and pricing of products and services.
- Demonstrate supply and demand relationships graphically.

NFTE Entrepreneurial Mindset Characteristic Focus

☑ Opportunity Recognition

National Entrepreneurship Standards

- **F.07** Explain the principles of supply and demand
- **F.08** Describe the concept of price
- **F.27** Determine the impact of small business/ entrepreneurship on market economies

Common Career Technical Core Standards

- **BM.1** Utilize mathematical concepts, skills and problem solving to obtain necessary information for decision-making in business.
- **BM-MGT.3** Apply economic concepts fundamental to global business operations.
- **CRP.5** Consider the environmental, social and economic impacts of decisions.

National Entrepreneurship Standards: Career Competencies

 K.12 Demonstrate spreadsheet applications

LESSON VOCABULARY

- consumers
- demand
- demand curve
- equilibrium point
- equilibrium price
- equilibrium quantity
- shortage
- suppliers
- supply
- supply and demand curve
- supply curve
- surplus

12.1 Opposing Forces of Supply and Demand

In the last chapter, you looked at what role entrepreneurs play in industries and economic systems. In this chapter, you will continue to investigate how economics and the idea of competition impacts your business decisions. This chapter will look at laws of economics and how they influence the price and availability of your products or service.

The Law of Supply and Demand

In a market economy, businesses provide goods and services because consumers will pay money for them. Businesses typically want to get the most money possible for the goods and services they offer. Consumers typically want to pay the lowest price possible for what they buy. These two opposing forces actually work together to make the market system operate efficiently.

Supply is the quantity of goods and services that a business is willing to sell at a specific price and a specific time. Demand is the quantity of goods and services that customers are willing to buy at a specific price and a specific time.

Suppliers control the amount of supply, that is, they decide what quantity of a good or service they are willing to sell at a particular price. Consumers decide how much they are willing to pay for a given good or service.

◀ **Figure 12-1**

Supply and Demand Relationships.

Prices of natural resources are constantly changing due to supply and demand relationships.

Applying Concepts.

Why do you think gas prices are constantly changing? What do you think influences that?

In a market economy, the price of a particular good or service is determined by supply and demand:

• When the supply is greater than the demand, the price goes down (e.g., an umbrella vendor on a sunny day)

• When the demand is greater than the supply, the price goes up (e.g., an umbrella vendor on a rainy day)

As you can see, both price and timing are important when considering supply and demand. For example, a garden store may have a supply of seeds and plants in the spring when the demand would be high and the price would also be high. But there would be substantially less demand for seeds and plants in the fall, when prices would be low (if, in fact, any consumers would even be interested in seeds or plants at all).

Apply Your Knowledge   How is the relationship between supply and demand made up of opposing forces? From your investigation, why does it seem that Nintendo incorrectly estimated on the demand for the system?

ENTREPRENEURIAL CASE STUDY: OPPORTUNITY RECOGNITION

 ## Andrea Dashiell— Honeecakes Bakery

Finding an Opportunity

Andrea Dashiell is the CEO and founder of Honeecakes Bakery (www. honeecakesbakery.com), located in Forestville, MD, outside of Washington, DC. Honeecakes Bakery provides homemade cakes, pies, cupcakes, and many other delicious desserts made to custom order. Recently celebrating its tenth anniversary in 2014, Honeecakes was started by Andrea while she was attending Suitland Senior High School in Forestville, Maryland. Initially, she took orders and produced homemade baked goods around her school schedule. Recognizing the huge opportunity behind her business, Andrea continued to run the business while she was attending college. Her hard work has paid off, as her successful business has been profiled in *Black Enterprise*, *Business Newsweek*, Fox5 DC, *The Gazzette*, and was honored by the National Coalition of 100 Black Women.

Entrepreneurial Balancing Act

While Andrea formally started her business as part of her entrepreneurship course sponsored by the Network for Teaching Entrepreneurship (NFTE), the seeds for Honeecakes had been planted many years before. Andrea

had been baking since childhood. It was a passion long before it became a lucrative business.

How lucrative a business it ended up being was somewhat of a surprise to Andrea, who continued to run the business while she was attending the University of Delaware. Said Andrea of the opportunity, "I had to do a lot of rearranging owning a business as an 18- or 19-year-old," Andrea said, "but it was definitely worth it."

Sometimes the demand for her product was greater than the amount she could produce. One time, she received the great opportunity to produce 200 mini-cupcakes for a company anniversary party. However, it was the same weekend that she was to attend homecoming at her alma matter.

Andrea Dashiell.

Because her company makes fresh baked goods, she could not make her product too far in advance. Andrea did not want to miss out on the opportunity. Instead, she found a way to complete the order by baking nonstop at a friend's house near campus. But this hard work did not sour her on the business. "That's when you realize your heart is really in it," Andrea said.

Infusing Business with Passion

As of 2014, Andrea continues to work on her business, while also looking for opportunities to further her education and stay involved in the community. She currently works for the International Broadcasting Bureau located in Washington, DC, and is attending Bowie State University to pursue her Master's degree in Organizational Communications. Knowing the importance of philanthropy, Andrea mentors in the HERStory Mentoring Program, and still is involved with NFTE. She currently serves on the NFTE e-Council, which assists students with their business plans, and lectures to high school and college students about youth entrepreneurship throughout the Washington, DC Metropolitan Area. Overall, it is her passion that continues to drive her forward. This is evident from the Honeecakes philosophy: "When you infuse your business with passion, opportunities will present themselves so it can sustain. It's important to create a business that not only fulfills you, but pushes you towards your purpose."

Thinking and Acting Like an Entrepreneur

- In what ways does Andrea balance her work with hobbies that she is passionate about?
- How do supply and demand principles impact how Andrea runs her food-based business?
- How does Andrea demonstrate the entrepreneurial mindset behavior of recognizing business opportunities?

12.2 Finding Equilibrium

Meeting in the Middle

How do entrepreneurs think about supply and demand? Imagine you are a potato farmer in Idaho. You are about to plant crops that you will eventually harvest and sell. When you are deciding how many potatoes to plant, you have to consider the following scenarios:

- **Scenario 1:** If the weather turns out to be just right, you and the entire country could end up with more potatoes than expected. This would be a **surplus**, or when the quantity supplied is greater than the demand. While this sounds great in theory, the demand for the potatoes will probably not change. People are not going to eat more potatoes just because there are more of them. To get rid of them, you would probably lower the price, and lose out on profit.

- **Scenario 2:** If the weather turns out to be lousy, you and the entire country could end up with a smaller crop of potatoes. Even when the weather is lousy, people will still want to eat the same amount of potatoes as the year before. So this scenario would be a **shortage**, or a time when the quantity supplied can't meet the demand. You might be able to charge more because more people want what is available, but you would miss out on sales that could have been made.

Neither scenario is beneficial to the entrepreneur. It is better to try to avoid having a surplus or a shortage by trying to establish an equilibrium point. An **equilibrium point** is the ideal quantity at a given price that a customer is willing to pay so that they can meet demand and maximize profits.

Finding the equilibrium point means determining an equilibrium quantity and equilibrium price.

- **Equilibrium quantity** is the quantity at which the supply equals the demand. If a supplier produces more than the equilibrium quantity, there will be a surplus of the item. The supplier will have to lower the price. If a supplier produces less than the equilibrium quantity, there will be a shortage of the item, and demand will not be satisfied.

- **Equilibrium price** is the price at which supply equals demand. It is the price that buyers are willing to pay and the supplier is willing to accept.

Finding an equilibrium point can help entrepreneurs decide whether or not to go into a particular business. As you will learn later in this unit, there are costs going into business that an entrepreneur must cover. At each potential price for a product or service, there must be sufficient demand for a product to make it worthwhile for a supplier to produce it. If the entrepreneur can't cover their costs and avoid a shortage/surplus, then it's not a worthwhile opportunity.

 **Apply Your Knowledge**   What causes a shortage? What causes a surplus? Which was present in the investigation of the Nintendo Wii?

CAREER COMPETENCIES

 ## Demonstrate Spreadsheet Applications

A spreadsheet is a grid of columns and rows used for storing data. Spreadsheets used to be written on paper; now, almost all spreadsheets are created with computer programs such as Microsoft® Excel®. Spreadsheets are used in any job that works with numbers—which is pretty much every job. Entrepreneurs can use spreadsheets to:

- Set up a budget for the business
- Create charts about research data
- Track sales data
- Forecast sales
- Analyze customer statistics
- Record results of trying new approaches

Spreadsheet programs have made workers more productive by automating tasks they used to do by hand. For example, they have features that let you set up equations or formulas so your computer can automatically perform calculations. The formulas might be simple, such as totaling a column of numbers, or complex, such as generating a chart based on data in multiple columns or rows. Workers can use the same spreadsheet in different situations by changing the values but keeping the formulas in place.

Career Skills in Action

Now try using a spreadsheet to reduce time on a longer task. Use a spreadsheet application to create a graph for the following data:

Selling Price	$5	$10	$15	$20
Quantity Demanded	80	70	45	20

Set up the data chart like the example provided.

- Use the automatic graphing tools to create a line graph of this data. You can search the Help feature of the program if you need more assistance, or find an online tutorial of the spreadsheet program you are using.

- If you are successful, you should produce a graph that shows a decreasing line graph.

12.3 Visualizing Supply and Demand

Supply and Demand Curves

So, how do entrepreneurs establish an equilibrium quantity and equilibrium price? A useful tool for determining this is to create a supply and demand curve, which shows the relationship between supply and demand graphically. To understand the supply and demand curve, let's look at each part separately.

A **supply curve** on a graph shows the quantity of a product or service a supplier is willing to sell at each price across a range of prices in a specified period of time. Quantity is shown on the x-axis, and price is shown on the y-axis. The supplier is willing to provide more as the price increases and less as it decreases.

A **demand curve** is a curve on a graph that shows the quantities that consumers are willing to buy at each price across a range of prices in a specific period of time. Once again, the quantity is shown on the x-axis, and the price is shown on the y-axis. Consumers are willing to buy more of a product at a lower price and less at a higher price.

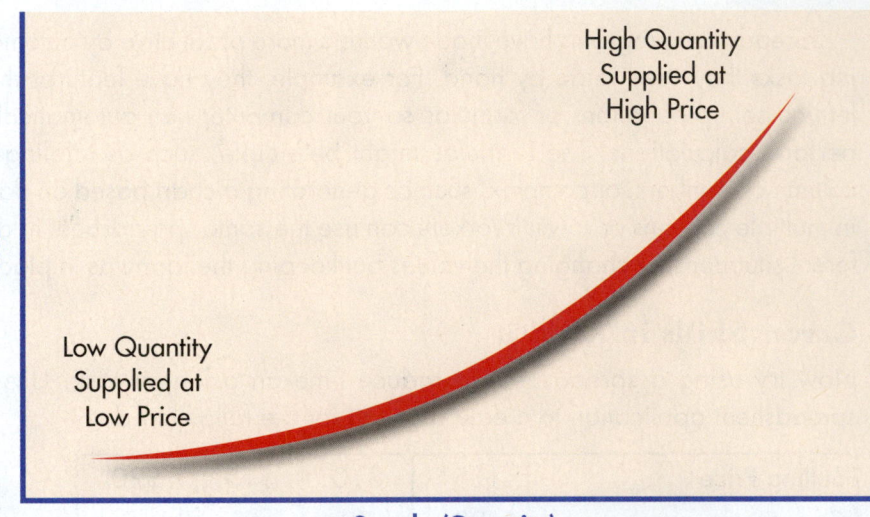

Figure 12-2 ▶
Supply Curve.

A supply curve shows the quantity and price relationship acceptable to suppliers.

Inferring.

Why is a supplier willing to supply greater quantities as the selling price increases?

High Quantity Supplied at High Price

Low Quantity Supplied at Low Price

Price

Supply (Quantity)

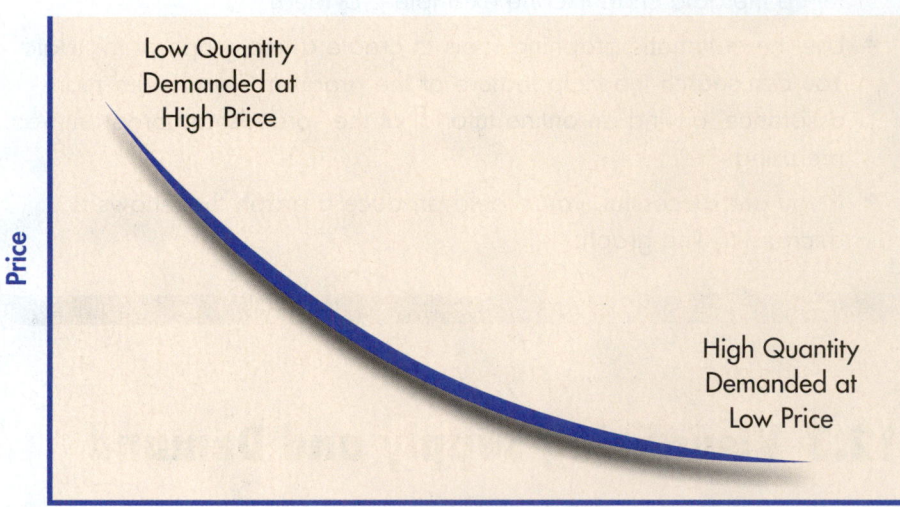

Figure 12-3 ▶
Demand Curve.

A demand curve shows the quantity and price relationship acceptable to consumers.

Comparing/Contrasting.

Why is the demand curve shaped so differently from the supply curve?

Low Quantity Demanded at High Price

High Quantity Demanded at Low Price

Price

Demand (Quantity)

A **supply and demand curve** is a graph that includes both a supply curve and a demand curve. It shows the relationship between price and the quantity of a product or service that is supplied and demanded. The **equilibrium point** is where the supply curve and the demand curve intersect. This is the point at which supply and demand are balanced.

- The x-axis coordinate of the equilibrium point identifies the equilibrium quantity.
- The y-axis coordinate of the equilibrium point identifies the equilibrium price.

Entrepreneurs can use supply and demand curves to determine how much quantity to produce at a specific price to make the venture profitable.

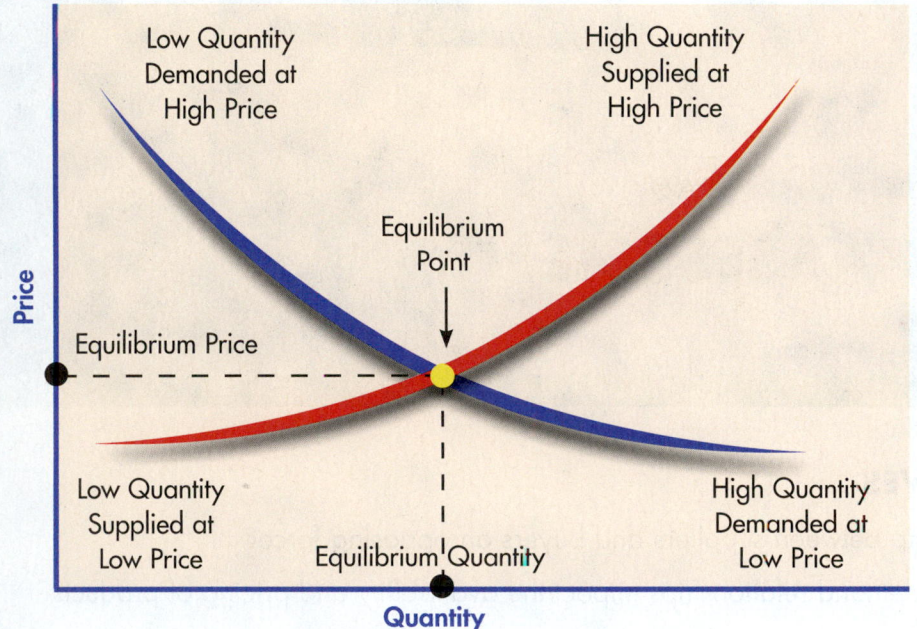

Low Quantity Demanded at High Price

High Quantity Supplied at High Price

Equilibrium Point

Price

Equilibrium Price

Low Quantity Supplied at Low Price

Equilibrium Quantity

High Quantity Demanded at Low Price

Quantity

Supply and Demand Curve.

A supply and demand curve shows the price relationship between the quantity supplied and the quantity demanded.

Interpreting Graphs.

Which portion of the supply curve indicates a surplus? What about a shortage?

Apply Your Knowledge   What do supply and demand curves tell entrepreneurs? Think back to your investigation of the Nintendo Wii. How could Nintendo have better used supply and demand curves with their launch?

✔ APPLICATION TO BUSINESS PLANNING

Availability of Product/Service

Use what you learned from this chapter about supply and demand to identify how much supply of your product or service you will make available. You should support your thinking using principles of supply and demand. Be sure to include:

- How much demand will there be for your product or service (low, average, or high)
- How available you plan to make your product/service (easy to purchase, or limited edition)
- Any limitations on providing large quantities of your product or service

12 ASSESSMENT

REVIEWING OBJECTIVES

1. How is the relationship between suppliers and buyers an opposing force?

2. How do supply and demand relationships impact the availability and pricing of products and services?

3. What do supply and demand curves tell an entrepreneur?

CRITICAL THINKING

Explain how supply and demand affect prices in the U.S. economy.

ENTREPRENEURIAL THINKING EXERCISE: OPPORTUNITY RECOGNITION

Think back to your investigation of the Nintendo Wii. If you were another business, what would you have done to take advantage of their mistake? How could you have made money off Nintendo's mistake? Be as explicit as possible.

12 ASSESSMENT

EXTENSION ACTIVITIES

Entrepreneurship & Mathematics Skills

Complete the following task to demonstrate your understanding of entrepreneurship:

Grades 9–12: Imagine that you are making custom t-shirts for your school's homecoming. You gather data on how much you would be willing to supply at each price to cover expenses and maximize profits at each price. You also research how many people will buy at each price. Use your data in the tables below to complete the following tasks:

T-shirts Supplied

Price	$5	$10	$15	$20	$25
Quantity	20	40	60	80	100

T-shirts Demanded

Price	$5	$10	$15	$20	$25
Quantity	130	100	70	40	10

• On the same graph, plot the supply curve and demand curve with the data given.
• Find the linear function that describes each of the curves.
• Find the y-intercept of the demand curve. What does this number represent?
• Find the intercept of the two curves. What does this number represent?

OBJECTIVES

- Identify various forms of competition.
- Determine market share for a business.
- Explain the role competition plays in the global economy.

NFTE Entrepreneurial Mindset Characteristic Focus

☑ Flexibility & Adaptability

National Entrepreneurship Standards

- **A.03** Assess global trends and opportunities
- **F.25** Explain the concept of competition
- **F.26** Describe types of market structures
- **F.28** Explain the nature of international trade
- **F.29** Describe small-business opportunities in international trade
- **F.30** Determine the impact of cultural and social environments on world trade
- **F.31** Explain the impact of exchange rates on trade
- **F.32** Evaluate influences on a nation's ability to trade

Common Career Technical Core Standards

- **BM.1** Utilize mathematical concepts, skills and problem solving to obtain necessary information for decision-making in business.
- **BM.2** Describe laws, rules and regulations as they apply to effective business operations.
- **BM-MGT.3** Apply economic concepts fundamental to global business operations.
- **CRP.5** Consider the environmental, social and economic impacts of decisions.

National Entrepreneurship Standards: Career Competencies

 D.24 Develop cultural sensitivity

 E.14 Communicate by computer

LESSON VOCABULARY

- competitor
- direct competitor
- exporting
- fair trade
- foreign exchange rate
- global economy
- importing
- indirect competitor
- market share
- quota
- strong direct competitor
- tariff
- trade barrier
- weak direct competitor

ENTREPRENEURIAL INVESTIGATION
Beyond the Box Lunch

Every day, millions of people leave their job or school to buy lunch. Imagine that you also needed to leave school to buy lunch. Perform the following investigation:

- List as many places near your school as you can where it is possible to buy any type of food. This does not have to be limited to restaurants. Use online search tools and business listings to help with your research. Once you have your list, organize the listings based on the type of business they are.

- Next, make a list of any other ways you could get food for lunch that don't include buying it from a business.

Be prepared to share and compile your responses as a class. Then, take a poll to get everyone's favorite lunch option from the list.

13.1 Identifying Your Competition

Now that you have a better understanding of economic systems and the law of supply and demand, let's look at some key players that influence those supply and demand relationships: your **competitors**. As you learned previously, a key entrepreneurial mindset skill is flexibility and adaptability. By understanding your competition, you can better adapt to what new things they bring to your industry, and keep up demand for your business.

Types of Competition

In addition to your target market, another critical area of market research involves identifying your competitors. They are the rival businesses with whom you are competing for the dollars that your target market spends.

Your research should include identifying two types of competitors:

- **Direct competitors.** Businesses in your market that sell a similar product or service to what your business provides are your **direct competitors**. McDonald's® and Burger King® are examples of **strong direct competitors** in the fast-food industry because they both sell a similar line of products. An ice cream shop that also sold hamburgers might also be considered direct competition for McDonald's and Burger King. However, the ice cream shop would be considered a **weak direct competitor**, because its main focus is on ice cream products. Hamburgers are only a sideline for the ice cream shop.

234 ● *Chapter 13*

- **Indirect competitors.** Businesses that sell a different product or service than your business provides, but that still fill the same customer need or want are your ==indirect competitors==. For example, Taco Bell® is in the fast-food industry, but it is an indirect competitor with McDonald's and Burger King because Taco Bell sells fast-food products, but not hamburgers. On a broader level, non-fast-food restaurants could also be considered indirect competition because the food they sell fills the same basic need.

	McDonald's	Burger King	Dairy Queen	Taco Bell
Main Product	Hamburger	Hamburger	Ice Cream	Taco
Secondary Product	Fries	Fries	Hamburger	Burrito

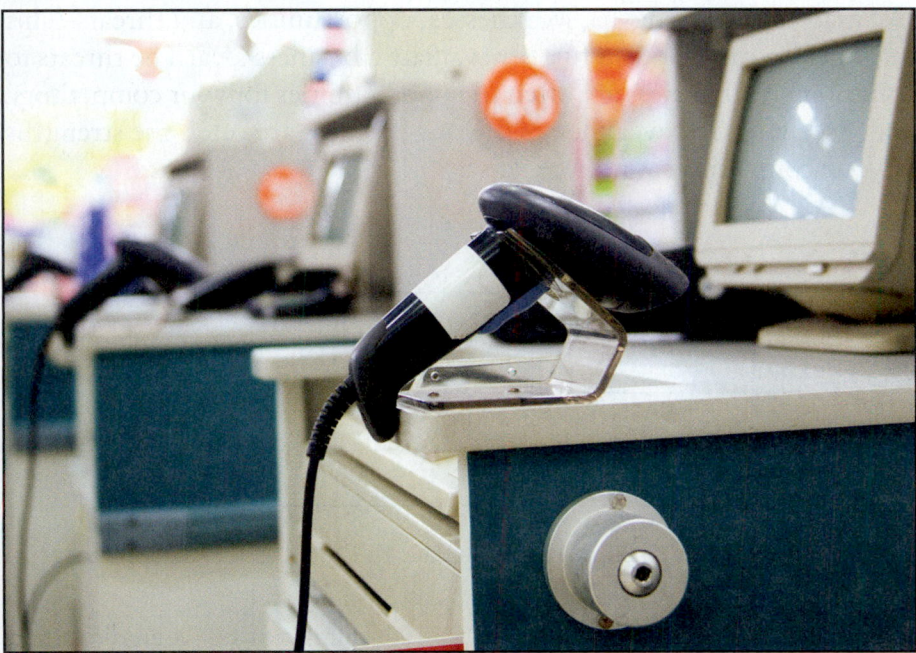

◀ **Figure 13-1**
Identifying Competition.
Large department stores offer many types of products.

Applying Concepts.
What are some businesses that compete directly with a large department store?

Other Forms of Competition

Keep in mind that your target customers may choose options other than buying from your business or your direct and indirect competitors. For instance, customers may decide to make a hamburger rather than buy it. Purchasing the parts or ingredients of a product may also be less expensive than buying a prepared version.

In tough economic times, customers may choose to provide a particular service for themselves rather than pay someone else to do it. Women who give themselves manicures, instead of going to a nail salon, are examples of customers who become the competition. Someone who changes the oil in their car, rather than taking it to a service station, is another example.

Indirect competition may include businesses outside your industry if they provide a product or service that has the same benefit as yours. Competition can also vary depending on the time of year or a temporary condition. For example, suppose you own a candy store. Around St. Valentine's Day, florists become your indirect competition even though they are not in the same industry because flowers or candy both fill a particular want—to present a gift to your Valentine.

Expand Your SWOT Analysis

You used a SWOT analysis in Unit 2 to test the feasibility of a business idea. As you obtain new data through market research, you can update and expand your SWOT analysis. Table 13.1 shows you a useful way to expand your SWOT analysis to include competitor data. Basically, this chart provides a way to translate the detailed data from your competitive matrix into strengths, weaknesses, opportunities, and threats. This information can help you further evaluate a business idea. The threats to your potential business are often the opportunities for your competitors, and vice versa. The weaknesses of your business are often the strengths of your competitors, and vice versa.

Table 13.1   Expanded Swot Analysis

Business	Strengths	Weaknesses	Opportunities	Threats
Your Business				
Competitor A				
Competitor B				
Competitor C				

 Apply Your Knowledge   What is the difference between direct and indirect competition? From the list you made during your investigation, can you find two businesses that would be your direct competitors? How about indirect competitors?

ENTREPRENEURIAL CASE STUDY: FLEXIBILITY & ADAPTABILITY

Maxine Clark— Build-A-Bear Workshop

Inspiration from a Friend

Maxine Clark is one of the true innovators in the retail industry. During her career, her ability to spot emerging retail and merchandising trends and her insight into the desires of the American consumer have generated growth for retail leaders, including department, discount, and specialty stores. In 1997, she founded Build-A-Bear® Workshop (www.buildabear.com), a teddy bear-themed retail-entertainment experience. Today there are more than 400 Build-A-Bear Workshop stores worldwide. Cumulative sales have exceeded $4.5 billion and over 125 million stuffed animals have been sold worldwide.

Maxine Clark.

Build-A-Bear Workshop was born from an idea that founder, Maxine Clark, and her friend Katie—who was 10 years old at the time—had when they were out shopping for stuffed toys. For the amount of businesses that sell stuffed toys, one would assume that they finished shopping with what they looking for. However, they couldn't find the stuffed toy that Katie wanted. Katie's response would soon inspire an entire company, "These are so easy, we could make them." Katie was thinking of a small craft project, but what Maxine heard was so much bigger.

Finding New Ways to Do Business

Maxine started thinking about how she could run a business that provided a better selection and higher-quality stuffed animals. Her first thought was to look around to see if she could buy a business, like a factory that made stuffed animals. She would then try to make it even more successful. While she found a few that made stuffed animals, no one wanted to sell.

Eventually, instead of opening a store that sold stuffed animals like everyone else, she decided to open a business where customers could make their own stuffed animal. As with many new ideas, there were people that did not get it at first. Every adult said it would never work, asking, "Why would anyone ever want to make their own stuffed animal?" But Maxine knew she was ahead of a trend, as every kid that heard about the idea said, "Where is it?" and "When can I do it?" Luckily for Maxine, she listened to her intuition, as her business was received with great success after its launch. Her business received national media attention and Maxine received numerous awards, among them being named one of The 25 Most Influential People in Retailing by Chain Store Age.

Helping Others Be Entrepreneurs

In June 2013, Maxine stepped down from her Chief Executive Bear role to apply her entrepreneurial skills to her passion for improving K-12 public education and to invest in and mentor women and minority entrepreneurs. Maxine is a Founding member of Prosper Women's Capital, a fund formed to invest in women entrepreneurs. In addition to generously giving her time to numerous local organizations in her community, Maxine is also a member of the Network for Teaching Entrepreneurship (NFTE) St. Louis advisory board.

Thinking and Acting Like an Entrepreneur

- How was Maxine's business like the existing competition? What made it different and better?
- Who might Maxine's competition be now that her business sells an experience and not just a stuffed animal?
- In what ways does Maxine demonstrate entrepreneurial mindset behaviors of flexibility and adaptability?

13.2 Market Share

Calculating Market Share

Another way to look at competition is in terms of market share. **Market share** is the percentage of a target market population that is buying a particular product or service from your business. To visualize this, imagine that you open up a shoe store in your town. You think your business will be successful because pretty much everyone needs to buy shoes. However, there may already be many other stores where people can buy shoes as well, and only so many pairs of shoes people are willing to buy. Figuring out what percentage of the town you can get to shop at your shoe store versus your competitors will help you analyze your business opportunity.

Determining a reasonable market share goal should be based on the level of competition in your target market. In most cases, you will be entering a market with many competitors. Or your market may have a few large competitors that hold most of the market share. Either way, don't

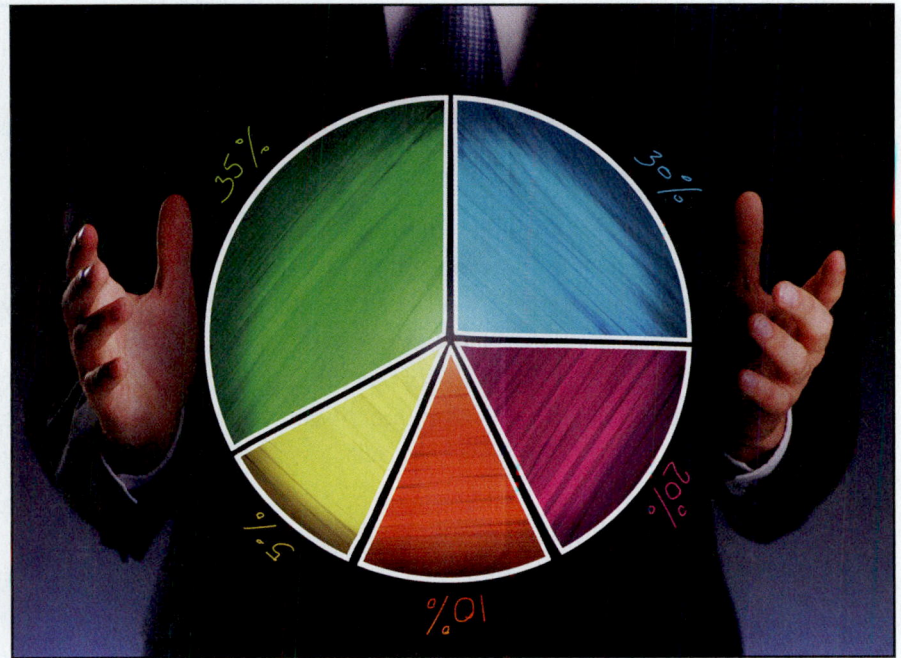

Communicating.

What is another way of illustrating market share in graphic form?

expect to grab much market share, at least in the beginning. However, if your business creates a unique product with no other direct competition, you will have a 100% market share for that product. That, of course, can change if any competitors create a similar product in the future.

Let's say you have a goal of selling $100,000 worth of your product or service in the first year. Based on research, you know that your target market buys about $2 million per year of this type of product/service from your competitors. Use the following formula to determine your estimated market share:

Total Sales ÷ Total Market Size = Market Share Percentage

$100,000 ÷ $2 Million = 0.05 or 5% Market Share

Depending on your business idea, if you feel that getting 5% of the potential customers to your business is feasible, then you will hit your goals. It's important to constantly monitor sales for your industry and your target market to re-evaluate where your business is in terms of market share.

Apply Your Knowledge   What does calculating market share tell you? From your investigation, why do these businesses selling food have to be concerned about market share on a daily basis?

CAREER COMPETENCIES

 ## Communicate by Computer; Develop Cultural Sensitivity

Entrepreneurs can benefit from the global economy. They can sell products or services that people in other countries need, or buy goods made somewhere else to sell in the United States. Many entrepreneurs today are using technology to buy and sell their products in the global market! One tool that entrepreneurs use is social networking websites. Many of the same websites that you use to keep in touch with your friends and share ideas are used by entrepreneurs to help build awareness and sell more of their products or services.

For example, a fashion designer may draw in new customers with her Facebook page with images of her new clothing or pictures of celebrities wearing her clothes. Or a restaurant could use Twitter to give discount information to customers. This information is available to people all over the world, helping the entrepreneur develop his/her business everywhere. Entrepreneurs need to be culturally sensitive in order to be successful with a global audience, meaning they need to understand what is appropriate in different countries.

Entrepreneurs who wish to engage in international trade need to show respect for the cultures of the people with whom they want to do business. Culture includes language, beliefs, attitudes, customs, manners, and habits. Obviously a nation can include people of many different cultures; however, there are often general cultural characteristics shared by many people within a country. In addition, business people within most societies follow particular social rules and customs called etiquette. Entrepreneurs should learn and follow the business etiquette practiced in foreign countries where they want to do business.

Entrepreneurs who fail to respect the cultures of foreign trading partners will often be unable to take advantage of business opportunities.

Career Skills in Action

Now think about your own business. Write a message about your business that you could communicate through social media to a worldwide audience. As you write your message, consider the following:

- What social networking websites would you use? How would you use each website?

- What would you include in your messages?

- How would you make sure your messages were culturally sensitive? What should you research about another country's culture before you construct your messages?

Predicting.
Would you be inclined to do business with someone who you felt did not show respect for your culture?

13.3 Competition and the Global Economy

The Global Economy

Although different countries have different economic systems, we share one economy across borders, the **global economy**, or the economy of the world. The global economy is the flow of goods and services around the world. As you learned in Chapter 11, scarcity is when there is not enough supply to meet the demand. Scarcity forces countries to buy goods and services from other countries. Most nations have developed supply specialties. They specialize in supplying particular goods and services to the rest of the world. Specialization helps countries make the most efficient use of their natural and human resources. Said Thomas Friedman in his book *The World is Flat*, "The ideal country in a flat world is the one with no natural resources, because countries with no natural resources tend to dig inside themselves. They try to tap the energy, entrepreneurship, creativity, and intelligence of their own people—men and women—rather than drill an oil well."

In nations with more of a command economic system, the government conducts and controls global trade. Individuals may have little to no opportunity to engage in international buying and selling. Countries with more of a market economic system, such as the United States, allow individuals much more access to the global economy. This provides business opportunities for entrepreneurs who wish to trade with people in other nations. Because of this, entrepreneurs must think globally when they are looking at their direct and indirect competition. Some time ago it mattered more to find out who was your nearest competitor. Now, the ability to buy/trade online and ship anywhere in the world has expanded how entrepreneurs think about competition. Direct and indirect competition may come from an entrepreneur operating hundreds of miles away!

Figure 13-4 ▶

Foreign Exchange Board.
Entrepreneurs who engage in international sales must be aware of up-to-date exchange rates.

Analyzing Concepts.
How does global competition impact local competition buying decisions?

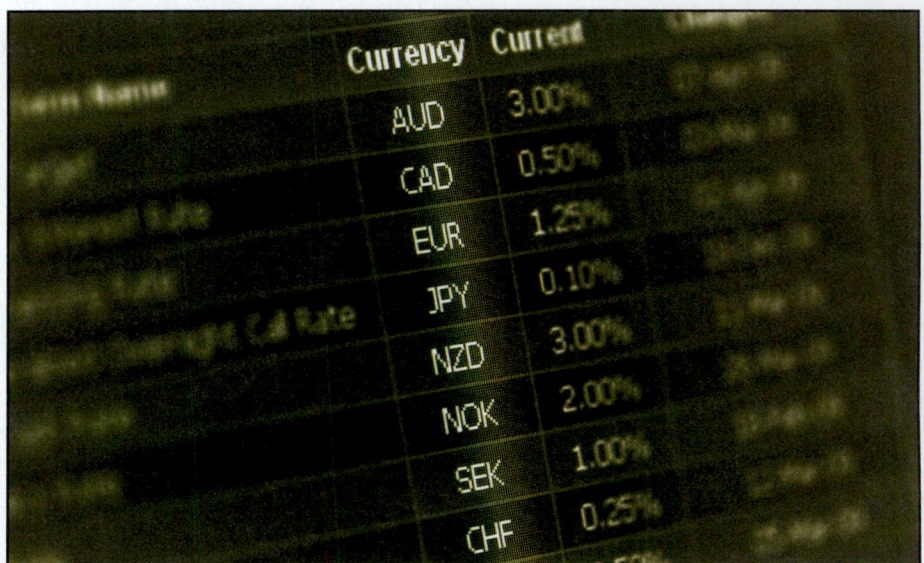

Currency	Current
AUD	3.00%
CAD	0.50%
EUR	1.25%
JPY	0.10%
NZD	3.00%
NOK	2.00%
SEK	1.00%
CHF	0.25%

Entrepreneurs and International Trade

Exporting is a business activity in which goods and services leave a country to be sold to foreign consumers. **Importing** is a business activity in which goods and services enter a country from foreign suppliers. Goods are physical objects, so they are imported and exported by shipping, for example, by truck, train, plane, or ship. Services are not physical objects. They are actions provided by people. For example, an engineering firm located in one country exports its services when it provides engineering services to customers in another country. Services can be exported and imported in various ways. People travel between countries to provide services. In addition, service businesses use traditional delivery methods (like the postal system) and telecommunication methods (phone, fax, e-mail, Internet, and so on) to help them work with foreign consumers. Not only do countries benefit from international trade, so do entrepreneurs.

Entrepreneurs can benefit from international trade by exporting goods or services that are in demand in foreign countries. Entrepreneurs may also benefit from importing. For example, they may import foreign goods to resell in their own country or they may import foreign materials that they then use to produce goods. These exchanges will only be financially beneficial to entrepreneurs if the supply and demand factors result in prices that the entrepreneurs are willing to pay.

There are business risks associated with international trade. In order to properly assess these risks, entrepreneurs must learn about the economic and monetary systems of the foreign countries in which they wish to do business. They also must learn about the government regulations relating to exporting and importing. In addition to financial and political challenges, there are also cultural challenges to doing business in foreign nations. Wise entrepreneurs examine all of the possible consequences (both good and bad) for their businesses before engaging in international trade.

Governments are very protective of the resources within their borders. Even nations with market systems typically put government restrictions on international trade. There are two main reasons for this. First, most nations want to give their domestic businesses a competitive advantage over foreign businesses selling the same good or service. Second, governments want to protect their consumers from foreign goods that might be unsafe or of poor quality.

A **trade barrier** is a governmental restriction on international trade. The most common trade barriers are tariffs and quotas on imports. A **tariff** is a fee, similar to a tax, that must be paid by importers on the goods they import. A **quota** is a limit on the quantity of a good that can be imported into a country. Countries use tariffs and quotas to give their domestic suppliers the best chance possible to try to meet demand within the country. Entrepreneurs must be aware of tariffs or quotas that apply to products they wish to import or export.

There are many types of money in use around the world. In general, each country or group of countries has its own currency. Examples include the U.S. dollar, the Japanese yen, the Chinese yuan, the Canadian dollar, the British pound, the Mexican peso, and the euro (the currency unit of the European Union, a group of European countries).

International sellers and buyers have to be able to translate one currency into another. To do this they need to know the **foreign exchange rate**. This is the value of one currency unit in relation to another. Imagine that one U.S. dollar has an exchange rate of fifty pence, or one-half of a British pound. This would mean that $1 has the same value as £0.50 (British pounds). Foreign exchange rates change often, even day to day, and must be monitored closely by entrepreneurs engaged in international trade. American and British businesses trading with each other would need to use the most current foreign exchange rate to convert prices between the two currencies.

Fair trade is a trading policy encouraged by private organizations with the goal of ensuring that small producers in developing nations earn sufficient profit on their exported goods to improve their working, environmental, and social conditions. Typical products include handmade crafts and farmed goods, such as coffee or bananas. Fair trade organizations help link small producers in developing countries with foreign merchants and consumers interested in encouraging fair trade. U.S. entrepreneurs interested in selling fair trade goods can coordinate with these fair trade organizations to import and resell goods to American consumers.

Apply Your Knowledge How does international trade impact local businesses? Let's return to our investigation of lunch options. Does international trade impact those businesses in any way? Why or why not?

APPLICATION TO BUSINESS PLANNING

Direct and Indirect Competitors

Use what you learned from this chapter about direct and indirect competition to identify the competition for your business. You should support your findings with research data. Be sure to include:

- A SWOT analysis that shows your main strong and weak direct competition
- Indirect and other competition that could fulfill the same needs
- Considerations on global competition

13 ASSESSMENT

REVIEWING OBJECTIVES

1. What are the various forms of competition? Provide an example for each.
2. How can you calculate the market share for a business?
3. What role does competition plays in the global economy?

CRITICAL THINKING

On the expanded SWOT analysis, why would your weaknesses often be a competitor's strengths and vice versa?

ENTREPRENEURIAL THINKING EXERCISE: FLEXIBILITY AND ADAPTABILITY

Think back to your investigation of the potential places to buy food for lunch around your school. Now that you have seen the competition, what recommendations would you make to your favorite lunch spot to get more market share? Be sure to list as many concrete adaptations you would make to the business.

EXTENSION ACTIVITIES

Entrepreneurship & Literacy Skills

Complete the following task to demonstrate your understanding of entrepreneurship:

1. Grades 9–10: Working with team members, find a source that details the primary exports and imports of the United States and the countries with which America trades. Write a short report that includes tables and charts that represents the data you found. In the report, discuss the following points: What is America's supply specialization? Who are America's primary trading partners? Who is America's biggest competition (provides similar exports)?

2. Grades 11–12: Working with team members, research the primary exports and imports of the United States and the countries with which America trades. Prepare a multimedia presentation that provides a visual representation of the data you found from at least three sources. In the presentation, discuss the following points: What is America's supply specialization? Who are America's primary trading partners? Who is America's biggest competition (provides similar exports)?

OBJECTIVES

- Examine how competition between consumers and suppliers impacts pricing.
- List the financial, social, and environmental benefits for generating a profit.
- Analyze the factors entrepreneurs must consider when pricing to stay competitive and cover expenses.

NFTE Entrepreneurial Mindset Characteristic Focus

☑ Comfort with Risk

National Entrepreneurship Standards

- **F.07** Explain the principles of supply and demand
- **F.23** Assess factors affecting a business's profit
- **F.25** Explain the concept of competition
- **L.35** Establish pricing objectives
- **L.36** Select pricing strategies

Common Career Technical Core Standards

- **BM.1** Utilize mathematical concepts, skills and problem solving to obtain necessary information for decision-making in business.
- **CRP.3** Attend to personal health and financial well-being.
- **MK.7** Determine and adjust prices to maximize return while maintaining customer perception of value.

National Entrepreneurship Standards: Career Competencies

☑ **E.17** Explain the nature of e-commerce

☑ **E.19** Develop basic website

LESSON VOCABULARY

- competition-based pricing
- economics of one unit
- overhead
- operating expense
- profit
- profit motive

14.1 Competition Between Suppliers and Consumers

So far in this unit, you have been trying to determine if there is anyone else in your industry that provides your product or service better than you do. Now that you have an understanding of supply and demand relationships, and how competitors fit into the economic system, let's take a closer look at how they specifically impact your pricing decisions. Finding the perfect price for your products or services is an important component to the entrepreneurial mindset skill of navigating business risk. Making a bad decision around this will encourage potential customers to visit your competition instead!

Competition in a Market Economy

Competition is common in a market economy. People are free to start and operate businesses that compete against each other, so suppliers often compete to sell similar products or services. Buyers are free to compete against each other to buy products they need and want. Competition between suppliers pushes prices downward. Competition between buyers pushes prices upward.

Competition Between Suppliers

If one supplier lowers the price of a good or service, consumers will typically buy from that supplier rather than from other suppliers. This assumes that only price changes, and all other aspects of the good or service are equal. The supplier who lowers his or her price offers an incentive for people to change their buying habits. The other suppliers will probably have to lower their prices to keep their customers. This is how competition pushes prices downward in a market economy.

Competition has another benefit. It encourages innovation and variety. Entrepreneurs introduce new and different goods and services in order to avoid (or at least delay) direct competition from other similar businesses This results in a wide variety of goods and services being offered for sale in a market economy.

Obviously competition between suppliers is good for consumers who want low prices and many choices. Competition between suppliers makes it tougher for businesses to succeed, but it forces them to work smarter and harder, just as competition in sports pushes athletes to perform better. Entrepreneurs use their cleverness and skills to outperform their competitors. In particular entrepreneurs look for ways to avoid competing solely based on price. They either offer new and different products or they ensure that their products have an advantage over similar products sold by other businesses.

◀ **Figure 14-1**
Competition.

Competition between consumers can drive the price of push prices upward

Applying Concepts.

Have you ever shopped around at a local mall due to the variety of products that you could choose from?

Competition Between Consumers

In a market economy there is not only competition between suppliers, but also competition between consumers. When consumers compete against each other to buy something, they push prices upward. For example, parents rush to stores in December to buy a popular toy as a holiday gift for their children. Consumers compete against each other to buy the limited supply of that toy. Suppliers can charge more for that toy in December than at other times of the year because demand is higher than usual. Customers are willing to pay more, so suppliers charge more. Competition between consumers for the same or similar products pushes prices upward in a market economy.

 **Apply Your Knowledge**   What role does competition play in a market economy? From your investigation of Amazon and Borders at the start of the chapter, how do you think customers responded when Amazon introduced a way to sell books that was cheaper and easier than Borders?

ENTREPRENEURIAL CASE STUDY: COMFORT WITH RISK

 **Ambar Romero— Styles by Ambar**

Entrepreneurial Spark

Ambar Romero, founder and CEO of Styles by Ambar (stylesbyambar.com), founded her business while in high school at Kolbe Cathedral High School in Bridgeport, Connecticut. Styles by Ambar is an online thrift shop that sells "pre-loved" women's clothes and accessories. Using a lean business model, Ambar is able to provide high-quality fashions at a low cost to customers and with a low environmental impact. Ambar used her experience in her entrepreneurship course, which was sponsored by the Network for Teaching Entrepreneurship (NFTE), to create a business plan for her business idea. She won first place with her initial idea in the 2014 NFTE Fairfield County, CT regional business plan competition.

Ambar Romero.

Ambar was born in Puerto Rico, and came to Connecticut soon after she was born. She was always unsure about what to study in college, but her NFTE class provided her with direction. "The most surprising thing about the NFTE class was how relevant and useful the information was. Unlike my history and science classes, I was able to use the information I learned in class that very same day. For the first time I was able to apply class notes to real life," Ambar says about her experience.

Responsibility to Community and Environment

Her inspiration to start her business came from her desire to have a positive social impact on the community and the environment through her business. Styles by Ambar is an online thrift store that sells previously owned women's fashion. The business accepts donations from previous owners to reduce the amount of clothes that end up in landfills. The business keeps costs low for customers by using pre-owned fashions, and doing all of its operations online. And after all of that, Ambar also makes sure to give extra profit back to the community. "We are committed to health education and career development support for women, so 15% of profits are donated to local organizations that help women in these areas," explains Ambar.

Ambar did not have to wait long to see if her business was a good opportunity. She started the business in July 2013 at the age of 15, getting help from NFTE mentors to finalize her plan and start her website. Ambar's business was a success out of the gate, generating over $500 in the first six weeks! Her business has been featured in *La Voz Hispana, Bridgeport Diocese News Paper* and she has had the opportunity to present her business at the National NFTE Business Plan Competition in 2014.

Plans for the Future

Even though her business has found some initial success, Ambar still plans to be a first generation college student, going to college for International Business Management and Marketing after high school. She says, "NFTE has definitely instilled in me the importance of resilience in the business world. Just always being confident and always trying your best, and trying your hardest. As a young entrepreneur, you're always going to be faced with challenges."

Thinking and Acting Like an Entrepreneur

- In what ways does Ambar's business demonstrate a social responsibility to the community and environment?

- Why is Ambar's business structured better than a traditional thrift shop?

- How Ambar demonstrate the entrepreneurial mindset behavior of being comfortable with challenges and risks?

14.2 Competition-Based Pricing and Profit Motive

Profit Motive

Because of the competition between suppliers and consumers, there are a few things to consider when determining a price for your product or service:

- Is this price competitive in the market? (Does it make sense for the market?)
- Is the price appealing to customers? (Is it too high for customers?)
- Am I making a profit? (Am I not charging enough?)

In very simple terms, a business makes a **profit** when the money coming in from sales is larger than the business's expenses. These are many times called **overhead**, or **operating expenses**, and can include rent for a storefront and paying staff. (You will learn more about calculating profit in later chapters.) Entrepreneurs choose how to use their profit. They can save it, spend it, invest it, or donate it to worthy causes

Businesses provide goods and services in an effort to satisfy consumers' demands. Profit is the businesses reward for successfully making this effort. If the business is unsuccessful in this effort, there will be no profits and the business is likely to fail. Consumers understand that the prices they pay for goods and services include a profit for the suppliers. Otherwise, the business would not be motivated to make the effort.

Profit is a very strong incentive in a market system. Starting a business is a risky thing to do. Some businesses will fail. The opportunity to earn a profit encourages entrepreneurs to accept the risks of starting new businesses. The **profit motive** is an incentive that encourages entrepreneurs to take business risks in the hope of making a profit.

As you will learn in the next chapter, businesses sometimes try to compete with each other by offering prices lower than their competition. Think about your experience as a customer. If there is an expensive item that you want to buy, you might shop around until you find the cheapest price. This strategy of charging more or less than what your competition is charging is called **competition-based pricing**. While it might be tempting to charge the extremely low prices to attract as many customers as possible, it is important to remember the goal of earning a profit while running the business. If you charge too low of a price, you run the risk of not making a profit after paying your operating expenses. For example, JC Penney, which used to be one of the nation's largest retailers, lost a ton of money after trying to lower its prices to compete with low-cost retailers like Wal-Mart.

Benefits of Profit

Although profit is a strong incentive, it is not the only goal that motivates entrepreneurs. In recent years, in addition to profit, businesses have also begun focusing on the social and environmental effects of their business. Some entrepreneurs refer to this approach as the "people, planet, profit" approach to business. Entrepreneurs with this approach try to be economically successful by making a profit, but they also try to ensure that their businesses have a positive impact on people and the planet.

◀ **Figure 14-2**
People, Planet, Profit.
People, Planet, Profit is a new approach to business that strives for positive impact on both people and the planet.

Drawing Conclusions.
In your area, what companies are using the people, planet, and profit approach for running their businesses?

Entrepreneurs who consistently make profits over time can build their own wealth and ensure their financial independence. This means they do not have to depend on others—family, friends, employers, or the government—for money. Prosperity and financial independence are goals for many people. Entrepreneurs must work hard and make wise business decisions to earn a profit, but the personal financial benefits can be very rewarding.

Many entrepreneurs use profit to benefit their existing businesses, start new ones, or invest in the businesses of others. Profit can be used to grow a business, for example, by offering more products or advertising to reach more customers. In addition, entrepreneurs can save profit for use when their businesses are not doing well financially.

Successful entrepreneurs also use profit to benefit society. Some businesses donate part or all of their profit to worthy causes. In 1982, actor Paul Newman started a business called Newman's Own, Inc. to produce and sell grocery items, like orange juice and popcorn. All of the profits from this business go to charitable causes. As of 2008, the profits donated by Newman's Own, Inc. add up to more than $200 million. These profits have been used to help people all around the world.

Apply Your Knowledge   What are the benefits of generating a profit? Of the two businesses from your investigation, which was able to generate more profit due to less operating expenses?

CAREER COMPETENCIES

 ## Explain the Nature of E-commerce; Develop Basic Website

Increasingly, people and businesses buy and sell goods online. This is called e-commerce. An e-commerce website can be a stand-alone business or the Web-based counterpart of a traditional storefront business. Some popular examples of e-commerce include: online banking, online retail sales, online travel resources, online ticket auctions, and so on. For instance, it used to be that in order to buy shoes, you needed to go into the store and try them on. Nowadays, you can buy shoes online and return them overnight if they do not fit.

An e-commerce business must rent space on the Web from a Web host— a business that stores the website information on its server computers. It also needs a commerce server, which is a computer that runs commerce-based applications, such as credit card processing and inventory management, and security programs to protect its customers' financial and personal information. Other expenses include marketing and promotions in order to attract customers to the site.

Starting and running an e-commerce website may be less expensive than starting a traditional bricks-and-mortar business. There is no rent to pay for store space and the business can run using fewer employees. Often, the business owner does not even have to store the goods, because they can be shipped directly from a warehouse or manufacturer to the customer. This means that the convenience of online shopping has unfortunately caused some small businesses to close. As a result, there may be fewer career opportunities in retail. However, there may be increased opportunities at online retail businesses.

Career Skills in Action

Identify a business that has a traditional storefront and a competitor that has an e-commerce website. Evaluate both on the experience of buying from each:

- How you rate each on the following criteria: ease-of-use, convenience, number of products, sales assistance, return policy, and visual appeal?
- Use a table to compare the features of each.
- Which model would you consider using for your own business?

14.3 Competition and the Economics of One Unit

Economics of One Unit

It is often helpful for entrepreneurs to calculate the profit they make on each individual good or service they sell. For instance, an entrepreneur could know that for every $20 tee shirt he sold, $2.20 was his profit. Another entrepreneur could know that for every $40 haircut, $3.80 was her profit.

The **economics of one unit** is a calculation of the profit (or loss) for each unit of sale made by a business. You calculate the economics of one unit by subtracting the costs for the unit of sale from its selling price.

In some cases, it's easy to figure out what a unit of sale is. Your business could make t-shirts, computers, or skateboards. A unit of sale would then be a t-shirt, a computer, or a skateboard. But what about a company that sells decorated toothpicks? Then a unit of sale might be a box of fifty toothpicks. A company that offers a service might charge for that particular service (such as a haircut or a shoe shine). However, other service companies might charge for an hour of babysitting, lawn mowing, or window washing. These are all examples of a unit of sale.

A unit of sale has a sales price to the consumer and a cost for the entrepreneur. The economics of one unit is the difference between the sales price and the cost. In other words:

$$\text{Sales Price} - \text{Cost} = \text{Profit (or Loss)}$$

If this equation results in a positive number, you've made a profit. If it's negative, you've sustained a loss. In order for a business to be successful financially, the economics of one unit must result in a profit. A business that cannot make a profit from one unit of sale will not make a profit selling many units of sale.

Another way to look at profit is as a percentage of the sales price. This calculation tells an entrepreneur the profit percentage based on sales. The formula per unit of sale is:

$$(\text{Profit}/\text{Sales Price}) \times 100 = \text{Profit \%}$$

If an entrepreneur made a profit of $2.20 for a $20 t-shirt, the entrepreneur would be making an 11% profit:

$$(2.20/20) \times 100 = 11\%$$

Figure 14-3 ▶

Economics of One Unit.

The economics of one unit is a calculation of the profit or loss from one unit of sale.

Analyzing Data

How could the entrepreneur make a larger profit?

Economics of One Unit

An entrepreneur buys plain backpacks and decorates them at home with handrawn art, stitching, buttons, and stickers before reselling them at the flea market for $25 each.

Because each backpack is different, the entrepreneur uses an average backpack as the unit of sale.

The expenses to the entrepreneur per unit of sale are:		
Plain backpack		$11.00
Ink, thread, buttons, etc.		3.00
Labor		6.00
Expenses per unit of sale		$20.00

The economics of one unit of sale are:		
Selling price per unit of sale	$25.00	
Expenses per unit of sale		20.00
Profit per unit of sale	$5.00	

The profit as a percentage of sales is:

$$\frac{\text{Profit per unit of sale}}{\text{Selling price per unit of sale}} \times 100 \qquad \frac{\$5.00}{\$25.00} \times 100 = 20\%$$

Figure 14-4 ▼

Staying Competitive.

Businesses find ways to change their expenses to stay competitive and profitable.

Drawing Conclusions.

What are the different ways to increase the profit for a unit of sale?

Doing calculations for the economics of one unit helps see how successful a business could be in generating a profit. Let's take a closer look at the backpack example shown here. Let's assume the entrepreneur wanted to make more profit with each sale. There would be a few approaches to adjusting the profit:

- Raising the selling price
- Using less expensive materials
- Find a way to pay less for labor

	Scenario 1: Less Expensive Materials		Scenario 2: Higher Selling Price		Scenario 3: Less Labor	
Plain backpack		$9.00		$11.00		$11.00
Ink, thread, buttons		2.00		3.00		3.00
Labor		6.00		6.00		4.00
Expenses per unit of sale		$17.00		$20.00		$18.00
Selling price per unit of sale	$25.00		$30.00		$25.00	
Expenses per unit of sale		$17.00		$20.00		$18.00
Profit per unit of sale	$8.00		$10.00		$7.00	

In doing any of these, the entrepreneur must also take competition factors into consideration:

- Can I decrease expenses without losing quality in the product or service?
- Can I increase the selling price without losing customers to competitors?
- Can I supply enough products to meet the demand produced by the economics of one unit?

Therefore, entrepreneurs must carefully consider both profit calculations and competition when pricing their product or service.

Apply Your Knowledge   What are the factors that influence pricing? Let's return to your investigation of Borders and Amazon. What are the materials and labor that each had to spend? Who do you think was able to charge lower prices?

APPLICATION TO BUSINESS PLANNING

Competitive Pricing

Use what you learned from this chapter about competition and pricing to identify a competitive price for your business. You should support your findings with data from research. Be sure to include:

- A comparison of price to other competitors
- An estimated economics of one unit that shows profit at that selling price

14 ASSESSMENT

REVIEWING OBJECTIVES

1. How does competition between consumers and suppliers impact pricing?
2. What are the financial, social, and environmental benefits for generating a profit?
3. What factors must entrepreneurs must consider when pricing to stay competitive and cover expenses?

CRITICAL THINKING

Why does supplier competition make it harder for an entrepreneur to be successful?

ENTREPRENEURIAL THINKING EXERCISE: COMFORT WITH RISK

Think back to your investigation of Borders Books and Amazon. Imagine you could go back to 2003 when Borders was at its peak. What recommendations would you make that would have helped them stay in business? Can you think of an even better model than Amazon that Borders could try? Be specific as possible in your recommendations.

EXTENSION ACTIVITIES

Entrepreneurship & Mathematics Skills

Complete the following task to demonstrate your understanding of entrepreneurship:

Grades 9–12: Return to the example economics of one unit table for the customized backpack from Section 14. Use that example to complete the following tasks:

- Write an equation that shows the relationship between selling price, expenses and profit for one backpack.

- Keeping the expenses per unit of sale constant, replace the selling price and profit per sale with variables.

- Graph this function with selling price as the independent variable (x-axis) and profit per sale as the dependent variable (y-axis). What is the relationship between these variables?

- Find the y-intercept of this graph. What does this number represent?

- Repeat the process keeping the selling price constant and making the expenses per sale a variable instead.

OBJECTIVES

- Explain how to gather competitive intelligence on other businesses.
- List potential differentiators that can act as a competitive advantage.
- Use a competitive matrix to determine a competitive advantage for a business.

NFTE Entrepreneurial Mindset Characteristic Focus

☑ Initiative & Self-Reliance

National Entrepreneurship Standards

- **O.02** Conduct competitive analysis
- **L.08** Determine unique selling proposition
- **L.35** Establish pricing objectives

Common Career Technical Core Standards

- **CRP.2**. Apply appropriate academic and technical skills.
- **CRP.7**. Employ valid and reliable research strategies.
- **BM-MGT.2**. Access, evaluate and disseminate information for business decision making.

National Entrepreneurship Standards: Career Competencies

☑ **D.13** Write persuasive messages

LESSON VOCABULARY

- competitive advantage
- competitive intelligence
- competitive matrix
- differentiator

15.1 Gather Competitive Intelligence

Over the course of this unit, you have been working to determine if your business is better than your competition. In this unit, you will look at how to utilize data around your industry and competitors to determine your edge over the competition. Determining this will get you one step closer to validating your idea as a true business opportunity. If you find that you need to adjust based on your competition, it will provide you with the opportunity to demonstrate your entrepreneurial mindset skill of adjusting plans to meet new goals.

Gathering Competitive Intelligence

Another critical area of market research involves identifying data on your direct and indirect competitors. The data you collect about your competitors is called **competitive intelligence**.

Competitive intelligence enables you to compare your competitors' strengths and weaknesses with your potential business. During this process you will be looking for unique ways to provide your product or service to your target market. You will be looking for your **competitive advantage**—something that gives your business an advantage over your competition.

Many sources of secondary data, or data that already exists from other sources, will help you gather competitive intelligence. Make sure to consider the various places where competitive products or services might be available to your target market. Some of your competition may be located nearby in physical stores, but they may also be on the Internet or in direct mail catalogs.

One way to gather valuable competitive intelligence is to pose as a customer and gain a sense of what it's like to buy your competitor's product or service (provided that you do not cause your competitor to exert a significant amount of effort if you don't intend to buy anything). Go at different times of the day and on different days of the week, and note which times were busiest and what kinds of customers were there. As you walk through your competitor's store, ask yourself these questions:

- What products do they carry? How are these products displayed? How much do they cost?
- What is their customer service like? Did staff offer to assist me? Were they friendly and helpful?
- How many other potential customers are in the store? What appears to be some of the customer demographics (age, gender, etc.)?
- Does the competitor offer any special purchasing terms such as credit with no interest? Do they provide any other special services, such as free delivery? What is their policy for returning products?

◀ **Figure 15-1**
Secret Shopper.

Going to a competitor as a customer is a great way to gather research data.

Applying Concepts.

Why is pretending to be a customer at a competitor's store one of the best ways to gather data?

Apply Your Knowledge   How does having a competitive advantage keep a business open? What do you think are the competitive advantages for the coffee-selling businesses in your investigation?

ENTREPRENEURIAL CASE STUDY: INITIATIVE & SELF-RELIANCE

 ## Jesus Fernandez-Ortiz & Toheeb Okenla—T&J Soccer

Reaching the American Dream

Chicago-area high school students Toheeb Okenla and Jesus Fernandez-Ortiz needed a business plan for their entrepreneurship class, which was sponsored by the Network for Teaching Entrepreneurship (NFTE) at Thornwood High School in South Holland, Illinois. They eventually designed a new soccer sock that featured a sewn-in pocket to allow players to insert the shin guard of their choice. From there, T&J Soccer was born. As the winners of NFTE's 2013 National Youth Entrepreneurship Challenge, Toheeb and Jesus have demonstrated their passion for soccer and business development.

Before they met and became co-founders and CEOs of T&J Soccer, both Jesus and Toheeb arrived in their NFTE course from very different backgrounds. Jesus's parents left the strawberry fields of Michoacán, Mexico in search of better opportunities for their chil-

Jesus Fernandez-Ortiz and Toheeb Okenla.

dren. Because a language barrier exists for them, they have always motivated him and taught him to work hard and be resilient. Toheeb came to the US from his native Nigeria at the age of 8 to reunite with his father, who had immigrated earlier. Sadly, Toheeb would lose his father a few years later. But his father's incredible strict work ethic became a model for how Toheeb lives his life.

Creating a Better Soccer Sock

After both families moved to the Chicago area, Toheeb and Jesus would meet and partner in their entrepreneurship course. When imagination failed them for finding a business idea, they turned to their shared interest and greatest passion: soccer. Jesus and Toheeb saw a need for a particular product first hand on the field as they witnessed multiple injuries. Inspired by this problem they faced on the soccer field, Jesus and Toheeb designed a new soccer sock that featured a sewn-in pocket that allows players to insert the shin guard of their choice. This prevents the shin guard from sliding around, providing better side-to-side protection than traditional methods. While they acknowledge that there are competitors that similar products, they point out that their business has a competitive advantage because you cannot change out the shin guard with the competitors' socks.

Leveraging New Opportunities

Since winning the national competition, Toheeb and Jesus are furthering the development of their business by using their earned venture capital. They are currently in the process of meeting with a textile manufacturer to develop the first iteration of their soccer sock. T&J Soccer would like to patent their technology to become the official sock used by youth soccer leagues in the Chicago area.

In addition, they both are furthering their education to gain additional business skills. Currently, both are attending the University of Illinois at Urbana-Champaign. Toheeb is a sophomore majoring in Information Systems and minoring in Computer Science Engineering at the School's College of Business and Engineering. Jesus graduated Thornwood High School as the class Valedictorian and has become the first person in his family to attend a four-year university, majoring in Computer Science. Both Toheeb and Jesus believe that, "thinking like entrepreneurs has helped us by strengthening our problem-solving and critical thinking skills. It has made us very competitive, which, in turn, has made us determined to be successful."

Thinking and Acting Like an Entrepreneur

- How did Jesus and Toheeb combine their skills and interests for their business opportunity?
- What competitive advantage does their business have?
- In what ways did Toheeb and Jesus demonstrate the entrepreneurial mindset behaviors of initiative and self-reliance?

15.2 Identify Your Differentiators

What Is a Differentiator for a Business?

Your competitive advantage could consist of one or more **differentiators**. These are unique characteristics that distinguish your business from other businesses. Ask yourself these four questions to help identify potential differentiators for your business:

- What product or service can your business provide that your competitors don't?
- What *mix* of products or services can your business provide that your competitors don't?

- What specialized selling or delivery method can give your business a competitive edge?
- Are there any unique ways that your business can meet customers' wants or needs?

Answering these questions can help you differentiate your business, setting it apart from your competitors. When thinking about your business, resist the temptation to copy exactly what other successful companies have done. The approach that works well for one particular business may not work the same for another. You can, however, learn helpful lessons and gain inspiration from the experiences of other businesses. Here are a few examples of successful companies that used differentiators to create a competitive advantage that set them apart from competitors:

- Apple's Macintosh computer and 3M's Post-It Notes are examples of ground-breaking products that were initially unique in their industry areas.
- FedEx Kinko's™ became very successful because it found a unique way to combine office products and business services (such as photocopying) in their stores.
- Amazon used an unusual mix of selling and delivery methods to set itself apart from competitors. It was the first business in its industry to sell a huge selection of music, books, and movies exclusively on the Internet. This enabled Amazon to sell their products at lower prices. Customer options include overnight delivery and, under certain conditions, free shipping. Customers also have the choice of buying new or used products.
- When the cable channel Black Entertainment Television (BET) was launched, it filled the needs and wants of a target market that hadn't yet been filled in the cable television market.

Figure 15-2 ▶
Ground-Breaking Product.

The Post-It Note was a ground-breaking product.

Drawing Conclusions.

How does 3M take advantage of being the first sticky notes on the market with Post-It Notes and stay competitive against new copycat products?

Apply Your Knowledge   What are examples of differentiators that can act as a competitive advantage for a business? What do you think are the differentiators for each of the coffee-selling businesses in your investigation?

CAREER COMPETENCIES

 ### Write Persuasive Messages

If you want to be able to attract potential customers to try your business over your competition, you will need to be able to write effective persuasive messages. A persuasive message is an attempt to get someone to do something. This might include telling a customer about why your business is better. Or, why they should buy from your business.

Here are some techniques suggested by CopyBlogger that can be used in persuasive messages:

- **Clarity:** Be sure that the desired message is clearly understood. Potential customers should know what your business does. They should also know that you want them to purchase from you.

- **Repetition:** Stating the most important point more than once can help people remember. This might be important for customers who might purchase from you on another date.

- **Solve Customer Problems:** Write your message so that you explain the problem your business is solving. Make sure customers know how they benefit from choosing you.

- **Use Data to Support:** Include any data or facts that support your argument. This will make you appear more credible.

- **Address Objections:** Try to stop customers from having concerns about buying your product or service. If you confront those head on, they will be more likely to choose your business.

Career Skills in Action

Now you try writing a persuasive message about your own business idea. After you're done:

- Evaluate your persuasive message against the listed techniques. Which techniques did you use?

- Read your message to a peer in your classroom. Would they be persuaded to buy your product or service?

15.3 Determining Your Competitive Advantage

Analyze the Competition

Just gathering market data is not enough. You must organize the data and then analyze it. Don't be surprised if your list of indirect competitors is much longer than your list of direct ones. Instead of listing indirect competitors individually, organize them into categories. For example, you could divide them up by industry type, or by the products or services they sell. After the indirect competitors are grouped, you can evaluate each category's level of competitiveness. That is, which groups will compete most often and most strongly with your business?

Analyzing direct competitors requires a more detailed and thorough approach. A helpful tool for doing this is a **competitive matrix**. This is a grid used to compare characteristics of your business with your direct competitors. To complete a competitive matrix, complete the following steps:

1. First, you'll pick the main direct competitors by reviewing the information you've been collecting.

2. Next, you'll plug selected data into the matrix.

3. Finally, you'll use the matrix to help pinpoint your potential differentiators that will act as your competitive advantages.

Using a Competitive Matrix

A competitive matrix can be formatted in various ways. The Table 15.1 provides a simple example. You can vary the factors you wish to compare depending the business opportunity you are exploring.

Table 15.1   Competitive Matrix

Factors	Your Business	Competitor A	Competitor B	Competitor C
Price				
Quality of Service				
Location				
Reputation/Brands				
Delivery Method				
Customer Service				
Unique Factors				

There are several reasons for creating a competitive matrix. It helps you to spot any holes or missing data in your research. It can also enable you to see patterns in the data. Most importantly, it helps you find out where your business fits in the marketplace.

Anticipate Future Competition

As you conduct market research on your competition, remember that businesses are constantly changing. Just because you have an advantage in your target market today doesn't mean it will last. One of your competitors could become aware of its weaknesses and find a way to improve. Once you start your business, all your current competitors could copy your business, eliminating your differentiating characteristics. In addition, new competitors could enter the market at any time.

As you've already learned, market research is an ongoing process. You need to continue to watch trends in your industry, and in the general economy. Stay alert to any customer needs and wants that may start to change. Continue to monitor what your current competition is doing. In particular, keep an eye out for any new direct competitors that begin selling to your target market.

Apply Your Knowledge   What can a competitive matrix help you determine? Let's return to our investigation of the coffee businesses. Complete a competitive matrix for two of the businesses. What are the competitive advantages of each business? How can both businesses sell coffee but still stay in business?

APPLICATION TO BUSINESS PLANNING

Competitive Advantage

Use what you learned from this chapter about gathering competitive intelligence to identify the competitive advantage for your business. You should support your findings with data from research. Be sure to include:

- A competitive matrix that shows your main competition
- The differentiators for your business
- An explanation of what sets your business apart

15 ASSESSMENT

REVIEWING OBJECTIVES

1. What are the steps to gather competitive intelligence on other businesses?

2. List potential differentiators that can act as a competitive advantage.

3. How does a competitive matrix help determine a competitive advantage for a business?

CRITICAL THINKING

Recognizing Patterns. When constructing a competitive matrix, many times it is not possible for a business to be the best in every category. For example, it would be difficult for a business to charge the lowest price, but also use the highest-quality materials. Why is this so?

ENTREPRENEURIAL THINKING EXERCISE: INITIATIVE AND SELF-RELIANCE

Think back to your investigation of the coffee-selling business. Imagine you were going to open a small business that also sells coffee. How would you demonstrate initiative in establishing a competitive advantage when competing with the established corporations? List as many approaches you would take to establish your competitive advantage.

15 ASSESSMENT

EXTENSION ACTIVITIES

Entrepreneurship & Literacy Skills

Complete the following task to demonstrate your understanding of entrepreneurship:

1. **Grade 9–10:** Working in groups of three, complete a short research activity for three restaurants in your local area. Have each member in your group identify their favorite local restaurant. Write a paragraph containing an argument for why they think it's the best. Identify the differentiators and competitive advantage for your restaurant in your argument. After writing your argument, construct a competitive matrix as a group for all three restaurants. Use the claims in your argument to complete the matrix. Analyze your matrix as a group to make sure all your claims are factual. Determine the competitive advantage for each and present your matrix to the class.

2. **Grade 11–12:** Working in groups of three, complete a short research activity for three restaurants in your local area. Have each member in your group identify their favorite local restaurant. Write a paragraph containing an argument for why they think it's the best. Use research data to support your claims in your argument. Identify the differentiators and competitive advantage for your restaurant in your argument using the data to support. After writing your argument, construct a competitive matrix as a group for all three restaurants. Use the claims in your argument to complete the matrix. Analyze your matrix as a group to make sure all your claims are factual. Determine the competitive advantage for each and present your matrix and research data to the class.

Unit 3: Competition

CHAPTER SUMMARY

11. Entrepreneurship and the Economy

Economics is concerned with how people satisfy their demand for goods and services when the supply of those goods and services is limited. An economic system is used by society to allocate goods and services for its people and to cope with scarcity. Economic systems answer the four fundamental questions of economics. There are three main types of economic systems: command economy, market economy, and a mixed economy. The United States and many other democratic nations are generally market economies. They feature voluntary exchange and freedom of choice. Entrepreneurs can play vital roles in both local economies and various industries as they work to achieve social and environmental goals.

12. Supply and Demand

Prices in a market economy are affected by supply and demand. If an entrepreneur supplies more than existing demand, there will be a surplus. If an entrepreneur produces less than existing demand, there is a shortage. Entrepreneurs use principals of supply and demand to determine an equilibrium, which is the ideal quantity to supply at a given price. Supply and demand can be graphed as curves, with the equilibrium point where the two curves intersect—indicating that supply and demand are balanced.

13. Direct and Indirect Competition

There are two types of competitors, direct and indirect. Direct competitors are businesses in the same market that sell a similar product or service. Indirect competitors sell a different product or service but one that fills the same customer needs or wants. When going against established competition, new businesses try to gain market share. Entrepreneurs also worry about global competition. The global economy encompasses the world. International trade consists of exporting and importing. The risks and challenges of international trade include trade barriers (tariffs and quotas), shifting foreign exchange rates, and cultural differences between nations. Entrepreneurs should practice the rules and customs of business etiquette in countries where they wish to do business.

14. EOU and Competitive Pricing

Competition affects supply and demand. Competition between suppliers drives prices down. Competition between buyers drives prices upwards. Competition-based pricing is an approach to pricing a product or service the less or more than as a competitor. Using this pricing approach comes with risk because businesses still have to make a profit after expenses. The profit motive is an incentive for entrepreneurs to take business risks in the hope of making a profit. The economics of one unit is a calculation of profit or loss from a unit of sale. Setting the selling price too low can mean reduced profits. Entrepreneurs have to find a selling price that covers their expenses, but is also competitive on the market.

15. Establishing a Competitive Advantage

The data you collect about your competitors is called competitive intelligence. After you gather data, you can use a competitive matrix and an expanded SWOT analysis to organize and analyze the information. The goal is to find one or more differentiators that can set your business apart from others. Any unique way that your business can meet customers' needs or wants is a potential differentiator.

UNIT 3 VOCABULARY

capital	demand curve	equilibrium quantity
capitalism	differentiator	exporting
command economy	direct competitor	fair trade
competition-based pricing	economic system	foreign exchange rate
competitive advantage	economics	free enterprise system
competitive intelligence	economics of one unit	global economy
competitive matrix	economy	importing
competitor	enterprise	indirect competitor
consumers	equilibrium point	industry
demand	equilibrium price	local economy

market economy

market share

mixed economy

North American Industry Classification System (NAICS)

operating expense

overhead

profit

profit motive

quota

scarcity

shortage

strong direct competitor

suppliers

supply

supply and demand curve

supply curve

surplus

tariff

trade barrier

voluntary exchange

weak direct competitor

CHECK YOUR UNDERSTANDING

Choose the letter that best answers the question or completes the statement.

1. Which of the following is a problem a nation might attempt to solve through its economic system?

   a. limited supply of goods and services

   b. democracy

   c. entrepreneur's profit motive

   d. all of the above

2. The equilibrium price is

   a. the price set by the government

   b. the price at which supply equals demand

   c. the price at which exports equal imports

   d. the price set by the foreign exchange rate

3. Profit is beneficial to entrepreneurs because

   a. profit builds wealth and financial independence

   b. profit is the equilibrium quantity on a supply and demand curve

   c. profit is a barrier to international trade

   d. profit is the answer to one of the fundamental questions of economics

4. A market economy is also called

   a. socialism

   b. capitalism

   c. free enterprise system

   d. b and c

5. The profit motive is

   a. the money left over after expenses are subtracted from sales

   b. the economics of one unit

   c. a reason entrepreneurs take on business risks

   d. profit calculated as a percentage of expenses

6. Which of the following statements about competition is false?

   a. competition motivates entrepreneurs to introduce new products to consumers

   b. competition between suppliers drives prices upward

   c. competition between consumers benefits suppliers

   d. competition occurs between suppliers and between consumers

7. Importing and exporting are activities primarily associated with

   a. nonprofit organizations

   b. the profit motive

   c. the economics of one unit

   d. the global economy

8. The economics of one unit is a calculation of

   a. the equilibrium quantity on a supply curve

   b. how many items an entrepreneur has for sale

   c. the profit or loss associated with a unit of sale

   d. foreign demand for an entrepreneur's product

9. The United States economy is best described as

   a. a pure market economy in which the government plays no role in the economy

   b. a pure command economy in which the government controls the economy

   c. a mixed economy in which suppliers and consumers play the primary role

   d. a socialist economy in which suppliers and consumers play the primary role

10. Which of the following challenges poses a business risk to entrepreneurs who want to conduct international trade?

   a. tariffs that must be paid to import goods

   b. cultural differences between nations

   c. trade barriers

   d. all of the above

11. A local economy is best described as

a. the flow of goods and services within a community

b. the flow of goods and services in international trade

c. an economic system based on foreign exchange rates

d. an economic system dominated by nonprofit organizations

12. A competitive matrix is used to compare your business with

a. direct competitors

b. indirect competitors

c. target markets

d. a and b

13. Competitors can

a. sell different products from yours

b. sell through direct-mail catalogs

c. both a and b

d. neither a nor b

BUSINESS COMMUNICATION

1. You want to do business in a foreign nation. Research business etiquette in that country and use a partner to demonstrate to the class at least three rules or customs an American entrepreneur should practice when meeting with businesspeople there.

2. You operate a nonprofit organization that benefits society. Imagine that your classmates are successful entrepreneurs gathered for a convention. Give a speech in which you try to convince them to donate some of their profits to your organization.

3. Imagine that you support fair trade and you import decorative fabric produced in a foreign village. You make jackets that you sell in your store. The U.S. government wants to put a high tariff on this type of fabric. Write a letter addressed to your congressperson about why you oppose this tariff.

4. Pick three competitive food products (for example, breakfast cereal or barbeque sauce) for a focus group. Prepare questions for the group and then conduct the focus group, having members see, taste, touch, and smell the products. Create a presentation that describes the results.

5. Working in groups of three, imagine that you own your favorite local restaurant. Create a competitive matrix for this restaurant compared to three local direct competitors.

BUSINESS MATH

1. Use the following supply and demand data for a cake business to draw a supply and demand curve. Circle the equilibrium point. How many cakes should the entrepreneur supply each week? Why? What price should the entrepreneur charge for each cake? Why?

2. Here are the expenses for your silk-screened t-shirt business: $5 for each plain t-shirt and $3 per t-shirt for ink, other supplies, and the cost of silk screening. You sell the t-shirts for $10 each. Calculate the economics of one unit of sale.

Supply

Quantity per week	2	4	6	8	12	14
Price per cake	$5	$10	$15	$20	$30	$35

Demand

Quantity per week	19	16	13	10	7	4
Price per cake	$10	$15	$20	$25	$30	$35

REVIEW & ASSESSMENT

BUSINESS ETHICS

1. You buy glow sticks for 50 cents each and sell them for $1 each at park concerts. One night a citywide blackout occurs. People at the dark concert want desperately to buy your glow sticks. Should you raise the price? Why or why not?

BUSINESS IN YOUR COMMUNITY

1. Working with several classmates, survey local businesses to compile a list of at least twenty products that are imported from foreign nations. Strive for variety in the products and countries. On a world map, draw an arrow from each foreign nation to your community. List the imported product above the line.

2. Interview a local entrepreneur or small-business owner whose enterprise involves producing goods and/or providing services. Determine the answers to the four fundamental questions of economics for that business. Write a one-page report summarizing the results.

INFORMATION TECHNOLOGY

Web Domains

The primary part of a website's address is its **Web domain**. (So, for www.website.com, the domain would be "website.") The Web domain, often referred to as the **domain name**, may be the name of the site itself, as is the case with Google (which has a Web address of www.google.com). A site has a **main domain**, also referred to as a **homepage**, and then a series of **subdomains**, such as individual product pages. Choosing a good Web domain is important. The domain name can mean the difference between success and failure. A domain name that is hard to remember may not become popular. Because many Web addresses have already been taken, Web businesses use creative spelling or invent new words—such as MySpace, YouTube, or Facebook.

Domain Registration

To get a domain name, a website owner must contact a **domain registrar**, such as GoDaddy.com, that manages domain names. Such sites provide a search engine where you can type in a name and see if it has been taken. For instance, you could type in the name "Joe Smith" and see if www.joesmith.com is available. Web addresses that have been bought but remain unused are called **parked domains**. The owner of the parked domain may be waiting to sell the name to the highest bidder. Purchasing a potentially popular Web name can cost thousands of dollars, which is why many businesspeople choose creative spelling over buying a parked domain.

Domain Suffixes

A **domain suffix** (such as .com) is the website's **top-level domain (TLD)**, meaning that these are the largest groupings of domains. International websites have domain suffixes based on the country of origin, such as .co.uk for the United Kingdom or .fr for France.

Common Domain Suffixes

Domain Suffix	Type of Website
.com	Commercial website
.net	Network—for commercial and noncommercial websites
.gov	Government website
.org	Organization—often the website of a nonprofit organization
.biz	Business—similar to .com

IP Addresses

In addition to a Web domain, each website is given an individual **Internet protocol (IP) address**. This is a unique string of numbers that identify the domain. For instance, the IP address for MySpace.com is 216.178.38.121. Typical users don't need to know the IP address, however. Think of it as the difference between a person's name and his or her Social Security number. When a computer accesses a website, it is actually a conversation between two IP addresses. IP addresses are regulated by the Internet Corporation for Assigned Names and Numbers (ICANN). Without them, our computers wouldn't be talking at all!

Tech Vocabulary

domain name

domain registrar

domain suffix

homepage

Internet Protocol (IP) address

main domain

parked domain

subdomain

top-level domain (TLD)

Web domain

Check Yourself

1. What does a domain registrar do?

2. Why might Web-owning businesspeople choose creative spellings for Web domains?

3. What does .com indicate?

4. What is an IP address?

What Do You Think?

Communicating. Why do you think domain names such as MySpace, Facebook, or YouTube are so effective?

CASE STUDY
Competition

EDGING OUT THE COMPETITION

Eva Tan is now the CEO and founder of Eva's Edibles. As you read about her challenges, consider how the lessons Eva learns might help you.

Scoping Out the Competition

Now that Eva had graduated school and was focused on starting Eva's Edibles, she looked back on her education to help with her business planning.

One of the first college courses Eva took was "Principles of Microeconomics." Considering topics such as supply and demand, the role of competition, and the profit motive made her think about the economy in and around Columbus.

To see if what chances for success her business had, economically speaking, she started researching how the city's current economy would impact a new event-planning business.

From her initial market research, she found that there was 15 personal chefs. Based on the growing population of busy professionals in the Columbus area, she felt that there was enough demand for her service to exist as well.

Building on her initial market research she set out to see how find out what other direct and indirect competitors she had. Eva made a list of established competitors and visited their websites. She also telephoned them to find out more about their services.

From this research, she was able to determine what would give her an edge in the market.

Her personal chef service was one of the only services that allows the customers to choose their own menus. This would appeal to customers who were health-conscious or had dietary restrictions.

Profit from a Loss

One of the other things that Eva learned from researching her competition was how to price her services. Most of her competitors had a price of $300 for a week of meals, so she decided to price her services the same. However, after making her first sales Eva discovered that she lost money instead of making a profit. In her desire to be competitive, she had made the price too low. Eva promised herself that, in the future, she would pay closer attention to her costs and make sure she made a profit!

Good Relationships

If Eva was going to keep her business profitable, she would have to find a way to control costs while keeping her pricing competitive. She decided to build relationships with vendors to get pricing lower.

When Eva found a vendor who did a good job at a reasonable price, she went back to that vendor when she needed the same product or service. By doing this, Eva found that she began to develop a good relationship with several vendors.

She approached these business owners and asked them if they would be willing to give her a discount in exchange for a certain level of repeat business. They agreed. In fact, some even said that they would recommend Eva to customers looking for an event planner. The negotiations ultimately benefited both Eva and her vendors.

What Would You Have Done?

1. **Writing.** When Eva tried to sell her services at the same price as her competition, she lost money because her expenses were too high. What would you have done if this happened to you? Would you have kept your expenses the same and raised the selling price instead? Explain your answer.

2. **Drawing Conclusions.** Eva felt that there was enough demand even with 15 other personal chefs in the Columbus area. Would you have felt comfortable starting a business with this many competitors? What would you have done differently?

BIG IDEA: DELIVERING VALUE TO CUSTOMERS

OBJECTIVES

- Compare and contrast marketing to a mass market versus a target market.
- List the components of a customer profile.
- Identify ways that a target market can be separated into market segments.

NFTE Entrepreneurial Mindset Characteristic Focus

☑ Critical Thinking & Problem Solving

National Entrepreneurship Standards

- **K.18** Determine underlying customer needs/frustrations
- **L.12** Explain the concept of market and market identification
- **L.14** Determine market segments
- **L.15** Select target markets
- **L.44** Determine customer's buying motives for use in selling
- **L.45** Differentiate between consumer and organizational buying behavior

Common Career Technical Core Standards

- **CRP.4** Communicate clearly, effectively and with reason.
- **MK.2** Implement marketing research to obtain and evaluate information for the creation of a marketing plan.
- **MK-MGT.4** Access, evaluate and disseminate information to aid in making marketing management decisions.
- **MK-RES.2** Design and conduct research activities to facilitate marketing business decisions.

National Entrepreneurship Standards: Career Competencies

☑ **D.08** Make oral presentations

LESSON VOCABULARY

- business-to-business (B2B) companies
- business-to-consumer (B2C) companies
- buying patterns
- customer profile
- demographics
- diversified market segment
- geographics
- market segments
- mass market
- multi-sided market segment
- niche market segment
- psychographics
- segmented market segment
- target market

ENTREPRENEURIAL INVESTIGATION
Profiled by Facebook

Do you or someone you know have a Facebook account? Even if you don't, you probably know what Facebook does. It's an online tool that connects you to your friends. You can share photos, posts, and find friends from different activities and elementary school.

When you are setting up your profile, you may notice that the online tool collects information including:

1. Birthday
2. Gender
3. Education
4. Relationship Status
5. Interests

In September 2014, Facebook was valued at $200 billion, more than established and larger companies like IBM, Coca-Cola, and AT& T! Even though Facebook is free to you, the company sells advertising and other services to businesses.

Do some research on Facebook and how they make money from advertisers. Afterwards, try to answer the following questions:

1. Why does Facebook ask for the listed information when you register?
2. Why would advertisers pay to get that information about Facebook users?

16.1 Mass Market vs. Target Market

In this unit, you will continue to validate your business opportunity. In Unit 3, you focused specifically on the competition and how you could ensure your business did something unique in the market. In this unit, you will look more closely at defining the people who will actually be buying your product or service. The goal of this unit will be to determine how your business can provide value to these people. Planning for this will require a great deal of utilizing the entrepreneurial mindset skills of critical thinking and problem solving.

You may be tempted to try to sell your product or service to as many customers as possible. This type of market is often called a **mass market**. Companies that are mass market are usually large and make products that fulfill general needs and have big budgets. For example, consumer electronic companies sell to mass markets and include companies like Samsung and Sony. For most small businesses, this approach isn't the best strategy. Selling to a mass market takes a great deal of resources—like time and money. Many entrepreneurs focus on identifying a **target market**, a limited number of customers who are most likely to buy the product or service. Focusing on a target market means you'll sell your product or service to anyone interested, but you'll spend your time and money on advertising to a specific or targeted group.

Target Market Customer Categories

Not all customers are created equal. You may recall from the discussion of market research in Chapter 9, it all depends on the type of business you decide to start. To identify and target the right customers, businesses develop customer profiles. A **customer profile** is a detailed description of your target market's characteristics. Consider the two main types of customers:

- **Consumers.** A company who sells to individuals is sometimes referred to as a **business-to-consumer (B2C) company**. B2C companies, are usually in retail or direct service and may include grocery stores, house cleaners, personal chefs—any business that sells directly to you the customer. The customer profile of a B2C company might include characteristics such as age, gender, occupation, and the neighborhoods where consumers live. Since there are so many different types of consumers, B2C companies often create multiple customer profiles. These companies also need to consider that most consumers' priorities also change as they get older or when major life events take place (such as getting married or having a baby).

- **Businesses.** A company who sells to other companies is called a **business-to-business (B2B) company**. In this case, the customer profile might include such details as company size, type of industry, and geographical location. Over time, businesses tend to be more consistent in their buying habits than consumers. They also tend to have larger budgets than individual customers.

◀ **Figure 16-1**

Business-to-Consumer Sale.

A retail store is a B2C business. Wholesale and service businesses are types of businesses that use B2C practices.

Applying Concepts.

What are the names of some B2C businesses in your community?

Figure 16-2 ▶

Business-to-Business Sale.

An example of a B2B business is a manufacturing and wholesale business.

Drawing Conclusions.

How would selling your product or service to another business be different than selling to a customer?

You do not have to choose just one of these customer categories. Your market research may indicate that it makes sense to target both types of customers. The product or service you provide to both consumers and businesses might be the same. However, you will probably need to approach each type of customer differently.

 **Apply Your Knowledge** Describe how mass market and target markets are different. Think back to your entrepreneurial investigation. Do you think Facebook focuses on a mass or target market? What customer category does Facebook interact with? Explain your answer.

ENTREPRENEURIAL CASE STUDY: CRITICAL THINKING & PROBLEM SOLVING

 ## Deena Kishawi— modestie

Solving a Problem in the Market

Deena Kishawi is the founder and CEO of modestie, a clothing business she runs as a college student at DePaul University in Chicago, Illinois. Her motivation to start her business came from her own frustrations with the fashion in the market. Looking for stylish clothing that also complied with her religious dress code as a Muslim, which includes wearing a scarf that covers the head and loose fitting clothes, always left her disappointed. "A countless number of times I'd go out somewhere and would be looking for a nice dress to wear to a wedding or a party," Deena said. "Because I wear the hijab, I have to find things that are long and loose. But the majority of the time, I found things that were frumpy. And for weddings, you always find strapless dresses, or ones with open backs." Her efforts have gotten the attention of customers and media outlets. In addition to being featured in Chicago news outlets, Deena was honored at the Network for Teaching Entrepreneurship (NFTE) 2014 Global Young Entrepreneur Awards.

Finding the Right Target Market

While Deena has been sewing her own clothes when she was in eighth grade, inspiration to start a serious business based on her fashions came after taking a NFTE entrepreneurship course at Whitney Young High School in Chicago. Initially she planned on Muslim women as her target market, but she soon realized that her fashions appealed to a much broader market.

Deena Kishawi.

"Many women complain about how the newest fashion trends are either too revealing or uncomfortably tight," explains Deena. "These same women who want more modest clothing tend to only find frumpy or old designs that comply with what they are comfortable wearing." Deena decided to design collections based on the needs of these women. Her line is "really for any woman who feels comfortable in the way she looks," she says. Deena studies the latest trends, the hottest styles, but most importantly, focuses on making her pieces modest and fashionable.

The result of this plan, modestie, a clothing line focused on young women, ages 16–28, who are comfortable in the skin they're in, took off during Deena's senior year of high school. Though most of the time and efforts spent on it have been expended during her first year in college. modestie was very time consuming—especially since every single piece in the collections is hand made by Deena. Stitch by stich, from the buying of the fabric, to cutting out patterns, to the final details and quality check. All done by her.

Growing the Business

Deena has made and sold many designs over the past few years, including through a pop-up boutique as part of the NFTE gala where she was honored. She is currently attending college, while working on launching a new collection and looking for other opportunities to grow her business.

Thinking and Acting Like an Entrepreneur

- How did Deena use her skills and interests to solve a problem with a business opportunity?
- What target market does Deena's business try to reach with her products?
- In what ways does Deena demonstrate the entrepreneurial mindset behaviors of critical thinking and problem solving?

16.2 Market Segments: Breaking Up the Customers

Customers are essential to the success of any business, and at first glance it feels like all customer needs and wants are different. But in reality most companies group their customers to create general types based on shared attributes or interest. These types are called market segments. A **market segment** is a grouping of consumers or businesses within a particular market that has one or more things in common. In a sense, the market segments are generalized customer profiles used to form a clear picture of your target market. A target market often includes more than one market segment. Here are some usual ways you can group customers into market segments:

- **Demographics.** **Demographics** are objective social and economic facts about people. Demographics for consumers include age, gender, marital status, family size (number of children), ethnic background, education, occupation, annual income, and whether they own a home or rent. Demographics for businesses include industry type, number of employees, and annual sales. You can find demographic information for a people on websites like the Census Bureau website: www.census.gov and information on companies from business profiles on industry websites.

- **Geographics.** Basing market segments on where consumers live or where businesses are located is called **geographics**. Groupings could include the nation, geographical region (such as the Northeast), individual state or province, county, city, neighborhood, and type of climate.

- **Psychographics.** Psychological characteristics of consumers, such as attitudes, opinions, beliefs, interests, personality, lifestyle, political affiliation, and personal preferences, are called **psychographics**. Psychographics for a person could include that she loves rock music and is fashionable. For a business, psychographics can be related to the "personality" of the business, like the company values, corporate culture, and how they interact with their customers. Psychographics of a socially responsible business might include that they will only partner with other socially responsible businesses, and that they require all employees to engage in community service.

Another way to group customers is by **buying patterns**. A buying pattern is the way people and businesses buy products or services, specifically related to quantity, timing, how often and whether they use credit or cash. For example, you can objectively measure how many times a year people buy airplane tickets, but they may be most likely to travel around holidays to spend time with family members, buy tickets well in advance, and use credit cards.

◀ **Figure 16-3
Customer Profile.**

It is important to put together a customer profile when targeting your market.

Drawing Conclusions.

What are the customer profiles in Figure 16-3?

Take a look at the customer profile shown in Table 16.1, which shows different segment factors for consumers and businesses as an example.

Table 16.1   Market Segments

Segment Factors	Consumer Profile	Business Profile
Demographics	Single, professional women Age: 25–40 Annual income: $80,000+	100+ employees $3.5 million in revenue per year Variety of tourist service industries
Geographics	Work or live in Manhattan's financial district	Orange County, Southern California
Psychographics	Liberal politics Fashion- and quality-conscious Read the *New York Times* daily	Customer-oriented Employee-oriented Focus on quality of service
Buying Patterns	Purchase airline tickets 7 to 9 times per year	Hire temporary contractors during summer months and holiday periods

Apply Your Knowledge   Describe how segmenting a market can help a business. Think back to your investigation at the start of the chapter and explain how Facebook helps their paying clients with providing information on similar profiles on its users. Why would a business be interested in obtaining this information from Facebook? Explain your answer.

CAREER COMPETENCIES

 ## Make Oral Presentations

Great speakers are rare and easy to recognize. Many of our U.S. presidents were great speakers. Why is that? Because being able to communicate is one of the most important skills needed in a career in politics. The best among the political communicators often become president.

Good news, you don't have to be the president to be an expert at using verbal communication. Here are a few steps on the way to becoming a great speaker.

- It is said that great speakers know their audience. But do you know what this actually means? It means you must know what your audience wants to hear. It also means that you must be considerate of the person (or persons) you are speaking to. What the president says to the American people—and how he says it—is usually different in tone and content from what he might say to a foreign leader.

- You must know what you are talking about. This seems obvious, but it actually takes a lot of work. Being a great speaker means that before you speak, you take the time to really consider what you say, what it means, and how it will be received. This means thinking before you speak.

- Never stop learning! The greatest speakers would all admit that they are always learning. You might sometimes think that you have learned all you need to know on a certain topic. But if you keep an open mind, you might find that you learn something new every day. The ability to keep an open mind and continually learn new things can make you a better speaker and person.

- Be comfortable being a little nervous. All speakers get nervous sometimes. The more you practice the better you'll get and you'll use that energy to improve.

- Practice your presentations in front of a mirror—this way you can see your facial expressions—or present to a friend/parent.

- Make notes, there's nothing wrong with preparing. Notes can help you be clear on the points; include pauses and pace your presentation.

Career Skills in Action

Now, you practice making a sales pitch to a target customer.

It's your job to sell your idea to this customer in two minutes. Write down your key points and what you would say to convince this customer to buy your product. Remember to include what's important to him/her. Practice and use the above tips to perfect your customer pitch. Present to your peers and teacher for feedback.

16.3 Not All Segments Are for Every Business

Once a business defines the general market segment factors, it's time to identify which segments to target, and a process that involves research. Most small or new businesses rely on their judgment to identify their segments to save time and other resources. Even with a little bit of research, an entrepreneur can use the following questions to identify target market segments.

- Does the company have the skills to serve the segment?
- Does the segment connect to the mission of the company?
- Is the segment big enough to pay off? This question is critical; the market segment(s) you choose should help it become profitable.
- Is the segment growing or have the potential to grow?

If the answer is no to any of the target market screening questions, the company may need to re-evaluate the market segmentation factors and how they identified the market segments. The market segment or mix of segments that the business targets informs how a company will tell customers about its product or service.

Niche Market Segment

A **niche market** is a narrow group of potential customers who share specific characteristics. Unlike the mass market, the niche market segment focuses on customer specialization. For example, a mass market service might be cleaning services, the niche cleaning service might be focused on the elderly or be organic.

Niche markets can be very attractive to entrepreneurs and small businesses for a few reasons:

- **Focus.** Since the business is narrow, entrepreneurs and small business owners don't need to spend additional time and energy trying to redefine their goals.
- **Little Competition.** Niche markets offer entrepreneurs opportunity to be "the big fish in a small pond." Because they can be so specific, there tends to be less competition in niche markets.
- **Strong Customer Relationships.** Businesses build customer loyalty and brand recognition quickly because of their focus.
- **Higher profits.** A narrow group doesn't mean less money. In fact, niche segment customers tend to be less sensitive to price because they feel they are getting the best product or service.

Niche markets can be risky and smart entrepreneurs must ensure that there is a good business case. Entrepreneurs also need to monitor potential customers and other niche market segments they could attract.

Applying Concepts.
How would you break the group in Figure 16-4 into smaller segments? What target market segments would you belong to?

Segmented Market Segment

The <mark>segmented market segment</mark> is similar to the niche market segment in that it focuses on specific customer group needs. The difference is businesses that use segmented market segment look at a larger market and then divide that market up into smaller segments based on customer needs and wants. For example, banks segment their customers based on the amount of money they have in their accounts. Based on the amount of money in an account, a client may receive additional services because they have additional needs. Segmented markets are generally good for all businesses but may be easier for larger businesses. Larger businesses have more resources to work with different segments of customers to customize experiences and build loyalty.

Diversified Market Segment

Unlike the niche and segmented, <mark>diversified market segments</mark> are "diverse" and serve two segments with different needs and wants. In general, companies that choose this segmentation are larger and more established businesses that may have started as niche or segmented. This can happen in different ways. For example, a business selling cosmetics through parties might also start selling jewelry. Or, a business that sells healthy soft drinks might also start producing smoothies through the existing business. The idea is that they are able to start selling an established brand to a new market segment, without starting a new business.

Multi-sided Market Segment

The <mark>multi-sided market segment</mark> focuses on multiple interdependent segments. These segments have different needs or wants from the same business. Businesses that use multi-sided market segmentation rely on one segment supporting the needs of the other. Websites or blogs are good examples for multi-sided market segments. Websites make money by charging advertisers for space on their websites, which are free to the public. This segmentation works well for small businesses and entrepreneurs.

Deciding on a targeted market segmentation strategy can help a business stay focused on its goals and customer needs. Entrepreneurs who spend time developing, analyzing, and reviewing how a strategy supports the business goals, profitability, and segment growth understand their customers. You're only in business if you have customers.

Apply Your Knowledge What are the different segments a business can separate its target market into? Let's return to your investigation on Facebook. What market segment(s) does Facebook cater to? Use evidence from your investigation to explain your answer.

APPLICATION TO BUSINESS PLANNING

Target Market Segments

Using what you learned about target market segments in this chapter, describe your target market and market segment characteristics. Use research to support your findings. Be sure to include:

- A clear description of your target market.
- Customer profile charts (similar to Table 16.1) for your market.
- Market segments that you will group customers into.

16 ASSESSMENT

REVIEWING OBJECTIVES

1. Compare and contrast marketing to a mass market versus a target market.

2. List the components of a customer profile.

3. Identify ways that a target market can be separated into market segments.

CRITICAL THINKING

Which of the following customer characteristics are considered demographics? Which are geographics? Which are psychographics? Characteristics: Likes to sew, three children in the family, married, earns $40,000 per year, works in Atlanta, 50+ employees, enjoys Chinese food, financially conservative, lives in Putnam County, 18 years old, customer service focus, Spanish heritage, outgoing personality.

ENTREPRENEURIAL THINKING EXERCISE:
CRITICAL THINKING & PROBLEM SOLVING

Think back to your investigation of Facebook. Imagine that you were a company that was going to hire Facebook to find information on a market segment that you were interested in. What information would you want to know? What would you do with that information?

16 ASSESSMENT

EXTENSION ACTIVITIES

Entrepreneurship & Literacy Skills

Complete the following task to demonstrate your understanding of entrepreneurship:

Grades 9–12: Identify a local business and interview the owner/entrepreneur. Ask the owner to describe his/her target market and market segment, and characteristics they share. Conduct your own research of an established business in the same industry online, identifying the target market and market segment characteristics. Compare the local business owner's market segment to the online business. Describe how many customer segments they each reach. Are they different? Is one better than the other? Write a two-page description of your findings and explanation.

CHAPTER 17

UNDERSTANDING THE NEEDS OF A CUSTOMER SEGMENT

OBJECTIVES

- Explain why customers buy benefits versus features.
- Describe how a business creates value for customers.
- Identify various value propositions that businesses can offer customers.

NFTE Entrepreneurial Mindset Characteristic Focus

 Flexibility & Adaptability

National Entrepreneurship Standards

- **D.04** Reinforce service orientation through communication
- **D.28** Show empathy for others
- **K.18** Determine underlying customer needs/frustrations
- **L.10** Build brand/image
- **L.43** Determine customer/client needs
- **L.44** Determine customer's buying motives for use in selling

Common Career Technical Core Standards

- **CRP.4** Communicate clearly, effectively and with reason.
- **MK-COM.4** Obtain, develop, maintain and improve a marketing communications product or service mix to respond to market opportunities.
- **MK-COM.5** Communicate information about products, services, images and/or ideas to achieve a desired outcome.
- **MK-SAL.2** Apply sales techniques to meet client needs and wants.

National Entrepreneurship Standards: Career Competencies

 D.02 Apply effective listening skills

LESSON VOCABULARY

- accessibility
- benefits
- brand
- brand mark
- convenience
- customization
- features
- mind share
- product mix
- product positioning
- value
- value proposition

17.1 What Matters—Benefits vs. Features

In the last chapter you learned about identifying a target market segment, which are your most important customers. In this chapter, we will explore how to show that target market the value of your business. **Value** is the relative worth of something—money, a product, or idea. The key word here is *relative*, as value is a judgment based on comparison and varies by market segment. Values can be tangible, such as price or size; or intangible, such as customer service. An entrepreneur needs to communicate the value of his/her business to potential customers.

To attract people in your target market, you need to choose a product that matches well with their needs or wants. When given a choice, consumers buy the product with the features and benefits that best meet their requirements.

The **features** of a product are what it does and how it appears to the senses (sight, sound, taste, smell, and touch). Features are factual statements about the product or service. Here are some examples of features:

- Open 24 hours
- Batteries included
- Organic cleaning supplies
- Fast food
- Custom Education Programs

Although features are important to potential customers, they do not influence them to buy.

The **benefits** of a product are the reasons customers choose to buy it. A benefit answers the question, "What's in it for me?", meaning the feature provides the customer with something of value to them. Here are a few examples of benefits: saving time, increasing social status, protecting the family, getting rid of a problem, improving a relationship, reducing worry, providing entertainment, and saving money. It may seem easy to identify benefits, but many entrepreneurs fall into the trap of describing their features in more detail. Benefits have to do with perceived value and about making the customer feel good about him or herself. For example, buying organic cleaning supplies makes a customer feel like a better person because she is contributing to saving our planet.

Businesses show customers the features and benefits in advertisements and in product packaging. The design and labeling of a bottle, box, bag, or other container is one way you can emphasize your product's features and benefits.

You may also choose to sell a combination of products that have similar or complementary benefits. The combination of products a business sells is called its **product mix**. The mix you choose will largely depend on the product image you want to communicate. It will also depend on the number and type of markets you are targeting. For example Samsung's product mix includes mobile phones, netbooks, tablets, televisions, refrigerators, microwaves, printers, and memory cards. These products are all consumer electronics but solve different problems but could be for the same market. While the features for these products are all different, they share benefits like giving customers piece of mind.

Apply Your Knowledge   Why do customers buy benefits? Think back to your investigation. Based on your research, what do you think the key benefits of a Dyson vacuum cleaner are?

ENTREPRENEURIAL CASE STUDY: FLEXIBILITY & ADAPTABILITY

 ## Luke Cooper—CEO & Founder, PeachMe

Overcoming Challenges

Luke Cooper is the CEO and founder of Baltimore-based Asurvest, Inc., DBA PeachMe (www.peachme.com). Through this business, Luke is focused on disrupting the $40 billion extended warranty market for the benefit of the average income consumers. The company, which operates under the name

Luke Cooper.

PeachMe, helps consumers to research and purchase extended warranty coverage for their favorite gadgets, smartphones, and electronics. The company's efforts have already been featured in *Forbes Magazine*, *Pando Daily*, *Black Enterprise Magazine*, and *Baltimore SmartCEO Magazine*.

There is a saying, "What you surround yourself with, you become." Luke Cooper proved this theory to be wrong at a young age. He grew up surrounded by poverty and crime. As a child, he had to provide a testimony that put his own father in jail. Life should have turned out differently for Luke. Luke attended an entrepreneurship course sponsored by the Network for Teaching Entrepreneurship (NFTE) in Bridgeport, CT. He went on to not only graduate from high school but also to attend Syracuse University College of Law and the F.W. Olin Graduate School of Business at Babson College.

Solving Socio-Economic Problems with Businesses

As a corporate lawyer for one of the largest national insurance companies, Luke had, for all intents and purposes, arrived. But he left the comfort of corporate America to make a bigger impact. His experience growing up has made him a rare entrepreneur, one who is not afraid to take risks. He decided to dedicate his life to businesses and nonprofit organizations that address important business and socio-economic problems. Not one to be scared of failure, Luke has led investments in more than a dozen new businesses.

Founded in 2013, Luke's most recent venture, Baltimore-based PeachMe, has been receiving an overwhelming positive buzz in its short existence. Many times when buying big ticket items, like electronics and cell phones, customers are offered extended warranties that do not make sense financially. The average customer who is unaware, buys them, and essentially wastes their money. PeachMe aims to translate the policies into plain English so consumers can make "peaches-to-peaches" comparisons when buying a warranty. Building the most advanced warranty analytics platform in the market, PeachMe can compare and summarize hundreds of policies in seconds. This helps customers by removing the friction and uncertainty when they face high-pressure tactics for warranty coverage. After being selected as a Techstars Rising Star, the company launched its first applications in November 2014.

Inspiring Success in Others

Luke is a dedicated philanthropist and spends considerable efforts to create sustainable academic achievement and economic growth within various inner cities around the country. As a Living Classrooms Foundation "Rising Star," he mentors the organization's core constituents through their outreach programs. Luke also works closely with Gather Baltimore, an organization that donates excess food from the weekly farmer's markets. Luke is a sought-after speaker and dedicates time helping to grow NFTE. In 2014, he was the honored with the NFTE Visionary Leader Award at the NFTE Fairchester 15th Anniversary event.

Thinking and Acting Like an Entrepreneur

- How does Luke use businesses and nonprofits to help solve business and socio-economic problems?
- What are the customer needs Luke identified, and how does PeachMe solve them?
- In what ways does Luke demonstrate the entrepreneurial mindset behavior of adapting (learning and acting from setback)?

17.2 Creating Value

As you learned earlier, value is a customer's perceived benefit. When an entrepreneur aligns the needs or wants of a customer segment to the product or service, he/she is creating value. The entrepreneur's **value proposition** is the short statement that summarizes all the benefits a company gives to its customers. Because the value proposition is specific to customer segments, they can vary by company and even within a company. For example, if your business targets a diversified market segment, you need to develop multiple value propositions to address each segment's needs. So how do you create value? In practice you can create new value or grow existing value.

Figure 17-2 ▶
Value.

Society places value on certain items but not everyone values items the same way. Would you spend money on a luxury item?

Applying Concepts.

What type of customer would make this purchase? What can you infer about their buying patterns?

Creating new value is the most challenging for any business. It means entering a whole new market and solving for needs that customers didn't even know they had. This type of value is generally created by inventions and discoveries. For example, cell phones created a whole new industry for communications.

A more common way to create value is to improve on how an existing product or service works. You may be able to make something less expensive, more efficiently or work faster. For example, Apple created value by pricing its new iPhones lower than previous version. This created more value for customers. A company like McDonald's improved on its value when it started the drive through window.

Companies can also offer better value through **customization**. Customization is personalizing products and services for the specific needs of customers. Many entrepreneurs create value through customization but it's important to think about how much you will customize. Too much customization can be costly to the business, so it's important to understand exactly what the customers want. For example, most shoes are made in a factory that repeats the same pattern, so having to create each shoe from scratch can be time consuming and expensive. To solve this problem, Nike came out with "NIKEiD," an online store where customers can select from existing colors and designs to buy personalized Nike shoes. By doing this, Nike let's people feel like they are creating personalized shoe, but by controlling the number of choices, Nike can keep the costs predicable." Likewise, a business can add value by offering extended product/service features, such as warranties, delivery and installation, training, technical assistance, and other service after the sale.

Whether you create new value or expand on existing values, it's important that your value proposition is clear and compelling to your customers. As a check, think about your value proposition as an equation:

$$\text{Value Proposition} = \text{Benefits} - \text{Costs}$$

Your benefits should outweigh any tangible and perceived costs your customers may have for your value proposition to be positive. There isn't one way to craft a value proposition, but here are some important components to include:

- Explanation of how your product solves customers' problems
- Specific benefits that are compelling to your customers. This should be measurable.
- Description of why your customer should buy from you not from the competition

Apply Your Knowledge Describe how customization and extended product features create value and help meet customer needs. Think back to your investigation of the Dyson vacuum cleaners at the start of the chapter. What is Dyson's value proposition to its customers?

CAREER COMPETENCIES

 ## Apply Effective Listening Skills

How is listening relevant to your career? It doesn't matter if you are a boss, an employee, or a co-worker, you will need to listen at some point. The better you are at it, the more successful you will be. Here are a few reasons why:

- Good listeners often pick up subtle—unmentioned or implied—cues in conversation. This means that a person's tone of voice or his word choice tell you more about what he thinks than what he says. In your career, you might have a great advantage if you can pick up these clues.

- Good listeners are often more trusted than bad listeners. If you listen carefully to what people tell you, you deliver the message that they are important to you. They are more likely to trust you and like you.

- Being a good listener will make you a better worker. When you listen carefully to instructions, for example, you are more likely to carry out your tasks without having to be reminded what to do. You are able to act to resolve problems that people tell you about so that your workplace is a more positive environment.

Listening involves being active and paying attention. With a little practice, anyone can become an active listener. Here are some ways to practice at home, school or with your friends.

- Show interest using eye contact and positive nonverbal messages.
- Let the other person finish speaking before you respond.
- Ignore distractions such as cell phones and other people.
- Set your preconceived opinions and emotions aside.
- Repeat the message that you hear out loud to make sure you received it correctly.

17.3 Value Is in the Eye of the Beholder

Now that you know how businesses create value for customers, let's explore value propositions that businesses offer their customers. Remember value propositions need to be specific to customer segment needs.

- **Helping Your Customer.** Creating value does not need to be difficult. A value could be helping customers get a task complete.

- **Brand.** A **brand** is a marketing strategy that can create an emotional attachment to your product in the mind of the consumer. This is because a brand is perceived in a certain way. It may be seen as excellent quality or high status—a premium brand. What matters here is how the consumer perceives it on a higher level. Companies who have well-known brands also use **product positioning**. Product positioning is a way of influencing potential customers to distinguish your brand's characteristics from those of the competition. Branding can cause customers to think of a particular company first. For example, what name do you think of when you want to buy a new pair of athletic shoes? Perhaps Nike, with its "Just Do It" slogan or "swoosh" **brand mark** (logo), comes to mind. **Mind share** is the awareness or popularity a certain product has with consumers. In addition to its name, you can use a symbol or other graphic design to identify a brand.

Figure 17-3 ▶
Branding.

A brand mark is a way to associate a symbol with a product and its qualities.

Drawing Conclusions.

What is an advantage of using a brand mark?

308 ● *Chapter 17*

- **Design.** Although not measurable, design is an important value for all creative businesses.

- **Price.** As we mentioned earlier, some customer segments may respond to lower prices for the same or similar value. Discount airlines like Spirit offers basic flight service with no frills at a cheap price.

- **Guarantees.** Most customers value reducing the risks of purchasing products or services. For example, Best Buy offers one- to three-year warranties on computers and other electronics. These warranties make customers feel less apprehensive about spending and provide an opportunity to return products with no questions.

- **Accessibility.** Innovative companies create value by providing access to products or services customers would not have otherwise. FedEx was built on providing customers rapid access to goods and documents from around the world through overnight shipping.

- **Convenience.** Companies can add significant value by designing or re-designing products to be easier to use or simply more useful.

There are many ways for companies to provide value to customers. The key as an entrepreneur is to determine which value propositions are suitable for your business while catering to the specific needs of your customer segment.

Apply Your Knowledge Name and describe two value propositions. What value does Dyson not appeal to? Do companies need to appeal to every value?

 **APPLICATION TO BUSINESS PLANNING**

Value Proposition

Using what you learned about creating value in this chapter, create value propositions for your customer segments. Be sure to include research data in your work. Remember, a value proposition should include:

- An explanation of how your product solves customers' problems
- Specific benefits that are compelling to your customers. This should be measurable
- A description of why your customer should buy from you and not from the competition

17 ASSESSMENT

REVIEWING OBJECTIVES

1. Explain why customers buy benefits versus features.

2. Describe how a business creates value for customers.

3. Identify various value propositions that businesses can offer customers.

CRITICAL THINKING

1. Consider iTunes' value proposition: *You've never been so easily entertained.* What value(s) do you believe Apple is offering its customers? What do you believe is most important to the customers?

2. How can branding create value for a business's product or service?

ENTREPRENEURIAL THINKING EXERCISE: FLEXIBILITY & ADAPTABILITY

Think back to your investigation of Dyson Vacuums. Imagine you're the CEO of Dyson and a large retailer calls to say that they will not carry your product due to the high price. How can you accommodate the retailer without compromising your core value proposition to customers? Explain your answer.

EXTENSION ACTIVITIES

Entrepreneurship & Literacy Skills

Complete the following task to demonstrate your understanding of entrepreneurship:

1. **Grades 9–10:** Do customers buy benefits? Interview 5–10 people in your school and ask each person to describe a product he/she purchased in the last week. Ask specific questions about features. For example, "Did you purchase the t-shirt because of the color?" Record your answers and write a short paragraph describing your findings. Compare your findings to the arguments match the claims in this chapter.

2. **Grades 11–12:** Do customers buy benefits? Interview 5–10 people in your school and ask each person to describe a product he/she purchased in the last week. Ask specific questions about features. For example, "Did you purchase the t-shirt because of the color?" Record your answers and write a short paragraph describing your findings. Compare your findings to the arguments match the claims in this chapter. If not, explain why you think the data did not support the claims.

18 DELIVERING VALUE TO A CUSTOMER SEGMENT

OBJECTIVES

- Know the function of marketing and the goals of a marketing plan.
- List the five P's of the Marketing Mix and examples of each.
- Explain how marketing strategies communicate value propositions to customers.

NFTE Entrepreneurial Mindset Characteristic Focus

 Future Orientation

National Entrepreneurship Standards

- **C.11** Describe marketing functions and related activities
- **F.08** Describe the concept of price
- **L.08** Determine unique selling proposition
- **L.09** Develop strategies to position product/service
- **L.10** Build brand/image
- **L.17** Explain the concept of marketing strategies
- **L.18** Describe the nature of marketing planning
- **L.20** Develop marketing plan
- **L.35** Establish pricing objectives
- **L.36** Select pricing strategies
- **L.37** Set prices
- **L.38** Adjust prices to maximize profitability

Common Career Technical Core Standards

- **CRP.4** Communicate clearly, effectively and with reason.
- **MK-COM.1** Apply techniques and strategies to convey ideas and information through marketing communications.
- **MK-COM.5** Communicate information about products, services, images and/or ideas to achieve a desired outcome.
- **MK.8** Obtain, develop, maintain and improve a product or service mix in response to market opportunities.
- **MK-RES.2** Design and conduct research activities to facilitate marketing business decisions.

National Entrepreneurship Standards: Career Competencies

 D.06 Address people properly

LESSON VOCABULARY

- bundling
- cost-based pricing
- demand-based pricing
- exclusive distribution
- intensive distribution
- markdown price
- marketing
- marketing mix
- marketing plan
- markup price
- promotion
- selective distribution

18.1 Setting Market Goals

In the previous chapters, you looked at the importance of identifying a target market segment, and determining a unique value proposition for those customers. In this chapter, you will look at putting together a plan for presenting your business, so that customers appreciate the value your business will provide. Being able to do this requires an entrepreneurial mindset characteristic of future orientation, as you will have to set goals that you want your business to achieve.

What Is a Marketing Plan?

As you've already learned, a market segment is a group of potential customers for a particular product or service. In this chapter, you will learn about marketing. **Marketing** is a way of presenting your business to your customers. It is one of the four main functions of a small business. The other three—operations, human resources, and finance—are discussed in Units 5 and 6.

The main purpose for marketing is to clearly communicate the value of your product or service. To do this successfully, you create a marketing plan. A **marketing plan** is a detailed guide with two primary parts:

- Marketing goals
- Strategies for reaching your goals (the marketing mix)

Every marketing plan is unique because each business has its own marketing goals. When you first begin creating a marketing plan, it's important to state what you want to accomplish. Write these items down so that you can refer to them as you develop marketing strategies. You can make adjustments to your goals later, as you consider your marketing strategies. You may also discover that some additional research is needed in the process.

Your marketing goals should be in agreement with your business plan's overall objectives. However, marketing goals are usually more specific and action-oriented. You should be able to measure them in practical ways. For example, "I want to increase the number of customers that come to my store" is too general. Adding the words "by 25%" to the end of this statement makes it more specific and measurable. Other ways to state goals in a measurable way is to specify the sales or profit goals you wish to reach.

Marketing goals also require a timeframe:

- **Short-Range Goals.** What do you want to accomplish within the next year? You may find it helpful to break one-year goals into even smaller periods such as a quarter (three months).
- **Mid-Range Goals.** What do you want to achieve within the next two to five years?
- **Long-Range Goals.** Where do you see your business ten or twenty years from now?

◀ **Figure 18-1**
Setting SMART Goals.
You will need to set marketing goals that are SMART.

Drawing Conclusions.
Use Figure 18-1 to create SMART goals for your business.

Some additional things to keep in mind when writing goals include:

- **Motive.** Think about why you want to reach each goal. How does each goal influence your messaging to your customer? Also, consider the opportunity cost of setting one particular goal rather than another.
- **Consistency.** Be careful not to write goals that conflict with one another. That will only create frustration. It will also decrease the possibility of accomplishing goals.
- **Cost.** Eventually, you will need to work out a budget for your marketing plan to check the feasibility of your goals. Cost not only includes money, but also your personal energy. Try to be as realistic as you can when writing goals. At the same time, remember that many worthwhile goals will require you to step outside your comfort zone and face the risk of potential failure with optimism.

Acting on Your Goals

Once you have your marketing goals written, it is time to put together a plan to act on them. Writing actions steps towards accomplishing each goal can help break down huge tasks into smaller chunks. For example, let's say your marketing goal was to have 100 subscribers to your e-mail blasts by the end of your first month of operations. Your action plan might consist of secondary and primary research aimed at finding out where to get contact info for your target customers. You might also break down the goal into smaller chunks, such as attending a different networking event and aiming to get at least five e-mails at each. Having specific action steps towards each goal will ensure your goals are achievable.

 **Apply Your Knowledge**   What are the main components of a marketing plan? Based on your Overstock.com investigation, would you say the company's short-range goals? Explain your answer.

 **ENTREPRENEURIAL CASE STUDY: FUTURE ORIENTATION**

Daymond John—CEO & Founder of FUBU, and Star of ABC's Emmy Award-Winning Series Shark Tank

Revolutionizing the Fashion World

As CEO & Founder of FUBU, Daymond John (www.daymondjohn.com) revolutionized the sportswear industry in the 1990s with a distinctive line of fashionable attire that transcended the underserved urban market and became wildly popular in the mainstream teen market. Over the past 20 years, Daymond has gone from sewing logos on hats in his basement to establishing an international clothing empire, earning himself the iconic title "Godfather of Urban Fashion." In addition to his success in style, Daymond John has become one of the world's most sought-after branding experts, authors, and motivational speakers.

Delivering Value to an Underserved Target Market

Daymond's first foray into the apparel market came in the early 1990's. Daymond and his friends were looking for a "tie-top hat," an accessory

Daymond John.

that was extremely popular in hip hop videos in the early 90s. But, after visiting the store, he was put off by the high prices. Taking this discovery as an opportunity, Daymond began to spend his mornings producing his own tie-top hats and his nights selling them on the streets of his Queens neighborhood of Hollis. Daymond recruited his friends to help him with the production, and after making an $800 profit in the first day of his new venture, it became clear that they had discovered an untapped market.

Recognizing that major fashion designers were not paying attention to the urban market, Daymond branded his company as FUBU, standing for "For Us By Us". The fashions proudly reflected its rap and hip hop roots, and the owners communicated this in their marketing efforts. Daymond and Co soon created the distinctive FUBU logo and began sewing it on hockey jerseys, sweatshirts, and t-shirts. Soon famed entertainer LL Cool J, a neighborhood friend of Daymond and music idol at the time, agreed to wear one of Daymond's shirts in a picture that would become the centerpiece of FUBU's first promotional campaign.

In 1992, FUBU premiered at the MAGIC fashion trade show in Las Vegas. The line of distinctively cut and vibrantly colored sportswear was an instant hit, garnering $300,000 in orders. By 1998, FUBU made $350 million in revenue and Daymond John's neighborhood tie-hat business was suddenly in direct competition with well-known brands like Donna Karan New York and Tommy Hilfiger. In 1999, FUBU the Collection became the first company to receive the ESSENCE Achievement Award.

Sewing Hats to Branding Genius

Daymond is now touted as a "branding genius" in the marketing world. His revolutionary contributions to fashion and American business have been recognized by many esteemed organizations that have honored him over the years. In addition, his services have been courted by Fortune 500 companies such as AT&T, Turner Networks, and Nike. In response to this demand, Daymond established the branding firm Shark Branding separate from his apparel businesses. Specializing in brand strategies, brand development, licensing, artist relations, and marketing, Daymond and Shark Branding have perfected the methods for communicating the value of a business to a particular customer segment.

His success and expertise as a branding genius has also allowed him to build a brand around the Daymond John name itself. In 2007, he entered the literary world, and has authored two best-selling books where he looks at topics such as celebrity-fueled brand loyalty, consumer impulses, and purchasing habits. Daymond's reputation in the field and experience with angel investing earned him a spot as an investor on the ABC reality television series Shark Tank, allowing him to help out up-and-coming entrepreneurs.

18.2 In the Mix: Where Will You Sell?

Every marketing plan has five main strategy areas, sometimes referred to as the "Five P's." How a company chooses to combine these areas is called its **marketing mix**. You may recognize some of the P's from previous chapters. In this chapter, we will focus on where you'll sell and for how much.

- **People.** Without a doubt, your target customers are the key to defining all the other strategies in a marketing plan. As you learned in Chapter 16, developing detailed customer profiles will keep your focus on the best prospects. You can also include a description of the people (employees) you will need to carry out the marketing plan.

- **Product.** What item(s) can your business provide that will best meet the needs of your target market? What is the value you are providing to your customer? This is a description of the product(s) or service(s) your company plans to offer and your value proposition.

- **Place.** This strategy refers to selling and delivery methods. How and where will customers be able to buy or receive your product or service? The location a business chooses can be a value to customers offering accessibility and convenience.

- **Price.** Pricing requires a balance between the price your target market feels is reasonable and staying profitable! Your pricing strategy may need to change over time depending on various factors, about which you'll learn later in this chapter.

- **Promotion.** The process you use to make potential customers aware of your product or service and to influence them to buy it is referred to as **promotion**. Some common examples of promotions are coupons, advertisements, e-mail blasts and customer rewards. Businesses plan promotional activities to support an overall marketing plan. You'll read about this in Chapter 20.

◀ **Figure 18-2**
Where and When to Sell.
A hot dog stand would be a great business on a college campus where students are looking for a cheap lunch in between classes.

Drawing Conclusions.
What type of customer would prefer a fine dining restaurant over a hot dog stand?

Where and When Will You Sell?

"Place" strategies need to include the selling location and the hours during which the product can be purchased. Examples of such strategies include the following:

- Choosing an excellent location for a physical store.
- Determining the days and hours when customers are most likely to shop.
- Taking online orders that customers can access any time, from anywhere in the world.
- Taking orders via a toll-free telephone number, with operators standing by 24 hours a day.

Remember, it is important that the strategy for your business aligns with the value proposition for your business. If your business is valued because of the convenience to your customers, then you might want to do online sales that customers can access at any time. If your customers value personalization, a face-to-face transaction might be better.

When determining your strategies, be sure to consider how widely you want to distribute your product. For instance, do you want to sell the item yourself, or do you want other business to sell your products for you? Do you want to use many sales outlets or only a few? Selling through partner locations (channels) such as third-party stores and wholesalers can result in lower margins but potentially higher sales as you leverage the scale and strengths of those partners. Directly owned channels such a company's own website or store have higher margins but also have higher operating costs and lack scale. When determining the places to sell through, a mix of these indirect and direct channels is critical to managing the customer experience and maximizing sales. Here are three basic options if you choose not to distribute your product yourself:

- **Exclusive Distribution.** This type of distribution is the most limited of the three basic options. ==Exclusive distribution== gives a specific retailer, or authorized dealer, the sole right to sell a product in a particular geographical area. An exclusive distribution agreement usually requires that the retailer or dealer cannot sell any competing products.

- **Intensive Distribution.** The opposite of exclusive distribution is ==intensive distribution==. The object of intensive distribution is to make a product available at as many sales outlets as possible. This means that the product will be sold at a variety of stores, many of which may compete with each other. For example, you can buy toothpaste at drug stores, grocery stores, large outlets such as Kmart or Wal-Mart, and small convenience shops at gas stations.

- **Selective Distribution.** Allowing a product to be sold at a moderate number of sales outlets, but not all, in a particular geographical area is called ==selective distribution==. Retailers/dealers are usually chosen based on a set of conditions, or criteria. For example, a car manufacturer may select dealers only if they have enough space and staff to provide a high level of maintenance and repair services.

How Will You Transport and Store Products?

Once you sell your products you need to make sure they get to the customers on time! Transportation is used to move a product from one point to another along a distribution channel. Ways to transport products include by airplane, train, boat, truck, or a mix of methods. The cost of shipping, as well as the speed at which the product needs to be delivered, are two key factors that affect transportation choices.

The type of shipping container used during shipment needs to be chosen to provide security and reduce damage. For example, if your product is fragile (such as glass), or spoils easily (such as fresh food or flowers), special transportation needs have to be considered. If a product cannot be shipped directly to its final destination, you will also need to decide where it will be temporarily stored along the way. You will learn more about managing the distribution of products and services to customers in Unit 5.

 **Apply Your Knowledge**   List the Five P's of Marketing and explain how each component communicates value to customers. Think back to your investigation of Overstock.com at the start of the chapter. Would brands using intensive or selective distribution sell through Overstock.com?

CAREER COMPETENCIES

Address People Properly

"You don't get a second chance to make a first impression."

Experts say it takes three to five seconds for a person to judge your appearance, body language, mannerisms, and dress. But what about how you greet and address people? What if you met the President of the United States? Or a famous musician? How would you address them? You might be more formal with the President and call him Mr. President, and you might refer to the famous musician by her stage name.

Knowing how to properly address people is a key skill for your life socially and professionally. Properly addressing someone shows your respect for her position and your sensitivity to offending her. As the global economy grows, cultural sensitivity is also important. Here are some tips for properly addressing people:

1. **Be observant.** Watch the people around you to read social cues and greetings.

2. **When in doubt, be formal.** It's better to play it safe and use Mr., Mrs., or Ms. Allow the person to invite you to use their first name or nickname that a friend would use.

3. **Once a person invites you to use his/her first name you should use it.** Going back to more formal address may seem come across as impersonal at that point. E-mail first impressions count too. Be formal in your first e-mail, "Dear Ms. Smith" and if the person asks you to use his/her first name do it.

4. **Use appropriate tone.** When communicating in a professional setting, it is important to communicate with assertive speech to people you meet for the first time. Avoiding aggressive and passive speech will help build a better first impression.

5. **Be sensitive to cultural norms and differences.** You should try to be sensitive to differences in how people communicate in various cultures. For example, if you are speaking to someone whose cultural norm is to not use first names in professional conversations, it might be a good idea to do the same. While it is impossible to know every cultural norm, you can use clues from the conversation to make sure you are using appropriate language.

6. **Do your homework.** If you know you're going to an event or starting to work with new people do some research. Ask your peers and look at professional social networks, so you can be prepared. Being prepared shows that you care and inspires trust. Now that's a great first impression!

18.3 Name Your Price

Companies spend a lot of time developing and re-analyzing their pricing strategies. There are many kinds of pricing strategies and techniques. The price of your product should ultimately be based on two main things: your target market and keeping your company profitable. As you learned in Unit 3, your product or service price should be low enough that customers buy from you rather than the competition. At the same time, your product's price must be high enough for your company to earn a profit. In this section, you will look specifically at determining pricing that aligns with your value proposition to customers. In Unit 6, you will look more closely at the financial factors that influence price.

The first step toward setting a price is to identify what you want achieve by it. For example, what do you want the price to say about your product? What do you want the price to accomplish for your business? When deciding price objectives, keep in mind your overall business plan goals, your marketing or brand goals, and what your target market will pay for the value your offer. Following are a few samples of price objectives:

Figure 18-3 ▶

Increase Sale Volume.

Prices are marked down to increase sales.

Applying Concepts.

Why would it be more important to know what time of year your target customer would be more willing to buy your product or service?

- **Build or Maintain an Image.** Prices can create or affect the image of a product in customers' minds. For example, customers may perceive lower-priced items as having a lower quality than similar items sold at a higher price.

- **Increase Sales Volume (Quantity).** Higher prices often lower the number of sales, and lower prices often increase the number of sales. However, you can charge a slightly higher price than the competition if you showcase the benefits.

- **Obtain or Expand a Market Share.** Sometimes an initial lower price can help a new business attract customers away from competitors. After a market share is obtained, prices can be increased slightly to improve profits.

- **Maximize Profits.** If you are introducing a new product into a market, a high price could be charged to maximize profits. Later on, if competitors mimic your product or find some other way to reduce its attraction, the price could be dropped.

After defining objectives, the next step is to pick a strategy for determining actual prices. There are three basic pricing strategies. Your decision about which strategy to use will depend on your product mix, your price objectives, and your target market.

- **Demand-Based Pricing.** A pricing method that focuses on customer demand—how much customers are willing to pay for a product—is called **demand-based pricing**. A demand-based pricing strategy is most useful when customers perceive your product as unique, or having greater value than other similar products. A maximum price can be determined by surveying potential target customers. An example for demand-based pricing is a new pair Nike athletic shoes. They are sold at a much higher price than other sneakers, because Nike's customers feel that their value is worth that much.

- **Competition-Based Pricing.** As you learned in Unit 3, a pricing method that focuses on what the competition charges is called **competition-based pricing**. After you find out your competitors' prices, you can decide to charge the same price, slightly more, or slightly less. Since the focus of this strategy is staying competitive, you will need to regularly review what your competitors are doing. This will allow you to make price adjustments if needed. Fastfood restaurants used competition-based pricing when McDonald's got the $1.00 menu, Burger King creates a $0.99 menu. Businesses use this strategy to get customers in, and then buy other products in addition (such as fries and a soft drink).

- **Cost-Based Pricing.** Setting a product's price based on what it costs your business to provide it, is called **cost-based pricing**. To use this strategy you need to understand your expenses to create your product or service per unit. After you figure out what your cost is for a single unit of your product, you must decide how much to add on to your product's price to ensure a profit.

In practice, a combination of all three of these strategies is ideal. In Unit 6, you will work on ensuring your price covers your expenses. For this unit, you want to make sure that your price aligns with your value proposition, what your customers are willing to pay for your product or services, based on competition in the market.

Allowing for Price Adjustments

If the distribution channel for a product is an indirect one, the price will get adjusted as it moves from the producer to the customer. When a retail store buys a product from a wholesaler, an additional amount is added to the wholesale cost in order to make a profit. This results in a **markup price**. Frequently, a percentage is used to calculate the markup price:

Wholesale Cost × Markup Percentage = Markup Amount

Wholesale Cost + Markup Amount = Markup Price (Retail Price)

A **markdown price** is set when a retailer wants to reduce the price of a product. Markdown prices are often used when a retailer is overstocked (has too much of a product). Or, perhaps the retailer needs to make room for new products. Another reason is a change in customer demand. For example, a clothing store will probably set markdown prices at the end of the summer to get rid of warm-weather clothing. To calculate the markdown price, use the following formulas. Keep in mind that to avoid losing money, the markdown price should not be less than the wholesale cost.

Retail Price × Markdown Percentage = Markdown Amount

Retail Price − Markdown Amount = Markdown Price ("Sale" price)

When your product is a service you provide to customers, time is a primary factor used to determine price. A service could be charged by the hour, as a physical therapist, business consultant, or marriage counselor might do.

Vendors such as car mechanics or electricians, commonly charge a separate fee for materials in addition to their hourly charge. This strategy provides flexibility for services that vary widely. For example, the job for a particular customer may require replacing expensive parts, inexpensive parts, or perhaps none at all.

Another way that businesses charge for services is based on a flat fee. Material costs, as well as time, are built into one price for a particular service. For example, consider a business that performs oil changes in cars. The amount of time it takes to complete an oil change, as well as the new oil and oil filter that's put in the car, are factored into one price.

Another technique to explore when setting prices is **bundling**. Bundling is the practice of combining the price of several different services (and/or physical products) into one price. The travel industry commonly uses bundling to create vacation packages that include airline services, hotel services, and car-rental services for one price.

◀ **Figure 18-4**
Bundling.
Bundling combines the price of several services and/or products into one price.

Applying Concepts.

How might computer stores use the technique of bundling?

Bundling can be a convenience factor for customers. But it also allows the business to sell services at a slightly lower price because customers are buying a greater quantity of goods or services.

Bundling might also be used to include optional services or product accessories with an item that's more in demand. This strategy is often used by vendors such as car dealers and appliance retailers. It helps them sell items that a customer may not otherwise buy if sold separately.

Apply Your Knowledge List two to three pricing objectives and describe the three pricing strategies. Consider Overstock.com's retail prices, what do you think is Overstock.com's pricing strategy.

✔ **APPLICATION TO BUSINESS PLANNING**

Marketing Mix

Use what you learned from this and previous chapters on the marketing strategies to develop your own marketing mix. Use data to support your work. Be sure to include:

- A list of your Five P's
- Specific strategies for place and pricing strategies
- A description how each strategy reinforces your value proposition

18 ASSESSMENT

REVIEWING OBJECTIVES

1. Explain the function of marketing and the goals of a marketing plan.

2. List the Five P's of the Marketing Mix and examples of each.

3. Explain how marketing strategies communicate value propositions to customers.

CRITICAL THINKING

Explain the differences between cost-based pricing and demand-based pricing. What would you say are the advantages and disadvantages of each?

ENTREPRENEURIAL THINKING EXERCISE: FUTURE ORIENTATION

Think back to your investigation of Overstock.com and imagine you're the CEO of a new competitor called Overflow.com. Describe the strategies from the marketing mix that would make you competitive.

EXTENSION ACTIVITIES

Entrepreneurship & Mathematics Skills

Complete the following task to demonstrate your understanding of entrepreneurship:

Grades 9–12: Imagine that you're a retailer who purchases a product at $2.50 per unit in January. Based on practices in your industry, you decide to use a 100% markup percentage. What will be the markup price (retail price) of this product? In May you realize the product is not selling and you are overstocked. You markdown the item by 20%. What is the new selling price? Finally in December you decide to sell all the remaining inventory at cost (at the purchase or wholesale price) during a clearance sale. What is the markdown percentage? Create a line graph, labeling the x-axis "months," and the y-axis "dollars." Chart the price changes and write a short paragraph describing the percentage changes. Explain why a business might choose to sell at each of the prices charted.

OBJECTIVES

- Explain the importance of personal selling and understanding customers' needs.
- List effective sales techniques for communicating a business's value proposition to customers.
- Identify the purpose and structure of an effective business pitch.

NFTE Entrepreneurial Mindset Characteristic Focus

☑ Communication & Collaboration

National Entrepreneurship Standards

- **B.01** Demonstrate honesty and integrity
- **B.17** Maintain positive attitude
- **B.18** Demonstrate interest and enthusiasm
- **D.01** Explain the nature of effective communications
- **D.02** Apply effective listening skills
- **D.05** Explain the nature of effective verbal communications
- **D.07** Handle telephone calls in a businesslike manner
- **D.17** Follow directions
- **L.42** Establish relationship with client/customer
- **L.43** Determine customer/client needs
- **L.44** Determine customer's buying motives for use in selling
- **L.47** Convert customer/client objections into selling points

Common Career Technical Core Standards

- **CRP.4** Communicate clearly, effectively and with reason.
- **MK.9** Communicate information about products, services, images and/or ideas to achieve a desired outcome.
- **MK-MGT.4** Access, evaluate and disseminate information to aid in making marketing management decisions.
- **MK-SAL.2** Apply sales techniques to meet client needs and wants.
- **MK-SAL.3** Plan, organize and lead sales staff to enhance sales goals.

National Entrepreneurship Standards: Career Competencies

☑ **D.30** Demonstrate negotiation skills

LESSON VOCABULARY

- business pitch
- cold call
- data mining
- elevator pitch
- objections
- prospect
- rapport
- referral
- sales account
- sales call
- sales force
- sales lead

19.1 It's Personal: Selling Your Business to Your Customers

In the previous chapter, you looked at putting together a marketing mix as a way of propositioning your value to customers. In this chapter, you will learn how to communicate your value directly to customers to get sales. Being able to talk about your business with customers requires a great deal of communication and collaboration, behaviors that are part of the entrepreneurial mindset.

As you learned in previous chapters, once you have a value proposition for your target customers, you need to find a way to clearly communicate that value to customers. One way to do this is to have a team of employees who sells your business's products or services to customers. This approach is a promotional technique used by a company's **sales force** and by every entrepreneur. Sales force is another term for salespeople or sales representatives. They are the company employees who are directly involved in the process of selling. As you learned in Chapter 17, customers seek companies that have compelling value propositions. In other words, customers want to buy from a company that meets their needs. Personal selling helps communicate the value proposition. In fact, for some customers, personal selling could be a benefit in value proposition.

Personal selling has several advantages over other types of promotion:

- **Helps Build Personal Relationships.** Personal selling involves contact by means of face-to-face meetings and telephone calls. Videoconferences are another way to speak with customers. Many people appreciate the opportunity to provide feedback as well as receive information.

- **Allows for Customized Communication.** Because personal selling is an interactive form of communication, salespeople have the opportunity to adapt their message to each potential customer. When someone has questions or objections regarding a product or service, the salesperson can address them individually and quickly. **Objections** are the reasons that a customer may be reluctant or cautious about buying. Non-personal forms of communication, such as media advertisements, cannot be easily adjusted, and making changes to them can be expensive.

Characteristics of Successful Salespeople

Developing an effective sales force is key to a business's success. That's why it is critical for the business owner to recognize what it takes to be a successful salesperson. Salespeople have various personalities and styles of selling. However, the most successful salespeople have the following characteristics:

- **Positive Attitude.** Successful salespeople focus on the positive, even when times are tough. When salespeople are genuinely excited about the product or service they are selling, their enthusiasm shines through in their conversation and actions. Choosing to keep an upbeat attitude makes work more productive, for the individual and for others in the sales force. It also has a positive effect on customers, which can lead to an increase in sales.

- **Good Listener.** Successful salespeople learn how to ask their customers quality questions and then listen closely without interrupting. The salesperson can then offer a solution for the specific situation. This flexible approach usually proves more effective than giving an identical sales pitch to everyone.

- **Persistence.** Selling is not easy. Salespeople often make many contacts before making a sale. Successful salespeople understand that they need to be patient and persistent to close a deal. It can be frustrating, especially for new salespeople with little experience. The good news is: the more you learn, the easier the selling process can become.

- **Hard Worker.** Salespeople who take responsibility for their own success make goals for themselves and then form strategies to reach them. They work hard to produce positive results.

- **Truthful.** Some salespeople tell customers only what they think they want to hear. This approach can lead to misunderstandings and deception. The result is often a breakdown in business/customer relationships. Reestablishing trust with a customer once it is broken can be difficult. It is important to remember that, in our ever-connected world, customers talk, chat, post comments to online message boards, and blog about negative experiences. This can cause an even greater loss of sales and a bad reputation.

Relating Concepts.

If you were interviewing a person for a sales position in your company, what characteristics would you look for?

- **Consistent.** To become successful, you need to be dependable. That means you don't promise something you cannot deliver within a reasonable timeframe. The customer may get annoyed and decide to buy elsewhere. Another form of consistency is keeping in touch with your customers. This could include sending thank you notes, birthday cards, newsletters, and such. Consistency builds trust, which leads to better customer relationships. In other words, it encourages customer loyalty to your brand or business.

Remember, the salesperson represents the company when they are dealing with customers. A customer often forms an opinion about an entire company based on the attitude and behavior of a single person. An entrepreneur needs to be thoughtful about his or her team, select the best representatives and train them to communicate the company's value proposition consistently.

In addition, salespeople need to help develop or be trained on the company selling process.

 Apply Your Knowledge Describe two advantages of personal selling. How difficult would it be for a company to personally sell through a website? How does Net Jets provide personal selling in its process?

ENTREPRENEURIAL CASE STUDY: COMMUNICATION & COLLABORATION

 ## Sylvester Chisom— Showroom Shine

Deciding to Be Your Own Boss

Sylvester Chisom is an author, inspirational speaker, and co-founder and co-CEO of Showroom Shine Express Detailing (www.showroomshinedetailing.com) in St. Louis, Missouri. Showroom Shine is recognized as an elite source for auto detailing, cleaning cars for government agencies, Fortune 500 companies, and cars that travel around the world. For their outstanding service, Showroom Shine has been featured in *The Wall Street Journal*, *The Huffington Post*, The *Steve Harvey Morning Show*, and more. Its success has also led to Sylvester Chisom and his partner being recognized as one of *Ebony Magazine*'s Top Young Entrepreneurs.

Sylvester Chisom.

Sylvester co-founded Showroom Shine with a water hose and a bucket at the young age of 17 with his friend and business partner, Arthur Shivers. While the two started washing cars as a side business to pick up extra money in high school, it since has grown into a full-fledged business. Initially, Sylvester attended and graduated from college with a degree in biology. However, after college, he and his business partner decided to go into business for themselves. "You can work at a job or you can actually try to see if it's something you can pursue yourself," explained Sylvester.

Delivering Value to Customers

In 2003, Showroom Shine started with very modestly with one location. As a way of attracting customers to their business versus other similar businesses, Sylvester and his team decided to focus on personalizing the experience for customers. They know that customers can choose any car detailing service, but they come to Showroom Shine because of the amazing customer experience. Showroom Shine offers a personalized touch, while focusing on building long-term relationships with their customers and their cars. To help communicate this value to customers, the entire team maintains a high level of customer service as a priority. The company also grew into a full-service detailing business with a small fleet of mobile units, for added customer convenience.

This intense focus on personalization and convenience for customers has paid off. Showroom Shine has continued to grow and expand as word-of-mouth spread. In addition to the growing mobile fleet and an additional three locations in St. Louis, they are building strategic partnerships with parking facilities at airports to expand across the country. Showroom Shine has also been recognized as the best auto detailing company in the nation four years in a row (2008–2011) by The Steve Harvey Hoodie Awards. Showroom Shine is the #1 rated auto detailing company on Angie's List (2005–2013).

Inspiring the Next Generation of Entrepreneurs

With the belief that it is important to always look for opportunities to do more, Sylvester has set out to inspire the next generation of entrepreneurs. He is the author of two books, including the best-selling, *The Young Entrepreneur's Guide to Success 2.0.* Both of his books are being used in school districts all across the country. As the founder of the National Association for the Advancement of Young Entrepreneurs (www.naaye.org), Sylvester has set out to create the largest social network of young entrepreneurs and entrepreneurial thinkers from around the world!

Thinking and Acting Like an Entrepreneur

- What value proposition does Sylvester's business have for customers?
- How does Sylvester's business deliver that value to customers?
- In what ways does Sylvester demonstrate entrepreneurial mindset behaviors of communication and collaboration?

19.2 Effective Sales Techniques

The phrase "selling process" is another way to refer to personal selling. This process is a cluster of activities used to obtain sales and build long-term relationships with customers. Although these activities are used for selling both products and services, the order in which they are performed may vary somewhat, depending on the particular situation.

The main steps in the selling process are:

- Finding and qualifying sales leads
- Preparing for a sales call
- Making the sales call
- Closing a sale and following up

Finding and Qualifying Sales Leads

The selling process starts by finding sales leads. A **sales lead** is a person or company that shares some characteristics with target market. These leads are obtained in several ways:

- **Promotional Responses.** Some sales leads come directly from people who respond to various types of promotion. For example, information is obtained when people fill out surveys, information request cards at trade shows, website forms, or mail-in postcards from magazines.

- **Referrals.** When a person provides contact information for someone else who may be interested in your product or service, it is called a **referral**. Satisfied customers will usually refer other potential customers. In some cases, a fee is paid to the customer if his or her referral turns into a sale.

- **Data Mining.** The process of using a computer program to search large collections of electronic information (databases) and look for patterns or trends is called **data mining**. When applied to the selling process, data mining can be used to sort through huge amounts of material and pick out sales leads based on selected factors.

- **Cold Calls.** When a salesperson contacts someone he or she does not know, and without prior notice, it is called a **cold call**. Another name for cold calling is *canvassing*. Various types of mailing and telephone lists are available for purchase from companies that have made a business out of gathering information, organizing it, and selling it to others. Salespeople use these lists for cold calls.

Salespeople investigate a sales lead's characteristics. If a sales lead has many of the characteristics of the target market, including some key characteristics, the sales lead becomes a **prospect**, or potential customer. Not every sales lead turns into a prospect. Salespeople are responsible for bringing in business and have limited time to spend on bad leads and to evaluate the opportunity cost. This process is called "qualifying the lead."

- **Know Your Product or Service.** The more a salesperson knows about a company's goods and services, the more comfortable (and convincing) they will be to a prospective buyer. As you learned, salespeople are the company's front line and communicate the value of the business to a target customers.

- **Develop an Overall Selling Strategy.** Research your prospect to determine the bestselling approach. Keep in mind the features and benefits of your good or service that will be the most appealing, and anticipate potential questions or concerns that you will need to respond to. Finally, be prepared to change your plan based on the interaction. Don't hold firmly to a plan if the prospect is giving you new information that contradicts what you previously believed about their needs.

Figure 19-2 ▶

Sales Presentations.
Sales presentations often include slides or a product display.

Inferring.
When making a sales presentation to a group, what can you do to make it more effective?

- **Write a Presentation Outline.** Plan what you want to say and what marketing materials you will show. Practice product demonstrations, if relevant, and if you bring an electronic presentation, always have a physical printed copy in case you encounter technical difficulties.

Making a Sales Call

Sales calls are a great personal selling technique, where the salesperson or entrepreneur can reinforce the company's value proposition. Giving a sales presentation does not mean you will take center stage and do all the talking. The most effective presentations allow for plenty of give-and-take between the prospect and the salesperson. Here are some suggestions for making your sales calls more successful:

- **Be on Time.** Being punctual shows that you respect your potential customer and don't want to waste your customer's time. Plan carefully so you aren't late. If, for any reason, you are running late, call. If you are late, make sure to apologize to your customer.

- **Build Rapport.** A word that comes from French, **rapport** (rah-POR) refers to an emotional connection between people, based on feelings of mutual trust and respect. To help build rapport, don't dive immediately into business talk when you arrive at a sales call. Take a little time to discover and talk about other things you may have in common. Sports, family, news events, and vacation plans are just a few possibilities.

- **Ask Questions and Take Notes.** As you talk about the benefits of your product or service, ask the prospect questions. Try not to ask questions that only require a yes or no answer. Ask about things that will help reveal what needs, problems, feelings, and objections the prospect may have. During this process, take notes on key points the prospect makes. This will help you later to remember what is most important to the prospect. Taking notes also shows that you are listening and that you care about what the prospect has to say.

- **Answer Objections.** Often a prospect shows resistance to buying, either in words or by body language. When this happens, it is best to identify with the prospect and then ask for more details. For example, you might say, "I can understand why you feel that way." Then ask for more information, suggest options, and discuss other ways of solving the problem. If you don't know the answer to a question, be honest and say, "I don't know, but I'll find out for you as soon as possible."

- **Ask for a Commitment.** Asking for a commitment is an important part of closing the sale. Often, an indirect approach works well. For example, you might ask, "Now that I've addressed your concerns, is there anything else that might affect your decision to buy?" Or, you might ask about the product quantity, or delivery options. Another way of securing a commitment could be to offer an incentive. For example, you could provide a special discount if an order is placed immediately. In any case, never try to force a sale. If a prospect does not want to buy, it may be that the timing is not right, but it could be in the future.

Closing a Sale and Following Up

Technically, the final closing of a sale occurs after a product or service is delivered or provided, the prospect is satisfied, and the payment is received. So after an order is taken, it is wise to follow up with the new customer to make sure that the entire process met his or her expectations. A happy customer will lead to a good relationship and additional sales.

Following up may also include asking a customer for referrals and written testimonials for use in promotional materials. Often your best sales leads come from existing customers. Routine contact with a ==sales account== (established customer) also helps a salesperson stay aware of possible changes in a customer's needs.

Being successful in sales is much more than a single presentation. It is an entire process that requires research, preparation, building relationships, and a lot of follow-up.

To evaluate the effectiveness of sales activities, business owners usually look at revenue (sales) for a specified time period. This information is tracked on the business's income statement. Many businesses also set sales goals or quotas for their salespeople and measure their effectiveness by the rate at which they convert leads into sales.

Apply Your Knowledge Describe the steps for making a sales call. Thinking back to your Net Jets investigation, what sales techniques could Net Jets employ to increase sales?

CAREER COMPETENCIES

 **Demonstrate Negotiation Skills**

Third graders swapping lunches and world leaders working out the complicated details of a peace treaty both involve negotiation.

Negotiation is a process in which two or more parties reach an agreement or solve a problem through communication.

For a negotiation to succeed, the parties must be willing to adjust their expectations in order to come to an agreement. Here are some tips to practice your negotiation skills:

1. **State your offer firmly.** As the saying goes, "You can't get what you don't ask for."

2. **Explain your position.** Explain and support your position rather than merely stating it. Give clear reasons why you cannot meet the other party's demands immediately, but suggest that your position may change in the future, in part as the result of this negotiation.

3. **Look for common ground.** Making progress on a lesser issue can create momentum or even light the way to a larger resolution.

4. **Be willing to make compromises.** A compromise is when all sides make concessions in order to reach an agreement. In fair negotiations, the trade-offs are roughly equal.

5. **Put the offers in writing.** Written offers makes it easier to compare the terms of each offer in their entirety. Eventually, for negotiations involving significant issues, you'll probably sign a written contract indicating the terms on which you've agreed.

6. **Weigh the long-term and the short-term consequences.** Exactly what do you need to get from this negotiation? Accepting less than what you hoped for in the short-term may produce good will that can assist you over the long-term. Conversely, getting ideal terms today can sometimes mean accepting terms that are not quite so good in the future.

7. **Take time off.** Taking a break can help introduce new ideas or perspectives. Particularly when in a stalemate, taking a step back can help both sides cool down while potentially conceiving new solutions, which may benefit both parties. This could lead to a new solution, one that could be better for everyone. Also, over time, the situation could change and the negotiations could change radically.

Career Skills in Action

Now it's your turn. Suppose you start a smoothie business. Your smoothies sales are off-the-charts because you get the sweetest berries from a local supplier. Yesterday the supplier contacted you to increase his per unit cost by $10/pint. He explains that he has no choice but you insist on meeting to discuss your options. You understand the supplier's position but cannot spend more than $5 extra/pint. He agrees to meet you. Using the tips above, prepare notes for your negotiation (Steps 1–6).

- Prepare a skit with a partner
- Decide who will be the supplier and who will be the entrepreneur
- Create a graphic that outlines what you are looking for and the potential compromises.

Be ready to negotiate in front of the class.

19.3 Pitching Your Business

To raise awareness and funding, entrepreneurs have to describe their businesses to bank loan officers, venture capitalists, or other potential investors. This is called a pitch. Much like a sales call, a pitch includes communicating the value proposition of a business. Investor pitches are usually crafted to persuade someone to buy something, where networking pitches are used to highlight opportunities for potential partners. Entrepreneurs usually memorize these one-minute pitches and are ready to present anywhere, even in an elevator.

This has led to the "elevator pitch" (so named because the pitch has to be succinct enough to be delivered during an elevator ride). In an elevator pitch, an entrepreneur has only 30 seconds. He or she must communicate in fewer than 150 words what the product does and how the consumer will benefit. Venture capitalists may ask entrepreneurs for an elevator pitch to weed out bad ideas immediately.

With micro-blogging websites such as Twitter—in which readers post updates of 140 characters or less—the "twitpitch" is the newest type of elevator pitch. Entrepreneurs post two-sentence business ideas to their accounts, efficiently getting through to time-crunched consultants and venture capitalists.

Whether in an elevator or to panel of investors, all pitches should include the following:

- **Name.** The name of the business
- **Description.** What the business does
- **Problem.** The problem that is solves with data to support the opportunity
- **Customer.** Who is the target consumer for the business
- **Value Proposition.** What are the benefits to the target consumer/customer segment
- **Cost.** How much the product or service costs

Figure 19-3 ▶
Elevator Pitch.

Why are business pitches called elevator pitches?

Applying Concepts.

Think of an idea for a new small business. Can you communicate that idea in 30 seconds?

Once an entrepreneur organizes his or her pitch, the next step is to make it engaging. Investors invest in people not ideas.

- **Attention:** Capture the audience's attention. Remember that you are competing against numerous distractions.
- **Excitement:** Once your audience is paying attention, get them excited about you and your company.
- **Engagement:** Once the audience is excited, help them imagine becoming involved with you and your company.
- **Action:** Get potential investors to spend time with you to learn about your company, your product, and the investment opportunity

Practice makes perfect. You should write your pitch down and present it to numerous people for practice before making a real pitch to an investor. Business pitches present the value a company gives to its target market.

Apply Your Knowledge Imagine you are pitching the concept of Net Jets to an investor. What points would you make in your elevator pitch?

APPLICATION TO BUSINESS PLANNING

Business Pitch

Use what you learned from this chapter about communicating your value proposition to write a one-minute (150-word) elevator pitch. Include the following and be ready to present to your class.

- Name
- Description
- Problem

- Customer
- Value proposition
- Cost

REVIEWING OBJECTIVES

1. Explain the importance of personal selling and understanding customers' needs.

2. List effective sales techniques for communicating a business's value proposition to customers.

3. Identify the purpose and structure of an effective business pitch.

CRITICAL THINKING

1. In developing a sales force, what qualities and characteristics would you recommend a business owner look for in a potential salesperson?

2. What could happen if you fail to follow up with a customer after a sale is made? What advantages might you gain from asking the customer for feedback?

3. What tools could a business owner use to determine the effectiveness of his or her sales force? How important do you think "relationship-building" is to the success of a business's sales activities?

ENTREPRENEURIAL THINKING EXERCISE: COMMUNICATION & COLLABORATION

Think back to your Net Jets investigation; imagine you are a salesperson at Net Jets speaking to a potential customer. What five questions would you ask to evaluate the costumer's needs and close the sale?

EXTENSION ACTIVITIES

Entrepreneurship & Literacy Skills

Complete the following task to demonstrate your understanding of entrepreneurship:

Grades 9–12: Choose a project or service and pretend you are a prospect for this item. Write a detailed customer profile and exchange yours with a partner. Read your partner's customer profile and provide written feedback. Revise your profile based on your partner's feedback and share with your teacher.

20 ATTRACTING AND RETAINING CUSTOMERS

OBJECTIVES

- List the elements of the promotional cycle.
- Describe the components of a Promotional Mix and examples of each.
- Explain the need for maintaining customer relationships.

NFTE Entrepreneurial Mindset Characteristic Focus

☑ Creativity & Innovation

National Entrepreneurship Standards

- **C.11** Describe marketing functions and related activities
- **L.11** Evaluate customer experience
- **L.17** Explain the concept of marketing strategies
- **L.18** Describe the nature of marketing planning
- **L.22** Describe the elements of the promotional mix
- **L.23** Calculate advertising media costs
- **L.24** Select advertising media
- **L.25** Prepare a promotional budget
- **L.26** Develop promotional plan for a business
- **L.32** Evaluate effectiveness of advertising
- **L.42** Establish relationship with client/customer
- **L.43** Determine customer/client needs
- **L.44** Determine customer's buying motives for use in selling

Common Career Technical Core Standards

- **BM-OP.2** Develop and maintain positive customer relationships.
- **CRP.4** Communicate clearly, effectively and with reason.
- **MK.9** Communicate information about products, services, images and/or ideas to achieve a desired outcome.
- **MK.7** Determine and adjust prices to maximize return while maintaining customer perception of value.

National Entrepreneurship Standards: Career Competencies

☑ **D.31** Handle difficult customers/clients

☑ **D.33** Handle customer/client complaints

LESSON VOCABULARY

- 360° marketing
- advertising
- AIDA
- blog
- channel partnerships
- CPM (cost-per-thousand)
- cross promotions
- direct mail
- infomercials
- media
- networking
- newsgroup
- personal selling
- pitch letter
- premium
- press release
- product placement
- promotional campaign
- promotional mix
- public relations (PR)
- publicity
- sales promotion
- social media
- telemarketing
- visual merchandising
- Web banner

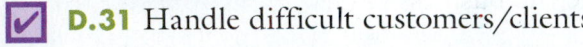

20.1 Promotions: Building Awareness, Making Sales, Keeping Customers

So far in this unit, you have looked at defining a customer segment, determining the needs of that customer segment, and communicating the value of your business to customers. In this chapter, you will look at specific strategies you can implement to attract customers and encourage them to make a purchase. Finding the best strategies that will be effective with your customers requires a great deal of creativity and innovation from the entrepreneurial mindset toolkit.

When you're on a website, do you ever notice the advertisements that pop up? Usually these advertisements are related to the topic you're reading about. For example, if you visit a health website like WebMD, you may find advertisements for Tylenol or other medicines. Why do you think the makers of Tylenol would advertise on a health website? As you learned earlier, it's because the companies share similar target markets and Tylenol uses the website to *promote* its products with advertisements.

Promotion is a type of communication and persuasion that is found throughout our daily lives. It is also one of the Five P's (people, product, place, price, and promotion) in your marketing plan. Businesses use promotions to achieve three main goals: build awareness, inspire customers to purchase, and retain customers. These businesses develop promotional plans where they identify strategies to attract customers. As their goals shift, businesses make adjustments to the plans that align to their overall marketing plans. Similarly, promoting products and services is an ongoing task just like the business plan.

For any business with a new product or service, the first step is to raise awareness. If people don't know about a product or service, they won't buy it. Building awareness is educating potential customers about a business and what it sells. For entrepreneurs, awareness promotions are even more important to differentiate their new business from established brands and competitors. The ultimate goal is to get potential customers to make a purchase.

AIDA is a popular communication model used by companies to plan, create, and manage their promotion to build awareness and get customers to buy products or services. The letters in AIDA stand for the following steps in any type of promotion:

1. **Attention.** The first step when introducing a new product to a market is to grab the attention of potential customers. For example, using a well-known celebrity to introduce a product may cause people to take notice.

2. **Interest.** After you get people's attention, you want to keep it. To hold a person's interest you need to focus your message on the product's features and benefits. Clearly communicate to customers how these specific features and benefits relate to them.

3. **Desire.** What can you do to make your product desirable? One way might be to demonstrate the product, or show how it works. Proving in some way that your product is a bargain is another tactic that may increase a person's desire to buy.

4. **Action.** Don't forget to ask customers to take action, to buy. You may also want to give them a reason why they should act right away. For example, a limited-time offer might motivate consumers to buy. Another important part of this stage is making sure it is easy and convenient for people to buy.

Once you get customers to buy, the next step is to keep them. Most companies rely on repeat sales from loyal customers. Retaining customers means forming relationships and knowing them.

◀ **Figure 20-1**
Sales Promotions.

Communicating a sale can generate awareness, interest, and desire to purchase all at once.

Drawing Conclusions.

Why do businesses have so many sales throughout the year?

Promotions that businesses use to maintain a customer relationship include:

- Rewards programs; e.g., frequent-buyer programs
- Special price offers; e.g., discounts for repeat customers
- Thank you notes or e-mails

Many companies focus on customer service as a retention tool in addition to the ones listed above. How a company relates to their customers is hard for competitors to copy, so this type of promotion can be great competitive advantage. Here are some examples of customer relationship building:

- **Personal Assistance.** Customers like to talk to people to ask questions and provide feedback. Customer service support provides customers with a great experience. People remember these types of experiences and often become repeat customers. For example, when you walk into an electronics store, there is usually a greeter who asks you how he/she can support you. In some businesses, repeat customers get a dedicated customer service experience. So anytime a customer calls he/she can talk to his/her own representative.

- **Automated Services.** While customers like personal touches, sometimes they may need to access information quickly. Many companies, especially online, help customers create profiles so they can log in to access their personal and customized information. The company can offer suggestions based on what the customer buys. One example of this is Netflix. When a customer views a movie, Netflix recommends similar movies and genres. These recommendations support the customer-business relationship.

- **Communities.** Customers like to feel a part of something bigger to share feedback, thoughts, and learn from other's experiences. When a company invests in building these types of communities, it shows customers that they want to hear feedback and develop customer trust. For example, YouTube allows users to post feedback and post their own videos online.

Retaining existing customers is a lot easier and less expensive compared to attracting new customers. Existing customers are also the best promoters and will often help bring in new customers.

Effective planning for promotion is designed to not only get customers to launch the business, but also to continuously attract new customers while retaining current customers.

 **Apply Your Knowledge**   What is the AIDA model and what is it used for? How do you think Zappos attracts new customers? What do they do to retain existing customers?

ENTREPRENEURIAL CASE STUDY: CREATIVITY & INNOVATION

 ## Mark Cuban— Dallas Mavericks

Innovating to Solve Problems

Mark Cuban is an entrepreneur, best-selling author, investor, and owner of the 2011 World Champion Dallas Mavericks (www.markcubancompanies. com). Since his acquisition of the Mavericks in 2000, he has overseen them competing in the NBA Finals for the first time in franchise history in 2006— and becoming NBA World Champions in 2011. In addition to owning the Mavericks, Mark appears as one of ABC's "Sharks" on the hit show *Shark Tank*, and is an investor in an ever-growing portfolio of businesses. Named a winner of the *GQ* "Men of the Year" in 2006 and included in *The New York Times* magazine's "Year in Ideas," Mark has been recognized as among the most influential people in both the cable and sports industries.

Mark Cuban.

Since the age of 12, Mark has been a natural businessman. Selling garbage bags door-to-door, the seed was planted early on for what would eventually become long-term success. After graduating from Indiana University—where he briefly owned the most popular bar in town—Mark moved to Dallas. After a dispute with an employer who wanted him to clean instead of closing an important sale, Mark created MicroSolutions, a computer consulting service.

He went on to later sell MicroSolutions in 1990 to CompuServe. Then, in 1995, Mark and long-time friend Todd Wagner came up with an Internet-based solution to not being able to listen to Hoosiers Basketball games out in Texas. That solution was Broadcast.com—streaming audio over the Internet. In just four short years, Broadcast.com (then Audionet) would be sold to Yahoo for $5.6 billion dollars.

Establishing Relationships with Fans

Mark took the money he earned from the sales of his businesses to buy the Dallas Mavericks in 2000. When Mark bought the Mavericks, they were a struggling team with a winning percentage of 40% in the previous 20 years, with a lukewarm fan response as a result. Mark decided that the key to turning the team around, and making it more appealing to fans, was to turn the team's home games into a total entertainment experience. Despite initial criticism, he added much more to the usual game-day experience options like the Mavericks ManiAACs. Mark became known for his passionate cheering for the team from the sidelines, creating a different relationship between the team owner and the fans. His successful efforts have brought a sense of pride and passion to the fans. Under his leadership, the Mavericks are currently listed as one of Forbes' most valuable franchises in sports.

Continued Innovation

After his success with the Mavericks, Mark has continued to grow his business portfolios in the sports and entertainment industries.

Mark co-owns the Landmark Theater chain, Magnolia Pictures, and Magnolia Home Video along with partner Todd Wagner. He is also the owner and chairman of AXS TV (www.axs.tv), the first TV network in the world to be programmed exclusively in high definition. Mark takes personal responsibility for the programming on the network, creating a unique schedule of innovative and original programs. Through these channels, Mark created the "Ultra VOD" platform, releasing movies to video-on-demand on both cable and satellite up to four weeks prior to their release in theaters. He has also been an investor in startups including Mahalo, JungleCents.com, motionlift.com, Filesanywhere.com, Naked Pizza, and 140Fire.com

Thinking and Acting Like an Entrepreneur

- What personal skills and unique knowledge did Mark use to identify his business opportunities?

- In what ways did Mark attract and keep customers in the Mavericks franchise?

- How does Mark demonstrate the entrepreneurial mindset behaviors of creativity and innovation?

20.2 It's All in the Mix

Not all promotions are the same. There are many forms of promotion to consider when developing your marketing plan. The combination of promotional elements that a business chooses to use is called its **promotional mix**. The elements in a promotional mix are varied, but also interconnected. All of them have common goals: to build a favorable awareness about your product and business, and to influence people to buy your product, come back for more, and tell others about it. The six elements in a promotional mix are:

- **Advertising** is a public, promotional message paid for by an identified sponsor or company.

- **Visual merchandising** is the use of artistic displays to draw customers into a store. It also refers to how products are visually promoted inside a store.

- **Public relations (PR)** consists of activities aimed at creating good will toward a product or company.

- **Publicity** is a form of promotion for which a company does not pay. It is sometimes referred to as "free advertising."

- **Personal selling** is the direct (one-to-one) effort made by a company's sales representatives to get sales and build customer relationships.

- A **sales promotion** is a short-term activity or buying incentive, such as providing coupons or free samples, or conducting product demonstrations. Think of sales promotions as temporary specials used to motivate potential customers.

Each element of the promotional mix has advantages and disadvantages. As you think about how to balance the various elements in your mix, try to visualize how each relates to the others. Look for ways that one type of promotion can be used to backup or support another type. This will help make the most of your promotional efforts.

◀ **Figure 20-2**
Promotional Mix.
To achieve your marketing goals, all forms of promotion should be considered.

Relating Concepts.
What factors determine the makeup of a promotional mix?

Forms of Advertising

The most common form of promotion is advertising. Advertising uses various **media**, or communication channels, to send promotional messages to potential customers. Advertising helps build a brand's image. For example, customers often perceive advertised products and services as being more valid or acceptable than non-advertised items. Advertising can be expensive, so it's important to focus on the types that will best reach your target market. The most common types of advertising are:

- **Print Advertising.** Ads placed in newspapers, magazines, school yearbooks, and trade association directories are all examples of print advertising. **Direct mail** is a form of print advertising, too. Direct mail is one-to-one communication. You can have it delivered specifically to individual customers in your target market. Brochures, print catalogs, fliers, postcards, sales letters, and newsletters are examples of direct mail.

- **Radio and Television.** This type of media has the advantage of reaching large amounts of people. It also has the added benefit of communicating with motion (in TV), and sound. However, it can be very expensive to create the advertisements and purchase the media time. Most radio and television commercials are short—around 15 to 30 seconds. **Infomercials**, usually produced as cable television shows, are product demonstrations that typically last from 30 minutes to an hour.

- **Product Placement.** This is a more subtle type of advertising. In **product placement**, a company pays a fee to have a product displayed during a movie or a television show in a prominent or obvious manner. There is no spoken or written message made about the product. The fact that a famous actor or other well-known person is using the product suggests to viewers that they, too, should buy it. When you see an actor drinking a bottle of Coca Cola® in a television show, that's product placement.

- **Web-based Advertising.** Sending e-mail messages to customers and creating an electronic catalog on a website, are ways of using the Internet to promote your product. Another way to encourage Internet users to go to your company's website is by using an electronic advertisement called a **Web banner**. You pay other companies or organizations to embed your Web banner on their sites. A Web banner includes a clickable link that sends potential customers to your website.

Figure 20-3 ▶
Marketing with Social Media.

More businesses use social media as a low-cost, effective promotional strategy.

Applying Concepts.

How is using social media as a marketing tool different than your personal use?

- **Outdoor Advertising.** This type of advertising includes signs on buses and taxis, billboards (posters) along streets or in subways, and banners or streamers carried by air blimps and airplanes. Outdoor advertisements aren't always print some are digital and on office buildings and are generally big to draw attention to an idea, brand or company.

Visual Merchandising

How you visually present and physically position your products is an important part of promotion. For example, how attractive are the displays in storefront windows? Is there an eye-catching sign outside? Another example of **visual merchandising** is when retailers position selected products at the ends of aisles or near checkout lines to draw customers' attention. Companies that provide services should also consider the visual impact they make. A place of business that looks clean and well-organized sends a more positive message than one with dirty floors and windows. Even the arrangement of the business furniture, and the comfort or pleasantness of a waiting room, can make a difference.

Public Relations and Publicity

Many companies have a public relations (PR) department to help build up and maintain a positive public image. As an alternative, sometimes a PR firm is hired to promote the goals of other businesses. In both cases, PR staff use publicity—unpaid advertising—to attract attention and create interest. Examples of activities and tools used to get publicity include the following:

- **News Articles and Announcements.** The PR staff works to develop good relationships with reporters in the local news media. They send a press release to the media whenever there is anything new or interesting involving their company. A **press release** is a written statement that typically consists of several paragraphs of factual information about a product or business. This information can be used by a reporter to create a printed news article or a feature story. Or, it may become a news report read by radio and television announcers. A cover letter, called a **pitch letter**, is often sent with a press release to introduce it. One or more photos may also be included.

- **Community Events.** Sponsoring an event that promotes a charitable cause can create favorable publicity. For example, a business may plan a dinner, entertainment, or sports event in which all the money from ticket sales goes to a local charity. A small amount of time during the program is sometimes used to provide information about the sponsoring company. Upcoming community events are also excellent reasons to send press releases.

Figure 20-4 ▶
Press Release.

When writing a press release, be sure to answer these questions: Who? What? When? Where? Why?

Analyzing Information.

Using this press release, identify the answers to the five questions.

FOR IMMEDIATE RELEASE
May 15, 20--
Contact: Maria Gonzales (555) 123-4567

Local High School Students to Teach Marketing Workshop for Community Teens

Anytown, NY — Wayne High School students Amy Chang, Tom O'Connor, and Brian Jones will be conducting a 5-day workshop for Anytown teenagers who want to learn how to market their own business.

The workshop will be held at the town hall June 16 to 20, from 7:00 to 9:00 PM. The workshop fee of $25 per person will include educational handouts. Participants will apply newly-learned information in small-group activities.

According to Mrs. Anita Andretti, a teacher at Wayne High School, "These students want the opportunity to share some of what they learned in the Entrepreneurship course last semester. They feel it's important to contribute to the community."

For more information, please contact Maria Gonzales at (555) 123-4567.

- **Contests.** Contests help create excitement about your product or business by offering prizes to winners. They also provide opportunities to learn more about customers, or to get their feedback. For example, ask customers who visit your store to drop a business card into a box for a contest drawing. Or enter people into a contest after they complete a short survey. Just like community events, contests provide another opportunity to send a press release.

Personal Selling and Sales Promotion

As mentioned earlier, sales staff meets and talks with customers person-to-person. This may occur on the phone, in the store, or at trade shows and conferences. Sometimes the sales staff visits the places where customers work or do business. For example, a textbook salesperson may visit teachers at their schools, or a medical supplies salesperson may visit doctors' offices and medical clinics.

When salespeople meet with customers they routinely leave a business card. They may also provide free samples of the company's product, or give them a **premium**. A premium is a "give-away" item or free gift that usually has the company's name, address, and telephone number printed on it. T-shirts, pens, note pads, coffee cups, and calendars are all examples of premiums.

Telemarketing, promoting or selling products or services one-to-one over the telephone, is another type of sales promotion. Telemarketing can be used two different ways. Sales staff can talk directly with potential customers. Or, a recorded sales message can be played over the telephone using an automated dialing system. Care must be taken when using telemarketing to avoid irritating potential customers. Calls made too frequently to the same numbers, or calling at the wrong times (such as dinner time), can annoy people.

The sales staff also uses a technique called **networking** to find new customers and promote products. Networking is a process of meeting new people though current friends and business contacts. People you know refer you to people they know. In turn, these new people introduce you to even more contacts. You can also meet new contacts at networking events. These are gatherings used by business people to meet and socialize with other entrepreneurs in their local area.

A form of electronic networking can be accomplished by using a newsgroup. A **newsgroup** is an online message board where people post information about a particular topic. These messages form an ongoing discussion. Although newsgroups are not used for advertising, they do help you meet new people and gain insights from potential customers.

Social Media

Today, entrepreneurs and big businesses are using social media to spread the word about their businesses. **Social media**, sometimes called viral media, uses community-based websites to spread an idea about a product. The goal is to literally get people talking about a product or service to create a buzz that will influence family and friends to purchase. What's different about social media is that customers can participate actively and provide feedback to business owners.

Entrepreneurs use social media because it is relatively inexpensive and reaches many users through their existing customers. When you think of social media, imagine a network or web of information. Millions of people make buying decisions based on social media. For example, if you "Like" a post on Facebook, your friends are likely to click on the link, too. Other popular social media sites are Instagram, Pinterest, Twitter, and YouTube.

Another form of social media is **blogs**. The Merriam-Webster dictionary defines a blog as a type of website that contains information that is updated regularly. It is short for "weblog," as in an online log. Blogs are great social media tools that promote ideas, get comments, and share information.

So how can one company do all this and be effective? A newer approach in marketing is called 360° marketing. This approach communicates with your prospects and customers from all directions; it blends low-tech and high-tech methods to deliver your message to customers in as many ways as possible. In some respects, 360° marketing can be a cost-effective method of marketing your product. Its goal is to take advantage of every means possible to put your message in front of prospects and customers.

A 360° marketing mix might include a company website, e-mails to existing customers, texts, direct-mail postcards and catalogs, instant messaging, and telephone calls to customers alerting them to new promotions. It might mean becoming involved with the local community for networking possibilities and referrals. It could involve face-to-face meetings with prospects and customers in nonbusiness settings. Entrepreneurs who practice this sort of marketing take networking seriously. They join clubs, organizations, and online social networks. They offer free consultations and demonstrations. An entrepreneur using 360° marketing might publish an online newsletter, write a blog, create a podcast, or host an online conference related to the company's product.

An entrepreneur does not need to use every element of the promotional mix, but should select ones that align with his/her business and marketing goals. The elements should reinforce the other promotional and marketing efforts.

Apply Your Knowledge What is 360° marketing and how does it relate to the promotional mix? Think back to your investigation of Zappos. What types of promotional strategies would be best for an online business?

CAREER COMPETENCIES

 ### Handle with Care: Dealing with a Difficult Customer

Customer relationships are key to the success of any business. There's the old adage that says, "The customer is always right." It's inevitable that one day you will face an unhappy or difficult customer. Difficult customers can be stubborn and at times just be plain rude.

Believe it or not you can actually change that customer's experience with how you handle him/her.

Here are some tips to handling a difficult customer:

1. **Stay calm.** If the customer is agitated, don't get upset or defensive. Instead try to calm the customer by speaking in a normal tone. Ask the customer to explain what the issue is from his/her perspective.

2. **Listen.** Don't interrupt when the customer is talking, even if you are right. Getting defensive could get the customer more upset.

3. **Confirm the concern.** Once you've heard the concern, confirm it by repeating it. For example, "I think you're concerned because…."

4. **Put yourself in the customer's shoes.** Once you understand their concern, think about how you would feel in the customer's position. Explain that you understand his/her feelings.

5. **Suggest a solution.** If you have a solution, present it politely. If you don't, ask the customer for his/her thoughts. By asking an opinion, you show you care about what he/she wants.

6. **Do something.** Once you decide on a solution, do something immediately. Explain the steps you're going to take and give a clear timeline.

7. **Follow up.** Once you've worked on the solution, follow up with the customer to make sure he/she is satisfied. This is an important step because you may think the concern is resolved but your customer may not or may need additional guidance.

8. **Learn from the experience.** Use the interaction to learn about customer needs and wants. You should also evaluate if the concern was something you can fix in the future. Get to the root of the concern.

Career Skills in Action

Now it's your turn. Imagine you are a baker. You have a large order from a customer and accidently write down the wrong number of cupcakes she needs. She needed 400 and you only made 200. She is very angry at your bakery. She demands you make 200 more.

- Write down the steps you would take to calm your difficult customer.
- Select a partner and create a skit to present to your class.

20.3 What's the Plan?

A promotional plan for a new business must take into consideration three stages of a business startup:

1. What promotions are needed *before* the business is opened?
2. What promotional adjustments need to be made when the new business is launched?
3. What ongoing promotional strategies are needed?

Creating Campaign Strategies

Breaking down each stage of your promotional plan into one or more campaigns will help focus your efforts. A **promotional campaign** is a group of specific promotional activities built around a particular theme or goal. Each campaign provides descriptions of the media to be used, dates, quantities, costs, and other details. For example, in Stage 1, your campaign may focus on:

- Establishing a favorable business image
- Educating your target market about the features and benefits of coming products
- Creating an awareness of where and when you will be opening

At Stage 2, your campaign may include announcements that you are now open for business. Stage 2 also usually includes sales promotions to get people to try a product or service.

As your customer base increases, your Stage 3, or ongoing plan, should add strategies for keeping current customers loyal.

Keep in mind that your ongoing plan may need to vary based on seasons or cycles in your business industry. You may also need to make adjustments along the way due to changes in the target market, business environment, and competition.

Measuring Promotion Effectiveness

In your promotional plan, include ways to track responses that result from specific types of promotion. Setting up some type of computerized database will make it easier to record and analyze data. This information will help you decide what forms of promotion to use in the future. Here are some examples of tracking strategies:

- Ask customers where they first heard about your business.
- Create an ad with a coupon or other clip-out feature. Include an individual code on each otherwise identical ad that is placed in different print media sources. When customers bring or send in the clip-out to your business, you can identify which advertising source provided the most response.
- Compare sales results with the time and place that a particular sales promotion was offered. See if you can detect any correlations between the two.
- Pretest potential advertisements before finalizing and submitting them to the media. For example, ask focus groups made up of your target market to view several versions of an advertisement. Their reactions and feedback can help decide which ad would be most effective.

Budgeting for Promotion

Your budget for promotion will determined by four factors:

- Your business industry
- The strength of your competition
- Which media best reaches your target audience
- The funds you have available

After you have conducted a number of promotional campaigns, you will have historical data available to help estimate costs. In the meantime, if you're starting a new business, you'll need to do some research. Following are a few strategies you can use:

- Contact sales managers at radio and television stations, newspapers, and magazines to request a list of their rates. As an alternative, you can pay a subscription fee to access databases at SRDS® (Standard Rate and Data Service) Media Solutions® (www.srds.com).

- When you buy a TV or radio spot, you are purchasing the ability to reach the number of people who are watching or listening at that specific time. The Nielsen Company (www.nielsenmedia.com) and Arbitron, Inc. (www.arbitron.com) publish guides that provide audience delivery estimates for television and radio. Ask your media salesperson to help you calculate the **CPM (cost per thousand)** using these guides. The CPM is the amount it will cost you to reach 1,000 potential customers with a particular advertising type and time slot.

- Factor in public relations and publicity costs. For example, if you plan to stage a community event, you may need to hire a catering service or other vendor.

- Research companies that produce sales promotion items and compare their prices. InkHead Promotional Products (www. inkhead.com), Superior™ Promos (www.superiorpromos.com), and Pinnacle Promotions (www.pinnaclepromotions.com) are just a few examples.

- Advertising agencies can help you create, plan, and manage advertising and other promotional activities. If you are planning to hire such an agency, you will also need to include its fees in your budget.

Consider Low-Cost Promotion Strategies

If your promotional budget is low, following are some potential ways to keep costs down:

- **Cross Promotional Partnership.** Many businesses might agree on **cross promoting** their business with others. For example, a kid's clothing store might offer a discount for shoppers at a nearby kid's hair salon. Or, two Web-based businesses might include links/advertisements on each others' pages.

- **Channel Partnerships.** A **channel partnership** involves partnering with another manufacturer or retailer who agrees to sell your product. This might be selling your organic cookies through a local cafe. This allows you to get your product in front of customers you wouldn't reach through your sales techniques.

Figure 20-5 ▶
Outline Your Budget.
Calculating an entire budget helps to create a feasible promotional pan for the business.

Drawing Conclusions.
Why is it important to set a limit on how much you will spend each month on promotions?

- **Testimonials and Endorsements.** If customers, news sources, or organizations praise your business for its products or services, ask if you can quote them in brochures or catalogs, or on your website. Even a membership in a trade organization, or in your local Better Business Bureau, is a type of backing that you can mention in promotional materials. You can also use membership logos on business stationery.

After collecting all your research data, make a list of priorities. Outline a budget that includes the items at the top of your priority list. But keep in mind that your budget will probably need to be revisited as you attract more customers and make more sales.

The right promotional plan means balancing your business and marketing goals, your potential customers and cost. A simple way to organize your promotional plan is in a chart like the one below.

Awareness	Purchase	Retention
Current & Short Term (1 month -6 months)		
What promotional mix elements will you use to get consumers to know you exist?	What promotional mix elements will you use to motivate people to buy your product/service?	What promotional elements will you use to build a long term relationship and get them to return?
Long Term (6 months-1 year)		
[Fill in your answer here]	[Fill in your answer here]	[Fill in your answer here]
Monthly cost, by phase:		$0.00
Awareness	Purchase	Retention

At the top are the goals for the business with timeline. In general, promotional strategies should be revisited every six months. How much you spend should link to your business goals. For example, if a t-shirt company just launched, they may want to spend more money on advertising to raise awareness about their brand. In this case the company should spend more promotional dollars on raising awareness over retention activities.

Apply Your Knowledge   Why is a promotional plan important for a company? In your opinion does Zappos have better promotions for new customers or existing ones? Describe the promotions and explain.

APPLICATION TO BUSINESS PLANNING

Promotional Plan

Use what you learned in this chapter about promotional strategies and planning to create a promotional plan. Use data to support your work. Your promotional plan should include the following:

- Promotional elements you will use. (Be specific, e.g., outdoor advertising-billboard)
- Categorize your element by purpose: awareness, purchase, or retention
- Costs associated with the strategies you selected
- Strategies for evaluating the effectiveness of individual promotional campaigns

20 ASSESSMENT

REVIEWING OBJECTIVES

1. List the elements of the promotional cycle (attention, purchase, retention).

2. List the elements of a promotional mix and examples of each.

3. Explain the need for maintaining customer relationships.

CRITICAL THINKING

Watch a popular recent movie or a successful sitcom. As you watch, keep a list of any product placement promotion that was used in the movie/show. Afterward, write a paragraph about how the target market for the product placement tied to the audience.

ENTREPRENEURIAL THINKING EXERCISE: CREATIVITY & INNOVATION

Think back to your investigation of Nick Swinmurn and Zappos. Imagine that you were hired to put together a promotional plan for the shoe store that initially lost his business. What could you have done to make sure that Nick did not leave the store empty handed and disappointed? Are there any strategies that Zappos use that the shoe store at the mall could have used?

EXTENSION ACTIVITIES

Entrepreneurship & Literacy Skills

Complete the following task to demonstrate your understanding of entrepreneurship:

1. **Grades 9–10:** As you learned in this chapter, promotions can be used to attract new customers, influence them to purchase, and retain existing customers. Write a short essay that compares and contrasts the promotional strategies you would use to attract new customers versus promotions to retain existing customers. Be sure to include data and evidence from this chapter to support your argument.

2. **Grades 11–12:** As you learned in this chapter, promotions can be used to attract new customers, influence them to purchase, and retain existing customers. Write a short essay that compares and contrasts the promotional strategies you would use to attract new customers versus promotions to retain existing customers. Be sure to include data and evidence from this chapter to support your argument. Also, include ways that you could test to make sure that those strategies are actually better suited for each group.

UNIT 4 REVIEW & ASSESSMENT

Unit 4: Delivering Value to a Customer

CHAPTER SUMMARY

16. Identifying a Target Market

Identifying a target market, rather than selling to a mass market, is usually the best approach for small businesses. Selling to a mass market can help entrepreneurs narrow their focus more effectively, while saving money and time in the process. Entrepreneurs do a great deal of research to determine how to split their target market into segments, which is a grouping of customers by a specific trait or commonalty. Some ways to split customers into market segments include a niche market, segmented, diversified, and multi-sided. Exploring market segments such as demographics, geographics, and psychographics can help you create a customer profile. This profile will provide a detailed description of your target market's characteristics.

17. Understanding the Needs of a Customer Segment

Once you have determined a market segment, it is important to understand what those customers value. Value is subjective and different people value different things. Creating a value proposition for your customer segments allows the entrepreneur to focus on what the customer wants to get out of the business. As part of their value proposition, entrepreneurs should focus on features and the benefits they offer customers. The features of a product or service are what it does and how it appears to the senses (sight, sound, taste, smell, and touch). Features are factual statements about the product or service. Benefits include the value the customer gets out of purchasing the product. Benefits might include convenience, accessibility or customization. The benefits that customers get out of purchasing the features should be the foundation of the value proposition.

18. Delivering Value to a Customer Segment

All interactions with a customer in a target market segment should remind the customer of the value they place on the business. To do this, entrepreneurs put together a marketing plan. A marketing plan is a detailed guide that includes marketing goals and strategies for meeting those goals. There are five main marketing strategy areas, called the Five P's: people, product, place, price, and promotion. How a company chooses to combine these elements defines the marketing mix. Your target market and employees make up the people element. To determine place strategies, you should decide what distribution channels to use, where and when you will sell your products, and how you will transport and store them. Developing price strategies involves identifying objectives, selecting a basic price strategy (demand-based, competition-based, or cost-based), and making adjustments.

19. Communicating Value to Customers

Personal selling is a promotional technique used by a company's sales force to help build customer relationships, address customer questions and objections, and reach business customers more effectively. Some of the characteristics of successful salespeople include having a positive attitude, being a good listener, being persistent, working hard, and being truthful and consistent. You start the selling process by finding and qualifying sales leads through promotional responses, referrals, data mining, and cold calls. Next, you prepare for a sales call, which includes setting up an appointment, learning about the prospect, knowing your product or service, developing an overall selling strategy, and writing a presentation outline. When meeting with the prospect, you try to build rapport, ask questions, take notes, answer objections,

and ask for a commitment. The last steps in the selling process are the closing of the sale and following up with the sales account. You do sales planning as you develop your marketing plan. To raise awareness and funding, entrepreneurs have to learn to pitch their businesses and its value proposition to bank loan officers, venture capitalists, or other potential investors.

20. Attracting and Keeping Customers

Building a product image involves attracting new customers and keeping current ones loyal. You use promotion to build a favorable awareness about your product and influence people to buy it. A communication model for planning, creating, and managing promotion is abbreviated as AIDA: attention, interest, desire, and action. The many forms of promotion that make up a company's promotional mix can include advertising, visual merchandising, public relations (PR), publicity, personal selling, and sales promotions. When developing a promotional plan, you should consider what promotions you will need before opening a new business, when it is first opened, and as ongoing strategies. It's also important to include methods for measuring promotion effectiveness in your plan.

UNIT 4 REVIEW & ASSESSMENT

UNIT 4 VOCABULARY

360° marketing

accessibility

advertising

AIDA

benefits

blog

brand

brand mark

bundling

business pitch

business-to-business (B2B) companies

business-to-consumer (B2C) companies

buying patterns

channel partnerships

cold call

competition-based pricing

convenience

cost-based pricing

CPM (cost-per-thousand)

cross-promotions

customer profile

customization

data mining

demand-based pricing networking

demographics

direct mail

diversified market segment

elevator pitch

exclusive distribution

features

geographics

infomercials

intensive distribution

markdown price

market segments

marketing

marketing mix

marketing plan

markup price

mass market

media

mind share

multi-sided market segment

networking

networking newsgroup

newsgroup

niche market

objections

personal selling

pitch letter

premium

press release

product mix

product placement

product positioning

promotion

promotional campaign

promotional mix

prospect

psychographics

public relations (PR)

publicity

rapport

referral

sales account

sales call

sales force

sales lead

sales promotion

segmented market segment

selective distribution

social media

target market

telemarketing

value

value proposition

visual merchandising

Web banner

CHECK YOUR UNDERSTANDING

Choose the letter that best answers the question or completes the statement.

1. Psychographics refers to such things as
   a. objective social and economic facts about customers
   b. where customers live or where businesses are located
   c. attitudes, opinions, beliefs, interests, personalities, lifestyles
   d. none of the above

2. Which of the following is not considered a one-to-one promotional strategy?
   a. telemarketing
   b. direct mail
   c. magazine advertisements
   d. personal selling

3. Which of the following is not considered a product feature?
   a. quiet
   b. colorful
   c. soft
   d. fun

4. The combination of products a business sells is called a
   a. value proposition
   b. brand mark
   c. bundle
   d. product mix

5. A group of specific promotional activities built around a particular theme or goal is called a
   a. promotional campaign
   b. community event
   c. contest
   d. none of the above

6. Combining the price of several different items into one price is called
   a. a package
   b. a flat rate
   c. a unit rate
   d. bundling

7. What is the term used when two companies share advertising costs?
   a. co-op advertising
   b. trade-out advertising
   c. combination advertising
   d. dual advertising

8. The four functions of a small business are
   a. advertising, promotions, public relations, and sales
   b. marketing, operations, human resources, and finance
   c. research, development, marketing, and sales
   d. recordkeeping, accounting, auditing, and finance

9. Which of the following is the least effective price strategy?

   a. Charge a slightly higher price than the competition when your product has more benefits.

   b. Set a high price when introducing a new, unique product into the market.

   c. After market share is gained, lower prices to improve profits.

   d. Lower prices to increase sales volume.

10. Which of the following is not a term related to radio or television advertising?

   a. trade-out

   b. premium

   c. infomercial

   d. CPM

11. The type of distribution that gives a retailer the sole right to sell a product is called

   a. intensive

   b. selective

   c. exclusive

   d. restrictive

12. The approach that gives you the most control over the selling process is

   a. external selling

   b. direct selling

   c. internal selling

   d. none of the above

13. A common term used to identify people who are directly involved in the selling process is

   a. sales callers

   b. sales force

   c. selling machine

   d. none of the above

14. All of the following are examples of sales support positions except

   a. trainers who teach and coach salespeople

   b. office assistants to salespeople

   c. retail clerks

   d. support people who perform follow-up after the sale

15. The most successful salespeople

   a. tell customers what they want to hear

   b. know how to listen and ask questions

   c. don't have to make many sales calls

   d. push until the prospect finally says, "yes"

16. A sale is closed when

   a. the salesperson asks for a commitment

   b. the product or service is delivered

   c. an order is placed

   d. the customer is satisfi ed and payment is made

BUSINESS COMMUNICATION

1. Design and draw a brand mark for a real or imaginary product, service, or company. Then develop a short presentation explaining why you created this design.

2. Work in a group of four. Each member should research the advantages and disadvantages of a different type of advertisement (such as newspapers, magazines, television, radio, Web banners, and so on). Together, create a chart on poster board that summarizes your combined research results.

3. Working with a partner, research techniques for improving active listening skills. Practice these skills with each other, with one person taking the role of speaker and the other the role of listener. For three to five minutes, the speaker should talk about a topic such as "What I want to do with my life" or "What I most enjoy doing." Afterward, the speaker should give feedback to the listener on the listening skills demonstrated. Then switch roles and repeat the process.

4. Research design tips to create effective PowerPoint slides. Create a slide show that demonstrates examples of good and bad design.

5. Research characteristics that help make a speaker successful. Then, listen to two talks by different speakers (on tape, television, or in person). Take notes on how well you think each speaker communicates. Afterward, make a list of things you think each speaker could do to improve.

BUSINESS MATH

1. Suppose you are calculating financial estimates for a new business. Based on research available to you, assume that the total sales your target market spends for your type of product is $500,000 per year. What annual sales amount will your company earn if it gains a 15% market share in its first year of business?

2. Suppose the sales tax rate in your state is 4.75%. What is the sales tax amount on a $155.02 purchase? A $2,549.99 purchase?

UNIT 4
REVIEW & ASSESSMENT

BUSINESS ETHICS

1. Work in groups of four. Research unethical advertising practices. Write a short presentation about these practices and how to avoid them. Develop ads that demonstrate these unethical practices. Ads can be on posters or magazine size. You can also create unethical television or radio ads that you would act out for the class. If your school has the capability, you could develop filmed or taped examples of unethical television or radio ads.

2. Write an essay on the topic of "How Lying Impacts the Selling Process." Explore reasons that salespeople who lie increase customers' resistance to buying rather than lowering it. Then work with a group to act out a scene in which a salesperson lies in the selling process. Finally, with the same group, act out the same scene, but this time show a salesperson acting ethically, without lying. Try to have the salesperson demonstrate all six characteristics of successful salespeople.

BUSINESS IN YOUR COMMUNITY

1. Working in a group, brainstorm an idea for a fundraising event at your school to benefit a local charity. Next, make a list of specific ways you may be able to get publicity for your event. What media resources should you contact? What local organizations might be willing to help spread the word? Then write a press release about your upcoming event.

2. Interview someone who works at a local advertising agency, or an individual who designs advertisements for a living. Find out what's involved in running their businesses and how they got started in advertising. Also, ask about the creative processes they use to produce actual advertisements. Then, develop a short presentation describing what you learned.

3. Attend a sales demonstration or presentation in your local community. What selling techniques were used? From a prospect's perspective, what do you think could have been done to make the demonstration more effective?

4. Interview a salesperson in your community. Find out what the salesperson likes best and least about the work. Also, ask about the preparation for a sales call or other interaction with potential customers.

INFORMATION TECHNOLOGY

Website Branding

Coca-Cola bottles, McDonald's Golden Arches, and the Nike "Swoosh" are ways companies have used to identify or brand their products. You know instantly which company it is and what it sells. Branding is a marketing strategy used to create an emotional attachment to a product or service. When it comes to website branding, Google is at the top! To "Google" has become part of our language. Everyone immediately knows that Google provides a way to find information online—it is a **Web search engine**. Google's name is one part of its branding strategy. Its logo is another:

Google

Names and logos as well as colors and **typefaces**—the design of printed characters (fonts)—are all elements in branding a company. Branding is important for websites, as for other businesses; each must create a unique presence online.

Domain Name Branding

Google can be found at www.google.com. Usually, a website's name is the same as its Web address. If the site's name and Web address are different, website branding is more difficult. So users can find them easily, businesses want to have the same Web address and site name. **Domain name registration** provides a way to reserve a Web address. The company then uses this address in all marketing materials and as an e-mail address for the business. If the website is www.goodstuff.com, for example, e-mail addresses for the business might be joe@goodstuff.com, jane@goodstuff.com, and so on. Web hosts—companies that rent out space online—can often set up both the website and e-mail accounts, with a series of e-mail addresses, all listed at the same location.

Logos and Slogans

Creating a website logo is an extremely important part of branding. People hire professional graphic designers to design an eye-catching logo. Logos need to be easy to read and distinct from logos that already exist online. A website's logo says a lot about the site—a toy store will have a different style of logo from that of a law office. A **website slogan** is a short phrase that describes what a company does. It, too, is an element of a company's brand. For example, the website eHow.com, which lists a series of how-to articles, has the slogan, "How to Do Just About Everything." The slogan appears just below the website's logo. A slogan becomes a **catch phrase**, a phrase that is repeated so often that people use it without knowing its original context. Some with which you might be familiar are "We bring good things to life." (GE) and "Snap™, Crackle™, and Pop™" (Rice Krispies).

Design Repetition

Design elements, such as the site logo, typeface, color, any unique graphics, and the company's slogan, should be repeated throughout the website. Consistency—repeating the same thing—is an important element of branding and helps consumers recall the company, product, or service easily. Generally, businesses use the same logo and slogan in all their materials, from the website to business cards, letterheads, printed brochures, and Web and TV advertisements. Another good place to put the company's logo and slogan is at the close of your e-mails, just after the signature. It's another opportunity to reinforce your branding.

Tech Vocabulary

catch phrase

domain name registration

typeface

Web search engine

website slogan

Check Yourself

1. Why is branding important?

2. What elements are included in branding?

3. What is a website slogan?

4. Why is brand repetition important?

What Do You Think?

Comparing/Contrasting. Research five companies that you like. Do they have logos and website slogans?

CASE STUDY

Delivering Value to a Customer

MARKETING & SELLING

When Eva started her business, she built a marketing plan and projected her first year's sales. Then the hard work began! She actually had to go out and sell her services—and, in the first three months, things didn't quite work out as she had planned.

A Recipe for Success?

Eva's initial concept was to have five clients. She planned to cook one day during the week for each customer. She figured it would take her about six hours per day to make five family-style dinners that the customer could reheat later. She had included all of this in her business plan.

Eva thought she had done everything right. For instance, she thought about the Five P's when creating her marketing mix:

1. **People.** Eva believed that her primary target market were busy professionals who didn't have time to cook dinner, but still wanted a healthy, affordable evening meal.

2. **Product.** Eva's Edibles planned to sell family-style dinners that clients could heat up. Eva developed a large selection of high-quality menus from which customers could choose. She adapted them so she could increase the quantity based on the number of people in her client's family. Eva made everything from scratch. Nothing came out of a can or box. And the food was delicious!

3. **Place (and Distribution).** Eva planned to cook in her clients' kitchens. Eventually she hoped she could rent a shared-space commercial kitchen.

4. **Price.** Eva planned to charge her customers $325 for five dinners. Based on her research, she thought her pricing was about right, and lower than that of many competitors. Her fee included the cost of ingredients, shopping, preparation, cooking, storage, and kitchen clean-up. She would consult with her clients to make sure they were happy with her menu choices. And she would focus on healthy food preparation using organic ingredients.

5. **Promotion.** Eva emphasized the convenience of her service. Her customers didn't have to cook allow them more time with family and friends and still provide the convenience and nutrition of home-cooked meals. Eva prepared a small but informative and colorful brochure. She also ordered business cards.

Then Eva began contacting satisfied customers of her event-planning business. She also contacted anyone recommended by her parents, other family members, or friends. She selectively mailed her brochure with a cover letter to local professionals, using a mailing list she purchased.

Eva planned to meet with potential clients to discuss her services. She figured that she would certainly have her five clients within one month. She even dreamed that there would be a waiting list.

Then reality set in.

Couples didn't seem to be that interested in her service. The biggest interest came from two-income families that had two or more children. And the kids wanted very different meals from those of their parents. This increased the amount of time cooking. She also didn't have many kid-friendly meal choices.

This wasn't at all what Eva was expecting. And it was taking her much longer to find clients than she had planned.

After three months, Eva knew she had to change her company's direction. She began marketing more specifically to double-income families with children. She changed her brochure and emphasized that she could prepare kid-friendly meals as well as "grown-up" food. The new approach seemed to work well and she had her first three clients.

Once she had satisfied customers, Eva asked them for referrals and recommendation letters. She also began to use other promotional methods to showcase her meals. This included giving out samples of her food at shopping malls, cultural fairs, and other family-oriented locations. By her fourth month, she had five clients and one on a waiting list.

What Would You Have Done?

1. **Comparing/Contrasting.** Eva discovered that she had misjudged her target market. What would you have done if this had happened to you?

2. **Predicting.** What other types of promotion might Eva have used once she had identified her appropriate target market?

UNIT 5

BIG IDEA: BUSINESS MODEL

21

CHANNELS OF DISTRIBUTION

"How do I get my product or service to customers?"

APPLICATION TO BUSINESS PLANNING:

☑ Distribution Channel

OBJECTIVES

- Provide characteristics and examples for each of the broad categories of businesses.
- Describe the progression of goods through distribution channels.
- List distribution considerations for delivering products or services to customers.

NFTE Entrepreneurial Mindset Characteristic Focus

☑ Opportunity Recognition

National Entrepreneurship Standards

- **C.03** Explain types of businesses
- **E.17** Explain the nature of e-commerce
- **E.18** Describe the impact of the Internet on business
- **F.01** Distinguish between economic goods and services
- **F.02** Explain the factors of production
- **F.08** Describe the concept of price
- **L.17** Explain the concept of marketing strategies
- **L.56** Analyze technology for use in the sales function
- **L.57** Manage online sales process
- **M.11** Select distribution channels
- **M.12** Develop and implement order-fulfillment processes

Common Career Technical Core Standards

- **BM-MGT.2** Access, evaluate and disseminate information for business decision making.
- **BM-MGT.4** Employ and manage techniques, strategies and systems to enhance business relationships.
- **BM-MGT.6** Plan, monitor and manage day-to-day business activities to sustain continued business functioning.
- **BM-MGT.7** Plan, organize and manage an organization/ department to achieve business goals.

LESSON VOCABULARY

- business model
- direct channel
- distribution chain
- distribution channel
- distribution management
- free on board
- indirect channel
- intermediary
- logistics
- manufacturer
- manufacturing business
- markup
- reseller's permit
- retailers
- retailing businesses
- service businesses
- trade businesses
- wholesaler
- wholesaling businesses

- **CRP.7** Employ valid and reliable research strategies.
- **MK.6** Select, monitor and manage sales and distribution channels.

National Entrepreneurship Standards: Career Competencies

 D. 25 Foster positive working relationships

ENTREPRENEURIAL INVESTIGATION
Not a Mom-and-Pop Store

What is the first image that comes to mind when you think of a small business? Does your image include a small storefront that the owner rents to sell products? Believe it or not, the use of technology in running businesses has made this setup less common. Websites like Etsy (www.etsy.com) allow anyone to sell products they created through the website, which is much cheaper and easier than owning a storefront. In fact, a 2013 study showed that 74% of Etsy users consider themselves a "small business owner."

Do some research on Etsy (and/or other e-commerce platforms that enable individuals or small businesses to sell directly to consumers) and reflect on the following questions:

- Why would it be easier to sell products through a website like Etsy versus having a store?
- What hidden costs other than rent go into having a storefront?
- As a customer, would you rather purchase something from a brick-and-mortar store, or an online store?

Be prepared to share your findings with your peers and teacher.

21.1 What Type of Business Do I Have?

Business Model Goals

In this unit of the business model validation process, you will be looking at how you will structure the actual business itself so that you will know how feasible your business would be. This is sometimes called the <mark>business model</mark> and includes looking at the details of how your business will operate. Figuring out your business model requires answering very important questions, such as: How will you get your product into the hands of your customers? How can you ensure that your product will be available to customers where and when they want it? Part of thinking like an entrepreneur is figuring out the opportunity that comes with a specific business model. In this chapter, you will look at <mark>distribution channels</mark>, which are the various ways through which a product can reach a customer.

Types of Businesses

Before you can plan the specifics on how your product gets to your potential customers, you need to understand what type of business you have. There are many different types of businesses. In general, businesses are divided into four broad categories, depending on their primary function and the kinds of products they sell.

Manufacturing Businesses

Manufacturing businesses (or **manufacturers**) are businesses that convert materials into goods and then sell those goods to others. Manufactured goods typically fall into two categories: industrial goods and consumer goods. Industrial goods are sold to other manufacturing businesses. Examples include metal and plastic parts, lumber, and heavy machinery. Consumer goods are goods that are sold to consumers.

Small manufacturing businesses that produce consumer goods sometimes sell directly to consumers. For example, small entrepreneurs making baked goods, silk-screened t-shirts, or jewelry often sell their products directly to consumers. Large manufacturing businesses that produce consumer goods may not sell directly to consumers. They may sell to wholesaling businesses. For example, Horween Leather Company is a leather manufacturer that sells leather directly to Wilson Sporting Goods so that they can make footballs and basketballs.

Wholesaling Businesses

Wholesaling businesses (or **wholesalers**) are businesses that buy goods in very large batches, typically from manufacturers, and resell the goods in smaller batches to customers other than final buyers. Wholesalers are also known as middlemen, go-betweens, distributors, or intermediaries, because they provide a link between manufacturers and businesses that sell goods to the final buyers. Wholesalers do not generally sell directly to consumers, but to retailing businesses. For example, an industrial goods manufacturer would produce plastic wheels, which it would then sell to a toy car company. The toy company would then install these wheels on its toy cars that they would sell to customers.

Retailing Businesses

Retailing businesses (or **retailers**) are businesses that buy goods, often from wholesalers, and resell the goods in small quantities directly to consumers, who are the final buyers. Retailing businesses are stores, supermarkets, shops, and boutiques. They sell groceries, clothing, shoes, household goods, computers, sporting goods, cosmetics, jewelry, and thousands of other consumer goods directly to final buyers. Retailing businesses include traditional stores that people visit in person and online stores that people visit on the Internet. Some retailers also sell to consumers through catalogs.

In most states, retailers must have a special permit (often called a **reseller's permit**) to purchase goods tax-free from wholesalers and collect sales tax from final buyers.

Wholesaling businesses and retailing businesses, together, are often referred to as **trade businesses**.

Retail businesses exist because it does not always make sense for a business to be a retailer themselves. For example, a business that makes granola bars probably would not open their own store that just sold granola bars. They would find more success selling through a grocery store. Usually retailers charge other businesses a fee to sell a product in their store. Entrepreneurs and salespeople from other businesses meet with retail store owners to convince them to carry their product.

Service Businesses

Service businesses are businesses that provide and sell services to customers. Service businesses provide a wide variety of professional, technical, and everyday services that people need and want. Examples include engineering, accounting, garbage pick-up, package delivery, dry cleaning, auto repair, babysitting, pet sitting, music lessons, tutoring, house cleaning, and landscaping.

Most states and some local governments have licensing requirements for people who provide particular services. This applies to professionals (doctors, dentists, engineers, lawyers, and so on) as well as other types of service providers, such as hair stylists, barbers, manicurists, automobile mechanics, athletic trainers, and daycare providers. In addition, some states require service businesses selling taxable services to have a permit to collect sales tax from customers.

Figure 21-1 ▶
Service Business.

A service business sells services to customers.

Classifying.

This entrepreneur owns a beauty salon. What other types of service businesses do you encounter on a regular basis?

Special Types of Businesses

Farming is a special type of business. Sometimes it is more like manufacturing if the agricultural products are used to create new products, as when grain is used to make bread. Farming is a combination of manufacturing and retailing when fruits and vegetables are sold directly to the consumer.

Mining is another special type of businesses. Often referred to as an "extraction business," mining takes resources from the environment and converts them into a form that can typically be sold to manufacturers. Examples of extraction businesses are copper mining, oil drilling, and harvesting sea salt.

Many businesses these days also do most, if not all, of their business online. While it might be tempting to create another category for these online companies, it's important to recognize that many of these online companies are still retailers or service businesses. They just do their business online. For example, Soap.com is a business that allows customers to order cleaning and beauty items online to have them delivered to their door. Since they are delivering single products to customers, they would be considered an online retailer. Another example, Intuit provides payroll and other accounting services online. This would be an online service business.

Sometimes businesses can be a combination of business types. Threadless.com is a company that manufactures and ships t-shirts to customers who purchase them online. They would be considered an online manufacturing/retail business. Non-tech business can be combinations as well. For example, a jewelry business that makes jewelry and sells to customers would be a manufacturing/retailing business.

When in doubt, use can use the steps outlined in Table 21.1 to determine what type of business you have.

Table 21.1 Determining What Type of Business You Have

Type of Business	Check 1: Creates Product	Check 2: Buys From	Check 3: Sells To	Check 4: Quantity Bought/Sold	Examples
Manufacturing	Yes	Manufacturer	Manufacturer or wholesaler	Large	Shoe factory Construction company
Wholesale	No	Manufacturer	Retailer or consumer	Large	Costco Sam's Club
Retail	No	Wholesaler	Consumer	Small	Foot Locker McDonald's
Service	Yes or no	Wholesaler or retailer	Consumer	Small	Barber shop Lawyer

Trends in Business Startups

Over the last fifty years, the business make-up of the United States has changed dramatically. In the 1950s, manufacturing was the country's dominant industry in terms of national income and number of employees. Wholesale and retail businesses were also important, but service businesses played a relatively minor role in the economy.

During the 1950s, America experienced a boom in business franchises. A franchise is a business arrangement in which an established company in one location sells the right for others to use the company's name and operating plan to sell products or services in other locations. Franchising became popular in the service and retail industries, particularly among fast food restaurants. McDonald's is probably the best known franchise company in the world.

From 1950 on, manufacturing lost its dominance in the U.S. economy. Service, wholesale, and retail businesses account for the majority of America's economic production. According to the U.S. Commerce Department, 90% of American companies with less than twenty employees are in the service and trade industries. In addition, the vast majority of businesses started in the 2000s have been service and trade businesses, with a large percentage of their operations being done online.

 **Apply Your Knowledge** What are the four main types of businesses? Think back to your investigation. What type of business is someone who makes and sells things to customers through Etsy? What type of business is Etsy itself?

Neil Blumenthal/Dave Gilboa.

 **ENTREPRENEURIAL CASE STUDY: OPPORTUNITY RECOGNITION**

Neil Blumenthal & Dave Gilboa— Warby Parker

Thinking and Acting Like an Entrepreneur

Neil Blumenthal and Dave Gilboa are co-founders and co-CEOs of Warby Parker (www.warbyparker.com), a transformative lifestyle brand that offers designer eyewear at a revolutionary price, while leading the way for socially conscious businesses. Started while the two were obtaining their MBAs from The Wharton School of the University of Pennsylvania, the two hoped to solve a large problem they saw in the market place: expensive eyewear. Puzzled by how a pair of eyeglasses could cost customers up to $700, they set out on a mission to make sure that anyone that needed a pair of glasses would be able to afford them. Others loved their idea as well, as they hit their first year sales target in three weeks.

Two Problems, One Solution

Warby Parker actually came from two separate problems that the two co-founders were initially trying to solve. Dave had left a pair of $700 eyeglasses on an airplane. "I couldn't figure out why this technology that has been around for hundreds of years should cost more than this magical, $200 iPhone," Dave said. "So I started talking to some of my classmates about it."

One of his classmates, Neil Blumenthal, had spent the past five years as Director of VisionSpring, a nonprofit social enterprise that trains low-income men and women to start their own businesses selling affordable eyeglasses to individuals living on less than $4 per day in developing countries. "Close to a billion people don't have access to eyeglasses," Neil said. "It has a profound impact on their ability to learn and to work." They wondered if there was a way that they could solve both problems by starting a business that could provide affordable eyeglasses to everyone.

After doing some research, they found the root of why eyeglasses were so expensive. In each step along the distribution channel, companies were marking up the price of glasses so that the final price for customers was very high. "After we learned there was no reason that glasses should be this expensive, we said, why don't we create a different model?" Dave said. "We can bypass the retail channel and sell them for a hundred dollars and still have a very viable business." They cut out the intermediary, by making, selling, and shipping their own glasses. This included keeping operating expenses low by selling online-only to start. With this new business model, customers could get stylish frames for only $95.

Buy a Pair, Give a Pair

When starting Warby Parker, Dave and Neil were determined to have a positive social impact with their business as well. Built into their business model was the idea of "Buy a Pair, Give a Pair." This meant that for every pair of eyeglasses sold, one would be distributed to someone in need. Through this initiative, Warby Parker has worked with organizations like VisionSpring to distribute over a million pairs of glasses as of 2014. Even with a successful business to run, the co-founders have also dedicated their time to helping other young entrepreneurs, with Neil serving on the board of the United Nations Foundation Global Entrepreneurs Council, and Dave sitting on the Entrepreneur Board of Venture for America, an organization dedicated to mobilizing graduates as entrepreneurs in low-cost cities.

Thinking and Acting Like an Entrepreneur

- How was Dave and Neil's business opportunity linked to their distribution channel?
- In what ways does their business demonstrate a commitment to the customers and the community?
- How do Neil and Dave demonstrate the entrepreneurial mindset behavior of recognizing problems as opportunities?

21.2 Understanding Distribution and Supply Chain Management

Distribution Chains

Now that you know a little bit more about the type of business you have, you can figure out where your business fits in getting a product to the final customers. (Note that the term "product" refers to physical goods, services, and intellectual property, including patents, copyrights, and trademarks.) A **distribution chain** is a series of steps through which products flow into or out of a business. The steps through which products flow into the business is often referred to as the supply chain. It's important to understand that the supply chain for one business can represent the distribution chain for another. One very common distribution chain begins with a manufacturing business producing a product. That product is sold to a wholesaling business and then resold to a retailing business. Each business is a link that serves a specific purpose in the chain.

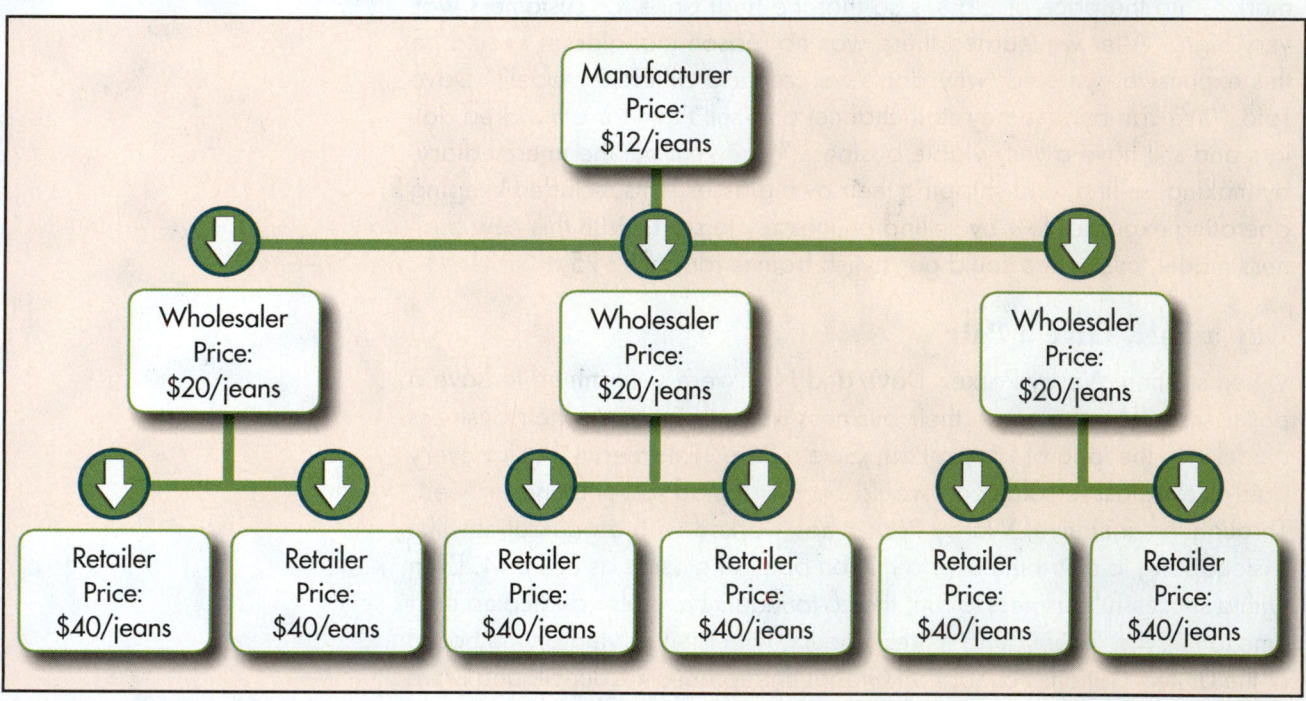

Figure 21-2 ▲
Distribution Chain for Jeans.

A distribution chain is a series of steps through which products flow into or out of a business.

Analyzing Data.

What was the markup from the manufacturer to the wholesaler? From the manufacturer to the retailer? From the wholesaler to the retailer?

What Channels Will You Use?

There are two kinds of distribution channels: direct and indirect. A **direct channel** is a pathway in which a product goes from the producer straight to the customer. Think of it as a trip with no stops in between the starting point and destination.

An **indirect channel** is a pathway in which the product goes from the producer to one or more intermediaries, before it reaches the customer. **Intermediaries** are the "middlemen" between a producer and a customer. They include agents, brokers, wholesalers, distributors, and retailers. The following is an example of an indirect channel in a consumer market:

1. A manufacturer produces millions of athletic shoes.

2. A wholesaler buys thousands of athletic shoes from the manufacturer.

3. A retailer buys one hundred of athletic shoes for his/her store from the wholesaler.

4. A consumer goes into the retail store and buys one pair of shoes.

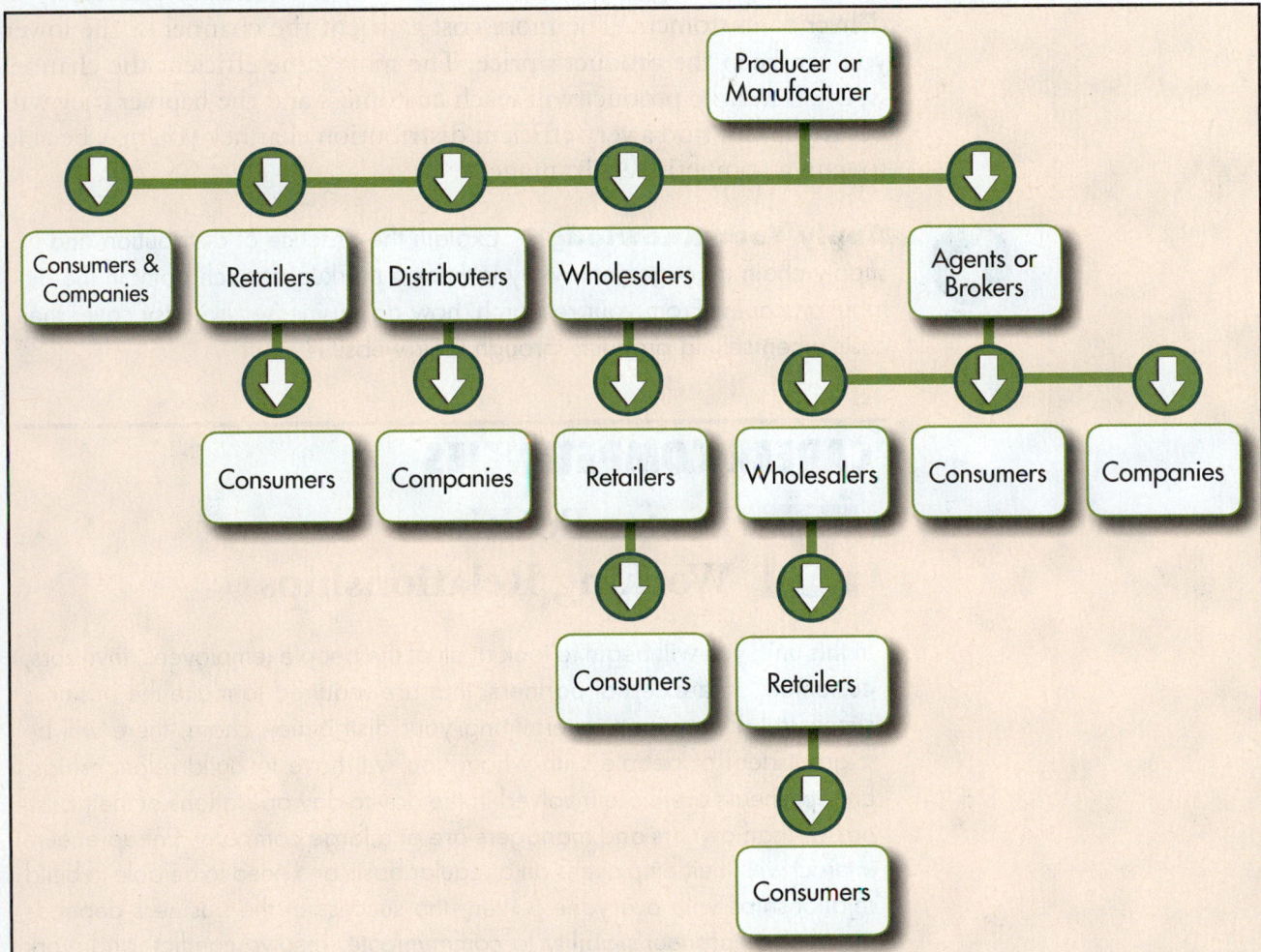

The businesses in each step of this chain have to figure out their supply chain, or where they are getting their products. All businesses need to figure out where they fit in this chain. A service business that decorates cell phone cases must determine how to get the art supplies and how to get the cases to the customer. Even a business that produces an app for cell phones has to determine where the customers will download the app from.

Determining Markup

Another fact to consider when determining a distribution chain is that the price of a product increases as it comes in through the supply chain and goes out through the distribution chain. A **markup** is a price increase imposed at each link in a distribution chain or channel. For example, the manufacturer sets a price based on his or her costs and desired profit.

Figure 21-3 ▲
Distribution Channels.

The path from producer to customer can take many different routes, both direct and indirect.

Recognizing Patterns.

What is an example of an item you've bought that flowed directly to you?

The wholesaler pays that price and then sets a higher price to cover his or her costs and to earn a profit. Likewise, the retailer adds a price markup to cover his or her costs and to earn a profit. These markups can be substantial. Thus, the price of a product in a retail store is typically much higher than the original manufacturer's price.

Finding the right distribution channel can influence what value you deliver to customers. The more cost efficient the channel is, the lower you can keep the product's price. The more time efficient the channel is, the faster the product will reach customers and the happier they will be. If you can find a very efficient distribution channel, you may be able to gain a competitive advantage.

Apply Your Knowledge   Explain the practice of distribution and supply chain management. Why is there a markup at each point in the distribution chain? From your research, how do businesses like Etsy cover their costs when selling products through their website?

CAREER COMPETENCIES

Foster Positive Working Relationships

In this unit, you will begin to look at all of the people (employees, investors, customers, and external partners) that are required to make the business successful. Even when determining your distribution chain, there will be a great deal of people with whom you will have to build relationships. Entrepreneurs are more involved in the day-to-day operations of their businesses than owners and managers are at a large company. Entrepreneurs interact with their employees on a regular basis and need to be able to build relationships with everyone. Often, the success of the business depends on the entrepreneur's ability to communicate, resolve conflict, and work together with his or her employees.

Relationships you build at work—like the relationships you build at school or at home—can have a major impact on your overall well-being.

- You have relationships with your co-workers and your supervisor, or your employees if you are an entrepreneur. As a team, you work together to achieve common goals. For example, you might work as a flight attendant. The other members of your flight crew are part of your team. You work together to make sure that you depart on time and arrive safely.

- You may also have relationships with customers or clients. You work to provide them with goods or services that satisfy their needs. The passengers are your customers. You work to provide them with information about the flight, drinks or snacks, and other things to make them comfortable.

You may have relationships with other people in your work environment, such as baggage handlers and cleaning crew. Knowing how to get along and avoid or solve conflicts is an important part of your career success. You can start building these skills today by how you build relationships with other students and teachers in your school or how you relate to family members.

All relationships are a two-way street. That means both people involved share the responsibility of keeping the relationship healthy.

When you have a relationship with someone, you exchange resources. That means you give and take. For example, you might exchange respect and support with co-workers. You might give advice to customers in exchange for money. You might give labor—your work—to your employer in exchange for salary and benefits.

When the exchange is equal—you give as much as you receive—both people are satisfied. When the exchange is unequal—you are either giving or receiving more than the other person—it may lead to problems.

Career Skills in Action

Try thinking about the relationships you will have to foster when setting up your chain of distribution. This might include: customers, investors, employees, and other businesses. For each, answer the following:

- What expectations would you have for each of these groups of people?
- What expectations would these people have of you?

Create a diagram that captures your thoughts. Share it with your teacher or a peer for feedback.

21.3 Shipping and Handling

Distribution Management

Once you have your distribution chain in place, you have to consider how these products will physically move through these chains. **Distribution management** is the management of materials and processes associated with incoming and outgoing products. The goal of distribution management is to ensure that products are handled, stored, and transported in an organized, safe, and cost-effective manner.

Transportation

Transportation of goods is a vital service in any distribution chain. Most goods are not manufactured and sold to consumers in the same immediate area. Some goods travel vast distances, even around the world, to reach their final buyers. **Logistics** is the handling and organizing of materials, equipment, goods, and workers. Transportation logistics is very complex for some businesses, particularly larger ones. Goods can be transported by ships, airplanes, trains, and trucks. Distribution managers make transport decisions based on the cost and schedule needs of their companies and their clients.

Shipping and Receiving

Most large businesses have a department devoted to the shipping and receiving of goods. A shipping department handles outgoing goods. These are goods moving to the next link in the distribution chain or to final buyers. A receiving department handles incoming goods. These are goods sent to the business by suppliers further up the distribution chain. In a small business, one individual may handle all shipping and receiving duties. Whatever the size of the business, it is vitally important that incoming and outgoing shipments are monitored and tracked carefully and that good records are kept. The products in incoming shipments should be checked against purchase invoices to ensure that all products are received as ordered and in good condition. Outgoing shipments should also be checked to ensure that orders are being properly filled.

Storage and Warehousing

Many products do not flow immediately down a distribution channel. They spend time in storage at each link along the way. Manufacturers and wholesalers can have very large inventories in storage at any one time. These businesses commonly operate warehouses, which are large buildings devoted to storing goods. Small businesses may not have warehouses, but typically have some area set aside for storage. In either case, stored goods must be kept safe from damage and organized so that they are easily accessible when it is time for them to be shipped out.

Figure 21-4 ▶
Storage and Warehousing.

Stored goods must be kept safe from damage or theft and organized to be easily accessible.

Applying Concepts.

What are the benefits of storing in a warehouse that outweigh the potential risks?

Materials Handling

Materials handling is a task of concern at every link in a distribution chain. All businesses in the chain must ensure that products are handled carefully to prevent them from becoming damaged or lost. Lost and damaged products represent lost profit to a business. As a result, care must be taken any time goods are handled by humans or equipment. Goods should be treated carefully and moved and stored in accordance with specific procedures. Materials handling involves more than the safety of the products. It is also concerned with moving goods in an orderly, efficient, and cost-effective manner.

Delivery Terms

Large products and large shipment orders are considered freight, meaning that they are transported by large vehicles, such as train cars or large trucks. Manufacturing and wholesaling businesses use specialized terms to describe their freight delivery options. One of these terms is "free on board." **Free on board** is a delivery term that is followed by a word or group of words that identify a physical location at which the ownership responsibility for the shipment switches from the seller to the buyer. Free on board may be abbreviated as FOB, fob, or f.o.b.

For example, a wholesaler in Chicago may use the delivery term "FOB Chicago." This means that as soon as the goods are loaded onto a transport vehicle in Chicago, they become the responsibility of the buyer. Thus, the buyer will ultimately be responsible for the shipping costs and bears responsibility for the goods while they are in transport. If they become damaged or lost during transport it will be the buyer's responsibility to file an insurance claim.

◀ **Figure 21-5**
FOB Delivery.
Determining an FOB can help with uncertain scenarios.

Solving Problems.
A wholesaler loaded five stoves onto this freight car in Albuquerque, NM. The stoves were intended for a retailer in Los Angeles, CA, "FOB destination." The car derailed and the stoves were damaged in the desert somewhere between the two cities. Who will file the insurance claim?

An FOB location identifier is not always the name of a place. The more general term "FOB origin" is also used. This indicates that responsibility for the shipment switches to the buyer as soon as the goods are loaded on a transport vehicle at their point of origin.

Likewise, the delivery term "FOB destination" means that responsibility for the goods switches from seller to buyer when the goods reach their destination. If the goods become damaged or lost during transport, it is the seller's responsibility to file an insurance claim.

It should be noted that the delivery term FOB has a different meaning outside of the United States and Canada. Entrepreneurs engaged in trade outside of these two countries should research the proper delivery terms for international freight transport.

 **Apply Your Knowledge** What is distribution management? Think back to your investigation of Etsy. In your opinion, would it be easier to outsource distribution, or to use traditional methods? Explain your answer.

APPLICATION TO BUSINESS PLANNING

Distribution Channel

Use what you learned from this chapter about types of business and distribution and supply chains to identify a distribution chain for your business. You should support your findings with data from research. Be sure to include:

- A description of the type of business you have
- The supply and distribution chain that will move major products through your business
- An explanation of how you and/or your customers will receive any products

REVIEWING OBJECTIVES

1. What are the characteristics for each of the broad categories of businesses?

2. Describe the progression of goods through distribution channels.

3. What are distribution considerations for delivering products or services to customers?

CRITICAL THINKING

1. Using the four business types, how would you classify the following: (a) restaurants, (b) construction companies, (c) a website that hosts music videos from new artists?

2. How can an efficiently operating distribution chain add value to the goods, services, and intellectual property you deliver to your customers?

ENTREPRENEURIAL THINKING EXERCISE: OPPORTUNITY RECOGNITION

Think back to your investigation of entrepreneurs who sell products through services like Etsy. Imagine that you have a friend who wants to start a business creating t-shirts. They are deciding between renting a storefront and selling their shirts online through a service like Etsy. Which would you pick as the better opportunity? Explain your answer.

EXTENSION ACTIVITIES

Entrepreneurship & Literacy Skills

Complete the following task to demonstrate your understanding of entrepreneurship:

1. Grades 9–10: Explain the complexity of distribution channels through an example in nature. Do research on the logistics involved in a wild honeybee hive and write a brief paper about it. Be sure to use language specific to this lesson (manufacturing, distribution channel, etc.) to explain the process of getting honey to its final customers. Be prepared to share your writing.

2. Grades 11–12: Explain the complexity of distribution channels through an example in nature. Do research on the logistics involved in a wild honeybee hive and write a brief paper about it. Be sure to use language specific to this lesson (manufacturing, distribution channel, etc.) to explain the process of getting honey to its final customers. You should also create analogies that explain distribution channels through this example. Be prepared to share your writing.

IDENTIFYING INTERNAL RESOURCES

OBJECTIVES

- Describe the different internal resources needed to run a business.
- Explain why it is important for entrepreneurs to have their intellectual property protected by law.
- Compare the advantages and disadvantages in hiring staff for a new business.

NFTE Entrepreneurial Characteristic Focus

☑ Creativity & Innovation

National Entrepreneurship Standards

- **A.13** Describe external resources useful to entrepreneurs during concept development
- **A.14** Assess the need to use external resources for concept development
- **A.15** Describe strategies to protect intellectual property
- **N.14** Explain legal issues affecting businesses
- **N.15** Protect intellectual property rights
- **A.23** Assess the costs/benefits associated with resources
- **A.24** Use external resources to supplement entrepreneurs' expertise
- **J.05** Delegate responsibility for job tasks
- **J.06** Determine hiring needs

Common Career Technical Core Standards

- **BM-MGT.5** Plan, monitor, manage and maintain the use of financial resources to ensure a business's financial wellbeing.
- **BM-MGT.6** Plan, monitor and manage day-to-day business activities to sustain continued business functioning.
- **BM-MGT.7** Plan, organize and manage an organization/department to achieve business goals.

National Entrepreneurship Standards: Career Competencies

☑ **B.24** Use time-management principles

LESSON VOCABULARY

- derivative
- financial resource
- human resource
- intangibles
- intellectual resource
- internal resource
- physical resource
- resume
- trade secret

22.1 Identifying Internal Resources

What Are Internal Resources?

In the previous chapter, you looked at setting up a distribution chain to get your product to your customer. Another important thing to consider when looking at a business model is the resources your business will need to operate. You may have heard the term "resource" before in other contexts, such as natural resources like oil and fresh water. In business terms, an **internal resource** is a supply of possessions managed by the business in order to function effectively. Resources can include:

- **Physical resource:** Any tangible asset that the business owns; can include a store location, warehouse, or equipment used to make products

- **Financial resource:** Money that the business uses in daily operations (for example, money to pay for deliveries), or money the business has in savings

- **Human resource:** People that help make the business run; can include people hired for a specific skill that not many others have (for example, someone with computer programming knowledge to support an online business)

- **Intellectual resource:** Unique inventions or processes that the business created that other businesses do not have access to

In later units, you will learn how to manage daily operations that includes managing all of these internal resources on a daily basis. In this chapter, you will begin to identify the important resources needed to get your business off the ground. You will also look at additional considerations around protecting and structuring your internal resources to ensure your business can operate feasibly.

The Benefits of Intellectual Property Law

As thinking like an entrepreneur includes engaging in creative thinking and innovating, some of your most important internal resources will be your own creations—an invention, a song, a slogan, or a name that you give a product or process. In Chapter 5, you learned that these innovations are referred to as intellectual property. While you may not think about these things as being something you "own," they are actually a very important piece to making your business successful. When planning your business, it is important to list anything that you have created for the purposes of the business. You'll then want to know what protection the law provides and how to secure it.

First, it helps to understand the thinking behind these laws. For hundreds of years, people have seen how granting legal ownership to creators of **intangibles**—things that have value but are not material goods— could benefit both the individual and society. The U.S. Constitution outlines the goal "to promote the progress of science and useful arts," which would be achieved "by securing for limited times to authors and inventors the exclusive right to their respective writings and discoveries." The Constitution's framers understood that creators are more motivated if they are guaranteed some control over their work and some profit from it. However, society also deserves to enjoy and benefit from that work. Thus, creators were given an "exclusive right," but for "limited

◀ **Figure 22-1**
The U.S. Constitution Protects Copyrights and Patents.

The U.S. Constitution understood that creators are more highly motivated if they are guaranteed control over their work and can profit from it.

Drawing Conclusions.

Do you think inventors or artists would create if they couldn't receive a profit from their work?

times." The doctrine of fair use, allowing other people restricted use of protected works, also balanced the rights of individual and society.

The wisdom of that reasoning is proven every day. The chance for personal and financial reward still drives entrepreneurs—and as you've read, much of the economy. Their success benefits society in other ways, too. Think of the songs and books that have become treasures of national culture. Think of the advances in medicine, food production, and other technology that have come in just your lifetime. Artists, inventors, and investors were willing to spend their time and money because they knew these discoveries might someday be profitable.

This understanding is having a global impact. In some countries, weak intellectual property laws drive talented entrepreneurs to leave for places that offer more protection for their ideas. Foreign businesses also avoid these markets. Now some governments have taken note and passed tighter restrictions. Safeguards for intellectual property have been written into recent trade agreements.

The law is also stretching to accommodate advances in technology and societal trends. For instance, the Internet search engine Google was sued over its practice of saving electronic copies of web pages in its archives for users to view. One author, whose work was saved, claimed copyright infringement; he argued that Google was making money by distributing a copy of his work. The court ruled against the author, saying he should have indicated that the material was not to be archived. This example shows why entrepreneurs have to completely understand intellectual property laws in the digital age.

Now, let's look more closely at what are considered unique internal resources and ways you can secure them.

 **Apply Your Knowledge** What are the internal resources an entrepreneur must identify? Think back to your investigation of Kentucky Fried Chicken's secret recipe. What type of resource is the recipe?

ENTREPRENEURIAL CASE STUDY: CREATIVITY & INNOVATION

 ### Sean Combs— Combs Enterprises

Make Your Own Opportunities

Sean Combs is the CEO and founder of Combs Enterprises, a multi-faceted entertainment powerhouse. With headquarters in New York and Los Angeles, Sean oversees one of the world's most preeminent entertainment companies, encompassing a broad range of businesses including recording, music publishing, artist management, television and film production, fashion, fragrance, spirits, and media properties. An entrepreneurial juggernaut, Sean was declared "One of the Most Influential Businessmen in the World" by *Time Magazine* and CNN.

Born in the Harlem neighborhood of New York City and raised in Mt. Vernon, New York, Sean demonstrated an entrepreneurial mindset at a very young age. At the age of 12, he was taking jobs to earn extra money. Sean explains, "My first job was a paper route. My next job was at a gas station. I was a busboy at a Mexican restaurant. I sold lemonade to people when it was hot outside. I have just worked hard all my life, and that is what I try to tell people—work as hard as you can, make your own opportunities."

Following Your Passion

While majoring in business administration at Howard University in Washington, DC, Sean continued to find ways to be entrepreneurial by running airport shuttles and producing weekly dance parties. However, music was always at the heart of his career. He left school to pursue a career in music, eventually creating the iconic music label Bad Boy Records. Sean recalls, "I wasn't too nervous about starting Bad Boy Records because I really believe that if you work hard enough and you truly believe in your vision, there is no way it won't come true. I am a bit of a dreamer—but also practical about what is required to be successful."

Sean Combs.

His hard work paid off. Bad Boy Records released its first album, the Notorious B.I.G's "Ready to Die," in 1994. The album went on to become an instant classic and one of the most influential rap records of all time. Bad Boy Records ushered in a new era that had a significant impact not only in the music industry, but also in pop culture as a whole. Today, he is recognized as an award-winning producer, solo artist, and performer, who has produced chart-topping hit songs for music superstars including Aretha Franklin, Sting, Jennifer Lopez, Mary J. Blige, Janet Jackson, and the Notorious B.I.G. Sean has also released four multi-platinum albums, and has won three Grammy Awards and two MTV Video Music Awards.

Expanding the Sean Combs Brand

Sean's success in music allowed him to find opportunities in other realms of entertainment. Expanding the portfolio of Sean Combs Enterprises, he continues to break new ground in the fashion industry. Since the inception of his label, Sean John Clothing, Sean has been praised for his innovative approach to fashion. His efforts were recognized in 2004 when he was awarded the prestigious "Perry Ellis Menswear Designer of the Year Award" from the Council of Fashion Designers of America (CFDA). He has had numerous acting and producing roles in movies, television, and live theatre. Notable performances have included a successful debut starring in the lead role of Walter Lee in the play, "A Raisin in the Sun," on Broadway. He also teamed up with MTV to find the next big hip hop group in the television series, "Making the Band II," which aired for three seasons. Recently, Sean announced his most ambitious project to date: a revolutionary partnership with Comcast and Time Warner Cable, two of the nation's largest cable television providers, to launch his own network, REVOLT, a music and news television channel influenced by social media.

Thinking and Acting Like an Entrepreneur

- How did Sean use his skills and passions to find business opportunities?
- What intellectual resources does Sean have to protect?
- In what ways does Sean demonstrate the entrepreneurial mindset behavior of creativity and innovation?

22.2 Protecting Intellectual Resources

Protecting Your Works

In 1988, the Los Angeles Lakers of the National Basketball Association had won two straight championships. One of the players described winning a third title as a "three-peat." Lakers coach Pat Riley saw the earnings potential of the term and registered it as a trademark for his company. The Lakers lost the championship that year, but Coach Riley did cash in on the trademark five years later. In 1993, after the Chicago Bulls had won their third straight title, Riley's company got a percentage of the sale of every item bearing the word, from key chains to collectible plates.

As that story shows, intellectual property law covers almost any creation. Depending on the work, you might take out a copyright, patent, or trademark. You may even protect a trade secret.

Copyright

As you read in the last section, copyright is the exclusive right to perform, display, copy, or distribute an artistic work. Copyright exists as soon as a work appears in a fixed, concrete form. A songwriter may play an original song on a guitar, for example, but holds the copyright only after recording it or writing it down. Copyright extends to **derivatives**, or works based on one or more existing works, such as a movie sequel or a translation in another language.

Copyright can be transferred to whomever the creator wishes. An illustrator might sign away copyright as part of a contract with a book publisher, for instance. Certain rights may be sold with conditions. Magazines typically require exclusive rights to an article for a limited time, after which the author is free to resell it. Even images you find on the Internet are protected by copyright laws, as the property of whoever created the image. This is why it is important to be sure that the creator has posted the image under free use, giving the rights to anyone else to use it. If not, then the image is not free for others to use.

Although copyright is automatic, many creators identify their works by using the © symbol, followed by the year and their name or company name. This informs or reminds others that the work can be used only with permission and possibly payment. Some creators take the additional step of registering their works with the Library of Congress's Copyright Office. Registering establishes a public record, which is evidence of ownership in cases of infringement. In fact, infringing on a registered copyright is a federal offense. Additionally, two international treaties, the Berne Convention and the Universal Copyright Convention, protect a work in almost any country its creator might travel.

In keeping with the goal of intellectual property law, copyright does have limits. Generally, the copyright exists for 70 years after the creator's death. After that, the work enters the public domain and can be freely used.

▲ **Copyright Symbol.**

◄ **Figure 22-2**

When Do You Hold a Copyright?
You only hold a copyright on a song when you record it or write it down.

Predicting.

If you were a musician and were working on a song, when would you write down or record it? Would you play the song to others?

Patents

Patents cover industrial works, things that are made by applying ideas. A patent gives the exclusive right to make, use, or sell the work for 20 years.

The U.S. Patent and Trademark Office (USPTO), the authorizing agency in the United States, grants three general types of patents: plant, design, and utility. Plant patents protect agricultural and horticultural products. Design patents concern the appearance or ornamentation of existing inventions. By far the most numerous patents issued are utility patents, which protect how an article is used and works. Utility patents are granted for these five types of inventions:

- **Articles of manufacture.** This category includes any tangible item.
- **Machines.** A machine's distinguishing feature is moving parts that do some kind of work.
- **Processes.** The process must lead to some tangible result. It may be a way to apply dye to fabric, or a series of exercises and drills to improve your basketball shooting skills. Since 1998, the definition has been expanded to encompass business methods, which a company uses to carry out business. An example is the system that online stores use to save a customer's information and automatically fill out the order form. The patent on this "one-click shopping" is held by the Internet retailer Amazon.com.
- **Compositions.** Compositions are combinations of two or more substances. You might patent a mixture of clay, gravel, and sand in cement, or a blend of odor-bearing molecules in a perfume.
- **Improvements on or new uses for existing inventions.** A patented invention can be the basis of another patent, if the improvement substantially changes the function of the original. For example, a skin lotion for people used as a flea repellent in pets might get an improvement patent. A shampoo for people to be used as a pet shampoo probably would not.

Not everything that fits into one of these categories can be patented. Unlike copyright, a patent must be earned. To qualify, the invention must be:

- **Novel.** It must be unique in some important way, or significantly different from anything that already exists.
- **Nonobvious.** Some relevant feature must be unexpected or out of the ordinary, given the trends and techniques at the time the patent was applied for. The USPTO must conclude that a person "having ordinary skill in the art" related to the invention would be surprised by its purpose or construction.
- **Useful.** The purpose may be as practical as the arrangement of rivets securing the blade and handle of a kitchen knife, or as frivolous as a singing hairbrush. This condition doesn't apply to plant or design patents, since they are based on inventions that have already been judged useful.

How do inventors know if their useful creation is also novel and non-obvious—that is, that no one has made something similar and is using it even now? One way to learn whether an invention is truly original is to conduct a prior art search for any information that is publicly available in any form that relates to an invention. One place to start is the USPTO online database, where you can search for registered patents by keyword at no charge. Many fee-based services search patent registries worldwide. You might also look for references to similar inventions in scientific or historical literature, such as early cookbooks or agricultural journals.

Finding prior art isn't necessarily a dead end. Examining the information may suggest a way to refine or adapt your own idea. You may see an element in the original creation that causes a problem, which your design corrects. The difference could be enough to qualify for a patent.

The next step is to file a patent application, which provides a painstaking description of the proposed invention. The title must identify the work explicitly. Detailed drawings, showing relevant parts from several angles, are required to indicate the appearance, design, and function. Drawings of the steps in a process patent may run a dozen pages.

The written description that explains the drawings must be equally precise—so complete, in fact, that a person of ordinary knowledge in the field could make or use the invention by reading the application. For example, consider this partial description from Patent #11,023, entitled, "Design for a Statue": "a female figure standing erect . . . the body being thrown slightly over to the left, so as to gravitate upon the left leg, the whole figure being thus in equilibrium, and symmetrically arranged with respect to a perpendicular line or axis passing through the head and left foot." Pages of details written in such language may not paint a clear picture to most people, but an engineer might recognize the description. It's the Statue of Liberty.

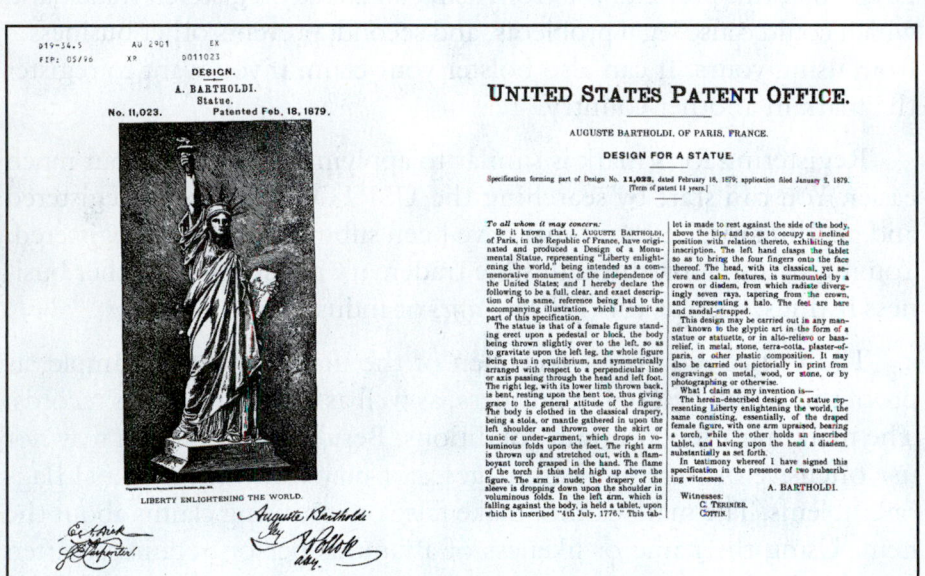

◄ **Figure 22-3**
Drawings Submitted with a Patent Application.

Drawings are the most important part of a design patent application, while the written description is central to a utility patent.

Drawing Conclusions.

How are detailed drawings evidence that an invention is the applicant's own idea?

At the USPTO, the application is thoroughly reviewed by a patent examiner, an authority in the area the invention pertains to. He or she conducts a more exhaustive search for prior art and analyzes the soundness of the ideas or processes. The examiner may contact the applicant several times to clarify details or get more information. Most applications are rejected on the first submission. The reasons range from design flaws to using an improper format. The applicant is free to correct the problem and resubmit.

This process can be expensive. Filing fees add up to several thousand dollars. Also, given the technicalities involved, most inventors hire a patent attorney or agent and a professional draftsperson who specializes in patent design.

Trademarks and Service Marks

As an entrepreneur, you try to deliver a quality product or service that you're proud of. You would not want a competitor to confuse or deceive customers with a similar or inferior item. To guard against this, you might use a trademark or service mark. A trademark is a word, phrase, or symbol that a manufacturer uses to identify its products. Likewise, a **service mark** is a word, phrase, or symbol that a service-based business uses to identify its services. When people refer to a product by its brand name, they are using its trademark or service mark. Both marks are types of source indicators; they indicate where an item or service came from. As you learned in Unit 4, having strong brand recognition with customers is an important marketing strategy for businesses. Utilizing trademarks and service marks appropriately can help with the communication of the value of the company's brand.

Although it's not required, trademarks and service marks give the most protection when they're registered with the USPTO (www.uspto.gov). First, this prevents you from using an already registered trademark, which could cause legal problems, and second, prevents other businesses from using yours. It can also bolster your claim if you want to register the mark in another country.

Registering for a mark is similar to applying for a patent, but much easier. You can start by searching the USPTO's database of registered and pending marks, those that have been submitted but not registered. You might also look through state trademark registries and other business listings, such as the *Yellow Pages* or industry directories.

The Office requires a specimen of the mark, or actual sample, as proof that it will be used in business, as well as a drawing for its records. The mark must meet certain conditions. Besides originality, it may not use offensive or stereotypical images, nor may it include national flags or emblems. The mark cannot make false or confusing claims about the item. Using the name or likeness of a famous person requires written permission.

▲ **Registered Trademark, Trademark, and Service Mark Symbols.**

◀ **Figure 22-4**

Using a Service Mark.
A service mark identifies a service rather than a tangible product.

Drawing Conclusions.
How could a promise for delivery under 30 minutes, or else the pizza is free, be an important service mark?

Trade Secrets

A **trade secret** is any information that a business keeps confidential in order to gain advantage over competitors who do not have that information. The information can take the form of a method, formula, or list of resources. In most states, trade secrets are protected under the Uniform Trade Secrets Act. There is no process to file the trade secret as such, but rather it protects the business if steps were taken to protect the secret and it still was leaked. The Act weighs certain factors in deciding whether the information qualifies as a trade secret. These factors include:

- **The information's value to the business.** The economic advantage, either actual or potential, must be real and significant.
- **The actual difficulty in obtaining the information.** The information must be something others could not learn through ordinary means.
- **The intention to keep the information secret.** Those who have the knowledge must make an effort to keep it a secret.
- **The business's role in developing the information.** The more the business contributed, the stronger its claim.

Apply Your Knowledge   What are the conditions for intellectual property to get a patent? Think back to your investigation of Kentucky Fried Chicken. Do you think the company should just get a patent and stop protecting the secret? Why or why not?

CAREER COMPETENCIES

 ## Use Time-Management Principles

As you start your business, one of your most important internal resources you will have to manage is your time. Time management is a skill you will need throughout life. Adults need to manage the time they spend at work and at home. As a student, you need to manage the time you spend at school and the time you spend studying. You also need to manage the time you devote to family, friends, and activities.

Time Management

Time can be a valuable friend or your worst enemy. You can never recapture misused or lost time. Learn to use time as a valuable resource. The way you manage this resource can make the difference between success and failure. Planning how to use your time is time management. It is a key element in your study habits. You are the only one who can plan and manage your time. Many people feel they don't have enough time, or they allow others to use up their time. The key to success is to make the best use of your time. If you are in the habit of wasting time, you can work to break the habit. Managing your time is not always difficult. Much of your time is planned for you. For example, your school hours are determined by your teachers and school officials. Your work hours are determined by your employer. But it is your job to manage the rest of your time. You might plan for the following activities:

- Uninterrupted periods for study
- Personal duties and chores
- Relaxation and fun

Did you ever run out of time and then wonder, "Where did the time go?" Most people don't know how they spend their time. A good way to find out is to keep a daily time log for two weeks. A time log is a written record of a person's use of time. After keeping a time log for two weeks, you may be surprised to see how you use your time.

Time Tips

The earth's timetable is fixed at 365 days a year, 24 hours a day, 60 minutes an hour, and 60 seconds a minute. How can you stretch this time? How can you get more time to do everything you want to do? The answer is to take these steps to make the best use of your time:

1. Write a To-Do List Each Day. What you don't write down, you can easily forget.

2. **Prioritize.** Priorities are things you consider most important. Tasks that have the highest priority should be done first. Categorize your tasks in order of (A) most important, (B) next important, and (C) least important. Check off the tasks as you complete them. Do the "C" tasks only if you have time.

3. **Focus on One Task at a Time.** Stay with one task and give it your full attention. Resist the urge to be distracted.

4. **Don't Procrastinate.** Do not delay or put off decisions or activities. Don't leave things until the last minute. Do a little each day on long-term assignments.

5. **Reduce Interruptions.** Beware of time thieves—instant messaging, social media, and phone calls will steal precious time and prevent you from completing tasks. Tell friends when you can be reached and try not to let anyone or anything interrupt your schedule.

6. **Establish a Regular Time and Place for Study.** This will help program your mind to stay on-task and discourage interruptions.

7. **Use Your Spare Time Wisely.** When you find yourself with some free time during the day, make it productive. Do some reading.

8. **Get a Good Night's Sleep.** You'll be better able to handle your tasks if you get the sleep your body and mind need.

9. **Make Time for Fun!**

Career Skills in Action

Now try creating a time log that you can use for a week. As you create it, consider the following questions:

- What are the major categories you need to track?
- What do you think you would spend the most amount of time on?
- Would there be anything you would be surprised to find out from the time log?

Share your work with a peer or teacher for feedback, then test it out for a week on your own!

22.3 Human Resources

Is It Time to Hire?

One of the other major internal resources are the people needed to help your business operate. You've probably heard the expression, "Entrepreneurs wear many hats," which means that they take on a lot of different roles in running a business. Often they're involved with producing a product or supplying a service, whether it's t-shirts or home security software. They may also act as their own store manager, advertising agent, sales representative, bookkeeper, tax advisor, and more. In truth, being an entrepreneur can feel like wearing a lot of hats at the same time. Balancing them all takes considerable effort. If one hat slips out of place, the rest may come tumbling down.

One solution is to hire someone to wear some of those hats. However, becoming a boss means taking on another role: human resource manager. **Human resources** are the people who work in a business, along with their skills and abilities. Bringing new people into a business can be like adding new members to the family: it changes everything.

Therefore, it's wise to consider simpler solutions first. Perhaps better time-management skills are needed. Improved organization and newer technology might streamline tasks, saving time and energy.

If these strategies are not enough, it may be time to take a closer look at expanding your workforce.

Advantages of Hiring Employees

The most obvious advantage of hiring employees, also called personnel, is having someone else to share the work. This choice is easier if the employee's job only duplicates the entrepreneur's own. If your one-person limousine service is overwhelmed with calls, you can hire another driver. If your gourmet pizza business can't keep up with demand, you hire another chef.

An employee can also be a valuable "second-in-command" when a business owner is called away from work. Caitlyn Impinto runs a garden shop from her rural home. Previously, taking a day off meant closing the shop and losing sales. Now she puts her two assistants in charge, and the receipts for that day almost equal their wages for the week. Knowing the shop is in trusted hands also helps her enjoy the time she takes off for family, hobbies, or volunteering.

Figure 22-5 ▶

Advantages of Hiring Employees.

Hiring the right people can be as valuable to the company as its intellectual property.

Drawing Conclusions.

How do you run a garden shop and find time to take a day off?

Employees can supply skills and qualities the entrepreneur lacks. A logical thinker who designs hacker-proof business software may not have the persuasive communication skills to sell it. New ideas may emerge when people of different backgrounds and personalities work together on a project.

Some entrepreneurs, meanwhile, leave the "nuts and bolts" of daily operation to employees in order to focus on the more challenging, rewarding aspects of their work. Hiring an administrative assistant to schedule appointments, for example, allows more time to research the market for a new service, tinker with improving a product design, or promote the company with potential investors. Some entrepreneurs are in demand for their unique talent. A music producer may hire dozens of people to operate studio equipment and record a CD, but it's the producer's artistic and commercial insight that makes the CD a hit.

Finally, many entrepreneurs take satisfaction in "seeding" future business owners by hiring entrepreneurially minded people. They themselves may owe a debt to an employer who inspired and showed faith in them.

Disadvantages of Hiring Employees

In any area of life, benefits usually come with responsibilities. Responsibilities of becoming a boss include added costs: not only employees' wages, but also taxes on those wages and premiums for insurance to cover on-the-job injury.

Dealing with these issues also entails a large amount of paperwork, beginning with the hiring process. First, an entrepreneur must send in Form SS-4 to the Internal Revenue Service (the IRS) to obtain an employer identification number (EIN). Additionally, many employers have job seekers fill out an application form and submit a **resume**, a written summary of work experience, education, and skills. Once an applicant is hired, the employer must fill out Form I-9, declaring that the employee has presented documents showing that he or she can legally work in the United States. In order to deduct taxes from the worker's wages, the employer must file a W-2 Form with the IRS. Records must be kept of the employee's hours worked, wages paid, and taxes withheld. If the worker is injured or files a complaint, this too must be documented.

Hiring employees may mean establishing more detailed workplace rules and policies. Developing an employee handbook is essential. As with a code of ethics, discussed in Chapter 5, these guidelines must be carefully written to be reasonable, understandable, and enforceable. That requires staying current on laws regarding fair treatment, employee rights, and workplace safety.

Figure 22-6 ►

Documents for Establishing Identity.

An employer must see one or more of these documents to check an employee's identity and eligibility to work. Keeping a copy of the documents on file is recommended.

Solving Problems.

Are electronic files the answer to the problem of paperwork? Why or why not?

Co-worker relations are another concern. Problems between employees are problems for the employer. Personal or professional conflicts can slow the workflow and sour the workplace atmosphere. If the problem involves illegal conduct or unfair treatment, the employer can be held responsible.

Looking at Yourself

After weighing all the options, advantages, and disadvantages, a few key questions remain:

- Is the business owner ready to be a boss?
- As an entrepreneur, could you make working in your business both enjoyable and productive?
- Do you have the people skills that are especially important in a small business?
- Do you know how to handle authority?
- Can you make difficult decisions, even at the risk of losing popularity?

At the same time, entrepreneurs must be able to share control. They must be able and willing to see when someone else can do a job better than they can. They must share credit for success, but accept ultimate responsibility when things go wrong.

Finding the right people that will be necessary to make your business operate is very important. Along with your intellectual, physical, and financial resources, human resources are some of a business's most important resources. You will learn more about managing the people that make up your human resources in a later unit.

Apply Your Knowledge What are some of the advantages of hiring employees? Disadvantages? Think back to your investigation of Kentucky Fried Chicken. What considerations do they need to take to keep their secret when the company hires anyone?

APPLICATION TO BUSINESS PLANNING

Internal Resources

Use what you learned from this chapter about managing internal resources to identify what physical, human, and intellectual resources you will need to run your business. You should support your findings with data from research. Be sure to include:

- A description of the resources you will need to run your business
- A plan for protecting any intellectual resources
- A list of human resources needed to help run the business

22 ASSESSMENT

REVIEWING OBJECTIVES

1. What are the different internal resources needed to run a business?

2. Explain why it is important for entrepreneurs to have their intellectual property protected by law.

3. What are the advantages and disadvantages in hiring staff for a new business?

CRITICAL THINKING

Suppose you buy a statue of a cat that someone else made. You then alter the statue to turn it into the base of a lamp. What type of intellectual property protection might your new creation qualify for? Explain your answer.

ENTREPRENEURIAL THINKING EXERCISE: CREATIVITY & INNOVATION

Think back to your investigation of Kentucky Fried Chicken's secret recipe. Imagine you were just hired by KFC to help think of innovative ways to protect the secret recipe from the public. What would you suggest? Provide specific examples using content from this chapter.

22 ASSESSMENT

EXTENSION ACTIVITIES

Entrepreneurship & Literacy Skills

Complete the following task to demonstrate your understanding of entrepreneurship:

1. **Grades 9–10:** Gather information from multiple sources to learn about a patented product of scientific research. Some possible topics include genetically engineered plants or animals, artificial body parts, automotive innovations, or advances in cosmetics—but feel free to investigate any area that interests you. Be sure to answer these questions: Who developed the invention? When and how? What issues had to be resolved before it was granted a patent? Be sure to cite your sources and an explanation of how you used each source to answer the questions.

2. **Grades 11–12:** Gather information from multiple sources to earn about a patented product of scientific research. Some possible topics include genetically engineered plants or animals, artificial body parts, automotive innovations, or advances in cosmetics—but feel free to investigate any area that interests you. Be sure to answer these questions: Who developed the invention? When and how? What issues had to be resolved before it was granted a patent? Be sure to cite your sources. Include a brief evaluation of each citation that includes how you used it to answer the questions, and how trustworthy you think each is.

GUIDING QUESTION:

"What activities will I need to perform to make this business work?"

APPLICATION TO BUSINESS PLANNING:

☑ Business Policies

OBJECTIVES

- Identify key operating activities performed by existing businesses.
- List examples of internal and customer-facing policies in place for business operations.
- Describe approaches for planning and managing inventory levels.

NFTE Entrepreneurial Mindset Characteristic Focus

☑ Communication & Collaboration

National Entrepreneurship Standards

- **A.25** Explain the complexity of business operations
- **A.27** Explain the need for business systems and procedures
- **A.28** Describe the use of operating procedures
- **C.12** Explain the nature and scope of operations management
- **C.13** Explain the concept of management
- **D.32** Interpret business policies to customers/clients
- **D.33** Handle customer/client complaints
- **I.10** Establish credit policies
- **I.11** Develop billing and collection policies
- **M.04** Establish operating procedures
- **M.06** Analyze business processes and procedures
- **M.12** Develop and implement order-fulfillment processes
- **M.22** Maintain inventory of products/supplies

Common Career Technical Core Standards

- **BM.6** Implement, monitor and evaluate business processes to ensure efficiency and quality results.
- **BM-OP.4** Plan, monitor and manage day-to-day business activities to maintain and improve operational functions.
- **BM-OP.2** Develop and maintain positive customer relationships.
- **BM-OP.3** Apply inventory tracking systems to facilitate operational controls.
- **CRP.7** Employ valid and reliable research strategies.

National Entrepreneurship Standards: Career Competencies

☑ **K.01** Explain the nature of business records

LESSON VOCABULARY

- credibility
- inventory investment
- inventory level
- inventory shrinkage
- inventory system
- inventory turnover
- inventory turns
- inventory value
- just-in-time (JIT) inventory system
- obsolescence
- operations
- operations management
- partial inventory system
- periodic inventory system
- perpetual inventory system
- pilfering
- policy
- repeat customers
- rework
- safety stock
- stock out
- visual inventory system
- warranty
- word-of-mouth

23.1 Operating Activities

What Are Operating Activities?

In the previous chapter, you learned about internal resources needed to make the business possible. In this chapter, you will look at some examples of operating activities, or operations. **Operations** are the everyday activities that keep a business running. Thus, **operations management** is management of the everyday activities that keep a business running. Large businesses often devote an entire department to a single operation, such as sales, human resources, or production. Some businesses, especially tech-based business, might even have a team of people dedicated only to developing software that makes the company website or application run smoother. Small businesses may have only one person overseeing all operations. In businesses that have employees, the operations manager will likely delegate some operational responsibilities to one or more employees. This gives the manager more time to devote to tasks that only he or she can handle.

In later units, you will learn how to manage daily operations that make sure all of these activities happen on a daily basis. In this chapter, you will begin to identify operating activities that will be critical once your business is off the ground. You use this information to determine operating policies in advance that shape the structure of your business.

As you learn about these activities, also consider how the entrepreneurial mindset behaviors of communication and collaboration are crucial to managing operating activities.

General Business Policies

A **policy** is a procedure or set of guidelines that specifies exactly how something should be done or handled. Many business policies are in written form. In order to ensure that operations proceed smoothly, businesses develop policies that govern how certain operational activities should be conducted. Operations managers are responsible for ensuring that these policies are implemented and followed for the good of the overall company.

Businesses develop policies for many different kinds of operations. However, there are some operating policies that are very general in nature and common to most small businesses. These policies involve hours of operation, extending credit to customers, handling returns and rework requests, and delivering products.

Hours of Operation

One important component of everyday operations is hours of operation. Many manufacturing plants operate around-the-clock, because it is typically more economical and productive to keep their machines running continuously than to stop and restart them over and over. Some wholesalers, retailers, and service businesses are also open all hours, especially in large cities. However, most businesses of these types choose limited hours to be open to customers. It is generally too costly for most businesses to be open around-the-clock. Instead, they choose hours that will best serve their own needs and the needs of customers. They may also be bound by local laws that prohibit businesses from operating at certain hours, for example, late at night.

◀ **Figure 23-1**
Hours of Operation.
Businesses must set their hours of operation.

Drawing Conclusions.
Why should you consider your customer profile when setting your business hours?

Extending Credit to Customers

Many businesses establish a credit policy as part of their operations management. A clear policy helps ensure that customers understand the conditions (if any) under which credit will be extended. Businesses often rely on three guidelines called the Three C's when deciding whether or not to extend credit to a particular customer. The Three C's are Character, Capacity, and Capital.

- Character is the financial trustworthiness of the customer. A customer's past payment history is considered a good indicator of this trait. A customer that has been extended credit in the past and paid those bills on time and in full is likely to do the same in the future.

- Capacity is the current cash inflow of the customer. A customer's current income is the best measure of this trait. Customers making good steady income are likely to pay their bills.

- Capital is the total financial assets of the customer. A customer that owns financial assets, such as a house or business or corporate stock or money in a savings account, is more likely to pay bills than a customer that lacks these things.

Returns and Rework Requests

Companies that sell products need to establish policies for handling situations when products are returned by dissatisfied customers. Returns due to product defects may be handled differently than returns due to other reasons. **Rework** is a manufacturing term that refers to work performed to correct defects in a product. Manufacturing businesses often set rework policies that clearly state the conditions under which they will correct defective products and how customers go about getting products reworked. All businesses should establish policies that establish whether or not they will exchange, repair, or replace returned products and/or refund customer money.

Figure 23-2 ▶
Returns.

Companies need to establish policies for returns.

Inferring.

Why might a company establish different procedures for returns for product defects than for returns because the customer is dissatisfied?

Service businesses do not sell products as their primary function, but some do sell products that are related to their work. As such, these businesses also need return policies. In addition, service businesses need to establish policies regarding how they will handle requests from dissatisfied customers who request that tasks be redone or that money be refunded.

Delivery Policy

Businesses that sell products need a delivery policy that covers the procedures involved in filling customer orders and delivering their products. Delivery policies make customers aware of their delivery options and the costs and time tables involved. Manufacturers and wholesalers commonly ship large orders using freight delivery services. Retail businesses sell much smaller orders. They may offer customers a choice of several delivery options, including the U.S. Postal Service or commercial delivery services, such as Federal Express or UPS.

A delivery policy may specify the amount of time between order placement and order shipment, for example, 24 hours. The policy should cover situations in which an order cannot be filled within the specified time, such as when items are out of stock. In addition, some delivery policies include a procedure to notify customers by e-mail when orders are shipped. Businesses may also provide customers with tracking information, so that packages can be tracked online while they are en route to their destination. A delivery policy should also make clear any delivery conditions or restrictions imposed by the seller. Some businesses do not ship outside of the country, for example, or will only deliver to street addresses, not to post office boxes.

◀ **Figure 23-3**
Delivery Policy.

E-commerce retailers may offer customers a choice of delivery options.

Applying Concepts.

Why would an online retailer need to have delivery options figured out before the first sale is made?

Every business needs to have policies in place that make sense for their business. For example, if your business model includes selling your product online, you will need to have delivery policies in place. If your business model includes a product or service that is very expensive for your customers, you may have to consider some sort of credit policy. Understanding operating activities will help you continue to determine the model for your business.

 **Apply Your Knowledge** What is a policy? Think back to your investigation of the best- and worst-rated businesses. What types of policies do the best-rated businesses have in place?

ENTREPRENEURIAL CASE STUDY: COMMUNICATION & COLLABORATION

 ## Teressa Moore Griffin— Spirit of Purpose

Helping Businesses Operate Better

Teressa Moore Griffin is an international speaker and the founder and CEO of Spirit of Purpose, LLC, and SoulWorks Publishing (www.spiritofpurpose. com). Spirit of Purpose is a consulting service that works with organizations to provide solutions for today's business leaders. These businesses hire her because they want to shape innovative people strategies that complement their business goals and drive day-to-day results from operating activities.

Theressa Moore Griffin.

Through her services, she helps executive leadership teams develop the inner confidence and outer skills that maximize effectiveness while working under conflicting priorities and unpredictable circumstances.

Selling Personal Skills and Characteristics

A graduate of Arcadia University, Boston University, and the Institute for Core Energetics, Teressa has been a personal development coach since 1987. Early in her career, Teressa did a self-analysis of her skills and personal characteristics. One thing she recognized was that she had strong interpersonal skills, which is the ability to communicate effectively with others. She also recognized that she was naturally professional and compassionate, and especially skilled at helping others determine what their strengths are. She decided to start a business where she could utilize these skills to help people flourish and businesses grow.

This led to her finding her niche in helping entrepreneurs and business executives be better leaders. Her process has guided hundreds of clients toward recognizing and acknowledging their unique gifts, identifying what they want to achieve, and eliminating beliefs that limit their success and satisfaction. She supports clients as they explore their personal depth and find the courage required to effectively embrace complex business challenges, move beyond perceived limits, and capitalize on pivotal opportunities. These efforts have helped her clients successfully manage organization-wide culture change and build strong leadership development programs.

Teressa's professional development offerings help businesses operate as effectively as possible. Her services include individual coaching for key executives, facilitation of customized learning events, and workshops and keynote addresses. Her client list includes Fortune-500 companies American Express, AT&T, Harley Davidson, Texaco, The Prudential, GlaxoSmithKline Pharmaceuticals, Consolidated Edison, Merrill Lynch, Pfizer, The United Negro College Fund, Forest Laboratories, and Barnett Banks.

Building a Brand

Through her business, Teressa has built her name into a recognizable expert in her field. Building on her services, Teressa is the author of *LIES That Limit: Uncover the Truth of Who You Really Are*. She publishes a widely read weekly blog and has written articles for WorkingMother.com, SheKnows.com, HealthyLiving.com, and numerous other outlets, all in support of her core services. Tapped for her expertise by NBC and CBS-TV, Teressa has also appeared on FOX Philadelphia's evening news and other radio and television outlets. She can be heard daily on CBS-KYW NewsRadio in Philadelphia. Her success has taken her from the board rooms of corporate America to television and radio studios and audiences around the world.

Thinking and Acting Like an Entrepreneur

- How did Teressa use her personal skills and characteristics to identify a business opportunity?
- Why would entrepreneurs want to improve their leadership skills as part of their operations?
- In what ways does Teressa demonstrate entrepreneurial mindset behaviors of communication and collaboration?

23.2 The Importance of Customer Service

Customer Service Policies

In the previous section, you looked at some customer-facing policies, such as extending credit and delivery policies. In addition, each business should have specific customer service policies determined in advance. All businesses from the first day they open have to interact with customers. Think about your own experiences. Have you ever visited a new business and then never returned after one bad experience? This happens all the time to new businesses who overlook the importance of customer service. As you can see, customer service is one of the most important aspects of operating a business.

There is a well-known saying that it costs more to gain a new customer than it does to keep an existing one. The goal of every business is to get **repeat customers**, that is, customers that buy from the same business over and over again, not just one time. Satisfied customers are likely to be repeat customers. They may tell others about their positive experiences with the company. **Word-of-mouth** means verbal marketing or publicity. Positive word-of-mouth about a company can bring in new customers. Dissatisfied customers also share their experiences with others. Negative word-of-mouth about a company can be very harmful to business.

Figure 23-4 ▶
Customer Service.

Happy customers are often repeat customers.

Applying Concepts.

Why should making sure that every customer is satisfied be part of your operations planning?

A customer service policy is designed to ensure that customers have good experiences whenever they deal with the company. As such, businesses set policies detailing how customers should be treated on a general basis and when particular problems arise.

- **Courtesy.** All customers should be treated politely, even if they are angry and not behaving in a courteous manner.

- **Respect.** Businesses show respect to customers through various means. Examples include a dress code and a code of conduct for employees to follow while they are at work. In addition, businesses should respect the personal and financial information of customers by safeguarding it.

- **Prompt Attention.** Customers do not like to be kept waiting, either on the phone or in person.

- **Knowledgeable Employees.** Customers want correct answers when they ask questions. Businesses must make an effort to handle every customer promptly and ensure that employees are knowledgeable about the company's business, so that they can answer questions and handle requests correctly.

- **Credibility.** The quality of being believable, trustworthy, or keeping one's promises is called **credibility**. A business with good credibility builds customer loyalty, because customers know that the business will keep its promises. A **warranty** is a statement from a seller, usually in writing, that promises that purchased goods and/or services meet certain standards and describes the conditions under which particular problems will be fixed by the seller at no cost to the buyer. Because a warranty is a legally binding document, it should be written with the help of an attorney.

Every customer service policy should include procedures for handling customer complaints. Even a company with very high standards for quality and customer service will get complaints. Complaints offer companies critical feedback that they can use to help refine and improve their policies and operations. Having pre-determined customer service policies in advance can also be helpful for businesses that do their business online, as customers won't have the opportunity to interact face-to-face with the entrepreneur. The basic components of everyday customer service—courtesy, respect, prompt attention, knowledgeable employees, and credibility—also apply to handling complaints.

Apply Your Knowledge   What is a customer service policy designed to do? Think back to your investigation of the best- and worst-rated businesses. Did you notice any customer service policies in place from your research? Explain why you think the best-rated businesses might have the best customer service policies in place.

CAREER COMPETENCIES

Explain the Nature of Business Records

One of the most important operating activities a business can perform is keeping detailed records. This can include any data on sales, customer information, employee information, or records of purchases made for the business. Even data from market research can come in handy when unexpected questions arises.

For example, as you will read in this chapter, maintaining the right amount of inventory is an important task for a business. Useful data can come from business records that include purchasing records, sales data and forecasts, and recorded lead times. Inventory managers must also consider the amount of space available for storage and the costs of buying and storing inventory. They can find this information from historical records of how much it cost to store inventory in the past.

Figure 23-5 ▶

Inventory Level Planning.

This graph illustrates inventory level planning based on past sales and purchasing data.

Interpreting Graphs.

Identify the points on the time line at which shipments are received.

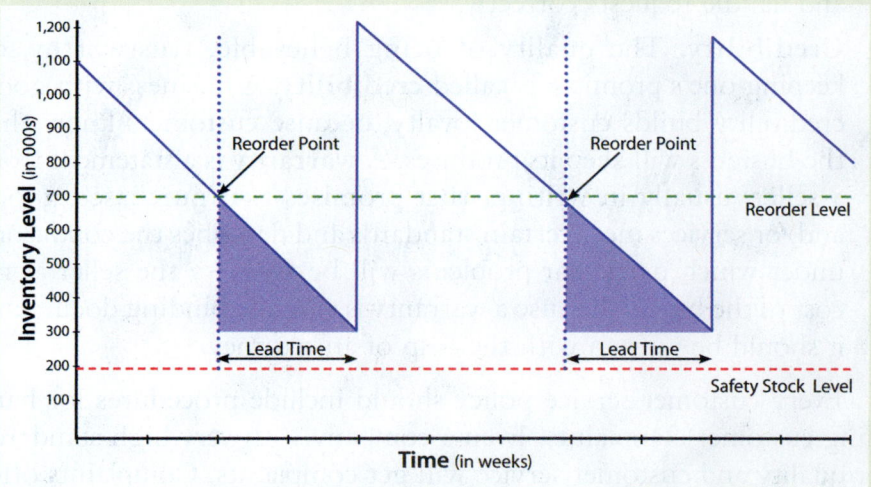

An ongoing business that keeps good records can rely on many data sources for inventory planning purposes. These include sales and cost data, vendor lead times, and losses of inventory due to damage and other reasons. Inventory managers can use this data to predict how inventory levels are going to decrease over time and decide when to reorder merchandise. Inventory management and purchasing management are closely linked activities.

Startup businesses do not have business records upon which to base inventory level decisions. However, wise entrepreneurs conduct market research and draw on it when they are ready to start their business. Proper planning allows new business owners to make reasonable estimates about expected sales during the first weeks or months after start-up. They also know how much cash and storage space they can devote to inventory. With all this information, they can estimate how much inventory to have for opening day.

23.3 Inventory Management

Why Manage Inventory?

Imagine this scenario: You have started a business where you make and sell souvenir key chains for large scale events. Your business starts doing so well that you get a ton of unexpected orders from schools during the prom season. However, you soon realize that you don't have enough key chains to fulfill the orders, and you don't have time to make more in the time that they need them. This could be avoided through ongoing inventory management.

Inventory actually has different meanings in business depending on the context in which the word is used. Inventory can be the merchandise itself, the quantity of the merchandise, or the monetary value of the merchandise. In this chapter, the word inventory refers to physical merchandise. The quantity of merchandise is called the **inventory level**, while the monetary value of the merchandise is called the **inventory value**.

Inventory management is concerned with the physical condition of inventory and the amount of space it takes up. The inventory level is also important, because it determines how well a business can meet customer demand. Inventory is a business asset; it has monetary value that affects a company's profitability. On the flip side, inventory has a cost. In addition to the money paid for inventory (which is called the **inventory investment**), there are costs associated with keeping inventory. Inventory managers try to maintain inventory at a level that satisfies customer demand, but minimizes costs.

The goal of inventory management can be summed up in one simple phrase: not too little and not too much. Too little inventory can be disastrous for a business. A **stock out** occurs when an item in inventory is completely gone. A merchandise stock out leads to lost sales and can cause disappointed customers to go elsewhere to shop. Desperate businesses may place emergency orders with vendors when stock outs appear likely, but will probably pay much higher prices than usual to get rush service and delivery.

Too much inventory is also a problem. Excess inventory ties up money that could be used for other purposes. Keeping inventory has material handling, labor, tax, and insurance costs. Inventory that becomes damaged during handling or storage may have to be discarded, adding to waste disposal costs. **Obsolescence** (ohb-suh-LESS-ence) is the process of becoming obsolete, which means no longer useful or desired. Retail inventory can go out of style, for example, as fashion trends change. Obsolete inventory has to be sold at a discount, maybe even for less than was paid for it. Obsolescence is much more likely to occur when excess inventory is kept, particularly for long periods.

Businesses often choose a minimum inventory level to keep at all times. This inventory level is chosen to cover typical sales and delivery situations and perhaps unusual situations, as well. **Safety stock** is inventory kept to protect against a stock out due to unusually high demand or unusually long lead times. In other words, safety stock is a minimum amount of inventory that protects a business against a stock out when sales are unusually high or a shipment is later than usual for some reason.

Imagine a business expects to sell an average of ten items per day and expects to experience a fourteen-day lead time each time an order is placed. However, from past data it knows that demand sometimes spikes to thirty items per day and some orders have been four to five days late arriving from the vendor. The safety stock level and reorder point are chosen to protect the business against a stock out when these unusual events occur. Every business has to determine its risk of a stock out and the measures it is willing to take to prevent a stock out from occurring.

Figure 23-6 ▶
Stock Out.

A stock out occurs when an item in inventory is completely gone.

Predicting.

How would you expect customers to feel about a store that has a stock out?

Calculating Inventory Investment

Inventory investment is money invested in inventory. Imagine a company that invests $1,200 per year in inventory. It may buy all its inventory at once or spread the purchases across the year. Each purchase represents an inventory investment. The average inventory investment for the year is calculated by dividing the total investment for that year by the number of inventory purchases that were made. For example, if the company made 10 inventory purchases in a year, the average investment was $1,200 ÷ 10 = $120.

$$\frac{\text{Total Investment}}{\text{Number of Investment Purchases}} = \text{Average Annual Inventory Investment}$$

$$\frac{\$1,200}{10} = \$120$$

Inventory turnover (or **inventory turns**) is the number of times during a given time period that inventory is completely sold out (and therefore replaced), or the number of times during a given time period that the average inventory investment is recouped (earned back). In reality, inventory should never be completely sold out, but inventory turnover is a useful mathematical tool for inventory planning. A low inventory turnover indicates that inventory is decreasing (selling) slowly. A high inventory turnover indicates that inventory is selling quickly. This is good, so long as that fast-moving inventory is not causing stock outs, because stock outs drive customers away and hurt future sales.

Businesses calculate inventory turnover in several different ways. One method divides the cost of the inventory sold during a time period by the average inventory investment during that same time period. Imagine a business that sold inventory last year for which it had paid $1,000. The average inventory investment was $250. Thus, the inventory turnover was calculated by $1,000 ÷ $250 = 4 times in that year.

$$\frac{\text{Total Cost of the Inventory}}{\text{Average Inventory Investment}} = \text{Inventory Turnover}$$

$$\frac{\$1,000}{\$250} = 4 \text{ Times per Year}$$

The business likes this inventory turnover rate and wants to achieve the same rate next year. It expects to spend $1,600 on inventory. The average inventory investment is calculated by $1,600 ÷ 4 = $400 inventory investment each time.

Controlling Inventory Level

Inventory shrinkage is any loss of inventory that occurs between the time the inventory is purchased and the time it is used or sold. Inventory levels shrink for a variety of reasons. Items may become damaged during handling or storage and have to be thrown away. In businesses with employees, there is also a risk of losing inventory to **pilfering** (PILL-fur-ring), which is stealing, particularly of small amounts over time. Retail businesses with walk-in customers lose inventory to shoplifting.

In inventory management there are two important values: the recorded inventory level and the actual inventory level. The recorded inventory level is the amount of inventory according to accounting records, for example, purchase and sales records. The recorded inventory level can differ from the actual inventory level for a variety of reasons, including human errors, poor recordkeeping, and shrinkage. One of the chief goals of inventory control is reconciling (comparing and bringing into agreement) the recorded and actual inventory levels.

Inventory Systems

An **inventory system** is a process for counting and tracking inventory so that inventory value can be calculated. Large companies often use electronic means for tracking inventory, for example, bar codes that are scanned when items enter or leave inventory. Electronic inventory systems often feed data to accounting software programs. Small businesses may rely on humans to physically count inventory items. This is known as a **visual inventory system** and is likely the system of choice for most new small business owners. Even companies using electronic inventory systems rely on occasional physical inventory counts to reconcile recorded inventory levels with actual inventory levels. Most businesses perform a physical inventory count at least once per year.

For accounting purposes, some businesses choose to update inventory value continuously and others choose to update it on a periodic basis. A **perpetual inventory system** is a system that tracks inventory on a continual basis and calculates the inventory value for accounting purposes after each inflow or outflow occurs. In other words, inventory is valued after every transaction. Large companies use electronic means, such as bar code scanning and sophisticated computer programs, to conduct perpetual inventory tracking. These systems provide a running total of inventory level and value.

A **periodic inventory system** is a system that calculates inventory value for accounting purposes at periodic times, for example, at the end of the month or end of the year when a physical inventory count is performed. A periodic inventory system does not keep a running total of inventory value.

A **partial inventory system** combines elements of the perpetual inventory system and the periodic inventory system. Businesses may use the perpetual inventory system to value their most important or most expensive items and use the periodic inventory system for their other items.

◀ **Figure 23-7**

Visual Inventory System.
Small businesses often rely on a physical counting of inventory.

Relating Concepts.

Why might a company that uses an electronic inventory system use a physical inventory count occasionally?

The **just-in-time (JIT) inventory system** is a system in which the goal is to maintain just enough inventory to keep the business operating, with virtually no inventory kept in storage. The JIT system first became popular in the manufacturing industry, but has since been embraced by other industries. This system requires precise planning and scheduling and very close cooperation with vendors to achieve a condition in which virtually no inventory has to be stored.

Warehousing

Some businesses use warehouses to store inventory, particularly if inventory levels are very large. Warehouses must be well organized and integrated into the inventory control system to ensure that inventory is counted properly. Inventory arriving at the warehouse should be logged into the inventory control system and then positioned in storage areas. Inventory leaving the warehouse, either to fill customer orders or to supply manufacturing processes or restock store shelves, must also be carefully tracked.

Apply Your Knowledge Why is tracking inventory important? Think back to your investigation of best- and worst-rated businesses. Have you ever been to a business that was out of something you wanted? How did that make you feel about the business? Do you think the best-rated businesses do a good job of managing inventory? Why or why not?

23 ASSESSMENT

REVIEWING OBJECTIVES

1. What are the key operating activities performed by existing businesses?

2. List examples of internal and customer-facing policies in place for business operations.

3. Describe approaches for planning and managing inventory levels.

CRITICAL THINKING

Why do you think companies typically have one policy for the return of defective products and a different policy for the return of products for other reasons?

ENTREPRENEURIAL THINKING EXERCISE: COMMUNICATION & COLLABORATION

Think back to your investigation of the best- and worst-rated businesses. Imagine you were hired to improve the image of one of the lowest-rated businesses. You have to develop a written statement about what changes the business will be making to better their operating policies and customer service. What would you include in the statement? Explain your rationale.

EXTENSION ACTIVITIES

Entrepreneurship & Mathematics Skills

Complete the following task to demonstrate your understanding of entrepreneurship:

Grades 9–12: Use what you learned in this chapter to represent inventory turnover as a linear equation that passes through the origin ($y = mx$). Assume the y-axis represents how much inventory is purchased by customers (cost of the inventory), and the x-axis represents how much of the inventory the entrepreneur could replace at a given time (average inventory investment).

a. Determine the slope of the line using the example in Section 23.2 ($y = \$1,000$ and $x = \$250$). What does this slope represent?

b. Write the linear equation that represents this relationship. Graph this function.

c. Imagine that this entrepreneur wanted to turn over inventory more quickly. What would the slope of this graph look like compared to your first line?

ESTABLISHING EXTERNAL PARTNERSHIPS

GUIDING QUESTION:

"What partnerships should I set up to make the business work?"

APPLICATION TO BUSINESS PLANNING:

☑ External Partnerships

OBJECTIVES

- Describe the importance of identifying key partnerships needed to run a business.
- Identify strategic partnerships that entrepreneurs establish to operate and protect the business.
- Explain the parts of an insurance policy and how it works.

NFTE Entrepreneurial Mindset Characteristic Focus

☑ Comfort with Risk

National Entrepreneurship Standards

- **A.13** Describe external resources useful to entrepreneurs during concept development
- **A.14** Assess the need to use external resources for concept development
- **A.24** Use external resources to supplement entrepreneur's expertise
- **A.26** Evaluate risk-taking opportunities
- **C.13** Explain the concept of management
- **D.25** Foster positive working relationships
- **F.24** Determine factors affecting business risk
- **I.08** Explain the purposes and importance of obtaining business credit
- **I.19** Establish relationship with financial institutions
- **I.26** Foster a positive financial reputation
- **M.06** Analyze business processes and procedures
- **M.16** Conduct vendor search
- **M.17** Choose vendors
- **N.02** Determine ways that small businesses protect themselves against loss

Common Career Technical Core Standards

- **BM.2** Describe laws, rules and regulations as they apply to effective business operations.

LESSON VOCABULARY

- business interruption insurance
- buying in bulk
- cash value
- catastrophic risk
- coverage
- deductible
- ergonomics
- insurance policy
- insurance premium
- law of large numbers
- liability insurance
- policy
- premium
- procurement
- property insurance
- purchasing
- purchasing managers
- pure risk
- quantity discount
- replacement cost
- rider
- risk reduction
- risk transfer
- sourcing
- speculative risk
- trade discount
- vendors
- volume buying
- worker's compensation insurance

- **BM-MGT.4** Employ and manage techniques, strategies and systems to enhance business relationships.
- **BM-MGT.6** Plan, monitor and manage day-to-day business activities to sustain continued business functioning.
- **BM-MGT.7** Plan, organize and manage an organization/department to achieve business goals.
- **CRP.7** Employ valid and reliable research strategies.

National Entrepreneurship Standards: Career Competencies

 N.07 Obtain insurance coverage

ENTREPRENEURIAL INVESTIGATION
Missed the Bull's-Eye

In 2014, retail company Target was involved in one of the largest data breaches in history. An outside computer hacker found a way into the company's data system and got access to credit and debit card information from millions of customers. While the company took quick action to make sure customers were notified, the damage was already done. While the company is still in business, their CEO resigned and a large customer base lost trust. Overall, even with insurance, shareholders of the business were charged $110 million because of the data breach.

Do some research on the Target data breach and reflect on the following questions:

- Was there anything that Target should have done differently?
- Do you feel comfortable shopping at Target after the data breach? Why or why not?
- Do you think this will hurt Target over the long term?

Be prepared to share your findings with your peers and teacher.

24.1 Determining External Partnerships

Types of Partnerships

So far in this unit, you have looked at both internal resources and operating activities that need to happen to make your business work. In this chapter, you will look outside of the business to see what other entities you can partner with to make your business be successful. These partners can be strategic partners that will help the business grow. For example, a kid-friendly hair salon might partner with the local kids clothing store to support and market each other's businesses. Or, a business that makes granola bars fresh every morning might partner with a local restaurant that only is open in the evening.

Sometimes services offered by external partners are only needed occasionally. A growing business might work with an employment agency to find seasonal help, or an advertising agency to develop a promotional campaign, or an administrative services agency to help with financial planning, bookkeeping, and record keeping. In these situations, working with an agency or bringing in professionals or skilled workers as needed is more cost effective than retaining their services full-time. Choosing an outside expert requires the same type of research as hiring a regular employee. Get recommendations from other business owners, especially those with needs like your own. Ask candidates for references from other clients. Check for consumer complaints through the Better Business Bureau. Check their credentials through a professional organization or state licensing or regulating agency. For professionals whose services will be used on an ongoing basis, such as tax advisors or legal experts, look for someone with whom you can establish a long-term relationship. As with a doctor or dentist, you may see them only once or twice a year, but you're trusting them with a valuable possession—your business's future.

When identifying these important partnerships, ask yourself the following questions:

- Do I need to rely on anyone to get supplies for my business?
- Would it be easier to share operations or resources with anyone?
- What services do I need that will help reduce the risk of running the business?
- What opportunities are there to help my business scale and grow?

In this chapter, you will begin to look at some external partnerships in action to determine what makes the most sense for your business.

Vendor Relationships

One of the most important partnerships to build is with **vendors**. Vendors (or suppliers) are businesses that sell products to other businesses. As you learned in Unit 4, these are B2B businesses. As you saw when you learned about channels of distribution, all businesses buy products for their own use. For example, office supplies, raw materials, or other items needed for everyday operations. Wholesale and retail businesses also purchase merchandise that they resell. **Purchasing** is buying materials, products, and services for business purposes, and **procurement** is the act of purchasing. Every business has many different purchasing needs.

Large companies typically have an entire department devoted to procurement. Persons that perform purchasing jobs are called buyers

Figure 24-1 ▶
Seasonal Factors.

Some businesses make purchasing decisions based on seasonal factors.

Recognizing Patterns.

Name other products that retail stores might have on hand for different seasons.

or **purchasing managers**. In small companies the business owner likely does all the purchasing. Whatever the case, buyers must be knowledgeable about the goods and services they purchase and the companies with which they do business.

Sourcing is choosing appropriate vendors to supply desired business goods or services. There are numerous factors involved in choosing a source or vendor. They include:

- Price
- Quality
- Lead time
- Location (local, foreign, etc.)
- Delivery and shipping options
- Reliability (for example, filling orders accurately)
- Customer service during and after order placement and after order delivery

Purchasing managers find and research potential vendors at trade shows or conferences, or by using the Internet, business directories, trade journals, or industry publications. Purchasing managers handle all communications with vendors and may negotiate contracts or agreements for particular prices and payment terms. Some buyers choose to work with a large number of vendors, while others prefer a small number of vendors with whom they can develop a close working relationship.

Many buyers planning to make a purchase, particularly a large or expensive purchase, ask several vendors to provide a price quote of what they would charge to fill the order. Some companies require their buyers to obtain and compare price quotes from a minimum number of suppliers before placing an order.

Drawing Conclusions.

What benefit is there in doing research on the best vendors or suppliers for a partnership?

Buyers also strive to get discounts from vendors. A ==quantity discount== is a discount given to buyers for purchasing a large quantity of a product or service from a vendor. Generally, the larger the order, the larger the quantity discount. ==Volume buying== (or ==buying in bulk==) means purchasing a large quantity from a vendor, typically to take advantage of a quantity discount.

A ==trade discount== is a discount given to resellers who are in the same trade, industry, or distribution chain as a vendor. Trade discounts often vary with the quantity purchased. In other words, a trade discount may also be a quantity discount.

Many small businesses are unable to take advantage of very large quantity discounts because they lack storage space for the goods or cannot possibly sell them in a reasonable amount of time. Small businesses should negotiate with vendors to get the best discount possible. For example, a vendor might give a quantity discount to a small business that commits to placing a large number of small orders over a long time period.

Identifying the right vendors, along with other strategic allegiances, will help your business operate more efficiently.

Apply Your Knowledge   In what ways can entrepreneurs use external partnerships with outside agencies or professionals? What factors should you consider when selecting an outside source or supplier? Think back to your investigation of the Target data breach. Do you think the event hurt any relationships with partners? Explain your answer.

ENTREPRENEURIAL CASE STUDY: COMFORT WITH RISK

Alice Niles— A.P. Orleans Risk Management

Outsourcing Risk

Alice Niles is the President of A.P. Orleans Risk Management (www.aporleans.com). A.P. Orleans specializes in helping entrepreneurs manage their business risk. As you have learned from your entrepreneurial studies, starting a business is full of many physical, financial, and emotional risks. Many entrepreneurs overlook getting insurance or finding external partners to outsource risk, often because they do not feel it is a priority. Alice's job is to help business owners understand how "at-risk" their business is, and then determine what steps they can take toward a risk-management program.

Gaining Experience

A lifelong resident of the Philadelphia area, she began her career in insurance underwriting after graduating from Saint Michael's College in

Alice Niles.

Burlington, Vermont. Insurance underwriters evaluate the risk of potential clients. Underwriters spend time getting to know the client, and determine how "at-risk" they are. It is their job to decide how much coverage the client should receive, how much they should pay for it, or whether or not the company can insure them. Underwriting involves measuring risk and determining the premium that needs to be charged to insure that risk. Her experience in underwriting automobile and homeowners insurance gave her the opportunity to speak with individuals and hear their concerns about the cost of insurance and how it impacted their household budgets.

Eventually, Alice moved to commercial lines underwriting, where she evaluated the risk involved for small business owners. This gave her the opportunity to service many different insurance agents and brokers and learn the differences in how they served their clients. As such, Alice became acquainted with exactly what insurance carriers expect from their independent agent partners and what qualities they look for in the companies and individuals they choose to insure.

Identifying New Opportunities

However, Alice's experiences made her realize that many mid-sized and startup businesses were underserved in the market. So in 2011, she made the decision to launch an independent insurance agency that had a vision and mission of helping mid-sized and startups navigate the complicated world of insurance. She was passionate about helping other entrepreneurs understand the importance of risk management and insurance as they built equity in their own companies. Alice now enjoys taking very difficult information and distilling it so that it makes sense to business owners. As a fellow entrepreneur, she is able to offer valuable, high-level advice that makes a difference.

Being involved in various roles within the Philadelphia insurance community for so long provided Alice with a unique ability to provide valuable insight to her clients. She also enjoys being active in community activities and not-for-profit organizations throughout the Philadelphia region. Her personal philosophy of making "deposits" before you take "withdrawals" is one that clients and friends admire.

Thinking and Acting Like an Entrepreneur

- How did Alice use career experience and personal skills to start a business?
- Why would entrepreneurs want to hire a business like Alice's as an external partner?
- In what ways does Alice demonstrate entrepreneurial mindset behavior of being comfortable with risk?

24.2 Outsourcing Risk Reduction

Reducing Business Risk

As you learned in previous chapters, many entrepreneurs will tell you that the element of risk, the possibility of loss, is part of the attraction of starting a business. In fact, as you'll remember, being comfortable with risk is part of having an entrepreneurial mindset. It might be closer to the truth to say that *managing* risk is the attraction—in particular, managing speculative risk, or risk that holds the possibility of either gain or loss. Speculative risk is undertaken freely. It can be partly controlled to improve the chance for gain and lessen the chance for loss. When Ben and Jerry's offers a new flavor of ice cream, they're taking a speculative risk: the new flavor could be a bestseller, or it could be a flop. They increase the chance for gain by first doing market research and taste tests. Then, they hope for the best.

Figure 24-3 ▶
Managing Risk.

A fire extinguisher helps
manage risk.

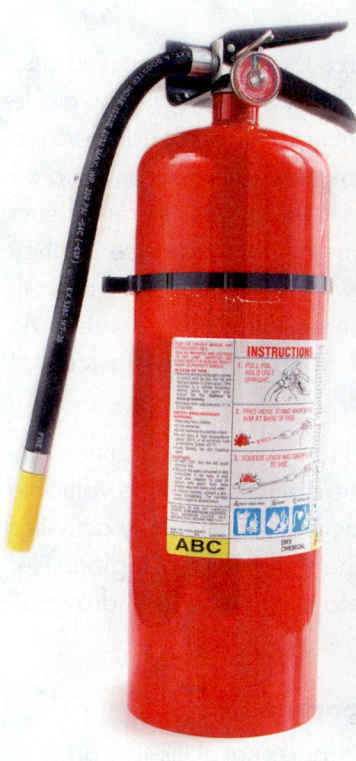

Applying Concepts.

What is the cost/benefit of
buying fire extinguishers, versus
paying for damaged property
due to a fire?

Running a business has other, less appealing risks. **Pure risk,** as the name suggests, is the chance of loss with no chance of gain. Managing pure risk consists of avoiding or reducing it—or, when those efforts fail, reducing the loss. For example, kitchen fires are a pure risk in running a restaurant. Restaurant owners can avoid the risk by serving only cold foods. They can reduce the risk by enforcing safety rules for using the stove. Knowing that fire is possible, however, they can reduce their losses by keeping fire extinguishers close at hand. They prepare for the worst.

As mentioned, external partners can be in the form of hiring professional services to help with **risk reduction**, or limiting the chances that something bad will happen. Practicing risk reduction pays in several ways. First, it avoids the cost of property repairs, legal fees, and other expenses resulting from the event. Also, practicing prevention tends to lower costs to buy insurance, which will be discussed in the next section. Next are a list of products and professional services that an entrepreneur could potentially invest in to help with risk reduction.

Securing Physical Property

Keeping buildings, supplies, and merchandise safe is an obvious place to start. A small workplace, like an artist's at-home studio, might need locks and alarms on doors and windows and surveillance cameras. Workplaces that see a large number of visitors often have sign-in policies or identification badges. Wireless systems let business owners monitor sensors via the Internet. Alerts are sent as e-mails or text messages. A professional security provider brings a physical presence of regular patrols and instant communication with an offsite monitoring station.

Good lighting, inside and out, also discourages crime. Spotlights protect vulnerable areas, such as parking lots, back doors, stairwells, and loading or receiving bays.

Personnel can be assets in security as well. Screen and hire employees carefully, then give them a solid code of ethics to work by. Train employees well. The better they understand their own and others' jobs, the better they can recognize possible signs of theft. Also teach them effective ways to act when they suspect theft by customers or clients. False accusations or attempts to stop an act of stealing can lead to lawsuits, injury, and ill will that can cost more than the price of the merchandise.

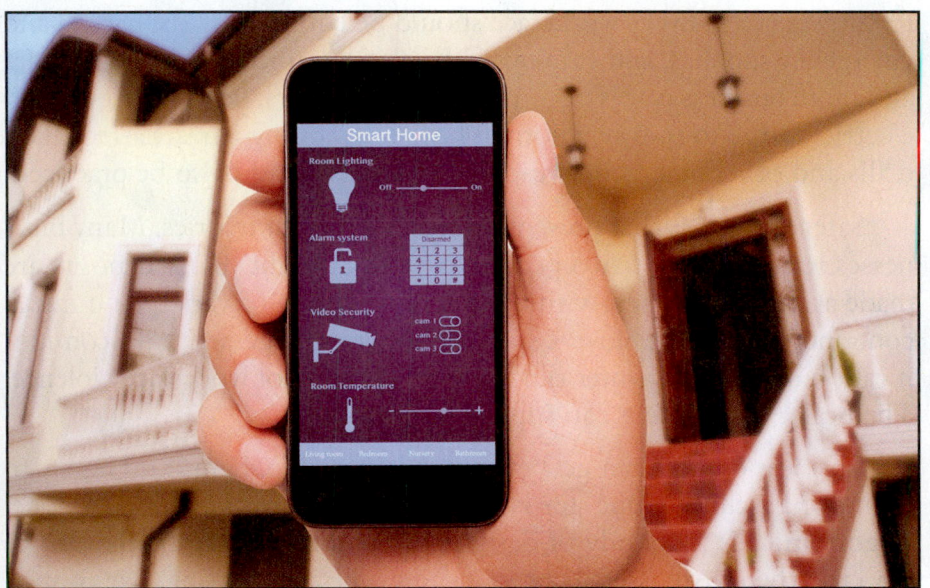

Applying Concepts.
What does the high number of available security systems available tell you about the value small business owners put on protecting their physical property?

Safeguarding Information

If sensitive information gets into the wrong hands, the consequences can be just as devastating as having a showroom ransacked. A business's own security is threatened, and it may be held responsible for customers' losses as well. Even so, many business owners use information and telecommunication technology without fully protecting against the risks that come with the efficiency and convenience. Thus, one critical component of any computer system or network is readily available technical support to explain how to use security features and handle breaches. Owners and employees should know how to use encryption software when sending electronic files. Web pages that take clients' personal and financial information need the same protection. Disks and other data storage units should be guarded like any other tangible property.

Businesses also need to guard information shared among employees. For example, suppose a manufacturer and a sales representative keep a file of memos on a merchant whom they suspect is underreporting sales and keeping the profits. That file is discovered and "leaked" by an unthinking employee, starting rumors about the merchant's dishonesty. The merchant's reputation and sales suffer. Those memos might then become evidence in the merchant's lawsuit against the manufacturer.

Promoting Health and Safety

It may be true that you can't put a price on good health. However, the price on bad health may be figured at around $87 billion. That's how much U.S. employers paid in workers compensation insurance and benefits in 2004. Keeping workers safe and healthy is sound financial preventive medicine.

Providing a safe workplace is an employer's legal and ethical responsibility. Safety training is required for certain high-risk jobs, from lab work

Figure 24-5 ▲

Providing a Safe Workplace.

Every workplace should be equipped with first-aid supplies

Applying Concepts.

What could happen to your business if you did not take precautions for the health, safety, and welfare of your workers and customers?

to cutting trees. Every workplace should be equipped with first aid and emergency supplies, and employees should be trained to use them. More and more business places now include defibrillators, devices that emit an electric charge to restore a normal heartbeat during a heart attack. Fire drills and other emergency response routines should also be practiced.

Safety practices that prevent crime also prevent injuries. Many businesses require at least two people to work at night. Bank deposits are made at irregular times, with the money carried in a variety of unusual containers. Some employers sponsor anger management and communication classes to counter the growing problem of workplace violence. The police department can supply other tips.

Business owners can go beyond preventing accidents and injury to promoting wellness. One step is to have an ergonomics assessment done. **Ergonomics** is the study of designing environments to fit the people who use them. An assessment will show whether lighting, use of storage space, and scheduling of tasks help maintain physical and emotional health. Some insurance companies offer wellness consultations to help business owners develop health and fitness programs. More and more employers are offering lower health **insurance premiums** to workers who complete wellness programs.

Less expensive measures can be useful as well. Vending machines might offer fresh fruit and juice. Health department workers may give flu shots on-site. Owners of health-related businesses, from organic grocers to physical therapists, are often happy to give talks on their field of work, which also promotes their business. Some businesses have even started investing in employee health through purchases like "stand up desks" that help with better posture. Research shows that stand up desks can promote healthier (and more productive) employees.

Figure 24-6 ▶

Healthy Food.

Vending machines that offer healthy food can be part of a company's effort to promote healthy eating.

Relating Concepts.

If healthy food or these vending machines cost more than the traditional vending machines or unhealthy snacks, how would a company justify the expense?

Apply Your Knowledge What security and worker health and safety precautions can an entrepreneur employ to minimize or eliminate risk? From your investigation, were there any products or services that Target should have considered to avoid the data breach?

CAREER COMPETENCIES

 ## Obtain Insurance Coverage

Buying Insurance

Deciding on an insurance package should be part of a business's start-up plan. The policies must be in effect before the doors open.

Choosing an Agent

Choosing an insurance agent is like hiring a very important employee. You want someone who is familiar with the particular needs of your type of business. You might first check with trade or professional associations. They sometimes have agreements with certain insurers to provide coverage that targets group members' needs. For example, antique dealers can get insurance through the Antiques and Collectibles National Association. Property insurance policies cover items they sell for private owners, whether in their shop or at a booth at a trade show.

Alternately, you can ask for advice from other business people in your field. They might recommend both exclusive and independent agents. Exclusive agents work for a single insurance company. They can usually get lower premiums by offering a package called a business owners policy (BOP). Of course, their choices are limited to the policies their company sells. An independent agent represents several insurers and can offer a wider range of policies. Whatever your choice, look at professional affiliations and credentials. For example, agents who specialize in business insurance and financial planning are identified by the designation CPCU, for Chartered Property and Casualty Underwriter.

Look for someone who inspires personal trust as well. Like medical doctors, insurance agents will ask for confidential information in order to assess a client's needs. They need to know about a business's assets and income, potential for growth, and ultimate goals in order to help the client make the most informed choice. They must be able to understand complex and important issues, and to give their best, most professional advice. Trustworthiness is especially valuable in independent agents, who may represent companies whose reputation and financial soundness are unknown to you.

Choosing Policies

The best insurance package is the one that most closely fits your needs. A newspaper owner has a special need for liability protection against

Establishing External Partnerships ● **441**

lawsuits due to careless or prejudiced reporting. The owner of the press that prints the paper is more concerned with worker injury from the noise and fast-moving machinery.

Some standard policies can be modified with the addition of riders. A **rider** is an amendment to a policy that changes the benefits or conditions of coverage. The owner of a trucking firm might need a rider to cover automobiles, precious metals, and other cargo with a high risk of theft.

Many owners of home-based businesses believe their personal home and auto insurance protects their business operation as well. They are mistaken. A one-person operation that has little customer traffic, such as a greeting card designer, might be well protected by a rider that simply increases the coverage provided by a homeowner's policy. A carpentry shop with three employees and expensive, potentially dangerous equipment would require an in-home business policy.

Some occupations have entire insurance packages designed just for them. Livestock producers, for example, need farm and ranch insurance that covers risks ranging from animal-vehicle collisions to milk loss from contamination or spoilage. Other businesses might pursue an "umbrella policy" that covers extra unforeseen future challenges not specifically outlined in the standard policy. For example, this might include protecting the business if one of its employees gets into legal trouble.

Figure 24-7 ▶
Special Insurance Situations.
Vendors at fairs and organizers of sports tournaments need short-term insurance policies tailored to their unusual situations.

Applying Concepts.
How might the insurance priorities of a food vendor who travels to fairs differ from those of a restaurant owner?

Career Skills in Action

Write an e-mail or place a phone call to an insurance agent. Contact them to answer the following:

- What parts of your business do you need insured?
- How much would the insurance policy cost?

Do a cost/benefit analysis to determine what would it cost to replace what is covered by the policy. Do you think the insurance policy is a good deal? Be ready to share your responses with the group.

24.3 Why Do I Need Insurance?

Understanding Insurance

Another important external partnership is with an insurance agent. Insurance agents have a saying: "Don't think you can't afford insurance. You can't afford *not* to have insurance." Those words aren't just a sales pitch. What threatens a business threatens everyone—owner, employees, customers, and community. Even if it were not required in some cases, buying insurance would still be a smart move, and a responsible one as well.

There's another saying that explains why a business needs insurance: "Hope for the best, but prepare for the worst." An entrepreneur wouldn't get far without both high hopes and realistic expectations. Insurance fits into that picture.

> ### Insurance
>
> Don't think you can't afford insurance.
>
> You can't afford *not* to have insurance.

Insurance As Risk Management

There is another option for managing pure risk: **risk transfer**. Risk transfer means shifting risk to another party. For business owners, that means getting business insurance. Taking on a client's risk is the service insurers provide.

Insurance companies are experts in risk management. They predict the likelihood of a pure risk, such as a kitchen fire, using the "**law of large numbers**." This theory says that if you want to predict how likely an event is to occur, you will get the most accurate answer by looking at the largest number of cases where it might occur.

For example, suppose a grocer wants to know how well the sauerkraut is selling. Over the course of one month, the grocer has 1,500 customers and sells 150 cans of sauerkraut. That averages to one can for every 10 customers. After three months the count is 5,250 customers, buying 420 cans. The average drops to one can for every 12.5 customers. After six months the totals are 10,400 customers and 1,095 cans of sauerkraut, for an average of one can per every 9.3 customers.

Which average is most accurate? According to the law of large numbers, it's the six-month figure, when the event—the sale of sauerkraut—has had the most chances to occur. Every customer represents one chance for occurrence. Thus, that's the pattern that is most likely to hold true. If you track sales for a year, the average will be more accurate still.

Insurance companies use the same principle. When they insure against a restaurant fire, they don't look at how often fires have occurred at a few restaurants over a few years, but at hundreds of thousands of restaurants over long stretches of time. They can predict how certain factors—such as safety training and keeping fire extinguishers—affect the risk and the extent of the loss.

Using this information, the company puts together its **insurance policies**. A **policy** is a written contract between the insurer and the policyholder. The policy details the **coverage**, which is the protection provided by the policy, and lists the **premium**, which is the amount of money the policyholder pays for coverage. It also shows the **deductible**, which is the amount the insured must pay before the insurance is required to chip in.

Types of Business Insurance

What does a business owner need to insure? Just about everything from the business's inventory to its intellectual property to the health of its employees. But there are some things that are uninsurable and may be difficult to protect against, such as damage to the business's reputation, a changing political climate, or even a pandemic. It's the business owner's job to choose the coverage the operation needs from among the many types available. The most common insurance needs and options are described here.

Property Insurance

Property insurance protects a business's possessions in the event of fire, theft, and damage from wind or rain. A basic policy covers the building and its furnishings, plus equipment, supplies, cash, and inventory stored there or offsite. Construction firms and home remodelers often leave equipment at the work site or clients' homes, for instance. Property can be insured for its actual worth, called **cash value**. However, experts recommend insuring property for its **replacement cost**, the cost of replacing it at current prices, which is usually higher. Property insurance also covers electronic data and software lost to physical damage or computer malfunction.

Vehicles owned by or used for business are insured under a separate policy. These policies provide additional coverage for damage and injury caused to, or by, the vehicle or driver. Personal auto policies don't apply to commercial uses.

Business owners who rent property need to protect those goods with renter's insurance. It's sometimes a condition of a lease or a loan. A landlord may require a renter to be insured against fire damage, for example. Business owners can also protect improvements they make to the premises that can't be removed, such as new roofing or a room addition.

Drawing Conclusions.

Why is it important to work with insurance agents to determine the insurance policy that your business would need?

Yet another option in a property insurance policy is **business interruption insurance**. This covers losses if a business can't operate due to a covered event, such as a storm or fire. The insurer uses company records to determine what the business would have earned during the shutdown, and covers ongoing expenses that must be paid despite the closure, such as utility bills. Some policies cover the cost of running the business from a different location. A hair stylist, for example, might rent space in another salon while her shop is closed to repair a broken water main.

Like other types of insurance, property insurance is limited in one important respect: basic policies protect only against events where the occurrence and loss are predictable. This is in keeping with the law of large numbers. A disaster like a hurricane or wildfire is classified as a **catastrophic risk**, an unpredictable event that causes severe loss to many people at the same time. In regions where a certain risk is most likely, coverage is often very expensive or not widely offered. As a result, business owners who most need the protection often go without it.

Liability Insurance

Of all the risks entrepreneurs face, the chance that their inexperience or negligence could hurt someone physically or financially is one of the worst. **Liability insurance** eases some of those concerns. It provides protection when a business's actions or lack of action injures another party. As with property insurance, different policies cover different risks. The three main types of policies are described next.

Figure 24-9 ▶
Catastrophic Loss.
In order to stay profitable, insurers charge higher premiums for disaster insurance.

Predicting.
Some people want the government to guarantee disaster insurance bought from private insurers. The government would promise to pay claims if the private insurers could not. What might be some advantages and drawbacks of this plan?

- General liability covers expenses related to injuries sustained on the business premises. It also covers injuries or damage due to employee carelessness at work. Suppose a lumberyard worker is using a hoist to load planks into a customer's truck. The worker misjudges the truck's position and drops the load on its roof. General liability insurance will pay for repairs to the roof. If the truck is the customer's business vehicle, the insurer may pay for lost income while the truck is unusable. If one of the planks falls on the customer's foot, the policy will pay the medical expenses.

- Product liability protects a business from losses caused by a product it produced or developed. This type of coverage is most important to manufacturers and food producers and processors.

- Professional liability covers harm done by a business's actions or failure to act. A well-known example is malpractice insurance, taken out by medical professionals. An error and omission policy would pay for stolen property if a self-storage business failed to hire enough security or used inferior locks.

Two other types of liability policies are becoming more common. One is identity theft insurance, which protects a business against damage done by the theft of sensitive information. It's recommended for companies that store a great deal of data electronically, which increases the opportunities for theft. A second type is called employment practices liability insurance. This policy covers claims of discrimination and other unfair treatment by employees and others a company does business with. This is a special risk for new businesses, where a code of ethics and hiring and firing procedures may not by fully in force.

Liability insurance covers losses caused by accident. Owners of service businesses may also have employees bonded. A bond is a type of liability insurance that covers losses due to dishonesty or failure to perform a contracted duty. An accounting firm owner, for example, might take out a fidelity bond to protect against an employee's theft of clients' funds.

Workers' Compensation

Workers' compensation insurance covers losses to employees due to job-related injury or illness. It's "no-fault" insurance, meaning it pays regardless of who is responsible. Workers' compensation is required in every state, and every state has its own terms. Generally, the policy pays employees' medical bills and reimburses them for lost wages. It pays for physical therapy or job training if the injury makes returning to the old job impossible. In case of death, the insurance covers funeral expenses and survivors' benefits to a spouse and dependents.

Requirements for employers vary also. In some states, very small businesses—those with five or fewer employees, for example—are exempt. In other states, it's needed for even one part-time employee. Business owners may be required to carry workers' compensation for seasonal or contract workers, such as a store owner who hires a company to patch and restripe a parking lot. Within the state, different rules may apply to different industries, such as agricultural and construction. Employers may carry workers compensation insurance regardless of their legal obligation because, in most cases, it protects them from lawsuits filed by employees.

◀ **Figure 24-10**

Workers' Compensation Report.

Employers must send in a form reporting claims of workers' compensation to the state government.

Drawing Conclusions.

Why do you think the government tracks workers' compensation claims?

Apply Your Knowledge What protections does insurance give? Think back to your investigation. Do you think Target would have made it through the data breach without insurance? Why or why not?

APPLICATION TO BUSINESS PLANNING

External Partnerships

Use what you learned from this chapter about the external partnerships you need to set up to run your business. You should support your findings with data from research. Be sure to include:

- Strategic partners that could launch and support your business operations
- Professional services or agencies you will need to hire
- Any part of the business that will require insurance coverage

24 ASSESSMENT

REVIEWING OBJECTIVES

1. Why is it important to identify the key partnerships needed to run a business?
2. List strategic partnerships that entrepreneurs establish to operate and protect the business.
3. Explain the parts of an insurance policy and how it works.

CRITICAL THINKING

1. Explain the difference between pure risk and speculative risk. Give an example of the human, natural, and economic risks that fall within each category.
2. Based on the information in this chapter, suggest two businesses that might need more property insurance coverage than liability coverage, and vice versa. Give reasons for your choices.

ENTREPRENEURIAL THINKING EXERCISE: COMFORT WITH RISK

Think back to your investigation of the Target data breach. Imagine that you were hired by Target to make sure that an event such as that one does not happen again. What risks would you advise Target to be aware of? What partnerships would you suggest to help protect the business? Explain your answers.

EXTENSION ACTIVITIES

Entrepreneurship & Mathematics Skills

Complete the following task to demonstrate your understanding of entrepreneurship:

Grades 9–12: Use statistics to determine which of the following is the best option (high-deductible, low-deductible, or no insurance):

a. Contact insurance providers to get costs of a high-deductible versus a low-deductible business insurance policy.
b. Assign reasonable probabilities of needing to use these insurance policies.
c. Calculate the amount that would be paid out-of-pocket for the same damages (for example, $100,000 in damages).
d. Make a claim about what is the best policy to have.
e. Repeat with various probabilities.

25 LEGAL STRUCTURES

"How do I structure my business to keep it protected?"

APPLICATION TO BUSINESS PLANNING:
- ☑ Legal Structure

OBJECTIVES:

- Identify the various legal structures that exist.
- Compare and contrast the advantages and disadvantages of the different legal structures.
- Describe steps to take in choosing and setting up a legal structure.

NFTE Entrepreneurial Mindset Characteristic Focus

☑ Initiative & Self-Reliance

National Entrepreneurship Standards

- **N.05** Determine business's liabilities
- **N.14** Explain legal issues affecting businesses
- **N.16** Select form of business ownership
- **N.17** Obtain legal documents for business operations
- **N.18** Describe the nature of businesses' reporting requirements
- **N.21** Develop strategies for legal/government compliance

Common Career Technical Core Standards

- **BM.2** Describe laws, rules and regulations as they apply to effective business operations.
- **BM-MGT.2** Access, evaluate and disseminate information for business decision making
- **CRP.7** Employ valid and reliable research strategies.

National Entrepreneurship Standards: Career Competencies

☑ **M.18** Negotiate contracts with vendors

LESSON VOCABULARY

- C corporation
- cooperative
- corporation
- dividend
- general partnership
- incorporate
- legal structure
- liability
- limited liability
- limited liability company
- limited partnership
- nonprofit corporation
- partnership
- partnership agreement
- share of stock
- shareholders
- sole proprietorship
- stockholders
- subchapter S corporation
- unlimited liability

25.1 Sole Proprietorships and Partnerships

Liability of Business Owners

In this unit, you have looked at the various things to consider when structuring your business. You looked at setting up distribution chains, as well as identifying internal resources, operating activities, and external partnerships to help run your business. In this final chapter, you will look at one final structure to consider for your business model. This is the **legal structure**, or the type of business ownership. These provide the entrepreneur another level of protection.

When considering the types of business ownership, one important consideration is the owner's **liability**. This is the legal obligation of a business owner to use his or her personal money and possessions to pay the debts of his or her business. These business debts could include loans that must be repaid, money owed to other businesses, and judgments resulting from lawsuits against the business.

Unlimited liability means that a business owner *can be legally forced* to use personal money and possessions to pay the debts of the business. **Limited liability** means that a business owner *cannot be legally forced* to use personal money and possessions to pay business debt. Business owners with limited liability risk only the money they specifically invested in the business. The level of liability for a business owner depends on the type of ownership structure used by the business.

Sole Proprietorship

A **sole proprietorship** (pruh-PRI-uh-tur-ship) is a legally defined type of business ownership in which a single individual owns the business, collects the profit from the business, and has unlimited liability for business debt. In the eyes of the law the owner and the business are one and the same. In other words, the owner personally bears all the legal and financial responsibility for the business. Many small businesses operate as sole proprietorships, particularly new small businesses. In fact, the vast majority of businesses in the United States are sole proprietorships.

Advantages

The sole proprietorship is the simplest and least expensive option for business ownership. Because the owner and the business are one and the same, business income and costs are reported on the owner's personal income tax return. This means less paperwork and easier tax accounting for the sole proprietor. The sole proprietor is also the sole decision maker, with complete control over the management of the business.

Disadvantages

In a sole proprietorship, only one individual is responsible for the business. That person has to carry a heavy workload and raise the financial backing to set up, operate, and expand the business. The sole proprietor also has *unlimited liability* for any debts of the business. This means that the owner's personal money and possessions (house, car, and so on) are at risk if they are needed to pay business debts.

Sole proprietorships often find it difficult to borrow money or attract investors. If the owner becomes unable to work or makes poor decisions, the business could fail. Loan institutions and investors are reluctant to take that risk. This lack of access to outside cash makes it difficult for sole proprietors to expand their businesses.

How to Set Up a Sole Proprietorship

For federal tax purposes, any business not organized under a more complicated ownership structure is considered a sole proprietorship. There are federal, state, and local government regulations that must be considered when setting up a sole proprietorship. Most communities require a business license, at least. In addition, there are often requirements for businesses with certain kinds of names and businesses that employ anyone other than the owner.

- **Naming Sole Proprietorships.** An entrepreneur may choose to use his or her name as the business name. For example, John Washington performs pet sitting using his name for his business name. He could also choose another name for the business, such as, Westside Pet Sitting, John's Pet Sitting, or Super Pets. Any business name other than the owner's name is called a trade name, fictitious name, or DBA (doing business as) name. Some states require sole proprietorships to register these names with a state or local government agency.

- **Sole Proprietorship Employees.** The federal government and some state governments require every business to have a taxpayer identification number. Typically, a sole proprietor can use his or her social security number for this purpose as long as the business has no other employees. A sole proprietorship with one or more other employees must obtain an Employer Identification Number (EIN). There are other situations in which sole proprietors must have an EIN, so entrepreneurs must research the requirements carefully.

Figure 25-1 ▶
Sole Proprietorship.

In a sole proprietorship, only one person is responsible for the business.

Comparing/Contrasting.

What do you think the advantages and disadvantages of this sole proprietorship would be?

Partnership

A **partnership** is a legally defined type of business organization in which at least two individuals share the management, profit, and liability of a business. The most common form of partnership is the general partnership. A **general partnership** is a partnership in which all partners have unlimited liability. Like sole proprietors, general partners are personally responsible for business debt. Because they assume personal financial risk, general partners usually take a very active role in a business.

A **limited partnership** is a partnership in which at least one partner has limited liability for the debts of the business and has no say in the management of the business. Limited partners want to invest money in a business, but are not involved in its day-to-day operation.

Advantages

A general partnership is much like a sole proprietorship as far as establishment and taxes are concerned. It is relatively simple and inexpensive to set up and maintain. It requires little paperwork compared to more complicated business structures.

The primary advantage of a general partnership compared to a sole proprietorship is that a general partnership can rely on the entrepreneurial skills and financial backing of at least two individuals, instead of just one individual. This makes it easier for a partnership to borrow money or obtain outside investors. Also, general partnerships can attract and motivate employees with the incentive of becoming a partner in the business at some point in the future.

Disadvantages

Because general partners have unlimited liability, they risk losing their personal money and possessions to pay business debt. There are three main disadvantages of a partnership compared to a sole proprietorship. First, any profit is split between partners. Second, each partner is responsible for the business-related actions of all other partners. And, third, partners may have trouble agreeing on how the business should be operated or managed.

Writing a Partnership Agreement

Entrepreneurs who wish to set up a partnership should develop and write a **partnership agreement** before they go into business together. A partnership agreement is a legal document that clearly defines how the work, responsibilities, rewards, and liabilities of a partnership will be shared by the partners. It also specifies what will happen if a partner dies or decides to leave the business. A well-written partnership agreement can help partners avoid conflicts and concentrate on managing and growing their business.

Apply Your Knowledge What are the main differences between a sole proprietorship and a partnership? Think back to your investigation of the gym. What type of legal structure did your business have?

ENTREPRENEURIAL CASE STUDY: INITIATIVE & SELF-RELIANCE

 ## Jacob Makoulian & Kaleb Smith— Makoulian Smith

Being Fashionable, Without Breaking the Bank

Jacob Makoulian and Kaleb Smith are co-founders and co-CEOs of Makoulian Smith. Makoulian Smith is a denim customization service that can distress and acid-wash jean pants, jackets, and other items. Their business was born while enrolled in their entrepreneurship course sponsored by the Network for Teaching Entrepreneurship (NFTE) at Piper High School in Sunrise, Florida. What started as a business plan created for their school work, has turned into a profitable business, making over $10,000 in net profits during the first year.

Jacob Makoulian and Kaleb Smith.

These two young men remember when they first imagined their business. Summer was coming to an end, and though they lacked the funds for it, they both wanted to own new back-to-school clothing. While attempting to upgrade their own old denim through bleaching and distressing, Makoulian Smith was born. The decided to start a business that specialized in bleaching pre-owned denim for other customers as well. Kaleb explains, "Basically we bleach clothes, in a way that's fashionable. We can take a shirt, jacket, a pair of jeans, a skirt, any article of clothing, and bleach it for you. There are over 7 billion people on the planet. They all have different styles. Our company allows them to be fashionable and unique, without breaking the bank."

Creating and Implementing a Plan

The collaboration between the two young entrepreneurs grew from a side project to a full-fledged business. The two wrote a business plan around Makoulian Smith and had the chance to present to their peers in NFTE business plan competitions at the school and regional level. Their plan was selected as one of the top student businesses, and was given the chance to present at the 2014 eMerge Americas Techweek at the Miami Beach Convention Center.

Both are appreciative of their opportunity to learn how to start a business at such a young age. From the hard work and problem-solving that Jacob and Kaleb experienced in formulating their business, they look toward the future with great confidence in their skills. Kaleb is now interested in majoring in business at Pennsylvania State University, and Jacob wants to own his own auto body shop.

25.2 Corporations and Other Business Structures

Corporation

A **corporation** is a legally defined type of business ownership in which the business itself is considered a "person" under the law, and limited liability is granted to the business owner(s). Although a corporation may have only one owner, most corporations have multiple owners. The owners of a corporation are called its **shareholders** or **stockholders**. A **share of stock** is a unit of ownership in a corporation. Corporations sell shares to raise money. They may limit share ownership (within a family perhaps), or sell shares to the general public. Shareholders are said to have equity (financial ownership) in the corporation. In other words, anyone who owns at least one share is an owner of the corporation. Each share can earn its owner a **dividend**, which is a portion of a corporation's profit. Most corporations are **C corporations**, which are taxed.

Most states require a corporation to have a board of directors consisting of one or more person responsible for making decisions about how the corporation should be operated and managed.

Advantages

Corporation owners have limited liability for business debt. Only the money they specifically invest in the corporation is at risk, not their personal money and possessions. Owners can end their ownership by simply selling their shares to someone else. Shares also trade hands when owners die. The life span of a corporation is not tied to the lifespan of its owners. There are many well-known corporations that have been in business for hundreds of years. All of these factors make it easier for corporations to raise and borrow money than sole proprietorships and partnerships.

Disadvantages

The primary disadvantage of corporations is that they are more difficult and expensive to set up and maintain than simpler business structures. Corporations are regulated under state laws, so to **incorporate** means to set up a corporation in accordance with the laws of the state where the business is located. States require corporations to follow very specific procedures for keeping records and selling shares. In addition, corporations are taxed differently than sole proprietorships and partnerships. Corporate profit is taxed twice. A corporation pays taxes on the profit it earns. Then, the shareholders pay taxes on dividends after they receive them from the corporation.

Subchapter S Corporations

A **subchapter S corporation** is a corporation that differs from a regular corporation only in how its income and loss are taxed by the government. This structure may offer some tax benefits to business owners, but it has many restrictions and is more complicated and expensive to set up and maintain than a regular corporation.

Limited Liability Company

A **limited liability company** is a legally defined type of business owner-ship similar to a corporation, but with simpler operating requirements and tax procedures and greater liability protection for the business own-ers (who are called members). Like a corporation, it is possible for a lim-ited liability company to be owned by only one person. In recent years the limited liability company has become a popular ownership option for small business owners because it combines the liability benefits of a corporation with the tax benefits of a sole proprietorship or partnership.

Nonprofit Corporations

A **nonprofit corporation** is a legally defined type of business ownership in which a corporation operates not to provide profit for its shareholders, but to serve the good of society and use any profit it earns to further that mission. Nonprofit corporations do not sell shares of ownership to raise money. The owners of nonprofit corporations have limited liability regarding corporation debts. This is one reason why nonprofit organiza-tions choose to incorporate.

Cooperative

A **cooperative** is a business owned, controlled, and operated for the mutual benefit of its members—people who use its services, buy its goods, or are employed by it. For example, farmers form cooperative businesses through which they sell their crops and buy farming equip-ment. In most states a cooperative is not a legal business structure, but a way of organizing and operating a business. Many cooperatives are incorporated as for-profit or nonprofit corporations.

◀ **Figure 25-3**
Cooperatives.

Farmers often form cooperatives to buy farming equipment.

Inferring.

Why might it make sense for farmers to form cooperatives to buy farm equipment?

Apply Your Knowledge What are the different types of corpora-tions? Think about your investigation of the gym. How could have setting up a different legal structure avoided liability for you?

CAREER COMPETENCIES

 ## Negotiate Contracts with Vendors; Business Contracts

From the discussion on intellectual property law that began earlier in this unit, it may sound like creating something for public use is making a deal with society: you share your work with society, and society ensures your right to profit personally. In a sense, you make a contract, a voluntary agreement between competent parties in which each party promises to take or avoid a specified action. Contracts play a big part in owning a business. Understanding how contracts and other legal procedures work is essential to succeeding as an entrepreneur.

What Makes a Contract Valid?

For a contract to be valid, or legally enforceable, all of the conditions mentioned in the definition must be met. Take a look at these one by one:

- **Agreement between the parties.** The parties must agree on the conditions, or the events or circumstances that must occur for the contract to be binding. One party starts by making an offer. The other party may make a counteroffer, agreeing to some but not all of the conditions. The agreement is fulfilled when one party makes an offer that the other party accepts.

- **Competence.** Competent, in the legal sense, means capable of understanding the terms of a contract and the consequences of entering it. Mental illness, the influence of drugs, and a lack of age (being a minor) are conditions that render a person legally incompetent.

- **Mutual exchange.** This is termed the consideration, or the benefit that each party provides for the other. This exchange of one thing for another is what distinguishes an enforceable contract from an unenforceable promise.

To illustrate these terms, imagine that the owner of an antique shop tells a carpenter that she wants a display case made for her showroom. The carpenter offers to build a case made of walnut for $2,500. The shop owner makes a counteroffer of $2,000. The carpenter says that $2,000 isn't enough for a walnut case. For that amount, however, he will build one of cherry wood. The shop owner accepts the offer. The two parties now have a valid contract.

Now suppose that the carpenter says he needs $300 to buy the cherry wood, and the shop owner gives him the money. The two parties would have an implied contract. An implied contract is made when the parties' actions demonstrate their agreement. However, these particular parties still have many other conditions to decide. They create an express contract, a contract in which the terms are explicitly stated either orally or in writing.

Notice that a verbal agreement can constitute a valid contract. However, putting things in writing is safer.

Types of Contracts

As the above example shows, a business owner will be at times either a buyer or a seller of goods or services. Thus, the need for sales and service contracts. The terms of these agreements include the service provided or items sold, the selling price and how it will be paid, and the date and location of the transaction. They also describe each party's rights and obligations. A landscaper's service contract may state that the company will replace any plants that die within 30 days, or that the customer will be charged a fee for canceling less than 48 hours in advance. Sales contracts typically give the buyer the right to inspect the goods and to refuse them, for sufficient reasons.

Leases are also common in business. A lease is a written contract in which a property owner gives temporary use of that property to another person or business. It's usually associated with real estate, but applies to any type of tangible item. Equipment may be needed only occasionally, for instance, or may be so expensive that it's worn or outdated before it's paid off. In these cases, renting may make better sense than buying, especially for a small business. Terms of leases include the length of the contract, the amount of rent and how often it's due. Limitations may be placed on the use of the property, and penalties imposed for damages or late payments.

Confidentiality or nondisclosure agreements usually concern employees, investors, and others with whom a business owner needs to share a trade secret or other sensitive information. A firm's marketing team may develop plans for a new product, for example, while investors need to know the business's financial soundness before financing the venture. Confidentiality and nondisclosure agreements bind parties to secrecy. They describe the types of information that are considered confidential and how the parties may and may not use what they know.

The discussion of contracts is not complete without mention of legal issues and procedures that impact them and other business operations. A *business tort* is an improper or intentional act that causes injury to another's business enterprise. These include:

- wrongful interference, where one party interferes with another party's ability to conduct business or develop business relationships.

- unfair competition, where one party infringes upon the patents, trademarks, service marks, and copyrights held by another party; or wrongfully discloses trade secrets or other confidential information; or markets a product or service that is confusingly similar to that of another party.

- disparagement, where one party makes false statements or fake claims about another party's product, service, or business, resulting in loss of business.

A business owner can take legal action against those whose conduct has caused them harm and seek monetary awards for damages done. The owner must be able to calculate with a reasonable certainty how the damages done translate into monetary value.

Career Skills in Action

Work with your teacher to get a copy of a business contract. Using this as an example, draft a sample contract that you could use with a potential vendor, employee, or business partner/investor as you set up your legal structure. Be sure to consider the business torts that could arise and the content you might add to the contract to protect your business against the wrongful or improper conduct of others. Share your work with someone with legal business knowledge to get their feedback on the validity of the contract.

25.3 Choosing the Best Structure

Learning about legal business structures can seem somewhat overwhelming to new entrepreneurs. It is important to focus on the key differences between the various options to help make your decision. Ask yourself the following questions:

- Do I care if I am the only owner, or would I be okay sharing ownership?
- Is it important for me to make all the decisions for the business?
- Will this business be too risky for me to start it alone?
- Do I have any personal assets that I want to make sure are protected?

Based on your responses, you can determine what is the most important for you to consider. You can then use the information shown in Table 25.1 to help you distinguish between the various options.

Once you have your decision, you will need your entrepreneurial mindset thinking to help determine how to set up the structure. Every state or county has different rules on setting up legal structures, so you will have to do research with your local chamber of commerce to determine the process that you would have to follow. Once you have the process, create an action plan to help you achieve the steps that you need to complete.

Regardless of which you choose, it is important to note that almost all businesses start as a sole proprietorship or general partnership. Once you start doing business, you are automatically considered one of these until you establish a formal structure. If you are not concerned about personal assets, and the business itself is not too much of a risk, there is

Figure 25-4 ▶

Pros and Cons of Legal Structures.

New entrepreneurs should weigh the pros and cons of each legal structure carefully.

Applying Concepts.

Is it possible for the best legal structure for a business to change over time?

Table 25.1 Types of Business Ownership

Ownership Issues	Sole Proprietorship	General or Limited Partnership	C Corporation	Subchapter S Corporation	NonProfit Corporation	Limited Liability Company
Who owns?	Proprietor	Partners	Stockholders	Stockholders	No one	Members
What is liability?	Unlimited	Limited in most cases	Limited	Limited	Limited	Limited
How is it taxed?	Individual rate (lowest rate)	Individual rate (lowest rate)	Corporate rate ("double taxation")	Individual rate (lowest rate)	None	Individual rate (lowest rate)
How are profits distributed?	Proprietor receives all	Partners receive profits according to partnership agreement	Earnings paid to stockholders as dividends in proportion to the number of shares owned	Earnings paid to stockholders as dividends in proportion to the number of shares owned	Surplus cannot be distributed	Members receive profits per agreed upon operating procedure
Who votes on policy?	Not necessary	Partners	Common voting stockholders	Common voting stockholders	Board of directors/trustees agreement	Members per agreed upon operating procedure
How long can company exist?	Terminates upon death of owner	Terminates upon death of partner	Unlimited	Unlimited	Unlimited through trustees	Variable
How easy is it to capitalize?	Difficult	Easier than sole proprietorship	Very easy (ownership is sold as shares of stock)	Same as partnership	Difficult (there is no ownership to sell as stock)	Same as partnership

nothing wrong with staying a sole proprietorship or general partnership at first. If you'd like more protection, you can register as an LLC or establish a corporation once you have gotten the business off the ground.

 **Apply Your Knowledge** What are the questions to ask in choosing a legal structure? Think back to your investigation of the gym. What legal structure would you have chosen if you could do it over?

APPLICATION TO BUSINESS PLANNING

Legal Structure

Use what you learned from this chapter about legal structures to determine what business structure would be best for you and your business. You should support your findings with data from research. Be sure to include:

- Which legal structure you chose
- Reasons for choosing your legal structure
- The legal procedures you will have to follow to set up your business structure

25 ASSESSMENT

REVIEWING OBJECTIVES

1. List the various legal structures that exist.

2. What are the advantages and disadvantages of each of the different legal structures?

3. Describe steps to take in choosing and setting up a legal structure.

CRITICAL THINKING

A sole proprietor owns two businesses: a furniture store and a skateboard outlet. Which business do you think most needs limited liability? Why?

ENTREPRENEURIAL THINKING EXERCISE: INITIATIVE & SELF-RELIANCE

Think back to your investigation of the gym that you opened with your friend. Imagine that you were going to take initiative and set up a partnership agreement ahead of opening the business. What would you include in it? What roles and responsibilities would you include for each of you? Be sure to explain your thoughts.

EXTENSION ACTIVITIES

Entrepreneurship & Literacy Skills

Complete the following task to demonstrate your understanding of entrepreneurship:

1. Grades 9–10: Using what you learned about legal structures in this chapter, create a simple flowchart that one could use to determine which legal structure is right for them. If you need to, re-read the section to determine the central ideas for each section. Be sure that your flow chart provides an accurate summary of each decision point.

2. Grades 11–12: Using what you learned about legal structures in this chapter, create a simple flowchart that one could use to determine which legal structure is right for them. If you need to, re-read the section to determine the central ideas for each section. Be sure that your flow chart provides an accurate summary of each decision point, but paraphrased in simpler terms.

Unit 5: Business Model

CHAPTER SUMMARY

21. Channels of Distribution

The four major types of business are manufacturing (manufacturers), wholesaling (wholesalers), retailing (retailers), and service. Manufacturing businesses convert materials into products for sale. Wholesalers purchase products in large quantities from manufacturers and resell them in smaller quantities to retailers. Retailing businesses sell small or individual products directly to consumers. Wholesale and retail businesses together are called trade businesses. Service businesses sell services (examples: doctors, babysitters, athletic trainers, and barbers). Over the past fifty years, service and trade businesses have replaced manufacturing as the primary industry in America. Service businesses are expected to dominate the U.S. economy for the foreseeable future. Products typically travel along a distribution chain (channel) that includes a manufacturer, wholesaler, and retailer. Distribution management is concerned with materials handling, logistics, shipping and receiving, storage and warehousing, transportation, and terms of delivery for products.

22. Identifying Internal Resources

To make sure that the business's model is feasible, entrepreneurs must identify the internal resources owned by a business. These internal resources might be physical, financial, human, or intellectual. Intellectual property law gives artists and inventors exclusive rights to their works for a specified length of time. Copyright, patents, trademarks, and service marks protect artistic work, invented items or processes, or proprietary business interests. A valid business contract is an agreement for an exchange between competent parties. Violators of intellectual property rights and contracts face legal consequences. Employees can bring needed help and new ideas to running a business. They can free entrepreneurs to focus on business expansion and development. Hiring employees, however, means added expenses and paperwork and new legal requirements.

23. Determining Operating Activities

Operations management is concerned with the daily activities that keep a business running. Policies are developed that specify procedures for handling particular operations. General operational policies address the hours of operation, extending credit to customers, handling product returns and rework claims, and delivering goods to customers. Customer service is one of the most important components of daily operations. The five fundamental elements governing the treatment of customers are courtesy, respect, prompt attention, knowledgeable employees, and credibility. Good customer service builds customer loyalty and spreads positive word-of-mouth about a business. Inventory management is concerned with having the right amount of inventory—that is, neither too much nor too little. Inventory managers strive to maintain inventory at a level that satisfies customer demand but minimizes expenses. They use purchasing records, sales data and forecasts, lead-time records, and space and cost considerations to plan inventory levels and investments. Inventory obsolescence and shrinkage due to damage or theft are also concerns. Inventory counting and control can be performed by people or by electronic and computerized systems. For accounting purposes, inventory value may be calculated continually or periodically.

24. Establishing External Partnerships

As part of setting up the business model, entrepreneurs should look at the external partnership and relationships they must build to get the business off the ground. The roles that these partnerships might play include: supplying materials, sharing operations and equipment, outsourcing professional services, and strategic partnerships. Managing purchasing is vital to a business because purchasing directly affects profits. Purchasing managers strive to buy goods and services of the right quality in the right amounts at the right time, and at the right costs and payment terms from the right vendors. Entrepreneurs also hire outside experts for services that are needed only occasionally, such as products and services that help navigate business risk. Insurance is a form of risk management that pays clients for losses due to unforeseen events. Business owners need to insure against property loss, liability, and work-related injury to employees. They should buy policies that meet their needs from a trusted agent. Businesses can also reduce risk by preventing theft and accidents and by promoting wellness.

25. Legal Structures

The major types of business ownership are sole proprietorship, partnership, corporation, and cooperative. Business structures differ primarily in terms of liability, taxes, who controls the business, and who shares its profits. Liability is the legal obligation of an owner to use personal money and possessions to pay business debt. There are significant legal restrictions and requirements associated with some types of ownership, particularly the corporation. Entrepreneurs that are just starting out should ask themselves about the level of risk and assets that are liable in helping decide which legal structure to set up.

UNIT 5 VOCABULARY

business model

business interruption insurance

buying in bulk

C corporation

cash value

catastrophic risk

cooperative

corporation

coverage

credibility

deductible

derivative

direct channel

distribution chain

distribution channel

distribution management

dividend

ergonomics

financial resource

free on board

general partnership

human resource

incorporate

indirect channel

insurance policy

insurance premium

intangibles

intellectual resource

intermediary

internal resource

inventory investment

inventory level

inventory shrinkage

inventory system

inventory turnover

inventory turns

inventory value

just-in-time (JIT) inventory system

law of large numbers

legal structure

liability

liability insurance

limited liability

limited liability company

limited partnership

logistics

manufacturer

manufacturing business

markup

nonprofit corporation

obsolescence

operations

operations management

partial inventory system

partnership

partnership agreement

periodic inventory system

perpetual inventory system

physical resource

pilfering

policy

premium

procurement

property insurance

purchasing

purchasing managers

pure risk

quantity discount

repeat customers

replacement cost

reseller's permit

résumé

retailers

retailing businesses

rework

rider

risk reduction

risk transfer

safety stock

service businesses

service mark

share of stock

shareholders

sole proprietorship

sourcing

speculative risk

stock out

stockholders

subchapter S corporation

trade businesses

trade discount

trade secret

unlimited liability

vendors

visual inventory system

volume buying

warranty

wholesaler

wholesaling businesses

word-of-mouth

worker's compensation insurance

CHECK YOUR UNDERSTANDING

Choose the letter that best answers the question or completes the statement.

1. Which type of business ownership provides limited liability for the owner(s)?

   a. corporation

   b. sole proprietorship

   c. general partnership

   d. all of the above

2. One advantage of a general partnership over a sole proprietorship is that a general partnership

   a. provides limited liability

   b. is a corporation

   c. provides unlimited liability

   d. can rely on more than one person for financial backing

3. A business owner with unlimited liability

   a. could have to sacrifice personal money and possessions to pay business debt

   b. is not personally responsible for the debts of the business

   c. is a shareholder of a corporation

   d. would not have to sacrifice personal money and possessions to pay business debt

4. One advantage of a corporation as compared to a sole proprietorship is

   a. a corporation is easier to set up and requires less paperwork

   b. a corporation provides limited liability for its owners

   c. a corporation has fewer shareholders

   d. a corporation has a partnership agreement

5. A nonprofit corporation

   a. provides unlimited liability to its members

   b. provides limited liability to its members

   c. is set up to make profits for its investors

   d. is set up to pay dividends to its shareholders

6. The special permit that allows retailers to purchase goods tax-free from wholesalers and collect sales tax from final buyers is called a

   a. reseller's permit

   b. retailing permit

   c. tax permit

   d. wholesale permit

7. Requiring food service workers to wash their hands before serving meals is a form of

   a. ergonomics

   b. risk reduction

   c. risk transfer

   d. infringement

8. A condition that will help earn a patent is

   a. non-obviousness

   b. speculative risk

   c. the law of large numbers

   d. none of the above

9. The most important quality in an insurance package is that it

   a. is inexpensive

   b. meets the policyholder's needs

   c. is sold by an exclusive agent

   d. covers catastrophic risk

10. A poem is in the public domain if

    a. the author has died

    b. it has not been published

    c. 70 years have passed since the author's death

    d. it wasn't registered with the Copyright Office

11. Which of the following would be considered an uninsurable risk?

a. natural disaster

b. a pandemic

c. workplace injury of an employee

d. none of the above

12. Liability insurance provides protection when

a. a business's action or lack of action injures someone

b. a business's vehicles are damaged

c. electronic data or software is lost due to a computer malfunction

d. a business has a fire or damage from the weather

13. How does the price of a product change as it moves along a distribution chain?

a. the price decreases to provide each business in the chain with a profit

b. the price increases to provide each business in the chain with a profit

c. the price decreases because the product quality decreases

d. the price increases because the product quality increases

14. The importance of courtesy is most likely explained in a

a. customer service policy

b. scheduling policy

c. production management policy

d. maintenance policy

15. Which of the following describes a typical distribution chain for a shirt?

a. manufacturer to wholesaler to customer

b. manufacturer to wholesaler to retailer to customer

c. wholesaler to manufacturer to retailer to customer

d. manufacturer to retailer to wholesaler to customer

16. A physical inventory count is

a. performed by people during a visual inventory

b. an inventory level calculated from accounting records

c. conducted by computers using barcode scanners

d. the number of inventory turns per accounting period

BUSINESS COMMUNICATION

1. You want to start a sole proprietorship retail business that employs several people. Research the steps necessary to comply with federal, state, and local government requirements for setting up your business. Summarize your research. Be creative. You can use a diagram, a flowchart, a 1-2-3 list, or any other method to summarize your research.

2. Write a patent description for a product feature or a process that you're familiar with—for example, the pull-tab top on a soda can, the design of a computer mouse, lacing up and tying a shoe, or the way a coffeemaker brews coffee. Describe the subject precisely and thoroughly so that someone who has never seen the subject could re-create it.

3. Carefully worded directions for use included with a product can save a business from a product liability lawsuit. Choose an item that you're familiar with, such as a backpack or shampoo. Write at least three directions for use that would protect the manufacturer from claims of selling an unsafe product.

4. Imagine that an unknown person calls your store one day and wants to buy an expensive item on credit. Make a list of at least five questions you would ask to help you determine whether you should extend credit.

5. Draw an inventory-level planning graph covering thirty-five days for a new business that is open every day of the week. Assume starting inventory and reorder quantity is 8,000 items, sales forecast average is 500 items per day, reorder level is 3,000 items, lead time is seven days, and safety stock is 1,000 items.

BUSINESS MATH

1. In 2002, the U.S. government spent $40,896,000 on processing copyright applications. That averaged out to $78.48 per application. How many applications did the government process that year? Each applicant paid a $30 application fee. How much did the government collect in fees?

2. Income exposure is the money lost due to business interruption. It's used to decide how much coverage is needed. A simple formula to estimate income exposure is Income Exposure = (Monthly Income + Operating Expenses) × Number of Months needed for recovery.

   A dry cleaner does $17,500 worth of business each month. Its operating expenses are $5,250. What would be the business's income exposure if it took seven months to reopen after a fire? If it needed an additional $1,580 per month to keep operating during that time, what would be the total amount of necessary coverage?

3. You have a twelve-pound package to ship to a customer who lives 500 miles away. Delivery company A charges $0.80 per pound plus $0.06 per mile. Delivery company B charges $10 per package for the first 8 pounds and first 400 miles. Additional pounds are $0.30 each and additional miles are $0.25 each. What is the total shipping price for each delivery company?

4. A manufacturer sells pens for $0.50 each. If the wholesaler adds a markup of 60% and the retailer adds a markup of 120% of the manufacturer's price, what is the final price of the pen?

REVIEW & ASSESSMENT

BUSINESS ETHICS

1. In a general partnership, do you think the partner who works the most hours is entitled to the largest share of the profits? Consider the partner who may have invested the most but doesn't put in nearly the same number of hours as the other partner. Also, consider how liability is shared. Come up with general rules that consider the amount each partner invests in the business and addresses how profit, liability, and work should be shared in a general partnership.

2. You own a catering business. The baker who supplies your bread has been teaching food service classes as part of a work-release program for low-risk offenders at a detention center. He urges you to hire some of his graduates. You support the program and you need the help, but your insurance agent warns you that the premiums on your property and liability insurance will go up if you hire these individuals. How would you respond to the baker's request?

3. Your business is running low on cash. A friend with her own business offers to pay you a large amount of money for a list of your customers' names and addresses so she can contact them about an investment opportunity. Your friend is reputable, has a very good business, and is often very helpful to people. You could really use the money right now because you have some expenses you could not otherwise pay. Should you sell her the list of your customers' names and addresses? Explain your answer.

UNIT 5 REVIEW & ASSESSMENT

BUSINESS IN YOUR COMMUNITY

1. Interview a local small business owner who has set up a sole proprietorship or general partnership within the past year or two. Make a list of the permits, licenses, identification numbers, and fees that were required for the business to open.

2. Working with a group of classmates, find five local retail businesses (as diverse as possible) that also offer one or more services to consumers (for example, a gas station that also offers oil changes). Prepare a short presentation for the class in which you describe the retail businesses and explain why they provide services as well as products.

3. Survey three local business owners about the types of insurance they purchase, the premiums, and the coverage. Make a chart of your findings.

4. Interview a local musician, painter, graphic artist, writer, or other individual involved in the arts about his or her experience with copyrights. Has the artist registered works with the Copyright Office? Has the artist had trouble with copyright infringement? If so, how was the problem resolved? If not, why do you think there hasn't been trouble?

5. Draw a map with your school at the center. Show the locations of at least five businesses that receive shipments from suppliers or ship packages to customers.

6. Interview a small business owner in your community whose business maintains an inventory. Find out what type of inventory management and control techniques are used at the business and report your findings to the class.

INFORMATION TECHNOLOGY

E-Commerce

Increasingly, people and businesses buy and sell goods online. This is referred to as **e-commerce**. You can typically recognize a website that focuses on e-commerce because it has ".com" as part of its online address.

E-Commerce Technology

An e-commerce website can be a stand-alone business or the Web-based counterpart of a traditional storefront business. Typically, running an e-commerce website is less expensive than running a storefront business. That's because the cost of renting physical space is usually much more than the cost of renting space on the Web from a **Web host**—a business that stores all the information for a website on its servers (computers with a large storage capacity that are connected to the Internet).

The site will also need a **commerce server**. This type of server runs commerce-based applications, such as credit card processing and inventory management. Credit card processing requires security measures, such as a secure **sockets layer (SSL)** that "locks" the site, making it secure so it cannot be read by outsiders. It is common to get a Web host, commerce server, and security program in one package.

Paying Online

E-commerce sites normally use credit or debit cards as the method of payment (although checks or cash can be used in some cases). E-commerce sites require a payment system to process orders. One of the most common is a **shopping cart**. This type of system asks shoppers to place selected items in a "virtual cart." When they are finished shopping, customers pay for the selected goods.

Affiliate Marketing

Sometimes website owners do not even store the products they are selling. What they sell is shipped from a location other than the website owner's personal location. An example of this type of process is **affiliate marketing**. With affiliate marketing, a website owner sells items from another store and takes a percentage of the profits.

Traffic and Conversion Rates

Website owners prize **Web traffic**, which is the number of visitors a site gets over a specific time period. However, a more important statistic is the website's **conversion rate**. This is the percentage of Web traffic that translates into sales. It is a measure of how many potential customers actually buy something. An e-commerce website owner uses a **Web analytics tool** to track daily traffic, length of stay on the site, sales, and conversion rates.

Tech Vocabulary

affiliate marketing

commerce server

conversion rate

e-commerce

secure sockets layer (SSL)

shopping cart

Web analytics tool

Web host

Web traffic

Check Yourself

1. Why is running a website typically less expensive than running a storefront business?

2. What is a commerce server?

3. What is affiliate marketing?

4. Why is Web traffic less important than its conversion rate?

What Do You Think?

Comparing/Contrasting. What are some ways a website can stand out from other sites?

CASE STUDY

Business Model

STRUCTURING THE BUSINESS

Eva's Edibles is ending its first year of business. After a slow start, she's making adjustments that she thinks will make her even more successful. Find out how Eva is structuring her business.

Growing and Changing

In the beginning, Eva's business was small enough that she did everything on her own. She did the cooking in her clients' kitchens. She used her own car for making trips to the grocery store. She had only needed to purchase small kitchen appliances, some utensils and basic supplies, and business cards and brochures.

But Eva wanted to grow her business. She wanted more clients.

Registering As a Business

First and foremost, Eva decided to make her business a legal entity. In her college course, Eva remembered learning about different business structures. She made a chart that compared the advantages and disadvantages of each. She decided to set up her part-time service business as a sole proprietorship. It seemed like the simplest and least expensive way to operate for the time being. She named her business "Eva's Edibles," filled out the necessary forms, and obtained a tax I.D. number.

Distribution Chain

Eva decided that in order to make the amount of meals that she wanted, she would have to lease a commercial kitchen. She could then deliver prepared dinners to her clients.

To shop for groceries and to make deliveries, Eva would also need a van that was outfitted with shelves and refrigerated storage compartments.

Finding External Partners

Eva realized that she would need additional financing to expand her operations. She applied for a loan from the teacher's credit union to which her mother belonged. Her parents were proud of Eva's success and agreed to co-sign the loan.

There was another aspect to building her business—Sylvia Watson joined Eva's Edibles. Sylvia was a chef who specialized in pastries and desserts (an area where Eva was not strong). Sylvia had skills and experience and also some cash savings that she could immediately invest. She was interested in joining an existing business rather than starting her own.

When Sylvia and Eva discovered they had similar philosophies, they decided to become business partners, with Eva having sixty percent of the shares and Sylvia forty percent. They also agreed to continue doing business as Eva's Edibles.

Improving Record Keeping

Eva noticed how often she became bogged down with paperwork. Using her generic spreadsheet software just wasn't working anymore. Sylvia, who had worked for a catering company at one time, was familiar with a specialized software package that could help Eva's Edibles be more efficient.

This software made figuring out the cost of a meal's ingredients much easier. Eva and Sylvia could calculate the cost of a meal by entering the price of each ingredient directly into the computerized recipes. They could also use the software to draw up contracts, track customer prospects, create invoices, and run customized reports.

Hiring Help

Eva and Sylvia felt they needed two part-time employees—one would help with prep work in the kitchen and the other with deliveries. Prepping the food took a significant amount of time and involved a great deal of trimming, cutting, peeling, chopping, weighing, and measuring. So Eva and Sylvia decided they would advertise for a cook who had excellent knife skills and was good with details. They also advertised for a part-time driver. They created job descriptions and agreed on the type and amount of compensation. Then they placed advertisements online and in the local newspapers. Eventually they found the right employees.

Protecting the Business

When Eva started the business, she had a small insurance policy to cover her few pieces of equipment and product liability in case a client became ill from the food. Now, with the leased commercial kitchen and employees, she needed additional liability and property insurance. Sylvia pointed out that Eva's Edibles might also need workers' compensation insurance if they kept growing.

What Would You Have Done?

1. **Inferring.** If you were Sylvia, would you have wanted to change the name of the company? Explain your answer.

2. **Comparing/Contrasting.** Compare specialized software programs for catering, such as CaterEdge (www.cateredgesoftware.com), CaterEase (www.caterease.com), and Visual Synergy (www.synergy-intl.com). Which would you recommend?

3. **Writing.** How would you write an ad for the prep-cook position that Eva and Sylvia wanted to fill?

4. **Applying Concepts.** Research product liability for a company like Eva's Edibles. What level of insurance would you choose? What might the annual premium be?

5. **Analyzing Information.** Would you buy a hybrid van because it was "green" and to get a special tax credit? Explain your answer.

BIG IDEA: FINANCIAL & EXPENSE MANAGEMENT

GUIDING QUESTION:

"What does it cost to make my product or deliver my service?"

APPLICATION TO BUSINESS PLANNING:

☑ EOU and Variable Expenses

OBJECTIVES

- Identify and categorize examples of variable expenses incurred by businesses.
- Describe the relationship between selling price, variable expenses, and contribution margin.
- Explain how to structure an Economics of One Unit of Sale (EOU) for various business types.

NFTE Entrepreneurial Mindset Characteristic Focus

☑ Critical Thinking & Problem Solving

National Entrepreneurship Standards

- **F.14** Describe the concept of economies of scale
- **F.23** Assess factors affecting a business's profit
- **G.03** Describe the sources of income (wages/salaries, interest, rent, dividends, transfer payments, etc.)
- **G.06** Explain the time value of money
- **I.13** Explain the nature of overhead/operating expenses
- **L.34** Explain factors affecting pricing decisions
- **L.37** Set prices
- **L.38** Adjust prices to maximize profitability

Common Career Technical Core Standards

- **BM.1** Utilize mathematical concepts, skills and problem solving to obtain necessary information for decision-making in business.
- **BM.3** Explore, develop and apply strategies for ensuring a successful business career.
- **BM-MGT.5** Plan, monitor, manage and maintain the use of financial resources to ensure a business's financial wellbeing.
- **BM-OP.4** Plan, monitor and manage day-to-day business activities to maintain and improve operational functions.

National Entrepreneurship Standards: Career Competencies

☑ **G.14** Open an account with a financial institution

LESSON VOCABULARY

- commission
- contribution margin
- cost of goods sold (COGS)
- cost of services sold (COSS)
- cost structure
- economy of scale
- expense
- labor
- salary
- unit of sale
- variable expense
- volume discount

26.1 What Is a Variable Expense?

Business Model Goals

In this unit of the business model validation process, you will be looking at financial and expense management. Any business you run, even nonprofits, will have money coming in and **expenses**, or things you will have to buy to keep the business running. Even the most basic of businesses, such as a lemonade stand, has expenses such as lemons, cups, and signs. This unit will help you set up a **cost structure** so that you can ensure you have a profit. Structuring your business so that it is profitable will require engaging in the entrepreneurial mindset behaviors of critical thinking and problem solving.

From your work in other units, you may already have some notes on items that you will need to buy. This unit will walk you through how to work all of these expenses into your planning based on the type of expense it is.

Variable Expenses

One of the first major expenses that you need to determine for your business are ==variable expenses==. Variable expenses are expenses that change based on the amount of goods or services a business sells. Essentially, they are always tied to the amount of product or service being sold. In the lemonade example, every customer that buys a cup of lemonade gets a cup. If you have no customers, you don't use any cups. On the other hand, if you have a lot of customers, you use a ton of cups. Variable expenses are called variable expenses because they vary with the amount of product or services sold.

◀ **Figure 26-1**
Variable Expenses.

The material to make a hat would be a variable expense for a hat business.

Applying Concepts.

What would be other variable expenses for the hat business?

When you are trying to make a profit off of a sale, you always need to consider variable expenses. For example, if a business named Matt's Hats pays its hat supplier $6.00 per hat, the $6.00 is a variable expense. If Matt's Hats sells 500 hats in November the total variable expense will be $3,000.00 (500 × $6.00). If Matt's Hats sells 600 hats in December, the total variable expenses will be $3,600.00 (600 × $6.00). Although the variable expenses per hat remained at $6.00, the total of the variable expense changed due to the difference in the number of sales. If Matt's Hats did not plan for the increase in its variable expenses, the owner would be disappointed when the profits were less than expected.

There are three types of variable expenses to consider:

- **Materials.** This variable expense includes the materials to make the product or provide the service. For a product, this should include any materials bought and consumed while making the product. A service should include all materials used while delivering the service. This can be anything from a hot dog for a hot dog stand to the soap used for a cleaning service.

- **Labor.** ==Labor== is a term that refers to the amount of money being paid in return for someone's time. When you are identifying variable expenses, you should include any labor expenses paid to make the product or deliver the service. You may pay employees for many different things. However, variable expenses should only include time specifically spent on making the product or delivering the service. (You will look more closely at other labor costs later in this section).

- **Other variable expenses.** This includes any other variable expenses not directly related to making the product or delivering the service, which can include paying UPS to package or ship a product, paying sales people to sell your product, or paying a fee to sell a product through an online website.

Because materials and labor are both related to making the product or delivering the service, they are together referred to as the **Cost of Goods Sold (COGS)** or **Cost of Services Sold (COSS)**. Let's return to the example of Matt's Hats to see its variable expenses.

Suppose you have purchased hats from a wholesaler for $6 per hat. Because you are buying a finished product (the hats), no labor or other materials are involved. Your cost of goods sold per unit is $6.

Let's say Matt's Hats prints interesting designs on hats you buy from a wholesaler. You would still have a variable expense for each hat of $6, but you also have printing expenses—labor and materials (ink). The cost of labor and materials is another variable expense added to your cost of goods sold. In this case they add another $2.50 per hat. You also have to pay shipping ($1) and handling ($0.25).

Knowing the variable expenses, you can calculate how much profit your business makes on each unit sold. Your goal would be to sell enough units each month to have profit left over.

Ledger 26.1 ▶
Cost of Each Hat.

Cost of Each Hat			
Cost of Good Sold			
Cost of Hat	$6.00		
Labor & Materials	2.50		
Total Cost of Goods Sold		$8.50	
Other Variable Expenses			
Shipping	1.00		
Handling	.25		
Total Other Variable Expenses		1.25	
Total Variable Expenses			$9.75

Variable or Not Variable?

For new entrepreneurs, it can be tricky to determine if an expense is variable or not. Let's look at an example of labor costs in a restaurant and why they would be considered variable or not variable.

Variable Labor:

• **Hourly.** Many employees are brought on as part-time employees, which means that they usually work less than a full 40-hour work week and only get paid for the amount of hours they work. In a restaurant, wait staff and hosts are typically part-time hourly employees.

• **Commission.** A **commission** is an amount paid based on the amount of products or services that a salesperson sells. Usually a commission is a percentage of the total amount sold. Since a salesperson on "straight commission" only gets paid if he or she sells something, this approach is directly tied to work performance and results. For example, that same restaurant might pay staff bonuses if they convince a customer to try a specific menu item. If they do not try it, the bonus is not paid. Some wait staff might even be paid an hourly wage plus commission of any sales that they make.

Not Variable Labor:

- **Salary.** A salary is a fixed amount of money that an employee is paid on a regular basis, such as weekly, bi-weekly, bi-monthly, or monthly. A salary is paid regardless of any sales made by the business. An example is the restaurant manager who is required to work regardless of how many customers there are. These are *not* variable expenses, and will be discussed in more detail in the next chapter.

The best way to tell whether an expense is variable or not is to ask yourself: "Would I still have to pay this expense if I had *zero* customers?" If the answer is no, then it *is* a variable expense.

Apply Your Knowledge   What is a variable expense? Think back to your investigation of Eli's Cheesecake. Was the vanilla bean a variable expense? What other variable expenses would be involved with making and shipping cheesecakes?

ENTREPRENEURIAL CASE STUDY: CRITICAL THINKING & PROBLEM SOLVING

 ## Ben Kaufman— Quirky

Making Invention Accessible

Ben Kaufman—Breaker, Maker, Founder, and former-CEO of Quirky (www.quirky.com)—makes inventions accessible. In 2009, Ben launched Quirky to break down the barriers to the invention process and allow creative people all over the world to invent together. He's helped hundreds of everyday inventors bring their product ideas to life and forged partnerships with the world's largest retailers to sell those products. While at Quirky, Ben worked to redfine the way the world thinks about product development and innovation.

Ben Kaufman.

Passion for Inventing

Ben started his entrepreneurial journey early while growing up in Long Island, New York. He was, he says, "a terrible student." But it was as a teenager attending school where he developed his first invention. Ben wanted to listen to his iPod while in class while not drawing attention from the teacher. "I went home and made a lanyard headphone that concealed the wires," he says. "It looked like I was just wearing a keychain, when I was wearing my iPod."

While probably not the best move for his grades, this event did spark a passion in Ben for innovation and inventing things. Ben soon recognized an opportunity to sell his invention to a larger market. He started his first business, Mophie, named after his golden retrievers Molly and Sophie, to sell his mobile accessories. However, Ben soon found that a good idea didn't mean it was easy to create a product. To get the $185,000 he needed to manufacture and distribute his product, he had to ask his parents to refinance their home. The risk paid off as Mophie was successful and grew into a full line of mobile accessories, but Ben still thought about how challenging it was to bring his idea to market. He thought about all of the innovative entrepreneurs with great ideas, but lacking in capital to have their products built. Ben knew he was on to a new opportunity.

Outsourcing the Cost of Doing Business

This inspired Ben to start Quirky. Quirky helps bring people's inventions to life by asking people to submit ideas to the website. It does not matter how detailed or realistic; anyone can submit. Then Quirky asks site visitors to vote and provide feedback on the ideas, so the inventors can perfect them. The best ideas, as decided by the market, get financed and put into production by Quirky. Instead of having to pay for the expenses of running the business, the inventors get a portion of the profit while Quirky runs the business operations. This model is perfect for those who enjoy inventing and creating, but would rather not take on the financial risk of starting and running a business.

As of 2014, the company had grown to almost 300 employees—with offices in Manhattan, San Francisco, Schenectady, and Hong Kong—and pushed almost 200 products to market that can be found in brick and mortar shops such as Best Buy, The Home Depot, and Target. With this success, Quirky has brought in over $175 million dollars in venture funding to grow the company as well. As the company grows, the company has dubbed Ben, "The World's Least Important CEO," to communicate the importance of the community that comes together to cultivate and fund innovation.

Thinking and Acting Like an Entrepreneur

- What problems did Ben solve with his business?
- Why would having Quirky build and sell a product be more appealing than traditional entrepreneurship for some people?
- How does Ben demonstrate the entrepreneurial mindset skill of critical thinking and problem solving?

26.2 The Economics of One Unit of Sale

What Is a Unit of Sale?

Entrepreneurs need to know their businesses are profitable. One important way to examine profitability is to look at how much profit the business makes every time it sells one item. But what exactly is the business selling? In some cases, this is easy to figure out. If you sell shoes, you would figure your profit from each pair of shoes. But what happens if you make buttons? Would it make sense to figure your profit based on a single button?

This is where the concept of one unit of sale comes in. A **unit of sale** is what a customer actually buys from you. It's the amount of product (or service) you use to figure your operations and profit. The unit of sale is really the basic building block of your business. If you were a retailer who sold athletic shoes, your unit of sale would be a single pair of shoes. But if you were a wholesaler and only sold a minimum of five pairs at a time, your unit of sale would be five pairs of shoes. The smallest unit a customer can actually buy from you isn't a single pair of shoes—it's a carton containing five pairs. So your unit of sale would be five pairs of shoes packed in a carton. (However, it would still be useful for you to know the cost of a single pair of shoes.)

If you were a manufacturer of buttons and sold them to other manufacturers, wholesalers, or large retail chain stores in cartons containing 1,000 boxes of 100 buttons each, your unit of sale would be one carton containing the 1,000 boxes. That's what your customer is actually purchasing. Figuring out a unit of sale for a service business is usually based on how a customer is charged. For example, if you run a hair salon, a unit of sale might be one haircut. If you are creating mobile apps, your unit of sale might be one download from an app store. If you run a lawn mowing company, your unit of sale might be mowing one lawn. But, because lawns are different sizes, you might have different rates for different sizes of lawns or you might charge by the hour. The easiest way to think about a unit of sale is to ask yourself this question: "What is it your customer is actually buying from you?" That is your unit of sale.

◀ **Figure 26-2**
A Unit of Sale.
A unit of sale might be a pair of customized gym shoes.

Drawing Conclusions:

Why should you define your unit as a pair or shoes, and not one single shoe?

The Economics of One Unit of Sale

Entrepreneurs use their profits to pay themselves, to expand their businesses, and to start other businesses. Entrepreneurs want to know how much the business earns on the products it sells. To do this, they study the economics of one unit of sale (EOU). You learned a little about the economics of one unit in Chapter 14. You learned the general formula:

Selling Price – Expenses = Profit (or Loss)

Now you will analyze the expenses involved in the economics of one unit of sale in more detail. This will enable you to see the profitability of your company more accurately.

To calculate the economics of one unit of sale, subtract the variable expenses for a unit from the selling price for the unit. Remember from the previous section that the variable expenses vary directly as a result of sales. The result is the **contribution margin**. This is the amount per unit that a product contributes toward the company's profitability.

Selling Price – Variable Expenses = Contribution Margin

When coming up with your Economics of One Unit of Sale, it is important that the contribution margin be as large as possible because other non-variable expenses need to be covered by this contribution margin. The higher the contribution margin, the higher your final profit.

Looking at the equation for the Economics of One Unit of Sale, you can increase your contribution margin either by:

- Raising the selling price
- Lowering the variable expense

When you raise the selling price, you will be bringing more money in, but as you learned in Chapter 14, you also risk losing sales from having too high of a price for the market, which is why you want to make sure your variable expenses are the lowest possible for your product or service.

Economy of Scale

Consider this strategy for keeping your variable expenses low. Check the prices of paper towels at your local supermarket. The price of three single rolls will be greater than the price of a three-pack of the same brand. The supermarket is offering you a lower price if you purchase a larger quantity of product. Typically in business the price per unit declines as you buy larger amounts. Similarly, as a business grows, it may be able to negotiate better prices from suppliers because it is purchasing larger quantities of goods. The cost reduction made possible by spreading costs over a larger volume is called an **economy of scale**.

◀ **Figure 26-3**
Economy of Scale.
Stores offer you lower prices when you purchase larger quantities.

Predicting.

Can you think of products where it would not make sense to buy in bulk?

You can get discounts from suppliers if you buy in quantity. (A discount for buying greater quantities is called a **volume discount**.) Typically, as your cost of goods sold per unit decreases, your profit increases. For example, normally Matt's Hats purchases 100 hats at a time at a price of $6.00 per hat. If Matt's Hats purchased 200 hats at a time, the price per hat would be reduced to $5.75 because of the volume discount.

In the next section, you will see how EOUs are calculated for the four types of businesses.

Apply Your Knowledge What is a unit of sale? From your investigation of Eli's Cheesecake, how did the more expensive vanilla bean impact the contribution margin for the business?

CAREER COMPETENCIES

 ## Open an Account with a Financial Institution

Functions of a Bank

Now that you will be making money and paying bills for your business, you will need to set up a bank account for your operations. A bank is a financial institution, which is a fancy way of saying a business that stores and manages money for individuals and businesses. The bank invests money or loans it to people and other businesses so the bank can earn even more money. There are basically three reasons to put your money in a bank: to keep it safe, to earn interest, and to make financial transactions easier. There are many types of banks and bank accounts that you will learn more about in Chapter 29. Understanding which bank provides the most conveniences and services that you need will help you choose the one that is right for you.

Banks keep track of the money you deposit and withdraw from your bank account. A bank statement is a record of the transactions between you and the bank. A bank account is a record of the transactions between you and the bank. When you deposit money, the amount is added to your current bank account balance. This is known as a credit. When you withdraw money, the amount is subtracted from the balance. This is known as a debit.

The most common types of personal bank accounts are checking accounts and savings accounts.

- **Checking accounts** are set up so that you can access your money by writing checks. You can also use a debit card or automated teller machine (ATM) card. Most people use checking accounts so they can pay for things without carrying cash. Checking accounts allow flexible payment options, such as writing a check for groceries, or, more commonly, using a debit card to pay for movie tickets. You must have enough money in the account to cover all of the checks and debit transactions.

- **Savings accounts** are not usually linked to checks or debit cards, although you may be able to deposit or withdraw money using an ATM card. Savings accounts earn interest, which means the bank pays you money that is a percentage of your balance—the amount of money in your account. That interest is an incentive for you to keep your money at the bank. People use savings accounts to save money for future use.

Opening a Bank Account

You open a checking or savings account by going to a branch, filling out some forms, and making a deposit. Each bank has different rules, but usually you meet with a manager or assistant manager to show a picture I.D., such as a student I.D., a driver's license, or a passport. You may also need a birth certificate or Social Security card. Then, you will do the following:

- Fill out a signature card that the bank will keep on file. A signature card helps keep your account safe, because it identifies the person authorized to use the account.

- Make the first deposit into the account when you open it. Some banks have a minimum deposit requirement, so it's a good idea to ask ahead of time how much money you will need.

- Fill out forms for ordering personalized checks. If you are opening a checking account, you will need to pick out your checks. The cost of the checks is automatically subtracted from your account balance, though some banks offer checks for free.

- Select personal identification numbers (PIN) for any debit or ATM cards, or for your online banking access.

Good practices and state laws dictate that entrepreneurs should open a separate account for their personal expenses and the business's expenses. That way, you will not have to worry about your own personal money

26.3 Calculating Your EOU

In Chapter 14, you looked at a basic EOU for your business. Now you will use your variable expenses to create a more detailed EOU. When structuring your detailed EOU, you have to take into consideration what type of business you have. Here are sample EOUs for each of the major business types.

EOU for a Manufacturing Business

Suppose a manufacturing business makes high school class rings and sells them wholesale for $40 each. We want to look at the economics of one unit based on a single ring. The materials used to produce a ring cost $3. Each requires one hour of labor at $15 per hour. So the cost of goods sold per unit would be $18 ($3 + $15). There are no commissions, and the expense of shipping and handling a single ring is $1.

◄ Figure 26-4 EOU for Manufacturing.

A class ring would be a product that is manufactured.

Applying Concepts.

What variable expenses would need to be covered when selling a ring?

In this example, the contribution margin per unit is $21. The manufacturer uses this information to make business decisions. One possibility would be to see if a new, less expensive supplier could be found. This would decrease the cost of the materials per unit from $3. Often manufacturers look at a single item as if that were the unit of sale. It can be a useful exercise, but they sell very large quantities of product. A manufacturer could then look at the unit of sale as 12 rings or 120 rings or even a larger number. If they do this, they are like wholesale businesses, which are described next.

Economics of One Unit: Manufacturing Business			
One Unit of Sale = 1 Ring			
Selling Price (per Unit):			**$40**
Variable Expenses			
Cost of Goods Manufactured & Sold			
Materials	$ 3		
Labor ($15/hour)	15		
Cost of Good Sold		$18	
Other Variable Expenses			
Commissions	0		
Shipping & Handling	1		
Other Variable Expenses		1	
Total Variable Expenses			19
Contribution Margin (per Unit):			**$21**

▲ **Ledger 26.2**
EOU for a Manufacturing Business.

▼ **Ledger 26.3**
EOU for a Wholesale Business.

EOU for a Wholesale Business

The method used to calculate the EOU for a wholesaler is similar to that of a manufacturing business. The difference is that the wholesale business buys finished products from a manufacturer, so its cost of goods sold per unit doesn't include labor.

In this example, the wholesaler buys rings from a manufacturer at $40 each. The wholesaler packages the rings in quantities of 12 per shipping carton. Shipping and handling for the carton is $16. Each carton with 12 rings is sold to a retailer for $1,200.

Economics of One Unit: Wholesale Business			
One Unit of Sale = 12 Rings in a Carton			
Selling Price (per Unit):			**$1200**
Variable Expenses			
Cost of Goods Sold			
Rings (12)	$ 480		
Cost of Good Sold		$ 480	
Other Variable Expenses			
Commissions	0		
Shipping & Handling	16		
Other Variable Expenses		16	
Total Variable Expenses			496
Contribution Margin (per Unit):			**$ 704**

The contribution margin per unit for the wholesaler is $704. This might seem high in comparison with the $21 contribution margin per unit for the manufacturer, but remember that the wholesaler's unit of sale is a *carton of 12 rings*, while the manufacturer's unit of sale is a *single ring*. The wholesaler's contribution margin for a single ring would be $58.66 ($704 ÷ 12). The wholesaler's contribution margin per ring is still more than twice that of the manufacturer.

EOU for a Retail Business

Using the same ring example, let's look at a retail business. The retailer purchases the rings for $1,200 for a carton of 12 rings and then sells the rings one at a time. The unit of sale therefore is one ring. The retailer's cost of goods sold per unit is $100 ($1,200 ÷ 12 rings). Like the wholesaler, the retailer buys finished products, so there is no labor expense. The retailer pays his salesperson a 15% commission on the sale of each ring. The ring is sold to high schools from a catalog and then shipped to each student purchaser. The price of shipping and handling is $7. The retailer sells each ring for $200.

These examples using class rings show a typical method of distribution. A product is produced by a manufacturer and sold to a wholesaler, who then sells the product to a retailer. The retailer then sells it to the ultimate user, the consumer.

▼ **Ledger 26.4**
EOU for a Retail Business.

Economics of One Unit: Retail Business			
One Unit of Sale = 1 Ring			
Selling Price (per Unit):			$200
Variable Expenses			
Cost of Goods Sold			
Rings (1)	$100		
Cost of Good Sold		$100	
Other Variable Expenses			
Commissions	30		
Shipping & Handling	7		
Other Variable Expenses		37	
Total Variable Expenses			137
Contribution Margin (per Unit):			$ 63

EOU for a Business Selling More Than One Product

A business selling a variety of products has to create a separate EOU for each product to determine whether it is profitable. However, when there are many similar products, you can develop a "typical EOU." For example, David sells four brands of candy bars at his booth at the local food market. The cost for each candy bar is similar (see Table 26.1).

Table 26.1   Costs for Candy Bars

Number	Brand	Cost
1	Chocolate Dee-Light	$0.36
2	Almond Happiness	$0.38
3	Fruit 'n' Joy	$0.42
4	Junior Chocolate Roll	$0.44

Figure 26-5 ▶
Selling More Than One Product.

Many businesses sell more than one product at a time.

Applying Concepts.

Which of the strategies for finding the EOU of multiple products would you use?

Rather than calculating EOUs for each of these similar products, David uses the average contribution margin of each transaction as his EOU. First, he adds up the cost of the four candy bars. Then he divides that total by four to get the average cost. The average cost is $0.40.

Chocolate Dee-Light	$0.36
Almond Happiness	0.38
Fruit 'n' Joy	0.42
Junior Chocolate Roll	0.44
Total	$1.60

$1.60 ÷ 4 = $0.40 (Average Cost)

There are other ways that David could calculate the cost of the candy bars. He could:

- Use the cost of the most expensive bar. That way he would slightly overestimate the average cost. This method would work best if he sold about the same number of each candy bar.

- Use the cost of the best-selling candy bar. This method would work best if he sold significantly more of the best-selling bar.

- Use the average cost weighted by volume. This way, the cost of the best-selling bar was given more weight in calculating the average cost; the next best-selling bar was given less weight, and so on.

Economics of One Unit: Business Selling More Than One Product			
One Unit of Sale = 1 Candy Bar (Average Cost)			
Selling Price (per Unit):			$1.00
Variable Expenses			
Cost of Goods Sold			
Candy Bar (Average Cost)	$0.40		
Cost of Good Sold		$0.40	
Other Variable Expenses			
Commissions	0		
Shipping & Handling	0		
Other Variable Expenses		0	
Total Variable Expenses			0.40
Contribution Margin (per Unit):			$0.60

David sells the candy bars for $1.00 each. The economics of one unit of sale (EOU) for David's business is developed by using the average of $.40 per candy bar. David doesn't pay a commission and he sells directly to the consumer, so there is no shipping or handling.

EOU for a Service Business

Manufacturing, wholesale, and retail businesses have one thing in common: they sell products. A service business typically doesn't sell products. Because of this, a different method of determining an EOU must be used. Sometimes figuring out what a unit of sale is for a service business is difficult. It might be one tutorial lesson, one lawn mowing job, or one income tax preparation. It could also be one hour of consulting, or a three-hour block of time. Cost of Goods Sold (COGS) does not apply, because no goods are actually being sold.

Instead, you would use Cost of Services Sold (COSS) when calculating an EOU. In the typical service business, you would calculate the cost of services sold by multiplying the number of hours the service takes to perform by the hourly wage of the person providing it. Sometimes, to perform the service, you must use supplies.

For example, if you were cutting hair, you might need hair gel, shampoo, conditioners, or other products. These would be variable expenses because they are directly related to the services being sold. For example, Joan Barry has her own hair styling business. She calculates an EOU based on each haircut. She estimates it takes her one hour to complete a hair styling job. She values her time at $30 per hour. She estimates that each job requires about $5 worth of supplies (shampoo, conditioner, gel, and so on). She charges $55 to style a customer's hair.

In this case, Joan is both the person providing the hair styling and the owner of the business. She will earn $30 as the hair stylist and $20 as the entrepreneur. If she could hire someone else to do the hair styling for $30 per hour, she would still receive the contribution margin of $20.

Figure 26-6 ▶
Service Business.

A service business also needs to keep track of the expenses involved in a unit of sale.

Drawing Conclusions.

How would you keep track of the supplies required for a dog grooming session?

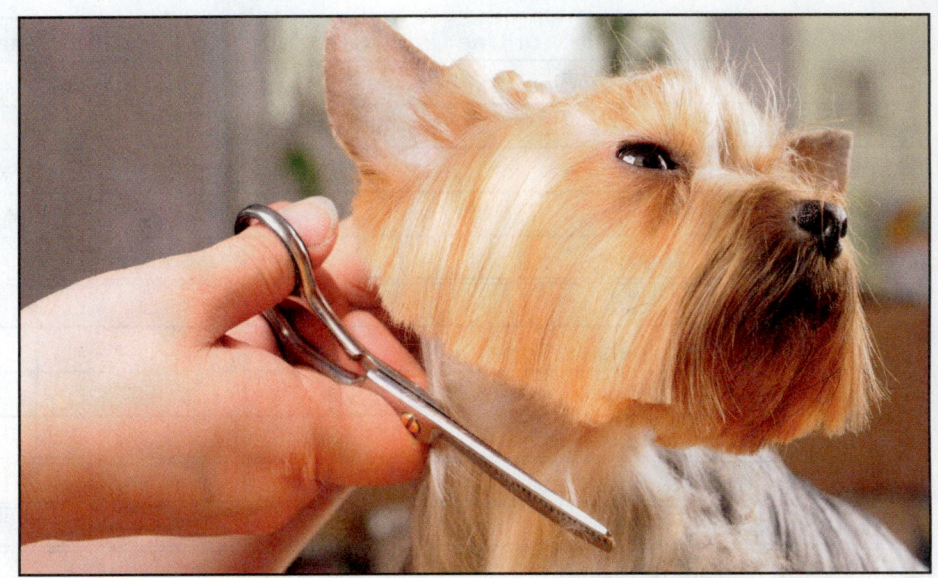

▼ **Ledger 26.6**
EOU for a Service Business.

Even better, if she could hire a stylist at $20 per hour, she would then have a contribution margin of $30 per styling job. Her cost of services sold per unit would be $25 and her contribution margin would be $30 ($55 − $25 = $30). By hiring additional stylists she would be able to increase the business's volume and also increase her profits. This is how you grow a business, which you'll learn more about in Unit 8.

Economics of One Unit: Service Business			
One Unit of Sale = 1 Hair-Styling Job			
Selling Price (per Unit):			**$55**
Variable Expenses			
Cost of Goods Sold			
Materials (Shampoo, etc.)	$ 5		
Labor ($30/Hour)	30		
Other Variable Expenses		$35	
Commissions	0		
Shipping & Handling	0		
Other Variable Expenses		0	
Total Variable Expenses			35
Contribution Margin (per Unit):			**$20**

EOU for Tech-Based Businesses

As you learned in Chapter 21, just because a company does the majority of its business online does not make it a separate type of business. A business selling its products through an online site is still a manufacturer. Any fees, shipping, and handling that go with each online sale would be accounted for in "Other Variable Expenses."

For online businesses, such as blogs or mobile apps, the EOU can get a little tricky. The key is to constantly ask yourself, "Who is the paying customer? What are they buying? What are the expenses with each purchase?" For a mobile app that is downloaded through an app store, there might not be any variable materials or labor, as you do not have to "make" the app with each download. However, you *would* have to pay a commission fee to Apple or Google Play for hosting your app to be downloaded. For a blog or website that is free to customers but makes money through advertising, your EOU would actually be the cost for other businesses to advertise on your website. Any variable expenses would be the time spent finding businesses to advertise.

▼ **Ledgers 26.7 and 26.8 EOU for a Tech-Based Business.**

Economics of One Unit: Tech-Based Business			
One Unit of Sale = 1 Paid Download for a Mobile App			
Selling Price (per Unit):			$2.99
Variable Expenses			
Cost of Goods Sold	$0.00		
Cost of Good Sold		$0.00	
Other Variable Expenses			
Commission per Download (Apple/Google Play Store)	$0.45		
Other Variable Expenses		$0.45	
Total Variable Expenses			0.45
Contribution Margin (per Unit):			$2.54

Economics of One Unit: Tech-Based Business			
One Unit of Sale = 1 Ad Banner for 1 Month			
Selling Price (per Unit):			$500
Variable Expenses			
Cost of Goods Sold	$ 0		
Cost of Good Sold		$ 0	
Other Variable Expenses			
Sales Commissions per Advertisement	$100		
Other Variable Expenses		$100	
Total Variable Expenses			100
Contribution Margin (per Unit):			$400

Apply Your Knowledge What does an EOU help you determine? Think back to your investigation of Eli's Cheesecake. How could they have used EOU calculations in helping with their decision?

APPLICATION TO BUSINESS PLANNING

EOU and Variable Expenses

Use what you learned from this chapter about variable expenses to structure your EOU for your main product or service. You should support your findings with data from research. Be sure to include:

- A list of your variable expenses
- A selling price that is more than your variable expenses (and reasonable for the market)
- An Economics of One Unit (EOU) that shows your contribution margin for each sale

REVIEWING OBJECTIVES

1. What are examples of variable expenses incurred by businesses?

2. What is the relationship between selling price, variable expenses, and contribution margin?

3. Explain how to structure an Economics of One Unit of Sale (EOU) for various business types.

CRITICAL THINKING

How does the method of calculating the contribution margin for a manufacturing business differ from that of a service business? From that of a mobile app business?

ENTREPRENEURIAL THINKING EXERCISE: CRITICAL THINKING & PROBLEM SOLVING

Think back to your investigation of Eli's Cheesecake. Create a list of pros and cons for each of the decisions. Make a recommendation on what the business should do based on your lists. Be prepared to explain your decision.

EXTENSION ACTIVITIES

Entrepreneurship & Mathematics Skills

Complete the following task to demonstrate your understanding of entrepreneurship:

Grades 9–12: Return to Ledgers 26.2 through 26.8 on pages 494–499 that show examples of economics of one unit. Use those examples to complete the following tasks:

- Convert the individual variable expenses into a percentage of the total variable expenses.
- Convert the total variable expense into a percentage of the selling price.
- Convert the total contribution margin into a percentage of the selling price.
- Write a polynomial equation that demonstrates how the contribution margin percentage of the selling price is a function of the total variable expense.

OBJECTIVES

- Identify examples of fixed expenses commonly incurred by businesses.
- Use a break-even analysis to help maximize the profitability of the business.
- Describe strategies for managing ongoing expenses.

NFTE Entrepreneurial Mindset Characteristic Focus

☑ Creativity & Innovation

National Entrepreneurship Standards

- **C.14** Explain the concept of financial management
- **F.23** Assess factors affecting a business's profit
- **I.03** Estimate cash-flow needs
- **I.13** Explain the nature of overhead/operating expenses
- **I.28** Supervise/implement regular accounting procedures and financial reports
- **L.33** Calculate breakeven point
- **L.34** Explain factors affecting pricing decisions
- **L.37** Set prices
- **L.38** Adjust prices to maximize profitability
- **O.07** Conduct break-even analysis
- **O.11** Develop expense-control plans
- **O.12** Analyze cash-flow patterns

Common Career Technical Core Standards

- **BM.1** Utilize mathematical concepts, skills and problem solving to obtain necessary information for decision-making in business.
- **BM.3** Explore, develop and apply strategies for ensuring a successful business career.
- **BM-MGT.5** Plan, monitor, manage and maintain the use of financial resources to ensure a business's financial well-being.

LESSON VOCABULARY

- break-even analysis
- break-even point
- break-even units
- burn rate
- cash flow
- cash flow statement
- cyclical
- depreciation
- depreciation expense
- disposal value
- fixed expense
- salvage value
- straight line method of depreciation

- **BM-MGT.6** Plan, monitor and manage day-to-day business activities to sustain continued business functioning.
- **CRP.3** Attend to personal health and financial well-being.

National Entrepreneurship Standards: Career Competencies

- ☑ **G.17** Develop spending plan
- ☑ **G.25** Develop personal budget

ENTREPRENEURIAL INVESTIGATION
Frugal Operations

Elementbars.com is a business that allows customers to go online and create their own energy bars. The bars are then baked and shipped out to customers. When the business was just starting, its founder, Jonathan Miller, decided to do most of the business online and out of his home to avoid paying expensive rent for an office building. When it came time to expand to a larger kitchen, he and his team looked at renting their own store to make and sell their bars. However, they soon decided to rent out space in a commercial kitchen that was not being used in the early morning. This allowed the new business to only pay a small fraction of the rent they would pay for their own kitchen. The business had a successful launch, and was even featured on ABC's *Shark Tank*.

Do some research on Jonathan and his business to answer the following questions:

- What do you think were the benefits of running a business from home instead of renting an office?
- Why do you think Jonathan decided to bake the bars in a shared space?
- What would you have done differently if you were in his shoes?

Be prepared to share your findings with your teacher and peers.

27.1 Fixed Expenses

In the previous chapter, you looked at expenses that were related to the unit of sale. In this chapter, you will look at the other expenses that you have to pay regardless of sales. In Chapter 14, you learned about these as operating expenses. Keeping these expenses to a minimum is another important strategy for maximizing the profit of your business. As you set up an action plan to identify and manage your expenses, you will be using your entrepreneurial mindset behaviors of initiative and self-reliance.

What Are Fixed Expenses?

In addition to your variable expenses, there will be other bills that you will have to pay regularly. These monthly expenses typically include rent, Internet access, salaries, and utilities (gas and electricity). An expense of this type is called a **fixed expense**—an expense that isn't affected by the number of items a business produces. The business will incur fixed expenses no matter how many products it sells. For example, if the rent for the space at Matt's Hats is $500 per month, it will remain $500 even if in September your business makes and sells twice as many items as it produced and sold in August.

Another way of looking at fixed expenses is that they are ongoing expenses a business must pay to be able to operate. The word "fixed" doesn't mean the expense will never change. It means only that an expense doesn't change in response to sales. For example, if Matt's Hats needs air conditioning, its electric bills will likely be higher in the summer than they are in the winter. The electric bills will fluctuate based on the season. However, they will not change according to sales. The business might even have more sales in the winter, when the electric bills are lower.

Here's another example. Suppose you are an automobile dealer. If you pay your sales manager $5,000 per month in salary, you will have to pay that same amount whether the business sells one automobile or a thousand. This is a fixed expense. Now, let's say that you decide to give the manager a raise to $6,000. Your business's fixed expenses will increase by $1,000 per month, but this figure has no direct bearing on the number of automobiles your business will sell.

The important thing to remember is that fixed expenses don't include expenses directly related to the products the business sells. These types of expenses would be variable expenses, as you learned from the previous chapter.

An easy way to remember eight of the most common fixed expenses is to remember the phrase:

I SAID U R + "OX"

This stands for:

- **Insurance.** Any premium paid for an insurance policy for the business. See Chapter 24 for more information on insuring your business.
- **Salaries.** As you learned in the last chapter, any employee that gets paid regardless of sales made is considered salaried. This could include paying managers to run your store, or tech support for your website.
- **Advertising.** Any paid advertising for your business. See Unit 4 for more information on advertising costs.

Predicting.

If you were starting a small business, would you rent or buy? Why?

- **Interest.** Interest that could be paid on loans for the business. See Chapter 29 for more information on loans.
- **Depreciation.** An accounting method of spreading cost of equipment over time. See below.
- **Utilities.** Utility bills such as gas, electric, telephone, and Internet.
- **Rent.** Rent for a storefront or work space.
- **Other Fixed Expenses.** Additional unique expenses such as a website hosting fee.

Depreciation

You have probably heard of many of these fixed expenses, or learned about them in your entrepreneurship course. One you may not have heard of is **depreciation**. It is an accounting method of spreading the total cost of the equipment a business buys over the number of years it will be used.

There are several depreciation methods a company can use. One of the most common ways of determining depreciation is the **straight-line method of depreciation**. The entrepreneur estimates how long the equipment will last and then figures what it could be sold for at the end of its business life (this is often referred to as the equipment's **disposal value** or **salvage value**). Next, to find the total depreciation, the entrepreneur subtracts the disposal value of the equipment from its actual cost. Then he or she divides that number by the estimated number of years during which the equipment will be used. The amount calculated per year is the **depreciation expense**.

For example, suppose a manufacturer buys a $25,000 machine. The manufacturer estimates that the business will use the machine for five years and then will sell it for an estimated $5,000 (this would be the disposal value). The total depreciation is $20,000 (the cost of the machine minus the disposal value). Using the straight-line method of depreciation, you would divide the total depreciation by the number of years the machine was used:

$$\text{Cost} - \text{Disposal Value} = \text{Total Depreciation} \div \text{Lifetime} = \text{Depreciation Expense}$$

$$\$25,000 - \$5,000 = \$20,000 \div 5 \text{ years} = \$4,000$$

A business can have many different types of expenses, including payments for materials, equipment, merchandise for resale (or inventory), rent, insurance, employee salaries and wages, sales commissions, and shipping and delivery. Managing expenses is a two-step process that involves:

- **Knowledge.** First, a manager must be knowledgeable about the expenses that a business incurs. These costs should be monitored, typically on a monthly basis.

- **Action.** Once a manager knows the extent of existing costs, he or she can act to reduce future costs. Cost cutting measures include buying used equipment, instead of new equipment; leasing buildings or company vehicles, as opposed to buying them; reducing energy usage (electricity, gas, oil, etc.); and hiring part-time or temporary workers, instead of full-time permanent employees. Spreading fixed expenses over as much output as possible is another way to gain economies of scale for your business. Typically, as your fixed expenses per unit decrease, your profit increases.

Apply Your Knowledge   List and explain some common fixed expenses of a business. Think back to your investigation of Elementbars. com. What are some fixed expenses that the business would have?

ENTREPRENEURIAL CASE STUDY: CREATIVITY & INNOVATION

 ## Dagim Girma— The Audible

The Social Sports Network

Dagim Girma is the founder and CEO of The Audible (www.theaudible.net). The Audible is a website through which high school sports fans can engage with one another through a social network platform. Dagim started this business while he was in his entrepreneurship course sponsored by the Network for Teaching Entrepreneurship (NFTE) at T.C. Williams High School in Alexandria, Virginia. For his business, Dagim was awarded the runner-up honors at the 2013 NFTE National Youth Entrepreneurship Challenge and Elevator Pitch Challenge, earning over $5,000 in education and venture grants.

Dagim Girma.

Combining Interests and Skills

Since he was young, Dagim's passion and interests have included technology and sports. Learning how to create websites at a young age, he used his knowledge to create websites around things that interested him. While working in his NFTE entrepreneurship course, Dagim was challenged to think about a business opportunity. In what seemed like a perfect opportunity for him to combine his interests into a business opportunity.

During this time, Dagim launched his website, "The Audible," as part of his business plan. The Audible was founded as a sports news website geared for the teenaged sports fan. Instead of traditional sports news reporting, Dagim planned on using social media and crowdsourcing to make the experience more interactive. The social element allows readers to receive the latest news from featured young writers, along with the opportunity to also try their own hands at sports reporting. Dagim's business was built around a lean cost structure, as he was able to create and maintain the website himself. Using up-and-coming reporters for the content also allowed him to keep personnel costs low as well.

Dagim entered his business plan in local business plan competitions sponsored by NFTE. After winning preliminary rounds, Dagim's business would be selected as among the best of 38 teen competitors from across the country. Judges loved how he used his unique knowledge and skills to create a business, and was able to run it with low fixed expenses. His business ended up taking second place in the 2013 NFTE National Business Challenge. He also received the opportunity to travel to the White House to pitch his idea to President Obama.

Getting Paid for Hobbies

After the competition, Dagim decided to continue to work on The Audible as his main priority. However, he is still working on other Internet startups in his spare time while he also attends Babson College. About his experience taking entrepreneurship in high school, "I am so grateful to NFTE for helping me do what I love to do and teaching me how to make money while doing it," Dagim said. "The National Youth Entrepreneurship Challenge has taught me to believe that I can achieve my dreams. Now I am looking forward to scaling my business and taking it to the next level."

Thinking and Acting Like an Entrepreneur

- How did Dagim use his skills and interests to identify his business opportunity?
- What are some reasons that Dagim is able to keep his fixed expenses low?
- In what ways did Dagim demonstrate the entrepreneurial mindset skills of creativity and innovation?

27.2 Breaking Even

What Is a Break-Even Point?

How can a manager be knowledgeable about the fixed expenses she or he incurs? One way to do this is do a break-even analysis.

Think about this: If you were running a business, what would happen if your expenses were exactly equal to your sales? There would neither be a profit nor a loss. The net income at the bottom would be zero. That is what's called the ==break-even point==, because the business has sold exactly enough units to cover expenses. A ==break-even analysis== is an examination of the income statement that identifies the break-even point for a business. A break-even analysis examines how many units of a product (or hours of a service) a business must sell to pay all its expenses.

For example, Matt would have a problem if Matt's Hats had sales of 500 hats and needed to sell 1,000 to break even (and pay his costs). Matt would have to make some decisions, because he wasn't selling enough hats to cover his expenses—let alone make a profit! He might decide to review his expenses to see if any could be reduced or eliminated. Or, he might find ways to increase sales. Frequently, business owners need to come up with combinations of methods to solve problems like this. The problems must be solved or the company will go out of business very quickly.

Break-Even Analysis

You use break-even analysis to determine how many units of a product a business must sell to pay all its expenses. Let's use Matt's Hats as an example of how to carry out a break-even analysis.

◀ **Figure 27-2**
Break-Even Analysis.
The number of units needed to break even for the business.

Applying Concepts.
What happens to the money brought in beyond the break-even units for a hat retailer?

In the month of July, Matt's Hats bought 1,000 hats at $6 each from a wholesaler. It sold the hats to customers at $10 each. At the end of the month, Matt determines the business had $3,000 in fixed expenses (rent, utilities, and salaries). Matt wants to know if that was enough to make a profit.

In this example:

- The unit of sale for Matt's Hats is one hat.
- The selling price per hat is $10.
- The variable expenses per unit is $6.
- The fixed expenses for the month is $3,000.

However, the full $10 brought in with each does not go directly to Matt. Because there were total variable expenses per unit of $6, Matt's Hats has a contribution margin of $4 per unit. Remember from the previous chapter, the contribution margin is used to pay the fixed expenses:

Selling Price per Unit – Total Variable Expenses per Unit = Contribution Margin per Unit

Using this information, Matt can calculate how many hats Matt's Hats has to sell each month to cover fixed expenses. These are its **break-even units**—the number of units of sale a business needs to sell to arrive at the break-even point (where the bottom line is zero). From this example, you can see Matt's Hats needs to sell 750 hats per month to pay its fixed expenses and break even.

Here's how to calculate break-even units:

Monthly Fixed Expenses ÷ Contribution Margin per Unit = Break-Even Units

$3,000 ÷ $4 = 750 Hats

If Matt's Hats sells fewer than 750 hats, it will lose money. If it sells more than 750, it will earn a profit. If it sells exactly 750, the company will cover its expenses and will have neither profit nor loss.

You can test if these break-even units are accurate by creating a monthly statement that figures out total sales, variable expenses, and profit after fixed expenses. For Matt's Hats in July, we know that the total sales were 1,000 making the total sales revenue $10,000.

Total Sales × Variable Expenses = Total Sales Revenue

1,000 hats × $10 per hat = $10,000

The Ledger 27.1 shows that Matt's Hats has fixed expenses of $3,000 for July. Taking the total revenue, total variable expenses, and total fixed expenses for the month shows that Matt's Hats made a profit of $1,000. This was expected with total sales of over 1,000 hats.

Ledger 27.1 ▶

Matt's Hats: Income Statement.

This shows a brief income statement for Matt's Hats for the month of July.

Analyzing Data.

If the selling price per hat is $10, how many hats did Matt's Hats sell in the month of July?

Income Statement for Matt's Hats (Brief Version)	
For the Month Ended July 31, 2017	
Revenue	$10,000
Cost of Goods Sold	6,000
Gross Profit	$ 4,000
Operating Expenses	3,000
Pre-Tax Profit	$ 1,000

The Burn Rate

Because you will be expected to cover fixed expenses in your first month of operation, most new businesses try to start with a surplus of cash. (You'll read more about the need for cash reserves in Chapter 29.) However, most new businesses also spend more money than they earn while getting off the ground. The question most beginning entrepreneurs need to know is: How long can I afford to lose money?

◄ **Figure 27-3**

Burn Rate.

Knowing the monthly fixed expenses can help you calculate the burn rate.

Applying Concepts.

Why is it a good idea to figure out how many months a new business could go without revenue?

The rate at which a company spends cash to cover overhead costs without generating a positive cash flow is called the <mark>burn rate</mark>. It is typically expressed in terms of cash spent per month. A burn rate of $10,000 monthly means that the business is spending that sum every month to cover rent and other fixed expenses.

Use the burn rate to calculate how long a company can go without revenue. If a business has $20,000 in cash and a burn rate of $2,000 a month, it can stay in business for 10 months without making any sales.

Cash on Hand ÷ Burn Rate = Number of Months Before Cash Runs Out

$$\$20,000 \div \$2,000 = 10 \text{ months}$$

Apply Your Knowledge   Why are break-even units important? From your investigation, why was the team at Elementbars.com concerned about break-even units as a new business?

CAREER COMPETENCIES

☑ ## Develop Spending Plan; Develop Personal Budget

Setting Up a Budget

To help manage your business's monthly fixed expenses, it is helpful to create a budget. Every budget has two main parts: income and expenses. All the money that comes in to you is income. Income includes the following:

- Wages and tips you take home from working
- Gifts you receive for birthdays, holidays, and special occasions
- Money you may receive from your family for helping with chores
- Interest that you earn on money in the bank

Expenses are all the ways you use your money. Expenses include the following:

- Purchases, including needs and wants
- Savings
- Charitable donations

You can set up a budget for any length of time, such as a week or a year. Most budgets are set up for a month. A month is convenient because most people pay expenses on a monthly basis, such as rent, telephone, and cable bills. They often receive income on a monthly basis as well.

When doing a personal budget, it is smart to start by listing all of your sources of income, then list your expenses. If you do not know the exact amount for one of the entries, you can estimate. Subtracting your expenses from your income should result in zero for a balanced budget, or more ideally more than zero to give a surplus. If your budget gives you a negative number, or a deficit, you should revisit your spending habits and savings goals.

Using a Budget to Manage Cash Flow

Budgeting for a business is similar to creating a personal budget. However, it is also used to make sure that the cash that is coming into a business will be sufficient to cover the cash that is flowing from it. A cash budget is a record on which a business owner forecasts (predicts) incoming and outgoing cash flows for an upcoming period (typically a month) and later compares actual cash inflows and outflows to the forecasted amounts. Making predictions about the future is difficult. However, business owners can use historical data and other records to make educated guesses about future cash flow.

Forecasting cash flow is a three-step process:

1. **List and Total Any Expected Incoming Cash Payments over the Next Month.** Orders from new, unknown, or unreliable customers that have been placed but not paid for yet should not be included in the cash forecast. There is an old saying, "Don't count your chickens before they hatch." Only cash receipts you really expect in the month should be counted. This includes, for example, checks from trusted customers or expected credit card payments.

2. **List and Total Expected Outgoing Cash Payments for the Next Month.** These include rent and any other expenses that will be paid in cash.

3. **Subtract Expected Cash Ouflows from Expected Cash Inflows.** The resulting sum will provide an estimate of the surplus (or shortage) of cash expected for the next month.

Cash Budget for the Month of January			
	Forecast	Actual	Difference
Cash Inflows			
Cash Sales			
Credit Collections			
Bank Loans			
Other Income			
Total Cash Inflows			
Cash Outflows			
Estimated Variable Expenses			
Insurance			
Salaries			
Advertising			
Interest			
Utilities			
Rent/Mortgage			
Other Fixed Expenses			
Total Cash Outflows			
Cash Available			

◀ **Ledger 27.2**
Cash Budget.

A cash budget shows forecasted and actual cash inflows and outflows.

Classifying.

Most of the fixed expenses are shown as possible cash outflows. Why wouldn't depreciation be a cash outflow?

Career Skills in Action

Now create a monthly budget and spending plan for your personal budget or your business. Be sure to include the following:

- All expected income for the month you are budgeting for
- All estimated expenses for the month you are budgeting for
- The resulting balance of your budget at the end of the month

Share your budget with your teacher or a peer for feedback. With the class, discuss the importance of budgeting.

27.3 Managing Cash Flow

Why Worry About Cash Flow?

A break-even analysis provides great targets for your business to hit monthly. However, what it does not take into consideration is the amount of cash you have on hand.

Cash for a business is like gasoline for an automobile—without it, the business does not have the necessary fuel to operate. Size doesn't matter. A compact car, a luxury sedan, or an 18-wheel semi-tractor cannot go anywhere on an empty tank. Similarly, it doesn't matter if a business is small or large—if it doesn't have enough cash to pay its bills as they come due, the creditors can force the business to close its doors.

For example, let's say that you do a break-even analysis for your business and determine that you have to bring in $3,000 in sales to cover your fixed expenses. However, just counting on those sales alone to cover your fixed expenses can be risky, because that might not necessarily be the amount of cash you received. Also, if some of your sales were made on credit, you may not get the money from those customers until October, or even later.

A company must have sufficient cash on hand to continue to do business. You must also continue to pay your suppliers, to pay for items you have purchased on credit, and to repay any loans you may have. If you are constantly short of cash, you could lose your business.

To ensure that you have enough money to operate, you must track your business's **cash flow**. Cash flow is the money received minus what is spent over a specified period of time.

The cash flow equation is:

$$\text{Cash Inflow} - \text{Cash Outflow} = \text{Net Cash}$$

Another example where monitoring cash flow is important are for businesses that have sales that are based on the time of year. For example, Matt sells hats in the summertime on the boardwalk and beach. Matt closes his business in the winter. If you were operating an ice cream stand, your sales during the summer months would be higher than in the winter. If you were selling scarves and gloves, your sales would almost certainly be higher in the cold weather.

Cash flow is **cyclical** for many businesses, meaning that it varies according to the time of year.

Other examples of businesses with cyclical cash flow are flower shops, bridal shops, and college book stores. Each of these businesses must carefully monitor cash flow in the months of low sales. Remember, you will have monthly expenses (fixed expenses) regardless of whether the month has typically high-sales or low-sales. This is especially important for retail businesses that do more sales in the holiday season. Some businesses get 50–70% of their yearly revenue between October and December. They must plan their cash flow for the less busy months as well.

Reading a Cash Flow Statement

To monitor cash flow, a business prepares a **cash flow statement**. This is a financial document that records inflows and outflows of cash when they actually occur. Besides preparing an income statement every month, a successful entrepreneur also prepares a cash flow statement.

Cash Flow Statement for Matt's Hats		
For the Month Ended August 31, 2017		
Beginning Cash Balance	$ 430	
Cash Inflow		
Sales	4,400	
Available Cash		$4,830
Cash Outflow		
Cash Purchases of Inventory	600	
Insurance Paid	200	
Interest Paid	300	
Rent Paid	200	
Telephone Paid	200	
Utilities Paid	75	
Total Cash Outflow		1,575
Net Cash		3,255

◀ **Ledger 27.3**

Matt's Hats: Cash Flow Statement.

This shows the August cash flow statement for Matt's Hats.

Analyzing.

What would happen if Matt didn't have enough cash on hand to pay for new inventory?

The format and headings for a cash flow statement may vary. Ledger 27.3 shows a typical cash flow statement prepared for Matt's Hats for August.

- **Beginning Cash Balance.** Matt started the month with $430 in cash.

- **Cash Inflow.** Matt received $4,400. Matt sells his hats on the boardwalk and only accepts cash payment. If Matt extended credit to his customers, he would show their payments as cash inflow. If Matt had any investments that increased in value, that would also be shown in this section.

- **Available Cash.** The beginning cash balance and the cash inflow for the month show the company's total available cash. In Matt's case, this is $4,830 ($430 + $4,400 = $4,830).

- **Cash Outflow.** This section notes the cash spent on purchases of additional inventory of hats ($600). The cash outflow section also includes money Matt spent on operating expenses. The total cash spent in August was $1,575.

- **Net Cash.** The last section shows the net change in cash flow. This tells the entrepreneur whether the business had a positive or negative cash flow that month. As you can see in Ledger 27.3, Matt's Hats had a positive net cash flow of $3,255 for the month of August.

Ways to Keep Cash Flowing

Here are five ways to avoid being caught without enough cash to pay your bills:

- **Collect Cash As Soon As Possible.** When making a sale, try to incentivize the customer to use cash rather than credit. Or, set up an electronic debit system that transfers cash to your business immediately. Be insistent on collecting overdue payments and adhere to any credit payment policies.

- **Pay Bills Close to the Due Date.** Always note the due date on your bills. Plan your payment to reach the creditor just before or on the due date. However, be careful not to send the payment so that it arrives after the due date.

- **Keep Track of Your Cash.** Check the cash balance every day. Always know how much you have. Keep track of the money your business earns and spends each day. Make sure you get and keep receipts for every purchase you make. You don't want to be surprised by a lack of cash.

- **Lease Equipment.** Often, a large down payment is required when you buy equipment. The down payment reduces your cash on hand. When feasible, don't buy equipment; lease it.

- **Keep Inventory to a Minimum.** Minimize the amount of inventory you stock unless it's part of your competitive advantage to offer customers a wide selection. Avoid large purchases of slow-moving inventory. Inventory ties up cash in two ways: the cash you use to purchase the inventory and the cash you spend in storing it.

 **Apply Your Knowledge** What is the purpose of a cash flow statement? Why is it important to monitor cash flow? Think back to your investigation of Elementbars.com. How was Jonathan more efficiently managing the business's expenses with his decision?

APPLICATION TO BUSINESS PLANNING

Fixed Expenses and Break-Even Units

Use what you learned from this chapter about managing fixed expenses to get an expense plan together. You should support your findings with data from research. Be sure to include:

- A list of your monthly fixed expenses (include any expenses identified from other units)
- The number of break-even units you need to sell to cover your fixed expenses (based on your contribution margin from the previous chapter)
- The amount of cash you will need on hand to keep the business open for at least three months of operations

ASSESSMENT

REVIEWING OBJECTIVES

1. What are examples of fixed expenses commonly incurred by businesses?

2. How can you use a break-even analysis to help maximize the profitability of the business?

3. Describe strategies for managing ongoing expenses.

CRITICAL THINKING

What are some methods that a business can maximize its profits through profit expense management?

ENTREPRENEURIAL THINKING EXERCISE: INITIATIVE & SELF-RELIANCE

Think back to your investigation of Elementbars.com. Imagine that you were hired as a consultant to help manage their expenses. Put together an action plan with achievable steps towards a goal of buying their own building. What do you think they would need to do to get there? Explain your answer.

EXTENSION ACTIVITIES

Entrepreneurship & Mathematics Skills

Complete the following task to demonstrate your understanding of entrepreneurship:

Grades 9–12: Return to the Matt's Hats break-even analysis from Section 27.2. Use that example to complete the following tasks:

- Write an equation with one variable that shows break-even units as a function of the contribution margin.

- Solve for the new break-even units if the sales increase by 30%.

- Solve for the new break-even units if the total variable expenses decrease by $1 a hat.

- Write an equation with one variable that shows break-even units as a function of the fixed expenses.

- Solve for the new break-even units if the fixed expenses increase by 25%.

28 REVENUE STREAMS AND SALES PROJECTIONS

GUIDING QUESTION:

"How much money can I plan on bringing in?"

APPLICATION TO BUSINESS PLANNING:

☑ Projected Income Statement

OBJECTIVES

- List potential revenue streams for a business.
- Explain the process for forecasting sales for a future period of time.
- Describe the parts and function of an income statement.

NFTE Entrepreneurial Mindset Characteristic Focus

☑ Future Orientation

National Entrepreneurship Standards

- **F.23** Assess factors affecting a business's profit
- **G.15** Set financial goals
- **G.19** Complete financial instruments
- **G.20** Maintain financial records
- **G.21** Read and reconcile financial statements
- **I.02** Prepare estimated/projected income statement
- **I.13** Explain the nature of overhead/operating expenses
- **I.28** Supervise/implement regular accounting procedures and financial reports
- **L.34** Explain factors affecting pricing decisions
- **L.37** Set prices
- **L.38** Adjust prices to maximize profitability
- **L.53** Plan strategies for meeting sales quotas
- **O.06** Forecast income/sales

Common Career Technical Core Standards

- **BM.1** Utilize mathematical concepts, skills and problem solving to obtain necessary information for decision-making in business.
- **BM.3** Explore, develop and apply strategies for ensuring a successful business career.
- **BM-MGT.5** Plan, monitor, manage and maintain the use of financial resources to ensure a business's financial wellbeing.

LESSON VOCABULARY

- calendar year
- fiscal year
- freemium
- income statement
- profit and loss statement
- revenue
- revenue stream
- sales forecast
- subscription
- syndication
- transaction fee

- **BM-MGT.8** Create strategic plans used to manage business growth, profit and goals.
- **CRP.3** Attend to personal health and financial well-being.
- **MK-SAL.1** Access, evaluate and disseminate sales information

National Entrepreneurship Standards: Career Competencies

 G.16 Develop savings plan

ENTREPRENEURIAL INVESTIGATION
There's No Business Like Show Business

Making and releasing movies is a multi-billion dollar industry for movie studios. In 2013, movies set an all-time record, bringing in over $10.9 billion through box office ticket sales. However, this is not the only money that this industry brings in. Choose a big blockbuster that was released recently, and consider the following:

- What type of items do you see being sold that are related to new movies in theaters?
- Do people pay if they want to see a movie a second time?
- How can movie studios make money from a movie after it leaves theaters?

Be prepared to share your findings with your peers and teacher.

28.1 Identifying Sources of Revenue

So far in this unit, you have been looking at the cost of doing business by investigating variable and fixed expenses. This has brought you one step closer to answering the business model validation question for this unit: does each sale make enough money to generate a profit?

In this chapter, you will start to look more closely at putting together a plan for bringing in the money needed to cover those expenses. You will also look at maximizing your profits over a long time frame, which will require a closer look at behavior of future orientation, an entrepreneurial mindset.

Revenue Streams

Throughout this textbook, you have seen or heard the term "revenue." In a business sense, **revenue** is the amount of money a business receives during a specific time period before expenses. It is usually calculated from the selling price of the product or services by the number sold. As you have already learned from the previous chapters, it is the entrepreneur's job to make sure that the business brings in enough revenue to cover all variable and fixed expenses, and make a profit.

In Chapter 26, you looked at the Economics of One Unit of Sale. You set a selling price for your main product or service, and determined how you defined that unit of sale. Doing this exercise is extremely important, as it determines the contribution margin for a one-time sale, and ensures that variable expenses are covered. But how can businesses also find other ways to bring in additional revenue? The answer is to look at revenue streams, or the individual methods by which money comes into a company.

Let's look at a real example: You are opening a gym that sells monthly memberships to its customers. It would be wise to do your EOU for one customer membership for one month, as that will be sure to cover your variable expenses per customer. However, your gym can also find additional revenue streams to bring in extra money:

- Charging customers for fitness classes or personal training
- Fees for equipment/locker rental
- Selling sports beverages and nutritional supplements

◀ **Figure 28-1**
Revenue Streams.
Businesses like a gym find many ways to bring in revenue.

Applying Concepts.
What are other ways that a gym could bring in extra revenue from customers?

When identifying sources of revenue streams, you should consider the following:

- **Subscription:** an ongoing fee for access to a service (gym membership, computer games with online access)
- **Advertising/Sponsorship:** money brought in for including advertisements through the business (Web banners, advertisements at sporting events)

- **Transaction/Usage Fees:** fee for using the business's services (fees at hotels, ATM fees)
- **Licensing and Franchise:** money brought in by allowing others to run new branches of your business
- **Renting/Leasing:** letting others use equipment or space that your business owns
- **Syndication:** allowing others to use your creative works at a cost (more frequent in TV and radio)

Non-Traditional Revenue Streams

Understanding how revenue is coming in to your business is very important for your financial planning. In fact, many businesses these days do not rely on traditional revenue streams, where customers paying money is the main source of revenue. Let's look at another example:

Pretend that you are creating a mobile app that acts as a personal organizer and to-do list. You decide to release it as a freemium model. A **freemium** model means customers can get a free version with limited features and/or advertisements, or pay for a version with all the features and/or no advertisements. In this model, you actually have two revenue streams:

- Customers downloading the freemium version for free and seeing advertisements
- Customers paying to download the full version

For this business, you would need to have an EOU for both scenarios to understand how the revenue coming into your business covers the variable expenses for each. You would also need to know how much of each you can expect to bring in, which we will investigate in the next section.

Apply Your Knowledge What are various types of revenue streams? Think back to your investigation of movie studios. Can you identify the numerous revenue streams they have with one movie?

ENTREPRENEURIAL CASE STUDY: FUTURE ORIENTATION

 **Dan Trepanier— The Style Blogger**

Finding a Niche Audience

Dan Trepanier is the founder, author, and Creator Director of Articles of Style (www.articlesofstyle.com). Part style diary and part practical dressing advice, Articles of Style aims to reach guys "somewhere between Kanye West and average Joe." The concept has found a receptive audience: Dan's website logs some 250,000 visitors from 195 countries every month. The business world has taken note, too. In the past year, Dan and his team have collaborated with a diverse roster of brands, including Ralph Lauren, Gillette, and Saks Fifth Avenue.

Unexpected Success

Dan's entrepreneurial beginnings started on a small farm outside of Windsor, Ontario, Canada, where he was born and raised. Two of his interests growing up would be the foundation for his career path: basketball and men's fashion. Dan eventually moved to New York City to attend Columbia University, where he was recruited to play basketball. He spent four years playing Division 1 basketball while pursuing a degree in Psychology. His teammates valued his skills on the court, but they also knew Dan was the go-to guy to get tips about personal clothing advice. After a while, Dan felt that maybe he could more efficiently communicate his style tips to his teammates and others. "I'll start a website and you can go there for your answers," he told them. Articles of Style (previously The Style Blogger) was born.

Dan Trepanier.

In 2009, Dan started the site as a hobby; two years later, it became a full-fledged business. "I saw a void for a guy's guide to style," Dan recalls. "Something for regular guys who aren't necessarily interested in fashion but want to improve the way they dress." Dan was not alone in his vision. Hundreds of thousands of visitors were suddenly coming to his website to hear his opinions. Overnight, he seemed to find Internet fame, being named Esquire magazine's "Best Dressed Real Man in America" the same year that his blog launched. Dan knew that he needed to capitalize on this opportunity that had been put in front of him.

Finding a Business Opportunity in Blogging

For the business to actually make money, Dan had to figure out how to pull in revenue from all of the visitors coming to his website.

While it would be hard to take money directly from customers for his advice, he instead decided on advertising as the main source of revenue for the business. Visiting Dan's website, as with most online media businesses, you will note that potential advertisers can find the demographics, psychographics, geographics, and buying patterns of the site's visitors. Through this approach, Dan can bring in revenue while customers receive advertisements that are targeted for their interests specific to the site, for example, clothes and grooming products.

For the future, Dan has plans for growth that include hiring more staff, creating higher-end content including video, manufacturing his own line of products, and reengineering the site to make it more interactive. And despite the overnight success of his business, Dan has remained focused on the mission for his readers: "I always want what we do to be authentic and relatable. That is the key. Be a trusted advisor, not a salesman."

Thinking and Acting Like an Entrepreneur

- How has Dan used his passion, interests, and skills to find a business opportunity for himself?
- What is the main revenue source for Dan's business?
- In what ways does Dan demonstrate entrepreneurial mindset behaviors of planning and acting on long-term goals?

28.2 Sales Forecasting

A **sales forecast** will be a key part of your company's financial planning process. A sales forecast is a prediction of the amount of future sales your company expects to achieve over a certain period of time. Think of a sales forecast as a tool to help evaluate the health of an established company or the feasibility of a new business venture. You should also consider doing a separate sales forecast for all the major revenue streams for your business.

Preparing a Sales Forecast

Sales forecasts for established companies are usually based on past sales performance. A forecast also takes into account such factors as the current economy, sales trends, company goals and capabilities, and what the competition is currently doing. There are four general steps in preparing sales projections:

1. Analyzing current conditions.

Analyze the current company and market conditions. Do this through market research and by updating your SWOT analysis chart to analyze strengths, weaknesses, opportunities, and threats.

2. Reviewing past sales.

Review your company's past sales figures. You can usually use past sales to project future sales. Sales often show seasonal variations. For example, you would sell more skis and sleds in the winter and more shorts and sandals in the summer. If you do not have past sales data because you are starting a new business, you will need to research general sales history for your industry. You can obtain this information from industry associations and by asking similar businesses outside your area.

3. Making educated projections about the future.

   Is there something in the future that could cause a change in your future sales? Will you need more or less promotion, or perhaps different types of promotion? Will you need more employees to accommodate these changes? Should you increase or decrease prices?

4. Estimating your future sales for a specific time period.

   Ask yourself if these sales will bring in more income than you expect to spend. Will these sales be enough to make a profit?

Sales Forecasting Techniques

There are many methods for estimating sales. Often, more than one technique is used to help make projections as accurate as possible because most techniques cannot take into account all of the factors that can impact sales.

If you plan to work with a bank to help finance your new business venture, you will probably want to make multiple sales forecasts. For example, make one that represents a best-case scenario, one for a worst-case scenario, and one for in-between. This will lend more credibility to your business plan.

Here are some common forecasting techniques:

- **Full Capacity.** This technique is pretty simple: you forecast selling as many products (or performing as many jobs) as you can. Often a young entrepreneur who is going to school has only so much time to devote to the business. For example, if you can spend 10 hours a week making candles, and you can make 20 candles an hour, your full capacity for a week would equal 200 candles. If it turns out that you can't sell all you can make, you'll need to adjust your forecast.

- **Observational Data.** One of the best ways to forecast sales is to observe your competitors' customers. For example, if you are opening a restaurant, you could sit in the restaurants your target customers frequent that are near your desired location. You could note such things as the number of customers who ate in the restaurant, how much they spent, and what they ate. This data would help you forecast your own sales.

- **Industry Standards.** To make a proper sales forecast, you will need to know how sales are estimated in your particular industry. For example, consultants, technicians, and designers are usually paid by the hour. In contrast, sales forecasts for retail stores are sometimes based on sales per square foot. (So, for a retail store's sales forecast, you would need to find out the annual sales per square foot for similar types and sizes of stores, in locations similar to yours. You would average the results, and then multiply that dollar figure by the estimated floor space of your business.)

Figure 28-2 ▶
Sales Cycles.
Florists are an example of an
industry greatly affected by
sales cycles.

Predicting.
In what months do you think
florists sell the most? Why?

- **Industry/Seasonal Cycles.** Keep in mind the particular buying phases that apply to your industry. For example, some retail businesses do about 50 percent of their annual sales from the end of October to the end of December. Fireworks companies, on the other hand, do almost all of their business around July 4th and January 1st. So vary your monthly sales estimates based on appropriate market cycles.

- **Team Effort.** Many businesses find that getting multiple groups of people involved in the forecasting process is helpful. You get a broader perspective on issues when you ask customers, salespeople, sales support, and company executives to all provide feedback.

- **Number of Customers versus Distance.** This technique is used primarily by businesses in which the customer must visit a physical store to make purchases. Examples include a hair or nail salon, a dry cleaning business, and a car wash. You would determine the number of households living within one mile of your business location that use your product/service. Then, estimate how much they will spend for these items per year. Estimate what percentage of money they will spend with you as compared with your competitors. You can use this technique with other distances, such as five miles and ten miles. Estimated sales figures usually get lower as the distance increases.

- **Market Share.** If the main portion of your goods is sold via the Internet or by catalog, you first estimate your market share in terms of customers in your shipping range. Then, calculate how often and how much the people in your market might buy from you per year. Your annual sales estimate could be calculated as:

Number of Customers × Number of Purchases per Year × Average Amount of Each Purchase

- **Proportional Scaling.** You should estimate sales separately for each product or service you sell. For each item, first estimate the quantity you think you will be selling six months from now. Then, calculate the total of all sales per day. Next, multiply the sales per day by the number of days per month that you will be open for business. This determines the total sales per month. Using this as your goal for month six, build up estimated monthly figures gradually, from little or no sales when the business first opens in month one to that monthly figure you calculated for month six. Then, gradually scale up your sales for months seven through twelve.

Apply Your Knowledge What are the four general steps to take in developing sales forecasts and projections? From your investigation, how do you think movie studios do their own sales forecasting?

CAREER COMPETENCIES

Develop Savings Plan

Differences Between Saving and Investing

Once your business starts making a profit, it can be tempting to spend that money immediately. However, smart business owners save the profit for future uses. Saving money is one of the most important steps toward financial security. You put the money someplace safe—such as a bank or a credit union—so that it is available when you need it for an unexpected expense (such as medical bills), a planned expense (such as education), or for retirement. As a bonus, the bank will pay you just for leaving the money in your account. The longer it stays in your account, the more money you will have to spend later.

You might decide to invest some of your savings. Investing is riskier than saving, but it also provides an opportunity to earn more money or to increase your savings at a faster rate. Saving and investing provide opportunities to increase your wealth, leading to financial security and freedom. There are a few options to consider when developing a savings plan:

- **Savings Accounts.** The safest, most reliable, and most convenient way to save is to deposit your money in a savings account at a retail bank or credit union. The money will earn a small amount of interest and be available when you need it. It is insured by the Federal Deposit Insurance Corporation (FDIC) or the National Credit Union Association (NCUA), so you won't lose the money. Savings accounts, and any other investment for that matter, earn interest in one of two ways. Simple interest is calculated based on the principal balance only. Compounded interest is calculated based on the principal plus any interest that has already been earned.

- **Investments.** Equity investments is a type of investment in which you purchase stock—or ownership—in a company. They can also be fixed income investments where you lend money to a business or the government in exchange for a bond that gains interest over time. Bonds are safer than stocks, but stocks allow for a larger return on the initial investment.

- **Tax-Deferred Savings Plan.** This is third savings method that, in a sense, combines saving and investing for the specific purpose of saving for retirement. Today, many companies let employees take a portion of their paycheck and set up an Individual Retirement Account (IRA), where money is set in a savings account, or a 401(k)/403(b) where employees can invest that same money. The positive is that this money is not taxed, as an incentive to use these plans. However, you cannot access the money in these accounts before you reach retirement age without incurring a penalty.

Most financial experts advise that you use a combination of saving and investing. Saving keeps your money safe and available, and investing gives you a chance to grow your wealth. The amount you save and the amount you invest depend on your financial goals, your financial resources, how old you are, and how much risk you are willing to take.

Career Skills in Action

Now create a savings plan to implement with the profit from your business. Do some research on savings account options in local banks. Be sure to include the following:

- How much money from your monthly budget you would be able save

- What percentage of your profit you would put in a savings account versus investing

- What financial goals you have (save over a long period of time versus try to grow wealth fast)

Share your plan with your teacher or a peer for feedback.

28.3 Income Statements

One of the most important documents for a business is an ==income statement==. An income statement is a financial document that summarizes a business's income and expenses over a given time period and shows whether the business made a profit or took a loss. That's why it's also called a ==profit and loss statement==, or P&L for short.

Many times entrepreneurs can use income statements to determine if their projected sales from all of their revenue streams together will cover expenses and produce a profit. If a business's sales are greater than its expenses, the income statement will show a profit. If a business's sales are less than its expenses, the income statement will show a negative number, or a loss.

When to Prepare an Income Statement

Because income statements show how a business is performing, they are prepared periodically.

- **Monthly.** Most small business owners should create a monthly income statement.

- **Quarterly.** Most companies generate an income statement showing income and expenses for the quarter. If you prepare statements monthly, it will be easy to put together quarterly statements.

- **Annually.** Most companies also prepare income statements on an annual basis that show how the company performed during the year. Preparing statements on a quarterly basis will make it easier to prepare an annual statement. A ==calendar year== is January 1 through December 31. However, your income statement might be based on what is called a fiscal year. A ==fiscal year== is any 12-month period you choose to treat as a year for accounting purposes. This would be the period you would use when figuring your taxes. Once you make a choice, you cannot change it, so give it some thought. For example, many retail companies have a fiscal year that starts February 1 and ends January 31 to reflect the holiday season.

◀ **Figure 28-3**

Determining a Company's Fiscal Year.

Many retail companies have a fiscal year that ends January 31 to reflect the holiday season.

Drawing Conclusions.

Why would a business that sells school supplies have a fiscal year that ends June 30th?

Differences in Income Statements

Income statements can vary in wording, but they all include the same basic information: revenue, expenses, and net income or loss. However, a significant difference in income statements is how businesses show their variable expenses. Based on the type of business, variable expenses will appear under these headings:

- **Cost of Goods Sold.** Merchandising businesses (wholesale and retail companies) keep track of the cost of their beginning inventory, the cost of any additional inventory they purchase, and the cost of their ending inventory. This allows them to calculate the cost of inventory sold during this period.

- **Cost of Goods Manufactured and Sold.** Manufacturing companies track the cost of both labor and materials. The two are added to arrive at the cost of the products they are selling.

- **Cost of Services Sold.** Service companies track materials involved in providing their services. Sometimes they include the cost of labor if the service can be easily broken down into segments. For example, a haircut could be separated into the cost of materials (shampoo, conditioner, etc.) and the time it takes to accomplish (say, 45 minutes). When labor is paid by the hour (for example, in a bike repair shop) or costs are based on projects (for example, with an event planner), the income statement wouldn't include this section.

Parts of a Typical Income Statement

Matt Washington has a summertime business. He sells hats on the boardwalk near the beach. He stores his hats in a large locker he rents from a local merchant. He runs the business from his parents' home and makes a contribution toward their utilities.

Matt needs to prepare an income statement for August. Because he has a retail business (selling hats purchased from a wholesaler), Matt uses Cost of Goods Sold to categorize his variable expenses. Ledger 28.1 uses Matt's Hats to identify the six parts of a typical income statement.

If you have a merchandising business (wholesaling or retailing), your income statement will be similar to Matt's.

- **Revenue.** This is the money Matt's Hats receives from selling its products. The revenue section includes gross sales (the total revenue from all the hats sold), return sales (the total dollar amount of the hats that were returned), and net sales (gross sales – return sales). Matt sells hats for $20 each. So, with gross sales of $4,800, Matt sold 240 hats ($4,800 ÷ 20 = 240).

- **Cost of Goods Sold.** This is the cost of all the hats Matt sold. It's calculated by subtracting the value of the ending inventory from the value of the beginning inventory (and any additional purchases of goods). The beginning inventory was $1,200 (Matt pays a wholesaler $6 a hat, so this means 200 hats: $1,200 ÷ 6 =

200). He paid $600 for an additional 100 hats in August (600 ÷ $6 = 100). At the end of the month, he had 80 hats left in inventory. Because each hat cost $6, this meant that his inventory had a value of $480 (80 × $6 = $480).

- **Gross Profit.** Gross profit is calculated by subtracting the cost of goods sold from the net sales.

- **Operating Expenses.** All of Matt's expenses in running his business are included in the operating expenses section. Only the expenses that apply are listed. Because Matt doesn't pay salaries or interest, for example, those aren't on the list. Often, accountants organize operating expenses alphabetically.

- **Pre-Tax Profit.** The pre-tax profit is calculated by subtracting the operating expenses from the gross profit ($3,080 − $650 = $2,430).

- **Net Profit (or Loss).** The net profit, also called net income, is calculated by subtracting taxes from the pre-tax profit. Taxes in this example are estimated at 15% of the pre-tax profit and are rounded off to the nearest dollar ($2,430 × 15% = $364.50, rounded to $365). The net profit is Matt's profit as an entrepreneur.

▼ **Ledger 28.1**

Matt's Hats: Income Statement.

This shows the income statement for Matt's Hats as of August 31.

Predicting.

If hats sell at $20 each, how many hats did Matt's Hats actually sell in August? (Hint: Use the Net Sales in your calculation.)

RETAIL BUSINESS: Income Statement for Matt's Hats			
For the Month Ended August 31, 2017			
Revenue			
Gross Sales	$4,800		
Sales Returns	400		
Net Sales			$4,400
Cost of Goods Sold			
Beginning Inventory	1,200		
Add: Purchases	600		
Total		$1,800	
Less: Inventory, August 31		480	
Cost of Goods Sold			1,320
Gross Profit			**3,080**
Operating Expenses			
Advertising	100		
Insurance	200		
Rent	150		
Telephone	100		
Utilities	100		
Total Operating Expenses			650
Pre-Tax Profit			**2,430**
Taxes (15%)			365
Net Profit			**2,065**

Income Statement for a Manufacturer

Ann Waverly sells t-shirts that she prints with her own designs and messages. Ann's is a manufacturing business because she buys supplies and, through her labor, converts those supplies into a new product.

Ann needs to prepare an income statement for March. As a manufacturing business, Ann will use Cost of Goods Manufactured and Sold in her income statement. Her statement is shown in Ledger 28.2.

If you have a manufacturing business, your income statement will be similar to Ann's.

- **Revenue.** Ann had gross sales of $7,500 in March, selling 500 t-shirts at $15 apiece. Her customers were very satisfied, as only 2 shirts were returned, so Ann sold 498 t-shirts.

- **Cost of Goods Manufactured and Sold.** Ann buys t-shirts from a wholesaler for $3 each. The total cost for t-shirts in March was $1,494 (498 × $3 = $1,494). In addition, Ann estimates that she spends $0.50 per shirt on inks and paints. The cost of these supplies in March was $249 (498 × $0.50 = $249). The total cost for materials was $1,743 ($1,494 for the t-shirts and $249 for the inks and paints). Ann spends 15 minutes printing each shirt. Because she wants to make $20 an hour, she estimates her labor at $5 for each shirt ($20 ÷ 4 = $5). So, the total cost of labor in March was $2,490 (498 × $5 = $2,490). The cost of goods manufactured and sold is $4,233, the cost of materials plus the cost of (Ann's) labor ($1,743 + $2,490 = $4,233).

- **Gross Profit.** The gross profit is calculated by subtracting the cost of goods manufactured and sold ($4,233) from net sales ($7,470). Ann's T-Shirts had a gross profit of $3,237 in March ($7,470 − $4,233 = $3,237).

- **Operating Expenses.** Ann sells her t-shirts to local specialty clothing stores who are long-time customers, so she doesn't need to do much advertising. She is paying interest on a loan her parents gave her to help get her business started. She rents a small room in the back of a customer's store. Her rent includes utilities. She pays a salary to a part-time employee who cleans her office and helps pack her t-shirts for delivery to customers.

- **Pre-Tax Profit.** The pre-tax profit is calculated by subtracting Ann's operating expenses from her gross profit ($3,237 − $1,600 = $1,637).

- **Net Profit (or Loss).** Again, taxes are estimated at 15% of the pre-tax profit and are rounded off to the nearest dollar ($1,637 × 15% = $245.55, rounded to $246). Ann had already paid herself $2,490 for her labor in printing the t-shirts. The net profit is Ann's revenue earned as an entrepreneur.

MANUFACTURING BUSINESS: Income Statement for Ann's T-Shirts			
For the Month Ended March 31, 2017			
Revenue			
Gross Sales	$7,500		
Sales Returns	30		
Net Sales			$7,470
Cost of Goods Manufactured and Sold			
Materials			
T-Shirts	1,494		
Inks/Paints	249		
Total Materials		$1,743	
Labor		2,490	
Cost of Goods Manufactured and Sold			4,233
Gross Profit			**3,237**
Operating Expenses			
Advertising	100		
Insurance	200		
Interest	300		
Rent	400		
Salaries	400		
Telephone	200		
Total Operating Expenses			1,600
Pre-Tax Profit			**1,637**
Taxes (15%)			246
Net Profit			**1,391**

Income Statement for a Service Business

Joan Barry styles clients' hair in their homes. She brings all her equipment to her appointments and styles hair for men, women, and children. Many of her customers work during the day and appreciate Joan's willingness to make appointments in the evening or on weekends. Often she styles an entire family's hair in one appointment.

Joan needs to prepare an income statement. She had 160 jobs. Joan will use a Cost of Services Sold section in her income statement, with an average price of $25 per job and an average cost of $1 for supplies.

She has a variety of prices for different types of jobs. Hair coloring or fancy styling costs more, but children's haircuts are less. Joan's income statement is shown in Ledger 28.3.

▲ **Ledger 28.2**

Ann's T-Shirts: Income Statement.

This shows the income statement for Ann's T-Shirts as of March 31.

Analyzing.

How much did Ann make in March? (Hint: Include her labor and her profit as an entrepreneur.)

SERVICE BUSINESS: Income Statement for Joan Barry Hair Styles		
For the Month Ended September 30, 2017		
Revenue		
Sales		$6,900
Cost of Services Sold		
Materials (Hair-Styling Supplies)	$ 160	
Labor (160 Jobs)	4,000	
Cost of Services Sold		4,160
Gross Profit		**2,740**
Operating Expenses		
Advertising	400	
Insurance	200	
Interest	300	
Rent	200	
Telephone	200	
Utilities	100	
Total Operating Expenses		1,400
Pre-Tax Profit		**1,340**
Taxes (15%)		201
Net Profit		**1,139**

▲ **Ledger 28.3**

Joan Barry Hair Styles: Income Statement.

This shows the income statement for Joan Barry Hair Styles as of September 30.

Analyzing.

Is it likely that Joan would make money in a month when her business showed a loss in net profit? (Hint: Remember that Joan pays herself for her labor and makes a profit as an entrepreneur.)

If you have a service business, your income statement may be similar to Joan's. However, many service companies, particularly those that don't use materials in their service, won't use a Cost of Services Sold section.

The net profit in an income statement like this would represent the profit for the entrepreneur's labor.

- **Revenue.** Joan had sales of $6,900 in September. In a service business, customers can't "return" the service. If a customer is disappointed, the business owner needs to find a way to provide satisfaction. This may include refunding the money the customer paid. Joan is an accomplished hair stylist. She didn't have to make any refunds in September.

- **Cost of Services Sold.** Joan worked hard in September, going to 160 appointments and charging a variety of prices. Because she estimates the average job at $1 for materials and $25 for labor, her price for materials is $160 (160 × $1 = $160) and her price for labor is $4,000 (160 × $25 = $4,000). The cost of services sold is $4,160 ($160 + 4,000 = $4,160).

- **Gross Profit.** Joan's gross profit is the revenue minus the cost of services sold ($6,900 − $4,160 = $2,740).

- **Operating Expenses.** Joan advertises her business by sending out flyers. Because she visits clients in their homes, she doesn't need a hair salon. However, Joan rents a room from her parents, where she keeps her hair-styling equipment. She also contributes to her parents' utility bills. Joan purchased a car because she needs to travel to her clients and bring heavy equipment and supplies. She is paying interest on the car loan.

- **Pre-Tax Profit.** The pre-tax profit is calculated by subtracting Joan's operating expenses from her gross profit ($2,740 − $1,400 = $1,340).

- **Net Profit (or Loss).** Taxes again are estimated at 15% of her pre-tax profit ($1,340 × 15% = $201). The net profit is $1,139 ($1,340 − $201 = $1,139). Joan already paid herself $4,000 in September as a hair stylist. The net profit is what she has earned as an entrepreneur.

Apply Your Knowledge What are the six parts of a typical income statement? Think back to your investigation of the movie studios. What would be the benefit of doing all of the income and expenses for each movie on different income statements? What would be the benefit of putting them all together on one?

APPLICATION TO BUSINESS PLANNING

Projected Income Statement

Use what you learned from this chapter about revenue streams and sales projections to put together a projected financial analysis for your first year of operations. You should support your findings with research data. Be sure to include:

- A list of your identified revenue streams
- Sales forecasts for each of your revenue streams
- A projected income statement for your first year that shows all revenue and variable/fixed expenses for your business

28 ASSESSMENT

REVIEWING OBJECTIVES

1. What are the potential revenue streams for a business?

2. What is the process for forecasting sales for a future period of time?

3. Describe the parts and function of an income statement.

CRITICAL THINKING

Look at any of the sample income statements in this chapter. What would happen to the net profit if the sales decreased by 100 units of sale? Does the business still make a profit that month?

ENTREPRENEURIAL THINKING EXERCISE: FUTURE ORIENTATION

Think back to your investigation of the movie studio releases. Many major movie studios plan their releases for at least three years in advance. What do you think the benefits of doing this would be? List all of the things they would need to consider to produce a movie over those three years.

28 ASSESSMENT

EXTENSION ACTIVITIES

Entrepreneurship & Mathematics Skills

Complete the following task to demonstrate your understanding of entrepreneurship:

Grades 9–12: Return to one of the sample income statements from this chapter shown in Ledgers 28.1 through 28.3. Use that example to complete the following tasks:

- Keeping the selling price and expenses constant, write an equation that shows the net profit as a function of the number of sales.

- Use your equation to determine the highest number of sales that generate a negative number. Explain what this negative number represents.

- Use your equation to determine the lowest number of sales the business can still make and generate a profit.

29 FINANCING THE BUSINESS

"How can I get money to start my business?"

☑ Start-Up Investment

OBJECTIVES

- Describe strategies for calculating start-up investment needs.
- Explain what a return on investment ratio means to an entrepreneur and/or investor.
- List potential ways that entrepreneurs obtain financing to start a business.

NFTE Entrepreneurial Mindset Characteristic Focus

☑ Comfort with Risk

National Entrepreneurship Standards

- **A.17** Distinguish between debt and equity financing for venture creation
- **A.18** Describe processes used to acquire adequate financial resources for venture creation/start-up
- **A.19** Select sources to finance venture creation/start-up
- **A.21** Describe considerations in selecting capital resources
- **A.22** Acquire capital resources needed for the venture
- **G.07** Describe costs associated with credit
- **G.10** Describe services provided by financial institutions
- **G.11** Explain legal responsibilities of financial institutions
- **G.12** Explain costs associated with use of financial services
- **I.12** Describe use of credit bureaus
- **I.14** Determine financing needed to start a business
- **I.15** Determine risks associated with obtaining business credit
- **I.16** Explain sources of financial assistance
- **I.17** Explain loan evaluation criteria used by lending institutions
- **I.18** Select sources of business loans

Common Career Technical Core Standards

- **BM.1** Utilize mathematical concepts, skills and problem solving to obtain necessary information for decision-making in business.
- **BM.2** Describe laws, rules and regulations as they apply to effective business operations.

LESSON VOCABULARY

- angel investor
- bank debt ratio
- barter financing
- bootstrapping
- collateral
- co-signer
- credit union
- crowdfunding
- customer financing
- debt financing
- emergency fund
- equity financing
- financing
- microloan
- payback
- reserve for fixed expenses
- return on investment (ROI)
- seed money
- start-up capital
- start-up expenditures
- start-up investment
- venture capital

- **BM.3** Explore, develop and apply strategies for ensuring a successful business career.
- **BM-MGT.5** Plan, monitor, manage and maintain the use of financial resources to ensure a business's financial well-being.

National Entrepreneurship Standards: Career Competencies

☑ **G.26** Build positive credit history

☑ **G.27** Improve/repair creditworthiness

ENTREPRENEURIAL INVESTIGATION
Lending a Helping Dollar

In many developing countries, entrepreneurs have a hard time getting money to start a business. Websites such as Kiva (www.kiva.org) have been established to connect people from around the world with people who are willing to lend $25 so that someone can start their business. They then pay the lender back after they make money. The website has been extremely successful. As of 2015, $747,539,675 in loans were given to 1,726,535 small business owners. The repayment rate is a staggering 98.66%, meaning over $737,000,000 was returned in full.

Do some research on Kiva, and answer the following questions:

- Would you lend someone money through this website?
- If you were trying to start a business but didn't have any money, would you use a site like this?

Be prepared to share your thoughts with peers and your teacher.

29.1 How Much Money Will I Need?

So far in this unit, you have looked at the variable and fixed expenses that go into running a business, and how to structure your business to cover those ongoing expenses. However, if you listed all of your expenses earlier in the unit, you may still have some one-time purchases that you might be wondering about.

To return to the lemonade stand example in Chapter 26, you can see how lemons, sugar, and cups would be variable expenses. But what about the things you only have to buy to start the business, such as a table, tablecloth, or cash register? These one-time items to get your business running are called start-up expenditures, which will be the focus of this chapter. Planning on what start-up expenditures you need, and how you find the money to pay for them, are another very important component of your financial plan when starting your business.

Start-Up Investment

Raising money for a business is called **financing**. Sometimes entrepreneurs can raise all the money they need to start and operate their businesses by themselves, through their earnings and savings. However, you may find that, to start your business, you need more money than you have. Or, after your business is up and running, you may need additional cash to expand it. You might want to add new products, or enlarge or remodel your store. At some point, most entrepreneurs are likely to need some type of financing.

How much money will you need to get your business going? **Start-up investment** is the one-time sum required to start a business and cover the start-up expenditures. The start-up investment is also called **seed money** or **start-up capital**.

The start-up investment for a new company has two components:

- Start-up expenditures
- Cash reserves (for an emergency fund and as a reserve for fixed expenses)

◀ **Figure 29-1**
Start-Up Investment.

Most startups, even one operating from a food truck, require a start-up investment.

Applying Concepts.

Aside from the items mentioned previously, what are some things you might include in your start-up expenditures if you were selling food from a truck?

Start-Up Expenditures

The start-up expenditures for opening a restaurant would be purchasing stoves, food processors, tables, chairs, dishes, silverware, and other items that won't be replaced frequently. The start-up expenditures might also be purchasing land on which to have the restaurant built or paying for the renovations needed for an existing space. Here's an example on a smaller scale. Caesar wants to start a new business called "Caesar's Smoothies." He plans on selling his smoothies from a cart. The start-up expenditures for Caesar's Smoothies might look something like what is shown in Ledger 29.1.

Start-Up Expenditures for Caesar's Smoothies	
Cart (plug-in, with refrigerator bins)	$3,000
License from the City	500
Starting supplies of fruits, yogurt, nuts, etc.	700
Business cards and flyers (advertising)	400
Commercial refrigerator, cabinets (to store food)	800
Total start-up expenditures	**$5,400**

Cash Reserves

When starting a business, an entrepreneur needs to set aside extra money for two purposes:

- **Emergency Fund.** The emergency fund is the amount of money a business should have available in the first three to six months for the emergencies that often arise when a company is just beginning. Some experts say it should be half the amount of the start-up expenditures. After the initial start-up period is over and things have settled down, an entrepreneur can decide how much money to keep in an emergency fund.

- **Reserve for Fixed Expenses.** Businesses usually set aside a reserve for fixed expenses. This is enough money to cover their fixed expenses for at least three months. The reserve for fixed expenses is maintained for the life of the business and is intended to be used to cover the business's fixed expenses (rent, insurance, etc.) if the company should experience a downturn in sales.

If you were going to the bank for financing, you would usually include your emergency fund and the reserve for fixed expenses as part of your start-up investment.

Start-Up Expenditures
+ Emergency Fund (½ Start-Up Expenditures)
+ Reserve for Fixed Expenses (Covers 3 Months of Fixed Expenses)
Start-Up Investment

If the total start-up expenditures for Caesar's Smoothies was $5,400, his emergency fund would be half of that amount, or $2,700. Let's say that the fixed expenses for Caesar's Smoothies for one month is $1,300, and Caesar wants to establish a 3-month reserve for fixed expenses, or $3,900. The total start-up investment for Caesar's Smoothies would be:

Start-Up Expenditures	$5,400
+ Emergency Fund	2,700
+ Reserve for Fixed Expenses	3,900
Start-Up Investment	12,000

Many small entrepreneurs aren't able to afford to set aside an emergency fund or a reserve for fixed expenses that follows the experts' recommendations. Nevertheless, it is important to consider both of these concerns in your business planning. It is also important to make a record of your complete start-up investment (and not just your start-up expenditures).

Return on Investment (ROI)

As you learned in earlier chapters, starting a business can be a big financial risk for an entrepreneur. Getting the money together to start the business can be a huge undertaking for the entrepreneur. They either need to get the money themselves or find others who are willing to lend them the money or invest. One thing that helps with the risk is finding the potential rewards from the initial investment. In other words, how much money will you make versus the amount of money you will need to start the business. If the potential profit exceeds the amount needed to start the business, it is more appealing to the entrepreneur or potential investors.

One approach to use to determine how profitable the business is in relation to the amount of money invested in it is called **return on investment (ROI)**. This shows the profit on the initial investment expressed as a percentage of that investment. It is calculated by dividing the net profit by the initial investment and multiplying by 100. For example, if the net profit is $1,500 and the initial investment was $10,000, the ROI is 15%.

(Net Profit ÷ Initial Investment) × 100 = Return on Investment (%)

($1,500 ÷ $10,000) × 100 = 15%

What this ratio means is that $1,500 was made from a $10,000 investment, or $0.15 for every dollar. It is also possible to have a ROI over 100%, which means more than the initial investment was made. The higher the percentage, the higher profit that will be made off the investment. Using ROI from your projected net profit is an important calculation to assure yourself and others that the risk is worth the investment, and should be part of any pitch to investors. The following sections of this chapter will look at these various investment sources.

Apply Your Knowledge   How is a return-on-investment (ROI) ratio calculated and what will the results tell you? From your investigation, what is the ROI for lenders with Kiva?

ENTREPRENEURIAL CASE STUDY: COMFORT WITH RISK

 ## Joe Mansueto— Morningstar

Humble, yet Ambitious, Beginnings

Joe Mansueto founded Morningstar (www.morningstar.com) in 1984. He has served as chairman since the company's inception and as chief executive officer from 1984 to 1996 and again from 2000 to present. Morningstar was founded on a specific mission: to create great products that help investors reach their financial goals. Today, investors around

Joe Mansueto.

the world turn to Morningstar's independent perspective as they make their investment decisions. Under Joe's leadership, Morningstar has grown into a globally renowned company and has twice been named to *Fortune* magazine's "100 Best Companies to Work For" list, in 2011 and 2012.

Joe developed an entrepreneurial spirit early on. While earning a bachelor's degree in business administration at the University of Chicago, Joe sold sodas and snacks to his dorm-mates to earn extra money. After graduating, Joe took a job as a securities analyst at Harris Associates. There, Joe worked with investors—people who spend money hoping to get more money in return. Investors may buy stocks or mutual funds or lend money to an entrepreneur. A good investment means making money, but a bad investment means losing money. It was during Joe's time at Harris Associates that he created an idea for a new business related to investing.

Focused on the Investor

From his experience as a stock analyst, Joe realized that investors lacked the information they needed about mutual funds to make intelligent decisions about how to invest their money. While he attended the University of Chicago Booth School of Business to pursue a master's degree in business administration, Joe made plans to launch a business that would provide quality investment research to investors. Driven by the same entrepreneurial spirit as NFTE students, Joe invested a small sum of money into a few early-model computers and launched Morningstar from his one-bedroom apartment in Chicago's Lincoln Park neighborhood.

He hired a few employees and began gathering data for Morningstar's first product, *The Mutual Fund Sourcebook™*. This quarterly publication contained information about approximately 400 mutual funds, which were growing in popularity at the time. Six hundred people subscribed to the publication in the first year, many in response to a Morningstar ad in *Barron's* magazine. It turns out Joe's intuition about the need for more investor-focused research in the market was correct. *The Mutual Fund Sourcebook*, which started as a bound publication of computer print-outs, eventually became the springboard for dozens of products and services not only for investors, but for the advisors and institutions that serve them. Since growing into a global company with thousands of employees in offices around the world, Morningstar has not changed its mission and still proves to be as intensely investor-focused as it was on the first day Joe launched the business.

Success from Honest Business Practices

Morningstar's mission of helping investors reach their financial goals has earned Joe and the company significant recognition. Morningstar has received numerous local and national awards. In 2010, Morningstar won the American Institute of Graphic Arts Chicago Chapter Corporate Design Leadership Award, which recognizes forward-thinking organizations that have advanced design by promoting it as a meaningful business policy. Joe has also received numerous awards for his influence on the investment industry, including *PLANSPONSOR* magazine's 2013 Lifetime Achievement Award. In 2010, Joe received the Tiburon CEO Summit award for challenging conventional wisdom and showing responsibility and intensive attention to consumers. In the same year, MutualFundWire.com named Joe ninth on its list of the 100 Most Influential People of the year and Chicago magazine listed him among its top 40 Chicago Pioneers over the past four decades. In 2007, *SmartMoney* magazine recognized Joe on an annual list of the 30 most powerful forces in business and finance.

Thinking and Acting Like an Entrepreneur

- How did Joe use his personal skills and career experience to identify a business opportunity?

- Why would Joe's customers rely on his business to figure out the return on an investment?

- In what ways does Joe demonstrate the entrepreneurial mindset of being comfortable with risk?

29.2 Sources of Debt Financing

Now that you have looked at what you need to start your business, you may be able to start a business with little or no start-up investment. You may also be able to fund the start-up investment yourself. However, if you need more money, you will have to find additional sources of capital. One method of obtaining more money is to borrow what you need. When you do that, you will increase your company's debt. This is called **debt financing**.

It is important to note that young entrepreneurs should weigh the advantages and disadvantages of debt financing carefully. When you are just starting out, it is probably a better idea to try to reduce the amount of start-up investment needed instead of borrowing more money than you need. Before seeking money through debt financing, ask yourself if the expense is something you really *need* for the business, or if you could start and grow later once you have more income.

Sources of debt financing include:

- Personal Savings
- Banks
- Credit unions
- Microloans
- Relatives and friends
- Credit cards

Personal Savings

Have you ever heard of the phrase "pulling yourself up by the boot-straps?" Basically, it means doing something completely on your own. As an entrepreneur, **bootstrapping** means starting a business by yourself, without any outside investment. This would typically be the most desirable way to start a business. However, unless you have a great deal of money, you would need to keep your start-up investment as low as possible. It often means starting your business with less money than you would like (as Caesar did).

Every business needs a different start-up investment, and some are lower than others. If your start-up investment is higher than the amount you have to invest, bootstrapping wouldn't be possible.

Figure 29-2 ▶

Using Personal Savings.

Using your savings or credit cards for start-up capital can lead to problems.

Applying Concepts.

What are the disadvantages of using your own savings versus a credit card?

Using your personal savings to finance your business is an ideal scenario. If you have enough money in your savings account for your start-up investment, you can be the sole owner of your business. All the profits will belong to you, and the only person you would "pay back" is yourself. However, this strategy has a major disadvantage. If your business fails, you will have lost all of the money you invested. Also, by taking your money out of the savings account, you will have lost the interest the money would have earned. You lose the ability to draw money from the savings account that you could have used for other purposes. For example, perhaps you could have used part of your savings to buy an automobile. Using your personal savings to start a business is a very serious undertaking. Weigh the advantages and disadvantages carefully.

Banks

The major source of debt financing for an entrepreneur is a bank. The money the bank lends you is referrred to as credit, and the bank is the creditor. The money you borrow and promise to pay back is referred to as debt, and you are the debtor. You will be required to make regular payments. Banks are very careful with their loans—they want to be as certain as possible that they will get their money back, with interest. One of the things a bank or other source of funding looks at when considering loaning money is the entrepreneur's credit score. It's hard to get approved without a credit score in the high 600s. The bank will also look for some sort of track record of success. As a minor, you would most likely not qualify for a small business loan on your own from a bank. If you felt that a bank was the only way to finance a business launch, you would need to talk with your parents or guardians and their financial advisors first.

To determine how much it might be willing to loan you, the bank will review your business's debt-to-equity ratio (discussed in Chapter 30).

The bank may also use a bank debt ratio. A **bank debt ratio** shows your monthly income compared to your debts.

(Monthly Debt Payments ÷ Monthly Income) × 100 = Bank Debt Ratio (%)

A good ratio is typically 40% or less. Banks have found that customers with debt ratios over 40% often become unable to repay their loans. Here's an example: Suppose Caesar's Smoothies has a monthly income of $5,000 and debt payments of $2,500 from his mortgage and student loan payments.

($2,500 ÷ $5,000) × 100 = 50%

In this example, Caesar's bank debt ratio would be 50%. The bank would probably not give Caesar a loan.

Banks also use the bank debt ratio to determine how much they will loan you. Let's say Caesar has a monthly income of $5,000 and debts of only $1,500. How much would they loan Caesar then?

($1,500 ÷ $5,000) × 100 = 30%

Because Caesar is already using 30% of his income to pay his existing debt, the bank might be willing to loan him about 10% of his monthly income. This is $500 ($5,000 × 0.1 = $500). Caesar could probably borrow an amount that would be repaid at $500 per month. This would allow him to spend 40% of his monthly income for debt payments, a percentage that is probably acceptable to the bank.

$$($2,000 \div $5,000) \times 100 = 40\%$$

The actual dollar amount of the loan would vary based on the length of time and the interest rate. But the bank would make sure that Caesar's monthly payment would not exceed $500. The bank debt ratio is sometimes used to determine affordable monthly payments for customers seeking mortgage loans.

The bank may ask Caesar for collateral against a loan. **Collateral** is property or assets that you pledge to a bank to secure a loan. If you fail to repay the loan, the bank will own your collateral and will resell it to get all or some of its money back. For example, if Caesar owned a truck that he used to pull his cart, the bank might ask him to use the truck as collateral. If he failed to repay the loan, the bank would take possession of the truck and sell it.

The bank may also ask Caesar to provide a co-signer for a loan. A **co-signer** is an individual who will sign a loan agreement to guarantee the payments in case Caesar, the first signer, is unable to make them. If Caesar asks relatives or friends to co-sign his loan and then isn't able to make the payments, they—the co-signers—will have to make them.

The biggest disadvantage of a bank loan for Caesar is what happens if he fails to repay it. The bank will probably bring a lawsuit against him. He is likely to lose his business and his credit rating could be ruined.

Entrepreneurs often use bank loans to start a business, but you need to be careful when assuming debt. Make sure you can make the payments.

Figure 29-3 ▶
Requesting a Loan.
The major source of debt financing is in the form of bank loans.

Inferring.
Other than the bank debt ratio, what do you think a bank looks for when making a loan to an entrepreneur?

Credit Unions

Another source of debt financing is the <mark>credit union</mark>. A credit union is a nonprofit cooperative organization that offers low-interest loans to members. Many entrepreneurs have financed their businesses through credit union loans. Credit unions, like banks, will loan you money for growing your business. However, credit unions may offer you lower interest rates than banks. Because most credit unions will only make loans to members, you must first join the credit union. If you do not meet the membership requirements, you cannot get the loan. A credit union, just like a bank, may ask for collateral or ask you to provide a co-signer. And, like a bank, if you fail to repay a loan, a credit union can bring a lawsuit against you.

Similar to credit unions, Small Business Investment Companies (SBICs) provide equity financing, as well as loans, for small businesses. SBICs are partially financed through guaranteed loans from the government. SBICs often accept lower interest rates than other sources of debt financing. There are hundreds of SBICs that specialize in equity investments and loans for small businesses. There are also additional SBICs that give money specifically to businesses owned by African Americans, Hispanics, Asians, women, and other minority groups. You can use the Internet to search for up-to-date information on SBICs.

Microloans

Today, there is another option other than banks for loans: the microloan. "Micro" means "small," and that's just what a microloan is: a small loan. A microloan is ideal for a small startup company that doesn't need much capital and has a limited credit history. (Credit history is a record of the ability of an individual or business to pay back a loan.) This history is what lenders consider when they decide whether to make a loan. Often, the entrepreneur applying for a microloan doesn't have enough collateral to qualify for a regular bank loan. A microloan is a relatively small amount of money, perhaps in the range of $10,000, and generally carries a higher rate of interest than a bank would charge. Microloans are usually extended to small business owners by nonprofit organizations through the Small Business Administration (SBA).

Relatives and Friends

The start-up capital for many businesses has come as a loan from the entrepreneur's relatives or friends. A large number of successful small businesses have begun this way. However, the major concern for you, as a new business owner, will be to earn enough revenue to pay back the loans—the hard-earned money of your friends or relatives. What happens if your business does not generate sufficient sales to make a profit, or it fails entirely? How would you feel if you had to tell your friends or relatives that you were unable to repay them? It would certainly be a stressful situation.

On the other hand, the advantage to borrowing from relatives or friends is that you have a willing source of capital for your new business. The pride and confidence they would have in you and your business venture is often worth the risk. You are offering them an opportunity to receive a return on their investment—if your business is successful.

Of course, if things don't go well, that's another story. If you are planning to borrow money from friends or relatives for start-up capital, you must thoroughly explain the risks and the opportunities of the business. Finally, everyone must agree to the interest rate that will be paid and when payments are expected. With proper communication on the parts of all parties involved, this strategy can be very effective.

Using Credit Cards

If all else fails, another strategy for funding the costs of starting a business is through your credit cards. Charging business items on your credit cards allows you to use the items while you are still paying for them. Although this certainly is an advantage, the strategy can also have some very significant disadvantages.

The major disadvantage is the interest rate charged by the credit card companies, which is often 20% or more on the outstanding balance. Unless your business is able make enough profit to pay the total amount you owe each month, the interest payments will add up very quickly. Also, if you reach the credit limits, you will not be able to use the cards for emergencies or for other opportunities. Keeping high balances on your credit cards also affects your credit rating. With a low credit rating, you may not be able to purchase merchandise from your suppliers on account. Other than in unusual circumstances, where you will very quickly earn back the money you borrow, using credit cards in your start-up investment is not a good idea.

Some entrepreneurs try to use credit cards with 0% introductory rates and 0% transfer fees to finance their business. However, such a strategy requires vigilance in locating and transferring balances to new credit cards when the introductory rate expires on the old ones.

Obtaining a credit card can be a huge decision for anyone. As a minor, you should have conversations with your family and their financial planner first for other sources of start-up funding that might be available before credit cards.

Payback

Naturally, most entrepreneurs would like to know when they can return the initial investment and begin to pay off in profit. That's the **payback**, the amount of time, measured in months, that it takes a business to earn enough in profit to cover the start-up investment.

To calculate payback, you will need to know your business's net profit per month. As you learned in Chapter 28, the net profit per month can be found on the income statement. (Remember: To find net profit, subtract the operating expenses from the gross profit.)

Once you know the net profit per month, you can calculate the payback by using this formula:

Start-Up Investment ÷ Net Profit per Month = Payback (in Months)

Let's continue with the example of Caesar's Smoothies. Let's say that Caesar obtained financing for $6,000 and was able to contribute an additional $4,000 of his own money. This wasn't the $12,000 he had hoped for, but it was enough to cover his start-up expenditures. He thought he would divide the remainder between an emergency fund and a reserve for fixed expenses.

So, Caesar's start-up investment was $10,000. Suppose he was projecting a net profit per month of $2,000. It will take Caesar approximately five months to pay back the start-up investment.

Start-Up Investment ÷ Net Profit per Month = Payback

$10,000 ÷ $2,000 = 5 Months

Apply Your Knowledge   What is debt financing? Explain the relationship between a creditor and a debtor. Think back to your investigation of Kiva. Is Kiva a source of debt financing? Why or why not?

CAREER COMPETENCIES

Build Positive Credit History; Improve/Repair Creditworthiness

The Role of Credit

Credit is the granting of extended time to pay off a debt. To buy on credit means buying now and paying later. A person or business that grants credit is called a creditor. Creditors set particular conditions, called credit terms, when they grant credit. These terms typically state the time limit when the debt must be paid and any interest charges that will apply.

As you are starting off your business, you may need to use a credit card or borrow money to pay for business expenses. Since you are just launching your career, the amount of money you will be able to borrow will be linked to how responsible you are with credit. To build a positive credit history, you should always use credit responsibly, which includes:

- Maintaining bank account balances and depositing paychecks
- Paying rent and bills on time
- Paying the entire balance due by the due date each month
- Only using it to buy items that you can afford
- Having only one or two credit cards in your name

Types of Credit

Although there are many types of credit, two types are of particular interest to business owners.

- **Trade Credit.** When one business gives another business an extended payment time for purchased goods or services, it is called a trade credit. Business owners take advantage of trade credit to postpone payment of their expenses. Trade credit is a useful tool for managing cash flow. Consider a retail store that buys merchandise by using trade credit from a wholesaler who allows 30 days for payment. The retail store sells enough of the merchandise within the 30-day period to pay the debt on time. In other words, the cash inflow is sufficient to pay the debt. Suppose the store has poor sales and does not earn enough cash in 30 days to pay the money back. This situation is known informally as a credit squeeze. The store will have to dip into cash reserves to pay the debt. Trade discounts are another consideration when extending credit to a business. A business owner might offer discounted pricing if the buyer pays within a shorter period of time; for example, 5 percent off the price if the bill is paid within 10 days instead of 30.

- **Consumer Credit.** When a business gives consumers an extended payment time for purchased goods or services, it is referred to as consumer credit. Businesses choose to offer consumer credit to the public to generate sales, which can, in turn, increase profits. For example, a furniture store might allow consumers up to twelve months to pay for a purchase. While this may make it easier for customers to buy from you, it also means that you will not have the cash on-hand until a later date, and may have to draw upon other cash reserves in the meantime. Although credit cards are a form of consumer credit, they are issued by banks. A business that wants to accept credit cards from its customers must set up a merchant account with a bank. That bank works with the bank that issued the credit card to process transactions. The business pays fees for this service and typically receive cash payments from the bank within a few days.

Granting Credit and Collecting Payments

As a business owner, you may also extend credit to customers. A sale made on credit is based on trust that the person or business will pay the debt in the future. Every person or business that has ever used credit has a credit history, which is a record of credit transactions and includes information about whether or not they were repaid in accordance with the credit terms set by the creditor. A credit bureau is a business that collects and maintains credit history records and sells the information under certain circumstances. Businesses can access credit records to help them determine if a credit applicant is likely to repay a future debt.

Many businesses follow specific procedures when deciding whether or not to grant credit to an applicant. The first step is to collect personal and financial information from the applicant—for example, employment and income histories. Next, the business can check the credit history of the applicant through a credit bureau. Many credit bureaus will provide a credit rating, or a number that rates the credit history of the applicant. If credit is granted, the federal Truth in Lending Act requires creditors to inform customers about the credit terms, including any finance charges.

Once credit has been extended to a customer, the creditor takes specific actions to make sure the debt is paid. The creditor starts by sending a routine bill to the customer when the debt is due. Unfortunately, some businesses and individuals who are granted credit will not pay as agreed. The creditor usually makes several attempts to contact the customer by letter or phone to remedy the problem. If these measures are not successful, the creditor may hire a business that specializes in collecting so-called uncollectible accounts. Debt collection businesses charge a fee, often a percentage of the amount collected, for providing this service. Business owners must understand that extending credit comes with risks. If customers don't pay, the company's profits and bottom line may be affected.

Career Skills in Action

Now do some research on credit options that a business might offer to its customers.

- Research a local business and the types of credit it offers to customers. These might be consumers like you or they might be other businesses. Would you recommend that the business change any of its credit offerings?

- What benefits might a small business realize by offering credit to customers?

- What are the disadvantages or risks of accepting and extending credit to a customer or another business?

- How can extending credit affect cash flow and profits?

Share your findings with your teacher or a peer for feedback.

29.3 Sources of Equity Financing

The other primary method of financing a startup business is to sell shares of ownership in the business. If you use this method, called **equity financing**, you will be giving up some of your company and perhaps some control.

The main sources of equity financing include:

- Relatives and friends
- Angels and venture capitalists
- Partners
- Customer financing
- Barter financing

Relatives and Friends

Sometimes start-up capital for a new business is obtained from relatives and friends as equity financing, in which they take a share of the company in payment for their investment. This is much the same as borrowing money from relatives and friends—with the same advantages and disadvantages—but with one big difference. Your friends and relatives now own part of the business. If they feel you are running it badly, or if they want to question a business decision, they have a right to tell you.

Angels and Venture Capital Companies

Some equity investors are referred to as "angels." An angel is an investor who is interested in financing startup ventures. Like any investor, an **angel investor** wants to make a profit, but may have additional reasons for investing. An angel investor might be interested in a specific type of business, or might want to support entrepreneurship in a certain community. Sometimes an angel takes an interest in an individual entrepreneur or might just want to be involved in something interesting. Because of a particular interest, an angel will often accept a lower return on an investment than other sources of equity capital. Typically, angel investors invest only on an equity basis; they don't make loans. Angels receive many requests for their capital, but fund only a small percentage. Finding an angel willing to invest in your business may be difficult.

Another source of equity financing, similar to angel investment, is venture capital. **Venture capital** is money that is invested in a potentially profitable business by a specialized company whose purpose is to invest in startups. Venture capitalists are only interested in equity financing. Unlike angel investors, venture capital companies create funds in which many people have invested. Because of this, venture capital companies are more structured and more heavily focused on high returns on investment than the typical angel investor. For this reason, venture capital companies want to invest in businesses that expect to return large profits. Venture capitalists invest in less than one percent of the businesses they consider. Because venture capital investment is a high-risk business, these investors typically seek to earn five to ten times their original investment over five years. Because they see so many business plans, venture capitalists are typically difficult to interest in anything but very promising business startups.

Figure 29-4 ▶
Venture Capital Company.

Typically a venture capital company wants to own a share of the business in which it invests.

Comparing/Contrasting.

How would sharing ownership with a venture capitalist be different from sharing it with a partner?

You can use the Internet to research venture capital firms and angels who might be interested in investing in your business. While you might not be sure who would be interested in funding your business, there are angel investors that specialize in certain niche markets. You might find a venture capitalist willing to fund your idea.

Partners

The most common source of equity financing is giving a percentage of the ownership of a business to a partner. When seeking a partner, you should do as much research as possible to be assured that the two of you will have the same basic principles and goals for the business.

You will be co-owners of the company. As with other forms of equity financing, adding a partner requires an entrepreneur to give up some ownership. Make sure you have a lawyer draw up a Partnership Agreement that carefully defines all aspects of the relationship.

Partners can bring new ideas and valuable expertise. But many partnerships fail because the partners disagree on how the business should be run.

Additionally, partners are typically personally liable for the actions taken in the business, and they are personally liable for paying debts or damages. If your partner incurs a debt on behalf of the partnership, you will be jointly responsible for paying it.

Unlike friends, family, angels, and some venture capitalists, a partner typically wants to play an active role in the operation of the business. For example, he or she may insist on approving all important business decisions. (See Chapter 25 for a review of the advantages and disadvantages of a partnership.)

Customer Financing

Your customers will get to know and appreciate your products or services. With this first-hand knowledge, they are often willing to provide capital for a business. **Customer financing** can be either debt or equity. Your customers might be more willing to make a loan to you than a bank would, and they might be willing to accept a lower interest rate. It all depends on your relationship with your customers and the profitability of your company. A customer who offers you equity financing will become a co-owner of the business. The customer will have information about your operations that once was private. This could cause problems.

Similar to customer financing, technology has allowed for entrepreneurs to turn to large groups of potential customers to raise start-up money. Many times, entrepreneurs might start a **crowdfunding** effort, where they try to fund their venture by raising monetary contributions from a large number of people online. This movement has linked borrowers around the world to private lenders through websites such as www.kickstarter.com and www.crowdfunder.com. These services allow entrepreneurs to obtain debt or equity financing that is spread out across many people.

Barter Financing

Barter financing is the trading of items or services between businesses. For example, your hardware store may sell lawn mowers while a land-

scaping business provides a lawn-mowing service. As the owner of the hardware store, you need to have your property properly land-scaped, so you make a deal with the owner of the landscaping business. You trade two of your lawn mowers to the landscaper for three months of landscaping services. The advantage of a bar-ter system is that both parties get what they want without spending any money. Of course, the major problem is finding a suitable trad-ing partner who does not want control of parts of your business in exchange.

Figure 29-5
Barter Financing.
Services such as landscaping can be offered in place of paying for services as a new business

Applying Concepts.
Why is barter financing usually less risky than debt financing?

 **Apply Your Knowledge**   What is equity financing? From your investigation, how could the Kiva model provide equity to the investors?

APPLICATION TO BUSINESS PLANNING

Start-Up Investment

Use what you learned from this chapter to put together a plan for your start-up expenditures and funding sources. You should sup-port your findings with data from research. Be sure to include:

- A list of your start-up expenditures (including cash reserves and emergency funds)
- A calculation of your ROI based on your net profit
- A list of potential sources you will use to fund your business

ASSESSMENT

REVIEWING OBJECTIVES

1. What are the strategies for calculating start-up investment needs?

2. What does a return on investment ratio mean to an entrepreneur and/or investor?

3. List potential ways that entrepreneurs obtain financing to start a business.

CRITICAL THINKING

Name five businesses you could start with little start-up investment. What do they have in common?

ENTREPRENEURIAL THINKING EXERCISE: COMFORT WITH RISK

Think back to your investigation of Kiva. Imagine that you were hired to help investors feel more comfortable about lending their money. How would you message the opportunity to the potential investors? Write a paragraph that convinces them to take the risk with lending the money.

EXTENSION ACTIVITIES

Entrepreneurship & Mathematics Skills

Complete the following task to demonstrate your understanding of entrepreneurship:

Grades 9–12: Use the bank debt ratio to determine which of the following businesses would be likely candidates for a loan based on the data for each. Explain your thinking:

- Bank 1: Monthly Income, $20,000; Monthly Debt Payments, $4,000
- Bank 2: Monthly Income, $75,000; Monthly Debt Payments, $8,000
- Bank 3: Monthly Income, $33,000; Monthly Debt Payments, $1,000
- Bank 4: Monthly Income, $65,000; Monthly Debt Payments, $6,000

30 FINANCIAL ANALYSIS

APPLICATION TO BUSINESS PLANNING:

☑ Financial Ratios

OBJECTIVES

- Describe how income statements are used for financial analysis.
- Identify the purpose and components of a balance sheet.
- Explain which financial ratios can be calculated from a balance sheet.

NFTE Entrepreneurial Mindset Characteristic Focus

☑ Flexibility & Adaptability

National Entrepreneurship Standards

- **F.23** Assess factors affecting a business's profit
- **G.19** Complete financial instruments
- **G.20** Maintain financial records
- **G.21** Read and reconcile financial statements
- **G.22** Correct errors with account
- **I.04** Prepare an estimated/projected balance sheet
- **I.05** Calculate financial ratios
- **I.21** Determine a business's value
- **I.28** Supervise/implement regular accounting procedures and financial reports

Common Career Technical Core Standards

- **BM.1** Utilize mathematical concepts, skills and problem solving to obtain necessary information for decision-making in business.
- **BM.3** Explore, develop and apply strategies for ensuring a successful business career.
- **BM-MGT.5** Plan, monitor, manage and maintain the use of financial resources to ensure a business's financial wellbeing.
- **BM-MGT.8** Create strategic plans used to manage business growth, profit and goals.

National Entrepreneurship Standards: Career Competencies

☑ **I.28** Supervise/implement regular accounting procedures and financial reports

LESSON VOCABULARY

- accounts payable
- accounts receivable
- asset
- balance sheet
- current assets
- current liabilities
- current ratio
- debt ratio
- debt-to-equity ratio
- financial ratio
- liability
- liquidity
- long-term assets
- long-term liabilities
- marketable securities
- operating ratio
- owner's equity
- quick ratio
- return on sales (ROS)
- same-size analysis

30.1 What Are Financial Ratios?

How do entrepreneurs know if a company is healthy? They often rely on information from financial records. But it's not always easy to analyze these records, to see the relationships, patterns, and the trends they show. From these financial records, they can apply their entrepreneurial mindset skills of flexibility and adaptability to change the business's course.

One of the most effective ways for entrepreneurs to analyze their financials is to use **financial ratios**. These are relationships between important financial data that are expressed as fractions or as percentages. Entrepreneurs calculate financial ratios by using the data from financial statements. All financial ratios are calculated by dividing one number by another.

An entrepreneur should *not* rely on just one or two ratios. Ratios are only indicators and each will shed light on a different aspect of the business.

Analysis Based on an Income Statement

As you've seen, entrepreneurs use income statements to show how their businesses are performing. The information contained in an income statement may sometimes need to be analyzed by using financial ratios or dramatized in charts and graphs. Income statements allow entrepreneurs to do two important types of analysis:

- Sales-data analysis
- Same-size analysis

Sales-Data Analysis

An income statement shows an entrepreneur the monthly sales totals at a glance. This helps determine how much the business can afford to spend on purchases and expenses. It also helps the entrepreneur determine whether the business can afford to hire additional personnel. As you saw in the example of Matt's Hats, you can also use monthly income statements to forecast future sales. Businesses often use bar graphs to display the sales data for several months, quarters, or years.

You can analyze the trends shown in bar graphs and use them to estimate future sales, just as Matt did. Combining income statement analysis and a knowledge of the industry (for example, slow periods, new competitors, or other factors that influence sales) will be very helpful in forecasting sales. An accurate forecast is an important factor in business success.

Same-Size Analysis

Besides using income statements for sales-data analysis, entrepreneurs also use income statements to measure how their cost of goods sold and operating expenses affect profits. They do this by using **same-size analysis**, which is a comparison of total revenue or other financial data against that same data converted into percentages.

You create a same-size analysis of an income statement by dividing a line item by the sales and then multiplying by 100, as shown in Table 30.1. This shows the line item as a percentage of sales. When calculating same-size analysis, many entrepreneurs just include the major items from the income statement.

Table 30.1   Same-Size Analysis

Income Statement	Amount	Calculation	% of Sales
Revenue (Sales)	$10,000	($10,000 ÷ $10,000) × 100	100%
COGS	$4,000	($4,000 ÷ $10,000) × 100	40%
Gross Profit	$6,000	($6,000 ÷ $10,000) × 100	60%
Expenses	$3,500	($3,500 ÷ $10,000) × 100	35%
Pre-Tax Profit	$2,500	($2,500 ÷ $10,000) × 100	25%

Same-size analysis makes it clear how each item affects the business's pre-tax profit. Entrepreneurs review the percentages and make changes to improve their profits. For example, an entrepreneur might know that the percentage for the average cost of goods sold in the industry is 30%. If the business has a cost of goods sold of 40%, any competing businesses will have an advantage. All things being equal, they will be 10% more profitable. The entrepreneur should attempt to lower the percentage to at least the industry average.

Same-size analysis also allows you to easily compare income statements from different months, quarters, or years. Even if the sales are different from month to month or quarter to quarter, a same-size analysis will show you patterns and trends. Look at the example shown in Table 30.2 from Matt's Hats, showing the major items in the income statement for January and February.

Table 30.2 Monthly Compairson Using Same-Size Analysis

JANUARY			FEBRUARY		
Income Statement	Amount	% of Sales	Income Statement	Amount	% of Sales
Revenue (Sales)	$50,000	100%	Revenue (Sales)	$40,000	100%
COGS	$19,000	38%	COGS	$10,400	26%
Gross Profit	$31,000	62%	Gross Profit	$29,600	74%
Expenses	$17,000	34%	Expenses	$15,200	38%
Pre-Tax Profit	$14,000	28%	Pre-Tax Profit	$14,400	36%

The comparison of sales for Matt's Hats shows that they dropped from $50,000 in January to $40,000 in February. However, in February, the business was able to reduce its cost of goods sold from 38% to 26%. As a result, the company had an increase in pre-tax profit over January, despite having a drop in sales. So which month do you think was better for Matt's Hats?

Income Statement Ratios

Sales-data analysis and same-size analysis are both based on the income statement. They are especially helpful for understanding how a business is doing over time. Some financial ratios that are based on the income statement are helpful for providing a "snapshot" of a specific aspect of a business. These ratios provide information you can use to monitor expenses, compare the performance of the company with competitors in the industry, and measure profitability.

The two most important financial ratios based on the income statement are:

- The operating ratio
- Return on sales (ROS)

Operating Ratio

One of the most significant ratios used by entrepreneurs is the **operating ratio**. It is the percentage of each dollar of revenue, or sales, needed to cover expenses. For example, if an income statement for Matt's Hats shows sales of $20,000 and an insurance expense of $1,000, Matt's operating ratio for insurance is 5%.

$$(\text{Expenses} \div \text{Sales}) \times 100 = \text{Operating Ratio (\%)}$$

$$(\$1,000 \div \$20,000) \times 100 = 5\%$$

Operating ratios are typically used to compare an entrepreneur's company with other businesses in the industry. Websites such as www.hoovers.com allow entrepreneurs to get industry data for comparison. For example, if Matt's Hats is paying $2,000 a month in rent and has sales of $10,000, its operating ratio for rent is 20%.

$$(\$2,000 \div \$10,000) \times 100 = 20\%$$

Matt could compare this 20% ratio with others in the industry. If 20% is higher than the industry average, Matt needs to make a decision: Should he remain in his present location or move to a less expensive one, where the rent would be lower? (Of course, there are usually many elements to consider before moving a business. For example, Matt's current location could be generating additional sales.)

Return on Sales (ROS)

Return on sales (ROS) is the financial ratio calculated by dividing net profit by sales. To convert that to a percentage, multiply the result by 100. ROS is an important measure of how profitable a business is, because it shows how much of each dollar of sales the company keeps as profit. ROS may also be called net margin, net profit ratio, net profit on sales ratio, or—most frequently—profit margin.

Here's an example of calculating return on sales: If the income statement for Matt's Hats shows sales of $30,000 and a net profit of $6,000, the ROS percentage for the business is 20%.

$$(\text{Net Profit} \div \text{Sales}) \times 100 = \text{Return on Sales (\%)}$$

$$(\$6,000 \div \$30,000) \times 100 = 20\%$$

A high ROS ratio is usually a good indicator of success for a business. However, the ROS percentage alone doesn't provide a total picture. A business selling high-priced items, such as luxury automobiles, can be very profitable with a 5% ROS, while a retailer like Matt's Hats who sells inexpensive items may need a 25% ROS or more. The ROS shown in Table 30.3 describe ROS ranges for various types of products.

Table 30.3   ROS (Profit Margin) for Various Products

ROS	Margin Range	Typical Product
Very low	2–5%	Very high volume OR very high price
Low	6–10%	High volume OR high price
Moderate	11–20%	Moderate volume AND moderate price
High	21–30%	Low volume OR low price
Very high	31% and up	Very low volume OR very low price

Figure 30-1 ▶
Return on Sales.
A business selling high-priced items, such as luxury automobiles, can be very profitable with a 5% ROS.

Drawing Conclusions.
How is a 5% ROS different for a $100,000 product than a $1,000 product?

 **Apply Your Knowledge**   What two ratios are calculated by using data from an income statement? Think back to your investigation of the record megastores. Who do you think had a lower return on sales, the record mega stores or online digital music? Explain your answer.

ENTREPRENEURIAL CASE STUDY: FLEXIBILITY & ADAPTABILITY

✓ Eddie C. Brown— Brown Capital Management

Building a Name in the Investment World

Eddie C. Brown is the Chairman, Chief Executive Officer, and Founder of Brown Capital Management (www.browncapital.com), the country's second oldest African-American owned investment management firm, located in Baltimore, Maryland. Eddie founded Brown Capital Management in 1983 in an effort to provide the highest-quality investment management services to institutional and individual clients. The firm seeks to provide the right management team, exceptional investment returns, and superior client service to help clients reach their investment goals.

Eddie earned a Bachelor of Science in Electrical Engineering from Howard University, a Masters of Science in Electrical Engineering from New York University, and an MBA from Indiana University School of Business. Prior to starting Brown Capital Management, Eddie worked in the financial sector. Eddie's innovative approach to investing is designed to provide a greater payoff over the longer term. It was founded on the desire to help others grow their current assets through smart investments.

Trusted to Manage and Grow Assets

Using his expertise in the financial sector, Eddie decided to start a firm focused entirely on the client. The firm grew quickly, thanks to performance outcomes, hard work, and Eddie's national exposure on "Wall Street Week with Louis Rukeyser," a nationally televised program. Over thirty years later, the firm is considered the "right choice" by savvy investors who entrust Brown Capital to manage and grow their assets. Brown Capital Management's only focus is to provide equity investment management services—ensuring no distractions by other lines of business. The firm works hard to attract and retain the most talented and experienced professionals, hiring only those dedicated to its investment methods, its culture, and its clients.

Eddie C. Brown.

Eddie's efforts have given him much recognition over the years. In 2003, he was selected as Ernst & Young's Entrepreneur of the Year in the financial services category for the State of Maryland. In April of 2004, he was inducted into the Maryland Chamber of Commerce Business Hall of Fame. In 2006, he was awarded the Marylander of Distinction Award by *Maryland Life Magazine*, and, in 2010, he was selected as the Business Leader of the Year by the Sellinger School of Business at Loyola University. In addition, Eddie was recognized as a Distinguished Alum by both Howard University and the Kelley School of Business, Indiana University.

Investing in the Community

Along with sitting on the boards of numerous local organizations, Eddie has found additional ways to support his community. In 2002, Eddie and his family announced the creation of the Turning the Corner Achievement Program (TCAP), an unprecedented educational initiative for African-American middle school students in Baltimore. TCAP provides youth with a unique combination of educational and personal support to prepare them for success in high school and beyond.

Thinking and Acting Like an Entrepreneur

- How did Eddie use his personal skills and career experience to identify a business opportunity?
- In what ways does Eddie demonstrate the entrepreneurial mindset behavior of flexibility and adaptability?
- How does Eddie's business help others navigate financial risk?

30.2 Balance Sheet

What Is a Balance Sheet?

Earlier in this chapter, you were introduced to two very important financial statements: the income statement and the cash flow statement.

This section will introduce another very important financial statement: the balance sheet.

A **balance sheet** is a financial statement that summarizes the assets and liabilities (debts) of a business. It shows how much a business is worth at a particular time. A balance sheet is like a snapshot of a business on a specific date. An income statement is more like a movie, reflecting changes in the business over a period of time.

A balance sheet answers the questions: What does the company own? To whom does it owe money? How much is the business worth?

The balance sheet focuses on the following fundamental accounting equation:

$$\text{Assets} - \text{Liabilities} = \text{Owner's Equity}$$

Another way to show this equation is:

$$\text{Assets} = \text{Liabilities} + \text{Owner's Equity}$$

Let's examine each of the terms in this equation:

- **Assets.** Everything owned by the business that has a monetary value is an **asset**. This could include such things as cash, inventory on-hand, equipment, and supplies.
- **Liabilities.** Any outstanding bill or loan that must be repaid is a **liability**.
- **Owner's Equity.** The value of the business on a specific date is referred to as the **owner's equity**. It's the value of the business if all the assets were sold and all the liabilities were paid.

Figure 30-2 ▶

What Does a Balance Sheet Show?

A balance sheet shows that assets are always balanced by liabilities and owner's equity.

Applying Concepts.

What does it mean when the liabilities of a business owner outweigh her or his assets?

The balance sheet shows you the value of your business on a specific date. For example, if you decided to close down your business, your first step would be to sell all your assets. The next step would be to pay off all your liabilities (debts). Any money remaining would be yours to keep. It's the value of your business, or your owner's equity.

Fiscal Year

Businesses often prepare a balance sheet monthly and most prepare one annually. As discussed previously, a business can choose to use a calendar year accounting period (January 1–December 31) or a fiscal year accounting period. A fiscal year is the 12-month period chosen by the business (for example, July 1–June 30).

Assets Are Owned

Assets are the items of value *owned* by a business: cash, inventory, furniture, machinery, and so on. On a typical balance sheet, assets are usually classified as either current assets or long-term assets.

- **Current Assets.** Short-term assets that can be converted into cash within one year are **current assets**. These include cash, inventory, marketable securities, and money owed the business by its customers (called accounts receivable). **Accounts receivable** is the amount of money owed to a business by its customers for credit sales.
- **Long-Term Assets.** Assets that usually take longer than one year to turn into cash are **long-term or fixed assets**. Examples of long-term assets are equipment, computers, furniture, machinery, buildings, and long-term investments.

Liabilities Are Owed

Liabilities are all sums of money *owed* by the business. One of the most common types of liability is **accounts payable**, which represents the amount of money a business owes to its suppliers for purchases made on credit. Other liabilities include bills owed for telephone, utilities, insurance, and taxes. Liabilities include such debts as short-term bank loans, mortgages, and loans from families or friends. On a typical balance sheet, liabilities are classified as either current liabilities or long-term liabilities.

- **Current Liabilities.** Short-term debts that must be repaid within one year are **current liabilities**. These include debts to suppliers for credit purchases (accounts payable), bank loans, and state sales taxes collected from customers and owed to the state.
- **Long-Term Liabilities.** Debts that usually take longer than one year to repay are **long-term liabilities**. The money owed on a mortgage, for example, is a long-term liability.

Preparing Balance Sheets

Balance sheets are divided into two sections. All the assets of the business are in the first section and the liabilities of the business and the owner's equity are included in the second section. Think of this second section as the creditors of the business, those to whom the business owes money, having the first claim on the assets. The owner receives any money remaining after all of the debts have been paid.

There are two formats for a balance sheet: one-column and two-column. Most large companies use the one-column format.

Matt Washington has been very successful over the past eight years. Matt's Hats now has a store that is famous for its large selection. Matt is preparing the annual balance sheet, as shown in Ledger 30.1. The accounting period for Matt's Hats is the calendar year.

- **Current Assets.** The first step in preparing the income statement is to determine the value of the company's assets. Matt's Hats has cash on hand of $25,000 and the value of the inventory is $100,000. Inventory is the value of the goods a business has on-hand and available for sale. Matt's Hats, for example, has a wide variety of hats available for sale. Customers owe the business $20,000 for sales made to them on credit. (This is Matt's accounts receivable.) Cash, inventory, and accounts receivable are classified as current asset accounts.

- **Long-Term Assets.** Matt's Hats owns its own building, which is worth $135,000. The company also has equipment for printing designs on baseball caps. The equipment is valued at $20,000. The building and the equipment are the only long-term assets owned by Matt's Hats.

- **Current Liabilities.** Next, Matt Washington has to determine the company's total liabilities. It has short-term bank loans of $25,000. The company also owes $40,000 to its merchandise suppliers for the inventory items purchased on credit, so the accounts payable total on the balance sheet is $40,000. The company also owes the state $5,000 for sales taxes it collected. So, the company's sales tax payable is $5,000. These are the company's current liabilities.

- **Long-Term Liabilities.** Matt's Hats has a mortgage loan on its building. The company owes the mortgage company $70,000 on the loan, so its mortgage payable is $70,000. This is Matt's only long-term liability.

- **Owner's Equity.** The final step is to determine the owner's equity. Owner's equity is calculated by subtracting the total liabilities from the total assets. The owner's equity account for Matt's Hats, shown on the balance sheet as Matt Washington, Capital, has a balance of $160,000. The word "capital" in accounting refers to the investment or ownership value of the business. Because Matt is the sole owner of the business, this account reflects the value of the business to Matt.

Balance Sheet for Matt's Hats		
December 31, 2017		
ASSETS		
Current Assets		
Cash	$ 25,000	
Inventory	100,000	
Accounts Receivable	20,000	
Total Current Assets		$145,000
Long-Term Assets		
Building	135,000	
Equipment	20,000	
Total Long-Term Assets		155,000
Total Assets		300,000
LIABILITIES & OWNER'S EQUITY		
Current Liabilities		
Bank Loans	25,000	
Accounts Payable	40,000	
Sales Tax Payable	5,000	
Total Current Liabilities		70,000
Long-Term Liabilities		
Mortgage Payable	70,000	
Total Long-Term Liabilities		70,000
Total Liabilities		140,000
Owner's Equity		
Matt Washington, Capital		160,000
Total Liabilities & Owner's Equity		300,000

Total Assets − Total Liabilities = Owner's Equity

$300,000 − $140,000 = $160,000

Not all businesses have all these accounts; however, the procedure for preparing the balance sheet (starting with assets and moving through liabilities to determine the owner's equity) will be similar to the procedure just outlined.

Analyzing Balance Sheets

A business usually prepares one balance sheet at the beginning of its fiscal year and another at the end. Comparing the beginning balance sheet to the ending one is an excellent way to determine whether the business is succeeding. For example, if the ending balance sheet shows that the owner's equity account has increased, it means that the business has gained value. Another method used to analyze balance sheets

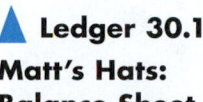

Ledger 30.1

Matt's Hats: Balance Sheet.

This shows the balance sheet for Matt's Hats at the end of the year.

Analyzing Data.

What would be the owner's equity if Matt's Hats increased its inventory to $150,000?

is often called a same-size balance sheet analysis. A percentage change column is added to a comparative balance sheet. This column provides a quick method of analyzing all the changes in the two balance sheets.

Comparative Balance Sheet

Ledger 30.2 shows a comparative balance sheet for Matt's Hats. The balance sheet on the right side was prepared last year on December 31. The balance sheet on the left side was prepared this year on December 31. Compare the two balance sheets to see what has changed after one year.

Current Assets

- **Cash.** Cash has decreased from $25,000 to $20,000. Businesses have cash coming in and going out all the time, so the decrease isn't necessarily bad—as long as there is sufficient cash for daily operations. Remember, a successful entrepreneur prepares and uses cash flow statements to assure that the business has enough cash on hand.

- **Inventory.** The inventory has risen from $100,000 to $125,000. Matt's Hats has purchased more hats, which it hopes to sell. Because inventory has value, this asset account has increased.

- **Accounts Receivable.** This asset has increased from $20,000 to $25,000. This means the amount owed by customers to Matt's Hats from sales on credit has increased.

Long-Term Assets

- **Building.** The building account has not changed.
- **Equipment.** Matt purchased more equipment for customizing baseball caps during the year, so equipment has risen from $20,000 to $25,000.

Total Assets

- **Total Assets.** The total assets for Matt's Hats have risen from $300,000 to $330,000. The company has increased its assets, but does that mean that Matt's Hats has had a successful year? Let's look at the liabilities.

Current Liabilities

- **Bank Loans.** The amount owed to the banks for the loans taken out by Matt's Hats was reduced from $25,000 to $20,000. Decreasing the amount a business owes to its creditors is a good business strategy.

Comparative Balance Sheet for Matt's Hats				
	December 31, This Year		December 31, Last Year	
ASSETS				
Current Assets				
Cash	$ 20,000		$ 25,000	
Inventory	125,000		100,00	
Accounts Receivable	25,000		20,000	
Total Current Assets		$170,000		$145,000
Long-Term Assets				
Building	135,000		135,000	
Equipment	25,000		20,000	
Total Long-Term Assets		160,000		155,000
Total Assets		330,000		300,000
LIABILITIES & OWNER'S EQUITY				
Current Liabilities				
Bank Loans	20,000		25,000	
Accounts Payable	30,000		40,000	
Sales Tax Payable	2,000		5,000	
Total Current Liabilities		52,000		70,000
Long-Term Liabilities				
Mortgage Payable	70,000		70,000	
Total Long-Term Liabilities		70,000		70,000
Total Liabilities		122,000		140,000
Owner's Equity				
Matt Washington, Capital		208,000		160,000
Total Liabilities & Owner's Equity		330,000		300,000

- **Accounts Payable.** The amount owed to the various wholesalers and manufacturers of hats decreased from $40,000 to $30,000. Despite adding inventory during the year, the amount owed to suppliers decreased. This shows that Matt made a deliberate business decision to reduce his liabilities.

- **Sales Tax Payable.** Matt's Hats collects sales tax for the state from its customers on every sale. It then makes payments to the state. Matt's Hats decreased the amount it owed the state from $5,000 to $2,000.

▲ **Ledger 30.2**

Matt's Hats: Comparative Balance Sheet.

This shows the comparative balance sheet for Matt's Hats on December 31, last year, and December 31, this year.

Predicting.

Based on this comparative balance sheet, how do you think Matt's Hats will do next year?

Long-Term Liabilities

- **Mortgage Payable.** The amount owed on the mortgage remained the same. This isn't unusual, because mortgages are structured so that payments in the early years of a mortgage are applied to the interest owed on the mortgage rather than to the principal. (The principal of a mortgage or any loan is the original amount borrowed, before interest is added.)

Owner's Equity

- **Matt Washington, Capital.** The owner's equity account of the business, named Matt Washington, Capital, increased from $160,000 to $208,000. That's good news for Matt, because it means that the business increased in value during that time period.

Despite having less cash at the end of the period, the comparative balance sheet contains very favorable financial information for Matt's Hats. The company has increased the amount of inventory it has available for sale, and it is owed more money from credit sales to customers.

The company has reduced all of its current liabilities. Amounts owed for bank loans, accounts payable, and sales tax payable all decreased. Remember:

$$\text{Assets} - \text{Liabilities} = \text{Owner's Equity}$$

By reducing liabilities, Matt Washington has increased his owner's equity, the value of his business. He reduced his liabilities by paying off some of the company's debt. Paying off debt is one of the smartest things a business can do with extra cash.

Same-Size Balance Sheet Analysis

Ledger 30.3 shows the comparative balance sheet for Matt's Hats, with an added column. This column shows all the changes from last year to this year as a percentage of last year's amounts. For example, cash received shrank from $25,000 last year to $20,000 this year. That's a 20% decline.

$$\$25,000 - \$20,000 = \$5,000$$
(Last Year) (This Year) (Difference)

$$(\$5,000 \div \$25,000) \times 100 = 20\%$$

The same-size balance sheet analysis statement provides a quick way to see how the business is performing. (Note that any value written in red and set in parentheses is a negative percentage.) A quick look at the percentages shows that Matt's Hats has increased both its inventory and

Same-Size Balance Sheet for Matt's Hats					
	December 31, This Year		December 31, Last Year		% Change
ASSETS					
Current Assets					
Cash	$ 20,000		$ 25,000		(20)
Inventory	125,000		100,00		25
Accounts Receivable	25,000		20,000		25
Total Current Assets		$170,000		$145,000	17.2
Long-Term Assets					
Building	135,000		135,000		0
Equipment	25,000		20,000		25
Total Long-Term Assets		160,000		155,000	3.2
Total Assets		330,000		300,000	10
LIABILITIES & OWNER'S EQUITY					
Current Liabilities					
Bank Loans	20,000		25,000		(20)
Accounts Payable	30,000		40,000		(25)
Sales Tax Payable	2,000		5,000		(60)
Total Current Liabilities		52,000		70,000	(25.7)
Long-Term Liabilities					
Mortgage Payable	70,000		70,000		0
Total Long-Term Liabilities		70,000		70,000	0
Total Liabilities		122,000		140,000	(12.8)
Owner's Equity					
Matt Washington, Capital		208,000		160,000	30
Total Liabilities & Owner's Equity		330,000		300,000	10

its accounts receivable by 25%. This reflects favorably on the business. Reducing all the current liabilities, especially the accounts payable, by 25% is another example of a good business strategy. The wise business decisions made by Matt are reflected in the 30% increase in his owner's equity.

Apply Your Knowledge A balance sheet consists of assets, liabilities, and owner's equity. Define each of these and then identify and explain the components that are recorded under assets and liabilities and how owner's equity is calculated. What two types of balance sheets are used to analyze how a business is doing? Think back to your investigation of the record stores. Tower Records borrowed $110 million dollars to expand before the sharp drop in sales. How did that impact their equity?

▲ **Ledger 30.3**

Matt's Hats: Same-Size Balance Sheet.

The same-size balance sheet analysis statement for Matt's Hats on December 31, last year, and December 31, this year, shows the percentage changes from one year to the next.

Drawing Conclusions.

Based on this statement, do you think Matt Washington made good business decisions during the year?

CAREER COMPETENCIES

Supervise/Implement Regular Accounting Procedures and Financial Reports

Another way entrepreneurs can see relationships, patterns, and trends is by using charts. Pie charts and bar graphs are very helpful in illustrating financial ratios. You can create either one in a computer software program such as Microsoft Excel. An entrepreneur often makes presentations on the financial status of the business. Showing financial data—including financial ratios—visually can be an effective way to help others understand the significance of your information.

Pie Charts

A pie chart has "slices" that represent portions of the whole. You could create a pie chart by using the information on the income statement for Matt's Hats (see Ledger 30.4).

The pie chart shows the cost of goods sold, operating expenses, and net income. The entire pie represents 100% of Mat's Hats sales in August—$10,000. Costs, operating expenses, and pre-tax profit are shown as percentages of this total. For example, because Matt's Hats had expenses of $3,000 in August, the percentage of expenses to sales is 30%.

Do you find it easier to review the status of Matt's Hats by using the pie chart or the income statement? They both give you the same information. In the future, Matt's Hats can use this percentage to evaluate whether its monthly operating expenses are in an acceptable range. Matt will know that, for his particular business, these expenses are about 30% of sales—at least for this current month. (The monthly percentage will probably vary—and every business will be different.)

Bar Graphs

A bar graph uses vertical or horizontal bars to show data. Bar graphs are good for demonstrating trends. For example, let's look at five monthly income statements for Matt's Hats. In January, the business had very little revenue ($300) because it was just getting started and didn't have many sales. Wisely, Matt had put aside some money that would take care of expenses for several months.

After the slow start, sales picked up. In February, they were $1,500; in March, $2,000. In April, sales reached $2,500, and they increased again in May to $3,000. Do you see a trend? Sales for Matt's Hats increased every month. This same information would have been found in Matt's income statements, but the bar graph made the trend easy to see at a glance. Matt can use this information to make predictions about future sales.

Income Statement for Matt's Hats			
For the Month Ended August 31, 2017			
Revenue			
Sales			
Cost of Goods Sold			
Beginning Inventory	1,200		
Add: Purchases	4,800		
Total		$6,000	
Less: Inventory, August 31		1,000	
Cost of Goods Sold			5,000
Gross Profit			**5,000**
Operating Expenses			
Utilities	450		
Salaries	700		
Advertising	500		
Insurance	400		
Interest	300		
Rent	500		
Telephone	150		
Total Operating Expenses			3,000
Pre-Tax Profit			**2,000**

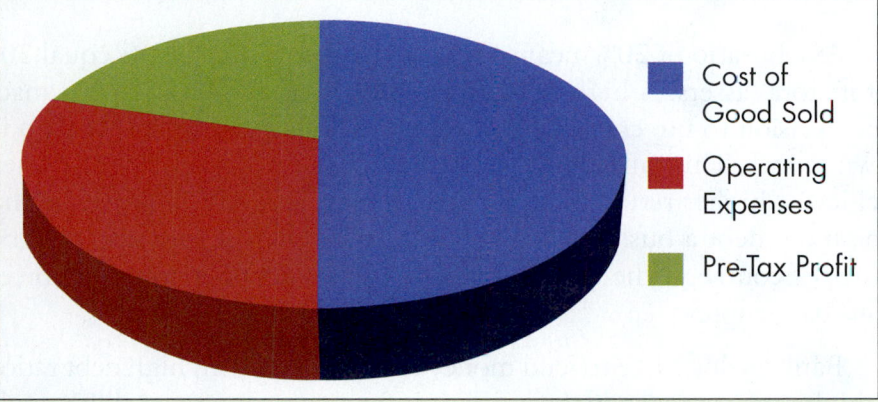

- Cost of Good Sold
- Operating Expenses
- Pre-Tax Profit

◀ **Ledger 30.4**

Income Statement and Pie Chart.

This pie chart shows the relationship of the COGS, operating expenses, and pre-tax profit.

Interpreting Graphs.

How would you know if this is a good split of costs and operating expenses to sales?

Career Skills in Action

Now try to use applications like charts or graphs to interpret the projected financial data for your business. Then answer the following questions:

- What data did you represent with a chart or table?
- What did you learn from presenting the data in this way?
- How does using tools such as these help entrepreneurs more efficiently supervise accounting procedures?

Share your work with your teacher or a peer for feedback.

30.3 Ratios from Balance Sheets

In addition to the financial ratios calculated by using the data on income statements, entrepreneurs also create ratios from the data on the balance sheets for their businesses. They then use these ratios to monitor debt, to compare debt with equity, and to make sure the business has sufficient cash to pay its debts.

The four most important financial ratios based on the balance sheet are:

- The debt ratio
- The debt-to-equity ratio
- The quick ratio
- The current ratio

Debt Ratio and Debt-to-Equity Ratio

A business needs to control its debts. If the business is unable to make the interest payments on its debt, it can be forced into bankruptcy. A ratio used to monitor the debts of a business is the **debt ratio**. This is the ratio of a business's total debt divided by its total assets. For example, if Matt's Hats has $100,000 in total debts (also referred to as its total liabilities) and total assets of $500,000, its debt ratio is 20%.

$$(\text{Total Debts} \div \text{Total Assets}) \times 100 = \text{Debt Ratio (\%)}$$

$$(\$100,000 \div \$500,000) \times 100 = 20\%$$

A debt ratio of 20% means that the debts for Matt's Hats equal 20% of its total assets. A high debt ratio indicates that a business has made the decision to use creditors and suppliers for financing, rather than its own money. This can be a good strategy, because it may help the owners achieve a higher return on their investment. The risk, however, is that the more debt a business has, the higher its interest payments will be. And, of course, if the business fails to pay its debts, it could be forced into bankruptcy.

Bankers don't like to lend money to businesses with high debt ratios. A high ratio may also make it difficult for a company to establish credit with suppliers. An ideal debt ratio is determined by the ability of the company to meet its loan payments, at an amount of debt considered acceptable in the industry. So when starting or operating your business, you will need to determine an ideal debt ratio based on your industry.

Another useful tool is the **debt-to-equity ratio.** This is the ratio of the total debts (liabilities) of the business divided by its owner's equity. For example, if Matt's Hats had debts of $100,000 and an owner's equity of $400,000, the debt-to-equity ratio would be 25%.

$$\text{(Total Debts} \div \text{Owner's Equity)} \times 100 = \text{Debt-to-Equity Ratio (\%)}$$

$$(\$100{,}000 \div \$400{,}000) \times 100 = 25\%$$

This means that, for every dollar of debt the business has, it has $4 of equity. *Because the value of a business is the owner's equity, you need to monitor the debt-to-equity ratio carefully.*

Quick Ratio and Current Ratio

The balance sheet also tells you about a business's liquidity. **Liquidity** is the ability to convert assets into cash. A business is illiquid if its assets cannot easily be converted into cash. Two ratios that help you keep an eye on liquidity are the quick ratio and the current ratio.

The **quick ratio** is the comparison of cash to debt, based on the concept that a business should have at least enough money on hand to pay its current debts. The quick ratio is calculated by adding the value of its marketable securities to the cash on hand. **Marketable securities** are investments, such as stocks or bonds that could be converted to cash quickly. Then that sum is divided by the current liabilities of the business.

For example, if a company has $50,000 in marketable securities, $150,000 in cash, and $100,000 in current liabilities, its quick ratio is 2 to 1 (which can also be shown as 2:1). Both quick and current ratios are calculated as ratios rather than as percentages.

$$\text{(Cash + Marketable Securities)} \div \text{Current Liabilities} = \text{Quick Ratio}$$

$$(\$150{,}000 + \$50{,}000) \div \$100{,}000 = 2 \text{ to } 1$$

The quick ratio tells an entrepreneur whether the business has enough cash to cover its current debts. Because a business should be able to pay its debts, the quick ratio should always be greater than 1 to 1.

A similar formula is the **current ratio**. This is current assets divided by current liabilities. For example, if Matt's Hats has current assets of $250,000 and current liabilities of $100,000, its current ratio would be 2.5 to 1.

$$\text{Current Assets} + \text{Current Liabilities} = \text{Current Ratio}$$

$$(\$250{,}000 + \$100{,}000) = 2.5 \text{ to } 1$$

Like the quick ratio, the current ratio provides information about the liquidity of the business. The current ratio indicates whether a business would be capable of selling its assets to pay its debts. Most businesses try to maintain a current ratio of 2 to 1.

Apply Your Knowledge   What are four ratios calculated from a balance sheet? From your investigation of the record stores, how could the businesses have used these ratios to determine the health of the business before things took a turn for the worse?

APPLICATION TO BUSINESS PLANNING

Financial Ratios

Use what you learned from this chapter on financial analysis to calculate financial ratios about your business. You should support your findings with research data. Be sure to include:

- A calculation of your ROS based on your projected sales and income
- A calculation of your operating ratio based on your projected sales and expenses
- An analysis of your balance sheet using the balance sheet ratios

REVIEWING OBJECTIVES

1. How are income statements used for financial analysis?
2. Identify the purpose and components of a balance sheet.
3. What financial ratios can be calculated from a balance sheet?

CRITICAL THINKING

1. Which do you think is more important to a business and why: the operating ratio or the return on sales?
2. Define the terms "liquid" and "illiquid" as they apply to a business's assets. Provide an example of each and explain why it is liquid or illiquid.

ENTREPRENEURIAL THINKING EXERCISE: FLEXIBILITY & ADAPTABILITY

Think back to your investigation of the record megastores. Album stores have more overhead expenses so their ROS are much lower than digital music, which have less direct expenses in downloading. If you were to go back in time and give them advice, what would you say that they should have done to adapt differently to the competition? Provide specific steps they should have taken.

EXTENSION ACTIVITIES

Entrepreneurship & Mathematics Skills

Complete the following task to demonstrate your understanding of entrepreneurship:

Grades 9–12: Use your understanding from this unit to determine how much return you would get in a month from investing $1,000 in each of the following:

- A business with monthly sales of $2,000 and operating ratio of 5%.
- A business with monthly sales of $3,000 and a return on sales of 5%.
- A savings account that has an annual interest rate of 15% (Hint: Use properties of exponents to calculate the approximate monthly interest rate.)

Unit 6: Financial & Expense Management

CHAPTER SUMMARY

26. The Cost of Doing Business

Entrepreneurs have two types of business expenses to consider: fixed expenses and variable expenses. Variable expenses vary based on the amount of product or services a business sells in a given time period. Variable expenses are divided into two categories: cost of goods sold per unit (COGS) and other variable expenses. The cost of goods sold per unit includes the cost of the labor and materials used to make a product. Other variable expenses could include commissions, shipping and handling charges, and packaging. A unit of sale is what a customer actually buys from a business. It is the amount of product or service a business uses to figure out its operations and profit. The equation for the economics of one unit of sale is selling price minus expenses equals profits. To find the contribution margin per unit, subtract all variable expenses for the unit from the selling price.

27. Expense Management

The fixed expenses of a business are expenses that are not affected by increases or decreases in the number of products a business sells. Common examples of fixed expenses are insurance, salaries, advertising, interest payments, depreciation, utilities, and rent. Depreciation is an accounting method of spreading the total cost of the equipment a business buys over the number of years it will be used. Despite being called "fixed," fixed expenses may vary from month to month. The break-even point is reached when costs and expenses are exactly equal to sales. At the break-even point, there is neither profit nor loss—the total at the bottom of the income statement is zero. To determine the break-even point, perform a break-even analysis. This shows exactly how many units a business must sell to pay all its expenses. A startup business needs to determine its break-even point to make sure it has enough money reserved to cover its losses early in the life of the company. When sales or expenses change, an entrepreneur should do a break-even analysis to make sure the company will remain profitable. Business owners manage their expenses, credit, and cash flow because these components are important to a business's financial health. Managing expenses requires knowledge of what they are and actions that should be taken to reduce them wherever feasible. To assure that enough cash is on hand, entrepreneurs prepare cash flow statements. These statements record cash inflows and cash outflows when they occur. Because of their importance, cash flow statements should be prepared monthly. In the beginning months of a new business, it is common that more money is spent than earned. The rate at which a company spends cash to cover overhead costs without generating a positive cash flow is called the burn rate.

28. Revenue Streams and Sales Projections

When preparing a financial plan for your business, entrepreneurs should look at how money, or revenue is coming into the business. Many businesses have multiple sources of revenue, called revenue streams. Potential revenue streams can include subscriptions, advertising, transaction/usage fees, licensing/franchising, and renting/leasing. You can make a sales forecast that predicts all of the revenue your company expects to bring in from its various revenue streams over a certain time period. It includes analyzing current company and market conditions, reviewing your company's past sales figures, making educated predictions about change and opportunity, and then estimating sales based on your research. An income statement includes sales and expense data as well as the net income or loss of a business. Income statements differ based on the type of business. Retailing and wholesaling use the category Cost of Goods Sold. Manufacturing companies use Cost of Goods Manufactured and Sold. Service businesses use Cost of Services Sold.

29. Financing the Business

Raising money for a business is called financing. Entrepreneurs need to figure out how much money they need to get the business going. This is the start-up investment, made up of the start-up expenditures and the cash reserves. Typically, the cash reserves consist of an emergency fund and a reserve for fixed expenses. Entrepreneurs need to figure out when their initial investment will begin to pay off in profits. This is referred to as payback. A ratio that is used to determine how well the business is doing in relation to the amount of money that has been invested in it is return on investment (ROI). When an entrepreneur starts a business alone, without any outside investment, it's called bootstrapping. Entrepreneurs can bootstrap a business by using personal savings and credit cards. Both are dangerous as sources of funding, however. If the company isn't able to pay these loans back, the entrepreneur will lose the money and, if credit cards are involved, could permanently damage his/her credit rating. Debt financing is borrowing the money needed for a business. The three main sources for debt financing are banks, credit unions, and relatives or friends. Banks use the bank debt ratio to determine whether a business is capable of borrowing additional funds. Typically, a good ratio is 40% or less. Banks almost always ask for collateral and sometimes a co-signer for a loan. Credit unions are nonprofit cooperatives that offer low-interest loans to members. A disadvantage to borrowing from relatives and friends is that, if the business is not successful, they could lose their investment. Equity financing is the selling of shares of ownership in a business to raise money. When an entrepreneur does this, he or she gives up some control of the company. The three main sources of equity financing are relatives and friends, angels and venture capitalists, and partners. Both debt and equity financing are available from specialized sources. Debt financing increases liabilities on the balance sheet and reduces owner's equity as a percentage of assets. Equity financing increases overall equity but also decreases the owner's equity as a percentage of assets.

30. Financial Analysis

Analyzing a company's records to see relationships, patterns, or trends isn't always easy. That's why entrepreneurs use financial ratios and charts. Two important types of analysis based on the income statement are sales-data analysis and same-size analysis. Two important financial ratios based on the income statement are the operating ratio and return on sales (ROS). A balance sheet is a financial statement that summarizes the assets and liabilities (debts) of a business. The balance sheet also shows the value of the business to the entrepreneur (owner's equity). The owner's equity is calculated by subtracting the total liabilities from the total assets. Entrepreneurs analyze balance sheets to help them determine how their businesses are performing. Comparative balance sheets and same-size balance sheet analysis statements are used by entrepreneurs to identify the changes in assets, liabilities, and owner's equity from one accounting period to another. Four ratios are based on the balance sheet: the debt ratio, the debt-to-equity ratio, the quick ratio, and the current ratio.

UNIT 6 VOCABULARY

accounts payable

accounts receivable

angel

asset

balance sheet

bank debt ratio

barter financing

bootstrapping

break-even analysis

break-even point

break-even units

burn rate

calendar year

cash flow

cash flow statement

collateral

commission

contribution margin

co-signer

cost of goods sold (COGS)

cost of services sold (COSS)

cost structure

credit union

crowdfunding

current assets

current liabilities

current ratio

customer financing

cyclical

debt financing

debt ratio

debt-to-equity ratio

depreciation

depreciation expense

disposal value

economy of scale

emergency fund

equity financing

expense

financial ratio

financing

fiscal year

fixed expense

freemium

income statement

labor

liability

liquidity

long-term assets

long-term liabilities

marketable securities

microloan

operating ratio

owner's equity

payback

profit and loss statement

quick ratio

reserve for fixed expenses

return on investment (ROI)

return on sales (ROS)

revenue

revenue stream

salary

sales forecast

salvage value

same-size analysis

seed money

start-up capital

start-up expenditures

start-up investment

straight line method of depreciation

subscription

syndication

transaction fee

unit of sale

variable expense

venture capital

volume discount

CHECK YOUR UNDERSTANDING

Choose the letter that best answers the question or completes the statement.

1. Expenses that are not affected by the number of products a business sells are called
   a. variable expenses
   b. fixed expenses
   c. contribution margin
   d. selling expenses

2. Expenses that change based on the quantity of goods a business sells in a given period of time are called
   a. fixed expenses
   b. variable expenses
   c. fluctuating expenses
   d. selling expenses

3. Which of the following is not used in determining the contribution margin?
   a. variable expenses
   b. fixed expenses
   c. cost of goods sold
   d. other variable expenses

4. In a service business, an entrepreneur charges $500 for a job, pays a commission of 10% of sales, and has a cost of services sold per unit of $100. What is the entrepreneur's contribution margin per unit?
   a. $350
   b. $300
   c. $395
   d. $400

5. In an income statement, subtracting the cost of goods sold from the net sales provides the
   a. revenue
   b. net operating income
   c. gross profit
   d. net income

6. A cost of goods sold section is included in a
   a. merchandising business income statement
   b. service business income statement
   c. cash flow statement
   d. balance sheet

7. The cash flow equation is

a. Cash Outflow – Cash Inflow = Net Profit

b. Cash Outflow – Cash Inflow = Gross Profit

c. Cash Inflow – Cash Outflow = Net Cash

d. Cash Inflow – Cash Outflow = Net Profit

8. Owner's equity is calculated by

a. subtracting total liabilities from total assets

b. dividing total liabilities by total assets

c. subtracting total assets from total liabilities

d. dividing total assets by total liabilities

9. Return on sales (ROS) is also called

a. net profit ratio

b. net margin

c. profit margin

d. all of the above

10. Total liabilities divided by total assets is the formula used to calculate the

a. debt ratio

b. current ratio

c. quick ratio

d. debt-to-equity ratio

11. If the net income of a business is $3,000 and the owner's investment is $10,000, the return-on-investment (ROI) percentage is

a. 300%

b. 30%

c. 3%

d. 0.3%

12. If the operating expenses are $5,000 and the gross profit per unit is $5, the number of break-even units is

a. 10

b. 100

c. 1,000

d. 10,000

13. The one-time investment of starting a business is called

a. financing

b. start-up investment

c. venture capital

d. working capital

14. Which of the following is the mathematical formula for payback?

a. start-up investment + net profit per month

b. net profit per month ÷ start-up investment

c. start-up investment ÷ net profit per month

d. net profit per month – start-up investment

15. Venture capital is typically a source of which type of financing?

    a. debt financing

    b. equity financing

    c. bootstrapping

    d. government-sponsored financing

16. The major source of debt financing is a(n)

    a. credit union

    b. angel

    c. customer

    d. bank

BUSINESS COMMUNICATION

1. Working in teams, prepare a presentation that traces a manufactured item through a wholesale business to a retail business. Prepare an EOU for the unit of sale for each of the three businesses in the chain.

2. Work with a partner. Imagine you operate a retail business selling disposable cell phones. First, decide on a selling price for the phones and prepare a list of the estimated fixed and variable expenses. You both want the business to increase its profit. One partner should suggest ways to lower the variable expenses; the other should suggest ways to lower the fixed expenses.

3. Partner with a classmate. You have an idea for a new energy drink. You need to raise capital to finance a test market in your area. Prepare an income statement that shows your plan. Role-play a presentation to a bank official, with a classmate playing the bank official. Then reverse roles.

4. Partner with a classmate. You own a sports equipment store with two partners. You've been in business for two years. You and another partner want to expand your product line. Prepare a presentation of your ideas. Use income statements, balance sheets, and cash flow statements to help you prove that the business will be financially capable of taking on the added risk. Make your presentation to the class, who will represent your third partner.

5. Working with a partner, prepare a balance sheet for a fictional business. From the data on the balance sheet, prepare the following ratios: debt ratio, debt-to-equity ratio, quick ratio, and current ratio.

6. Split into two teams. Each team will be starting a new business. Each will develop a list of what is necessary to begin the business. Then the team members will determine the start-up capital required. One team will be using equity financing to obtain the start-up capital; the other will be using debt financing. Each team will prepare a short presentation to convince their sources of financing to provide start-up capital. While one team presents, the other will play the role of the funding source.

BUSINESS MATH

1. A wholesale business sells pen and pencil sets to retailers for $12 per dozen. The wholesaler pays the manufacturer $0.50 for each individual pen and pencil set. The wholesaler pays its salespeople a commission of 10% of sales. The wholesaler has packaging expenses of $0.30 for each unit of 12 sets. What is the wholesaler's contribution margin per unit?

2. Dana Wright operates an airport limousine service. He owns the limo and does his own driving. He values his driving time at $25 per hour. He pays a commission fee of $10 to the person who brings him the business. A trip to the airport takes three hours and uses $25 worth of gasoline. If Dana charges each customer $200, what is his contribution margin per unit of sale? How much does Dana make on each trip as a driver? As the owner of the business?

3. Last year's balance sheet showed an owner's equity of $400,000 and this year's balance sheet showed owner's equity as $500,000. What is the percentage increase?

4. In a monthly income statement, if the gross profit is $10,000, the total operating expenses are $4,000, and the taxes are 15%, what is the net profit? If the total operating expenses double next month, what is the percentage change in net profit from this month to next month?

5. The income statement for your business shows sales of $50,000 in June. The operating expenses for the month totaled $20,000. What is the operating ratio percentage for June?

6. Your skateboard-painting business has operating expenses of $3,600 per month. The gross profit for each skateboard you paint is $12. How many skateboards do you need to paint to reach the break-even point?

7. The start-up investment for your business is $36,000. Your net income per month is $6,000. What is the payback period for your investment?

8. Your local bank requires its customers to have a bank debt ratio of 40% or less before approving a loan. Your entrepreneurial business provides you with an income of $4,200 per month. Your business has monthly debts of $1,500. Will you qualify for a loan at that bank?

BUSINESS ETHICS

1. You own a retail business that sells clocks, which you purchase from a local wholesaler. Your typical order is for 12 dozen clocks at a cost of $100 per dozen. The salesperson for the wholesaler offers you a special deal. She says that if you double your order to 24 dozen, she will give you one-half her commission on the extra clocks. This deal would lower your contribution margin per unit and you think you would be able to sell the extra clocks. However, you feel uneasy about the offer. Write a short report describing what you would do in this situation. Include an EOU for the current ordering amount and the special deal.

2. You own an electronics store. While taking inventory, you notice that five cell phones are missing. Last month you hired a part-time worker who has access to the cell phones. You aren't absolutely sure that the new employee stole the phones, but you can't think of any other

explanation. You can't afford to continue losing inventory. Do you confront the employee with your suspicions? How would you resolve your problem? With a partner, role-play the situation. Then reverse roles.

3. You badly need a bank loan to be able to pay your operating costs. But you are aware that the bank requires a bank debt ratio of less than 40% before they will grant a loan. By your calculation, your ratio will be 42%. One of your friends loaned you some start-up money. Knowing that the total amount of debt will make your bank debt ratio too high, he makes a suggestion. He recommends that you do not include your payments to him in the bank loan application. He says he has confidence in you and your business and that the bank should be willing to loan you the money because your bank debt ratio is just slightly over the 40% limit. What should you do?

BUSINESS IN YOUR COMMUNITY

1. Working with three or four classmates, prepare a survey to be completed by two owners of retail businesses in the community. The survey should ask the owners to identify their major fixed and variable expenses. Collect and tabulate the surveys. Write a report comparing the results and present them to the class.

2. Interview two service business owners in your community. Ask them how they calculate their fixed and variable expenses. Write a short report summarizing the results of your interviews and present your findings to the class.

3. Interview two entrepreneurs or small business owners in your community. Ask them if they use break-even analysis in their financial planning. Also ask each of them how long it took the business to become profitable. Write a short report comparing the results of your interviews.

4. Working in teams of three or four, prepare a questionnaire on how local small businesses financed their startups. It should include questions on sources of start-up investment, types of debt financing, equity financing, and any other types of funding the businesses use or have used. Present the questionnaire to the owners of small businesses in your community. As a team, prepare a short presentation based on the results of the questionnaire.

5. Interview individuals from at least two sources of debt financing (banks, credit unions, etc.) in your community. Ask them what criteria they use to determine whether to grant a loan. Ask how they calculate the maximum amount of money they will loan an applicant. Write a short report summarizing the results of your interviews.

INFORMATION TECHNOLOGY

Competing Online

What is your most important goal if you are an e-business owner? Easy! It's getting customers to visit your site. Just as with a traditional store, customers can't buy something without first walking through the door. An e-business owner has to think about **site traffic**, the number of visits a website gets over a specified period.

But how do potential customers find your website? Considering all the websites on the Internet, how do they come to yours? You probably already know the answer. Many potential customers find websites by using a search engine, such as Google. Because of this, an e-business owner is very interested in **search engine ranking**, the order of specific words or groups of words in a particular search engine. The goal is to be on the first page of search results. No business wants to be buried on the tenth page. Very few customers would have the patience to find the company.

Deciding to Compete

With a traditional store, it is relatively easy to determine whether you should open in a particular neighborhood. You need to determine if there are competing businesses in the area and whether the neighborhood needs the products or services you are offering. For an e-business, it's a bit more complicated. You need to know how many other websites are offering similar products or services.

What Makes a Business Special?

Once you know how many websites are selling a similar product or service, you need to figure out what will make your business stand out from the others. One way to do this is to check which of the competing online businesses is getting the most traffic. You can do this by visiting a **site-ranking portal**, which lists top-ranking sites. One site-ranking portal is Alexa.com.

Once you know which of your possible online competitors is getting the most traffic, you will need to figure out why. Some questions are: Is this site's design especially engaging? Is it easy to navigate? What about it sets it apart from competitors? What makes it special? Often, analyses of competing websites are undertaken by an outside consultant.

Setting Goals

Once a website is up and running, the e-business owner sets goals for daily Web traffic. Having researched the site traffic at competing websites, you will likely have a realistic expectation for your Web traffic. Most new e-businesses take a while to begin to generate optimal Web traffic. You can typically plan for lower traffic for the first few months until the business begins to generate the amount of traffic it should. Even with extensive planning, a startup business may not see a profit in the first year or more. Businesses that aren't well funded sometimes cannot make it through this initial period and are shut down when their traffic goals are not met.

Tech Vocabulary

search engine ranking

site traffic

site-ranking portal

Check Yourself

1. Why is traffic important for any store?

2. Why is a high search engine ranking important for an e-business?

3. How would a prospective e-business owner use a site-ranking portal in the business planning process?

What Do You Think?

Solving Problems. What would you do if you did not meet your projected traffic goals for a new e-business?

CASE STUDY

Financial and Expense Management

ANALYZING THE FIRST YEAR

It's the end of the first year. Things didn't work out quite as Eva Tan projected. But she realized this and she made adjustments. Sometimes doing that can be as important as having a good business plan. Eva took some time to reflect on her first year in business as she generated her first annual income statement.

The Best-Made Plans

Eva hadn't been able to locate any clients in her first month of business. It had taken her four months to gain five clients. The market for her service wasn't at all what she had expected. It turned out that single professionals and two-income couples weren't that interested. However, two-income families were very interested.

Her advertising budget was affected when she had to redo her brochure, her cards, and her website to promote her new kid-friendly focus. And her car had also needed new tires.

Over the year she bought many more cooking supplies than she had expected. Among other things, she bought portable coolers that plugged into her car and some small portable cooking equipment.

She also had to increase the variety of meals she cooked. The kids didn't want the same things as the grown-ups. This increased the overall cost of groceries by $10 but didn't increase her time cooking. After realizing this, Eva increased the price of a 5-dinner plan from $325 to $350, beginning in June.

You Can't Please Everyone

Eva even had one client she just couldn't please. After providing three free meals, Eva decided she needed to establish a policy about when to cancel an agreement with a client. She cancelled the client but wasn't able to sign up a replacement for two months.

After one year in business, Eva has put together the first annual income statement for Eva's Edibles (see the next page).

What Would You Have Done?

1. **Comparing/Contrasting.** Prepare a comparative balance sheet for Eva's Edibles, using her projected income statement. How did Eva do in her first year?

2. **Analyzing Information.** How do the ROS and ROI after the first year compare to those in her projected business plan?

New Economics of One Unit (End of Year 1)		
One Unit of Sale = 5-Dinner Plan		
Selling Price (per Unit)	$ 350	
Variable Costs	264	
Contribution Margin	$ 86	
Eva's Edibles		
Annual Income Statement: Year 1		
March 31, 2017		
REVENUE		
Sales		
(186 Days Cooking; 56 @ $325/Plan, 130 @ $350/Plan)	$ 62,400	
Total Revenue		$ 62,400
COST OF SERVICES SOLD		
Materials (Groceries @ $110/Plan)	$ 20,460	
Labor (@ $150/Plan)	27,900	
Cost of Services Sold		48,360
GROSS PROFIT		$ 14,040
OPERATING EXPENSES		
Advertising	$ 2,550	
Depreciation	200	
Insurance	1,400	
Telephone	1,200	
Other Operating Expenses (Auto-Related)	2,100	
Other Operating Expenses (Cooking-Related)	1,900	
Total Expenses		9,350
PRE-TAX PROFIT		$ 4,690
Taxes (15%)		704
NET PROFIT		3,986

BIG IDEA: OPERATING THE BUSINESS

31

MANAGING THE BUSINESS

GUIDING QUESTION:

"What do I need to do to operate my business on a daily basis?"

APPLICATION TO BUSINESS PLANNING:

☑ Organizational Chart

OBJECTIVES

- Learn about the four main management functions.
- Compare types of organizational structures.
- Understand the importance of a healthy business environment.

NFTE Entrepreneurial Mindset Characteristic Focus

☑ Communication & Collaboration

National Entrepreneurship Standards

- **A.09** Describe entrepreneurial planning considerations
- **A.10** Explain tools used by entrepreneurs for venture planning
- **A.20** Explain factors to consider in determining a venture's human-resource needs
- **A.28** Describe the use of operating procedures
- **B.06** Recognize others' efforts
- **B.15** Evaluate personal capabilities
- **B.16** Conduct self-assessment to determine entrepreneurial potential
- **C.13** Explain the concept of management
- **D.23** Treat others fairly at work
- **D.34** Explain the nature of organizational change
- **J.01** Develop a personnel organizational plan
- **J.16** Exhibit leadership skills
- **N.12** Establish parameters for staff responsibility/authority
- **O.08** Develop action plans

Common Career Technical Core Standards

- **BM.6** Implement, monitor and evaluate business processes to ensure efficiency and quality results.
- **BM-HR.5** Plan, staff, lead and organize human resources to enhance employee productivity and satisfaction.

LESSON VOCABULARY

- authoritarian leadership style
- company image
- controlling
- delegating leadership style
- democratic leadership style
- directing
- interpersonal skills
- line organization
- line-and-staff organization
- management
- operational plan
- organizational structure
- organizing
- planning
- project organization
- quality control program
- strategic plan
- tactical plan
- team building
- workplace climate

- **BM-HR.6** Plan, monitor and manage day-to-day business activities to foster a healthy and safe work environment.
- **BM-OP.4** Plan, monitor and manage day-to-day business activities to maintain and improve operational functions.
- **CRP.9** Model integrity, ethical leadership and effective management.

National Entrepreneurship Standards: Career Competencies

 D.11 Write informational messages

ENTREPRENEURIAL INVESTIGATION

A Happy Company Is a Profitable Company

Many entrepreneurs and managers have to deal with the challenge of employee turnover, or, in other words, employees leaving their positions and needing to hire new ones. The retail industry has an average employee turnover rate of 59% annually, with the supermarket industry being even higher. Training new employees costs these businesses more than 40% of their profits.

Jim Sinegal was the co-founder and CEO of Costco Wholesale Corporation for 30 years. Under his leadership, Jim kept the employee turnover rate down to 12% annually, which helped his company grow. His strategies for managing employees included: listening to employee feedback, making changes based on employee suggestions, and offering employee the best benefits and perks.

Do some research on Jim Sinegal and Costco, and answer the following questions:

- Do you think Jim's approaches encouraged employees to stay at Costco? Why or why not?
- Do you think Jim's management approach plays into the success of the business? Why or why not?

Be prepared to share your work with a peer or your teacher.

31.1 What Is Management?

In the previous units of this textbook, you looked at validating a business opportunity through ongoing market research. At this point, you should have a fully vetted opportunity that you can start operating. This unit will provide content and suggestions to consider when making your business operational.

Once an entrepreneur creates a business and gets it running, he or she takes over management of the business. **Management** is the skillful use and coordination of all the business's resources—money, facilities, equipment, technologies, materials, employees—in a systematic and effective way to achieve clearly defined goals. A manager has authority over employees and is ultimately responsible for their work. He or she must use many skills in this role but, mostly, a manager is a creative problem solver. The purpose of management is not just to achieve business goals but to achieve them with the greatest efficiency. This means maximizing the amount of work done by employees while minimizing expenses. Experts break down the job of a manager into four general functions:

- Planning
- Organizing
- Directing
- Controlling

Planning

Planning is an ongoing process of setting goals, deciding when and how to accomplish them, and determining how best to accomplish them.

A *plan* is a systematic process for achieving a specific goal. Three types of plans are used in business management:

- **Strategic Plan.** A **strategic plan** lays out a broad course of action to achieve a long-term goal, typically three to five years in the future. These plans are usually created by top-level managers with a big picture view of what needs to be done and the general way in which it will be accomplished.

- **Tactical Plan.** A **tactical plan** outlines specific, major steps for carrying out the strategic plan. Tactical plans typically cover a time period of less than a year and include target dates for accomplishing goals. Tactical plans are usually laid out by mid-level managers who analyze the big picture of the strategic plan and choose the steps to take to achieve it.

- **Operational Plan.** An **operational plan** details the everyday activities that need to be accomplished in order to achieve the goals laid out in the tactical plan (and thus, ultimately, the strategic plan). Operational plans are short-range, covering days, weeks, or at most, months. These plans are typically drawn up by low-level managers—usually supervisors—who are very familiar with the actual day-to-day workings of the business. Supervisors know the capabilities of their employees and the exact tasks that will be required to accomplish the goals of the tactical plan.

Organizing

Organizing is an ongoing process of arranging and coordinating resources and tasks to achieve specific goals. Organizing creates structure. It puts the people and other resources of a business in the right places and in the right combinations to maximize output and minimize expenses.

One of the most important aspects of organizing is choosing and hiring the best employees, training them properly, and assigning them authority and responsibilities. Managers create organization charts that outline the chains of command within the business and the working relationships between different groups of people. Physical resources must also be organized. These include raw materials, machinery and other equipment, and inventory. Lastly, managers organize all the processes, duties, activities, and everyday operations that make a business successful.

Planning and organizing are interrelated. Planning a project is pointless if you cannot obtain and organize the people and materials needed to make it work. On the other hand, you cannot organize people and materials effectively without proper planning.

Figure 31-1 ▼
Organizational Chart.
Organizing creates structure. An organization chart shows the chain of command and the relationships between departments.

Interpreting Illustrations.
Which manager is directly responsible for the warehouse?

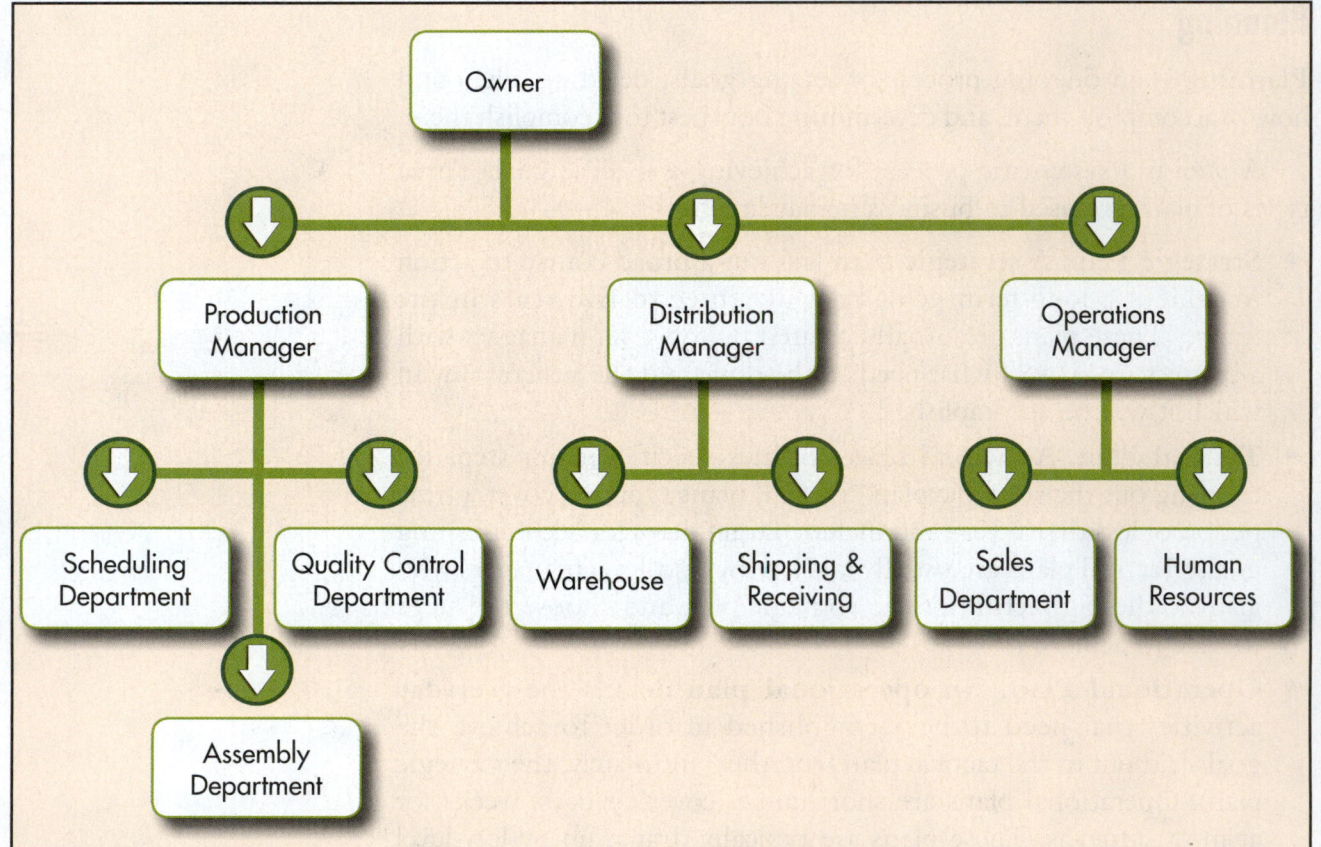

Directing

Directing is an ongoing process of leading, influencing, and motivating employees so they will work together to achieve specific goals. Leaders must have good **interpersonal skills**. These are skills used by people as they interact with others, particularly in a one-on-one setting. They include communicating clearly, listening, having a positive attitude, and behaving politely. Communication skills are particularly important. Leaders who communicate well with their employees build connections that help ensure the success of the business.

The ultimate goal of directing is **team building**, which is motivating individuals in a group to work together to achieve a shared goal. Leaders build teams. A good manager is not necessarily a good leader. Employees may obey a manager because he or she has authority. Employees willingly follow a leader because they have confidence in that person and share the leader's vision for the future.

Although there are as many leadership styles as there are leaders, the three basic ones are:

- **Authoritarian.** The **authoritarian leadership style** (aw-thor-uh-TEHR-ee-un) is practiced when a leader tells employees what needs to be done and how to do it, without seeking their advice. This style is only appropriate in certain situations. New employees are often directed in an authoritarian manner because they lack the information and experience needed to make important decisions. A leader may also use the authoritarian style when something needs to be done quickly and without discussion (as in an emergency).

- **Democratic.** The **democratic leadership style** is practiced when a leader seeks input from employees about what tasks need to be done and how to do them but ultimately makes the final decisions. This style is appropriate when employees are experienced and knowledgeable about their jobs. Their input may be valuable to the leader, but the leader, as the manager, bears final responsibility for the success of their performance.

- **Delegating.** The **delegating leadership style** is practiced when a leader gives employees complete freedom to decide what tasks need to be done and how to do them. Obviously this style will only prove successful with experienced and knowledgeable employees who have demonstrated their ability to think and work independently. A leader who delegates responsibilities to trusted employees is able to tackle other, more pressing matters. This can be a very effective time-management tool.

In reality, good leaders choose and adjust their leadership styles depending on the situation. For example, they might lead a new employee in an authoritarian manner to ensure that he or she learns how to perform a task properly. They might use a democratic style and ask more

experienced employees for suggestions about how to improve a task. And they might delegate a task to the most skilled and trusted employees and ask them to accomplish it as they see fit.

Planning, organizing, and directing are all interrelated. A group of well-organized people with a solid plan will only be successful with good leadership. They must become a team with a shared goal and have a leader they want to follow.

Controlling

Controlling is an ongoing process of setting performance standards, measuring actual performance, comparing actual performance to the standards, and taking corrective action if actual performance does not meet the performance standards.

A business has many components for which performance standards can be set: production, expenses, customer service, employee actions, equipment, finances, inventory levels, product quality, profits, and sales. In all cases, the standards and the components to which they apply should be numeric and specific. For example, this might include the number of sales per day per employee. That way, actual performance can be compared easily to a standard.

Many businesses use the controlling management function to monitor the quality of the goods or services they sell. A **quality control program** is a program used by a business to ensure that its products or services meet specific quality standards. For example, a clothing manufacturer might set a quality standard for the number of straight seams sewn in a garment.

The most difficult component of controlling is usually implementing the appropriate corrective action. Equipment that is not meeting standards may be easy to fix, but most business tasks are accomplished by people, not machines. This explains why controlling is closely related to the other three management functions. Effective leadership of an organized team with a sound plan helps ensure that corrective action is applied successfully.

Apply Your Knowledge What are the four functions of management? From your investigation of Costco, what type of management style do you think Jim Sinegal used?

ENTREPRENEURIAL CASE STUDY: COMMUNICATION & COLLABORATION

 ## Kirsten Kelly & Anne de Mare— Spargel Productions

Highlighting Societal Problems

Kirsten Kelly and Anne de Mare are the co-founders of Spargel Productions, LLC (www.spargelproductions.com). Spargel Productions is a film and documentary production company based in New York City. It was founded in 2002 by filmmaker and theater artist Kirsten Kelly and her partner, Anne de Mare. They have a strong interest in the curious, quirky, and wondrous stories of life in the U.S. and the shifting definition of what it means to be an American. With backgrounds in theatre, including character and story development, they share a dedication to projects in which the individual human experience illuminates the face of society as a whole. In other words, they try to use the stories of individual people to highlight problems being faced by many.

Kirsten Kelly (top) and Anne de Mare (bottom)

While in her final year of the Master's Directing Program at The Juilliard School in New York City, Kirsten began working with playwright Anne de Mare. She wanted to do a project based on her hometown, Shelby, Michigan, which was the Asparagus Capital of the Nation. Rural farmers in this Western Michigan town were scrambling to keep their prized crop in the face of pressure from increased imports due to globalization. This project became the team's first feature documentary.

Initial and Continued Success

To produce the film, Anne and Kirsten created Spargel Productions. Their movie, *Asparagus! Stalking the American Life*, premiered at the Full Frame Documentary Film Festival in 2006 and went on to win Best Documentary and Audience Choice Awards in festivals across the country, as well as the W.K. Kellogg Good Food Film Award.

Building on their newfound success, Kirsten and Anne continued making films under the name of Spargel Productions. They soon produced and directed short documentaries projects for The Juilliard School and The Park Avenue Armory. Their film work was also featured in projects at Lincoln Center with the Music Technology Center at Juilliard. However, they soon wanted to do another film that would continue the work of highlighting larger social problems through film. In 2010, they began work on researching and producing The Homestretch, a new feature film about homeless teens in the Chicago Public Schools. They decided to film the stories of three homeless teenagers as they braved Chicago winters, faced the pressures of high school, and lived life alone on the streets to build a brighter future. The Homestretch premiered at the Hot Docs Canadian International Documentary Festival in 2014 and was broadcast nationally on PBS's *Independent Lens* in 2015.

Managing a Film Production Company

While Kirsten and Anne are driven to make their films through their passion, it takes entrepreneurial thinking to be able to run a movie production business. Creating a movie can require managing a great deal of financial resources, such as the sound and camera equipment, and human resources, such as people hired to do the filming, editing, and distribution of the film. Anne and Kirsten have found great success in managing these moving pieces to get their movies made. They also rely on the financial contributions of various foundations, such as the Sundance Institute, The MacArthur Foundation and the Chicago Community Trust, to help cover their start-up expenses and make their vision come true.

Thinking and Acting Like an Entrepreneur

- How did Kirsten and Anne use their skills and passion to identify a business opportunity?
- What specific challenges come with managing a business in the media or entertainment industries?
- In which ways do Anne and Kirsten demonstrate an entrepreneurial mindset behavior of communication and collaboration?

31.2 Organizational Structures

Do you remember your first day of school? You may have had no idea what was expected of you or who all those adults were. Gradually you learned you were expected to be in class at a certain time and do the work assigned. The adults were the principal, teachers, maintenance crews, and cafeteria workers.

You also figured out the relationships between authority figures. You were answerable to all adults, but especially to your teachers concerning your assignments. Your teachers answered to the principal but not to the maintenance crew, although they wisely heeded the maintenance chief's warnings about a leak in the hallway.

These elements—groups of people, responsibility, and authority—are found in a business as well. They are part of its ==organizational structure==, a system for dividing work, authority, and responsibility within a company. When you hire employees, you will need to develop an organizational structure that suits the business.

Traditional Structures

The simplest structure is ==line organization==, a direct chain of command through levels of personnel who are directly involved in a business's main occupation. To use the school comparison, line organization describes the relationship between principal, teacher, and student.

An expanded version of a line organization is the ==line-and-staff organization==. In this type of structure, staff members advise, assist, or support the work of line personnel. In the school example, that's where the maintenance crew fits in.

Figure 31-3 ▼
Organizational Structures.

(a) Line Organization and (b) Line-and-Staff Organization.

Applying Concepts

What is the main difference between the line organization and line-and-staff organization?

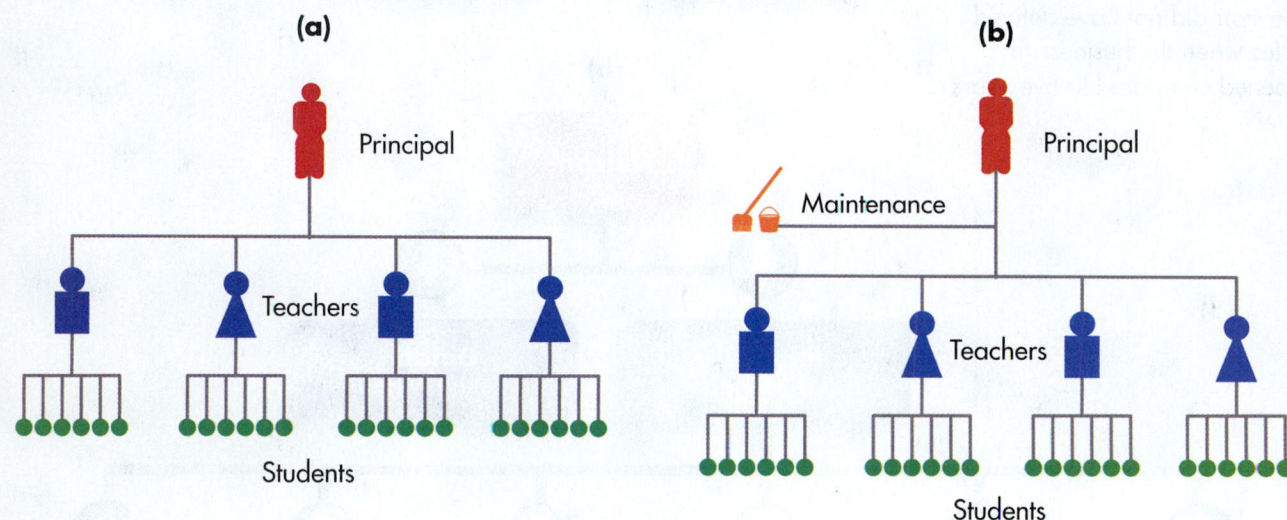

(a)

Principal

Teachers

Students

(b)

Principal

Maintenance

Teachers

Students

A business's organization often changes as the business grows or the market changes. For example, consider Nelson Ortega's independent bookstore. Nelson opened it with two employees, Mitchell Folse and Dinah Madrigal. All three were responsible for waiting on customers, ordering books, taking deliveries, and stocking the shelves. So the basic structure when the store opened was a line organization, with both Mitchell and Dinah reporting to Nelson.

Five years later, the business has moved to a larger space and grown considerably. Nelson has hired six salespeople to work in the store. These employees became part of the line. As the business grew, Mitchell and Dinah took on more specialized tasks. Mitchell became the sales manager, with all salespeople reporting to him. Dinah became the marketing manager. She looks for ways to publicize the store and analyzes trends in publishing and book buying.

Dinah is now a manager. She doesn't take part in the business's revenue-generating work. Instead, she provides input that is needed to make the revenue-producing work more profitable. The final authority to make decisions, however, remains with Nelson.

Figure 31-4 ▶

Nelson Ortega's Bookstore.

(a) Organization of Nelson Ortega's bookstore at opening, and (b) Nelson's organization five years later.

Drawing Conclusions.

Why might be a reason that the staff did not have defined roles when the business first opened compared to five years later?

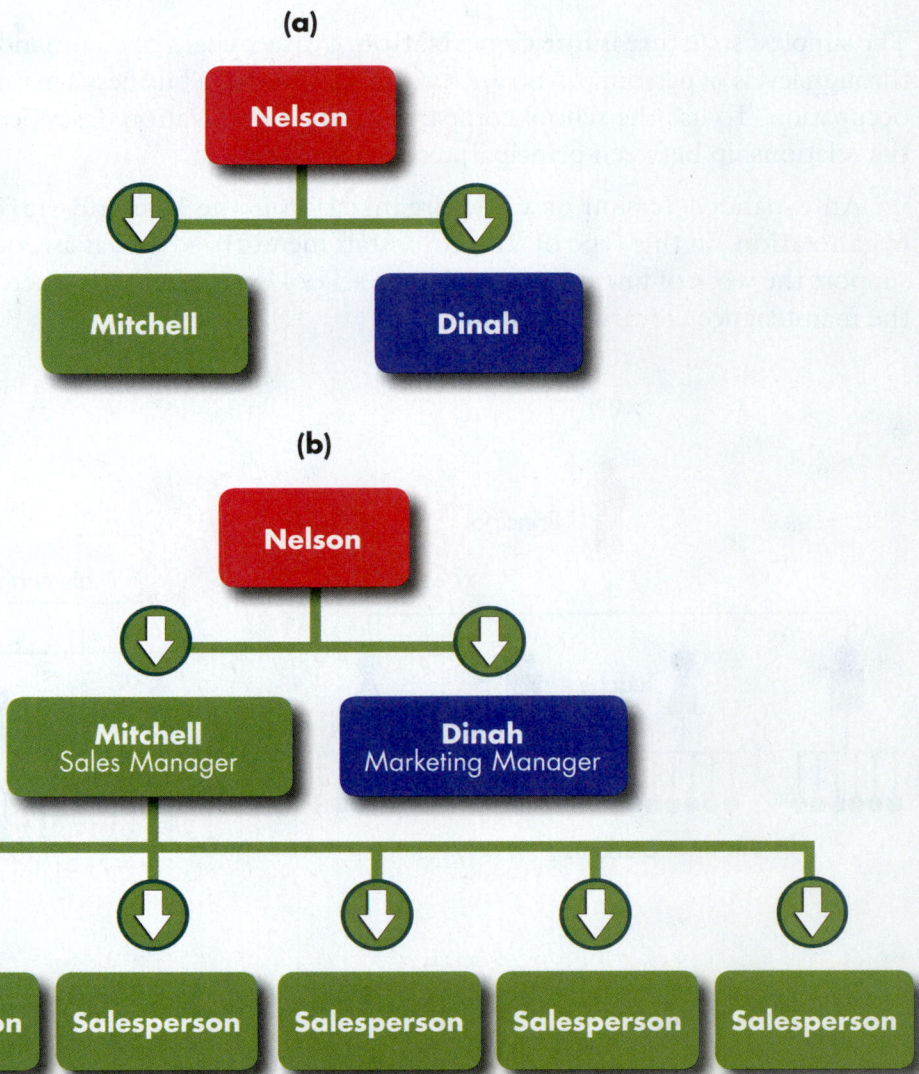

At certain times, a business may use a **project organization**, in which employees from more than one department work as a team on a specific goal. Project organization ends once the project goal is reached. For example, at Sea Breeze Restaurant, Tim, the owner, wanted to develop a line of healthy frozen meals. He asked the executive chef and the marketing manager to work with an outside dietician on this project. Tim also participated and took on the responsibility of trying to finance the initiative through loans and investors.

Sea Breeze Project

◀ **Figure 31-5**
Project Organization Chart.

Sea Breeze Restaurant used project organization to plan a strategy for marketing healthy menu items as frozen foods.

Interpreting Charts.

Do you think all participants in this project have equal importance?

Trends in Structures

Although they are useful, traditional organizational structures don't always fit today's rapidly changing, global economy. To stay competitive, entrepreneurs are stretching traditional structures and inventing new ones. Clearly defined roles and responsibilities are giving way to interdepartmental teams and networks that can be put together as the need arises. Larger companies especially need this flexibility.

New communication technology is playing a role in this evolution. Electronic communication has created a virtual workplace where project members meet by using only the Internet or cell phones.

These trends can open doors for small entrepreneurs such as Darren Novak. The owner of a small chemical analysis lab in Nevada, Darren was contacted by a fertilizer manufacturer in Texas. The fertilizer company was concerned when its chemists found unusually high amounts of pollutants in the water discharged as a result of the manufacturing process. Through teleconferences with other experts the company had assembled, Darren was able to track down a flaw in the sampling method, which had led to incorrect results. Now the fertilizer manufacturer uses Darren's company to randomly double-check its own chemists' findings.

Apply Your Knowledge What are the different ways to organize your employees? Think back to your investigation of Costco. What type of organizational structure do you think they might have used in their stores?

CAREER COMPETENCIES

 ## Write Informational Messages

Memos

A memo (short for memorandum) is a brief note that informs employees about a business-related matter. A letter is written to people outside the business, and a memo is written to people within it. Compared to business letters, memos are typically shorter and less formal. They share relevant news or information employees need to perform a task. The subject might range from a reminder of an office birthday party to a marketing trend that will affect a company's profits.

A memo has two main parts:

- **Heading.** The heading consists of the lines that identify the recipients, the sender, the date, and the subject of the memo. A precisely worded subject line lets recipients know how the message applies to them and how quickly they should respond. Be careful to match the message to the audience. Information meant for only a few should be sent in separate memos to those individuals. This is a matter of privacy as well as relevance.

> TO: Baxter's Bakery Sales Associates
> FROM: Ginny Baxter
> DATE: May 15, 20--
> SUBJECT: Organic Chocolate Ingredients
>
> As of June 15, Baxter's Bakery will be using only organic, sustainably grown chocolate in its baked goods. This includes baking cocoa, baking chocolate, and semi-sweet chocolate chips.
>
> I've ordered promotional pamphlets. Please place one in every bag with customers' purchases. Also read a pamphlet yourself, so you can promote the cause of sustainable agriculture (and our tasty baked treats!) and help answer customers' questions.

- **Body.** The body contains the message. Memos tend to cover only one subject. However, you may still want to break down the topic with separate paragraphs or a list for easier reading. Word processing software usually includes memo templates. Often, word processing software has "families" of templates. Each family has a common name and a similar look. For example, the software might have a "Professional" family of templates, with a "Professional" letter template and a "Professional" memo template. Another style might be designated "Classic" and would have a "Classic" letter template and a "Classic" memo template. If your software has families of templates, use the memo version from the same family as your letter template for a consistent look in communications.

E-Mail

As you know, an e-mail is a message that is sent and received electronically over a computer network. E-mails are a common type of communication for business because they are easy. You can read and respond to the message on your own schedule. You can send and forward it to others without paying postage. Also, if you do not print the message, it's environmentally friendly, with no paper or empty ink cartridges to be recycled. Unfortunately, speed and ease of use also make e-mail a potential hazard. You may not take as much care writing e-mails as you would for a letter or a memo. It's easy to send an e-mail to the wrong person or to respond too quickly without fully thinking through your response. It's also easy to send an e-mail without the attachments you intended. Once you have sent a message, you usually cannot retrieve it. In business, the consequences of a badly written, sloppy, or poorly conceived e-mail can be dramatic. You should write an e-mail with the same care you would give to a business letter. Practicing the following guidelines will not only prevent potential trouble but will also help you slow down and give the e-mail proper consideration:

- Write a short, but useful, description in the subject line.
- Learn what format to use for your attachments and make sure they are a manageable size; anything over twenty five (25MB) is likely to be rejected at some point as it travels over the Internet. Keeping attachments under ten megabytes (10MB) is usually safe.
- Consider using a signature. This is information you have keyed that is added automatically by the word processing software at the end of your e-mail. A signature often consists of your name, the company name, the company phone number, and sometimes a company slogan.
- To avoid sending an e-mail before you mean to, compose it offline first. Fill in the "to" field last, just before sending.
- Use discretion before forwarding an e-mail.
- If you send the e-mail to many people, hide their addresses by using the "bcc" (blind courtesy copy) feature. This respects their privacy and saves them from scrolling through a long list of names to get to the message. Using "reply" automatically creates a message thread, which shows every previous message in the correspondence. Over time, these may become unnecessary. You might want to start a fresh thread, summarizing the most recent, relevant messages.
- If the information is sensitive, write a business letter instead.

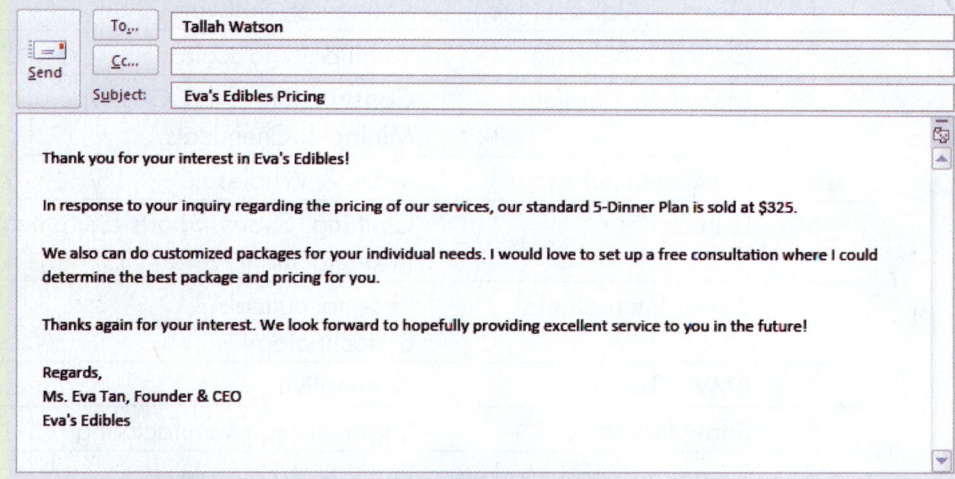

Career Skills in Action

Now, you try creating an informational message that you would have to send as the manager of your business. Be sure to create the appropriate header and body content. Share your letter with a peer or your teacher for feedback.

31.3 Maintaining a Healthy Business Environment

Workplace climate refers to the general feeling in a business, and is shaped by the psychological states and attitudes of the people who work there. Workplace climate is affected by many circumstances, including such things as interpersonal relationships, job security, and pay levels. Managers play a major role in shaping the workplace climate. Businesses that successfully implement the four management functions—planning, organizing, directing, and controlling—are much more likely to create a healthy environment.

A **company image** is the perception (thoughts, attitudes, opinions, and beliefs) that the public holds about a company. Companies build image every time they interact with the public. Logos, signs, websites, store layout, business cards and letterhead, product choices and packaging, advertising, publicity, customer relations—even the way employees dress—contribute to a company's image. Companies try to create and foster images that fit the vision of how they want to be identified in the marketplace. A good company image is not only good for business, it also makes employees proud to be associated with the company and contributes to a positive workplace climate.

Table 31.1   Best Companies to Work For

Rank	Name	Industries
1	Google (Alphabet Inc.)	IT, Internet, Software & Services
2	Costco Wholesale	Retail & Wholesale
3	Marathon Petroleum	Construction, Oil & Gas Operations, Mining & Chemicals
4	The Container Store	Retail & Wholesale
5	LL Bean	Clothing, Shoes, Sports Equipment (Manufacturing & Retail)
6	Baxter International	Pharmaceuticals & Biotechnology
7	BMW Group	Automotive
8	Shaw Industries	Engineering, Manufacturing
9	Wegmans Food Markets	Retail & Wholesale
10	Harley-Davidson	Automotive

2015 Rankings from Forbes.com.

Apply Your Knowledge   What is a workplace climate? From your investigation of Costco, do you think the low turnover rate meant that the business environment was healthy for employees?

 **APPLICATION TO BUSINESS PLANNING**

Organizational Structures

Use what you learned from this chapter on management to create an organizational structure chart as part of your implementation and growth plan. You should support your findings with data from research. Be sure to consider:

- The hiring needs will you have for the business
- The type of management style you think fits your personality
- The type of management style will be the best for your business environment

ASSESSMENT

REVIEWING OBJECTIVES

1. What are the four main management functions?

2. Compare and contrast the different types of organizational structures.

3. Why is maintaining a healthy business environment important?

CRITICAL THINKING

Scheduling tasks would be classified as which management function?

ENTREPRENEURIAL THINKING EXERCISE: COMMUNICATION & COLLABORATION

Think back to your investigation of Costco. Imagine that you were working as a consultant to Costco's competition to help their managers be better at their jobs. What main points would you want to communicate? What do you think would be the best approach for teaching good management skills to others?

ASSESSMENT

EXTENSION ACTIVITIES

Entrepreneurship & Literacy Skills

Complete the following task to demonstrate your understanding of entrepreneurship:

Grades 9–12: Research what motivates people to follow a leader. Prepare a presentation to the class about various theories about leadership and motivation. Make sure you discuss how this would apply to business, to normal social interactions, and to politics. Be sure to use and cite numerous sources while attempting to answer the question.

GUIDING QUESTION:

"What regulations do I need to follow when operating my business?"

APPLICATION TO BUSINESS PLANNING:

☑ Business Compliance Plan

OBJECTIVES

- Understand the role of government regulation.
- Identify laws that impact business operations.
- Describe government resources that help small business comply with regulations.

NFTE Entrepreneurial Mindset Characteristic Focus

 ☑ Flexibility & Adaptability

National Entrepreneurship Standards

- **F.26** Describe types of market structures
- **H.03** Explain the rights of workers
- **I.08** Explain the purposes and importance of obtaining business credit
- **N.10** Establish safety policies and procedures
- **N.17** Obtain legal documents for business operations
- **N.19** Adhere to personnel regulations
- **N.20** Implement workplace regulations (including OSHA, ADA)
- **N.21** Develop strategies for legal/government compliance

Common Career Technical Core Standards

- **CRP.1** Act as a responsible and contributing citizen and employee.
- **CRP.9** Model integrity, ethical leadership and effective management.
- **BM.2** Describe laws, rules and regulations as they apply to effective business operations.
- **BM-HR.1** Describe and follow laws and regulations affecting human resource operations.
- **BM-OP.1** Describe and follow laws and regulations affecting business operations and transactions.

National Entrepreneurship Standards: Career Competencies

☑ **D.10** Write business letters

LESSON VOCABULARY

- adulterated
- antitrust laws
- Fair Labor Standards Act
- license
- monopoly
- Occupational Safety and Health Administration (OSHA)
- permit
- price discrimination
- price fixing
- recall
- severance pay

32.1 The Role of Regulation for Employees

Entrepreneurs and government share a history in the United States that goes back to colonial times. If you wanted to start a company in the British colonies, you needed a charter from the British monarch. A charter was similar to today's articles of incorporation. It granted legal permission to carry out specified business activities. For example, the Hudson's Bay Company was founded in 1670. Its charter gave it "the whole, entire and only... Privilege of Trading and Trafficking to and from the Territories, Limits, and Places"—in other words, exclusive trading rights—with "all the Natives and Peoples inhabiting... within the Territories."

The charter also described the composition of the board of governors—whose head was also governor of the colony—and their duties. It spelled out members' voting rights and how they were to elect successors. It also forbade the Company from doing business in territories granted to another company without that governor's written permission, and authorized punishments for breaking the charter's rules.

◀ **Figure 32-1**
Industrialization.

Industrialization in the mid-1800s brought rapid growth in industry—and in wealth.

Relating Concepts.

Why might rapid growth and the possibility of great wealth lead to unsafe workplaces and worker abuse?

In the newly independent United States, business was largely free from government oversight. No one wanted to stifle active trade and production. This freedom formed the basis of America's economic strength. In the 19th century, rapid growth through industrialization brought wealth. It was the mid-1800s version of today's technological revolution.

However, with this growth came abuses. Starting in the late 1800s, the U.S. government began to exert some control over industry. It did this to protect smaller businesses from larger ones, to protect workers from unsafe work sites, to protect the health of the public, and to protect the environment. The process continues to this day. Not only has the federal government attempted to control industry, but states have often passed their own laws, some of which have been stricter than the federal laws on which they were based.

Some entrepreneurs feel that regulation is an obstacle to growth. Some argue that the laws that seem to hinder the entrepreneur's dream are the same as those that promote the rights of the individual and thus make the realization of entrepreneurial dreams possible. The remainder of this chapter discusses the laws and legal issues governing businesses.

Employee Protection

Hazards in the workplace have always existed. However, they became more common, and more serious, as the United States went from a farming economy to one that was factory-based. The workforce has also grown more diverse, and employers have not always welcomed this diversity. It gradually became apparent that laws were needed to ensure both workers' physical health and their career-advancement opportunities.

Workplace Safety

The **Occupational Safety and Health Administration (OSHA)** is the federal agency responsible for setting and enforcing standards of safety in the workplace. OSHA sets general standards that employers are expected to adjust to their own situations.

Some regulations that apply to many businesses include:

- Providing needed tools and equipment in good working order, and the training to use them.

- Supplying appropriate safety gear and garments.

- Documenting serious work-related illnesses, injuries, or accidents, their causes, and the number of workdays missed.

- Displaying posters telling employees of their right to work in a safe, healthful environment and to report possible violations.

- Giving workers access to records related to illness, injuries, or possible exposure to harmful substances in the workplace.

OSHA enforces its rules through workplace inspections. An inspection may be part of routine oversight or triggered by a complaint. Minor violations might bring only a warning. Serious offenses can easily result in thousands of dollars in fines, with follow-up inspections to ensure the problems have been corrected.

Employers have certain rights that go along with their responsibilities. They can contest inspectors' reports or ask to be exempted from certain standards. OSHA also has a nonretaliation policy, which states that employers who ask about health or safety policies are neither more nor less likely to be inspected for violations.

Figure 32-2 ▶

Promoting Workplace Safety.

OSHA provides posters like the one shown here to help employers comply with agency regulations.

Communicating.

Besides using posters, how can employers communicate safe procedures to employees?

Fair Treatment

In 1840, President Martin Van Buren made a sweeping proclamation that, without any reduction in their current pay, federal employees could be made to work no more than ten hours a day. The proclamation was progressive for its time.

The concept of fair treatment has grown considerably since then. The Equal Employment Opportunity Commission (EEOC) enforces laws that promote a level playing field in the workplace. Fittingly, one of the first laws it enforced dealt with hours and wages. The **Fair Labor Standards Act**, a federal law, guarantees most hourly workers a minimum hourly wage, a maximum number of hours worked, and extra pay for working overtime. Some states have a minimum wage that is higher than the national level and add requirements for lunch and rest breaks, pay periods, and severance pay. **Severance pay** is an amount of money given to employees when they are terminated for reasons other than performance. Employees are also due time off. The Family Medical Leave Act gives them up to 12 weeks of unpaid leave a year after the birth or adoption of a child or the placement of a foster child. In cases of serious illness, they can take the same amount of time to care for a spouse, child, or parent—or themselves.

Employee protection against discrimination has grown as well. Landmark legislation, including the Civil Rights Act of 1964 and the Age Discrimination in Employment Act of 1967, outlaws discrimination based on age, gender, religion, race or ethnicity, or national origin. The Americans with Disabilities Act (ADA) of 1990 requires employers to provide reasonable accommodations to make the workplace and job duties more accessible for qualified workers with disabilities.

◀ **Figure 32-3**
Exceptions to the Rules.
Some federal protections don't extend to employees in very small businesses or in certain agricultural jobs.

Drawing Conclusions.
Why might an employer offer these protections even if not legally required to do so?

Antidiscrimination laws have had a far-reaching impact. For example, the Civil Rights Act forbids employers from making hiring decisions based on the assumption that married candidates are more responsible than unmarried ones. They cannot pass over an individual from a minority group for promotion. Employers are also responsible for creating an atmosphere of tolerance and respect in the workplace. Job ads that imply that older workers are not qualified for a position violate the Age Discrimination in Employment Act. The ADA also prevents employers from asking, during a job interview, how a candidate became disabled. They can't make taking a medical exam a condition of being hired unless it's required of all employees.

Apply Your Knowledge   What are some health and safety protections for employees set out by government regulations? Think back to your investigation of the oil spill. How could have the employees that died been better protected by the company?

ENTREPRENEURIAL CASE STUDY: FLEXIBILITY & ADAPTABILITY

 ## Mercy Hernandez— EDGE Charitable Foundation

Responsibilities to the Community and Environment

Mercy Hernandez is the founder and President of the Early Development of Global Education (EDGE) Charitable Foundation (theedgecf.com/about-us).

Mercy Hernandez.

She is an entrepreneur, early childhood education specialist, humanitarian, environmentalist, and author, as well as the owner and founder of several prominent businesses in the South Florida area, one of these being the EDGE and the EDGE Charitable Foundation, a 501(c)3 nonprofit charitable organization. As the first humanitarian and environmental education program of its kind targeted to children, the EDGE is presently impacting the lives of over 20,000 children worldwide through humanitarian services, education, and environmental advocacy.

Building a Better Tomorrow

Mercy was born in New York and raised in Miami, Florida. As an active and passionate community advocate, she decided to pursue a career that would allow her to help children in need worldwide, while also teaching environmental responsibility and leadership skills to as many young students as possible. This mission led her to establishing and directing the first eco-friendly preschool in the nation for over 20 years, the Old Cutler Academy Learning Center. While happy with her running her eco-friendly businesses, Mercy wanted to be able to make a larger-scale positive impact on the environment.

Working towards this goal, she stared the EDGE Charitable Foundation in order to provide leadership, education, services, and advocacy that will assist in revolutionizing a global humanitarian movement of environmental education and awareness through partnerships with families, teachers, schools, and our global communities. Since 2007, The EDGE Charitable Foundation has impacted thousands of children by encouraging the care of our precious planet from an early age to encouraging children to give back to those less fortunate.

Working to Solve Local Problems

Along with a family of caring and dedicated professionals, schools, and businesses, EDGE teaches environmental education and social responsibility. To do this, Mercy co-authored The EDGE Curriculum, a science-based early childhood curriculum infused with important environmental issues and socially responsible, developmentally appropriate practices. They also work specifically with children from South Florida that come from low income families, migrant families, victims of domestic violence, and victims of human trafficking. Through strong community partnerships with schools and businesses, they are able to provide services such as toy donations, food drives, and flu shots for migrant families. Funding for these efforts comes from private donations made from individuals, corporate donations, fundraising events, and in-kind donations, which is a donation of services instead of money.

Mercy has received numerous awards for her efforts. Some of her most recent accomplishments include the Hispanic Police Officer's Association Community Advocate Award of 2011, several county and town proclamations to both Old Cutler Academy Learning Center and the EDGE, which includes one from Congresswoman Ileana Ros-Lehtinen, and EDGE awarded Chamber South's first Green Business of the Year Award in 2011.

Thinking and Acting Like an Entrepreneur

- How did Mercy use her skills and passions to identify business opportunities?
- What specific government regulations must Mercy follow as a nonprofit organization?
- In which ways does Mercy adapt her efforts to solve new found problems?

32.2 Customer and Environmental Protection

Treating customers fairly is not only good business sense—it's the law. As a business owner, you are bound by laws regulating how you sell your goods or services, whether the customer is an international corporation or an individual consumer.

Labeling

Many people only remember a time when product labels were covered with information. Some of this is legally required as a way to help customers make informed choices. The Fair Packaging and Labeling Act requires that all product packaging identify the item, its manufacturer, and the quantity, either in weight or number. The Food, Drug, and Cosmetic Act and its various amendments forbid any false or deceptive labeling. A product is also considered mislabeled if it leaves out essential information.

Other requirements vary depending on the product. Most packaged foods require an ingredients list and nutrition facts. Any health-related claims must meet the definition set by the Food and Drug Administration (FDA) and the U.S. Department of Agriculture (USDA). The label must warn if the product contains, or may have had contact with, foods that are major allergens (allergy-causing ingredients).

Products that contain hazardous substances, from laundry detergent to pesticides, must be labeled with safety-related information. Manufacturers must describe the dangers associated with the product, its proper use and precautions, and first-aid or emergency treatment if it's misused or mishandled.

Product Safety

The FDA and the USDA are also concerned with food and drug safety. They forbid the sale of adulterated products—those containing harmful substances, processed in ways that may be harmful to health, or modified to mask poor quality. Some cases of adulteration that you may have heard of are meats or vegetables contaminated with the *E. coli* bacteria and pet foods containing the poisonous chemical melamine.

The task of regulating most other products falls mainly to the U.S. Consumer Product Safety Commission (CPSC), which sets standards for about 15,000 consumer goods. (Along with food products and drugs, major exceptions are motor vehicles, alcohol, and medical devices.) For example, CPSC requires that infants' toys must have no small parts that could pose a choking hazard. Fabrics must be flame-resistant. Packaging for drugs must be child-resistant.

◀ **Figure 32-4**
Product Safety.
The FDA and USDA are
concerned with food safety.

Applying Concepts.

Why is it important for
entrepreneurs who work with
food to know FDA and USDA
guidelines?

If a manufacturer learns that one of its products does not meet these standards, whether by design or from some defect or flaw, it should issue a recall. A **recall** is a notice for customers to return a product that poses a risk of injury or illness. Recalls are not required, but businesses that learn of problems and don't act to correct them face serious consequences. The CPSC may ban the item from the market and the business can be held liable for the harm it causes. The damage to the firm's reputation may be beyond repair.

Fair Competition

A free market needs competition, and fair competition needs honest, accurate advertising. The Federal Trade Commission (FTC) enforces detailed truth-in-advertising laws that cover promotion in all of its forms, including endorsements, testimonials, sales, and special pricing. The FTC requires ads to be:

- **Truthful and Nondeceptive.** An ad must not mislead customers on any significant point that would affect their buying decision. For example, an item shown must be available for sale.

- **Supported by Evidence.** Business must have proof of any stated or implied claims. Health claims must be backed by scientific research. Letters from "satisfied customers" must be made available to confirm that the writers actually exist.

- **Fair.** An ad must not lead customers to "substantial injury," such as by not mentioning possible dangers, conditions or requirements, or unwanted outcomes that customers could not have foreseen. Customers must be told about any added fees that increase the advertised price.

Price fixing is another anticompetitive practice. **Price fixing** refers to competing companies agreeing to set the price of goods or services or the terms of business deals. All of the growers at a farmers market might decide to charge the same price for their produce, for instance, or to give the same discount to restaurant buyers.

A similar practice is price discrimination. **Price discrimination** is charging competing buyers different prices for the same product. This is illegal only when used intentionally, to favor one customer over another. It would not be illegal to charge different prices to buyers in different parts of the state to stay competitive with the market in each area.

A monopoly is another illegal obstacle to fair competition. A **monopoly** describes the situation where a single supplier becomes a market's only provider of a certain product. This is sometimes called "cornering the market."

To combat monopolies and similar schemes, the FTC uses **antitrust laws**, laws that forbid anticompetitive mergers and business practices. (A trust is a type of business ownership that used a legal technicality to evade laws against monopolies.) The oldest is the Sherman Act of 1890, which outlaws "every contract, combination, or conspiracy in restraint of trade or commerce." The Clayton Act of 1914 and several later laws have reinforced those restrictions.

Although antitrust laws are not used often, the penalties can be severe. Fines start at a million dollars for an individual, with prison sentences up to ten years.

Licenses and Permits

Many business owners need some kind of license. A **license** is a legal document issued by a state or local government that allows a business to provide a regulated product or service. They give consumers assurance that a business or individual meets standards of professionalism and reliability, such as a beauty salon or a physician. Certain highly regulated industries require national (federal) licenses. These include broadcasting, investment consulting, and meats preparation.

Licensing usually requires some type of certification, either from the state or a professional group. For example, some states require athletic trainers to be accredited by a Board of Certification for the Athletic Trainer. To become a licensed building contractor, you may need to pass a state exam testing your knowledge of engineering, electrical systems, and carpentry.

A **permit** is a legal document that allows a business to take a specific action. As a homebuilder, you might need several permits for a house: one for putting in a driveway, perhaps, and another to close street lanes in the construction area. Permits are generally issued by local governments.

Zoning Laws

Zoning laws, also called ordinances, are designed to help ensure that businesses are good neighbors in the community. Some laws determine the areas where a business can locate and the activities it can carry out there. A sheep farm would be located in an agricultural zone, while a textile factory that turns the wool into fabric operates in an industrial zone. A shop that sells the fabric would be sited in a commercial zone. A seamstress who makes clothing from the fabric for individual clients might run the business from home, in a residential zone. Other laws relate to a property's physical appearance, including the building's size, the number of parking spaces, and the type of signage allowed.

A recent trend in city planning is the creation of "walkable" cities, where small businesses are placed within walking distance of homes. The goal is to strengthen the sense of community, reduce the need and impact of motor traffic, and increase opportunities for physical exercise.

◀ **Figure 32-6**
Zoning Laws.
Zoning laws determine where certain types of businesses can be located.

Drawing Conclusions.
How might zoning laws help businesses? Consumers? Neighbors? The locality?

Environmental Protection

Business owners must be aware of laws designed to reduce the harmful impact they may have on the environment. Many of these regulations are set by the U.S. Environmental Protection Agency (EPA). These cover a wide range of business activities in almost every field.

- Under the Clean Air Act, for example, factories with smokestacks are limited in the types and amounts of chemicals they are permitted to release into the atmosphere.

- Farmers must learn whether they can burn crop stubble in their fields without damaging air quality.

- The owner of a road-construction firm has to avoid causing traffic delays that increase pollutants over the legal level.

- The Clean Water Act may require a business to get a permit to discharge wastewater (water left over from almost any human activity, including washing hands). Receiving permission depends on the amount of water released and the substances it contains.

- Builders who want to develop land near a wildlife preserve may need to submit plans to lessen the impact on the plant and animal life, in accordance with the Endangered Species Act.

Punishment for violating EPA laws can be costly. A business can be fined thousands of dollars each day until it meets standards.

 **Apply Your Knowledge** Why is it important for a business owner to be familiar with consumer and environmental protection laws? From your investigation of BP, why do you think the EPA got involved with the accident?

CAREER COMPETENCIES

 ### Write Business Letters

Business letters are used for longer or more official messages. For example, you would use a letter to answer a customer's inquiry or to ask for information about a product. A business letter should be typed in an easy-to-read font, not a fancy script. Following an accepted form shows professionalism and attention to detail.

The well-developed business letter includes the following elements:

- Include the date in the upper-left corner.

- Skip a line or two and type the recipient's name and address below the date. Use the same name and address you use on the envelope.

- Skip a line and type the salutation, or greeting, starting at the left margin. "Dear" is the accepted greeting, followed by the person's title (Mr., Ms., or Dr., for example), the last name, and then a colon. Use the first and last name without a title if you're not sure whether the recipient is a man or woman. Use a comma only if you are on a friendly basis with the recipient.

- For the body of the letter you can either indent the first line of each paragraph or skip a line between paragraphs.

- Start a new line at the left margin for the closing. "Sincerely," is the usual closing. If you use a phrase such as "Sincerely yours," capitalize only the first word. End every closing with a comma.

- Skip a few lines and type your name, position, and address (unless your address is shown on your stationery—your letterhead).

- Sign your name in the space you left above your typed name. Sign your name as you typed it unless you are on a friendly basis with the recipient—then sign only your first name.

- In some cases, you might also include a reference line under the date. This would begin with the abbreviation "re:" (for "regarding") and summarize the subject of the letter, much like the subject line in an e-mail.

- If you're sending a copy of the letter to others, skip a line below your address and type "cc:" (for "courtesy copy") at the left margin. Then, add the names of the people who are receiving a courtesy copy.

- If you are enclosing a document, such as an ad to be run in a newspaper, you would type "enc:" (for "enclosed") below your name and address (and below the cc: line, if there is one) at the left margin. Then, you would add a short description of the document. Once you establish a working relationship with someone, you might drop some formality. Remember the qualities of good communication, however, and always keep the letter brief and organized.

Word processing software usually includes various templates to use for letters. You can pick the one you think most effectively conveys the look you want for your business. Addressing an envelope is easy. Put the recipient's address in the center of the envelope and put your address (referred to as the "return address") in the upper-left corner. Put the stamp in the upper-right corner.

Career Skills in Action

Now, you try writing a business letter that you would write to a government regulating organization to describe how your business is compliant to a regulation of your choosing. Be sure that your letter contains the formatting outlined in this section, as well as the relevant content from the chapter. Share your letter with a peer or your teacher for feedback.

32.3 Help for Small Business

Following all these regulations established by agencies and departments of the government could be an overwhelming task for many new entrepreneurs. Many businesses often need to hire lawyers with expertise in administrative law to help ensure they are complying with regulations and rules. Fortunately, some exceptions exist for small businesses. For instance, employers with fewer than ten employees are not required to document minor workplace accidents. Businesses with fewer than fifteen workers are exempt from some provisions of the Americans with Disabilities Act. Food sellers with less than $50,000 a year in sales don't need to include all nutrition information on labels.

As mentioned earlier, tax credits are available for businesses that follow sustainable practices, which help them meet EPA standards. Other tax credits offset some of the expenses of complying with the Americans with Disabilities Act.

The conditions for these and other types of aid can be complex. It's wise to consult the enforcing agency for exact details. Small business owners may also find these agencies their best resources for learning how to meet particular regulations.

Regulating agencies sometimes look to small businesses to assist them in developing rules and guidelines. OSHA, for example, has set up Small Business Advisory Review Panels to hear business owners' input on developing safety standards. The Equal Employment Opportunity Commission recognizes that small businesses are often the best setting for disabled workers, especially those looking for their first job. The agency can suggest affordable ways to make the workplace accessible.

 **Apply Your Knowledge** Why is it important to understand the rules and regulations established by agencies and departments of the government? What three general types of aid help small businesses comply with government regulations? Think back to your investigation of the oil spill. BP is a huge company with a lot of resources to help in the case of an accident. Why is being compliant with government regulations even more important for small businesses?

✔ APPLICATION TO BUSINESS PLANNING

Business Compliance Plan

Use what you learned from this chapter on government regulations to summarize administrative laws that affect your business and create a compliance plan as part of your implementation and growth plan. You should support your findings with data from research. Be sure to include:

- Employee regulations specific to your business (for example, OSHA standards for equipment used)
- Regulations that will affect customers (labeling, product safety, etc.)
- Environmental protection considerations

REVIEWING OBJECTIVES

1. What is the role of government regulation?

2. Describe examples of administrative laws that impact business operations.

3. How do government resources help small business comply with regulations?

CRITICAL THINKING

Given the purpose of licensing, explain why each of the following should have a license: a teacher, a lawyer, a restaurant owner, an auto mechanic.

ENTREPRENEURIAL THINKING EXERCISE: FLEXIBILITY & ADAPTABILITY

Think back to your investigation of the BP Oil spill. If you were one of BP's competitors in the oil industry, how might you adapt your practices after the accident? What regulations would you pay the most attention to so that no accident happened like that with your company?

EXTENSION ACTIVITIES

Entrepreneurship & Literacy Skills

Complete the following task to demonstrate your understanding of entrepreneurship:

Grades 9–12: With a partner, identify some concerns that a homeowner might have about a small business opening in the neighborhood—for example, noise and traffic. First, identify the type of business that would be opening. Then, devise a plan that a business owner could carry out to address the potential problem areas. Include supporting details from this chapter in your work.

GUIDING QUESTION:
"How I can best keep track of my financial records?"

APPLICATION TO BUSINESS PLANNING:
☑ Financial Records

OBJECTIVES

- Differentiate between various financial records.
- Discuss the advantages and disadvantages of computerized accounting systems.
- Describe the issues associated with the use of accountants and bookkeepers.

NFTE Entrepreneurial Mindset Characteristic Focus

☑ Comfort with Risk

National Entrepreneurship Standards

- **A.27** Explain the need for business systems and procedures
- **G.10** Describe services provided by financial institutions
- **G.20** Maintain financial records
- **G.21** Read and reconcile financial statements
- **I.01** Explain accounting standards (GAAP)
- **I.08** Explain the purposes and importance of obtaining business credit
- **I.28** Supervise/implement regular accounting procedures and financial reports
- **K.01** Explain the nature of business records
- **K.02** Maintain record of daily financial transactions
- **L.51** Process sales documentation
- **M.03** Document business systems and procedures
- **M.06** Analyze business processes and procedures
- **N.03** Establish controls to prevent embezzlement/theft
- **O.13** Interpret financial statements

Common Career Technical Core Standards

- **CRP.2** Apply appropriate academic and technical skills.
- **CRP.3** Attend to personal health and financial well-being.

LESSON VOCABULARY

- accounting
- accounting controls
- auditor
- bank reconciliation
- chart of accounts
- checking account
- double-entry accounting
- duality
- embezzlement
- Federal Deposit Insurance Corporation (FDIC)
- general journal
- internal audit
- payee
- purchase order
- receipt
- sales invoice
- savings account
- source document
- T-account
- transaction

- **CRP.11** Use technology to enhance productivity.
- **BM-BIM.1** Describe and follow laws and regulations affecting business operations and transactions.
- **BM-BIM.2** Plan, monitor, manage and maintain the use of financial resources to ensure a business's financial well-being.
- **BM-BIM.3** Access, evaluate and disseminate information for business decision making.
- **BM-BIM.4** Plan, monitor and manage day-to-day business activities to sustain continued business functioning.

National Entrepreneurship Standards: Career Competencies

 E.13 Demonstrate file management skills

ENTREPRENEURIAL INVESTIGATION

Transparent Clothing

It is not required for businesses to make every detail about their operations public. However, because of this, some businesses unfortunately engage in unethical behavior and keep it a secret. To encourage ethical business practices, fashion designer Bruno Pieters launched Honest by (www.honestby.com) in 2012. In addition to running the business to be environmentally friendly, he decided to make every financial transaction known to his customers. This allows his customers to see what the business pays for materials, and what they charge customers for the final product. His goal is to allow customers to make informed purchases.

Do some research on Honest by to answer the following questions:

- Do you think that Honest by's customers appreciate Bruno's willingness to share financial details?
- Do you think that more businesses should be required to share all financial transactions? Why or why not?

Be prepared to share your thoughts with a peer and your teacher.

33.1 Financial Records

Entrepreneurs need to know exactly how much money is coming in to and going out of the business. In fact, one of the major reasons that businesses fail is the owner's lack of financial management skill. This includes not keeping good financial records. The more you know about recordkeeping, the more you increase your odds of being a successful entrepreneur.

Having business accounts at a local bank is important for an entrepreneur. You'll be able to discuss your savings and checking accounts directly with a bank representative. As a bank customer, when you apply for a loan, your application will typically receive preferential treatment over a non-customer's application.

One concern for your money is safety. Your money is obviously much safer in a bank than in your purse or wallet. Money in a bank account is insured, in case the bank goes out of business. The **Federal Deposit Insurance Corporation (FDIC)**, created in 1933, is an independent agency of the federal government that insures savings, checking, and other types of deposit accounts.

As an entrepreneur you'll certainly need a checking account soon after your start your business.

Savings Accounts

A **savings account** is a bank account in which you deposit money. The bank pays interest on the amount in your account. Typically, the rate of interest a bank pays on a savings account is low. However, because the FDIC insures savings accounts, you have virtually no risk of losing your money. Banks earn their profits by using the money in the savings account as a basis for making loans. The interest rate they charge on their loans is higher than the interest rate they pay you on your savings account.

Checking Accounts

A **checking account** is a bank account against which you can write checks. You can also remove money from your account by using a debit card. When you write a check, you authorize the bank to pay the holder of the check from the money in your account.

When you pay someone with a check, that person (the **payee**) goes to their bank and either cashes your check or deposits it in their own account. The payee's bank sends the check back to your bank, at which point your bank takes the money out of your checking account and pays the other bank.

Once your bank has paid the check, the check is cancelled. The bank may send the cancelled checks back to you. They provide proof that the payees received their money. To save on expenses, many banks now keep your cancelled checks instead of mailing them to you. You have access to them in person at the bank or through the bank's website.

Banks have taken advantage of modern technology. Online banking allows a bank's customers to use a secure website for transacting their banking business. It is available 24 hours a day. You can monitor your accounts, transfer money from one account to another, pay monthly bills online, and even input information from your online bank statement directly into recordkeeping software on your computer.

You can use an ATM (automatic teller machine) card to access your money at many locations at any time of day. With a debit card, you can withdraw money directly from your checking account without having to write a check. When you use a debit card to make a purchase, the amount is automatically deducted from your checking account.

Don't forget to subtract the amount of the debit card purchase from your checkbook. Once a month, your bank sends you a checking account statement. The statement includes a list of all the deposits and checks you've written that have cleared. It also shows the ending balance in the account.

The ending balance on the bank statement may not match the balance shown in your checkbook, however. The two main causes for this are outstanding checks and outstanding deposits. Outstanding checks are checks that haven't been cashed. Outstanding deposits are funds you have put in the bank but the bank hasn't yet recorded. Other differences between your account balance and the bank balance could include bank service charges and fees.

Figure 33-1 ▶
ATMs.

Automatic teller machines (ATMs) allow you to access your money at many locations at any time of the day.

Predicting.

What method would you use to make sure you kept receipts from ATM withdrawals?

Bank Reconciliation

One of the best ways to maintain good control over cash is to reconcile your business checking account with the bank statement each month. A **bank reconciliation** is the process of verifying that your checkbook balance is in agreement with the ending balance in your checking account statement from the bank.

Here's an example of bank reconciliation.

Assume that the end-of-month balance in your business checkbook is $2,500. Your bank statement, however, shows a balance of $3,180. Follow these steps to reconcile your checkbook with your bank statement:

1. Compare your checkbook activity with the transactions listed in the bank statement to see if there are any outstanding checks. In our example, let's assume Checks #327 and #330 haven't yet cleared the bank. The total amount of these checks is $1,700.

2. Compare your checkbook with the deposits shown in the bank statement to see if you made any deposits that aren't listed on the bank statement. Let's say you made a deposit on the last day of the month for $1,000. It wasn't recorded by the bank until the next day and isn't shown on the statement.

3. Finally, check to see if the bank statement shows any bank charges or fees. You notice that the bank charged your account $20 to have new business checks printed.

Your bank reconciliation would look like that shown in Ledger 33.1.

Reconciliation Example		
Explanation	**Checkbook**	**Bank Statement**
Balance on October 31	$2,500	$3,180
Less Outstanding Checks		−1,700
Plus Unlisted Deposits		1,000
Less Bank Service Charges/Fees	−20	
Actual Cash Balance	$2,480	$2,480

◀ **Ledger 33.1**
Bank Reconciliation.

A bank reconciliation is the process of verifying that your checkbook balance is in agreement with the ending balance in your checking account statement from the bank.

Analyzing Information.

What kinds of fees might be shown on a bank statement?

If the totals still don't agree:

1. Look for items on the bank statement that you haven't entered in your checkbook, such as other service charges, interest earned on your account or ATM withdrawals.

2. Check the amount written on each check against the amounts shown in your checkbook. A common mistake is a transposition error, which is reversing two numbers. For example, you might have written a check for $73 and written $37 as the amount in your checkbook.

Business Documents

When you start a business, you need to establish recordkeeping procedures. These procedures will typically involve receipts, purchase orders, and invoices.

Receipts

A **receipt** is the detailed written proof of a purchase. When you make a sale, always give the customer a receipt and always keep a copy for yourself. Write down the date, customer name, what the customer purchased, and how the customer paid.

Be sure to get a receipt when your business pays for goods or services. When merchandise is shipped to you, the receipt, or packing slip, is usually in one of the packages. Check to see that the shipment includes all the items on the receipt. The receipt will be helpful if you have a problem with the order or need to return merchandise. Save all receipts. Your purchases might qualify for a tax deduction. These deductions will save you money in taxes, but you need to save the receipts as proof of the expenses.

Various styles of receipt booklets are available at local office supply stores or discount retailers.

Purchase Orders

A **purchase order** (often referred to as a PO) is a detailed written record of a business's request for supplies or inventory. When purchasing supplies, write up a purchase order that contains a description of what you are ordering, from whom, at what price, and who is taking the order. Also, be sure to date and number the purchase order. Give the supplier the purchase order number when you place the order.

The purchase order system is highly reliable. A purchase order clearly states what you want to buy. The seller has a document that clearly states what you want. There is no confusion. Another advantage of this system is that it helps you record your business's purchases. Employees who make purchases from suppliers know that they must prepare a purchase order. They also know that the owner must sign the purchase order before it is sent to the supplier. The PO system helps prevent unauthorized purchases.

Purchase order forms are available in office supply stores or from discount retailers. You can also download purchase order templates and adapt them for your business.

Sales Invoices

You use a purchase order when you buy supplies or inventory. But what should you use when you sell goods or services? A **sales invoice** is an itemized list of goods delivered or services rendered and the amount due.

If your business offers credit terms, you agree to let the customer pay you later. When payment is due, you need to send the customer an invoice. The invoice contains much of the same information included on a receipt. It also includes the date when the payment should be made, to whom the check should be made out (for example, your business name), and your business mailing address. Depending on your business, the invoice may include additional information, such as the amount the customer will be charged for a late payment.

Once you receive the customer's payment, write or stamp "Paid" on the invoice. File all invoices, either by invoice number (in numerical order) or by customer name (in alphabetical order).

As with other receipts and purchase orders, invoice forms are available at many office supply stores and discount retailers. Invoice templates are also available online and can be downloaded and adapted for your business.

Apply Your Knowledge   What are some examples of financial records? Think back to your investigation of Honest by. If they are showing the costs of their materials, what financial records are they making viewable to the public?

ENTREPRENEURIAL CASE STUDY: COMFORT WITH RISK

Sam Zell— Equity Group Investments

Building an Investment Empire

As Chairman and founder of Equity Group Investments (www.egizell. com), Sam Zell is a self-made billionaire, visionary, and macroeconomist. In 2014, Forbes estimated his net worth at $4.9 billion. While Sam's investments span industries across the globe, he is most widely known as a founding father of the modern commercial real estate industry. His leadership and active investments helped steward the industry in the U.S. from a total of $9 billion in 1990 to $800 billion today. He did this in the form of pioneering real estate investment trusts (REITS), which enabled real estate companies to list in the public markets. He created the three largest REITs in their respective sectors: office

Sam Zell.

buildings, apartments, and manufactured homes. In 2007, Sam sold his first office REIT, Equity Office, which he had taken public ten years prior, for $39 billion in the largest leveraged buyout (LBO) in history at the time.

The son of Polish immigrants, Sam was born in 1941 in Chicago three months after his parents arrived in the U.S. The family had barely escaped their homeland in Poland days before the Nazi invasion. Sam learned early on that economic success was equated with freedom, and he was raised with a deep appreciation for this country. As a result, Zell credited his immigrant origins with much of his life philosophy and success.

Taking a Risk on New Opportunities

Sam began his career as an undergrad at University of Michigan when he started managing student housing apartments. He learned from a friend that the building he lived in was to be torn down so a new student apartment building could be developed. Out of the blue, Sam suggested to his friend that they pitch to the owner that they manage the building in exchange for free apartments. He had no experience, but believed they knew what appealed to students and could use that knowledge while they learned along the way. The owner agreed and within a few years gave Sam and his friend two more buildings to manage. A few years later, when Sam was in his second year of law school, he bought his first building. Then, he bought another and another. By the time he graduated law school, Sam's company was managing 40,000 apartments and he personally owned dozens of buildings.

After graduating from law school, Sam sold his local business to his fraternity brother, Bob Lurie, and moved to Chicago. Three years later, Bob joined Sam at the new investment firm he had created, and together they proceeded to build what today is known as Equity Group Investments (EGI). The firm was the genesis for an investment empire. Today, Sam serves as chairman for five public companies traded on the New York Stock Exchange, as well as chairman for his two private investment firms. His holdings include companies in a wide range of industries, including: apartment building ownership and management, office building ownership and management, oil and gas, energy-from-waste and power generation facilities, manufacturing, logistics, and communications.

Fostering an Entrepreneurial Spirit in Others

Sam believes that entrepreneurs built America and that encouraging entrepreneurism is critical to our country's future. He is a primary sponsor of programs to promote higher education in the areas of entrepreneurialism, risk management, and real estate, among others. His significant beneficiaries include the Zell/Lurie Entrepreneurial Center at the University of Michigan, his alma mater; the Center for Risk Management at Northwestern University's Kellogg School of Management; the Samuel Zell/Robert Lurie Real Estate Center at the University of Pennsylvania's Wharton School; and the Zell Entrepreneurship Program at the Interdisciplinary Herzliya Center (IDC), a private higher education institute in Israel.

33.2 Accounting Principles

Keeping good records is a crucial part of any business. Without good records, business owners can't be confident that their income statements, cash flow documents, and balance sheet are accurate. The IRS also insists that you keep accurate records for tax purposes.

Accounting is the system of recording and summarizing business and financial transactions and analyzing, verifying, and reporting the results. Fortunately, as an entrepreneur, you aren't expected to perform all these accounting tasks personally.

When you start your business, you will probably pay an accountant to prepare the required financial statements. However, you should have a basic understanding of accounting so you know what information to collect for your accountant. Your accountant will need certain information to prepare monthly and annual financial statements, as well as for filing your taxes properly.

Before choosing an accounting system, you should know the various types available and how they differ. Accounting systems are categorized as either manual or computerized, but with today's technology, most small businesses use some type of computerized system.

Both manual and computerized accounting systems have basic similarities. All use some method of recording every business transaction. Any payment or any income received is a **transaction**.

A journal or an accounting database is used to record each transaction as it occurs. The information that's recorded comes from source documents. A **source document** is the original record (source) of a transaction. Source documents include receipts, cancelled checks, invoices, bank deposit slips, and other records.

At a minimum, an entrepreneur must carefully track:

- All cash inflows (receipts)
- All cash outflows (payments)

The accounting requirements usually become more complex as a business grows. However, most small businesses can use a relatively simple system that requires only a journal or an accounting database.

All accounting systems make use of what is called **double-entry accounting**, which basically means that every business transaction affects at least two accounts.

Chart of Accounts

The first step in double-entry accounting is to create a chart of accounts. A **chart of accounts** shows all the accounts used in the business. For example, it includes all assets, liabilities, owner's equity, income, and expense accounts. Each account is numbered. Ledger 33.2 shows an example of a chart of accounts for Matt's Hats.

Ledger 33.2 ▶

Chart of Accounts.

This is an example of a chart of accounts for Matt's Hats.

Analyzing Data.

When might Matt Washington use account C302?

Matt's Hats Chart of Accounts	
Accounts	**Account Codes**
Assets	
Cash	A101
Inventory	A102
Accounts Receivable	A103
Liabilities	
Bank Loans	L201
Accounts Payable	L202
Sales Tax Payable	L203
Owner's Equity	
Matt Washington, Capital	C301
Sales Revenue	R401
Utilities Expense	E501
Insurance Expense	E502
Interest Expense	E503
Rent Expense	E504
Internet Service Expense	E505
Matt Washington, Withdrawal	C302

The next step in double-entry accounting is to record transactions. All transactions must be recorded and must affect at least two accounts. There are two approaches to recording transactions:

- **Single-Column, Database Approach.** This is a simple method. Most computerized systems use it.

- **Double-Column Approach.** This method uses a left-hand (debit) column and a right-hand (credit) column for each account. Most manual accounting systems use a double-column method.

No matter which of the two you use, it depends on the same basic principle:

$$\text{Assets} = \text{Liabilities} + \text{Owner's Equity}$$

You first encountered this basic accounting equation in Chapter 30 when you were introduced to the balance sheet. The most important thing to remember about recording transactions is that, just as with a balance sheet, any change on the left side of the equation *must* equal a change on the right side.

Single-Column, Database Approach

Suppose Matt Washington buys a new computer for Matt's Hats, using $4,000 cash. The asset Cash would be reduced by $4,000, and the asset Office Equipment would be increased by $4,000. Each transaction in this example happened on the left side of the equation, dealing with assets. Therefore, there's no need to make an entry in the liabilities/ owner's equity side of the equation.

This transaction can be shown as:

Cash	Office Equipment
−$4,000	+$4,000

What would happen if, instead of paying cash, Matt's Hats bought the new computer on account? Here, Cash wouldn't be affected. Instead, Office Equipment would go up by $4,000 on the assets side of the equation. And on the other side, a liability (Accounts Payable) would also go up by $4,000. The equation would balance.

A single-column accounting database, which is especially suited to computerized systems, shows the equation this way:

Office Equipment	=	Accounts Payable
+$4,000		−$4,000

Double-Column Approach

Manual accounting systems use the double columns of debits and credits. Each account has a left-hand and a right-hand column. The left-hand column is the debit side, and the right-hand column is the credit side.

Here's the key to understanding this approach:

- Increases in assets are recorded on the debit side.
- Increases in liabilities and owner's equity are recorded on the credit side.
- Decreases in assets are recorded on the credit side.
- Decreases in liabilities and owner's equity are recorded on the debit side.

This is a summary of the earlier transaction in which Matt's Hats purchased office equipment for $4,000 cash.

Cash		Office Equipment	
Debit	Credit	Debit	Credit
+	−	+	−
	$4,000	$4,000	

This sort of double-sided presentation is called a **T-account**. Here, we can see that Cash, an asset account, is credited because it decreased, and Office Equipment, another asset account, is debited because it increased. Most transactions can be entered formally in what is called a **general journal**, an accounting record that shows all the transactions of the business. The purchase of the office equipment for cash would look like this as an entry in the general journal:

General Journal					Page: 1
Date	**Explanation**		**Ref.**	**Debit**	**Credit**
Aug. 2	Office Equipment			$4,000	
	Cash				$4,000
	Bought new computer on account				

What would a T-account look like if Matt's Hats bought the computer on account?

Office Equipment		Accounts Payable	
+	−	−	+
$4,000			$4,000

Rather than using T-accounts, you could make this entry in the general journal:

General Journal					Page: 1
Date	**Explanation**	**Ref.**	**Debit**	**Credit**
Aug. 2	Office Equipment		$4,000	
	Accounts Payable			$4,000
	Bought new computer on account			

Here, office equipment increased, so you debit that account. Accounts payable, a liability, also went up, so you credit that account. Remember that debits must *always* equal credits when you record a transaction.

Duality

No matter which approach you use, you are employing a key accounting concept called <mark>duality</mark>. In the single-column method, duality means that, for any transaction, all changes on the asset side minus all changes on the liability/owner's equity side must equal zero. In a computerized system, a transaction is entered only once and all journals and ledgers are updated automatically. At the end of each reporting period, the account balances are totaled and transferred to the financial statements.

In the double-column method, duality means that for any transaction posted to the general journal (and any special journals), all debits must equal all credits. At the end of each day, the general journal entries are posted to each respective account in what is called a general ledger. At the end of the accounting period, the general ledger balances are used to prepare financial statements.

Basic Process

No matter which approach you use, the end result produces the same set of financial statements. Although the number and types of accounts may increase and the approach may vary, the process used in a simple double-entry accounting system has five basic steps:

1. Prepare a chart of accounts.
2. Record all business transactions in an accounting database or journal, using source documents.
3. Total each account in the database or journal at the end of the accounting period.
4. Prepare an income statement and statement of cash flow.
5. Prepare a balance sheet using the ending balances in each asset, liability, and owner's equity accounts.

The last two steps can be reversed. The order for preparing the balance sheet, income statement, and statement of cash flow doesn't matter.

 **Apply Your Knowledge** The equation Assets = Liabilities + Owner's Equity is the underlying principle of double-entry accounting systems. What does this mean in terms of recording transactions? What are the steps in a double-entry accounting system? Think back to your investigation of Honest by. Do you think any of these steps should be made available to customers? Explain your thoughts.

CAREER COMPETENCIES

 # Demonstrate File-Management Skills

Large or small, any business must keep careful track of all the financial statements it receives so that it can record every single transaction, or instance of buying or selling, in its accounting books. The reason for this level of accounting detail is that for a business to be successful, it must always know precisely how much money it currently has and how much it currently owes. The only way to accurately keep track of this is to know exactly how much money comes in as revenue and how much goes out as expenses. And if a business is seeking a loan, would-be investors typically look at the business's financial statements to determine if it is a good risk. For these reasons, financial statements are one of the most important parts of accounting—or the system of recording, summarizing, and reporting business and financial transactions.

Although many businesses hire accountants to keep track of financial information, collecting, understanding, and saving financial statements will be up to you if you decide to start your own business. For this reason, learning to recognize and understand them will serve you well. Even if you do not plan on starting your own business, you will encounter financial statements in your life at some point. For instance, if you have a bank account, then you have already been given a financial statement in the form of a bank deposit slip. Finally, the Internal Revenue Service (IRS), the government agency that collects federal taxes, also insists that you keep accurate records for its tax-collecting purposes.

Coding and Accessing Files

Even small companies have a large number of financial records. As these records accumulate, they become harder to find and access when needed. You can imagine how this issue becomes more challenging as a company grows.

To solve this problem, a wise accountant will use some type of system to keep track of where all the records are. This is called a coding system, a method of keeping track of files through unique names.

A coding system has two components. The first is the labels. For every file that goes into storage, a special label with a unique name goes on the file. This name can have any number of formats, as long as it is given to that specific file only. For instance, it can be a color, number, or name.

The second part of a coding system is an index, a list of the names given to each file and a corresponding location for each. So, if a certain file is put in one filing cabinet, the index would record the name of the file as labeled and where it went. That way, an accountant can easily find exactly where that file is located. Computerized systems make access to files much easier. In fact, the computer applies the coding system for you. The difficult part of computerized systems is inputting the financial records into the computer in the first place (unless they are already computerized). Most records are entered manually, but some are scanned.

Career Skills in Action

Now, you take what you have learned about file management to apply it to operating your business. Use your own business idea to do the following:

- Identify categories of financial records you will accumulate (consider any customer or vendor interactions)
- Come up with an list of names that you would use for your business
- Put together an index of your transaction categories for quick access

Share your final index with a peer or your teacher for feedback.

33.3 Computerized Accounting vs. Human Accountants

In the remainder of this section you'll learn the advantages and disadvantages of computerized accounting systems. Many accounting software programs are available. Some programs are meant to be used by entrepreneurs who have no knowledge of accounting, while others require the user to have a strong accounting background.

There are several accounting software packages for small businesses. Among the more popular products are QuickBooks, Peachtree, Business Works, and Mind Your Own Business. Entrepreneurs with only a basic understanding of accounting can use these software programs. They are often called general ledger programs and are similar in operation.

The programs all provide simple instructions, and most provide templates. They provide accounts common to most businesses, such as sales revenue and accounts payable. You can change the names of the accounts on the templates to match the actual names of the accounts in your business. You can also easily add additional accounts to the chart of accounts.

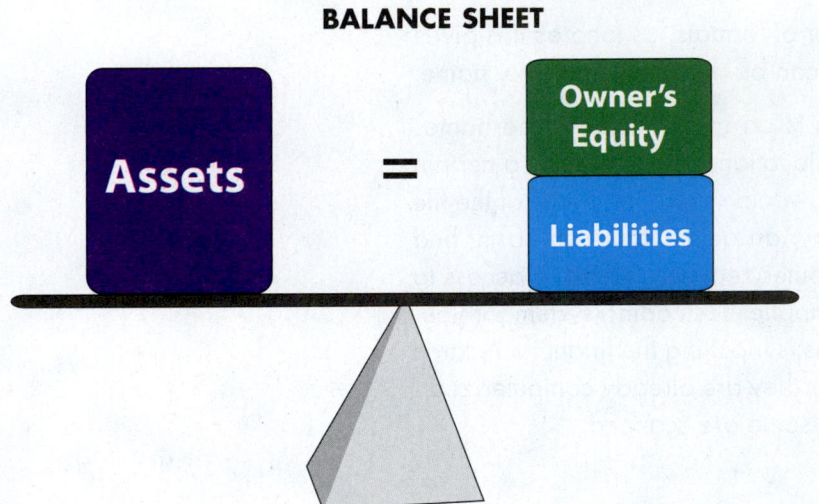

BALANCE SHEET

Assets = Owner's Equity + Liabilities

▲ **Figure 33-2**

Assets = Liabilities + Owner's Equity.
Whether you use a computerized accounting system or a manual system, any change on the left side of the equation must equal any change on the right side.

Recognizing Patterns.
If Matt's Hats bought more inventory on credit, what would happen to Matt's assets and his liabilities?

Although the method of entering transactions in these software programs may vary somewhat, they are basically similar. Most provide examples of how to enter typical business transactions. In some programs you would simply enter a transaction by using the name of the account involved. With this type of program, you don't have to be familiar with spreadsheet software or terms such as debit and credit that are needed with manual systems.

The tremendous advantage of this type of computer accounting system compared to a manual one is that a computerized system prepares financial statements automatically. In a manual system, the user must do the calculations by hand. Computerized accounting systems automatically prepare income statements, balance sheets, and other financial statements. This feature saves time and prevents mathematical errors. Furthermore, computer accounting systems don't generally require the user to have extensive knowledge of accounting procedures.

The major disadvantage of an accounting software program, like many computer programs, is the amount of time it takes to learn how to use it. Also, although accounting software programs are fine for inputting typical transactions, they often lack clear instructions for inputting unusual (atypical) transactions. For example, if you have to change a transaction because of an error, often called a correcting entry, the program may not have clear instructions on how to input the change.

Accounting software programs are available in a range of prices. Some are free and others can cost hundreds of dollars. Many entrepreneurs contract with accounting firms to prepare their financial reports. The employees of these firms use professional software programs, like those mentioned earlier, to keep the books and prepare reports.

Using Accountants and Bookkeepers

Many entrepreneurs don't keep their own records. They feel their time is better spent managing the business rather than doing recordkeeping work. This is especially true if the entrepreneur has little or no background in accounting.

Some entrepreneurs pay a part-time accountant or bookkeeper to maintain their books. This of course is an additional business expense.

Having someone else keep the records for your business presents another potential problem. If the accountant has the authority to write checks and also does the bank reconciliation, there is the possibility of embezzlement. **Embezzlement** is the crime of stealing money from an employer. To avoid this, entrepreneurs need to have proper accounting controls in place. **Accounting controls** are checks and balances established so that accounting personnel follow procedures that will avoid potential problems. These procedures allow the owner to have better control of the financial operation of the business and also help prevent embezzlement. An example of an accounting control would be to require that all checks, purchase orders, and invoices have the owner's signature.

Some entrepreneurs pay an auditor to check their books. An **auditor** is an accountant who examines a company's financial records and verifies that they have been kept properly. This type of audit is often called an **internal audit**. It shouldn't be confused with the kind of audit performed by the Internal Revenue Service (to check an individual's or a business's income tax declarations).

Whether an entrepreneur keeps his or her own records or hires a bookkeeper or accountant, they should be aware of updates to accounting standards that are issued by the Financial Accounting Standards Board (FASB). These updates provide simplified accounting alternatives for some or all private companies and relate to a variety of accounting practices, ranging from leasing arrangements to goodwill accounting.

Apply Your Knowledge   What is one of the disadvantages of using an accountant or bookkeeper to maintain your books? From your investigation of Honest by, how does having transparent operations avoid some of the ethical concerns with using accountants?

 **APPLICATION TO BUSINESS PLANNING**

Financial Records

Use what you learned from this chapter about recordkeeping to create a plan for tracking financial records as part of your implementation and growth plan. You should support your findings with data from research. Be sure to include:

- What financial records you will have to track for your business
- Plan for who will be completing accounting tasks
- Accounting controls you will put in place

REVIEWING OBJECTIVES

1. Differentiate between various financial records.

2. Discuss the advantages and disadvantages of computerized accounting systems.

3. Describe the issues associated with the use of accountants and bookkeepers.

CRITICAL THINKING

Which do you think you would prefer, a manual accounting system or a computerized accounting system? Why?

ENTREPRENEURIAL THINKING EXERCISE: COMFORT WITH RISK

Think back to your investigation of Honest by. Many companies would not want to share their financial records because there is a risk if the business underperforms or does something a customer does not agree with. How would you convince them to be comfortable with that risk? What potential benefits would you say come along with increased financial transparency?

EXTENSION ACTIVITIES

Entrepreneurship & Mathematics Skills

Complete the following task to demonstrate your understanding of entrepreneurship:

Grades 9–12: Use your knowledge of reconciling bank statements to complete this task. Imagine that you know the following about your bank account:

Bank statement balance from last period: $6,400

Outstanding payments: $330, $275, $151

Outstanding deposits: $1,500, $1,000

- Using this information, write an equation that defines your current balance as the unknown variable.
- Solve for the unknown variable to find your current bank balance.
- Insert this information in a table to check your answer.

34 ACCOUNTING SYSTEMS

GUIDING QUESTION:
"Which accounting systems will I use for my business?"

APPLICATION TO BUSINESS PLANNING:
☑ Accounting System

OBJECTIVE

- Learn the parts of an accounting worksheet.
- Describe how to use a single-column accounting worksheet.
- Create financial statements based on a single-column accounting worksheet.

NFTE Entrepreneurial Mindset Characteristic Focus

Critical Thinking & Problem Solving

National Entrepreneurship Standards

- **A.27** Explain the need for business systems and procedures
- **G.20** Maintain financial records
- **G.21** Read and reconcile financial statements
- **I.13** Explain the nature of overhead/operating expenses
- **K.12** Demonstrate spreadsheet applications
- **M.06** Analyze business processes and procedures
- **O.13** Interpret financial statements

Common Career Technical Core Standards

- **CRP.2** Apply appropriate academic and technical skills.
- **CRP.3** Attend to personal health and financial well-being.
- **CRP.11** Use technology to enhance productivity.
- **BM-BIM.1** Describe and follow laws and regulations affecting business operations and transactions.
- **BM-BIM.2** Plan, monitor, manage and maintain the use of financial resources to ensure a business's financial wellbeing.
- **BM-BIM.3.** Access, evaluate and disseminate information for business decision making.
- **BM-BIM.4** Plan, monitor and manage day-to-day business activities to sustain continued business functioning.

National Entrepreneurship Standards: Career Competencies

 D.21 Respect the privacy of others

 D.22 Explain ethical considerations in providing information

LESSON VOCABULARY

- financing activities
- investing activities
- operating activities
- Pacioli check column
- posted

34.1 Using an Accounting Worksheet

You have learned the basics of recording accounting transactions using a single-column approach and a double-column approach. In this section, you will use the single-column approach, which can be done manually or with a computer spreadsheet program like Microsoft Excel.

The Accounting Worksheet

A simple accounting system is especially helpful to entrepreneurs starting their businesses. Often beginning entrepreneurs will use a single-column accounting worksheet. An accounting worksheet relies on one main database. After each transaction is **posted** (written in the accounting worksheet) in an accounting period (such as a month), an entrepreneur can immediately determine the effect the transaction has on the financial statements. In other words, an accounting worksheet is "real-time." It allows a business owner to make immediate decisions regarding the financial health of the enterprise. At the end of the accounting period, it is easy to prepare an income statement, statement of cash flows, and balance sheet.

An accounting worksheet is primarily a cash-only accounting system. The only time you will make entries that don't affect cash is when you remove inventory upon a sale of goods, or when you estimate your tax expense based on the current period income before taxes. All other worksheet entries will increase cash when it's collected or decrease cash when it's paid.

If you keep an accounting worksheet by hand, the entries should be made in pen so that there is a permanent record of your work. Write neatly. Since an accounting worksheet has many rows and columns, you can use a long ruler when inputting numbers to assure that you are placing the numbers on the correct line.

Preferably, however, you will use an accounting worksheet constructed with spreadsheet software (such as Excel) to record your transactions. The accounting worksheet template supplied with this text is shown in Figure 34-1.

If You Aren't Familiar with Spreadsheet Software

- Search for "Free Excel Spreadsheet Tutorial" on Google or Yahoo.
- Find a tutorial that looks helpful and invest about an hour in learning Excel basics.

This will allow you to use the accounting worksheet template in a more informed way. It will also help with such activities as preparing budgets, preparing financial statements, and projecting cash flows.

Parts of the Accounting Worksheet

At the top of the accounting worksheet template is a heading for you to key such information as Company Name, Student Name, Class/Section, and Teacher, along with the relevant accounting period.

Cell References

Like any spreadsheet, the accounting worksheet has many columns and rows. An easy way to refer to a cell is to list the column of the cell first, and then the row of the cell. For example, the first cell in a spreadsheet is cell A1 (column A, row 1).

Here's an explanation of some of the important parts of the accounting worksheet template:

- **Check or Deposit Number, Date, and To/From Columns.** Beginning in cell A11, and running across the first three columns, are the columns for the Cash account. These are very much like the columns you would see in a checkbook.

◇	A	B	C	D	E	F	G	H	I	J	K	L	M
1	Company Name:				Month/Day/Year:								
2	Student Name:												
3	Class/Section:												
4	Teacher:												
5										E			A= L+E
6	←		Total Assets			→		= Liabilities	+	Equity			
7										(Net Worth)			
8	←		Cash Account →		← Other Assets →								
9	Ck #	Date	To/From	Cash	Inventory	Capital Equipment					A/C Code	Explanation for Equity Change	Pacioli Ck **
10	Balance Sheet Numbers, Beg. of August												
11													
12													
13													
14													
15													
16													
17													
18													
19													
20													
21													
22													
23													
24													
25													
26													
27													
28													
29	Balance Sheet Numbers, End of August												
30													

Figure 34-1

Transaction Portion of the Accounting Worksheet.

The accounting worksheet is organized according to the accounting equation: Assets = Liabilities + Owner's Equity.

Applying Concepts.

Can you explain the concept in row 7 as it applies to the accounts in rows 9 and 10?

- **Accounts.** The business accounts, beginning with Cash, in cell D10, run across columns D through J. Columns D through F show the Other Assets accounts. Columns G and H show the Liabilities accounts. And column J shows the Equity account. The Other Assets account titles have a green background. The Liabilities account titles (such as Loans Payable and Income Tax Payable) have a red background. The Equity account title has a blue background.

- **Equity.** Take a close look at the cells in column J under Equity (most are colored orange). As you will see a bit later, most changes in Owner's Equity (otherwise known as Net Worth) are due to revenues and expenses. Revenues increase Owner's Equity, and expenses decrease Owner's Equity.

- **A/C Code.** In column K, beginning in cell K10, the appropriate Chart of Account Code is shown for each transaction. The code is taken from the Chart of Accounts (which begins in cell A32.) The Chart of Account Code is a convenient way of labeling all revenues and expenses. This makes it easier to prepare your income statement.

- **Explanation for Equity Change.** In column L, beginning in cell L10, you can provide an explanation for the change in equity. This serves as a handy reminder of the type of each revenue and expense item.

- **Pacioli Check.** Column M, beginning with cell M10, is the ==Pacioli check column==. The column is named after the father of modern-day bookkeeping, Luca Pacioli (pa-CHO-lee). Pacioli was a Franciscan monk from Sansepolcro, Italy. In 1494 he wrote the first textbook describing the duality aspect of accounting. This column will ensure that the accounting equation always balances after each transaction.

Entering Transactions

The following example shows you how to use the accounting worksheet for a merchandising business called Jean Waverly's T-Shirts. It's a sole proprietorship selling t-shirts.

Let's start with Transaction 1. Jean started her business on August 2, 20-- by contributing $2,000 of her personal savings to open a business checking account. When she deposited this money in the business account, she would make the following entry in the accounting worksheet.

Ck #	Date	To/From	Cash	Inventory	Jean Waverly, Capital	Pacioli Ck **
Balance Sheet Numbers, Beg. of August			0	0	0	0
Deposit	8/2/20--	Jean Waverly	2,000		2,000	0

Only the affected accounts are shown.

To get a bit more practice, let's look at Transaction 2. Here, the business purchased 200 blank t-shirts for $3 each from ACME T-Shirt Supply. The total cost of $600 is subtracted from Cash and added to Inventory (Check 101).

Ck #	Date	To/From	Cash	Inventory	Jean Waverly, Capital	Pacioli Ck **
Balance Sheet Numbers, Beg. of August			0	0	0	0
Deposit	8/2/20--	Jean Waverly	2,000		2,000	0
101	8/2/20--	ACME T-Shirt Supply	-600	600		0

Only the affected accounts are shown.

Note that Jean's current balance in Cash is $1,400, and her balance in Inventory is $600. You can determine the account balance for any account by adding up the numbers from the beginning of the period to the current date. This is what makes the accounting worksheet real-time.

 **Apply Your Knowledge** In an accounting worksheet, what role does the Pacioli check column perform? From your investigation of Enron, how does something like a Pacioli check help auditors see if something is entered incorrectly?

ENTREPRENEURIAL CASE STUDY: CRITICAL THINKING & PROBLEM SOLVING

 **Lang Dobson— Newsies Clothing Co.**

Fashion for the Urban Movement

Lang Dobson is the founder and CEO of The Newsies Clothing Co., LLC, a fashion line for the urban movement. Lang started his business while he was in his entrepreneurship course sponsored by the Network for Teaching Entrepreneurship (NFTE) at his high school in North Miami Beach, Florida. After his experience in his NFTE course, Lang continue to grow and run his business past graduation and while attending college. In April 2014, Lang was honored as South Florida's Entrepreneur of the Year at the NFTE Global Gala in New York City for his accomplishments in growing his business.

Turning an Idea into an Opportunity

Lang Dobson faced seemingly unsurmountable odds in high school, from dealing with temporary homelessness to academic challenges. Growing up in both New York and Miami, he was witness to what could happen to people without the proper guidance or motivation. A mentor once told

Lang Dobson, "You must figure out what in life you love so much that you'd be willing to do it for free, then figure out how to get paid for it. That is the meaning of a meaningful life." Thanks to his passion for the arts, Lang realized that there was an opportunity to start a business designing clothes for the urban movement.

With the help of NFTE and his own drive to create his own future, Lang decided to combine his love for art and desire to deliver more positive messages to our youth. The business that grew out of these two passions is an urban fashion company, Newsies Clothing Co. Lang worked on this business idea while in his entrepreneurship course. He soon realized that this opportunity would be one that he could actually launch into a true business opportunity.

Entrepreneurial Thinking

Launching this business quickly taught Lang that he needed to think outside of the box. For example, when he was challenged with the task of increasing his sales and attaching more customers, instead of using typical and more expensive advertising tactics, he decided to collaborate with local artists to reach more potential customers. Lang has continued to be innovative in his designs and marketing to expand his reach and differentiate Newsies from its competition. He has also been inspired to use his role models to promote the brand.

Lang Dobson.

Lang continues to run his business while studying at the Miami Ad School and working a full-time job while he runs his company. He credits his success to learning entrepreneurship at a young age: "NFTE showed me that with the right networking and the proper drive, even the youngest people can become successful entrepreneurs. I am inspired to use my art to rise above the status quo."

Thinking and Acting Like an Entrepreneur

- How did Lang use his skills and passion to identify a business opportunity?
- What challenges did Lang have when trying to make his business operational?
- In which ways does Lang demonstrate the entrepreneurial mindset behavior of critical thinking and problem solving?

34.2 Using the Accounting Worksheet

Let's start from the beginning for Jean Waverly's business. After she wrote a business plan and studied the market, Jean decided to open a merchandising business selling t-shirts. She began her business on August 2, 2017.

The first thing she did was to prepare a Chart of Accounts for her business and open a business checking account at a local bank. Jean pays the supplier of her t-shirts $3 for each shirt. She sells the shirts for $10 apiece.

The first step in using the accounting worksheet is to enter all the transactions. As an example, here are the business transactions for Jean's T-Shirts in August, 2017:

August 2   Jean Waverly invested $2,000 from her personal savings account to provide start-up financing for the business. She opened up a business checking account at her local bank.

August 2   The business purchased 200 t-shirts from ACME T-Shirt Supply (200 × $3 = $600.00). This is Check 101.

August 8   The business sold 50 t-shirts at $10 each (50 × $10 = $500). This transaction requires two entries. First, you record the sales revenue. Add $500 to Cash and $500 to Jean Waverly, Capital (as Revenue). Second, you record the Cost of Goods Sold (COGS) expense. The cost per shirt is $3. Thus, the COGS Expense is $3 × 50 shirts = $150.

> Each sale of inventory requires two entries: one to record the sales revenue and one to record the COGS expense.

August 9   The business paid $100 for advertising flyers. (Check 102)

August 10   The business paid $500 for a new Office Machine, a cash register. (Check 103)

August 11   The business paid its monthly rent of $300 to Ron's Real Estate. (Check 104)

August 15 The business sold 100 t-shirts at $10 each for the week (100 × $10 each = $1,000). The cost of each t-shirt is $3. Thus, COGS expense is 100 shirts × $3 = $300.

August 15 The business purchased 400 more t-shirts from ACME T-Shirt Supply (400 × $3 = $1,200). (Check 105).

August 16 The business paid its utility bill to Atlantic Electric Co. for $225. (Check 106).

August 22 The business sold 150 t-shirts for the week (150 × $10 = $1,500). The cost of each t-shirt is still $3. So COGS expense is 150 shirts × $3 = $450.

August 24 The business paid a salary of $125 to a part-time worker, Mary Smith. (Check 107)

August 25 The business paid its $200 insurance bill for the month to ABC Insurance Co. (Check 108)

August 26 The business sold 200 t-shirts for the week (200 × $10 = $2,000). The cost of each t-shirt is $3. So COGS expense is 200 shirts × $3 = $600.

August 31 The business calculated pre-tax net income for the period by adding all revenues and subtracting all expenses. Pre-tax net income is $2,550. At a 15% income tax rate, a tax liability, tax expense is calculated to be .15 × $2,550 = $382.50.

Figure 34-2 shows the completed accounting worksheet for Jean's T-Shirts after all the transactions have been entered for August.

Apply Your Knowledge   What is the first step in completing an accounting worksheet? Think back to your investigation of Enron. Why is it important to have accountants who will complete accounting worksheets honestly?

Company Name:	Jean Waverly's T-Shirts
Student Name:	John Doe
Class/Section:	NFTE Ent 101/01
Teacher:	Mr. Killebrew

Month/Day/Year: 4/8/20--

A = L + E

| | | | ← Total Assets → | | | = Liabilities | | + E Equity (Net Worth) | | | |
| | | | Cash Account | ← Other Assets → | | | | | | | |
Ck #	Date	To/From	Cash	Inventory	Capital Equipment	Loans Payable	Income Tax Payable	Jean Waverly, Capital	A/C Code	Explanation for Equity Change	Pacioli Ck**
Balance Sheet Numbers, Beg. of August			0	0	0	0	0	0			0
Deposit	8/2/20--	Jean Waverly	2,000					2,000			0
101	8/2/20--	ACME T-Shirt Supply	-600	600							0
Deposit	8/8/20--	Dep. Cks. from Sales	500					500	R1	Sales Revenue	0
				-150				-150	VE1	COGS Expense	0
102	8/9/20--	Corner Print Shop	-100					-100	FE1	Adv. Expense	0
103	8/10/20--	Otto's Office Machines	-500		500						0
104	8/11/20--	Ron's Real Estate	-300					-300	FE2	Rent Expense	0
Deposit	8/15/20--	Dep. Cks. from Sales	1,000					1,000	R1	Sales Revenue	0
				-300				-300	VE1	COGS Expense	0
105	8/15/20--	ACME T-Shirt Supply	-1,200	1,200							0
106	8/16/20--	Atlantic Electric Co.	-225					-225	FE3	Utilities Expense	0
Deposit	8/22/20--	Dep. Cks. from Sales	1,500					1,500	R1	Sales Revenue	0
				-450				-450	VE1	COGS Expense	0
107	8/24/20--	Mary Smith	-125					-125	FE4	Salary Expense	0
108	8/25/20--	ABC Insurance Co.	-200					-200	FE5	Insurance Expense	0
Deposit	8/26/20--	Dep. Cks. from Sales	2,000					2,000	R1	Sales Revenue	0
				-600				-600	VE1	COGS Expense	0
	8/31/20--						638	-638	VE5	Income Tax Expense	0
Balance Sheet Numbers, End of August			3,750	300	500	0	638	3,913			0

▲ **Figure 34-2**

Transactions for Jean Waverly's T-Shirts.

All the transactions for August have been entered in the accounting worksheet.

Predicting.

From the data in this accounting worksheet, do you think that Jean's T-Shirts was profitable in August?

CAREER COMPETENCIES

 ## Respect the Privacy of Others; Explain Ethical Considerations in Providing Information

Storing Records

Keeping accurate records might be the most important part of business financial management. Considering how important it is to keep good records, and the large amount of records a business accumulates over time, a good filing system is critical. Yet this is only one of the concerns about maintaining financial records for a company. Other issues include security and access.

Since companies must keep records of all financial transactions, these issues are concerns for even the smallest of businesses. This also means that as companies grow in size, the issues become more complicated and important.

Maintaining the Security of Financial Records

If a company is publicly traded—owned by members of the general public, called shareholders, who pay to own a certain percentage—financial records must be made public. But privately owned companies, particularly those with many competitors, might not want investors, competitors, and others to access sensitive financial data.

For instance, would you buy a product from a company if you thought the company was failing? Would you be more interested in opening a shoe store if you knew the only other shoe store in town was doing very well?

There are two ways a company must store its financial records. If the records are physical files and documents, they must be physically secured by being put in a locked location. Moreover, only trusted individuals should be allowed access to them, as information contained within them must not be released. If the records are on a computer, they must be encrypted, or digitally secured so that only authorized people can access them. Encryption uses complicated mathematical algorithms (programs or formulas designed to solve problems) to turn regular data into unreadable data that can be transformed back with a special password, called a "key." These days, financial records are usually both physical and computerized, so both methods of security are necessary.

Accountants are perhaps the most trusted people in any company. This is because they deal directly with all of the money that a company makes and spends. An accountant must never abuse the trust placed upon his or her position by making false documents or stealing money. This is called embezzlement, and it is a serious crime.

Here are wrong and right ways to deal with situations if you are an accountant and entrepreneur managing financial transactions.

DO NOT

- Tell your friend who works in a competing business about the financial status of your company.
- Borrow money from your company's income for your own personal use.
- Fail to record some transactions.
- Falsify sales numbers so the business looks better.

DO

- Make careful, detailed records of all the business income and expenses.
- Keep all of the income safely locked away.
- Report any problems with the financial records.

Career Skills in Action

Now, you take what you learned about respecting the privacy of financial records to put together a plan for protecting financial records in your business. Be sure to include a list of potentially sensitive data that will require a higher level of security. Share your plan with a peer or teacher for feedback.

34.3 Creating Financial Statements

After the transactions for a period are correctly entered into the accounting worksheet, you can prepare the balance sheet, income statement, and statement of cash flows. It doesn't matter which financial statement you start with. See Figure 34-3.

Balance Sheet

First, look at row 34. These are the ending balances in each of the accounts in the Assets, Liability and Owner's Equity portions of the balance sheet. They are the basis for preparing the balance sheet in the accounting worksheet.

Look at the Owner's Equity part of the balance sheet. Compare it to the Balance Sheet at the beginning of the month. Jean Waverly, Capital had a zero balance on August 1 because the business was just beginning.

On August 2, Jean financed the business by contributing $2,000 of her personal money to the business. Jean's T-Shirts earned a net income of $1,913 during August. So, the August 31 ending balance for Jean

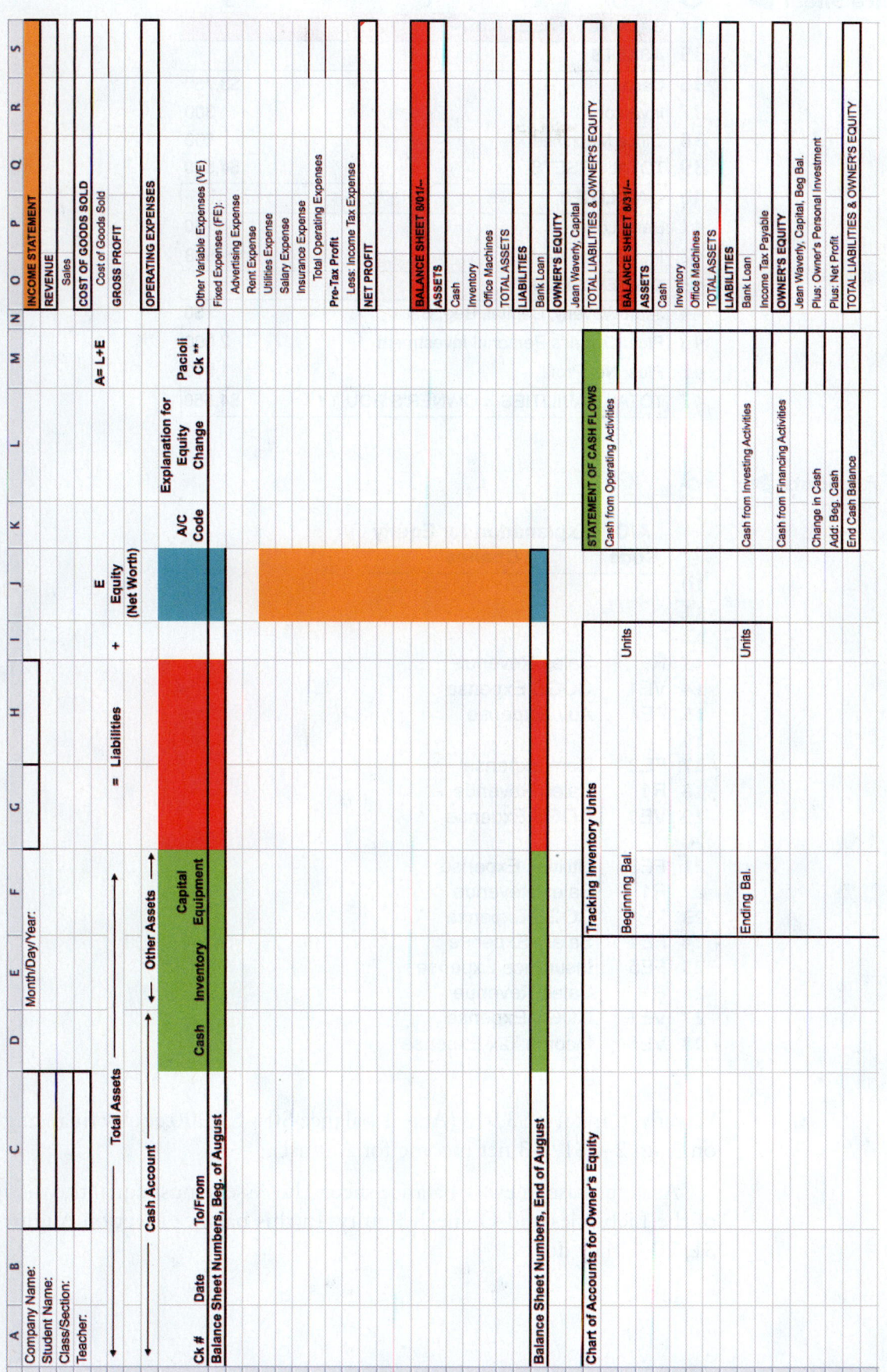

▲ **Figure 34-3**

Bank Accounting Worksheet.

The complete worksheet shows an income statement, a beginning and ending balance sheet, a statement of cash flows, and an inventory report.

Predicting.

Which financial document would you prepare first?

Balance Sheet ▶

◇	O	P	Q	R	S
34	**BALANCE SHEET 8/31/--**				
35	**ASSETS**				
36	Cash				$3,750
37	Inventory				300
38	Office Machines				500
39	TOTAL ASSETS				$4,550
40	**LIABILITIES**				
41	Bank Loan				$0
42	Income Tax Payable				638
43	**OWNER'S EQUITY**				
44	Jean Waverly, Capital, Beg. Bal.				$0
45	Plus: Owner's Personal Investment				2,000
46	Plus: Net Profit				1,913
47	TOTAL LIABILITIES & OWNER'S EQUITY				$4,550

Chart of Accounts ▶

◇	K	L
9	**A/C Code**	**Explanation for Equity Change**
10		
11		
12		
13	R1	Sales Revenue
14	VE1	COGS Expense
15	FE1	Adv. Expense
16		
17	FE2	Rent Expense
18	R1	Sales Revenue
19	VE1	COGS Expense
20		
21	FE3	Utilities Expense
22	R1	Sales Revenue
23	VE1	COGS Expense
24	FE4	Salary Expense
25	FE5	Insurance Expense
26	R1	Sales Revenue
27	VE1	COGS Expense
28	VE5	Income Tax Expense

Waverly, Capital is $3,913 (Aug. 1 balance $0 + $2,000 equity financing on Aug. 2 + $1,913 net income for August).

As is the case in every balance sheet, the Assets must equal the total of the Liabilities and Owner's Equity. In this balance sheet on August 31, 20--, they do.

Income Statement

For the income statement, begin by looking at cell K9, labeled "A/C Code" (which stands for Account Code). This code allows you to classify revenues, variable expenses, and fixed expenses.

Using the Account Code, you can add all the accounts for the month to the Income Statement portion of the accounting worksheet. For example, for your Sales (account R1), add all the R1 transactions:

- From 8/8, add $500
- From 8/15, add $1,000
- From 8/22, add $1,500
- From 8/26, add $2,000

So Jean Waverly's total sales revenue for the month of August is $5,000. Add that amount to the Income Statement under Revenue, Sales in cell S3.

Here's another example: For Cost of Goods Sold (account VE1), add all VE1 transactions:

- From 8/8, add $150
- From 8/15, add $300
- From 8/22, add $450
- From 8/26, add $600

Jean Waverly's total COGS for the month of August is $1,400. Add that amount to the Income Statement under Cost of Goods Sold in cell S5.

Continue in this way for all the accounts with entries in August. Some, such as Office Equipment, will only have one entry (on 8/10, when Jean bought a cash register). Others, like Jean Waverly, Capital, will have multiple entries that you'll need to add up.

Here, to the right, is the final income statement.

The Net Profit of $1,913 in the income statement is also reported on the balance sheet as an increase in Owner's Equity.

▼ **Income Statement**

◇	O	P	Q	R	S
1	INCOME STATEMENT				
2	REVENUE				
3	Sales				$5,000
4	COST OF GOODS SOLD				
5	Cost of Goods Sold				-1,500
6	GROSS PROFIT				$3,500
7					
8	OPERATING EXPENSES				
9	Other Variable Expenses (VE)				$0
10	Fixed Expenses (FE):				
11	Advertising Expense				-100
12	Rent Expense				-300
13	Utilities Expense				-225
14	Salary Expense				-125
15	Insurance Expense				-200
16	Total Operating Expenses				-950
17	Pre-Tax Profit				2,550
18	Less: Income-Tax Expense				-638
19	NET PROFIT				$1,913

Statement of Cash Flows

In relation to the statement of cash flows, there are three basic types of business activities:

- **Operating activities.** Day-to-day activities are called **operating activities**. Most cash changes fall into this category.

- **Investing Activities.** When a business buys assets that will last more than one year, they are called **investing activities**. Jean's only investing activity is the purchase of a cash register for $500 on August 10.

- **Financing Activities.** The third category is **financing activities**. It consists primarily of debt and equity financing. Jean's only financing activity in August is the $2,000 she personally invested to provide start-up equity financing for her business.

Jean can now prepare the statement of cash flows by adding all the changes in the Cash column (Column D) under the appropriate head, as shown here.

Statement of Cash Flows ▶

◇	K	L	M
32	**STATEMENT OF CASH FLOWS**		
33	Cash from Operating Activities		
34		Cash Sales	$5,000
35		Cash Pd. for Supplie	-1,800
36		Cash Pd. for Advert.	-100
37		Cash Pd. for Rent	-300
38		Cash Pd. for Utilit.	-225
39		Cash Pd. for Salary	-125
40		Cash Pd. for Insur.	-200
41	Cash from Investing Activities		
42		Purch. of Equip.	-$500
43	Cash from Financing Activities		
44		Jean's Personal Co	2,000
45	Change in Cash		$3,750
46	Add: Beg. Cash		0
47	Cash Balance, 8/31/--		$3,750

The ending cash balance of $3,750 is the same number as the cash balance reported on the balance sheet. For businesses that are more complicated than Jean's, it is often a good idea to create a separate Chart of Accounts for all changes in cash (just as with changes in Owner's Equity). You could create a code column next to cash with three labels: "O" for operating activities, "I" for investing activities, and "F" for financing activities.

Figure 34-4

Completed Accounting Worksheet.

A completed accounting worksheet includes a completed income statement, a beginning and ending balance sheet, a statement of cash flows, and an inventory report.

	A	B	C	D	E	F	G	H	I	J
1	Company Name:		Jean Waverly's T-Shirts		Month/Day/Year:		4/8/20—			
2	Student Name:		John Doe							
3	Class/Section:		NFTE Ent 101/01							
4	Teacher:		Mr. Killdrew							

Total Assets — Cash Account → ← Other Assets → = Liabilities + Equity (Net Worth) • A = L + E

	Ck #	Date	To/From	Cash	Inventory	Capital Equipment	Loans Payable	Income Tax Payable	Jean Waverly, Capital	A/C Code	Explanation for Equity Change	Pacioli Ck **
10	Balance Sheet Numbers, Beg. of August			0	0	0	0	0	0			0
11	Deposit	8/2/20—	Jean Waverly	2,000					2,000			0
12	101	8/2/20—	ACME T-Shirt Supply	-600	600							0
13	Deposit	8/8/20—	Dep. Cks. from Sales	500					500	R1	Sales Revenue	0
14					-150				-150	VE1	COGS Expense	0
15	102	8/9/20—	Corner Print Shop	-100					-100	FE1	Adv. Expense	0
16	103	8/10/20—	Otto's Office Machines	-500		500						0
17	104	8/11/20—	Ron's Real Estate	-300					-300	FE2	Rent Expense	0
18	Deposit	8/15/20—	Dep. Cks. from Sales	1,000					1,000	R1	Sales Revenue	0
19					-300				-300	VE1	COGS Expense	0
20	105	8/15/20—	ACME T-Shirt Supply	-1,200	1,200							0
21	106	8/16/20—	Atlantic Electric Co.	-225					-225	FE3	Utilities Expense	0
22	Deposit	8/22/20—	Dep. Cks. from Sales	1,500					1,500	R1	Sales Revenue	0
23					-450				-450	VE1	COGS Expense	0
24	107	8/24/20—	Mary Smith	-125					-125	FE4	Salary Expense	0
25	108	8/25/20—	ABC Insurance Co.	-200					-200	FE5	Insurance Expense	0
26	Deposit	8/26/20—	Dep. Cks. from Sales	2,000					2,000	R1	Sales Revenue	0
27					-600				-600	VE1	COGS Expense	0
28		8/31/20—						638	-638	VE5	Income Tax Expense	638
29	Balance Sheet Numbers, End of August			3,750	300	500	0	638	3,913			0

Chart of Accounts

R1 = Revenue Source #1	
VE1 = Cost of Goods Sold (a Variable Expense)	
VE2 = Sales Commission (a Variable Expense)	
VE3 = Utilities	
VE4 = Salary	
VE5 = Income-Tax Expense (also a Variable Expense)	
FE1 = Advertising Expense (Flyers)	
FE2 = Rent Expense	
FE3 = Utilities Expense	
FE4 = Salary Expense	
FE5 = Insurance Expense	
FE6 = Registration Fee for Market Booth	
FE7 = Business Cards	
FE8 = Flyers	
FE9 = Rent	

Tracking Inventory Units

August 1 Beginning Bal.	0 Units
August 2 Purchase	200 Units
August 8 Sale	-50 Units
August 15 Sale	-100 Units
August 15 Purchase	400 Units
August 22 Sale	-150 Units
August 26 Sale	-200 Units
August 31 Ending Bal.	100 Units

STATEMENT OF CASH FLOWS

Cash from Operating Activities	
Cash Sales	$5,000
Cash Pd. for Supplies	-1,800
Cash Pd. for Advert.	-100
Cash Pd. for Rent	-300
Cash Pd. for Utilit.	-225
Cash Pd. for Salary	-125
Cash Pd. for Insur.	-200
Cash from Investing Activities	
Purch. of Equip.	-$500
Cash from Financing Activities	
Jean's Personal Co.	2,000
Change in Cash	$3,750
Add: Beg. Cash	0
Cash Balance, 8/31/—	$3,750

INCOME STATEMENT

REVENUE	
Sales	$5,000
COST OF GOODS SOLD	
Cost of Goods Sold	-1,500
GROSS PROFIT	$3,500
OPERATING EXPENSES	
Other Variable Expenses (VE)	$0
Fixed Expenses (FE):	
Advertising Expense	-100
Rent Expense	-300
Utilities Expense	-225
Salary Expense	-125
Insurance Expense	-200
Total Operating Expenses	-950
Pre-Tax Profit	2,550
Less: Income-Tax Expense	-638
NET PROFIT	$1,913

BALANCE SHEET 8/01/—

ASSETS	
Cash	0
Inventory	0
Office Machines	0
TOTAL ASSETS	0
LIABILITIES	
Bank Loan	0
OWNER'S EQUITY	
Jean Waverly, Capital	0
TOTAL LIABILITIES & OWNER'S EQUITY	0

BALANCE SHEET 8/31/—

ASSETS	
Cash	$3,750
Inventory	300
Office Machines	500
TOTAL ASSETS	$4,550
LIABILITIES	
Bank Loan	$0
Income Tax Payable	638
OWNER'S EQUITY	
Jean Waverly, Capital, Beg. Bal.	2,000
Plus: Owner's Personal Investment	$0
Plus: Net Profit	1,913
TOTAL LIABILITIES & OWNER'S EQUITY	$4,550

** Pacioli Check - Named after Luca Pacioli, the father of double-entry accounting. This ensures accounting transactions always balance.

Predicting.

In your opinion, how useful would this accounting worksheet be to you if you were a beginning entrepreneur?

Tracking Inventory

Every time inventory is purchased, you should record the type of inventory, number of units purchased, and its cost. Also, every time inventory is sold, you should make a note of the type of inventory and number of units sold. At any one time, your accounting records should agree with the number of units on hand. This is a crucial accounting control to make sure customers or employees aren't stealing merchandise from your business.

Thus, in the accounting worksheet, you see that there should be 100 t-Shirts on hand at the end of August. If there are fewer than that, you have a problem. Customers or employees may have stolen t-shirts, or there may be an accounting error.

The inventory of t-shirts has a dollar value. At the end of the month, the balance in Inventory is $300 (100 t-shirts × $3). See Figure 34-4.

Using a Computerized Spreadsheet

If you use an electronic spreadsheet, such as Excel, you can easily keep track of transactions and prepare financial statements. There are three major features of a spreadsheet program that are particularly useful when using a spreadsheet accounting worksheet:

- **Linking Numbers from One Part of the Worksheet to Another.** One of the main advantages of a computer spreadsheet is that you can link numbers from one part of a spreadsheet directly to another part of the spreadsheet. For example, the amount in cell D29 for Cash is $3,750. This amount will also be shown on the balance sheet in cell S36 ("Cash"). To have the spreadsheet software place the amount in cell D29 into the cell at S36, you can click in cell S36, and then in the Formula Bar type "=d29". This tells the computer to take the amount in cell D29 and put it in cell S36.

- **Adding Columns of Numbers.** You can also have the spreadsheet software total columns of numbers for you. For example, you could add the Cash totals shown in column D. To do this, place the cursor in the cell where you want to place the sum of the column, in this case cell D29. Then, in the Formula Bar, type "=sum(d11:d28)" and press Enter. The software will place the sum for cells D11 through D28 into cell D29.

- **Adding Comments to Cells.** You can add comments for specific cells. You can easily remind yourself about a number in any cell by inserting a comment using the Insert/Comment command from the main menu of the spreadsheet program. See Figure 34-5 on the next page.

	Ck #	Date	To/From	Cash	Inventory	Capital Equipment	Loans Payable
9							
10		Balance Sheet Numbers, Beg. of August		0	0	0	0
11	Deposit	8/2/20--	Jean Waverly	2,000			
12	101	8/2/20--	ACME T-Shirt Supply	-600	600		
13	Deposit	8/8/20--	Dep. Cks. from Sales	500			
14					-150		
15	102	8/9/20--	Corner Print Shop	-100			
16	103	8/10/20--	Otto's Office Machines	-500		500	
17	104	8/11/20--	Ron's Real Estate	-300			
18	Deposit	8/15/20--	Dep. Cks. from Sales	1,000			
19					-300		
20	105	8/15/20--	ACME T-Shirt Supply	-1,200	1,200		
21	106	8/16/20--	Atlantic Electric Co.	-225			
22	Deposit	8/22/20--	Dep. Cks. from Sales	1,500			
23					-450		
24	107	8/24/20--	Mary Smith	-125			
25	108	8/25/20--	ABC Insurance Co.	-200			
26	Deposit	8/26/20--	Dep. Cks. from Sales	2,000			
27					-600		
28		8/31/20--					
29		Balance Sheet Numbers, End of August		3,750	300		0
30							
31							
32		Chart of Accounts					Units
33							

Note that the formula bar reads: =sum(D11:D28), which adds up all numbers in this range of cells. The total is $3,750.

Figure 34-5

Adding Comments to an Accounting Worksheet.

You can add comments to specific cells.

Inferring.

Why might you add comments to specific cells?

Apply Your Knowledge What are the three main types of business activities captured in financial statements? From your investigation of Enron, how could have making accurate financial statements available to employees and stockholders changed the outcome?

APPLICATION TO BUSINESS PLANNING

Accounting Systems

Use what you learned from this chapter on accounting systems to decide which accounting system you will use as part of your implementation and growth plan. You should support your findings with data from research. Be sure to include:

- Whether you will use a manual or computerized accounting system
- Which accounting system you will use

REVIEWING OBJECTIVES

1. What are the main parts of an accounting worksheet?

2. Describe how to use a single-column accounting worksheet

3. How can one create a financial statement based on a single-column accounting worksheet?

CRITICAL THINKING

How would you record the following transaction using the accounting worksheet template shown in this section? Your business purchased $200 of advertising brochures using the business's debit card.

ENTREPRENEURIAL THINKING EXERCISE: CRITICAL THINKING & PROBLEM SOLVING

Think back to your investigation of Enron. Pretend that you were an accountant or auditor working with Enron right before the scandal broke. What would you have done if you thought you found errors in the financial records? Who would you have talked to? How would you have brought evidence to support your thoughts that something was off?

34 ASSESSMENT

EXTENSION ACTIVITIES

Entrepreneurship & Literacy Skills

Complete the following task to demonstrate your understanding of entrepreneurship:

Grades 9–12: Research Luca Pacioli, the father of modern-day bookkeeping. Report on any of the following: Pacioli's life, the early history of bookkeeping, the development of the concept of duality, Pacioli's early texts on accounting, or how business was conducted in Pacioli's time. Present your report to the class.

CHAPTER

35 TAXES AND YOUR BUSINESS

GUIDING QUESTION:

"How will I be sure my business pays the appropriate taxes?"

APPLICATION TO BUSINESS PLANNING:

☑ Plan for Filing Taxes

OBJECTIVES

- Explain how the government uses tax money.
- Describe the purposes of business taxes.
- Suggest ways that businesses can reduce their taxes.

NFTE Entrepreneurial Mindset Characteristic Focus

☑ Initiative & Self-Reliance

National Entrepreneurship Standards

- **B.02** Demonstrate responsible behavior
- **F.20** Describe the relationship between government and business
- **F.21** Assess impact of government actions on business ventures
- **I.06** Determine and deposit payroll taxes
- **K.03** Record and report sales tax
- **K.04** Develop payroll record keeping system

Common Career Technical Core Standards

- **BM-BIM.1** Describe and follow laws and regulations affecting business operations and transactions.
- **BM-BIM.2** Plan, monitor, manage and maintain the use of financial resources to ensure a business's financial wellbeing.
- **BM-BIM.3** Access, evaluate and disseminate information for business decision making
- **BM-BIM.4** Plan, monitor and manage day-to-day business activities to sustain continued business functioning.
- **CRP.1** Act as a responsible and contributing citizen and employee.
- **CRP.3** Attend to personal health and financial well-being.

National Entrepreneurship Standards: Career Competencies

☑ **G.05** Read and interpret a pay stub

LESSON VOCABULARY

- deduction
- enterprise zone
- excise tax
- FICA
- infrastructure
- intrastate sales
- pass-through businesses
- sales tax
- subsidy
- tax avoidance
- tax credit
- tax evasion
- taxes
- tax-increment financing

ENTREPRENEURIAL INVESTIGATION
Paying Uncle Sam

In the U.S., every citizen that earns an income is generally expected to pay a portion of that to the government in the form of an income tax. While no one wants to give up part of their income, everyone agrees to pay these taxes because the money goes to fund important necessities. Things funded by taxes include: national defense, health care, education, and law enforcement. Not paying taxes is breaking the law.

Businesses and entrepreneurs are no exception to the rule. However, some entrepreneurs have tried to avoid paying taxes from their business. The largest taxes ever evaded was from Walter Anderson, an entrepreneur who lied about earning over $350 million so that he would not have to pay taxes. After getting caught, Walter had to pay back taxes with interest and serve time in federal prison.

Do some research on Walter Anderson to answer the following questions:

- Do you think it is as important for businesses to pay taxes as citizens do?

- Should entrepreneurs face penalties as Walter Anderson did for not paying taxes? Why or why not?

Be prepared to share your thoughts with your peers and teacher.

35.1 Why Do Businesses Pay Taxes?

Oliver Wendell Holmes, Jr., a Supreme Court Justice in the early 1900s, is credited with the statement, "I like to pay taxes. With them I buy civilization." Few people can claim they like paying taxes, money required by the government to support its various functions. Yet taxation is so important to the nation that it was authorized in the Constitution.

Article I of the Constitution states, "The Congress shall have Power To lay and collect Taxes, Duties, Imposts and Excises, to pay the Debts and provide for the common Defence and general Welfare of the United States." Some 239 years later, taxes—and the reasons for paying them—remain. Taxes may not "buy civilization," but they do buy government services, from trash collection to medical care.

The U.S. government raises money by taxation or by borrowing. It can be a problem when the government borrows money. Future generations must pay back this debt—and the interest on it.

◀ **Figure 35-1**
Oliver Wendell Holmes.
Oliver Wendell Holmes once said, "I like to pay taxes. With them I buy civilization"

Drawing Conclusions.
What does it mean to "buy civilization" through paying taxes?

Public Services

Life in the United States is built on the public services that taxes provide. Tax dollars support the **infrastructure**, the system of organizations, public systems, structures, and services that a society needs to function and be productive. For example, did you have clean water to wash your face this morning? A regional sanitary district probably maintains the pipeline and water treatment plants and the health department tests the water quality. Further up the governmental ladder, human and environmental health is protected by state and federal agencies, ranging from the Centers for Disease Control to the National Weather Service.

Local and federal taxes also help you get across town and across the country. Workers who lay the roads are hired through government contracts. City buses, commuter rail services, and Amtrak (the national rail passenger carrier) are given subsidies by the government to keep

◀ **Figure 35-2**
Tax Dollars Support the Infrastructure.
Local and federal taxes are used to build roads.

Relating Concepts.
Without adequate funding, roads and bridges fall into disrepair. How would this hurt our business and personal life?

fares low and encourage ridership. A **subsidy** is financial aid from the government to support an industry or public service. Other agencies oversee travelers' safety. Cities install traffic lights. State departments of motor vehicles test drivers and issue licenses. Local and state police enforce the laws.

Your education, too, is at least partly funded by the government. Public schools depend wholly on taxes for salaries, maintenance, and other expenses. You may use books and other resources from public libraries or attend programs at publicly supported museums. Later you may get a government loan or grant to help pay for college, where you may take part in research or other programs that receive government money.

Taxes support the life of the community through public parks and recreation areas. You might swim at a community pool, skate in a local park, or meet the local wildlife at a nature center.

Some tax money goes to maintaining the money supply. Taxes fund the work of the United States Treasury, which includes regulating national banks, printing money—and collecting taxes through the Internal Revenue Service.

Social Programs

Starting with the Great Depression in the 1930s, the government has taken an ever greater role in weaving a social safety net for people who can't meet their basic needs. Today, social services account for almost half of all federal government spending. Some programs are carried out by state or regional offices with funds from a federal agency. Others are supported by matching funds at each level of government.

The largest and oldest of all social programs is Social Security. The program's full name—Old Age, Survivors, and Disability Insurance Program—gives a clue to its scope. Social Security provides benefits for retired workers, dependents of deceased workers, and workers who have disabilities and their dependents.

Another agency dependent on taxes is the Department of Health and Human Services (HHS). The HHS fills a range of needs that include early childhood education, immunizations, and programs to combat domestic violence and drug dependency. Through Medicare and Medicaid, it provides health insurance for one-quarter of all Americans.

The Department of Agriculture (USDA) offers similarly varied assistance through its Cooperative State Research and Education Extension Service at state universities and colleges. The USDA further works to ensure healthful diets with its Fresh Fruit and Vegetable Program for low-income school districts and the Senior Farmers' Market Nutrition Program, which provides vouchers to buy food from local producers at recognized markets.

◀ **Figure 35-3**
Tax Dollars at Work.
Providing for the armed forces accounts for about 20% of the federal budget.

Classifying.

What other services does the armed services provide beyond fighting in wars?

Defense

The Department of Defense (DOD) is a prime recipient of tax money. Providing for the armed forces takes about 20% of the federal budget.

For their money, taxpayers get more than national security. The armed services also provide education and career training. Many commercial airline pilots, for example, learned their skills in the military. The armed forces assist in nonmilitary actions. The National Guard and the Coast Guard aid in disaster relief, drug enforcement, rescue operations and environmental protection. To care for wounded service personnel, the DOD has funded medical research, from surgeon training to developing artificial limbs. The Global Positioning System (GPS) that helps drivers find their way in traffic uses DOD satellites.

Business

Some tax money returns to business as resources for growth and development. The Small Business Administration (SBA) is a federal agency that provides information, advice, government contracts, and loan guarantees for operations that fall within its size restrictions. It emphasizes underserved business owners, such as women, teens, military veterans, Native Americans, and other minority groups.

Subsidies for public transportation make it more affordable and available, help lower-income citizens, and reduce stress on the roads and the environment. The owner of a commercial property may qualify for a low-interest construction loan by including energy-efficient features in the new building.

Cities and states subsidize entrepreneurs, too, by creating enterprise zones. An **enterprise zone** is a geographic area in which businesses receive economic incentives to encourage development there.

Figure 35-4 ▶
Subsidized Agriculture.

The USDA subsidizes loans for producers of grains, dairy foods, and other basic agricultural goods.

Inferring.

What are the pros and cons of subsidized loans for agricultural goods?

Entrepreneurs might be awarded grants to improve a property or tax credits for hiring employees.

Another way business taxes are used to influence the economic climate is through tax-increment financing. **Tax-increment financing (TIF)** is the strategy of spending taxpayer money to encourage businesses to locate to an area or improve their property there, with the goal of starting a cycle of growth and prosperity. TIF designation is saved for areas in serious decline. It is somewhat riskier than establishing an enterprise zone, and the benefits take longer to realize. The designation usually lasts around 20 years.

For a TIF designation, the local government first raises money by selling bonds, just as a company raises capital by selling shares. The money may be used to upgrade the infrastructure, buy rundown properties, or reimburse entrepreneurs for their expenses. Businesses move into the TIF district and generate sales and property taxes. The taxes go to pay off the bonds, with interest, and also to fund public services. Potentially the city looks more attractive to other businesses, which promotes continued growth.

Business also benefits indirectly from government programs. Good roads make ground transportation more efficient. Sports arenas, museums, and tourist attractions bring customers to area merchants. Telecommunication networks use satellites built by the space agency NASA. And think how many businesses owe their existence to the Internet, which was created in the 1960s by the Department of Defense.

 **Apply Your Knowledge** What kind of social services are paid for by taxes? Think back to your investigation. Do entrepreneurs and businesses benefit from these social services?

ENTREPRENEURIAL CASE STUDY: INITIATIVE & SELF-RELIANCE

Onyekachi C. Ekeagwu— Solar Powered RC Toys

Clear Vision for the Future

Onyekachi Ekeagwu is currently an undergraduate studying engineering at Morgan State University in Baltimore, Maryland. Prior to this, he was a high school student taking an entrepreneurship course sponsored by the Network for Teaching Entrepreneurship (NFTE) at Patterson High School in Baltimore.

By developing a well-organized business plan, he and his business partners won several business plan competitions, including first place in the 2013 NFTE Baltimore Business Competition, the Consolation Energy NFTE/MESA Competition, The Johns Hopkins University Baltimore Robotics Cup, and 2nd place in the Mathematics Engineering Science Achievement (MESA) Regional Virtual Robotics Competition.

Onyekachi C. Ekeagwu.

Pursuing a Dream

Onyekachi's entrepreneurial spirit was fostered at a young age. He was born in Nigeria in a remote village called Ezeogba. Being the son of a resourceful farmer, he had to spend many hours not at school, but on the farm, just to have a meal on the table for that day. It was during this time that he discovered his natural gift for engineering. Onyekachi explains, "All my energy was channeled towards what I thought to be critical thinking. As a young child, all my time was spent figuring out how most appliances work and how to fix them when broken." During his free time, he would scavenge for broken and discarded electronic devices at the nearest dumpster just to play with them and try to fix or restore them back to their normal working condition.

While on course to graduate as a senior in Nigeria, Onyekachi left for the United States hoping to fulfill his career goals of becoming an engineer. While he spoke three languages, he did not speak or understand English when he arrived in the U.S. and enrolled in high school. The school put him in Advanced Placement (AP) classes, while he was also taking prerequisite classes needed for high school graduation and English Speakers of Other Languages (ESOL) courses. It was there that he was introduced to Project Lead the Way (PLTW) and Foundation of Technology (FOT) classes through chatting with a friend.

35.2 What Taxes Do Businesses Pay?

As many parents will tell you, having a child changes life in ways they never could have imagined. Parents must meet all of a child's many needs, every day, including some they didn't expect. For instance, did you know that even a one-year-old needs to see a dentist?

It's fitting then that entrepreneurs often feel like parents to their businesses, especially when it comes to taxes. Paying taxes is a daily reality. They must be included in every sale that is made and paycheck signed. There are many business taxes, some of which many people don't know about. For example, did you know that some limited liability corporations have to file a tax return even if they never open their doors for business?

There is another important similarity between parents and entrepreneurs: Just as parents are responsible for their children's actions in the eyes of the law, entrepreneurs are responsible for their business's taxes before the IRS. Trying to avoid paying taxes through illegal or deceptive means is called **tax evasion** and is a federal crime. It's punishable by fine, seizure of property, or even imprisonment.

Payroll Taxes

As you learned earlier, retirement and disability insurance is one of the biggest items in the federal government's budget. The government pays for these by using Payroll taxes, also referred to as FICA. **FICA** is the acronym for the Federal Insurance Contributions Act, the law that requires employers and employees to share the cost of the federal government's insurance and retirement program through deductions from wages and income.

Although both employers and workers contribute to the tax, the employer is responsible for calculating and sending the payments to the IRS. FICA tax is composed of two separate deductions: a larger one for Social Security and a smaller one for Medicare. They are figured as a percentage of the employee's wages or salary and withheld from each paycheck. The employer's own contribution equals the contribution of the employee.

Most states also require employers to deduct state income taxes from an employee's paycheck. This amount is sent to the state government.

Here's an example of how to calculate the FICA for an employee making $20,000 a year, with a Social Security amount of 6.2%, and a Medicare amount of 1.45%.

Employee's Gross Salary	$ 20,000
Social Security ($20,000 × .062)	– 1,240
Medicare ($20,000 × .0145)	– 290
Employee's Net Salary	$ 18,470

This example shows two important things:

- As an employee, your gross salary is always reduced by your Social Security and Medicare payments.

- As an employee, you paid $1,530 in taxes. Your employer will deduct this from your paycheck in each pay period and send it to the government. Your employer will also pay an *additional* $1,530 in taxes to the government to match the amount you paid.

Federal Unemployment Tax

Just as payments to Social Security are technically called FICA taxes, payments to fund unemployment insurance are called FUTA, for the Federal Unemployment Tax Act. As the name tells you, the FUTA tax aids workers who have lost a job. It is also a percentage of employee wages; however, unlike FICA taxes, the FUTA tax is paid solely by the employer. Also, it's paid only on the first few thousand dollars an employee earns each year.

The FUTA fund is run jointly by the federal and state governments. Depending on individual state law, employers may or may not be required to make payments to the state, as well. If they are, the tax is divided, with the state's portion applied as a credit toward the federal government's share. Payments are typically sent in quarterly.

Consumption Taxes

As a consumer, you're probably well aware that most of the goods and services you buy are taxed. Because these things are used, or consumed, such taxes are called consumption taxes.

Lawmakers decide which goods and services are taxed, and at what rate. Business owners who sell these items decide who pays the tax. They either absorb the entire amount themselves or pass some or all of it on to the customer.

The most common consumption tax is a <mark>sales tax</mark>. Some local and state governments require this, so entrepreneurs may need to calculate taxes for a variety of situations. For example, a state may impose a sales tax on merchandise, such as a frying pan. However, merchandise that is bought to be resold later may be tax-free. So, if a restaurant equipment wholesaler sells a shipment of frying pans to a department store, the wholesaler wouldn't be liable for sales tax—the department store would be. However, the store would probably not collect a sales tax if it sold the pans to a church for use in its soup kitchen, because sales to nonprofit organizations are usually tax-exempt.

Even figuring the tax on a single product can be complicated. In some states, food products are tax-free. However, a bakery owner might have to collect a tax on a birthday cake based on candles, decorations, and other inedible elements if they make up over half of the cake's retail value.

Figure 35-5 ▶
Sales Tax.
A baker may have to pay taxes on the decorations, but not on the cake.

Applying Concepts.
Why might food products be tax-free over any other product on the market?

Additionally, certain items are subject to excise taxes. An **excise tax** is a tax on a specific product or commercial activity. Federal, state, and local governments often impose excise taxes to control consumption or raise money for a project. A city may have a tax on restaurant sales to pay for a civic center, for instance. Excise taxes on large commercial trucks, diesel fuel, and truck tires help pay for highway maintenance. Taxes on alcohol help fund state programs to treat alcoholism.

Laws on taxing goods sold via the Internet are still evolving. Generally, these sales are exempt from sales tax. The main exception is **intrastate sales**—that is, sales made within the state where the company is physically located.

Goods that are traded internationally may be subject to tariffs. Some governments impose tariffs on imported goods to protect or strengthen a domestic industry by discouraging foreign competition. Exports may be taxed to encourage producers to satisfy the market at home rather than sell overseas. These taxes are sometimes controversial because they can restrict trade.

Business Income Tax

In many cases, income earned as a business owner is taxed in the same way as income earned as an employee. The business's income is the owner's personal income as well. This is true for sole proprietorships, partnerships, S corporations, and limited liability corporations (LLCs). For this reason, these types of businesses are called **pass-through businesses**.

The main difference, once again, is that the business owner is responsible for calculating and sending in these payments—not once a year, as an employee does, but throughout the year, even as they are earning income.

This is described as paying estimated taxes. Entrepreneurs predict what they will owe in income and payroll taxes and send in their payments each April, June, September, and January. Many business owners estimate conservatively, sending in the smallest amount necessary, to keep more money available for their business. They can also skip a payment if they believe they have no liability for that period. However, they need to be cautious or they may be penalized for underpaying. At year's end, they file a tax return, like any employee, to receive a refund or pay the balance of what they owe on their actual earnings.

For corporations other than S corporations and LLCs, taxation is more complex (and some believe less fair). C corporations are, in effect, taxed twice. First, a corporate income tax is assessed on the business's earnings. Then shareholders pay personal income tax on any corporate dividends received.

Property Tax

Entrepreneurs who own the land or building where their business operates are also subject to an annual commercial property tax. As with personal property, the tax rate for commercial property is set by the local government. Each government sets rates according to its own formula. In some areas, taxes are based on both the property's actual and potential value. Values rise in areas where homebuyers are building and the infrastructure is being improved, for example.

In addition, some states assess a tax on personal property used in business, including furniture, fixtures, supplies used for daily operations, and inventory held for sale.

Figure 35-6 ▶

Business's Contribution to the Budget.

Business taxes support various government functions at the local, state, and federal level.

Interpreting Graphs.

To what part of the federal budget do businesses contribute most? To what part of state and local budgets?

U.S. Federal Revenue

Individual Income Tax (45%) Social Security & Medicare Tax (34%) Corporate Income Tax (14.5%) Excise Tax (2.5%) Tariffs (1%) Other (3%)

State & Local Revenues

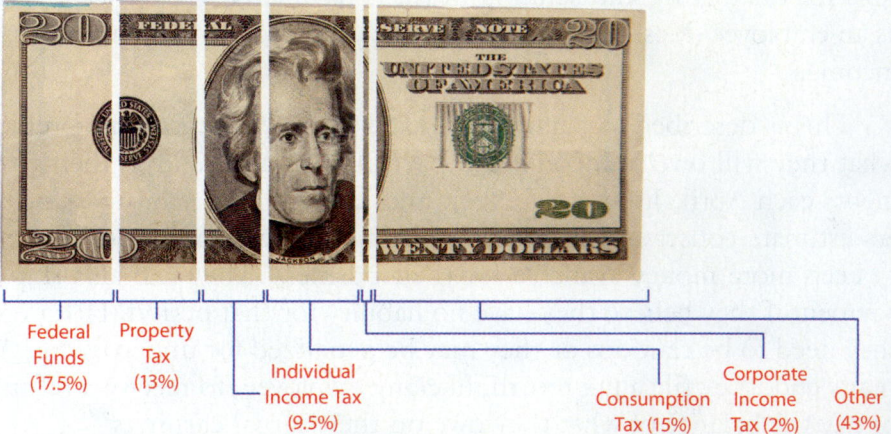

Federal Funds (17.5%) Property Tax (13%) Individual Income Tax (9.5%) Consumption Tax (15%) Corporate Income Tax (2%) Other (43%)

 **Apply Your Knowledge** How does the government use payroll taxes? Think back to your investigation. Why is it important for entrepreneurs to provide the appropriate amount in payroll taxes?

CAREER COMPETENCIES

 ## Read and Interpret a Pay Stub

When running a business, you will most likely eventually have an employee working for you. In order to make sure that you are compliant with taxes, it is a good idea to pay these employees with paychecks. To look at how taxes impact paychecks, let's look at the components of a paycheck.

Understanding Your Paycheck

A paycheck looks like a personal check you might write. Most paychecks include the following:

- Your employer's name and address in the upper-left corner
- A check number
- The date of the check
- Your name as the recipient, or payee
- The amount of the check written in numbers and spelled out
- The signature of a person authorized by your employer in the lower-right corner

Your paycheck is just a piece of paper until you deposit it or cash it. You must endorse—sign—the back of the check to make it valid. It's a good idea to sign it at the bank, because once you sign it, anyone can cash it or deposit it.

There are two types of endorsements.

- A blank endorsement is when you just sign your name. The check can then be cashed or deposited by anyone, for any purpose.
- A restrictive endorsement is when you sign your name and below it write how the check should be used. For example, you can write "For Deposit Only," if you want the check to be deposited, or you can write "Pay to the Order of Jack Smith" if you want the check to be used by Jack Smith.

If you lose your paycheck, you will have to follow your company's procedure for canceling it and issuing a new one.

Understanding Your Pay Stub

A pay stub is attached to the paycheck and provides a lot of information about the money you earned. It has no cash value, and you cannot exchange it for money at the bank. Most pay stubs have four sections.

- Personal information about the employee. This usually includes the check number and date, the starting and ending dates of the pay period, your name, and your employee number.

- Information about earnings. This usually includes the number of hours you worked, your hourly wage, and the amount you are being paid this pay period.
- Information about deductions. Employers withhold state and federal taxes, as well as FICA, which is social security. They may also withhold local taxes. The amount of these deductions is based on a percentage of how much you earn. You might have other deductions, such as contributions to a health care plan or to a savings account.
- Information summarizing earnings and withholdings. You usually get this information for the current pay period and the year-to-date (YTD), which is since January 1 of the current year. In this section, you can see your gross income, which is your pay before withholdings, and your net income, which is your pay after withholdings. Some people call net pay take home pay, because it is the amount you actually take home.

It is important to look closely at your pay stub to make sure the information is correct, particularly the number of hours worked. If there are any errors, you will have to follow your company's procedure for correcting them.

It's also important to note that even teenagers have to pay taxes. Age doesn't matter when it comes to paying taxes. If you receive a paycheck from a company, that company will withhold taxes and social security. If you make over a certain amount, you will even have to file an income tax form. Even money earned by running a business, or even babysitting or mowing lawns, is potentially taxable. This is considered self-employment income. If you earn more than $400.00 in self-employment income in a year, you are required to report it to the Internal Revenue Service (IRS).

Career Skills in Action

Now, use what you learned in this section to look at a sample paycheck and determine what percentage of pay is taken out for taxes. If you do not have a part-time job where you are paid with a paycheck, ask your teacher to provide you an example.

35.3 Tax-Saving Strategies

So far in this section, you've seen examples of how governments write tax laws to promote or discourage certain behaviors—by creating enterprise zones or taxing imports, for instance. When a government does this, it creates opportunities for **tax avoidance**, which amounts to using legal strategies to reduce one's tax liability. Unlike tax evasion, tax avoidance is taking advantage of what the law offers, and the law offers a lot to entrepreneurs who know where to look.

Taking Deductions

A **deduction** is an item or expense subtracted from your gross income in a tax return. Deductions reduce your taxes. Expenses that are considered "ordinary and necessary" for operating a business are typically tax-deductible. Utilities and rent, for example, are common business expenses. Others include:

- **Employees' Compensation.** You'll recall that compensation includes pay and benefits. Employers can deduct the wages and payments to retirement plans they offer employees.

- **Costs of Goods Sold.** A producer or wholesaler can deduct the cost of raw materials, labor, and storage of items sold.

- **Travel.** Reasonable deductions for transportation, meals, and lodging are all permitted.

- **Vehicle Use.** This includes the expense of maintenance, repairs, and mileage for business vehicles, and for personal vehicles when used for business purposes.

- **Taxes.** Business taxes, including consumption and property taxes, are themselves tax deductible.

- **Insurance.** Premiums for business insurance can be deducted. This includes, for example, policies that are associated with certain types of businesses, such as special insurance for employees who work in clients' homes.

- **Depreciation.** As you learned in Chapter 26, depreciation is a tax deduction that allows business owners to recover the cost of property used in the business. Any property that is used for over one year and loses value through wear or because it becomes outdated can be depreciated. A computer can be depreciated, for example, as can computer software.

◀ **Figure 35-7**

Vehicle Use As a Tax Deduction.

Business owners and staff can deduct vehicle-related expenses if used for the business.

Drawing Conclusions.

If using a personal vehicle for a business, why might it be a good idea to keep detailed records of all trips?

In addition, new entrepreneurs can deduct start-up expenditures for up to five years after opening the business. That includes money spent on market research and scouting locations. Also, sole proprietors who aren't covered by an employer's insurance plan can deduct 100% of the premiums of private insurance. If you use part of your home to carry out any or all of your business activities, you can deduct a percentage of utilities and certain home-maintenance expenses.

Entrepreneurs who understand how deductions work can time spending and receipts to their advantage. For example, suppose your business is having a very profitable year and you expect a large tax liability. You could lighten the load by increasing the number of deductions. You might buy a needed copier this year rather than next, or put more money in a retirement plan. You could also reduce income by asking customers who owe money late in the year to delay payments until January.

Using Tax Credits

A **tax credit** is a dollar-for-dollar reduction in taxes owed. While a deduction lowers taxable income, a credit lowers the tax itself. Tax credits can be taken for a variety of business activities, from using green energy sources, to donating goods to a charitable group, to hiring those who are reentering society after serving time in prison. A small business may take a credit for making the workplace accessible to disabled workers, as required by the Americans with Disabilities Act.

Figure 35-8 ▶

Mine Rescue Team Training Credit.

Staying current on tax credits that are useful only to a specific industry can pay off for an entrepreneur.

Solving Problems.

Some business activities are eligible for either a deduction or a credit. How would you go about making a decision about which to use?

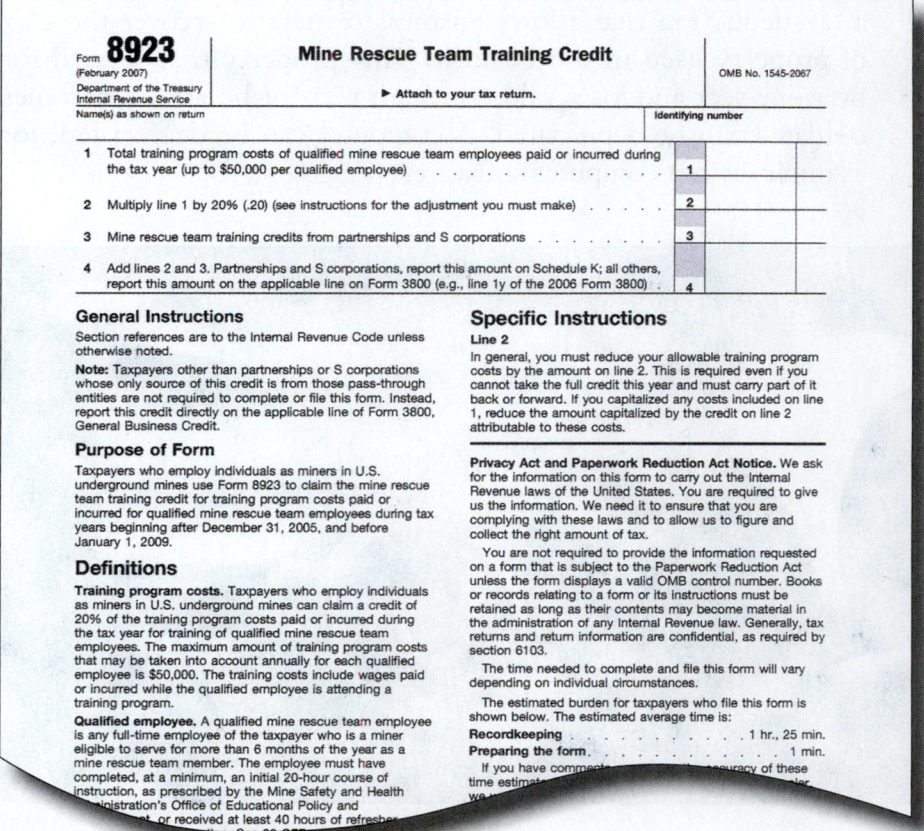

Tax credits tend to be less permanent than deductions. Standard deductions may remain the same from year to year. Credits are subject to phasing out, depending on how popular they are with taxpayers or how valuable they are to an industry.

Apply Your Knowledge What is a deduction? Think back to your investigation. Why is it better for entrepreneurs to seek out deductions and credits versus not paying taxes altogether?

 ## APPLICATION TO BUSINESS PLANNING

Plan for Filing Taxes

Use what you learned from this chapter on taxes to create a plan for filing your taxes that you will use as part of your implementation and growth plan. You should support your findings with data from research. Be sure to include:

- What taxes you will have to pay for your business
- Which deductions and credits your business qualify for
- An action plan to make sure you are able to get your taxes filed on time

CHAPTER 35 ASSESSMENT

REVIEWING OBJECTIVES

1. How does the government use tax money?
2. What are the purposes of business taxes?
3. How can businesses reduce their taxes?

CRITICAL THINKING

Many people believe that some services provided by government could be better handled by the private sector (for-profit businesses). Give arguments for and against this position, discussing specific agencies or departments.

ENTREPRENEURIAL THINKING EXERCISE: INITIATIVE & SELF-RELIANCE

Think back to your investigation of entrepreneurs paying taxes. How could you make sure that your business is compliant with paying taxes in full and on time? Put together an action plan with achievable steps that could help you follow the appropriate steps for determining and filing taxes on time.

EXTENSION ACTIVITIES

Entrepreneurship & Literacy Skills

Complete the following task to demonstrate your understanding of entrepreneurship:

1. **Grades 9–10:** Using examples from the chapter, explain how taxation can be used for political power. Find examples of politicians from local/national elections discussing their position on taxes. Use these examples to explain why a politician's position on increasing or decreasing taxes might affect his or her ability to gain votes.

2. **Grades 11–12:** Using examples from the chapter, explain how taxation can be used for political power. Find examples of politicians from local/national elections discussing their position on taxes. Use these examples to explain why a politician's position on increasing or decreasing taxes might affect how entrepreneurs would vote in elections.

UNIT 7 REVIEW & ASSESSMENT

Unit 7: Operating the Business

CHAPTER SUMMARY

31. Managing the Business

Business managers skillfully use and coordinate resources, such as money, facilities, equipment, technologies, materials, and employees, in a systematic manner to achieve particular goals. Managers have authority over their employees and are ultimately responsible for their work. Managers must be creative problem solvers to achieve business goals while minimizing costs. A good manager exercises the four management functions of planning, organizing, directing, and controlling and also works to build a positive company image and workplace climate.

32. Government Regulations

Governments regulate business to make the free market more open and fair and to protect workers, customers, and the environment. Business owners are legally bound to create a workplace that is free of physical hazards and discriminatory practices. They must give customers accurate information to make informed choices and safe products. They cannot use tactics that prevent free and fair competition or act in ways that threaten the environment.

33. Recordkeeping

Entrepreneurs must keep accurate financial records. The first step a new business owner should take is to go to a bank and open both a business checking account and a savings account. Every month you should reconcile the bank's checking account statement with your checkbook balance. The next step in setting up a business is to install a recordkeeping system using business documents such as receipts, invoices, and purchase orders. All accounting systems make use of double-entry accounting which means that every business transaction affects at least two accounts. There are two approaches to recording transactions: the single-column, database approach and the double-column approach. Both approaches use the concept of duality—all changes on one side of the accounting equation must equal all changes on the other side.

UNIT 7 REVIEW & ASSESSMENT

34. Accounting Systems

An accounting workbook relies on one main database. After each transaction is posted, an entrepreneur can determine the effect the transaction has on the financial statements. An accounting worksheet includes a balance sheet, an income statement, a statement of cash flows, and an inventory report. Using a computerized spreadsheet makes preparing an accounting worksheet simpler.

35. Taxes and Your Business

Businesses pays taxes for government services. These include public transportation and highways, social programs, national defense, and assistance for business itself. Business payroll taxes fund workers' insurance and retirement; unemployment taxes aid workers who have lost their jobs; sales taxes are collected on products and services sold and sent to state governments. Businesses pay income tax on their profits and property tax on buildings and inventory. Businesses can reduce their tax payments by taking deductions and using tax credits.

UNIT 7 VOCABULARY

accounting

accounting controls

adulterated

antitrust laws

auditor

authoritarian leadership style

bank reconciliation

chart of accounts

checking account

company image

controlling

deduction

delegating leadership style

democratic leadership style

directing

double-entry accounting

duality

embezzlement

enterprise zone

excise tax

Fair Labor Standards Act

Federal Deposit Insurance Corporation (FDIC)

FICA

financing activities

general journal

infrastructure

internal audit

interpersonal skills

intrastate sales

investing activities

license

line organization

line-and-staff organization

management

monopoly

Occupational Safety and Health Administration (OSHA)

operating activities

operational plan	project organization	subsidy
organizational structure	purchase order	T-account
organizing	quality control program	tactical plan
Pacioli check column	recall	tax avoidance
pass-through businesses	receipt	tax credit
payee	sales invoice	tax evasion
permit	sales tax	taxes
planning	savings account	tax-increment financing
posted	severance pay	team building
price discrimination	source document	transaction
price fixing	strategic plan	workplace climate

CHECK YOUR UNDERSTANDING

Choose the letter that best answers the question or completes the statement.

1. The most common reason that the ending balance on a bank's checking account statement doesn't match the balance you show in your checkbook is

   a. a bank math error

   b. banker fraud

   c. employee embezzlement

   d. outstanding checks

2. When you pay someone with a check, that person is the

   a. payer

   b. payee

   c. debtor

   d. depositor

3. A detailed written proof of a purchase is called a(n)

   a. receipt

   b. purchase order

   c. invoice

   d. purchase slip

4. An itemized list of goods delivered, or services rendered, and the amount due is called a(n)

a. receipt

b. invoice

c. purchase order

d. packing slip

5. An accounting term used to describe where all the transactions of a business are recorded is an accounting database or an accounting

a. ledger

b. journal

c. chart of accounts

d. entry book

6. The process of entering data into a database or journal is called

a. deducting

b. capitalizing

c. transferring

d. posting

7. The first step in creating a bookkeeping system for a business is to create a

a. general journal

b. general ledger

c. chart of accounts

d. transaction summary account

8. Checks and balances established by a business to provide employees with mandatory procedures are called

a. accounting controls

b. auditing controls

c. management controls

d. recording controls

9. Lawful tax deductions for entrepreneurs include

a. cost of goods sold

b. your personal car

c. your children's education expenses

d. a spouse's retirement fund

10. Taxes pay for

a. roads

b. the National Guard

c. unemployment insurance

d. all of the above

11. The goal of government regulation is to

a. control business development

b. balance the rights of different groups in society

c. favor certain industries over others

d. discourage competition by foreign companies

12. To avoid fines from the EPA, a business owner should

  a. pay required sales taxes

  b. rearrange work areas to accommodate workers with disabilities

  c. use green business practices when possible

  d. randomly check product labels for accuracy

13. FICA taxes are paid by

  a. sole proprietors

  b. corporations

  c. employees

  d. all of the above

14. Good interpersonal skills are most important to a manager who is

  a. planning a project

  b. directing employees

  c. controlling equipment

  d. improving cash flow

15. Which of the following is a planning activity?

  a. setting goals

  b. granting credit

  c. directing employees

  d. using interpersonal skills

16. Controlling is an ongoing process of

  a. using the authoritarian management style

  b. avoiding the democratic delegating style

  c. setting and measuring performance standards

  d. delegating to experienced employees

17. A positive workplace climate is associated with

  a. high pay for managers

  b. a poor company image

  c. happy employees

  d. credit bureaus

18. Setting performance standards is closely associated with which management function?

  a. planning

  b. directing

  c. organizing

  d. controlling

BUSINESS COMMUNICATION

1. You want to start a dog walking business. Using a piece of paper, prepare a simulated accounting worksheet for your first month of business, assuming you invest $500 in the business. The worksheet should include column titles you would need for your business.

2. Using Internet search engines, prepare a list of some potential accounting programs. Make a chart showing the advantages and disadvantages of each program. Rank each program based on its usefulness for a small business. Report your results to the class.

3. Partner with a classmate. You and your partner own a sporting goods store. You need an accounting system. One of you wants to use a manual system; the other, a computerized system. Each of you should prepare a list of the advantages of their choice and the disadvantages of the other choice. Then you will debate in front of the class.

4. Working with a partner, obtain a copy of an IRS tax form for business and the instructions for filling it out (available online at irs.gov). Examples are Form 1120S (U.S. Income Tax for an S Corporation) and Form 1040, Schedule F (Profit or Loss from Farming). In a brief report, explain the purpose of the form and any problems you would have if you were a business owner filling it out. Then write suggestions for making the form easier to use.

5. OSHA requires employers to eliminate recognized hazards, which it describes as "causing or likely to cause death or serious physical harm." Look around school. Do you find any hazards? List and rank these in order of dangerousness.

6. Read print ads or take notes while watching television advertising. Evaluate them on the three criteria set forth by the FTC. Are the ads truthful? Fair? Are the claims supported? Choose one written and one televised ad and write a critique of each.

7. Many leadership styles are used besides the three described in Chapter 31. Using the Internet or other source, study other leadership styles and describe five of them to the class, using examples of famous people to demonstrate each one.

UNIT 7 REVIEW & ASSESSMENT

BUSINESS MATH

1. The owner of a costume shop pays the supplier $5 for each mask purchased. In turn, the owner sells the masks for $15 each. In the month of October, the business had mask sales revenue of $2,250. What was the cost of goods sold (COGS) for October?

2. An accounting worksheet showed the beginning inventory for December as $30,000. During the month, the business made two additional purchases—one for $6,000 and the other for $5,000. The COGS for the month was $20,000. What is the value of the ending inventory?

3. The current FICA tax rate is 6.2% for Social Security and 1.45% for Medicare. If you employ one worker at an $18,000 annual salary, what amount is deducted from your employee's salary and sent to Social Security? To Medicare? How much will your company pay for each of these? What is the total amount you will be sending to the government?

4. In one state, the annual fee for a business license is $65 plus $1 for every $800 in gross receipts. Imagine you own an apiary (a honeybee colony). You earned $26,000 in honey sales last year. Sales of bee-themed merchandise brought in another $1,700. Beeswax candles added another $1,100. What were your gross receipts? What was your annual license fee?

BUSINESS ETHICS

1. You work at a hardware store. You have become friends with the accounting clerk. After a few months, she tells you that she wants to "alter" the accounting system to create a fictitious vendor to whom the hardware store owes money. She plans to write checks to this vendor, who is really her sister-in-law. She asks you to submit fake invoices to the hardware store in order for her to "pay" the bill. She promises you that you'll get 15% of what she "makes." What should you do?

2. You are a restaurant owner. The city council is considering increasing the excise tax on alcohol, with the added money going to a program to educate teens on the dangers of drinking. Alcohol sales account for a large portion of your income. Paying the tax will cut into your profits. You could raise your prices to help pay the new tax, but you're afraid this may hurt your business. You're torn! You strongly believe that teens must make educated choices about drinking. The local restaurant association asks you to speak against the proposal at the next city council meeting. What would you tell them, and what is your position on the proposal?

BUSINESS IN YOUR COMMUNITY

1. Working with three classmates, brainstorm how to start a business in your community that would provide accounting services to entrepreneurs. Investigate companies in your community that perform accounting services. What kinds of services do they perform and how do they charge for their services? What services would your company perform and how would you charge for your services? Write a description of your services and pricing policies, and share them with the class.

2. Interview two small-business owners in your community. Ask each of them what kind of accounting system they use in their business and why they chose to use that specific system. What do they feel are the advantages and disadvantages of the system? Write a short report with the results of your interviews.

3. Interview area business owners about the impact of local, state, and federal laws on their business decisions. For example, have property taxes or sales taxes affected their choice of location? Has complying with safety and ADA requirements influenced workplace design and daily routines? Have labeling and safety laws influenced their choices about what products and services they offer?

4. Ask a local business owner for a cost analysis of complying with one of the laws described in Chapter 32. For example, how much time does he or she spend calculating and sending in payroll taxes? What costs are involved in maintaining safety standards? What are the business's productivity costs of granting family and medical leave?

INFORMATION TECHNOLOGY

Web Hosts

Think of a traditional business renting a "brick-and-mortar" storefront. The business owner rents the space and pays a landlord every month. Web hosting works in a similar fashion. The owner of a website rents space online from a Web host. A traditional storefront needs floor space, shelves for merchandise, and a cash register. A website owner needs a place for Web graphics, such as pictures, video, and text. The website owner can upload (transfer) new graphics, text, or video to the Web host. Just as the owner has a key to the store, the website owner logs in to the Web host using a unique username and password so no one else can access the site.

Web hosts commonly provide tools that help someone set up a site. These tools typically include Web design tools, e-mail accounts, and domain name registration. For e-commerce sites—sites that are selling a product—Web hosts also typically include shopping cart technology.

Keeping Web Servers Online

Web hosts use Web servers to store information for every site using that Web host. In a sense, a Web server is the Web host's brain. If a Web server stops working, due to a malfunction or other problem, no one can access the site. To prevent this, the Web host typically uses several Web servers at the same time, all containing the same information and often placed in different locations. If there's a problem at one Web server location, another server will make sure the site is still up and running. The amount of time a website is online is called **uptime**. Web hosts generally promise that a website will be online 99.9% of the time.

Types of Web Hosts

There are many opportunities to set up a website by using a **free Web host**. Blogging software, such as Blogger, is free to use, as is setting up a page at Myspace.com. Most free Web hosts are limited in the types of websites you can create. For instance, MySpace allows you to create a MySpace page, which is different from creating a unique, independent website.

Shared Web hosting is the process of sharing server space with other websites. Compare this to a **dedicated server**, which gives a website its own server space. Very large, complicated sites may need a dedicated server. Most personal and small-business websites use shared Web hosting.

Web Hosting Costs

For a small website, renting space on a Web host can cost as little as $5.00 a month. However, it can cost the website owner more if the website gets a lot of visitors. For example, a Web hosting package may allow for 5,000 visitors a day (these are also called **Web hits**). If the site goes over 5000 hits, the website may go offline so that it can't be accessed unless you pay an additional fee. This is similar to a cell phone plan that has a limited number of minutes, after which you incur extra charges. If a website starts getting a lot of "traffic" (yet another word for visitors), the owner of the website will need to upgrade to a different plan—usually with the same Web host.

Tech Vocabulary

dedicated server

free Web host

shared Web hosting

uptime

Web hits

Check Yourself

1. How is a Web host similar to a landlord?

2. What is uptime and why is it important?

3. What are the three types of Web hosts?

4. What is one important factor influencing the cost of renting space on a Web host?

What Do You Think?

Solving Problems. What would happen if you had an e-commerce site on a Web server that stopped working?

CASE STUDY
Operating the Business

MANAGING FOR SUCCESS

After refining her business opportunity, business is booming at Eva's Edibles. Eva Tan and Sylvia Watson, came up with a long-range plan that involved leasing a commercial kitchen that had a small storefront. Watch as Eva's Edibles moves into its new space and continues to grow.

The Big Picture

In taking Eva's Edibles operational, Eva and Sylvia worked together to develop a strategic, or "big-picture," plan for the business. They made a list of their goals for the company over the next five years.

Both women pictured Eva's Edibles becoming a large commercial kitchen with a small storefront for retail. This would enable them to expand their offerings of packaged meals. Sylvia also wanted a place where she could showcase her cakes to the public. She wanted to sell cakes both whole and by the slice.

To help accomplish this, Eva and Sylvia divided the business responsibilities. Eva focused on hiring and directing employees, handling business promotions, and building a favorable company image.

Sylvia, a talented pastry chef, was responsible for the baking. Sylvia also had experience in purchasing and inventory management, so she handled those areas.

Eva and Sylvia developed a day-to-day operational plan for achieving their overall objectives. They also resolved to review their strategic progress every year.

"Let's make sure we are always happy with our direction," said Sylvia. "If we don't plan it, it won't happen!"

Location, Location, Location

The first step in achieving their goal was to locate a commercial kitchen with a small storefront. To encourage walk-in customers, Eva and Sylvia wanted an easily accessible location with parking. An area near both the Ohio State University and the downtown Columbus business center seemed best.

They discovered the perfect location. It was a two-story brick building with a storefront, a modern commercial kitchen, and a large walk-in refrigerator. The building was in an area zoned for commercial use. They wanted to lease the building and use the upstairs as an office.

Although they had been putting away money for the initial payments (first and last month's rent and security deposit), they needed more funding. Sylvia had some savings and she agreed to lend the company the necessary cash. Eva and Sylvia hired a lawyer to write an agreement that specified the repayment terms.

Moving into the building brought new management challenges. They changed the layout to maximize the kitchen's efficiency and created a small, cheery front retail space where walk-in customers could buy prepared meals and bakery items.

They posted their hours of operation: Monday through Saturday from 10 a.m. to 5 p.m., and Sunday from 12 p.m. to 4 p.m.

Eva's Edibles had found a place of its own.

Buying Smart

When Eva's Edibles began, purchasing was pretty easy. Eva bought what was needed to make each customer's meals for a week. She had no storage or inventory issues. Now that the company had grown, Eva and Sylvia wanted to start buying in volume to reduce costs.

Because she was responsible for inventory management, Sylvia had to consider the lead time required for certain foods. Groceries needed to arrive in time to fill orders but not too long before that. Spoilage was an issue with fresh ingredients. Sylvia couldn't afford to order too much at one time.

Storage space was also limited. So Sylvia adopted a just-in-time inventory system for fresh items and a periodic inventory system for dry ingredients that had a long shelf life.

Controlling costs was also important. Eva suggested they could save money by doing their own cutting and trimming of meat, poultry, and fish instead of paying a higher price for items that were already prepped. "We have this huge walk-in refrigerator," Eva said. "Let's use it."

Sylvia began buying whole poultry, fish, and large cuts of meat. Frank, the cook they hired to help them, learned how to butcher. Eva's Edibles reduced its costs and increased its profits.

Things were definitely going well.

Keeping the Government Happy

Eva and Sylvia hired an accountant with business expertise to review their financial records regularly and make sure their taxes were paid on time. They wanted to take advantage of all the tax deductions for which their business was eligible. Eva wanted to buy a hybrid van for the business, not just because it was "greener" but also because she heard they could get a special tax credit.

What Would You Have Done?

1. **Predicting.** Imagine you were Eva or Sylvia beginning to take Eva's Edibles operational. What would be your goals for the company?

2. **Relating Concepts.** What other production, distribution, or operation issues might Eva or Sylvia have needed to address after moving to their new location and selling prepared foods and bakery items to walk-in customers?

3. **Solving Problems.** During a holiday season, Eva's Edibles ran out of a key ingredient used to make its specialty cakes. What would you have done to solve this problem and prevent it from happening again?

BIG IDEA: GROWING THE BUSINESS

PLANNING FOR BUSINESS GROWTH

GUIDING QUESTION:

"How can I be prepared for the challenges in growing my business?"

APPLICATION TO BUSINESS PLANNING:

☑ Growth Plan

OBJECTIVES

- Investigate business growth strategies.
- Explore product life cycles.
- Study the practical challenges of growing a business.

NFTE Entrepreneurial Mindset Characteristic Focus

☑ Creativity & Innovation

National Entrepreneurship Standards

- **A.33** Create processes for ongoing opportunity recognition
- **A.34** Adapt to changes in business environment
- **A.35** Explain the need for continuation planning
- **M.02** Determine equipment needs
- **M.04** Establish operating procedures
- **O.04** Develop company goals/objectives

Common Career Technical Core Standards

- **BM.3** Explore, develop and apply strategies for ensuring a successful business career.
- **BM-MGT.7** Plan, organize and manage an organization/ department to achieve business goals.
- **BM-MGT.8** Create strategic plans used to manage business growth, profit and goals.
- **CRP.3** Attend to personal health and financial well-being.

National Entrepreneurship Standards: Career Competencies

☑ **G.07** Describe costs associated with credit

LESSON VOCABULARY

- core business
- debt capital
- diversification growth strategy
- equity capital
- horizontal diversification
- horizontal integration strategy
- integrative growth strategy
- intensive growth strategy
- market development
- market penetration
- market share
- micromanager
- organic growth
- perpetual life cycle
- product development
- product life cycle
- self-financing
- synergistic diversification
- vertical integration strategy

36.1 What Is Business Growth?

In the previous unit, you looked at some considerations that entrepreneurs should make when operationalizing their business. In this unit, you will look at how to accomplish the goal of growing your business from its initial operations.

To grow a business means to make changes that result in greater sales. A business grows, or expands, in two ways: internally and externally. Internal growth is achieved when a business expands by adding new products or services for sale—which is often called **organic growth**. External growth is achieved by buying other businesses or merging with them. Most small businesses experience organic growth rather than acquiring other companies.

When a business thrives, the owner must eventually decide whether to maintain the original strategy or take a bold step to grow the business. Because entrepreneurs are ambitious by nature, the question is often not whether to grow, but when and how to grow.

Growth, like any business move, must be carefully thought out. A smart entrepreneur develops a carefully researched business plan before launching a business. Business growth also requires a great deal of planning. The original business plan should be updated or an entirely new one developed. In either case, the plan should outline steps for implementing the growth strategy and look at the possible consequences for the business.

Deciding When to Grow

Three factors affect the decision to grow a business:

- **Condition of the Business.** A business is ready to grow when it has a solid base of customers and makes sales that meet or exceed forecasts and contribute to a satisfactory net profit. The business has become good at what it does. It makes a consistent profit and achieves quality standards and customer satisfaction targets. The owner does not struggle to keep up with the day-to-day demands of the business but has enough time to devote to growth.

- **Economic Climate.** The economic climate in which the business operates is also important. Owners planning for growth must consider economic conditions at the local, national, and perhaps even global levels. Economies tend to follow cycles of upturns and downturns. A downturn is not necessarily a bad time to expand a business. It depends on the business and its markets.

- **Life Goals of the Business Owner.** Growing a business is not only an economic move, it's a personal one as well. An owner who decides to grow a business takes on new pressures and demands. Growth will require more time and money and introduce new risks. Owners who want to grow their businesses should schedule growth with their life goals in mind.

◀ **Figure 36-1**
Life Goals.

The decision to grow a business also depends on the life goals of the business owner.

Predicting.

How would various life goals, such as marriage, children, or relocation, affect the decision to grow a business?

Product Life Cycles

A **product life cycle** is a series of stages—introduction, growth, maturity, and decline—that a product may pass through while it is on the market. This concept can be applied to a product type or industry (for example, automobiles), to a specific brand (for example, Ford), and to a particular product (for example, the Ford Explorer).

Product Life Cycle Stages

Each stage in a product life cycle has specific cost and profit considerations. A conventional product life cycle curve is shown in Figure 36-2.

- **Introduction.** When a product is introduced, the marketing effort is devoted to building product awareness—that is, making consumers aware of the product. This is typically an expensive phase with high advertising and promotional expenses. Profits may be low at first.

- **Growth.** Sales and profit increase steadily as the product is embraced by consumers. Competitors may be few at this stage, allowing the business to expand distribution and take advantage of strong demand.

- **Maturity.** This is the stage during which sales and profits stop growing. They level off and may begin to decline. By now, the product probably faces stiff competition. The business may have to lower prices or enhance the product in some way to give it a new competitive advantage and extend its life.

- **Decline.** During the decline stage, product sales and profits fall steeply and don't recover. The product loses its appeal to consumers. In some cases, the decline is due to technological advances or governmental regulations. For example, the VCR has given way to the digital video recorder.

Figure 36-2 ▶

Product Life Cycle Curve.
A product life cycle typically includes various sales stages.

Interpreting Graphs.
During what stage do sales reach their peak?

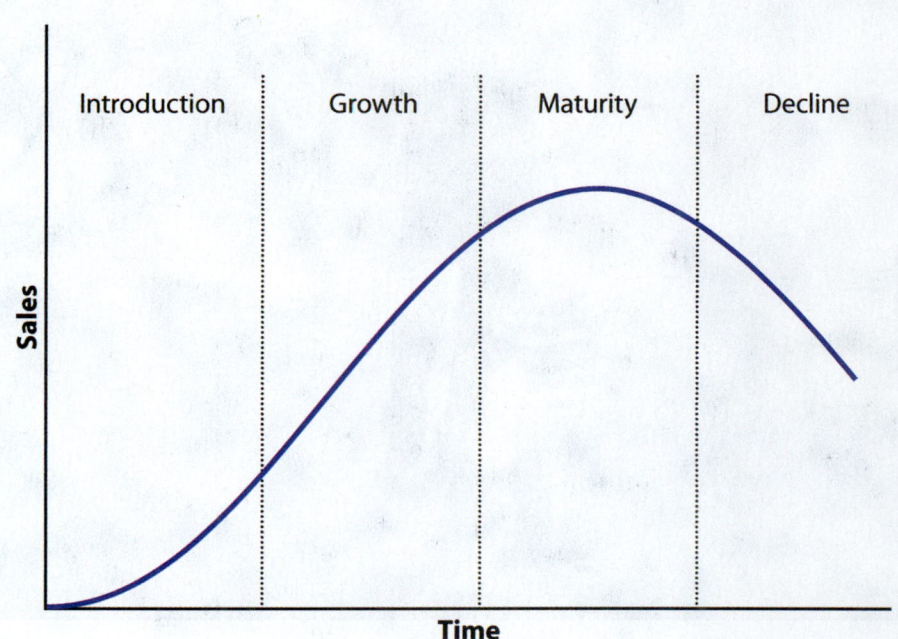

Product life cycle curves have many variations. Some products are immensely and immediately popular. Their sales rocket upward but then decline quickly. This cycle is common in the fashion and entertainment industries.

Other products endure for long periods. A **perpetual life cycle** is a product life cycle in which a product never undergoes a final decline, because it remains in the maturity stage forever. Basic food products, such as bread and other items in everyday use, are said to have a perpetual life cycle. However, individual brands and products within the bread industry can certainly decline.

Product Life Cycle in Growth Planning

The product life cycle is a useful concept for planning growth strategy. One way for a business to grow is to provide a product (or service) that it has not offered before. This product will be new to the business but may not be new to the market. It could be similar to other products already being offered. If you want to add a new product to your company's offerings, you must understand the product group's stage in the product life cycle. This knowledge will help you determine the level of competition you will face and the costs and marketing strategies that will be required to make the new offering successful.

The product may be completely new and different, with no competition. This is an introductory stage offering. The product may be similar to others that are in a growth phase. In this case, the new offering probably needs to be innovative to set itself apart from competitors. A business may decide to introduce a copycat product when the overall life cycle for that product group is in the maturity stage. At this point, price or product enhancements may be the competitive advantage. Introducing a product that is part of an existing product group in the decline stage typically wouldn't be a wise business move. However, the decline stage is an excellent time to introduce a replacement product for the one that is in decline.

◀ **Figure 36-3**
Product Life Cycles.

A business must understand a product group's stage in the product life cycle.

Drawing Conclusions.

A company is considering offering a DVD player that is new to the company. Would this be a wise move in relation to the product group's stage in the product life cycle?

Businesses also have to consider the costs and risks of introducing a new product that competes against their existing products. For example, a business with an existing product in the maturity stage may find it difficult and expensive to lure customers away from that product to a new, but similar, offering.

 Apply Your Knowledge What are the four stages of a typical product life cycle? From your investigation of Groupon, what would the curve of their product life cycle look like?

ENTREPRENEURIAL CASE STUDY: CREATIVITY & INNOVATION

 ### Abi Mandelbaum— YouVisit

Identifying the Problem

Abi Mandelbaum is the co-founder and CEO of YouVisit (www.YouVisit.com). YouVisit is a technology company that develops first-of-a-kind, life-like virtual guided walking tours complete with rich media, video content, and 360-degree panoramic views. YouVisit creates virtual tours for companies and institutions in varied industries. Under Abi's leadership, YouVisit has become the world's most robust virtual tour platform. As such, leading organizations throughout the globe, from the world's best universities to Fortune 500 companies, work with YouVisit to create interactive experiences that captivate and engage online visitors.

Abi Mandelbaum.

Originally from Colombia, Abi came up with the idea for YouVisit with two of his college roommates, Taher Baderkhan from Jordan, and Endri Tolka from Albania. They met while attending Brandeis University in Massachusetts, and while discussing how difficult and frustrating it had been to research colleges from afar, they came up with the initial idea for a business that made the college matching process easier for both students and colleges.

Building and Revisiting the Model

Recognizing how difficult it is for students to get a better feel for what it is like to live and study at different colleges and universities, they decided to create a virtual walking tour platform that would allow students and parents to explore college campuses as if they were physically there. To see if they their idea would be feasible, they worked on developing a prototype of their technology to showcase to other people. While also working full-time jobs, they worked long nights and got together during the weekends to build the walking tour platform from the ground up, utilizing the computer science skills they had learned in college. When they finally got to show their prototype to colleges and universities throughout the country, the reaction and feedback was overwhelmingly positive. After realizing this was an unmet need for not only international students, but also for out-of-state students, they established YouVisit in 2009.

YouVisit makes the virtual walking tours available for students and parents on YouVisit.com as well as on the college's website. They also scaled their initial model to include tours on Facebook, mobile devices, and virtual reality platforms such as Oculus and Google VR, creating the world's most robust virtual tour ecosystem. YouVisit has had great success. The company has created thousands of virtual tours in the real estate, healthcare, and travel sectors, as well as for colleges, hotels, restaurants, and factories across five continents, making it the global leader in virtual tours.

Inspiring Young Entrepreneurs

Seeing how entrepreneurship has changed his life, Abi is a fervent advocate for youth entrepreneurship and serves as a mentor for the Network for Teaching Entrepreneurship (NFTE). He has a great deal of advice for young entrepreneurs working on innovative ideas. "Too many potential entrepreneurs worry too much about others stealing their ideas, but what they don't realize is that it's all in the execution, and great execution isn't easy. Talk to as many people as you can about your ideas. They will help you improve them and put you in touch with other people who may be able to help and steer you in the right direction."

Thinking and Acting Like an Entrepreneur

- Why was it important that Abi and his team test their assumptions about their idea?
- What do you think YouVisit had to consider when growing into new markets/industries?
- In what ways does Abi demonstrate the entrepreneurial mindset behavior of creativity and innovation?

36.2 Growth Strategies

Businesses can follow many growth strategies when they wish to expand. These strategies typically focus on new products and/or new markets. (In this discussion, services are referred to as the products of a service business.) Three broad categories of growth strategies are:

- Intensive growth strategies
- Integrative growth strategies
- Diversification growth strategies

Intensive Growth Strategies

An **intensive growth strategy** is a growth strategy that focuses on cultivating new products or new markets, and sometimes both. Businesses use an intensive growth strategy when they believe they haven't fully realized their strengths or their markets. This strategy is best described as "doing more of what you are good at doing." The three most common types of intensive growth strategies are:

- Market penetration
- Market development
- Product development

Market penetration is an intensive growth strategy that emphasizes more intensive marketing of existing products. This strategy has two goals: sell more to existing customers and sell to new customers in existing markets. Both goals require extensive, and expensive, marketing (advertising, promotions, and so on). However, market penetration is a way for a business to increase its profits by taking advantage of its existing skills, experience, and knowledge about its target markets. It is a popular growth strategy for small businesses.

Figure 36-4 ▶

Market Penetration.

A company that sells a cleaning product at a store might send a salesperson to offer coupons and samples at the store as part of a market penetration strategy.

Applying Concepts.

How can companies encourage customers to try their product through market penetration strategies? How can you tell if a market penetration strategy is effective or not?

Existing customers may be convinced to buy more of a product if the business advertises new uses for that product. The makers of dry soup mixes could, for example, publish recipes for party dips made from their products. Businesses can also try to convince existing customers to buy a product more often. Toothbrush manufacturers advertise that dentists recommend replacing a toothbrush every three months. Existing customers may also buy more and buy more often if they are offered incentives, such as frequent-buyer programs.

◀ **Figure 36-5**
Product Development.
A product development strategy enhances existing products.

Drawing Conclusions.
What is the benefit of developing an enhanced version of an existing product to increase sales?

Market penetration can also involve pursuing new customers in current target markets. Basically, the business uses marketing tactics to try to gain customers from its competitors. **Market development** is an intensive growth strategy that focuses on reaching new target markets, such as customers in another geographic area or customers who have different demographics from current customers. A retail store might open a branch in a new city or develop a website to sell its products online.

Product development is the process of creating and bringing a new product to market. Enhancements may include bonus features or new packaging for products. For example, they could add small toys to cereal boxes. Product development is typically costly for a business but can be a successful means of growth if the new or enhanced offering is popular with customers.

A business can evaluate the effectiveness of these intensive growth strategies by looking at **market share**, which is the percentage of the total sales captured by a product or a business in a particular market. In other words:

$$\frac{\text{Sales by Business}}{\text{Total Sales in Market}} \times 100 = \text{Market Share Percentage}$$

If a company sells $1,000 worth of tennis rackets in a town where total sales of tennis rackets are $5,000, the company has a one-fifth, or 20%, market share.

$$\frac{\$ 1,000}{\$ 5,000} \times 100 = 20\%$$

Through successful market penetration, sales by your business would increase as a percentage of the total market. Through successful market development, you would create a bigger market for your business to target. Through product development, you increase both sales and target market.

Integrative Growth Strategies

An **integrative growth strategy** is a growth strategy that emphasizes blending businesses together through acquisitions and mergers. Integrative growth strategies are typically more expensive than intensive growth strategies and are usually practiced by mature businesses with large amounts of capital. There are two types of integrative growth strategies:

- **Vertical Integration.** An integrative growth strategy in which one business acquires another business in its own supply chain, *but not at the same supply chain level*, is a **vertical integration strategy**. An example of this type of growth strategy is when a retail store buys a wholesaler. Another example is when a manufacturing business buys a retail store in which its products are sold.

- **Horizontal Integration.** An integrative growth strategy in which one business acquires another business *at the same supply chain level as itself* is a **horizontal integration strategy**. When one manufacturing company buys another manufacturing company, that's a horizontal integration strategy. The acquired business may be a competitor or a business in a completely different industry. For example, if the dry soup business purchased the toothbrush company described previously, that would be considered a horizontal integration strategy. The businesses do not have to even be in the same industry, but both earn the parent company business at a retail store.

Diversification Growth Strategies

Every business has a **core business**, which is the most important focus of the business. For example, the core business of McDonald's is selling fast food. A **diversification growth strategy** (die-ver-sih-fih-KAY-shun) is a growth strategy in which a business grows by offering products or services that are different from its core business. There are two types of diversification growth strategies:

- **Synergistic Diversification.** A growth strategy in which a business adds new products or services that are related to its existing products or services is a **synergistic diversification** (sin-er-JIS-tic). A clothing store that begins selling shoes practices this type of growth. So does an event-planning business that begins to offer catering services.

- **Horizontal Diversification.** A growth strategy in which a business adds new products or services that are not related to its existing products or services but appeal to its existing target market is called **horizontal diversification**. Recently some large grocery stores have begun offering credit cards to their customers. This is an example of horizontal diversification. Another example would be a gasoline station that sells food.

 **Apply Your Knowledge**   Name three broad categories of growth strategies. From your investigation, which growth strategy do you think Groupon followed?

◄ **Figure 36-6**

Horizontal Diversification.

A grocery store that offers credit cards to its customers is practicing horizontal diversification.

Recognizing Patterns.

Can you name other types of products or services that a grocery would offer that would be examples of horizontal diversification?

CAREER COMPETENCIES

 ## Describe Costs Associated with Credit

When to Use a Credit Card

A credit card lets you use credit—a loan—to buy now and pay later. Every time you use a credit card, you are borrowing money from the business that issued the card, such as the bank, store, or credit card company. The business pays for the purchase, and then you repay the business by paying your credit card bill.

Credit cards may be convenient because you do not have to have enough money to pay at the time you make the purchase. You can also make a lot of purchases, and then pay them all at once with a single check or electronic fund transfer by paying your credit card bill. This is especially appealing for entrepreneurs who need to buy more equipment and materials to grow their operations. However, if you don't pay your credit card bill in full each month, you will be charged interest on the balance. You can end up spending a lot more than the original purchase price.

Dos and Don'ts of Credit Card Use

While credit cards can be convenient, they can also be dangerous. Think about how you will use a credit card once you get one.

DOS

- Choose credit cards with the lowest interest rates.
- Choose credit cards with no annual or hidden fees.
- Pay the balance off in full each month.
- Only make purchases that you know you will be able to pay for in the very near future.

DON'TS

- Pay only the minimum amount each month.
- Charge much more than you can reasonably expect to pay off.
- Pay your credit card bill late.
- Apply for a new credit card when the first has reached its spending limit.

Using an Installment Plan

If credit cards can be risky, then how do entrepreneurs and everyday people get big items that they need in an emergency that they might not have the full amount for at that time? Another payment option—especially for items that you can't afford to pay for up front—is installment buying. With this method of payment, you buy something, such as a car or a piece of furniture, on credit, with a series of future payments to be made at specified intervals. Of course with such a payment plan, you don't actually own the thing you purchased until your last payment is made, and if you fail to make your payments, the seller can take that car or couch back. While most often used with automobiles and major appliances, many stores offer layaway programs that also allow you to pay for items over time.

Career Skills in Action

Now, you apply what you learned about credit card usage to scaling the operations of your business. Do some research to find out the average interest rate of a credit card and do the following:

- Identify the cost of a large item you might need to scale your operations (for example, a computer, a van, etc.)
- Figure out the length of time and payment amounts of installment buying over 3 years.
- Determine how much the item would cost with interest if it was put on credit and paid off over 3 years. Use the interest rate on the credit card you researched.

36.3 Challenges of Growth

Entrepreneurs excel at identifying business opportunities and finding resources to transform innovative ideas into reality. This is ideal for starting a business but may not be as useful when it comes to growing the business.

Business growth often requires the owner to give up some personal control over the business. This may be difficult for someone who has been the driving force and creative center of the business and largely responsible for its success. A **micromanager** is an individual who interferes too much in the decisions and tasks of associates or employees. He or she constantly scrutinizes and criticizes everything they do, or automatically dismisses their ideas and opinions as inferior. A micromanager does not trust others to get things done or to do them right. A business owner prone to micromanagement, or reluctant to delegate responsibilities, may become overwhelmed by the added demands of business growth. Entrepreneurs must truthfully examine their personal feelings about giving up some control for the chance to grow the business.

Also, business growth increases risk. The growth effort may fail; it may even put the overall business in jeopardy. Entrepreneurs who are considering growth should carefully examine the risks involved and weigh them against their personal capacity for taking on that risk.

Obviously there are personal challenges and potential negative consequences associated with business growth. However, growth that is successful can be rewarding to a business owner. It will probably bring greater personal income and financial stability and a sense of accomplishment. Business owners must ultimately make the decision about whether to grow or not, based on their life goals.

◀ **Figure 36-7**
Successful Growth.

Successful growth can be rewarding to a business owner.

Inferring.

People say that the greater the risk, the greater the reward. How would you relate that to growth that was very rewarding?

Practical Challenges of Growing a Business

Growing a business involves six practical challenges. Each should be addressed in the revised business plan you will develop.

- **Space.** A growing business usually requires more physical space. If the existing building or rooms are not large enough to handle the expansion, you will have to find additional space.

- **Business Structure.** You may need to change the organizational structure of your business—for example, from a sole proprietorship to a limited liability company or corporation.

- **Materials and Equipment.** Growth may require you to purchase more materials, equipment, and office furniture and supplies. A manufacturing business that wants to grow must be sure the supply chain will be able to accommodate the new demands.

- **Information Technology (IT).** This is the use of computer systems, hardware, and software to store and manage information. IT demands for accounting, purchasing, inventory, payroll and other operations will increase as the business grows and expands its recordkeeping.

- **People and Skills.** A growing business almost always needs more employees, especially at the management level. Existing staff may have to be trained in new skills that will be necessary to make the growth effort successful.

- **Money.** Business growth requires financing. This money may come from the company itself or from outside sources.

Self-financing means obtaining the funds for growth from existing operations, for example, by reinvesting cash reserves (profits). External sources of money include **debt capital**, which is money obtained by a business through a loan, and **equity capital**, which is money obtained by a business from an investor in exchange for a share of ownership (equity) in the business. Whatever the source, you must carefully consider the financial risks and obligations as part of your growth strategy. To review the various types of financing available, return to Chapter 29 and the discussion of financing a startup.

Can a Business Grow?

The success of business growth will be more certain if you follow a strategic plan. It is also important to know as much as possible about your business: what works well, what could be improved, what drives profitability, and so forth. An effective tool for accomplishing this task is a SWOT analysis.

The SWOT analysis introduced in Chapter 8 was used for evaluating the prospects of starting a business. A SWOT analysis assesses strengths, weaknesses, opportunities, and threats for a startup. However, a SWOT

▲ **Figure 36-8
Materials and Equipment.**

Growth often requires purchasing more office furniture and supplies.

Applying Concepts.

Why would it be a good idea to calculate the cost of supplies you will need to provide a new hire, alongside their salary?

analysis is also useful for established businesses when analyzing growth opportunities. An established business that keeps good records should be well aware of its strengths and weaknesses. Customer surveys can also provide valuable feedback. The threat component of the SWOT analysis is, in large part, the competition. Business owners need to learn as much as possible about the strengths and weaknesses of potential competitors and the market share their actual competitors have. It's also important to be aware of any new or potential regulations that may impact growth.

When you know your business's capabilities, limitations, and threats, you can better select an appropriate growth opportunity. Many small businesses choose to grow by opening a new location that offers the same products or services as their original location. But the factors that made one location successful may not work in another location. A business owner with multiple locations must also be careful that the original customers are not ignored during the growth process. Another possible choice is to expand the product offerings in the existing location. No matter what strategy a business owner selects, a completely new business plan should be prepared to assess all aspects of the situation.

Apply Your Knowledge   How is a SWOT analysis used to analyze a growth opportunity? Think back to your investigation. How could Groupon have used a SWOT analysis to find its growth challenges before the rapid growth started?

◀ **Figure 36-9**
Multiple Locations.
The factors that made one location a success may not exist in a new location.

Comparing/Contrasting.
What kinds of factors might exist in one location but not in a second location?

✓ APPLICATION TO BUSINESS PLANNING

Growth Plan

Use what you learned from this chapter to create growth strategies as part of your implementation and growth plan. You should support your findings with data from research. Be sure to include:

- Any product life cycle to consider for your business
- Growth strategies that are appropriate for your business
- Foreseeable challenges with growth and an action plan to overcome them

36 ASSESSMENT

REVIEWING OBJECTIVES

1. What are strategies for business growth?

2. Describe a product life cycle.

3. What are some of the practical challenges of growing a business?

CRITICAL THINKING

1. How can intensive growth strategies, such as market penetration, market development, and product development, contribute to the success of a business's marketing program?

2. Classify each of the following plans as a type of growth strategy: (a) a retail shoe store that wants to buy the manufacturing plant that makes its shoes; (b) a bookstore that wants to sell packs of flavored coffee; (c) a landscaping business that plans to advertise in another part of the state.

ENTREPRENEURIAL THINKING EXERCISE: CREATIVITY & INNOVATION

Think back to your investigation of Groupon. Imagine that you have been hired by the company to introduce a new service that would bring growth back to Groupon. What approaches would you take to determine options? Be specific in how you would help the company create a new growth plan.

36 ASSESSMENT

EXTENSION ACTIVITIES

Entrepreneurship & Literacy Skills

Complete the following task to demonstrate your understanding of entrepreneurship:

1. Grades 9–10: Working with three classmates, develop a poster showing the four stages in a product life cycle, with two products, product groups, and brands or industries that fall into each one. Each member of the group should write a paragraph as part of the presentation for each stage of the product cycle.

2. Grades 11–12: Working with three classmates, develop a poster showing the four stages in a product life cycle, with two products, product groups, and brands or industries that fall into each one. Each member of the group should write a paragraph as part of the presentation for each stage of the product cycle. Be sure to use supporting details from the chapter to explain how entrepreneurs can use this information to help with planning for growth.

37 GROWING OPERATIONS

OBJECTIVES

- Learn about the site selection and layout planning.
- Examine the tasks and tools of production management.
- Explore factors in purchasing management.

NFTE Entrepreneurial Mindset Characteristic Focus

☑ Initiative & Self-Reliance

National Entrepreneurship Standards

- **A.09** Describe entrepreneurial planning considerations
- **A.27** Explain the need for business systems and procedures
- **C.06** Describe crucial elements of a quality culture/ continuous quality improvement
- **C.07** Describe the role of management in the achievement of quality
- **C.13** Explain the concept of management
- **F.02** Explain the factors of production
- **F.09** Explain the concept of productivity
- **M.01** Plan business layout
- **M.02** Determine equipment needs
- **M.06** Analyze business processes and procedures
- **M.07** Implement quality improvement techniques
- **M.10** Select business location
- **M.13** Explain the buying process
- **M.14** Describe the nature of buyer reputation and vendor relationships
- **M.15** Establish company buying/purchasing policies
- **M.16** Conduct vendor search
- **M.17** Choose vendors
- **M.19** Place orders
- **M.23** Organize shipping/receiving

LESSON VOCABULARY

- automation
- cash discount
- demand forecasting
- division of labor
- e-procurement
- Gantt chart
- green procurement
- law of diminishing returns
- layout
- lead time
- maintenance
- milestone
- nonperiodic reordering
- packing slip
- periodic reordering
- PERT chart
- product specification
- production management
- productivity
- purchase order
- quality circle
- sales forecasting
- value analysis
- zoning laws

Common Career Technical Core Standards

- **CRP.11** Use technology to enhance productivity.
- **CRP.12** Work productively in teams while using cultural/global competence.
- **BM-OP.3** Apply inventory tracking systems to facilitate operational controls.
- **BM-OP.4** Plan, monitor and manage day-to-day business activities to maintain and improve operational functions.

National Entrepreneurship Standards: Career Competencies

 D.07 Handle telephone calls in a businesslike manner

ENTREPRENEURIAL INVESTIGATION
Whole Lot of Ice Cream

Cold Stone Creamery is one of the largest and best-known sellers of ice cream in the U.S. Under its former CEO, Doug Ducey, the business grew from 74 locations to over 1,440 locations. He achieved that amazing growth by changing the business model to allow franchisees to buy into the company.

However, in 2014, it was reported that a larger percentage of Cold Stone Creamery franchisees went out of business. In a *Wall Street Journal* article, these business owners claimed that the Cold Stone Creamery business model made it hard to make money. The cost of the goods to run the business made them charge high prices. While the parent company achieved its growth goals, some of the franchise owners were not profitable. But, as a whole, the business is still growing and generating a profit.

Do some research on Cold Stone Creamery to answer the following question:

- What are your thoughts on Cold Stone Creamery's growth strategy?
- Is it more important to have as many locations as possible, or should growth be limited so that every owner has a chance to make their business succeed?

Be prepared to share your thoughts with peers or your teacher.

37.1 Managing and Scaling Operations

In the previous chapter, you looked at putting together a plan to grow your business. An important part of your growth plan should be about how you can scale operations. For example, it does not matter how many people want to buy your product if you do not have the processes in place to produce enough for the demand. As you read through the operational considerations in this chapter, try to think how you could structure the operations of your business to create more product or deliver to more people if needed.

Site Selection and Layout Planning

One of the first actions entrepreneurs must take is to choose a site (location) for the business. Then, once the site is chosen, they must decide how to use the space.

Site Selection

The choice of location depends partly on the type of business. Retail and service businesses that expect walk-in customers need locations that are easily accessible and have adequate parking. A manufacturing firm that uses machinery or other kinds of equipment will likely require a large space. The same is true for wholesaling businesses that carry extensive product inventories.

Some entrepreneurs choose to operate their small businesses from their homes. This choice has some advantages. It is convenient and saves the expense of buying or renting another location and commuting. In addition, certain expenses associated with operating a home business can be deducted from personal income tax. However, some entrepreneurs prefer to locate their businesses away from home so they can keep their home and business lives separate.

Most cities and communities have **zoning laws**. These are local laws that specify the types of development and activities—residential, commercial, industrial, or recreational—that can take place on a particular property. Some zoning laws forbid businesses in residential areas. If home businesses are allowed, there may be restrictions on the types of businesses that can be operated, the number of employees, the use of streets for customer parking, and the hours a business can be open to the public. A business that cannot be located at home needs a space in an area that is appropriately zoned. As mentioned earlier, this introduces additional expenses, such as rent, utilities, and commuting.

Figure 37-1 ▶

Zoning Laws.

Some zoning laws forbid businesses, even home businesses, in residential areas.

Drawing Conclusions.

Why might some communities restrict home businesses in residential areas? How would you feel if you had a home business?

Layout Planning

A **layout** is a physical arrangement of objects and spaces. Layout considerations differ by type of business. A manufacturing business needs to arrange machines and processes so production proceeds as efficiently as possible. Having adequate storage space for incoming materials and outgoing products is also important. Wholesaling businesses are very concerned with storage layout, as they often have large inventories of products that must be well organized and readily accessible. Retail and service businesses that have walk-in customers need an appealing, customer-friendly layout.

Layouts must be custom designed to meet specific needs. Entrepreneurs may choose to do their own layout planning. If the business is complex, hiring a consultant can make sense. Using a consultant will certainly add to the cost of setting up a business. However, it could also end up saving money through efficiency. Or, it may bring in more money in the long run by attracting more customers.

As you think about growing your operations, it is important to consider your long-term growth plans. If you think you may be growing rapidly, you will need a space that the business can grow into. If you think your growth will be slower, you should consider a transitional space in the meantime.

 **Apply Your Knowledge** What are zoning laws? Think back to your investigation of Cold Stone Creamery. Why would being aware of zoning laws be important for opening a retail business?

ENTREPRENEURIAL CASE STUDY: INITIATIVE & SELF-RELIANCE

Marcelo Claure— Brightstar

Tapping into the Entrepreneurial Spirit

Marcelo Claure was named Sprint President and CEO in August 2014. Prior to this, he was founder and CEO of Brightstar (www.brightstar.com), a company he launched in 1997. Under his leadership, Brightstar became the largest global wireless distributor and one of the leading service companies in the telecommunications industry. As of August 2014, it had delivered its products and services to more than 90,000 customers in over 125 countries. Brightstar was also recognized as the largest Hispanic-owned business in the United States from 2007 through 2009 and again from 2011 through 2013.

Marcelo Claure.

While raised in Bolivia, Marcelo eventually traveled the world with his father, who worked various jobs across the Americas and Africa as a geologist with the United Nations. Even though the family was constantly traveling, Marcelo's father was sure to enroll him in great schools to get a good education wherever they went. "I always complained that my friends always had a lot more money than we did," Marcelo remembers. "My dad said, 'The only thing I can give you is a good education, so I spend everything on that." As he bounced from school to school, Marcelo found he was not the best student in a traditional sense, nevertheless, he found ways to tap into his entrepreneurial spirit. Even as young as six, he was selling marbles in the schoolyard to other kids for a profit.

Overwhelming the Client with Service

While attending Bentley University in Massachusetts, he started a business buying unused frequent-flyer miles and selling them to make extra money. After college, he had a brief stint working for the Bolivian Soccer Federation, but he felt like he wanted to build another venture of his own. He returned to Boston to explore opportunities. While looking to purchase a cell phone, Marcelo struck up a conversation with the store owner and learned that the owner was tired of running the business. Marcelo offered to buy the business from him and pay him in monthly installments. Within a year, Marcelo had grown that store to be one of the largest cell phone franchises in Massachusetts.

They achieved this goal by implementing an "impulse-friendly" technique. Marcelo hired salespeople to be stationed in cars across the state outside of convenience stores. As soon as a customer would call for information, they would send the nearest sales representative to make the sale. Marcelo explained, "You could buy a cell phone from us faster than you could get a pizza. My goal was to remove every possible barrier between an impulse and a purchase." This approach of "overwhelming the client with service" has not changed for Brightstar. They have just found ways to scale their operations to do the same for customers around the globe.

Exponential Growth

In 2013, Forbes Magazine listed Brightstar as the 55th largest privately held company in the U.S., with its global sales bringing in over $10 billion in gross revenue. Named a Young Global Leader by the World Economic Forum, Marcelo has been recognized as a "bold, brave, action-oriented and entrepreneurial individual committing both time and talent to make the world a better place." He is a member of Ernst & Young's Entrepreneur of the Year Hall of Fame and in 2010 was included in the Global Telecoms Business 40 under 40.

Thinking and Acting Like an Entrepreneur

- What problem did Marcelo want to solve with his business opportunity?
- How do you think Brightstar was able grow its operations into a global business?
- In what ways does Marcelo demonstrate the entrepreneurial mindset behavior of initiative and self-reliance?

37.2 Production Management

Production management is management of the processes that produce goods and services. The goal of production management is to use materials and resources efficiently to produce the desired quantity and quality of goods and services while meeting cost and schedule requirements. Large companies, particularly manufacturing companies, often employ a production manager to perform this function. In small companies, the business owner typically oversees production management. As business grows, entrepreneurs need to be more attuned to production management as more people will be required to make more products or deliver more service.

Production managers typically focus on three issues:

- Scheduling
- Productivity
- Quality

Scheduling

Scheduling is a key activity in every business. Manufacturers make schedules for their production processes. Wholesalers and retailers make schedules for their orders and deliveries. Service businesses make schedules of the activities they intend to perform for customers. However, making a schedule and keeping it are two different things. It is the responsibility of the production manager to ensure that schedules are kept.

A schedule is not a wish list; it is a plan for achieving goals. Like any good plan, a schedule should reflect reasonable expectations. Production managers need to know how long it will take to make a product, perform a task, get an order from a supplier, or serve a customer. Established businesses rely on past data to make these predictions. New businesses have to make sensible estimates, using the best information available.

Production managers use tools to create schedules. One tool is a Gantt chart, a bar chart that shows schedule goals for a list of tasks and the duration (length of time) of each task. A Gantt chart may also show the progress made at achieving each task. Although Gantt charts have many variations, a typical example includes a timeline across the top and a list of tasks down the left side. Bars indicate the start and end dates of each task. The timeline may list actual dates or chunks of time (for example, "Week 1"). A diamond shape is used to indicate a milestone—a significant point of progress. Bars and diamonds are outlined on a proposed schedule and then darkened as tasks are completed. If a particular task is finished late (or early), the start and end dates of future tasks and milestones may have to be adjusted.

This Gantt chart shows the schedule for opening a retail book store. Week 3 has just ended.

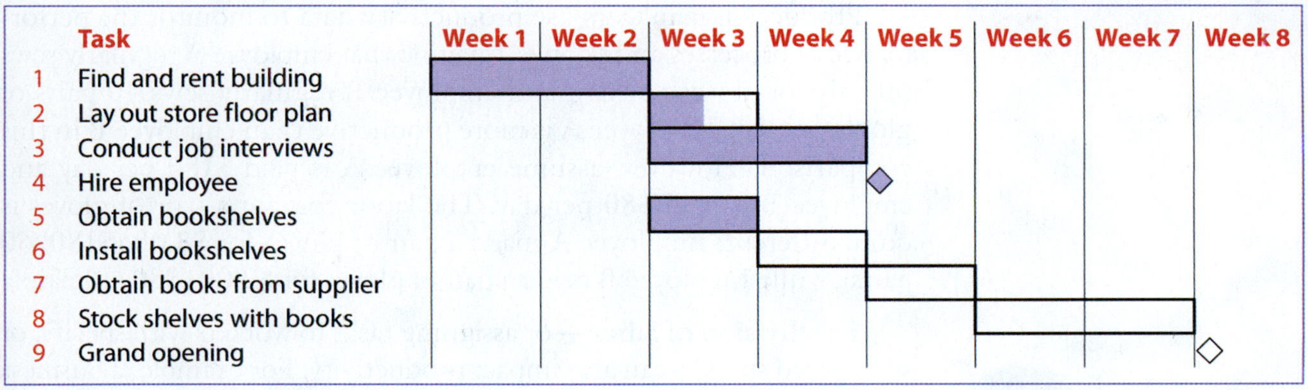

▼ **Figure 37-2**
Gantt Chart.
A Gantt chart shows the schedule of goals for a list of tasks.

Interpreting Graphs.
Which task is behind schedule? Which task is ahead of schedule?

	Task	Week 1	Week 2	Week 3	Week 4	Week 5	Week 6	Week 7	Week 8
1	Find and rent building								
2	Lay out store floor plan								
3	Conduct job interviews								
4	Hire employee				◇				
5	Obtain bookshelves								
6	Install bookshelves								
7	Obtain books from supplier								
8	Stock shelves with books								
9	Grand opening								◇

Another scheduling tool is the Program Evaluation and Review Technique (PERT) chart. A **PERT chart** is a scheduling diagram that shows tasks as a sequence of steps and illustrates how those steps are dependent on each other. In other words, PERT charts show which tasks must be completed before others can be started. A basic PERT chart uses circles to represent completed tasks. Arrows between the circles illustrate the order in which tasks should be completed.

The illustrated PERT chart covers the same nine tasks that were included in the Gantt chart. The PERT chart makes it obvious that the building should be rented (task 1) before any other tasks take place. Store layout (task 2), job interviews (task 3), and obtaining bookshelves (task 5) can proceed at the same time. They are not dependent on one another. However, hiring an employee (task 4) should be completed before the bookshelves are stocked with books (task 8), so the employee can help with the stocking.

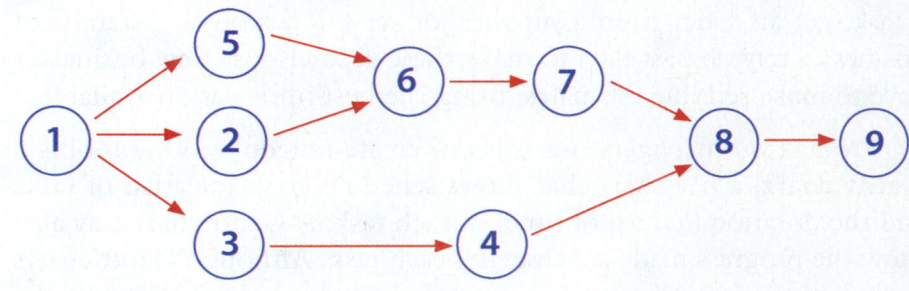

Figure 37-3 ▶
PERT Chart.

A PERT chart shows tasks as steps in a sequence and illustrates how they are dependent on each other.

Interpreting Graphs.

Task 6 is dependent on which other tasks? Why?

Productivity

Productivity is a measure of business output compared to business input. An example of productivity is the number of items produced per employee or the number of customers served per day. Productivity is a ratio of one numerical value to another numerical value. It can be measured in time intervals (hours, days, or weeks) or labor increments (employee, department, or division). The most common measures of productivity for a small business are: output per employee, output per unit of time, and output per dollar of cost.

Production managers use productivity data to monitor the performance of processes and people. Imagine that employee A regularly sews 60 pairs of gloves per day, and employee B regularly sews 40 pairs of gloves per day. Employee A is more productive than employee B in this comparison. However, assume employee A is paid $180 per day and employee B is paid $80 per day. The labor cost for a pair of gloves is quite different. Employee A made a pair of gloves for $3.00 ($180/60 pairs), while Employee B made a pair of gloves for $2.00 ($80/40 pairs).

The **division of labor**—or assigning tasks to workers with specific or specialized skills—can also impact productivity. For example, a business that makes violins might have one worker assemble the body, another who places the fingerboard, neck, and scroll, and a third who adds the pegs and strings. This type of labor specialization can streamline production by eliminating the downtime that occurs when a single worker has to switch from task to task.

Productivity is also affected by the **law of diminishing returns**, which holds that if one factor of production (worker training, for example) is increased while others remain constant, the incremental improvement in productivity will tend to fall off, or "diminish," at some point. That's because the opportunity for further improvement lessens once the initial gains are achieved from changes in any single factor.

▲ **Figure 37-4**
Automation.
Robotic machines now do many tasks that people used to do.

Comparing/Contrasting.
What are the benefits of robotic machines? What are the disadvantages?

Automation is the use of machines to perform tasks normally performed by people. In the manufacturing industry, robotic machines now do many of the tasks (assembling, painting, and sorting goods) that people used to do. Automation is less common in other types of businesses, but it does occur. Examples include automatic car washes and ATMs at banks. Automation is used when machines can do the same job as people. Of course, sophisticated machines are very costly. The extra cost of automation has to be weighed against the potential savings. Most businesses, no matter what kind, rely on equipment to some degree. This includes industrial machines, electrical tools, company vehicles, computers, and other electronic devices. **Maintenance** is the upkeep and routine care of equipment to keep it in good working order. All businesses want to keep their equipment working productively. A maintenance schedule helps ensure that equipment gets the attention it needs to keep serving the business.

Quality

Controlling quality is one of the primary functions of business managers. Most entrepreneurs strive to provide high-quality goods and services to satisfy customers. However, quality can be difficult to define and measure. High quality may mean different things to different people. Production managers set quality standards for their businesses based on the types of goods and services they are providing. These standards are part of their overall quality control program. Regular quality inspections ensure that standards are being met.

Quality inspections can be conducted at stages during the production process or when a service or product is completed. Manufacturing businesses use quality inspections to make sure their goods meet specified production standards. For example, a product may need to meet certain standards for appearance or strength. Service business managers conduct inspections to make certain that a task has been performed properly. For example, a car wash employee may inspect a vehicle after it has been washed to make sure the job met the company's standards.

Quality control is not just the responsibility of managers. Employees sometimes take an active role in quality control programs. A **quality circle** is a group of employees who provide input and suggestions about ways to improve the quality of the goods or services they produce. Although quality circles are most often associated with manufacturing businesses, they can benefit any type of business.

Apply Your Knowledge   What are the three issues on which production management focuses? From your investigation of Cold Stone Creamery, how do you think the parent company uses productivity measures in the evaluating the various locations?

CAREER COMPETENCIES

Handle Telephone Calls in a Businesslike Manner

Telephone Calls

With wireless technology, making business calls is more convenient than ever, but receiving them is not always convenient. Here are five tips for making effective phone calls:

- Identify yourself immediately. Even people who know you might not recognize your voice at first.
- Ask if the person has time to talk.
- If you're put on hold, be patient.
- If asked to leave a message, be sure to include enough information to help the recipient prepare a response and return your call.
- When someone can take your call, give the conversation your full attention. Provide feedback by saying things like "Yes," "OK," or "Uh-huh" to indicate you are listening. Show the same courtesy when you receive calls. If you can't give the other person the attention needed, find a time that's more convenient for you both.

Remember to record a helpful and professional-sounding message on your answering machine or voice mail. For example, say, "I'm in the office from eight to five o'clock. In an emergency, I can be reached at home between seven and nine o'clock." Check your messages often and return calls promptly. With the increasing use of caller ID, make your business calls from a phone number that is appropriate for a return caller to call.

Conference Calls

A conference call allows three or more parties in different locations to speak to each other over the same phone line. For example, someone at the home office in Chicago might arrange a conference call between a salesperson in Nashville and a writer in a satellite office in New York who is writing a brochure.

Scheduling is absolutely necessary to coordinate a conference call. If the callers are located in different time zones, everyone must be sure of the time. Three o'clock in Portland, Maine, for example, is noon in Portland, Oregon.

A quiet setting is important for focusing on several callers at the same time. Land phones are preferable to cell phones, which tend to pick up background noise. Using the "mute" button to silence the line when you are not speaking can also help the other participants hear each other if the lines are noisy.

If any charts, contracts, or other written materials will be required in the conference call, send copies to all parties in advance.

Videoconferences

A videoconference is a meeting in which participants in different locations see and hear each other through monitors, cameras, microphones, and speakers. However, videoconferences cannot duplicate the experience of face-to-face meetings. A videoconference takes some getting used to and some special preparation.

A videoconference room usually has two monitors. The party you're talking to appears on one monitor. You and your party appear on the other. This helps you communicate effectively. If you hold up a chart, for instance, you can see whether it's legible on the receiving end. But seeing yourself on camera can be distracting. Bright colors and detailed patterns in clothing can appear more vibrant on camera. White garments and glittery jewelry can reflect light and create a glare. Neutral colors and subtle patterns, such as solid tan or blue-gray pinstripes, are easier on the eyes.

You also need to be concerned about the audio aspect of videoconferencing. Microphones magnify any noise you make. Habits such as shuffling papers or tapping a pen on the table can quickly become irritating.

Career Skills in Action

Now, you apply what you learned about communicating through telephone communication systems to scaling the operations of your business. Put a plan together on how you could use telephone communication, conference calls, and videoconferences to manage people and operations remotely. Share your plan with a peer or your teacher for feedback.

37.3 Managing Purchasing

The goal of procurement management is to buy goods and services of the right quality in the right amounts at the right time, and at the right cost and payment terms from the right vendors. Managing purchasing is extremely important, because every purchase has a cost, which directly affects the profitability of a business.

The goals of procurement management generally fall into the following categories:

- Quality
- Amount
- Time
- Vendors
- Cost
- Terms

Selecting the Right Quality

Quality covers many aspects of a product or service. For material things, quality can involve appearance, function, artisanship, or other properties of importance to the buyer. Wholesale and retail buyers may care about who produces the merchandise (for example, name brand companies), where the merchandise is produced (for example, locally made or American made), or how the merchandise is produced. **Green procurement** is the act of purchasing goods and services that are environmentally friendly in some way. Examples include recycled-content printer paper or a cleaning service that uses all natural products.

One of the tools used by procurement managers to make decisions about quality is called **value analysis**. This is a process for assessing the performance of a product or service relative to its cost. Performance includes any quality characteristic that is important to the buyer. Value analysis is particularly helpful when comparing products. When two items are equivalent in performance, the less costly item should be purchased.

Selecting the Right Quantity

Sales forecasting (**demand forecasting**) is predicting future sales based on past sales data (or other available information) and expected market conditions in the future. Purchasing managers use sales forecasting to help them determine the right quantities to purchase. They also rely on inventory data—that is, information on the number of such items the business already has in stock. The purchase quantity may also be influenced by vendors. Manufacturers and wholesalers typically sell merchandise in very large batches. Purchasing managers must consider all of these factors when deciding what quantities to buy.

Timing Purchases

Sales and inventory data help purchasing managers schedule the best times to place reorders. Items that are used or sold at a relatively constant rate are likely be reordered at regular time intervals. This is called **periodic reordering**. Other items may be reordered at irregular time intervals. This is called **nonperiodic reordering**.

Lead time is the period between starting an activity and realizing its result—for example, the time between order placement and receipt of shipment. In this case, lead time includes how long it will take for a vendor to process an order, pack it, and ship it. Purchasing managers should keep records of the lead times associated with every purchase they make from every supplier. This information will be useful for timing future purchases from these vendors.

Some businesses make purchasing decisions based on seasonal factors. Retail stores, for example, may time their purchases to have certain types of merchandise on hand for cold weather, hot weather, or holiday shopping. Most businesses should also consider cash flow and tax consequences when timing their purchases.

Getting the Right Payment Terms

Businesses that sell to the general public typically demand payment at the time of purchase. However, business-to-business purchases are often handled differently. Many vendors allow established business customers extra time to pay for purchases—for example, 30 days or 60 days.

As we have learned, trade credit is extended payment time given by one business to another business for purchased goods or services. A common trade credit term is "Net 30," which means payment is due within 30 days of purchase. If the buyer pays after that time, the vendor may charge extra fees or refuse to give trade credit to the buyer in the future. Another trade credit term is "Net EOM." EOM is an abbreviation for "end of month," meaning payment is due at the end of the month.

Buyers must be very clear about when a trade credit period begins. The starting date is often called the reference date. The reference date may be the date the goods or services are purchased or received by the buyer, the last day of the month, or some other date designated by the vendor.

Vendors who allow trade credit often provide a small discount to the buyer if full payment is made early and in cash. A **cash discount** is a discount given to buyers who pay for purchases in cash, either at the time of purchase or within a set time period after purchase. A cash discount typically ranges from 1 to 3% of the total.

For example, the term "2/10 Net 30" means full payment is due within 30 days but a 2% discount is given if the bill is paid within the first 10 days of that period. If the amount due is $1,000, a 2% discount totals $20. The buyer can pay $980 to satisfy this debt as long as payment is made within the first 10 days. The Table 37.1 gives examples and definitions of some common trade credit terms.

Table 37.1 Trade Credit Terms

Term	Meaning
Net 10	Payment is due within 10 days.
1/10 Net 30	Payment is due within 30 days. A 1% discount is given for full payment within the first 10 days.
2% EOM	A 2% discount is given for full payment before the end of the month.
3% EOM 10	A 3% discount is given for full payment before the 10th day after the end of the month (that is, the 10th day of the following month).
1% prox 10	A 1% discount is given for full payment before the 10th day of the following month. The abbreviation "prox" is short for proximo, which means "in the next month."

Receiving and Following Up on Purchases

Purchasing managers are responsible not only for making good purchasing decisions but also for making sure that purchased goods and services are received on time and in the proper quantity and condition. When goods are received, the buyer should double-check the shipment to make sure that all items ordered were received. Any problems, such as delivery delays or incorrect shipments, should be discussed with the vendor as soon as possible. Bills received from vendors should also be carefully checked to make sure they match what was ordered and that payment terms are those agreed upon before the purchase.

The Process of Purchasing

Proper purchasing management requires good recordkeeping. Several types of paperwork are common to the purchasing process.

- **Product Specification.** A <mark>product specification</mark> is a written, detailed description of the characteristics (size, shape, capabilities, etc.) of a product. Businesses may develop product specifications for items they intend to purchase, particularly those that are expensive or crucial to their operations. Buyers use product specifications to guide their purchases and vendor selections and make sure that products meet their quality standards. Suppliers develop product specifications to provide buyers with information about products they have for sale.

- **Purchase Order.** A <mark>purchase order</mark> is a document issued by a buyer to a vendor that lists the items to be purchased, their quantities and prices, and other relevant information, such as delivery or payment terms. Once a vendor accepts a purchase order, it becomes a binding agreement between the two parties to complete the purchase. A purchase order is a financial commitment. Businesses with employees should have policies that specify exactly who within the company has the authority to issue purchase orders and whether there are any spending limitations.

- **Invoice.** An invoice (bill of sale) is a document issued by a vendor to a buyer on fulfillment of a purchase order. An invoice typically lists the items purchased, their quantities and prices, and other information such as date of shipment and payment terms. Vendors should issue a receipt after each invoice is paid.

- **Packing Slip.** Another vendor-issued document is the <mark>packing slip</mark>, which is a list of all items in a shipment. Purchasing managers should make sure that invoices, receipts, and packing slips are accurate and match the original purchase orders.

Prior to the computer age, most purchasing was accomplished through paper catalogs and phone calls. Purchasing over the Internet or any other digital platform is called <mark>e-procurement</mark>. Many vendors operate e-procurement systems that allow buyers to access product information and specifications, fill out purchase orders, and make purchases online.

◀ **Figure 37-5**
Packing Slip.
Purchasing managers should make sure a packing slip is accurate and matches the original purchase order.

Solving Problems.
What would you do if the packing slip didn't match the original purchase order?

Apply Your Knowledge What is the goal of procurement management? Think back to your investigation of Cold Stone Creamery. Do you think successful franchise owners have done a better job with managing their expenses? Why or why not?

APPLICATION TO BUSINESS PLANNING

Plan for Scaling Operations

Use what you learned from this chapter to put together a plan for scaling operations as part of your implementation and growth plan. You should support your findings with research data. Be sure to include:

- A location for your business that will allow your business to grow over time
- Productivity systems so you can produce more products if needed; be sure to consider automation, maintenance, division of labor and specialization, and the law of diminishing returns
- Purchasing relationships that allow you to gain economies of scale

REVIEWING OBJECTIVES

1. Learn about the site selection and layout planning.

2. Examine the tasks and tools of production management.

3. Explore factors in purchasing management.

CRITICAL THINKING

1. How is productivity related to profit?

2. Why would a vendor offer a discount to buyers who pay in cash at the time of purchase or within a short amount of time after the purchase?

ENTREPRENEURIAL THINKING EXERCISE: INITIATIVE & SELF-RELIANCE

Think back to your investigation of Cold Stone Creamery. Imagine you were hired to be a consultant to new franchise owners. Your job is to help them set up the location's operations so they fit with the model of the larger business. Put together an action plan with achievable goals that you would implement with the franchise owner.

EXTENSION ACTIVITIES

Entrepreneurship & Literacy Skills

Complete the following task to demonstrate your understanding of entrepreneurship:

Grades 9–12: Work with three classmates. Imagine you are a group of entrepreneurs with a paper airplane business. Within your group, determine a process to produce large quantities of paper airplanes at a high quality output. Prepare a written presentation for the class in which each member of the group explains their role in the production process.

GUIDING QUESTION:

"How can I most effectively grow the number of employees I have?"

APPLICATION TO BUSINESS PLANNING:

☑ Hiring Needs

OBJECTIVES

- Describe the process of recruiting employees.
- Compare various methods of employee training and development.
- Explain various methods of motivating, evaluating, promotion, and dismissing employees.

NFTE Entrepreneurial Mindset Characteristic Focus

☑ Communication & Collaboration

National Entrepreneurship Standards

- **A.20** Explain factors to consider in determining a venture's human-resource needs
- **A.24** Use external resources to supplement entrepreneur's expertise
- **C.15** Explain the concept of human-resource management
- **D.18** Explain the nature of staff communication
- **G.03** Describe the sources of income (wages/salaries, interest, rent, dividends, transfer payments, etc.)
- **J.02** Develop job descriptions
- **J.03** Develop compensation plan/incentive systems
- **J.05** Delegate responsibility for job tasks
- **J.07** Recruit new employees
- **J.08** Screen job applications/resumes
- **J.09** Interview job applicants
- **J.10** Select new employees
- **J.12** Dismiss/fire employee
- **J.13** Orient new employees (management's role)
- **J.14** Conduct training class/program
- **J.18** Recognize/reward employees
- **J.20** Ensure equitable opportunities for employees
- **J.23** Provide feedback on work efforts
- **J.24** Assess employee performance
- **J.25** Take remedial action with employee
- **L.55** Train staff to support sales efforts

LESSON VOCABULARY

- accreditation
- benefits
- compensation
- flextime
- job description
- job enlargement
- job enrichment
- job shadowing
- orientation
- protégé
- recruit
- salary
- telecommuting
- wage

- **M.03** Document business systems and procedures
- **M.21** Schedule staff

Common Career Technical Core Standards

- **CRP.4** Communicate clearly, effectively and with reason.
- **CRP.9** Model integrity, ethical leadership and effective management.
- **BM-HR.1** Describe and follow laws and regulations affecting human resource operations.
- **BM-HR.2** Access, evaluate and disseminate information for human resources management decision making.
- **BM-HR.3** Motivate and supervise personnel to achieve completion of projects and business goals.
- **BM-HR.4** Plan, monitor and manage the use of financial and human resources to ensure a business's financial well-being.
- **BM-HR.5** Plan, staff, lead and organize human resources to enhance employee productivity and satisfaction.
- **BM-HR.6** Plan, monitor and manage day-to-day business activities to foster a healthy and safe work environment.
- **BM-HR.7** Plan, organize and implement compensation, benefits, health and safety programs.

National Entrepreneurship Standards: Career Competencies

 H.09 Interview for a job

ENTREPRENEURIAL INVESTIGATION
Good Help Is So Hard to Find

Google is known for being one of the best companies to work for. According to an interview in Forbes, Google claims a great deal of its success is because of the talent it recruits. In that same article, Google executives outlined some important tips for recruiting and hiring the right people:

- Find people who are passionate and interesting
- Make sure the interview tells you if the person is someone you can work with
- Have a hiring committee that makes an objective decision on hiring based on past performance

Do some research on Google and their hiring processes to answer the following questions:

- Do you agree or disagree that hiring the right people is important to a business's success?
- Do you think Google's interviewing tips would be effective? Would you add anything else?

Be prepared to share your thoughts with peers and your teacher.

38.1 Managing and Scaling Operations

In the previous chapter, you looked at considerations for growing your operations. In this chapter, you will look at increasing the number of people you have on staff, along with providing them with the appropriate training and development.

Staffing

It is usually good news when a small business needs to hire employees. Imagine you're an entrepreneur and you have been doing everything either on your own or with a partner. After a while, you might want to cut back on your hours a bit. When the business gets strong enough, you feel you could pay someone to grow and improve your operation. But how can you make sure you get the best possible candidate?

Entrepreneurs have many tools available to them for hiring new people. Many small business owners rely on word-of-mouth or hire someone they already know. But if very specialized or unusual skills are required, you might need to look in other places. Some companies turn to online classified advertisements through their local newspapers or websites such as LinkedIn or Indeed.com.. These companies then interview potential new hires on their own. Other companies use staffing agencies, such as Kelly Services or Adecco. Having someone else do your hiring will save significant time but may not ultimately result in the best fit for a small business.

To **recruit** means to find and hire qualified candidates for a job. Recruiting is an investment: the thought and preparation put into the process is repaid by the quality of the workers you hire. In small businesses especially, the impact of a single hiring decision can be felt throughout the company. Experts calculate that replacing an employee can ultimately cost three or four times that person's salary. This is a result of lost productivity, customer loyalty, company morale, down time without a replacement, hiring a replacement, training the new employee, and many other factors. So choosing employees wisely is critical to a small business.

Writing a Job Description

You can't fill a position until you can tell applicants what it entails. That's the purpose of writing a job description, an explanation of a position's purpose, tasks, and responsibilities and the qualifications needed to perform it.

To attract only qualified applicants, a **job description** should list specific activities and qualifications and rank their importance. A description for an assistant might read: "Answers phones, schedules appointments, and maintains office equipment. Must have experience with database and Internet research; familiarity with accounting software preferred."

Any required training or credentials should also be included. A childcare provider may need training in CPR and other emergency procedures, for instance.

The description should also reflect how responsibilities might grow in the future. If you hope the assistant hired today will advance to become the office manager of tomorrow, you might note: "Experience in personnel management desirable."

ROUTE DELIVERY DRIVER

RESPONSIBILITIES:

- Deliver products in good condition to customer.
- Merchandise, display, and rotate products according to company standards.
- Invoice and collect monies due.
- Pick up company property.
- Ensure compliance with regulatory and company policies and procedures.
- Settle all accounts daily.

QUALIFICATIONS:

- Valid Class A Driver's License.
- MVR in accordance with company policy.
- Familiarity with DOT regulations.
- 1–3 years of general work experience.
- 1+ years of commercial driving experience preferred.
- Local delivery experience preferred.
- Prior grocery store and/or consumer products
- Experience a plus.

Figure 38-1 ▲

Job Description.

A job description provides the basis of an ad when the position needs to be filled.

Inferring.

This description doesn't mention personal qualities; however, based on the requirements, what qualities do think this employer is looking for?

Determining Compensation

Compensation refers to the money and benefits an employee receives in exchange for working. For employers, it's a balancing act between three main factors:

- What workers need and deserve based on their qualifications
- What the business can afford
- What other, similarly sized businesses in the same field are paying

How employers pay depends partly on the type of job. Work that requires a set number of hours or items produced is generally paid as a **wage**, payment to employees per hour worked or piece of work completed. A **salary**—a weekly, bimonthly, or monthly payment—is more typical for jobs where the hours and schedules vary. Some employers offer stock in the company as partial payment. This option adds an incentive to employees by making them owners as well—their income rises or falls based on the company's success.

Benefits are types of compensation other than salary or wages. Some benefits, such as family and medical leave, are required by law. Many more have become standard, especially health insurance, paid vacation, sick days, and investment plans for retirement saving.

New entrepreneurs often worry that they can't match the compensation offered by larger established firms. However, compensation isn't the only benefit of working for a business. Location, scheduling flexibility, on-site day care, the company's culture, and possibilities for advancement are just some of the factors that may increase a company's desirability to a prospective employee.

Locating Job Candidates

Ideally, you'll create a list of potential candidates before the need to hire becomes pressing. Take note of people you meet whose talents or work ethic you admire, including current employees of customers and the competition. When Mimi was recruiting a sales representative for her organic pet foods, she offered the job to the assistant manager of a pet store that carried her products. Mimi knew he was knowledgeable about animal nutrition and experienced at selling.

College and university placement offices connect employers to job-seeking students and graduates. College counselors keep up with the regional job market, using input from employers to help students prepare for their careers. They often coordinate with teachers to send students to companies as unpaid interns to gain experience and credit for coursework. At the placement office's website, employers can post job openings and read student resumes at no charge. They can register to recruit on campus at job fairs or at information sessions with interested students. Employment agencies run by a state's Department of Labor or Commerce offer similar services.

Other useful sources are trade association websites and publications. Some have online job banks or resources for employers. Leads might be found through association members' forums and blogs. Linda Joseph is a member of the American Saddle Makers Association. When she wanted to hire a skilled leather worker, she phoned a master saddle maker who was listed on the group's website. Sometimes it is useful to advertise your job

◀ **Figure 38-2**
Locating Job Candidates.
How would you locate a skilled leather worker?

Drawing Conclusions.

Based on the fact that businesses need to find workers with specific skills, why do you think many cities are known for having many businesses in one industry (e.g., finance in New York City, technology in San Jose)?

on general help wanted types of websites. The problem with these more general sites is that you could receive many applications, which would increase the work a business would need to do to locate an appropriate employee. Consider using the most specific online job listing you can.

Employers can eliminate some of the work of recruiting by hiring a personnel agency to locate and recommend candidates for them. The hefty fee—often a percentage of the employee's first year's wages, which can amount to several thousand dollars—makes this an option of last resort for most small business owners.

Screening Candidates

Taking applications or resumes is the most practical and most fair way to evaluate job candidates. Those documents, along with the job description, provide a fair, fixed standard for comparing potential employees.

What can applications and resumes tell you about a job seeker? Correct spelling and grammar show basic language skills and attention to detail. Applicants who stress their recent experience and training in relevant skills show an understanding of the position. A job description for a sales associate in a clothing store might not include a background in fashion, for example. A candidate who highlights her degree from design school shows an understanding that leads her to mention that added qualification. It also suggests initiative.

Applications and resumes can also raise "red flags" that warn against hiring someone: unexplained gaps in the work or education history, for example, or holding a series of unrelated jobs without advancement.

Figure 38-3 ▶

Interviewing Candidates.

Putting the candidates at ease during the interview can help them answer any questions you have for them.

Applying Concepts.

What types of questions would you want to ask when interviewing a candidate?

You should contact the most promising applicants for interviews. Be sure to prepare for each interview. Make a list of questions you plan to ask. Focus on relevant information that expands on the facts given in the application or resume. You cannot legally ask questions about age, race, sexual orientation, marital status, religion, or other personal matters.

Try to put candidates at ease during the interview. Give them time to answer questions and explain statements or information in their resumes. At the same time, notice how they handle stress or difficult questions. For example, a common question is, "What do you see as your biggest weakness?" A response such as, "Sometimes I talk without thinking, so I'm working at listening better" shows not only honesty but also problem-solving skills. Other questions that focus on the applicant's behavior might be, "Tell me how you solved a problem at work." Or, "Describe a situation where you resolved a customer complaint."

Get a feel for overall personality, as well. An employee should be enjoyable to work with and have traits that fit the workplace atmosphere. Recall, however, that diversity in philosophy and thinking style can be an asset for problem solving and creativity. Make written notes of all these impressions; don't rely on your memory.

Also realize that while you are judging the applicant, the applicant is also judging you as an employer. It will benefit both of you if you encourage questions about the job and the company. Be positive—but honest—about what you can offer and what you expect. Communicate respect for what a new employee can bring to the workplace.

If an applicant seems like a good match, check his or her references before offering the position. Learning about the candidate's relationship with former co-workers, teachers, or classmates can provide added insight. Also, more and more employers are taking the precaution of checking an individual's background for financial problems or criminal activity. This is required for certain positions, especially in healthcare, childcare, and security services.

Table 38.1 Possible Interview Questions

Question	What It Reveals
How did you get interested in this line of work?	Their interest in the position
What achievements are you most proud of?	Their past work experience
What would you like to learn from this job?	Their expectations of the job
What are your career goals for the next five years?	How long they plan to stay with the company

Hiring Outside Professionals

Some very important services are needed only occasionally. A growing business may require advice on financial planning or legal help. In these situations, bringing in professionals, consultants, or skilled workers as needed is more cost effective than retaining their services full time. The expense associated with these specialists will usually be more than the hourly wages of your employees. Their payment will usually be established by a contract that spells out what is expected and the compensation.

Choosing an outside expert requires the same type of research as hiring a regular employee. Get recommendations from other business owners, especially those with needs like your own.

Ask candidates for references from other clients. Check for consumer complaints through the Better Business Bureau. Check their credentials through a professional organization or state licensing or regulating agency.

For professionals whose services will be used on an ongoing basis, such as tax advisors or legal experts, look for someone with whom you can establish a long-term relationship. As with a doctor or dentist, you may see them only once or twice a year, but you're entrusting them with a valuable possession: your business's future.

 **Apply Your Knowledge** List four sources of potential job candidates. Think back to your investigation of Google candidates. What is something they might be looking for when they screen candidates?

ENTREPRENEURIAL CASE STUDY: COMMUNICATION & COLLABORATION

 **The Tattoo Team— Henoo**

When five 14- and 15-year-old girls at the Skinners' Company's School, in London, were asked to come up with some concepts for starting a business, their first step was testing ideas to see which would attract more customers. They did a feasibility study as part of their market research, asking other girls in the school, teachers, family, and friends which product they would be most interested in purchasing. The answer: henna tattoos that could be applied in a matter of hours and would wear off within a few weeks. Their company, Henoo, was born.

The girls knew each other before they started Henoo, but they were classmates rather than friends. How were they able to form a successful team without the problems that usually occur when working with partners?

Team Building: Communication

According to the girls, communication was vital. "We had to listen to each other's ideas and make sure everyone had a chance to express her thoughts and opinions on the business ideas. We learned how to work together as a team, making important decisions, problem solving, and taking risks."

The Henoo team.

All the girls took a Belbin® Team Role Test, which is widely used in Great Britain, to find out their skills and strengths in various areas. The developer, Meredith Belbin, discovered that the most successful teams are those that are balanced in team roles. With the results of the tests, the girls divided responsibilities according to individual strengths.

Each Team Member Has a Role

With so many team members, the business could not have been successful without effective collaboration skills. Arooj Akhtar was responsible for keeping track of expenses, revenue, and profit, and Duygu Atas was responsible for customer service—making sure customers were satisfied and handling any complaints.

Karess Laidley handled human resources, training, and stock control. She made sure there was enough henna and that the working area was clean and safe.

Maimoonah Teladia did the marketing and advertising. Henoo had business cards, posters, a catalog showing all their designs, and an informational magazine containing everything a customer would need to know about henna. Kasanah Shalders-Gayley became the team manager, ensuring that business operations ran smoothly.

Even though the girls had different responsibilities, they helped each other. Three of the girls were experts at applying the henna. While they worked, the other two made sure the customers were satisfied and that they paid for the designs.

The Henoo Team was remarkable, according to their advisor, Ms. Selda Kurtuldu. "There were no problems at all. They worked really well as a team."

Thinking and Acting Like an Entrepreneur

- What are the differences between working by yourself and working with partners?
- What's the most important thing when working with partners?
- Which of the jobs at Henoo would you prefer?

38.2 Employee Training and Development

By successfully completing elementary school, you were qualified to start middle school. However, you still had some things to learn on your way to becoming a capable middle school student—perhaps how to handle new freedoms and responsibilities or which foods to avoid in the cafeteria.

The same is true of employees. Qualified candidates may have the necessary skills but need to learn how to apply them. A new job might involve different responsibilities from the last one or follow a different routine. In a growing number of fields, rapid advances in technology make updating skills an ongoing necessity. Training builds employee enthusiasm and eases the normal concerns of starting a job or assuming new duties.

Not all training is skill related. Workplace safety, business ethics, and coworker relations are a few areas where employers need to explain their rules and policies.

A company focuses on specific training and development needs and then figures out the best way to fill them. It marks progress by using definite, measurable goals. Such a program saves time, money, and other resources.

Learning relevant skills makes employees feel that they—and their employer—have spent their time well. Ideally, employees come away with a sense that their value as individuals has increased. They also feel they've learned something that makes them more valuable in the job market. For example, some training confers **accreditation**, certification by a professional group that an individual possesses certain skills or a specific level of expertise. Having accredited employees enhances a company's reputation as well as the employees' professional status.

Figure 38-4 ▶
Workplace Safety.

A company needs to train employees about workplace safety.

Predicting.

What would happen if a company didn't train employees in necessary workplace safety?

In-House Programs

Some training and development takes place within the firm, involving only its own employees. These are referred to as in-house programs. In a smaller company, the owner and a few key employees might take care of the training. A large corporation might dedicate an entire division of the human resources department to this need.

Whatever the size of the business, training for a new employee starts with orientation. **Orientation** is the process of gradually integrating an employee into a workplace. During this stage, employees might tour the facilities, learn the company's policies and procedures, and meet the people with whom they'll be working. Equally important, they start on-the-job training. In a two- or three-person business, this may be as simple as learning how to access files on the company's computers. It also may involve **job shadowing**, a process of learning a job by watching an employee perform the job over a period of time. In a larger business, a new manager might spend several weeks learning to perform jobs in each department.

A business with many employees might offer a mentoring program. As you may remember from Chapter 1, a mentor is a person of greater experience or knowledge who guides and supports another person in developing as a professional. A mentoring relationship is typically a long-term relationship. Besides practical knowledge about the job and career, a mentor can impart lessons on life management—setting and reaching goals, for example, or the rewards of giving back to the community.

Informal mentoring is common in a workplace. If employees are interested in starting a formal mentoring program, business owners can show support by providing time, facilities, training, and a budget. Employees can set program goals that promote the company's values. Encourage all employees to take part in the program, with mentors chosen based on a set of objective requirements.

Mentors should be:

- **Interested in a Mentoring Relationship.** The individual must be willing to take on the responsibilities of mentoring. He or she makes time to meet with the **protégé** (PRO-tuh-zhay), the person who receives guidance in a mentoring relationship. Mentors offer useful ideas and find resources for resolving a protégé's questions.
- **Enthusiastic about Their Careers.** They genuinely care about the work they do and believe in its importance.
- **Positive and Constructive Communicators.** Good mentors recognize and encourage a protégé's strengths and explain any improvement needs.

- **Respected Role Models.** They exhibit the traits of professionalism, especially a strong sense of ethics.
- **Trusted by Their Protégés.** Mentor and protégé should share qualities. The mentor should understand the protégé's situation, and should make him or her feel comfortable and understood.

Training and Development Providers

Although in-house programs can help new employees adapt to the workplace, an entrepreneur might sometimes need outside advice for special training and development issues. Suppose, for example, you're a landscaper who needs to know how to accommodate workers with disabilities at a job site. You could talk to individual experts or read magazine articles, but this advice and information might not be complete. Instead, the solution may be a professional training and development provider.

There are many types of training and development providers. A large consulting company might address a range of public relations skills, from leadership to telephone etiquette. An individual expert may specialize in time management. Programs can range from simple to sophisticated. Sales staff might attend a day-long multimedia presentation, using role-playing activities to improve selling skills. A catering crew might spend an hour with a local florist learning how to arrange flowers for banquet tables.

Training and development providers educate employees, as well as employers, in a variety of settings:

- **Classes.** Classes may be offered individually or in a series, at the workplace or elsewhere. Online classes are popular because of their convenience and economy.

- **Workshops.** In a workshop, a small group of people gathers to learn through discussion, demonstration, and practice. A workshop may be a single session lasting a few hours or several sessions on related topics spread out over a few days.

- **Seminars.** At a seminar, participants in small groups exchange information and discuss topics in a selected field. If you attend a seminar, you will be expected to actively contribute to the discussion. Seminars often have an audience, which usually has an opportunity to ask questions of seminar participants.

◀ **Figure 38-6**
Seminars.
If you attend a seminar, you will be expected to participate actively in the discussion.

Relating Concepts.
How can participation in a seminar help you gain greater understanding of the topic you are discussing?

- **Conferences and Expos.** A conference or an expo (short for exposition) can be a robust learning experience. These events, which usually run several days, may offer classes, workshops, or seminars at one site, along with panel discussions, vendors' booths, and representatives from professional associations. Attending a conference or expo can be costly in travel, lodging, and time taken off from work. Yet the expense can pay dividends in learning new techniques and keeping up with the latest developments—to stay ahead of the competition. Above all, conferences and expos can be excellent places to network and build new relationships with others in the same industry.

Apply Your Knowledge   What are five qualities of good mentors? Think back to your investigation of Google. What do you think their mentoring program might look like?

CAREER COMPETENCIES

 ## Interview for a Job

What happens when an entrepreneur needs to hire employees for the business? She or he gathers resumes of potential qualified candidates and invites them in for an interview. A job interview is a formal meeting between a job seeker and a potential employer—the interviewer. The job interview helps the potential employee and the interviewer make important decisions regarding the position at stake.

The interviewer decides if the job seeker is the best person for the position. The job seeker decides if the position is the one he or she really wants. Both can use the job interview to get to know each other. They learn information that you cannot learn from a cover letter or resume. For example, the interviewer learns whether or not the job seeker has the appropriate interpersonal skills. The job seeker learns if people at the company are friendly. A job interview is successful if the job seeker convinces the interviewer to offer her or him the job. It is also successful if they learn that the position would not be the right fit.

Whether as an employee or an entrepreneur, you will definitely participate in a job interview at some point in your life. Knowing tips for preparing for interviews will help you on your own interviews and in determining your expectations when hiring employees.

Preparing for a Job Interview

A test is always easier if you are prepared. A job interview is like a test—if you pass, you are offered the job. Use these four steps to prepare for a job interview:

1. Research the company or organization where you are interviewing. Talk to someone who works there. Visit the company's website.

2. Make a list of questions an interviewer might ask you. Common questions include, "Tell me about yourself," "Why do you want to work here?" "Do you have the skills to get the work done?" and "Why should I hire you?"

3. Prepare answers to the questions. Be specific. Emphasize your strengths, skills, and abilities. Explain how you solved a problem, made an important decision, or showed responsibility. Mention your goals, and briefly explain how you plan to achieve them.

4. Make a list of five to ten questions you can ask the interviewer. Ask about the company, the work environment, and the position. Common questions include, "What kinds of projects or tasks will I be responsible for?" "Is there opportunity for advancement?" "What are the hours?" "What is the salary range?" and "When will you make a hiring decision?"

Making the Most of the Job Interview

- Many interviews are ten to fifteen minutes long. How can you best use that time to get a job offer?
- Arrive ten minutes early.
- Introduce yourself to the receptionist, and explain who you are there to meet.
- Be polite and respectful to everyone you meet.
- Shake hands with your interviewer when you arrive and before you leave.
- Listen carefully, using positive body language. For example, smile and lean forward slightly when the interviewer is talking.
- Use proper English when you speak; no slang.
- Avoid chewing gum.
- Turn off your cell phone. If you forget and it rings or vibrates, apologize and ignore it or turn it off without checking to see who called.
- At the end of the interview, shake hands again, and thank the interviewer. Ask for a business card, so you have the interviewer's contact information.
- Write a thank you note within 24 hours of the interview. Refer to something specific that you discussed during the interview.

Career Skills in Action

Now you and peer should apply what you learned in this section to practice your interviewing skills. Take turns with each other being the interviewer and the job seeker. Hold your interviews as if you were hiring an employee for your own business. Have a third group member act as an observer to give feedback to both of you afterward.

38.3 Motivating and Evaluating Employees

Milton Hershey, founder of the Hershey Chocolate Company, was a progressive-minded entrepreneur who believed in taking care of the people whose work helped build his fortune. He was also a shrewd businessman who understood that people are motivated to work harder when they feel appreciated. In the early 1900s, he developed the town of Hershey, Pennsylvania, as a model community for his employees. It included good housing, quality schools, parks and recreation facilities, and a trolley for transportation.

Most entrepreneurs can't match Hershey's scale of employee appreciation. Yet all entrepreneurs can follow his example of employee motivation.

They can recognize their employees' value and importance to the business and encourage them to realize their potential. Not all motivational techniques are expensive. In fact, some of the best forms of motivation cost nothing at all.

Performance-Based Rewards

Imagine that your teacher gave everyone in the class $25 for being a "good student." At first you might be thrilled. Then you might start to wonder: What made you a good student? Was it something you could do again? If you were an even better student, would you get more money? Could your teacher afford to be that generous?

Performance-based rewards, when carefully thought out, avoid such confusion. First, the reward is linked to a specific, achievable goal and is related to the work involved—in other words, the greater the achievement, the greater the reward. An employer must also be able to afford it. A small reward employees can be sure of receiving will motivate them better than a large one that is doubtful. Withdrawing rewards that have been promised can be demoralizing. Also, the reward should be something the employees would value.

These guidelines allow for a lot of possibilities. Suppose you own a trucking firm. You could award points for every mile driven without an accident or ticket. The points could be redeemed as a gift card from a business of the driver's choice.

Or imagine you own a home cleaning service. You might offer a finder's fee to workers who bring in new customers—or if you're hiring, for new employees. When a customer reports a cleaning crew's outstanding service, you could give the crew credit points that they could exchange for rewards.

Membership in professional groups is another valued reward. A sales associate in Gemma Gottlieb's quilt shop is also the store's webmaster. When the site recorded its one millionth hit, Gemma bought the associate a year's membership in the American Webmasters Association, which entitled him to discounts on online Web design courses and other benefits.

Flexible Work Arrangements

When employees are asked what they value most in a job, it isn't always pay or benefits. It's often flexibility. Having more choices about when and how to work helps them find a time (or place) for focusing on the job. One way to take advantage of this is to offer **flextime**, or flexible work schedules. Some employees might start and finish work one hour earlier or later than others, or alternate between working four days and five days a week. Or employees could split duties through job sharing.

▲ Figure 38-7
A Useful Reward.
This watch might be appreciated by a sales executive.

Solving Problems.
What would you do if only a few employees were earning your business's performance-based rewards?

Another possibility is **telecommuting**, working from a location other than the business site, linked by telecommunication technology. Through telecommuting, a company can profit from the talents of people who otherwise would not be available—people with disabilities, parents of young children, and those who live far from the workplace.

Workplace flexibility isn't an option for all businesses or all employees, of course, but it may be practical for small operations. For instance, beginning entrepreneurs may not be able to pay high wages, so flextime allows employees to hold other jobs. A business may start out with only basic supplies and equipment. Through flextime and telecommuting, schedules can be arranged so workers share, rather than compete for, its limited resources.

Policies on flextime and other arrangements should be clearly described in an employee handbook. For example, a store may need a certain number of workers at certain hours. Telecommuters might be required to work on-site one or two days a week.

Delegating Responsibility

One trait entrepreneurs can appreciate in employees is the desire to take on more responsibilities. Two practices capitalize on this quality: job enlargement and job enrichment. Both practices motivate by delegating (assigning) more responsibility to workers.

Job enlargement means adding responsibilities to a position. For example, one restaurant worker's duties typically included cleaning and preparing fruits and vegetables, preparing salad dressings, and assembling these ingredients into salads. Job enlargement might involve adding new salads to the menu, requiring the salad maker to learn new recipes—and possibly new techniques. The basic tasks are the same, but additional responsibilities have been added.

◀ **Figure 38-8
Job Enlargement.**
Mastery of one responsibility might lead to job enlargement.

Applying Concepts.
What is the benefit of job enlargement for an employer? An employee?

Related to this technique is **job enrichment**, which means increasing the depth or involvement of a job. Here the restaurant worker might have to order the salad ingredients, based on cost, local availability, and the other items on the menu. She would gain new knowledge, develop new skills, and work in new relationships to play a greater role in the business. With job enrichment, the basic position changes.

Of course, job enlargement and enrichment should not simply mean more work for the employee. Instead, lesser tasks can be reassigned—ideally, to expand or enlarge another employee's job.

A Positive Environment

Did you know that enjoying yourself is a recognized psychological need? It's associated with learning, laughter, and a sense of belonging—all of which have proven emotional benefits. It's no surprise then that people are motivated by an atmosphere that meets their need for enjoyment and value recognition. Creating such a workplace makes good business sense.

First, work is more enjoyable when the physical environment is designed for efficiency and safety. Employees should have ready access to needed tools, such as insulated gloves or graphic arts software.

Employees also need to feel confident that they're doing their job well. A good training program and job description help provide this assurance. Giving employees reasonable, yet challenging, goals and deadlines will help them decide where to direct their efforts. Providing the opportunity for frequent, informal feedback helps employees feel confident.

Equally important is personal recognition, especially for unexpected or little-noticed contributions to the workplace (or to the community). Think of the motivational impact of giving an Employee of the Month Award to an employee who handles a difficult situation in an ethical way. Think of a workplace where recognition is given to the employee who was named Scoutmaster to the National Boy Scout Jamboree or who donated blood to the American Red Cross.

Figure 38-9 ▶
A Positive Environment.
A pizza party can be motivational.

Applying Concepts.
What type of approaches would motivate you at your job?

Also, don't forget the motivational value of employer-sponsored fun, tailored to employees' tastes and your resources. This could mean something as simple as having a pizza party at the end of work on a Friday or providing tickets to a local event. Showing that you value your employees in such a way will increase their loyalty and enthusiasm.

Evaluating Employees

Students are sometimes asked to review each other's work. For example, classmates might give their opinions of your essay. You might check a classmate's solution to a math problem. Giving and accepting this kind of feedback may be difficult. However, both parties can benefit when the judgment is formed with care and expressed with consideration.

The same applies to evaluating employees. Judging employees' work can help improve both their performance and your workplace, if handled with objectivity and respect.

Performance Evaluations

Performance evaluations are regular employee reviews, usually given at least annually. Some companies give formal quarterly or semiannual reviews to reinforce good performance and alert employees to improvement needs in a timely fashion. The review process is handled by the business owner, the employee's supervisor, or a human resources specialist. Performance evaluations have two goals:

- **To point out how well the employee is meeting the job requirements and expectations.** This is done by filling out an evaluation form. A well-written job description is valuable because it provides an objective standard for judgment.

- **To improve not only the employee's performance, but also the employer's.** Usually the employee and evaluator meet one-on-one to discuss the evaluation.

Suppose you notice that a sales representative is just barely reaching his sales quota each month. In discussing the problem, you find that his sales area overlaps that of a well-established competitor. Perhaps the employee could learn effective tactics by working with a more experienced representative. Maybe revising your training to include better education on your products and the competitor's would help your salespeople sway potential customers. If many salespeople have the same problem, it might point out a flaw in your hiring practices.

Both the reviewer and employee sign the performance-evaluation form, indicating that they've had the discussion. They may write out and sign a list of goals and a plan for improving employee performance and job satisfaction. Some employers have employees fill out a form that asks what tools, training, or changes in the work environment would help them do their job better.

Figure 38-10 ▶

Performance-Evaluation Form.

Some evaluation forms break down and rate job duties in detail. Others describe and grade duties broadly as either acceptable or unacceptable.

Recognizing Patterns.

Why can comparing performance evaluations from one year to the next be helpful?

Performance Evaluation Form						
Criteria	Not Applicable	Excellent	Good	Fair	Unsatisfactory	Comments
Meets work quality standards						
Completes assignments reliably						
Shows initiative in problem solving and decision making						
Adapts well to changing circumstances						
Shows willingness and ability to learn new skills						
Arrives on time and prepared to work						
Effectively gets desired results from subordinates						

General comments on employee's performance:

Promoting Employees

When a higher-level, better-paying job becomes available, promoting an existing employee has advantages. It shows recognition and respect for the people whose work and commitment helped build the company. It means the company's philosophy and values will be carried out in the higher position. It also saves resources spent on training someone from outside. For these reasons, publicizing a job opening within your own company makes sense.

However, employees should be promoted for the same reason they are hired: for being the best candidate for the job. It's a mistake to assume that success at one position automatically translates into success at a higher level. One important difference is that a promotion usually involves greater responsibility for managing people and other resources. Relationship skills become especially important. Employers need to ask whether the employee has shown these skills or shown an interest and aptitude in developing them. Can the employee see beyond his or her department in relation to issues that affect the entire business? Does he or she have the sense of initiative needed in a leader?

If you think an existing employee who would be a good prospect hasn't applied for a position, you might urge that person to do so. You might see skills and qualities in someone that could be successfully developed in a higher position. On the other hand, people may know themselves and their priorities better than you do. For example, they may not want to miss family time if the job involves travel. The decision ultimately must be theirs.

Once the job has been filled, make sure other employees understand why they weren't chosen. This will allow them to work toward preparing for the next opening, if they wish. Or they may decide their future lies with another company. That decision, too, is theirs to make.

Dismissing Employees

Dismissing an employee may be the entrepreneur's most difficult responsibility. Firing an unproductive or troublesome worker may be necessary for the business's survival. Good employees deserve competent coworkers. However, losing a job can be devastating to an individual's self-image and their financial situation. For the employer, it means added time and expense to hire and train a replacement. It could also open the company to legal action. Dismissals due to financial troubles in the business can shake workplace morale. Thus, the decision to fire should be made only after other options have been tried.

Before considering dismissal, tell the employee how he or she is failing to meet your expectations. The conversation might yield a solution. The job's duties may have changed, for example, and the employee might need retraining or other support to adjust. Perhaps those duties could be reassigned, to develop and better use the employee's strengths. Or the worker's skills might be better utilized, and the worker might be happier, in a different position.

Make sure employees who are dismissed for economic reasons know that losing the job was not their fault. Make sure their former co-workers know this as well. The dismissal should be planned to give the employee a fair amount of time to make the transition and find another job. In this situation, you can also help by writing a recommendation or using business and personal connections to generate employment leads.

Whatever the reasons for the firing, be sure the reasons are legally justified. Double-check your policy and employee handbook—the grounds for dismissal should be clearly stated and enforceable. All discussions and actions should be documented and retained in the employee's file. Firing someone due to personal feelings or bias is not only illegal, it's unwise. To dismiss an employee who has the potential to help your business is your loss—and possibly the competition's gain.

 **Apply Your Knowledge** What are two goals of performance evaluations? Think back to your investigation of Google. What do you think their performance evaluations might look like?

APPLICATION TO BUSINESS PLANNING

Hiring Needs

Use what you learned from this chapter to determine your business's hiring needs as part of your implementation and growth plan. You should support your findings with data from research. Be sure to include:

- The various positions you will have to fill for your business
- The plan for recruiting talent to these positions
- The vision for training and developing your employees

38 ASSESSMENT

REVIEWING OBJECTIVES

1. Describe the process of recruiting employees.
2. What are the various methods of employee training and development?
3. Explain the various methods of motivating, evaluating, promotion, and dismissing employees.

CRITICAL THINKING

How are benefits different from performance-based rewards?

ENTREPRENEURIAL THINKING EXERCISE: COMMUNICATION & COLLABORATION

Think back to your investigation of Google's hiring practices. Imagine that you are working with Google to find candidates that are passionate and have performed well in previous jobs. What types of questions would you ask in an interview to determine this? Write a list of questions that you would ask. Practice your interviewing skills by asking a peer to be a job seeker.

EXTENSION ACTIVITIES

Entrepreneurship & Literacy Skills

Complete the following task to demonstrate your understanding of entrepreneurship:

1. Grades 9–10: Working in a small group, develop an orientation program for new students at your school. Cover the formal aspects of student life, such as the location of classrooms. Also include insider tips about teachers, courses, the food in the cafeteria, sports, extracurricular activities, and so on. Use a group sharing application to share your work with other students and teachers at the school, and make updates based on their input and feedback.

2. Grades 11–12: Working in a small group, develop an orientation program for new students at your school. Cover the formal aspects of student life, such as the location of classrooms. Also include insider tips about teachers, courses, the food in the cafeteria, sports, extracurricular activities, and so on. Use a group sharing application to take a poll of students and teachers to see if your information is accurate. Update your work based on the poll findings.

GUIDING QUESTION:

"What are additional ways I can increase my reach and profits?"

APPLICATION TO BUSINESS PLANNING:

☑ Franchising and Licensing Revenue

OBJECTIVES

- Investigate franchising a business.
- Examine the advantages and disadvantages of being a franchisor.
- Explore brand licensing.

NFTE Entrepreneurial Mindset Characteristic Focus

☑ Opportunity Recognition

National Entrepreneurship Standards

- **A.33** Create processes for ongoing opportunity recognition
- **A.34** Adapt to changes in business environment
- **M.03** Document business systems and procedures

Common Career Technical Core Standards

- **BM.3** Explore, develop and apply strategies for ensuring a successful business career.
- **CRP.3** Attend to personal health and financial well-being.
- **CRP.10** Plan education and career path aligned to personal goals.

National Entrepreneurship Standards: Career Competencies

☑ **B.19** Make decisions

LESSON VOCABULARY

- brand equity
- brand licensee
- brand licensing
- brand licensor
- Federal Trade Commission (FTC)
- franchise agreement
- franchise disclosure document
- franchise fee
- franchise operations manual
- franchise royalty
- indemnification

39.1 Franchising a Business

As you learned in Unit 2, a franchise is a business arrangement in which an established company sells others the right to use the company's name and operating plan to sell the products or services in other locations. The franchisor is the owner of the established company. A franchisee is an individual who uses the company's name and operation to run the same business in another location. The franchisee pays the franchisor for this privilege. These payments typically include:

- **Franchise Fee.** The **franchise fee** is an upfront charge that is usually sizeable—from many thousands of dollars to more than a million—and allows the franchisee to join the franchisor's system.
- **Franchise Royalty.** The franchisee pays the franchisor a regular, ongoing payment called a **franchise royalty**. This is typically a percentage of the sales the franchisee earns. Basically, royalty fees are payments made to stay in the franchisor's system. They may be made monthly, quarterly, or on some other time schedule set by the franchisor.
- **Franchise Advertising Fee.** Many franchisors operate an advertising fund on behalf of their franchisees. This fund pays for the creation and distribution of marketing, advertising, and promotional materials that benefit all franchisees. For example, a franchisor might buy national radio or television commercials. Franchisees are often required to pay into this advertising fund based on a percentage of their sales.

◀ **Figure 39-1**
Franchises.
Franchises are copycat businesses in various locations.

Predicting.
Do you think there is a limit to the number of franchises a franchisor can establish?

Franchising Documents

Franchisors must provide three documents to any franchisee:

- Franchise disclosure document
- Franchising agreement
- Operations manual

Franchise Disclosure Document

A **franchise disclosure document** is a legal document that provides detailed information to potential franchisees about the franchisor. Typically, the document must be given to a potential franchisee at least ten days before the franchisee signs a franchise agreement or pays the franchise fee.

The **Federal Trade Commission (FTC)** is a U.S. government agency that administers consumer protection laws and regulates certain business practices. A federal law called the Franchise Rule regulates what must be included in a franchise disclosure document. State laws may include additional requirements. The FTC requires the document to include:

- Background information about the franchisor
- The costs of entering the franchisor's system
- The legal obligations of the franchisor and franchisee
- Notice of any recent lawsuits filed against the franchisor
- Statistics and detailed financial information about the franchisor's company (including all locations)

If the franchisor makes any statements about the existing or projected financial performance of the company, the statements must be backed up with specific information.

Franchise Agreement

A **franchise agreement** is a legally binding contract between a franchisor and franchisee that lists the rights and responsibilities of each party. A well-written franchise agreement includes:

- Detailed information about fees, royalties, and other payments (such as taxes or rent) to be paid by the franchisee
- Information regarding the use of the franchisor's patents, trademarks, service marks, copyrights, signs, and systems by the franchisee
- Description of the geographic territory in which the franchisee will operate
- Indication of the term of the franchise agreement (for example, ten years)
- The availability of training, technical support, marketing and advertising support, and other services to be provided by the franchisor
- Any requirements regarding specific vendors the franchisee must use
- Other financial and operational considerations
- Legal requirements, including the terms for renewal or termination of the agreement

Franchise Operations Manual

A **franchise operations manual** is a manual produced by a franchisor that gives detailed instructions to a franchisee about how to operate, staff, and manage a franchise unit. The manual should cover hiring and training employees, management practices, marketing, and operating procedures and systems (such as computer software). Because a franchise operations manual is considered the property of the franchisor, the franchise agreement will probably include a requirement to keep its contents confidential.

The operations manual must be detailed and precise so that franchisees can closely duplicate the practices and systems that have made the franchisor's business a success. Franchisors typically update the operations manual frequently.

 **Apply Your Knowledge** What are the three types of documents associated with franchising? From your investigation of Subway, why do you think that new Subway owners also have to fill out similar documents?

◀ **Figure 39-2**
Training.
A franchise operations manual must be very detailed and precise so franchisees can closely duplicate the practices and systems that have made the franchisor's business a success.

Drawing Conclusions.

Why is it important to duplicate the practices and systems of the original franchisor?

ENTREPRENEURIAL CASE STUDY: OPPORTUNITY RECOGNITION

 ## Kevin Plank— Under Armour

There Has to be Something Better

Kevin Plank is the founder and CEO of Under Armour (www.ua.com). Under Armour started when Kevin had the idea for a t-shirt that would better absorb sweat and keep athletes cool, dry, and light. Since its launch in 1996, Kevin has grown the business into a multi-billion dollar global brand with over 8,000 employees. Under Armour athletic performance apparel, footwear, and equipment are sold worldwide and worn by athletes at all levels—from youth to professional—on playing fields around the globe. Kevin has received a wide variety of professional accolades that demonstrate his growing influence within the industry.

It all started in 1995 when Kevin Plank, then the special team's captain on the University of Maryland football team, noticed that the cotton t-shirts he and his teammates wore underneath their pads were always soaked and heavy with sweat. He had become frustrated by having to change his t-shirt over and over again during practices, and the idea hit him: "There has to be something better." He didn't realize it then, but that one, simple statement would soon launch the performance apparel industry.

Kevin Plank.

Building and Growing the Business

Upon graduating from college with a bachelor's degree in business administration, Kevin started making that idea a reality and changing the way athletes dress. He set out to make a superior t-shirt—one that stayed light in even the most severe heat. After driving through the night to New York's famous garment district for fabric samples, Plank built his first prototype, which he then gave to his Maryland teammates and friends who'd gone on to play in the NFL. With their feedback, he went back to work, quickly emerging with a revolutionary new t-shirt built from microfibers that wicked moisture and kept athletes cool, dry, and light.

With his design nearly perfect, Plank needed funds to launch his apparel line, so he maxed out his credit cards to the tune of $40,000 and set up a company in his grandmother's basement in Washington, DC. With his new shirts in the back of his beat-up Ford Bronco, Kevin proceeded to phone every equipment manager in the Atlantic Coast Conference and reached out to his former football teammates, giving them samples and asking them to spread the word about his innovative product. Twelve months later, he made his first team sale to Georgia Tech. Other major Division I teams followed in droves, along with two dozen NFL teams. The company soon moved its headquarters to South Baltimore where it developed its now-famous gearlines, which included HeatGear®, ColdGear®, and AllSeasonGear®.

Revenue through Brand Recognition

Today, the Under Armour brand is instantly recognized as the world's most innovative performance footwear, apparel, and accessories. After strategic placement in two high-profile football movies and having their clothes worn by some of the world's most elite athletes, it has become a mainstay on athletic fields, courts, pitches, gyms, and rinks everywhere. Capitalizing on the popularity of the brand, the business has expanded its revenue streams to include money from direct sales and licensing fees to sell products with the Under Armour brand.

Thinking and Acting Like an Entrepreneur

- What problems did Kevin solve with his business?
- Why is a licensing strategy effective for a business such as Under Armour?
- In what ways does Kevin demonstrate the entrepreneurial mindset behavior of opportunity recognition?

39.2 Advantages and Disadvantages for Franchisors

A business can expand geographically in two ways: either by opening multiple company-owned units or by franchising the business. Franchising represents a great opportunity for business owners who want to expand their business but lack the money, time, or personnel to open numerous company-owned units.

Advantages for Franchisors

Franchising provides five major advantages to a franchisor:

- **Increased Revenue.** The franchisor earns a substantial upfront fee and regular royalty payments from each franchise.
- **New Locations without Financial Responsibility.** The franchisee, not the franchisor, takes on the financial responsibilities for loans, leases, and other expenses needed to get a franchise unit up and running.
- **Franchisee Investment.** Because franchisees invest their own money, they are highly motivated to make their franchise units profitable. This may not be the case for company-hired managers who run company units. Also, company-hired managers may quit at any time. A franchise agreement requires a franchisee to commit to a specific number of years.
- **No Liability.** A franchisor is not directly liable (legally and financially responsible) for the acts of the franchisee's employees, or accidents that take place on franchisee premises.
- **Builds Brand Awareness.** Franchising builds brand awareness for the franchisor's products or services.

◀ **Figure 39-3**
Franchise Advantages.
Franchises build brand awareness.

Drawing Conclusions.
What are the pros and cons of opening a franchise versus starting your own fried chicken restaurant?

Disadvantages for Franchisors

Franchising has five major disadvantages for a franchisor:

- **Regulatory and Legal Requirements.** There are substantial government regulations and legal restrictions.

- **Extensive Preparation.** Preparing a business for franchise, assembling the needed documents, and finding and training qualified franchisees can be time-consuming and expensive. Many franchisors hire professionals to help with the legal and accounting matters associated with franchising.

- **Substantial Upfront Investment.** All of the expenses involved in setting up a franchise have to be made before a single franchise fee is ever earned. This represents a substantial investment from the franchisor.

- **Time-Consuming.** Franchising is also time-consuming. The franchisor must prepare a thorough and detailed operations manual and provide technical, marketing, and other forms of support throughout the franchise arrangement. Franchisors risk spending so much time and money on their franchising activities that they neglect their original business. An established business should have more than one company-owned location before attempting to franchise. This helps prove to potential franchisees that the business concept and operations are repeatable.

- **Requires Certain Types of Businesses.** Franchising can only be successful for businesses that are in solid financial condition, easily duplicated, and not dependent on the personal characteristics of their owners. A business owner with a struggling business shouldn't consider franchising. Likewise, a business whose success is due primarily to its owner's personal contacts, charisma, or skills isn't a good candidate for franchising.

 **Apply Your Knowledge**   What are the five major advantages and disadvantages to a franchisor in relation to franchising a business? Think back to your investigation of Subway. Which of these advantages and disadvantages would apply to opening a Subway store?

CAREER COMPETENCIES

 ### Make Decisions

Six Steps to a Decision

You can take some of the uncertainty and doubt out of decision-making by turning it into a process. A process is a series of steps that leads to a conclusion.

1. Identify the decision to be made. Make sure you recognize and understand the choice. Define the decision as a goal—what do I want to achieve with this choice?

2. Consider all possible options. You usually have lots of options for each decision. Try to think of as many as you can, and write them down. Don't just consider the obvious choice; some of the best options might seem pretty bizarre at first. Consider your available resources and what you are trying to achieve.

3. Identify the consequences of each option. Each option will have consequences—some positive and some negative; some long-term and some short-term. Recognizing all the consequences will help you predict the outcome of your decision.

4. Select the best option. Once you consider the options and identify the consequences, you have the information you need to make your decision.

5. Make and implement a plan of action. Making the decision is not the end of the process. You must take steps to make it happen. Until you do, the decision is just an idea or thought in your head.

6. Evaluate the decision, process, and outcome. After you have acted on your decision, you can look back and evaluate it, based on your values and standards. Did you achieve the goal you defined in step 1? Did you miss any possible options? Did you correctly identify the consequences? Did you make use of your resources? Was the outcome what you hoped for?

Making Financial Decisions

A financial decision is a decision about how to manage your money. A basic financial decision might be what you should buy for lunch. A more complicated financial decision might be how much money to save for college. To make healthy financial decisions, you must consider your financial needs and wants, as well as how much money you have available.

You can use the decision-making process for financial decisions. For example, your bicycle might be broken. How can you decide what to do about it?

1. Identify the decision to be made. Do you need a new bicycle? Do you need to have your old bicycle repaired?

2. Consider all possible options. You could buy a new bike. You could buy a used bike. You could have your old bike fixed. You could use your brother's bike. You don't need a bike.

3. Identify the pros and cons of each option. If you buy a new bike, you will spend a lot of money. You will have less money available for other things. It will cost less to buy a used bike, and less than that to have your old bike fixed. If you have your old bike fixed, it might just break again.

4. Select the best option. You decide to have your old bike fixed.

5. Make and implement a plan of action. You call a few bike shops to find out what they charge for repairs and how long it will take. You select a shop and take your bike there.

39.3 Licensing a Brand

A brand is more than a name. It's a name with a specific worth in the marketplace. It has this worth because of the reputation of the product, company, or individual associated with the brand. **Brand equity** is the perceived monetary value of a brand. Entrepreneurs who build brand equity can benefit financially by selling the right to use their brand name to other businesses. This is referred to as licensing a brand, or brand licensing. **Brand licensing** is granting permission to some person or company to use your brand. The purpose of brand licensing is to associate a new product with an existing and popular brand name.

The company or person who owns the brand is the **brand licensor**. The company or person who is granted permission to use the brand is the **brand licensee**. A brand licensee pays the brand licensor for the privilege of using the brand name. The licensee is then responsible for producing and marketing the branded product. The licensee may pay an upfront fee and then pay regular royalties based on sales of the branded product. The licensor retains control over how the licensee can use the brand name and image.

Brand licensing has been popular for years in the entertainment and sports industries. Marketing new products can be expensive and time-consuming for companies. Associating a new product with the name or image of celebrities past or present (Babe Ruth and Michael Jordan are good examples), fictional characters (such as Mickey Mouse), or company brands (Harley-Davidson, Levi's, Caterpillar) helps gain recognition and acceptance in the marketplace. Basically, licensees are renting brand names to give their products a particular image and a marketing advantage. Licensees hope that customers who are already familiar with an existing brand will have positive feelings toward new products bearing the same brand.

▲ **Figure 39-4**
Brand Licensing.

Brand licensing has been popular for years.

Applying Concepts.

What are some logos that you see on different products?

Licensing Agreements

Brand licensing is accomplished through a written licensing agreement between a licensor and a licensee. The licensing agreement grants limited rights to the licensee. The licensor maintains ownership of the brand name and any trademarks or other marks associated with it.

The typical components of a licensing agreement are:

- **Time and Termination.** A licensing agreement specifies the length of time the agreement will be in effect and the conditions under which it can be ended.

- **Financial Terms.** These are the amounts and payment schedules for upfront fees and royalties.

- **Licensee Performance Standards.** The licensee may need to meet specific business performance standards during the licensing term—for example, sales or earnings targets.

- **Licensing Restrictions.** The licensor may impose restrictions on the licensee in such areas as pricing, the markets in which the licensed brand can be sold, distribution methods (and marketing techniques (such as how and where the licensed brand may be advertised and how much will be spent on advertising them).

- **Quality Control Criteria.** The licensee may have to provide regular samples of the branded products so the licensor can make sure they meet quality control standards.

- **Indemnification.** The licensor typically requires protection in the agreement from any legal action, fines, or other damages resulting from the licensee's actions. This is referred to as **indemnification** (in-dem-nih-fuh-KAY-shun).

- **Ownership Assurances.** The licensor must provide reasonable assurances to the licensee that the licensor is actually the legal owner of the brand name or trademark being licensed.

- **Confidentiality.** The licensee must keep confidential any trade secrets, quality standards, or other technical information provided by the licensor.

- **Multiple Licensees.** Many licensors want to be able to lease their brands to multiple companies. A non-exclusive licensing agreement is one in which a licensor maintains the right to lease the brand, only the licensee has the right to use the brand.

Advantages and Disadvantages of Licensing

Successful companies that have worked hard to build a positive brand name or image in the marketplace can benefit greatly from licensing.

The two biggest advantages are:

- **Increased Revenue.** The licensor typically receives substantial upfront fees and royalties from licensees.

- **Brand Enhancement.** Ideally, the branding process should increase customer awareness and enhance the positive reputation of the original brand.

These advantages will only be realized if the licensor chooses reliable licensees and makes wise decisions about which products to license. Some of the potential problems with licensing are:

- **Misbranding.** Some brand concepts do not transfer well across industries or across product groups. Misbranding is choosing the wrong product to brand. There are many famous examples of misbranding, including the failed efforts of the Harley-Davidson motorcycle company to extend its brand name to a cake decorating kit!

- **Over-Branding.** Over-branding occurs when licensors sell a brand name to so many licensees that the original brand concept becomes muddied and unclear to consumers.

- **Risk to the Brand.** Licensors risk losing the good name and image associated with their brand if they license it to products or services that disappoint consumers.

- **Lack of Marketing.** Licensees may mistakenly assume that a well-known brand name will sell their products on its own. As a result, they may shortchange their advertising campaigns. The licensor needs to be knowledgeable about the marketing techniques and intentions of licensees and should insist on minimum advertising standards and expenses as part of the licensing agreement.

- **Expense.** Licensors often hire brokers to find and qualify potential licensees for their brands. This can be an expensive process.

Market Saturation

In 2004, Starbucks seemed to be on an unending growth spurt, opening new stores at a rate of 4 per day for a total of 1,344 new stores. But in 2008, the company announced the closing of 600 stores across the United States. What happened?

One possibility is market saturation. Market saturation means that a product has been completely distributed in its market. For example, most households in the United States own a stove and only need one. So future growth in the stove industry will only come from population growth or from one manufacturer of stoves taking business from another manufacturer. In many cities, it is the same with coffee. Starbucks opened new stores quickly. They were followed by competition such as Caribou and Barnies, and now even McDonald's is getting into the premium coffee market. Everyone who wants fine coffee is covered. So what does a savvy entrepreneur do in the face of saturation? Starbucks is getting back to basics, eliminating its line of breakfast sandwiches and focusing on the quality of its core product. It is also pursuing growth overseas in newer markets, such as China.

Product innovation is also a core strategy in saturated markets. For example, it is true that most households have a washer and dryer. But not every household has a high-efficiency front load machine—in red.

 **Apply Your Knowledge** What is brand licensing? Think back to your investigation of Subway. How could Subway licenses its brand to make extra revenue?

✔ APPLICATION TO BUSINESS PLANNING

Franchising and Licensing Revenue

Use what you learned from this chapter to determine revenue that you can earn from licensing and franchising as part of your implementation and growth plan. You should support your findings with data from research. Be sure to include:

- Potential opportunities for licensing your brand
- Potential opportunities for making your business a franchise

ASSESSMENT

REVIEWING OBJECTIVES

1. What steps go into franchising a business?

2. Explain the advantages and disadvantages of being a franchisor.

3. What are the benefits of brand licensing?

CRITICAL THINKING

Why do successful businesses try to license their brands?

ENTREPRENEURIAL THINKING EXERCISE: OPPORTUNITY RECOGNITION

Think back to your investigation of Subway. Imagine that you were hired by a Subway competitor to grow their company. They currently manage all of their locations. What franchising or licensing opportunities would you propose? Be clear with your recommendations on how they would proceed to achieve their goals.

EXTENSION ACTIVITIES

Entrepreneurship & Literacy Skills

Complete the following task to demonstrate your understanding of entrepreneurship:

1. Grades 9–10: Using information in this chapter and other sources, research the popularity of franchising fast food restaurants such as McDonald's during the 1950s and 1960s. Based on your research, give a brief presentation describing how—and why—this period in history witnesses the birth of fast food in America.

2. Grades 11–12: Using information in this chapter and other sources, research the popularity of franchising fast food restaurants such as McDonald's during the 1950s and 1960s. Based on your research, give a brief presentation describing how—and why—this period in history witnesses the birth of fast food in America. Be sure to also discuss why the explanation for this boom seems unclear or uncertain.

CHAPTER 40

EXIT STRATEGY

OBJECTIVES

- Study methods for valuing a business.
- Investigate exit strategies for business owners.
- Understand how to build wealth.

NFTE Entrepreneurial Mindset Characteristic Focus

 Future Orientation

National Entrepreneurship Standards

- **A.35** Explain the need for continuation planning
- **A.38** Develop exit strategies
- **D.27** Demonstrate self control
- **G.06** Explain the time value of money
- **G.15** Set financial goals
- **G.16** Develop savings plan
- **I.22** Establish financial goals and objectives

Common Career Technical Core Standards

- **BM.3** Explore, develop and apply strategies for ensuring a successful business career.
- **CRP.3** Attend to personal health and financial well-being.
- **CRP.10** Plan education and career path aligned to personal goals.

National Entrepreneurship Standards: Career Competencies

 B.28 Set personal goals

LESSON VOCABULARY

- book value
- compounding
- diversification
- emergency fund
- employee stock ownership plan (ESOP)
- future value of money
- goodwill
- harvesting
- Individual Retirement Account (IRA)
- initial public offering (IPO)
- liquidation
- liquidity
- management buyout
- multiple of earnings method
- net worth
- owner's equity
- Rule of 72
- volatile

40.1 When to Leave a Business

One of the goals of owning a business is to build personal wealth. In fact, business ownership provides a unique opportunity for doing so. Regular profits earned during the lifetime of a business can provide a very good income and a comfortable living for the owner. But when an entrepreneur leaves his or her business, a much more valuable asset is involved. It's the accumulated and potential worth of the business itself.

Liquidity is the ease of converting a non-cash asset (such as a business) into cash. A successful business is a very valuable asset, but actually selling it is not always an easy process and must be timed carefully. The owner should consider three factors when deciding to sell a business:

- Personal considerations
- Condition of the business
- Condition of the economy

Entrepreneurs thrive on creating and growing innovative businesses. However, there may come a time when a business owner decides to sell the business. This decision is often prompted by personal reasons. The entrepreneur may wish to retire or pursue other business opportunities, or may have health or family issues. Selling a business can take months or even years. The new owner may insist that the old owner stay for a while after the deal is closed to help smooth the transition process. A business owner must consider these possibilities when selling a business.

◀ **Figure 40-1**
Personal Factors.
The decision to sell a business is often prompted by personal reasons.

Communicating.
What types of personal reasons might make an entrepreneur want to sell an existing business?

The condition of the business and the economy are also important in timing when to sell. The business will be worth more if it's growing and thriving when it goes up for sale. It needs to be operating smoothly and should not be dependent on the owner's extensive day-to-day involvement. Overall economic conditions are also important. A business will probably sell more quickly and for more money when the national and local economies are doing well.

How to Value a Business

Determining the value of a business can be difficult. You need to consider such factors as the business type, the length of time the business has been operating, its sales and profits, its cash flow, its liabilities or debts, its tangible assets (such as buildings, furniture, inventory, and equipment), and its reputation and prospects for growth. Obviously some of these factors are easy to express in numbers, but others, such as reputation, are not as easy to calculate.

There are no simple formulas for calculating the value of a business. There are, however, methods for calculating amounts that are considered benchmarks or reference points in the valuation process. These methods usually use numbers from the income statement or balance sheet. They don't completely give the worth of a business, but they do provide a starting point from which to begin an analysis of the business's value.

A business that is not doing well may be valued purely on the tangible assets it owns. **Liquidation** is a process in which the tangible assets of a business are sold. Liquidation often occurs when a failing business declares bankruptcy, or the owner decides the business itself is not worth selling. The owner (and any investors or creditors) may be able to recoup some of the money they have put into the business over its lifetime.

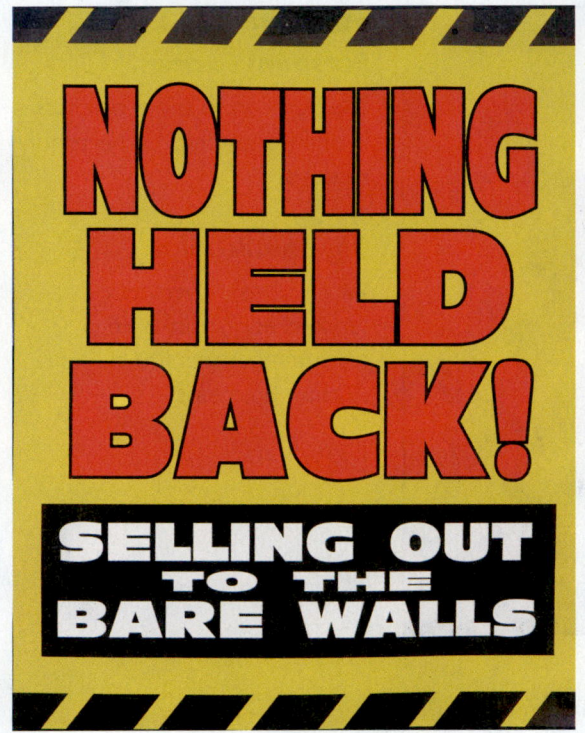

Another business valuation method is based on the book value of the business. **Book value** (also known as the **net worth** or **owner's equity**) is an accounting term that means the total assets minus the total liabilities according to a company's balance sheet. Experts believe that the book value isn't generally a good indication of the overall value of a business, but it does serve as a point of reference.

Total Assets − Total Liabilities = Book Value

The **multiple of earnings method** is a method of valuing a business in which the amount of business earnings over a specific time period (usually one year) is multiplied by a number, typically 3 to 5, to determine a reasonable sales price for the overall business. Use the annual net income as "earnings" in this calculation. For example, if the annual net income for a business is $230,000 and you are using a multiplier of 3, the value of the business would be $690,000.

▲ **Figure 40-2**
Liquidation.

Liquidation is the process in which the tangible assets of the business are sold.

Net Annual Income × Multiplier = Value of Business

$230,000 × 3 = $690,000

Inferring.

When would a business liquidate its assets? When wouldn't a business want to do this?

Other business-valuation methods use multiples—for example, multiples of cash flow or multiples of book value.

Some business-valuation methods consider both historical earnings and tangible assets. The value of tangible assets is also important to an owner who wants to leave a successful business. A prospective buyer may be more interested if the business owns a substantial amount of tangible assets. Additional methods for business valuation include estimating future earnings or future cash flow, the known value, or sales price for similar businesses in the industry.

All the valuation methods described here deal with aspects of a business that can be easily calculated. But one thing in the valuation process can't be calculated: goodwill. **Goodwill** is a business term that encompasses the intangible positive aspects of a business, such as location, employee knowledge and skills, brand awareness, intellectual property, relationships with suppliers and customers, and reputation in the community and the industry. The actual value of a business, therefore, depends on factors that can be calculated and factors that cannot be calculated.

In all cases, the business will be more valuable if a new owner is confident that the business already includes both the tangible and intangible aspects needed for success.

Apply Your Knowledge Why would a business owner want to sell or liquidate his or her business? What are the three factors to consider when deciding to sell or liquidate a business? From your investigation of PayPal, did the owners seem to take these into consideration? Why or why not?

ENTREPRENEURIAL CASE STUDY: FUTURE ORIENTATION

 ## Andres Cardona— Elite Basketball Academy

Solving a Problem in the Community

Andres Cardona is the founder and CEO of Elite Basketball Academy (www. eliteballacademy.com). Elite Basketball Academy was a business that he started as a high school student in his entrepreneurship course sponsored by the Network for Teaching Entrepreneurship (NFTE). Even at age 14, Andres Cardona recognized the lack of affordable options for youth to improve their basketball skills in South Miami. Andres loved the game so much he decided to start Elite Basketball Academy, where he teaches basketball fundamentals to youth in the area. For his efforts, he was named a 2012 NFTE Global Young Entrepreneur.

Andres Cardona.

Andres excels at basketball. Unfortunately, his community offers few basketball leagues for young athletes, and personal training is too expensive for most families. With such limited options for kids to hone their basketball skills, Andres decided it was up to him to provide an affordable, quality alternative. He used the skills he was learning in the NFTE course to start to put together a plan for a basketball academy that would be more financially reasonable for families in the community.

Creating Your Own Job

About the same time as taking his NFTE course, Andres's mother lost her job. Though she never asked him for help, he knew she needed it. When he couldn't find a job either, he decided to create one. He took a personal inventory of his knowledge, strengths, weaknesses, and experience, and ultimately saw the wisdom in following his passion. "After days of thinking about other businesses and really critiquing their chance of success, I came to the conclusion that I should only launch a business where I knew I was going to love what I was doing, regardless of its profitability or demanding work hours."

After a lot of hard work and with support from NFTE, Andres launched his business to immediate success. Andres feels that much of the business's success was due to the experience. "The difference between my business and that of my competitors is that we don't just 'coach,' we focus on our athletes individually," says Andres. "We give every single client our undivided attention, which allows us to build long lasting relationships that extend beyond the basketball court." Furthermore, Andres recognizes a direct correlation between the discipline that is necessary on the court and the work ethic that informs academic success. He has made it a point to stress that with his clients, who are at risk of spending more time on the street than in the classroom.

Seeing Problems as Opportunities

Andres's academy's launch was so successful a competitor quickly wanted to buy it! Andres, however, had no interest in selling his business, as he wants to continue to let kids who have had trauma in their lives have an accessible outlet. He continues to run the academy while attending Florida International University, double majoring in finance and marketing. Andres also continues to pursue his entrepreneurial spirit, recently launching his second business, PublicizeUs.com, to help small businesses develop websites and e-commerce. "Thinking like an entrepreneur helps you see problems for what they truly are: opportunities," Andres explains.

Thinking and Acting Like an Entrepreneur

- How did Andres use his skills and passion to identify a business opportunity?
- What are some ways that Andres could potentially grow his business to have an impact on more youth?
- In which ways does Andres demonstrate an entrepreneurial mindset behavior of having a future orientation?

40.2 Strategies for Leaving the Business

Planning how to sell a business is just as important as planning how to start a business. The process of exiting a business and gaining the value of the business in cash when you leave is referred to as **harvesting** the business. It's sometimes called cashing in or cashing out because it involves turning a non-cash asset (the business) into cash.

An exit strategy should be part of an entrepreneur's initial business plan. Thinking about exiting a successful business someday helps entrepreneurs focus on their goals for the business and determines the measures they will use to define business success. Potential investors will be keenly interested in an entrepreneur's exit strategy. It represents a

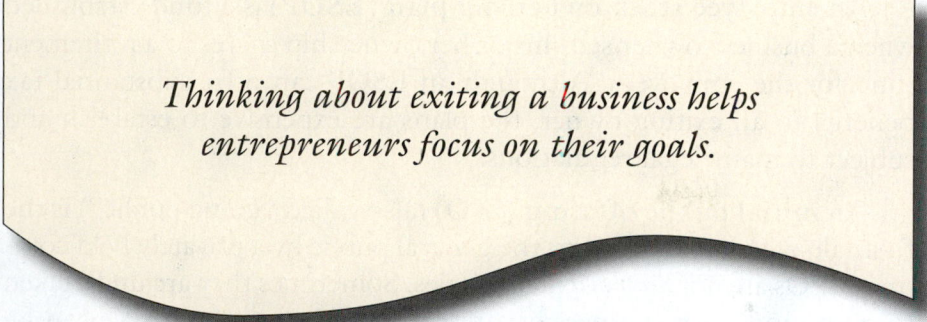

Thinking about exiting a business helps entrepreneurs focus on their goals.

future opportunity for them to recoup their investment and potentially gain additional profit beyond their initial investment.

Harvesting Value from a Business

Several methods exist for harvesting value from a successful and growing business. Most methods account not only for the past success of the business but also for its future potential to make money. For most entrepreneurs, the desired exit strategy is selling the business, or at least selling their ownership interest in the business.

Some successful business owners choose to sell their business to another company, merging it into the other company in the process. Often, competing businesses have an interest in such sales. The terms acquisition and merger are often used interchangeably to describe the financial union of two companies. However, the first indicates the outright purchase of one company by another, and the second is a mutual decision by two companies to join together. In both cases the deal results in an exchange of money (or stock) and changes in ownership control. An owner that chooses to sell to, or merge with, another company must be prepared for close scrutiny by the other firm.

▲ **Figure 40-3**
Selling a Business.

Businesses can be sold just like any product.

Drawing Conclusions.

How would you put a price on the business you created?

Most small businesses, and many large ones, are privately held, meaning their shares are held by a small number of people—maybe only by one individual (the owner) or by the owner and family members or a handful of investors (and not traded publicly). Typically the company's founder/owner is the sole or majority shareholder. By selling those shares, the owner gives up ownership in the company in exchange for a cash payment.

A **management buyout** is an exit strategy in which a business owner sells his or her ownership shares to the business's managers. The managers then take over ownership of the business. The management buyout is popular with entrepreneurs who wish to transfer business ownership to people they already know and trust to lead the company in the future.

An **employee stock ownership plan (ESOP)** is a fund established when a business owner sells his or her ownership shares to a retirement fund for the employees. Although an ESOP can offer substantial tax benefits to an exiting owner, the plans are expensive to establish and subject to many legal regulations.

An **initial public offering (IPO)** (also called "going public") is the first sale of shares of stock to the general public by a privately held company. IPOs are not always exit strategies. Sometimes they are undertaken to raise money for business expansion. In either case, an IPO can be risky. The stock may be popular with the general public, or it may not. There's no way to tell until the IPO is actually executed. An exiting business owner is also bound by government regulations that restrict company executives from selling their shares within a certain time period after an IPO is initiated.

 **Apply Your Knowledge**   Explain three exit strategies for leaving a business. Think back to your investigation of the sale of PayPal. What exit strategy did Elon and his co-founders use?

CAREER COMPETENCIES

 ### Set Personal Goals

Most successful people say that the secret to their success is setting goals. When you set a goal, you decide what you want to accomplish. Goal setting enables you to focus on your dreams and turn them into reality. By setting goals, you create a path for your future success. Learning how to set goals is a valuable lesson you'll use throughout your life.

Start with a Dream

Everyone has wishes and dreams. This is the starting point for success. The idea is to convert a wish or dream into an achievable goal. Sometimes a wish or a dream is a long-term goal, something you'll make happen in a few years. You can also set short-term goals to achieve right now. For example, you might dream of being the owner of a successful company. To achieve this, you might set a series of short-term goals—each of which can take you a step closer to your final destination.

As with any journey to a specific destination, you need a roadmap. Setting goals lets you map out exactly where you're going and how you'll get there. Each goal becomes a manageable step along the way. And accomplishing each short-term goal helps you keep your focus on the long-term goal.

Where do you begin? You begin by identifying your dream. What do you desire? In what area do you want to be successful? What do you want to change, improve, or achieve in your life? Allow your imagination to dream big! Dare to dream!

Think Positively

When we identify a dream, we often come up with excuses that prevent us from reaching our goals.

We think about the work involved and the challenges and before long we're using words like no, can't, won't, never, maybe, impossible, and later. To achieve a goal, you need to develop an "I will make it happen" attitude. Get out of your own way and start planning your future. Surround yourself with people who will support your dream and cheer you on. You may encounter roadblocks along the way, but a positive attitude will help you figure out how to overcome each challenge.

The Goal-Setting Process

When you begin the process of setting a goal, you need to make sure you are working with a SMART goal. A SMART goal is one that is:

- **Specific.** Your goal statement spells out exactly what you want to achieve, in simple language.
- **Measurable.** You must be able to measure your progress.
- **Action-Oriented.** You must list the actions required for reaching your goal and commit to them.
- **Realistic.** Your goal must be manageable. Do you have everything you need to achieve it?
- **Time-Specific.** Goals need to have a target date for completion.

SMART goals are focused and achievable. You decide what you want, you agree to the steps involved, and you control the outcome. You are in the driver's seat.

Career Skills in Action

Try it. Set a goal for yourself by following these steps:

1. **Goal Statement.** Decide what it is you want and then write a goal statement. Make sure it is a SMART goal. Write the goal in the form of a positive "I will" statement.
2. **Action Steps.** Below the goal statement, write a numbered list of the action steps required for completing the goal.
3. **Completion Date.** Below your list of action steps, write the date when you want to complete your goal.

40.3 Building Wealth

Building a successful small business is a fine achievement. What you do with your earnings, however, determines whether you will have a secure financial future or will always be struggling to get by.

The key to a secure financial future is saving money and investing it. Whether you have a career as an entrepreneur or work as an employee, you need to learn how to invest your money so it can earn more money.

Importance of Saving

When you earn money, what do you do with it? If you're like most people, you use it to pay bills and buy things. Here's an idea: pay yourself first. Get into the habit of automatically saving 10% of your income. This is the first step toward building wealth.

If you don't make a great deal of money, this may sound hard— even impossible. But try it. You'll discover ways to get by without that 10%. Let's say that you pay yourself $200 from sales made by your small business this month. First thing, put $20 into your savings account. Don't even think about it. You'll still have $180 to use for bills and purchases.

Time Value of Money

If you start saving now, you'll have money for such goals as buying a house or financing a comfortable retirement. Investing some of your savings will help you, too. Safe investments usually grow slowly. Riskier ones may grow faster, but you could lose your money. If you are counting on your investment for your future, a good policy is to invest most of your funds in a relatively safe way.

Remember, all investments involve some risk, meaning that you could lose money. And remember this principle as well: The greater the potential reward of an investment, the more risky it is likely to be.

High Reward = High Risk

This implies that if an investment has little or no risk, the reward will probably not be high.

Low Risk = Low Reward

Invested money grows by **compounding**, which means that you earn interest on your interest. The younger you are when you start saving and investing, the more compound interest you will accumulate.

The **Rule of 72** is a quick way to figure how long it will take to double your money at a given rate of return. Here's how it works: Divide 72 by the interest rate (or return rate) to find the number of years needed to double your money. Some examples are shown in Table 40.1.

Table 40.1   The Rule of 72

Growth Rate	Years to "Double"
4%	18
6%	12
8%	9
10%	7.2
12%	6

For example, how long would it take for you to double $1,000 if you were earning 8% interest?

72 ÷ Interest or Rate of Return = Number of Years to Double Money

$$72 \div 8 = 9 \text{ Years}$$

The government allows you to set up a retirement account called an IRA (Individual Retirement Account). This type of investment is tax free, meaning that you typically won't have to pay taxes on the money in the account until you withdraw it. The goal is to save this money, allowing it to compound, so you'll have money after you retire.

One type of retirement account, the Roth IRA, can be a good choice for a young person because it allows you to make a one-time withdrawal of funds to buy a house. With the Roth, you can save not only for your retirement but for buying a house as well.

The government establishes a maximum amount of money that you are allowed to save in an IRA each year. To encourage people to save, the government has been steadily increasing that figure.

Future Value of Money

The future value of money is the amount to which a given sum will increase over time through investment.

The Future Value of Money chart, shown in Table 40.2 on the next page, shows you how much one invested dollar will be worth over time at a given interest rate. Take a look at the table. Can you see that $1 invested for 10 years at 10% will grow to $2.59? (So $100 invested at 10% for 10 years will increase to $259.)

Risk Factors: Time and Liquidity

Two factors affect the risk associated with an investment:

- **Time.** The longer someone has your money, the greater the chance that your investment could somehow be lost. The longer you have to wait for the payback on your investment, the greater the return should be.

Table 40.2 Future Value of Money

Period (in years)	1%	2%	3%	4%	5%	6%	7%	8%	9%	10%	11%	12%
1	1.0100	1.0200	1.0300	1.0400	1.0500	1.0600	1.0700	1.0800	1.0900	1.1000	1.1100	1.1200
2	1.0201	1.0404	1.0609	1.0816	1.1025	1.1236	1.1449	1.1664	1.1881	1.2100	1.2321	1.2544
3	1.0303	1.0612	1.0927	1.1249	1.1576	1.1910	1.2250	1.2597	1.2950	1.3310	1.3676	1.4049
4	1.0406	1.0824	1.1255	1.1699	1.2155	1.2625	1.3108	1.3605	1.4116	1.4641	1.5181	1.5735
5	1.0510	1.1041	1.1593	1.2167	1.2763	1.3382	1.4026	1.4693	1.5386	1.6105	1.6851	1.7623
6	1.0615	1.1261	1.1941	1.2653	1.3401	1.4185	1.5007	1.5869	1.6771	1.7716	1.8704	1.9738
7	1.0721	1.1487	1.2299	1.3159	1.4071	1.5036	1.6058	1.7138	1.8280	1.9487	2.0762	2.2107
8	1.0829	1.1717	1.2668	1.3686	1.4775	1.5939	1.1782	1.8509	1.9926	2.1436	2.3045	2.4760
9	1.0937	1.1951	1.3048	1.4233	1.5513	1.6895	1.8385	1.9990	2.1719	2.3580	2.5580	2.7731
10	1.1046	1.2190	1.3439	1.4802	1.6209	1.7909	1.9672	2.1589	2.3674	2.5937	2.8394	3.1059
11	1.1157	1.2434	1.3842	1.5395	1.7103	1.8983	2.1049	2.3316	2.5084	2.8531	3.1518	3.4786
12	1.1268	1.2682	1.4258	1.6010	1.7959	2.0122	2.2522	2.5182	2.8127	3.1384	2.4985	3.8960
13	1.1381	1.2936	1.4685	1.6651	1.8057	2.1329	2.4098	2.7196	3.0658	3.4523	3.8833	4.3635
14	1.1495	1.3195	1.5126	1.7317	1.9799	2.2609	2.5785	2.9372	3.3417	3.7975	4.3104	4.8871
15	1.1610	1.3459	1.5580	1.8009	2.0789	2.3966	2.7590	3.1722	3.6425	4.1773	4.7846	5.4736

- **Liquidity.** As you remember from Chapter 30, liquidity refers to the ability to convert assets into cash. You always want to know how liquid your investment is. Can you get your money out in twenty-four hours? Or do you have to commit your investment for a specified period?

The longer the time frame, the riskier the investment. The less liquid, the riskier the investment. The easier your money is to retrieve, the lower your return will probably be.

Tolerating Risk

Here is one more factor to consider when deciding on the risk and potential reward an investment offers: How do you feel about risk?

Everyone has a different tolerance for risk, and there is no level of tolerance that is "right" for everyone. Some people prefer safe investments that offer lower rates of return and minimal risk. Others prefer to take greater chances with their money in hopes of earning higher returns.

You need to know how you feel about risk before you make a decision about investing. You don't want to enter into investments that will keep you awake at night worrying!

Investing

Once you have saved some money and have determined your risk tolerance, you are almost ready to invest.

Before you actually make the investment, be sure you have enough cash saved to cover your personal expenses (food, clothes, rent, transportation, and so on) for at least three months. This is your **emergency fund**. It will protect you from having to sell off investments if an emergency prevents you from being able to earn money for a while. Keep your emergency fund in a savings account (or in some investment that can be turned into cash within twenty-four hours).

Once you have established an emergency fund, you are ready to invest. Choose from these possibilities:

- **Cash.** Cash investments can be retrieved in twenty-four hours. There is almost no risk that you will lose money in a savings account, so savings accounts typically pay a very low rate of interest. Treasury bills are another cash investment. Treasury bills are short-term loans issued by the U.S. government. The government pays you a fairly low interest rate but guarantees your money. You can sell treasury bills on the market for cash within twenty-four hours. You can also turn stocks and bonds into cash fairly quickly by selling them, but the price may be lower than what you paid. Securities (stocks and bonds) are riskier than cash.

- **Bonds.** Bonds are also riskier than cash, but less risky than stocks. Bonds are interest-bearing loans. Corporations issue bonds to borrow money that they agree to pay back on a specific date. If you buy a bond, you will be paid interest. When the bond comes due, the money you paid for it will be returned to you. Bond prices fluctuate and can be traded (bought and sold) on the bond market.
- **Stocks.** Stocks represent equity shares of a company. If you own stock in a corporation, you own a piece of the business, however small. Stocks may pay dividends, which are a share of the company's profits. You can trade stocks on the stock market. Stocks tend to be more risky (and potentially more rewarding) than bonds or cash.

Volatile Investments

Investments can be affected by world events. If war breaks out, stock prices usually fall. Bad news often drives the stock market down. A stock's price may also change in reaction to news about the company that issued the stock. Because stock prices change in reaction to information, they are considered to be **volatile** investments. This means they can change frequently and unpredictably.

When there is uncertainty, people tend to move their money into cash and other low-risk, highly liquid investments, even if it means taking a loss.

Diversification

Protect yourself from volatility by spreading your money over different types of investments. This method of decreasing risk is called **diversification**. It is the opposite of "putting all your eggs in one basket."

If you have $10,000 and you invest it all in the stock of one company, you will lose all your money if that company goes out of business. It is wiser to diversify: buy small amounts of many different stocks. When you own $1,000 worth of each of ten stocks, you'll only lose a small part of your investment if one company fails. Because the stock market and the bond market tend to behave differently, it is good to diversify by owning both. When the stock market goes down, bonds usually rise, and vice versa.

What Would You Do with Wealth?

This chapter has provided an overview of the strategies for exiting a successful business and suggested ways to build personal wealth. Your decisions in building a business and in building your wealth will cause you to think about your long-term life goals. If you do accumulate wealth—from the continued performance of your business or from exiting the business one day—what would you do with that wealth?

Many entrepreneurs use their wealth to start a second business. In this way, over time, individuals have built great fortunes. Others use their money to go back to school. Still others become philanthropists and focus on helping others.

The most important lesson entrepreneurship can teach is that you have the power to think for yourself and to create an exciting and fulfilling life. When you use your imagination and skills to grow a small business, you prove to yourself that you can create something real and valuable from an idea.

Whether you become a lifelong entrepreneur or choose another career entirely, remember that you will always be stronger by thinking and behaving entrepreneurially.

Never stop asking:

- What kind of life do I want?
- How can I make my community a better place?
- What makes me happy?
- How can I help others be happy?

> *Use your imaginaton to grow not only the business of your dreams, but also the **life** of your dreams. Dare to dream!*

Apply Your Knowledge   What are some ways of building wealth? How did Elon and the founders of PayPal build wealth through starting and selling their business?

APPLICATION TO BUSINESS PLANNING

Exit Strategy

Use what you learned from this chapter to determine revenue that you can earn from licensing and franchising as part of your implementation and growth plan. You should support your findings with data from research. Be sure to include:

- The estimated value of your business before you would consider selling it someone else
- The exit strategy that is appropriate for your business

REVIEWING OBJECTIVES

1. What are the methods for valuing a business?

2. Describe exit strategies for business owners.

3. What are different ways to build wealth?

CRITICAL THINKING

How might having an exit strategy help an entrepreneur focus on the business?

ENTREPRENEURIAL THINKING EXERCISE: FUTURE ORIENTATION

Think back to your investigation of Elon and the sale of PayPal. Imagine that you were trying to convince a fellow entrepreneur to put in the eventual sale of their business as an exit strategy. What would you argue to convince them of the long-term investment? Be clear and use examples from this chapter to support your argument.

EXTENSION ACTIVITIES

Entrepreneurship & Mathematics Skills

Complete the following task to demonstrate your understanding of entrepreneurship:

Grades 9–12: Use your knowledge of interest rates on saved money from this chapter to complete the following task:

- Create an equation that demonstrates the Rule of 72. Have the interest rate be the dependent variable and the number of years to double the money be the independent variable.

- Plot this function on a graph.

- What type of curve does this produce? Describe what this graph represents.

Unit 8: Growing the Business

CHAPTER SUMMARY

36. Planning for Business Growth

Growing a business means making changes that are expected to result in increased sales. Growth should be well planned and timed based on the condition of the business, the overall economy, and the life goals of the business owner. When introducing a new product to the market, it is important to know the product's life-cycle stage for the product group. Growth strategies fall into three broad categories: intensive, integrative, and diversification. Intensive growth strategies include market penetration, market development, and product development. Integrative growth strategies include horizontal and vertical integration. Diversification growth strategies may be synergistic or horizontal. Growing a business poses both personal and practical challenges to the business owner. The personal challenges include less control but more risk for the entrepreneur as a business grows. Any plans for growth must be carefully timed with the entrepreneur's life goals in mind. Practical challenges relate to space, organizational structure, materials and equipment, information technology, people and skills, and money. The funds needed for growth can be raised through internal or external means—from cash reserves (profits) or by borrowing or selling equity. A SWOT analysis should be performed to assess the strengths and weaknesses of the business, the threat posed by competitors, and the growth opportunity.

37. Growing Operations

One of the largest challenges for businesses that what to grow is being able to continue operations at a higher rate. Entrepreneurs must structure operations so that more products or services can be produced if needed. Before a business begins scaling its operations, it must choose a site and plan its layout that will accommodate growth. Production management is concerned with the processes that produce goods and services. Three major tasks are scheduling, controlling productivity, and controlling quality. Gantt charts and PERT charts are common scheduling tools. Buyers use sales and inventory data, sales forecasts, and information on lead times to help them make purchasing decisions. Price and payment terms are particularly important factors. Discounts are often offered to buyers who buy large quantities, pay their bills early, or are in the same trade as the vendor. Good recordkeeping is an essential element of the purchasing process.

38. Recruiting and Training Staff

Entrepreneurs can recruit potential employees from professional contacts and competitors, colleges, and websites of professional organizations. Through taking applications and resumes and conducting interviews, they can choose the best candidate for the job. Entrepreneurs also hire outside experts for services that are needed only occasionally. Entrepreneurs train and develop employees in-house through orientation and mentoring. Outside providers include classes, seminars, workshops, and conferences. Entrepreneurs can motivate employees by offering flexible work arrangements, performance-based rewards, and a positive work environment. Regular performance evaluations are a tool to improve employee performance and the business's practices and policies. The decision to promote or dismiss an employee should be made carefully and objectively, based on what's best for the business.

39. Franchising and Licensing

Setting up and running a franchise operation is expensive for the franchisor but can provide significant benefits if the franchise units are successful. The franchisor earns cash from fees and royalties paid by the franchisees, and benefits from wider brand awareness in the marketplace. Franchising does pose substantial legal, accounting, and regulatory challenges to the franchisor. Brand licensing is the granting of legal permission to others to use your brand name to sell something. The licensor maintains ownership over the brand name but earns income by leasing its use to other companies that wish to take advantage of the brand's existing public name awareness and good reputation.

40. Exit Strategies

Exit strategies are ways of leaving a business and harvesting as much cash as possible. You should include an exit strategy in your original business plan. Exit timing will be governed by personal considerations and the state of the individual business and the economy as a whole. The value of a business can be roughly estimated by using financial records, such as the income statement or balance sheet. The actual evaluation should take into account the intangible, goodwill aspects of the business. Owners often exit unsuccessful businesses by selling off tangible assets. Possible exit strategies for owners of thriving businesses include acquisitions and mergers, management buyouts, establishing employee stock ownership plans, or making an initial public offering of stock. When you invest money, it compounds and builds wealth. The future value of money is the amount to which it will increase over time.

UNIT 8 VOCABULARY

accreditation

automation

benefits

book value

brand equity

brand licensee

brand licensing

brand licensor

cash discount

compensation

compounding

core business

debt capital

demand forecasting

diversification

diversification growth strategy

division of labor

emergency fund

employee stock ownership plan (ESOP)

e-procurement

equity capital

Federal Trade Commission (FTC)

flextime

franchise agreement

franchise disclosure document

franchise fee

franchise operations manual

franchise royalty

future value of money

Gantt chart

goodwill

green procurement

harvesting

horizontal diversification

horizontal integration strategy

indemnification

Individual Retirement Account (IRA)

initial public offering (IPO)

integrative growth strategy

intensive growth strategy

job description

job enlargement

job enrichment

job shadowing

law of diminishing returns

layout

lead time

liquidation

liquidity

maintenance

management buyout

market development

market penetration

market share

micromanager

milestone

multiple of earnings method

net worth

nonperiodic reordering

organic growth

orientation

owner's equity

packing slip

periodic reordering

perpetual life cycle

PERT chart

product development

product life cycle

product specification

production management

productivity

protégé

purchase order

quality circle

recruit

Rule of 72

salary

sales forecasting

self-financing

synergistic diversification

telecommuting

value analysis

vertical integration strategy

volatile

wage

zoning laws

CHECK YOUR UNDERSTANDING

Choose the letter that best answers the question or completes the statement.

1. The recruiting process includes

   a. resumes and interviews

   b. promotions and dismissals

   c. mentors and protégés

   d. seminars and workshops

2. The purpose of orientation is to assess a worker's performance over the

   a. past year

   b. locate potential job candidates

   c. acquaint a new employee with co-workers and job duties

   d. determine whether a worker should be dismissed

3. To be effective, a performance-based reward should be

   a. withheld occasionally

   b. shared by all employees

   c. linked to a specific, achievable goal

   d. fairly expensive

4. An employee's compensation includes

   a. only wages or salaries

   b. wages or salaries and benefits

   c. wages or salaries and performance-based rewards

   d. only wages; salaries are not considered compensation

5. You buy $5,000 worth of lumber on credit from a vendor. The vendor offers you a 2% discount on the price if you pay the full amount within 10 days. What is the discounted price you will pay for the lumber?

   a. $4,900

   b. $4,800

   c. $4,500

   d. $4,200

6. How could a SWOT analysis be used when planning business growth?

   a. to assess the threat posed by the competition in a new market

   b. to assess a company's existing strengths and weaknesses

   c. to assess a specific growth opportunity

   d. all of the above

7. The stages of a product life cycle are

   a. introduction, growth, maturity, and decline

   b. space, materials, people, and money

   c. vertical and horizontal

   d. intensive, integrative, and diversification

8. A fast food restaurant that begins selling toys is following which growth strategy?

   a. market development

   b. vertical integration

   c. horizontal diversification

   d. micromanagement

9. A product with a perpetual life cycle is

   a. a product in the introduction stage of the product life cycle

   b. a product in the growth stage of the product life cycle

   c. a product with rapidly declining sales

   d. a product with relatively constant sales

10. An integrative growth strategy is best described as

   a. developing new markets for existing products

   b. buying other companies in the same industry

   c. developing new products for existing target markets

   d. introducing products in the decline stage of the product life cycle

11. If one factor of production is increased while others remain constant, the incremental improvement in productivity will tend to fall off at some point. This is known as

   a. the division of labor

   b. the law of diminishing returns

   c. indemnification

   d. liquidation

12. A franchise royalty is

   a. the same as a franchise fee

   b. the fee for filing a franchise disclosure document

   c. a regular ongoing payment based on the franchisee's sales

   d. a regular ongoing payment made to the Federal Trade Commission by the franchisor

13. The Rule of 72 tells you

a. how much a dollar is worth over a specified amount of time at a given return rate

b. how much to save for an emergency fund

c. when your money doubles at a given return rate

d. when to cash in stocks and bonds

14. Which of the following is an advantage of franchising to the franchisor?

a. selling a franchise can help a struggling business

b. the franchisor must pay legal fees to prepare a franchising document

c. the franchisor collects a fee and royalties from the franchisee

d. selling a franchise is an inexpensive process

15. The book value of a business is equal to

a. the overall value of the business

b. net worth minus owner's equity

c. a multiple of business's earnings

d. total assets minus total liabilities on the company's balance sheet

16. One of the primary goals when exiting a business is to

a. have exclusive licensing agreements

b. have nonexclusive licensing agreements

c. convert the business to cash

d. prepare a franchise disclosure document for the new owner

BUSINESS COMMUNICATION

1. Using the Internet, find five large companies that offer products or services that differ from their respective core businesses. Present your findings to the class.

2. Work in a group of five. One person plays the owner of a successful pet-sitting business and the others are employees in the business. The owner wants to expand by offering dog obedience classes but doesn't want to hire anyone new. Role-play the situation when the owner tells the employees that they will need to become dog trainers.

3. Imagine that you operate a successful retail store and wish to grow your business by using an intensive growth strategy. Choose one of the strategies and write a letter to your local bank manager explaining how you plan to grow.

REVIEW & ASSESSMENT

4. Research the Federal Trade Commission's Franchise Rule and create a table showing a list of the items that must be included in a franchise disclosure document and a brief description of each item.

5. Write an exit strategy for an imaginary business. Include both the business and personal goals you hope to fulfill when you leave.

6. Working with three or four classmates, develop a written list of fifteen branded products for which the industry or product group associated with the original brand name is different from the present industry or product group of the branded product. Share your list with the class.

7. Write a help wanted ad for the job of being a high school student. Include at least six points detailing the position's purpose, tasks, and responsibilities; the education needed; and the qualities of an ideal candidate.

8. Throughout this text, you used the Entrepreneurial Discovery Process (see table at the end of Chapter 5 in Unit 1) to explore and develop the sections of a business plan. Using what you have learned, finalize your business plan and present it to the class, explaining each section and how you addressed the key questions during each phase of its development.

BUSINESS MATH

1. Total sales of athletic shoes amounted to $3 million last year. Tip Top Shoes had a 30% market share, while Might-ee Shoes had a 45% share. The remaining market share was split evenly between Super Glide and Hoopster Shoes. Calculate last year's sales for each company.

2. A small car wash business makes $5 in profit for each car washed. It performs an average of 200 car washes per month. For the past twenty months, the owner has been saving 50% of the profit. She wants to buy a new machine that costs $12,500. How much money has she saved so far? How many more months until she has enough to buy the machine?

3. You must pay a franchise royalty of 5% on monthly sales up to $20,000 and 7% on monthly sales greater than $20,000. (For example, if your sales were $23,000, you would pay 5% on $20,000 and 7% on $3,000.) If your monthly sales for the past three months were $18,500, $20,100, and $27,200, how much did you pay in franchise royalties per month and in total?

4. You have received two offers to buy your business, which has a book value of $93,500 and annual earnings of $108,500. Company A has offered to pay $20,000 plus four times the book value. Company B will pay $23,500 plus three times annual earnings. How much is each company offering? Which offer will you take?

5. In 1960, employers in the United States spent $36 billion on employees' health insurance premiums. In 1980, they spent $201 billion. How does the later figure compare to the earlier one as a percentage? In 2006, health insurance premiums cost employers $465 billion. How does that amount compare, as a percentage, to the 1980 figure? During which time period was the rate of increase faster?

6. Major League Baseball imposes a competitive balance tax on teams whose players' salaries and benefits in a year exceed the maximum allowed. The tax equals 40% of the sum over the limit. In 2007, the maximum was $148 million. The New York Yankees' payroll was $207.7 million. How much did the Yankees pay in competitive balance tax? The Yankees averaged $24.32 million in taxes each year. How does the 2007 payment compare to that average?

BUSINESS ETHICS

1. Your family gave you money to start your business five years ago. In exchange, you gave them 20% ownership in your company and a share in the decision-making. The business is doing well, and you want to add some new products to your line. Your family is opposed to the idea because of the risk. An outside investor will provide the cash you need to grow, but only if you buy back your family's share of the business, putting them out of the decision-making process. Should you take the money from the outside investor? Explain your reasoning.

2. You are an entrepreneur with a successful and profitable business that employs twenty-five people, some of whom have been with you for many years. You want to sell the business and invest the cash in another opportunity. Should your employees be a consideration in your decision? Should you tell your employees you are planning to sell the business? If so, when? Describe your decision and the steps you would take with your employees.

3. You have a business credit card that gives mileage points that can be used toward airfare or other travel expenses. You have ten employees. You announced that the company would award these points to the employee who missed the fewest days of work during the year, to help pay for a well-earned vacation. Now you find employees are coming in sick when they should, perhaps, have stayed at home. You have also been told that some employees are coming to work and missing family engagements or community responsibilities. Your performance-based reward doesn't seem to have worked out the way you wanted. How would you respond to this situation?

BUSINESS IN YOUR COMMUNITY

1. Interview a local small business owner who has a physical store in your community and also operates a website from which customers can order the business's products. Find out how the company's marketing efforts differ in targeting its potential walk-in and online customers.

2. Working with a group of classmates, choose a small business in your community. Think of seven specific ways that the business might be able to grow—using three intensive growth strategies, two integrative growth strategies, and two diversification growth strategies. Present your ideas to the class.

3. Working with a group of three classmates, research three existing franchises that do not have locations in your community but which you believe would be successful. Report your findings to the class and explain why these franchises might do well in your locality.

4. Interview a successful entrepreneur in your community and ask for a description of the goodwill aspects of his or her business.

5. With three or four other students, survey three area businesses of different types and sizes on their organizational structure. Are they traditional or modified? Has their organizational structure changed since the business began? Make a short presentation of your findings to the class.

6. Survey at least three business owners on cost-effective ways to motivate employees. How do they determine whether a method is successful? For example, do they see increased productivity? Fewer sick days taken? Happier customers? Describe the results of your survey to the class orally.

INFORMATION TECHNOLOGY

Internet Promotion

As you've learned, promotion is used to build favorable awareness about your product and influence people to buy it. There are many forms of promotion—including advertising, public relations, publicity, and word-of-mouth.

Every business, whether e-commerce or brick-and-mortar (or some combination of these), needs to advertise its products. E-commerce companies use Web ads as well as traditional means of advertising—such as print, television, and radio—to help find new customers and boost sales. Brick-and-mortar businesses use traditional means along with business websites and Web advertising. There's a great deal of crossover. For example, although mcdonalds.com sells apparel and accessories online as an e-commerce business, the main purpose of the website is to promote the McDonald's restaurant chain.

Internet Advertising

Banner ads are probably the most common type of Internet ad. A **banner ad** is typically a horizontal ad at the top of a Web page; however, banner ads can also appear as vertical ads at the side of the page. Banner ads can have multiple pages and include animation. When a banner ad appears in a vertical format at the side of a Web page, it is often called a **sidebar ad**. A **pop-up** is an ad that appears, or "pops up," in its own window on top of a Web page. An **interstitial ad**

appears in its own window before a Web page loads. "Interstitial" means in between, and these ads often have a link that says "Skip to website" to bypass the ad. A **floating ad** floats or flies over the Web page for five to thirty seconds. A **unicast ad** is a TV/Web commercial that appears in its own window.

By clicking on a Web ad, you're automatically taken to a page on the advertiser's website. The **click-through rate** shows how many customers have clicked on a Web ad. The more people who click on the ad, the more effectively it sells a company's product or brands the business. Each type of ad has a different level of click-through. Generally, according to research done by DoubleClick, a provider of digital marketing technology and services, interstitial ads had more than ten times the click rate of plain banner ads, while floating and pop-up ads had close to fifty times the click rates of banner ads.

Viral Marketing

Word-of-mouth promotion on the Internet has become known as **viral marketing**. Companies use e-mails, blogs, and social networks to promote a product and pass along brand awareness. Some things, such as a news clip or a YouTube video, can "go viral" on their own, without any forethought. This means that, for example, the same video will pop up on hundreds of sites within hours or days. Advertisers try to create buzz with viral campaigns. One company e-mailed existing customers an offer to join its consumer panel where they would get free products to review. But to join the panel, the customers had to get the most nominations from their friends. Customers used their own online social networks, such as MySpace or Facebook, to spread the word and get nominations. The advertiser found that this approach produced a response rate three times higher than banner ads or standard e-mail campaigns.

Tech Vocabulary

banner ad

click-through rate

floating ad

interstitial ad

pop-up

sidebar ad

unicast ad

viral marketing

Check Yourself

1. Name three types of Web advertisements.

2. What is the difference between a pop-up and an interstitial ad?

3. What is a click-through rate?

4. What is viral marketing?

What Do You Think?

Analyzing Concepts. Which type of ad do you find most appealing when you use the Internet?

CASE STUDY

Growing the Business

EXITING THE BUSINESS

Eva's Edibles has been in existence for eight years. It has had its share of ups and downs. But, with detailed planning, lots of hard work, and strategic adjustments along the way, the company is making a good profit. Continue the journey with Eva Tan as she thinks about leaving the company she founded.

New Opportunities for Growth

Eva's Edibles had a solid base of customers. It had a satisfactory, consistent net profit. It had a loyal, efficient group of employees. But Eva and Sylvia wondered if the business could continue its growth. Maybe they had grown it as much as they could.

Then something happened.

In a routine staff meeting, people began mentioning the lack of cuisines that reflected their various backgrounds. Eva missed Filipino food. Frank, the cook, complained about not being able to find good Jamaican food. Sylvia wished she could have French bistro fare. Paul, another cook, said that there was no Brazilian food in the area. Suddenly Sylvia said, "This might be a business opportunity!" After some discussion, they agreed that there might be a market for prepared foods for national and cultural groups whose preferred cuisines weren't locally available.

Eva and Sylvia began researching this idea in more detail. They became convinced that there were real possibilities in this market. They thought they could maintain their current successful menus while gradually creating new ones that were more ethnically diverse. These new products could also be marketed to current customers who might want to try new foods.

Another idea for growth was to sell packaged frozen meals to gourmet supermarkets. Sylvia pointed out that if they were successful in establishing a recognizable brand in the Columbus area, they could then possibly expand statewide and perhaps even nationally.

Eva also proposed the idea of providing cooking classes, a service that was outside their core business. She had discovered that training their employees in cooking techniques was a personally satisfying task, and she wanted to do more of this type of work. She could conduct classes in the kitchen at Eva's Edibles or in clients' homes.

Knowing When to Leave

After much research and planning, and some additional investment, Eva's Edibles began adding a few new specialty meals every month. Products that were successful were included in their future product offerings. Those that weren't successful were dropped.

Eva also began conducting cooking classes. She loved the work, but in Sylvia's opinion, it took Eva away from the more profitable aspects of the business that needed her help and expertise. Sylvia strongly believed that Eva's Edibles should focus on what it did best: making great packaged meals for a reasonable price.

Over time, Eva saw the wisdom of Sylvia's views about the cooking classes. Promotional costs and Eva's time investment in teaching them weren't in the best interest of the company. Reluctantly, Eva agreed to discontinue the classes and turn her attention back to promoting the company's new line of prepared meals.

But Eva just wasn't happy. She remembered how she and Sylvia had always said they needed to be happy with the direction of the company. She wondered if continuing to run Eva's Edibles was the best choice for her, personally.

When another entrepreneur, Daniel Ross, approached Sylvia and Eva about selling the company's frozen meals on a national basis, Eva found that her heart just wasn't in the business anymore.

After much thought, Eva talked with Sylvia. She told her that her real interest was teaching cooking. She wondered how Sylvia would feel if she left the business. Sylvia wanted Eva to be happy and suggested they might ask Daniel if he had any interest in Eva's part of the business.

Eva and Sylvia approached Daniel and asked him if he wanted to buy Eva's share of the company. Daniel was interested and figured out a fair value for Eva's percentage. Eva agreed and sold him her share. As part of the negotiation, Eva agreed to continue working at Eva's Edibles part-time for six months to help make the transition easier.

While working part-time, Eva returned to school. She transferred her credits to the Ohio State University and eventually earned a four-year degree in Technical Education and Training. After graduating, Eva was hired as a full-time teacher at a vocational school, teaching entrepreneurship and culinary skills.

Eva is happy teaching, but she has another dream now. It's an idea for starting another business: her own culinary school. And Eva knows that, to make it a reality, the only thing she needs to do—the only thing any entrepreneur needs to do—is dare to dream.

What Would You Have Done?

1. **Drawing Conclusions.** In your opinion, did Eva do the right thing in discontinuing the cooking classes? Explain your answer.

2. **Relating Concepts.** What methods would you have recommended for Eva to determine the value of her portion of the business?

APPENDIX A
EVA'S EDIBLES—SAMPLE BUSINESS CANVAS

Competition: Is there someone else providing my product or service better than I can?	Value Proposition: Will customers value my product or service enough to buy it?

Who are Eva's Edibles competitors?

1. At-Home Chef
2. Chef d'Jour

Why? Because they are also personal chefs who cook healthy meals in Columbus

What are the features of my product?

1. Healthy
2. Fast
3. Tasty
4. Customized 5 meals (3 courses)

At-Home Chef:

- Prepares meals in customer homes, too
- Based in Columbus
- Price: $400/5 dinners
- Chef has training in health and developed standard plan
- Taste matters—for kids, too

Chef d'Jour:

- Similar to At-Home Chef standard meal plan prepared in customer homes
- Price $500/5 dinners—can charge more because the chef is a certified personal chef and has been working for the past 3 years with the same customers

This gives customers the benefits of . . .

1. Less time spent planning and shopping for dinners
2. Less time spent in the kitchen cooking and cleaning up
3. The convenience of eating dinner whenever the client wishes

Additional information from USPCA:

- 15 personal chefs in Columbus area
- Focus on healthy meals

Are there other competitors?

- Home cooks
- Fast food

Business Model: Can I actually operate my business given the appropriate resources?

What are all the steps customers need to take?

1. Consult with potential client to determine what types of meals he or she likes best
2. Travel to supermarket to shop for groceries for clients' meals
3. Shop for and purchase groceries
4. Travel to client's home
5. Organize kitchen and groceries
6. Clean and chop vegetables
7. Cook clients' meal package
8. Clean up kitchen
9. Return home

What do I need?

1. Car
2. Customer kitchen
3. Cooking supplies—knives, measuring cups, pots
4. Training/license

Who can I ask for help?

1. My mom
2. Kate
3. Another personal chef

What do I need help with?

1. Finding customers
2. Cooking—Who can I ask?

Cost Structure: Does each sale make enough money to generate a profit?

What is my unit of sale?

1. Meals (1, 2–5?)
2. Hours
3. Customers

How much should I charge?

- Competition charges $400–$500
- I want to charge less because I'm new, but will it be enough?

Expenses:

1. Groceries
2. Time cooking
3. Advertising (fixed)
4. Car (fixed)
5. Insurance (fixed)
6. Computer (fixed)
7. Cell phone (fixed)

Unit of Sale: 5 meals — How long does that take?   10 hours

How much per hour do I want to make? $50

Per Unit Cost:

5 meals

$400 − [(groceries estimated $50) + ($50 × 10)] = ($150) (negative)

Can I charge more? How can I change my per unit costs?

APPENDIX B
EVA'S EDIBLES—SAMPLE PLAN

Executive Summary

Company Background

Business Description: Eva's Edibles is a personal chef service that sells packages of five, freshly cooked, gourmet dinners to business professionals who don't have time to cook for themselves. Eva's Edibles is structured as a Limited Liability Corporation (LLC).

Business Model: Eva's Edibles will prepare homemade dinners for clients. Each dinner will be based on a client's personal preferences. Dinners will be cooked in clients' kitchens, with all cleanup performed by Eva. The dinners will be stored in a client's refrigerator or freezer. Clients can reheat the dinners when it's convenient. It is estimated that this service will save a client nine to ten hours per week by reducing shopping, meal preparation, and cleanup.

Mission Statement: Eva's Edibles, a personal chef service, will provide busy clients with healthy and delicious dinners that are based on clients' preferences and prepared in their kitchens. Dinners are stored in clients' refrigerators or freezers to be reheated at their convenience.

Market Opportunity

Opportunity: Columbus, Ohio has a large population of professionals with substantial amounts of disposable income, but busy schedules that do not afford them time to prepare dinner. On average, these professionals eat out or order in four out of five workdays each week. Eva's Edibles seeks to provide these individuals with a healthy, homemade, and affordable alternative to ordering from area restaurants.

Target Market: Business professionals, couples, and families with an annual household income of more than $50,000. These individuals live hectic lives and rarely cook, but they want healthy and convenient meal options that won't break the bank.

Contact Information
Eva Tan
614-555-6208
eva@evasedibles.com

Eva's Edibles
303 Olentangy River Rd
Columbus, OH
43202

Year Founded
2016

Number of Employees
1

Investment Opportunity
$4,073

Annual Operating Costs*
$5,916

Annual Sales*
$81,900

Annual Profit*
$10,180

Return on Sales*
12.4%

Return on Investment*
250%

Breakeven Units/Month*
7 units

_____
*Projected amounts.

Industry Overview: According to the American Personal and Private Chef Association (APPCA), about 9,000 personal chefs are currently serving some 72,000 clients nationwide. Those numbers are expected to double over the next five years.

Market Research: Of the 301,800 Columbus households having two or more people, 36.7% have annual, combined incomes of over $50,000. The people in this market have busy lifestyles and want healthy dinners. In general, the target households go out to dinner or order in four out of five workdays each week.

Leadership

Eva Tan, CEO: Eva Tan has an associate's degree in Business Management from Columbus State Community College, and was Assistant to the Director of the Campus Dining Services at Ohio State University. She also ran her own event planning business, Eva's Entertainment Services, for four years. Eva has completed an intensive training course offered by the U.S. Personal Chef Association (USPCA), and has received the federally recognized trademarked designation of Certified Personal Chef (CPC).

Business Plan

1. Business Idea

See Chapter 1, pages 2–15.

1.1 Problem Identification

In Columbus, Ohio there is a large population of young professionals in finance, marketing, and healthcare services. Individuals from these professions earn $50,000 or more per year, providing them with substantial amounts of disposable income. What these individuals have in terms of income, they lack in terms of time. As a result, they go out to dinner or order in four out of five workdays each week.

Eva's Edibles seeks to provide these individuals with a healthy, homemade, and affordable alternative to ordering from area restaurants.

See Chapter 2, pages 16–31.

1.2 Personal Characteristics/Skills

Eva Tan has many personal characteristics and skills that are particularly valuable in the personal chef business, including: a passion for cooking, attention to detail, organizational skills, flexibility, creativity, sociability, ability to multi-task, high physical energy, and endurance.

See Chapter 3, pages 32–59.

1.3 Career Cluster

Eva's Edibles is part of the Hospitality & Tourism industry. As the dining habits of Americans has changed over time, there is opportunity to think entrepreneurially about how to help busy professionals eat healthily.

1.4 Mission Statement

Eva's Edibles, a personal chef service, will provide busy clients with healthy and delicious dinners that are based on clients' preferences and prepared in their kitchens. Dinners are stored in clients' refrigerators or freezers to be reheated at their convenience.

Eva's Edibles will use natural, organic, and locally grown ingredients whenever possible. The company's code of ethics directs that the business be as "green" as possible. It will choose vendors who are environmentally and socially responsible.

In addition to helping her potential customers, Eva will give back. Eva's Edibles will provide internships for interested culinary students in the community. In the future, Eva Tan hopes to volunteer at local elementary schools to speak with students about healthy eating and lifestyle choices. After three years, Eva's Edibles plans to contribute 1% of yearly net profit to a local food bank.

See Chapter 4, pages 60–81.

1.5 Qualifications

Eva has an associate's degree in Business Management from Columbus State Community College. As Assistant to the Director of the Campus Dining Services at Ohio State University, Eva acquired experience in the management of various types of food-service operations, as well as catering. She also ran her own event-planning business, Eva's Entertainment Services, for four years. Eva has completed an intensive training course offered by the U.S. Personal Chef Association (USPCA), and has received the federally recognized trademarked designation of Certified Personal Chef (CPC).

See Chapter 5, pages 82–103.

2. Opportunity & Market Analysis

2.1 Business Idea

Eva's Edibles is a personal chef service that sells packages of five, freshly cooked, gourmet dinners to business professionals who don't have time to cook for themselves.

See Chapter 6, pages 118–131.

2.2 Business Opportunity

Columbus has a large population of professionals with substantial amounts of disposable income, but busy schedules that do not afford them time to prepare dinner. On average, these professionals eat out or order in four out of five workdays each week. Eva's Edibles seeks to provide these individuals with a healthy, homemade, and affordable alternative to ordering from area restaurants.

See Chapter 7, pages 132–149.

See Chapter 8, pages 150–163.

2.3 Opportunity Screening

The personal chef business is a viable opportunity for the Columbus area, as shown by the initial research data on the opportunity. Columbus has a large population of professionals, primarily from the business and medical spheres that is growing steadily. Of the 301,800 Columbus households having two or more people, 36.7% (110,760) have incomes of $50,000 or more.

Figure B-1 ▶

Annual Combined Household Income.

Total: 301,800 Columbus households having two or more people.

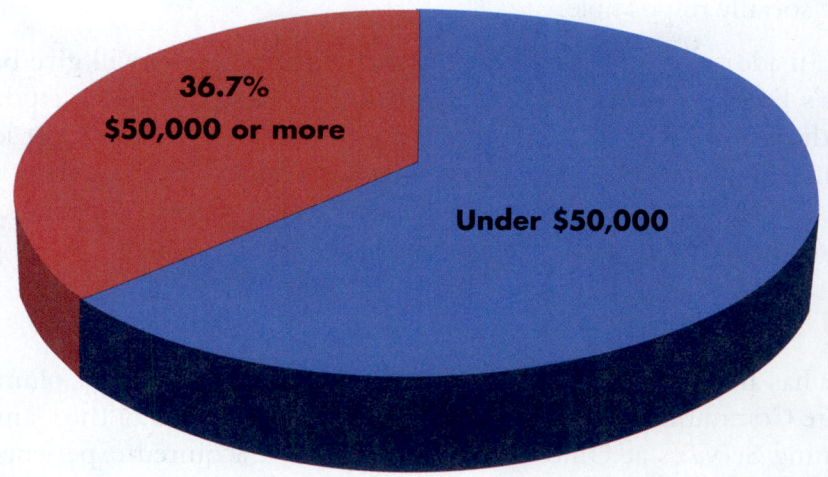

People in this market have busy lifestyles and want healthy dinners. The target households go out to dinner or order in at least four days each week. Based on research conducted by Eva's Edibles, this market represents approximately 25% (27,690) of the households having combined household income of over $50,000. Eva's Edibles will provide people an opportunity to stay healthy without compromising a busy and productive lifestyle.

Figure B-2 ▶

Households Eating Dinner Out or Ordering In.

Total: 11,760 Columbus households of two or more people with a combined income of $50,000 or more.

- ■ Four or more days per week
- ■ Three days per week
- ■ Two days per week
- ■ One day per week
- ■ Don't eat out or order in

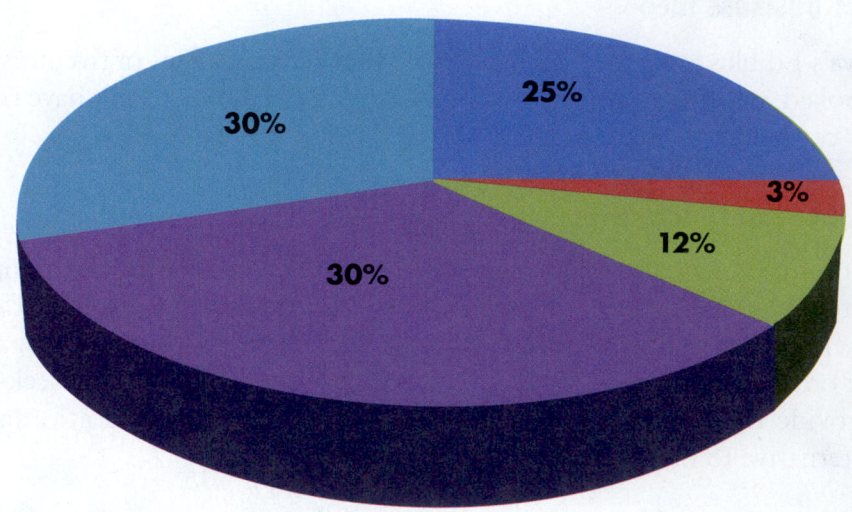

2.4 Market Research Questions

Based on the initial research data found, the personal chef business is a valid business opportunity for the Columbus area. However, to make sure that Eva's Edibles is best aligned to the opportunity, and continues to be aligned with the current trend, ongoing market research will be done. Questions that will be asked to current and potential clients on an ongoing basis will include:

See Chapter 9, pages 164–179.

- What is your current household income?
- How many hours a week do you work?
- How many times a week do you eat out?
- How much do you spend on average per meal?
- How much would you pay to have additional time freed up during the week?
- How much would you pay to have more convenient, healthier food options?

2.5 Market Research Tools

Since the target customer for Eva's Edibles are busy professionals, ongoing market research should be done with a busy schedule in mind. Eva's Edibles will use the following approaches to gather research data:

See Chapter 10, pages 180–193.

- E-mail surveys using online survey tools
- Questions through social media posts during rush hour commute times
- Brief survey during consultation/order process with reward attached

3. Competition

3.1 Industry & Industry Statistics

The personal chef business is one of the fastest-growing segments in the food-service industry. According to the American Personal and Private Chef Association (APPCA), about 9,000 personal chefs are currently serving some 72,000 clients nationwide. Those numbers are expected to double over the next five years.

See Chapter 11, pages 208–219.

3.2 Availability of Product/Service

There are currently fifteen personal chefs, or businesses performing some type of personal chef service, in the greater Columbus area. Of these, only seven advertise that they are members of one of the professional personal chef associations. Based on the growing professional population in Columbus, there should be enough demand for another personal chef business in the market.

See Chapter 12, pages 220–231.

See Chapter 13, pages 232–245.

3.3 Direct & Indirect Competition

Direct Competitors: Based on website research, only one direct competitor is federally recognized as a Certified Personal Chef. Only two indicated specifically that they were focused on preparing healthy meals.

Indirect Competitors: Columbus area restaurants, including fast food and takeout establishments, will indirectly compete with Eva's Edibles. The upscale restaurants are generally expensive and will not be an everyday option. The majority of lower-priced, "family-style," and fast food restaurants offer meals much lower in quality and nutrition than the dinners that will be provided by Eva's Edibles.

See Chapter 14, pages 246–259.

3.4 Competitive Pricing

On average, similar personal chefs in the Columbus area charge between $300 and $500 for their chef services. Groceries are an additional cost. Eva's Edibles will charge $325, including groceries, making its pricing very competitive.

See Chapter 15, pages 260–271.

3.5 Competitive Advantage

Eva's Edibles has three major competitive advantages:

1. It will focus on customer service by allowing clients to choose their menus.

2. It will focus on preparing healthy versions of client favorites and, after consultation with clients, will tailor dinners to meet their special dietary needs.

3. Eva Tan is one of the few personal chefs in Columbus to have the federally recognized designation of Certified Personal Chef. Eva Tan is an active member of the United States Personal Chef Association (USPCA).

	Eva's Edibles	At-Home Chef	Chef D'Jour
Factor 1: Price	$325/5 dinners	$400/5 dinners	$500/5 dinners
Factor 2: Quality	Custom meals, healthy	Meals from chef's plan, not focused on health	Meals from chef's plan, healthy
Factor 3: Unique Knowledge	Certified Personal Chef, event planning	Focuses on "kid-friendly" meals	Certified Personal Chef, knows customers

4. Delivering Value to Customers

4.1 Target Market Segment

See Chapter 16, pages 286–299.

Based on research conducted by Eva's Edibles, the company estimates the total market segment includes 27,690 households. Eva's Edibles target customers share the following characteristics:

- **Demographic Information:** Professional couples and families, with household incomes of over $50,000.
- **Geographic Information:** Greater Columbus, Ohio, area
- **Psychographic Information:** Desires healthy food, often dual-income households living hectic lives, hardworking, would like to spend more time at home without increasing time in the kitchen cooking and cleaning up
- **Buying Patterns:** Eats out often (4 times a week) but would like to reduce the cost of eating out. These customers buy using credit more often than cash.

4.2 Value Proposition

See Chapter 17, pages 300–311.

Value Proposition: Spend more time with your family and friends, and let Eva's Edible's prepare customized, home-style meals in your kitchen. To attract potential customers, Eva's Edibles will highlight key benefits that include:

1. Less time spent planning and shopping for dinners
2. Less time spent in the kitchen cooking and cleaning up
3. The convenience of eating dinner whenever the client wishes
4. Delicious and healthy dinners tailored to the client's personal choices
5. Less money spent eating out
6. More time to spend with friends
7. Dinner choices that can be tailored for diabetics, vegetarians, and those who need low-cholesterol or low-sodium meals

4.3 Marketing Plan

See Chapter 18, pages 312–327.

Product Strategy: Eva's Edibles will use a 5-Dinner Plan, cooking five dinners for one household per day. Clients can select dinners from a list of healthy home-style meals offered by Eva's Edibles or come up with others in consultation with Eva. The dinners will be stored family-style in the client's refrigerator or freezer in appropriate containers, with reheating instructions.

Pricing Strategy: Eva's Edibles will price based on demand and competition. As a member of USPCA, Eva has access to standard pricing and services. Eva's Edibles will charge $325, including groceries. Eva decides to price her product competitively to create a reputation and gain market share.

Personal Selling: Eva's Edibles will depend heavily on personal selling. This involves contacting past customers of the event-planning business and pursuing business contacts through the Ohio State University.

Direct mail pieces and the brochure will have a mail-back card to capture a prospective client's e-mail address and telephone number. Eva Tan will follow up on all mail-back cards personally by e-mail or phone. Future selling strategies will include asking customers for referrals and recommendations of potential clients. Again, Eva will get in touch with each prospect personally.

Steps a consumer follows to purchase my service:

1. Customer will contact Eva by phone or e-mail for a free meal plan consultation.
2. Customer will schedule an appointment for Eva to cook one meal package (five dinners)—customers must be at home during first visit so that Eva can be let in. (Homeowners will not need to be present during subsequent visits if they choose to give Eva a spare key so she can let herself in.)

4.4 Business Pitch

See Chapter 19, pages 328–341.

"It's the beginning of the week and America's hardworking professionals and families are busy juggling work, kids, traffic and all the other things that drive us crazy throughout the day. When they finally get home, they're faced with the daunting task of putting a full meal together for dinner. There just aren't enough hours in the week to juggle their work, buy groceries, cook and clean up afterwards. Imagine having five home cooked meals of your choice prepared for you or your family every week. Not only does it save time and money, but you'll also gain peace of mind! Well I'd like to introduce you to Eva's Edibles: a personal chef service that provides packages of five freshly cooked, gourmet dinners to busy families and business professionals."

4.5 Promotional Plan

See Chapter 20, pages 342–361.

Eva's Edibles will engage in five types of promotional activities:

1. Establishing a website
2. Maintaining a referral listing on the USPCA website
3. Hosting in-store promotions
4. Promotions at local events
5. Developing strategies for retaining current clients

Company Website: Eva's Edibles will construct its own website, which will provide full information about services and display a selection of dinner menus. The website will offer monthly catering promotions and offer a sign-up list for prospective clients. Sample dinners will be show-cased. The website will promote Eva Tan as one of the few personal chefs in the Columbus area who has the federally recognized designation of Certified Personal Chef. It will indicate that Eva Tan is an active member of the United States Personal Chef Association (USPCA).

USPCA Referral Website: Eva's Edibles will use a referral listing pro-vided by the USPCA. Because of her membership in the USPCA, Eva Tan can access its referral listing at www.hireachef.com. Eva's Edibles will be able to create and modify its listing and track listing statistics. According to the USPCA, this service "is the most effective, efficient method to put customers and personal chefs in touch with each other." Annually, hireachef.com logs over 500,000 listing views and 95,000 clicks for more information. These statistics represent more than simple Web-page hits, which can be deceiving. Clients in the hireachef.com system review personal chef pages and make contact. Inquiries from potential clients are sent directly to the chef's e-mail account.

In-Store Promotions: Eva's Edibles plans to offer in-store promotions at local cookware shops on a regular basis. One store, The Wire Whisk, has agreed to host an hour-long presentation by Eva Tan every other week. The presentation will be dedicated to healthy eating and feature the company's dinners. At each event the company will offer sample menus and a brochure describing its philosophy.

Promotions at Local Events: Eva's Edibles will also participate in local events at shopping malls, cultural fairs, environmental exhibits (Earth Day), and other appropriate venues. It will offer free samples, gift baskets, and discount raffles. Eva's will offer its brochure at each of these events as well.

Strategies for Retaining Current Clients: Eva's Edibles will provide current clients with extras for their loyalty—for example, free snacks and desserts after purchasing three 5-Dinner Plans. Another strategy will be to offer current customers a 10% discount when they refer Eva's Edibles to a potential client who signs a contract with the company.

5. Business Model

See Chapter 21, pages 376–391.

5.1 Distribution Channel

Eva's Edibles is a service business that will prepare food at clients' homes. The only distribution involved will be the transportation of groceries to the clients' homes.

A typical delivery of service includes the following steps.

1. Consult with potential client to determine what types of meals he or she likes best
2. Travel to supermarket to shop for groceries for clients' meals
3. Shop for and purchase groceries
4. Travel to client's home
5. Organize kitchen and groceries
6. Clean and chop vegetables
7. Cook clients' meal package
8. Clean up kitchen
9. Return home

See Chapter 22, pages 392–411.

5.2 Internal Resources

The company has started the process of trademarking "Eva's Edibles" as a brand name. Eva will also copyright her brochures and all printed materials.

Eva Tan will be the only person employed full-time by Eva's Edibles during the first year. If sales increase as projected, it may become necessary to hire part-time assistance in the second year. As the business grows, Eva's Edibles anticipates offering internships to local culinary college students.

See Chapter 23, pages 412–429.

5.3 Operating Policies

Customer Agreements: Eva's Edibles will have a written contract with each of its clients that will specify the dates on which the service will be performed, the menus chosen by the client, and any dietary requirements. The contract will also set out provisions for the cancellation of services by either party.

Hours of Operation: Eva's Edibles will typically work at a client's home from 11:00 a.m. to 5:00 p.m. Eva Tan will shop for groceries in the morning, buying in bulk for multiple clients whenever possible.

Rework Requests: If a customer is unhappy with a dinner, Eva's will work carefully with that client to establish the reason for the dissatisfaction, and the company will provide two additional dinners to the client free of charge.

Client Satisfaction: Eva's will depend on word-of-mouth referrals. Clients must be pleased at all costs. Customer service will be critical to the success of Eva's Edibles.

Inventory Management: Eva's Edibles will keep a minimum inventory of frequently used ingredients, such as condiments and spices, in a cooler and a storage container in her car. The company will use a just-in-time inventory strategy. This means items will be purchased as needed, and long-term storage will not be necessary.

5.4 External Partnerships

In case of illness, the company has entered into a reciprocal agreement with James Martin, a personal chef in Columbus, who will prepare dinners for Eva's Edibles clients on short notice.

See Chapter 24, pages 430–449.

Eva's Edibles will purchase groceries on an as-needed basis in the mornings, according to client needs. Eva Tan will buy in bulk whenever possible, choosing vendors for both price and quality. Some ingredients, such as meat or produce, will be purchased as needed to avoid spoilage. Eva's Edibles will cook dinners with seasonal ingredients. In addition, the company will build relationships with local organic farmers to ensure the highest quality and best price.

Eva's Edibles will use outside services for legal and accounting/tax needs. In addition, Eva will seek the mentorship of colleagues who are also members of USPCA. USPCA liability insurance costs $600 annually for members. It is a standard general liability policy with clauses that cover food products, personal injury, advertising injury, and property damage. The company will also pay for automobile insurance for Eva Tan.

5.5 Legal Structure

Eva's Edibles will be a Limited Liability Company (LLC), wholly owned and operated by Eva Tan. The LLC status will protect Eva Tan's personal assets and allows the company to enjoy some tax benefits.

See Chapter 25, pages 450–465.

6. Financial and Expense Management

See Chapter 26, pages 482–501.

6.1 EOU & Variable Expenses

Definition of One Unit: One unit is defined as cooking five dinners for a client in the client's kitchen.

Variable Expenses:

Materials				
Material Description	**Bulk Price**	**Bulk Quantity**	**Quantity per Unit**	**Cost per Unit**
Misc. groceries (specific ingredients vary from client to client)	$100.00	5 dinners	5 dinners	$100.00

Labor		
Cost of Labor per Hour	**Time (hrs) to make one unit**	**Total Labor Cost per Unit**
$25.00	6 hours	$150.00

EOU		
Material Costs	**Labor Costs**	**Total EOU**
$100.00	$150.00	$250.00

EOU:

Selling Price per Unit			$325.00
Variable Expense per Unit			
Cost of Goods Sold			
Material	$100.00		
Labor	150.00		
Total Cost of Goods Sold		$250.00	
Other Variable Expenses			
Commission	$0.00		
Packaging	0.00		
Other	4.00		
Total Other Variable Expenses		$4.00	
Total Variable Expenses			$254.00
Contribution Margin per Unit			$ 71.00

6.2 Fixed Expenses & Break-Even Units

See Chapter 27, pages 502–517.

Expense Type	Monthly Cost	Explanation
Insurance	$117.00	As a food services business, it is imperative that Eva's Edibles is insured to protect against liability
Salary	0.00	Eva will be paid an hourly wage
Advertising	146.00	Advertising will include direct mailings and postage, as well as marketing collateral and samples to be distributed at in-store promotions local events
Interest	0.00	Eva's Edibles has a financing strategy that does not include repaying loans with interest
Depreciation	23.00	Eva will depreciate her cooking equipment over a 5-year period of time ($1,373 over 60 months)
Utilities	100.00	Because Eva cooks in her client's kitchens, the only utility she will pay will be service for her mobile phone.
Rent	0.00	Because Eva cooks in her client's kitchens, she will not incur costs related to rent
Other Fixed Expenses	107.00	These costs are associated with automobile maintenance and gas to drive to promotional events
Total Fixed Expenses	**$493.00**	

$$\frac{\text{Fixed Monthly Expenses}}{\text{Contribution Margin}} \rightarrow \frac{\$493.00}{\$71.00} = 6.94 = 7 \text{ Units}$$

See Chapter 28, pages 518–537.

6.3 Revenue Streams & Sales Projections

Revenue Streams: The main source of income for Eva's Edibles will be the sale of 5-meal dinner plans. After a couple of years, once she has built up a team, Eva will also plan on bringing in additional income catering large-scale events and selling cookbooks.

Sales Projections: Eva's Edibles forecasts sales by analyzing the factors in the following chart.

Factor	Influence on Sales
Market Analysis	Given the large number of target households in the Greater Columbus area (27,690 households), Eva must only sell to less than 0.08% of this potential market to meet her sales estimates. Eva believes this is highly feasible.
Maximum Capacity	Eva has a maximum capacity of 7 units per week (42 hours), which means she can serve a maximum of 28 customers per month. As a result, Eva's sales estimates are aligned with her maximum capacity.
Breakeven Units	Eva must sell at least 7 units per month to cover her operating expenses. Eva's sales estimates are above her breakeven point.
Seasonality	Eva's business will not be affected by seasonality because her clients will continue to eat dinner, regardless of the time of year.

Sales estimates for the first two years are shown in the following chart. Each 5-Dinner Plan represents cooking five dinners for one household in the client's kitchen. Eva's Edibles will be available to cook every weekday and on some weekends, when required.

	Year 1		Year 2	
	5-Dinner Plans	Monthly Sales	5-Dinner Plans	Monthly Sales
January	20	$6,500	22	$7,150
February	20	6,500	22	7,150
March	20	6,500	22	7,150
April	20	6,500	22	7,150
May	21	6,825	22	7,150
June	21	6,825	23	7,475
July	21	6,825	23	7,475
August	21	6,825	23	7,475
September	22	7,150	23	7,475
October	22	7,150	23	7,475
November	22	7,150	24	7,800
December	22	7,150	24	7,800
Annual Totals	252	$81,900	273	$88,725

Projected five-year sales estimates are shown in Figure B-3. The projections assume that Eva's Edibles moves to a commercial kitchen in its third year. That will allow the company to deliver meals to clients, rather than to cook in their kitchens, thus significantly increasing the number of 5-Dinner Plans the company can provide.

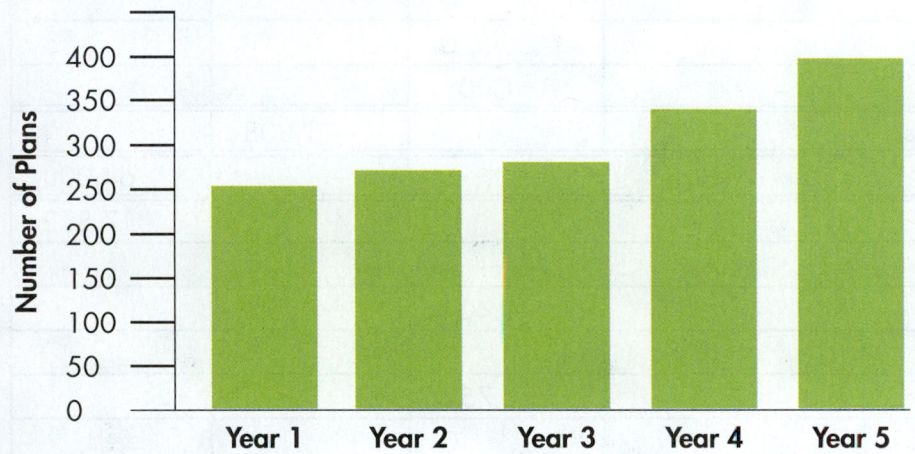

◀ **Figure B-3**
Projected Five Year Sales—Number of Plans.

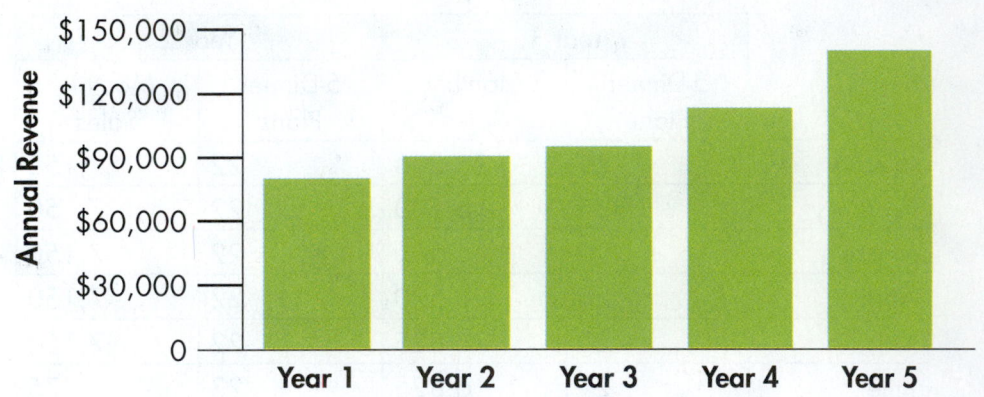

Figure B-4 ►
Projected Five Year Sales—Revenue.

Projected Income Statement for First Year of Operations			
REVENUE			**$81,900**
Gross Sales	$81,900		
Sales Returns	0		
Net Sales			81,900
VARIABLE EXPENSES			
Cost of Goods Sold			
Materials	25,200		
Labor	37,800		
Total Cost of Goods Sold		63,000	
Other Variable Expenses			
Commission	0		
Packaging	0		
Other	1,008		
Total Other Variable Expenses		1,008	
Total Variable Expenses			64,008
CONTRIBUTION MARGIN			17,892
FIXED OPERATING EXPENSES			
Insurance	1,404		
Salaries	0		
Advertising	1,752		
Interest	0		
Depreciation	276		
Utilities	1,200		
Rent	0		
Other Fixed Expenses	1,284		
Total Expenses			5,916
PRE-TAX PROFIT			11,976
Taxes (15%)			1,796.40
NET PROFIT			10,179.60

6.4 Start-Up Investment

See Chapter 29, pages 538–557.

Eva Tan will invest $5,000 of her own money in the company. This will be the beginning equity for Eva's Edibles and cover her start-up investment.

Item	Why Needed	Vendor	Cost
Victorinox Swiss Army Cutlery Set (8 Piece)	Needed to chop vegetables and trim meat	Macy's	$618.00
Anolon Nouvelle Copper Hard Anodized Nonstick 10-Piece Cookware Set	Needed for basic cooking	Amazon.com	450.00
Misc. cooking equipment	Need specialty equipment for preparing gourmet meals	Amazon.com	305.00
Spices, oils, etc.	Needed to season food	Whole Foods	100.00
Wheeled cart	Needed to transport all cooking supplies and groceries	Globalindustrial.com	269.00
Total Start-Up Expenditures			**$1,742.00**
Emergency Fund (½ of start-up expenditures)			871.00
Reserve for Fixed Expenses (covers 3 months of fixed expenses)			1,479.00
Total Start-Up Investment			**$4,092.00**

6.5 Financial Ratios

See Chapter 30, pages 558–579.

Return on Sales (ROS):

$$\frac{\text{Annual Net Profit}}{\text{Total Annual Sales}} \rightarrow \frac{\$10,179.60}{\$81,900.00} = 12.4\% \approx \$0.12$$

Return on Investment (ROI):

$$\frac{\text{Annual Net Profit}}{\text{Total Start-Up Investment}} \rightarrow \frac{\$10,179.60}{\$81,900.00} = 12.4\% \approx \$0.12$$

Growth and Implementation Plan

7. Operating the Business

See Chapter 31, pages 596–613.

7.1 Organizational Structure

Eva's Edibles currently is operated solely by Eva Tan, who performs all shopping, cooking, and sales functions in the business. Her title will be President. As Eva hires more employees, she will implement a line organization structure, with Eva managing all of her employees who will perform specific business functions.

See Chapter 32, pages 614–629.

7.2 Business Compliance

To run her business, Eva has become federally recognized as a Certified Personal Chef and is an active member of the United States Personal Chef Association. Currently, there are no government regulations concerning a personal chef cooking in a client's home. In the future, if the company leases a commercial kitchen, Eva Tan will investigate all appropriate license and inspection protocols.

See Chapter 33, pages 630–649.

7.3 Recordkeeping

Running Eva's Edibles will require a great deal of tracking and storing a great deal of financial and customer records. Eva will use computer software programs to keep detailed records of financial transactions secure and confidential. These records will include:

- Purchases from food and other vendors
- Customer sales transactions
- Payments to employees and delivery services
- Customer payment information
- Payments to external partners for additional services

See Chapter 34, pages 650–671.

7.4 Accounting Systems

Eva's Edibles will use the latest version of QuickBooks accounting software. Offsite backups of the business accounts and records will automatically be made every day.

See Chapter 35, pages 672–691.

7.5 Taxes

Eva's Edibles will pay self-employment tax and collect sales tax. Workers' Compensation will be made available should three or more full-time employees be hired.

8. Growing Your Business

8.1 Growth Plan

In its first year, Eva's Edibles plans to build a profitable customer base so that, by the end of the year, it will be cooking in clients' kitchens 22 days in every month. The business will be manageable at this level, and will allow the company to reach its revenue goal of $81,900. To obtain this growth, Eva will rely on promotional strategies outlined in her initial marketing plan, as well as obtaining at least three references from each current customer.

See Chapter 36, pages 706–723.

8.2 Plan for Scaling

Eva's Edibles anticipates that, after a profitable customer base has been built, the company will develop an intensive growth strategy. Eva's intends to increase its market penetration by leasing or buying a commercial kitchen. This will allow increased storage and allow the company to serve more clients, thereby increasing its revenues and profits. Dinners will then be delivered to customers.

See Chapter 37, pages 724–741.

8.3 Hiring Needs

To support growth, Eva's Edibles will need to change its business model and lease or buy a commercial kitchen to increase the number of clients. This, in turn, may require additional financing and will almost certainly require additional employees with cooking skills. She will recruit through the college she attended where she obtained her degree in hospitality and food administration. At this point, she will focus her attention on managing her employees, and allowing the additional chefs cook the meals.

See Chapter 38, pages 742–765.

8.4 Franchising and Licensing

Although premature to plan for, Eva's Edibles may represent a business that could be franchised in other cities with large upscale populations of professionals.

See Chapter 39, pages 766–781.

8.5 Exit Strategy

After establishing itself as a viable business with a stable roster of clients, it is likely that Eva's Edibles could be valued as a desirable business operation for a chef looking for a single-person business. However, Eva Tan has no plans to leave the business in the foreseeable future.

See Chapter 40, pages 782–799.

360° marketing—Approach to marketing that communicates with your prospects and customers from all directions; it blends low-tech methods and high-tech methods to carry your message to customers in as many ways as possible.

A

Accessibility—An approach to communicating value to customers by providing access to products or services customers would not have otherwise (e.g., overnight shipping).

Accounting—System of recording and summarizing business and financial transactions and analyzing, verifying, and reporting the results.

Accounting controls—Checks and balances established to provide accounting personnel with procedures that will avoid potential problems.

Accounts payable—Amount of money a business owes to its suppliers for purchases made on credit.

Accounts receivable—Amount of money owed to a business by its customers for credit sales.

Accreditation—Certification by a professional group that an individual possesses certain skills or a specific level of expertise.

Active content—Web content that changes frequently, such as the current time and temperature.

Active listening—Listening consciously and responding in ways that improve communication.

Adulterated—Containing substances or processed in ways that may be harmful to health, or modified to mask poor quality.

Advertising—Public, promotional message paid for by an identified sponsor or company.

Affiliate marketing—Process used by website owners who sell items from another store and take a percentage of the profits.

Affiliate network—Intermediary between affiliates and merchants with affiliate programs.

AIDA (attention, interest, desire, and action)—Popular communication model used by companies to plan, create, and manage their promotions.

Angels—Equity investors who finance startup ventures in which they have a particular interest.

Antitrust laws—Laws that forbid anticompetitive mergers and business practices.

Applications—End-user programs.

Apprenticeship—Internship in which a technical or trade skill is taught. See also internship.

Aptitude—Natural ability to do a particular type of work or activity well.

Asset—Everything owned by the business that has a monetary value.

Assumption—Something that you assume is true about your business and what the customer wants; entrepreneurs test these during the market research process.

Attitude—Way of viewing or thinking about something that affects how you feel about it.

Auction site—Website where buyers and sellers come together to buy or sell goods and services.

Auditor—Accountant who examines a company's financial records and verifies that they have been kept properly.

Authoritarian (aw-thor-uh-TEHR-ee-un) **leadership style**—Practiced when a leader tells employees what needs to be done and how to do it, without seeking their advice.

Automation—Use of machines to perform tasks normally performed by people.

B

Balance sheet—Financial statement that summarizes the assets and liabilities (debts) of a business.

Bank debt ratio—Your monthly income compared to your debts.

Bank reconciliation—Process of verifying that a checkbook balance is in agreement with the ending balance in the checking account statement from the bank.

Banner ad—Ad at the top or side of a Web page.

Bargaining in good faith—An honest intention to resolve differences in a way that is acceptable to all.

Barter financing—Trading of items or services between businesses.

Benefits—Reasons customers choose to buy a product; types of compensation other than salary or wages.

Bidding—Making an offer on an item.

Blog—Personal journal. Short for "weB LOG."

Book value—Accounting term that means total assets minus total liabilities according to a company's balance sheet. Also referred to as net worth or owner's equity.

Bootstrapping—Starting a business by yourself without any outside investment.

Bounce rate—Percentage of visitors who visit the landing page and exit without visiting another page.

Brainstorm—A creative thinking technique where one thinks of as many possible answers to a question, no matter how ridiculous, as quickly as possible.

Brand—Marketing strategy that can create an emotional attachment to your product(s).

Brand equity—Perceived monetary value of a brand.

Brand licensee—Company or person who is granted permission to use the brand.

Brand licensing—Granting of legal permission to someone or some company to use your brand.

Brand licensor—Company or person who owns the brand.

Brand mark—Symbol or other graphical design that can be used to identify a brand.

Breach of contract—Failure to carry out the required conditions of a contract.

Break-even analysis—Examination of the income statement that identifies the break-even point for a business.

Break-even point—Point at which the total at the bottom of the income statement is zero because the business has sold exactly enough units for sales to cover expenses.

Break-even units—Number of units of sale a business needs to sell to arrive at the break-even point.

Bundling—Combining the price of several different services (and/or physical products) into one price.

Burn rate—Rate at which a company spends cash to cover overhead costs without generating a positive cash flow.

Business—Organization that provides products or services, usually to make money.

Business broker—Someone who is licensed to sell businesses.

Business canvas—An alternate tool to traditional business planning that allows you to make changes to your opportunity as more information is gathered.

Business environment—Any social, economic, or political factors that could impact your business including global, national, and industry-related factors.

Business ethics—Moral principles applied to business issues and actions.

Business interruption insurance—Covers losses if a business can't operate due to a covered event, such as a storm or fire.

Business model—A description of how you will structure the business itself so it will work.

Business model validation—Used to prove, through ongoing market research and data analysis, that your business idea is truly a business opportunity.

Business opportunity—Consumer need or want that might be met by a new business.

Business pitch—A pitch designed to present the value a company gives to its target market. See also elevator pitch.

Business plan—Statement of your business goals, the reasons you think these goals can be met, and how you are going to achieve them.

Business risk—Possibility of loss that comes with operating the business; entrepreneurs take efforts to navigate foreseeable business risk.

Business-to-business (B2B) company—Company that sells to other companies.

Business-to-consumer (B2C) company—Company that sells to individual people.

Buying in bulk—Purchasing a large quantity from a vendor, typically to take advantage of a quantity discount. Also referred to as volume buying.

C

C corporation—Corporation that is taxed as an entity by the federal government.

Calculated risk—Risk in which potential costs and benefits are carefully considered before starting a business.

Calendar year—January to December.

Call center—Operation where a group of people answer phone calls and offer help—often part of an outsourced customer service.

Call to action—Part of the ad copy that tries to get the website visitor to perform a specific action, such as registering for the site or buying a product.

Capital—Another name for the cash and goods a business owns.

Capitalism—Another name for a free enterprise system.

Carbon footprint—Amount of carbon you use and thus release into the atmosphere.

Career cluster—A classification of specific jobs and industries into similar categories done by the National Association of State Directors of Career Technical Education Consortium (NASDCTEc).

Carbon offset—Practice of "buying" a certain amount of carbon to help offset your carbon footprint.

Carrying capacity—Maximum number of companies an industry can support based on its potential customer base.

Cash budget—Record on which a business owner forecasts (predicts) incoming and outgoing cash flows for an upcoming period (typically a month) and later compares actual cash inflows and outflows to the forecasted amounts.

Cash discount—Discount given to buyers who pay for purchases in cash, either at the time of purchase or within a set time period after purchase.

Cash flow—Money received minus what is spent over a specified period of time.

Cash flow statement—Financial document that records inflows and outflows of cash when they actually occur.

Cash value—Actual worth of a property.

Catastrophic risk—Risk of an unpredictable event that causes severe loss to many people at the same time.

Catch phrase—Slogan or phrase that is repeated so often that people use it without knowing its original context.

Cause-related marketing—Partnership between a business and a nonprofit group for the benefit of both.

Central processing unit (CPU)—Unit that does all the actual computing in the computer.

Characteristic—Describes a quality or behavior of a person; can include determination, honesty, and patience.

Chart of accounts—Shows all the accounts used in a business, including assets, liabilities, owner's equity, income, and expense accounts.

Chat room support—Type of online customer service in which the support staff communicates with the customer using instant-messaging software.

Checking account—Bank account against which the account holder can write checks.

Click-through rate—Shows how many customers who saw a Web ad actually clicked on it.

Co-signer—Individual who signs a loan agreement to guarantee the loan payments in case the first signer is unable to make them.

Cold call—Sales call to someone not known, and without prior notice; also called canvassing.

Collateral—Property or assets pledged to a bank to secure a loan.

Command economy—System in which the government controls the production, allocation, and prices of goods and services.

Commerce server—Type of server that runs commerce-based applications, such as credit card processing and inventory management.

Commission—Amount paid based on the volume of products or services that a salesperson sells.

Company image—Perception (thoughts, attitudes, opinions, and beliefs) that the public holds about a company.

Compensation—Money and benefits that an employee receives in exchange for working.

Competent—In the legal sense, capable of understanding the terms of a contract and the consequences of entering it.

Competition-based pricing—Pricing method that focuses on what the competition charges.

Competitive advantage—Something that puts your business ahead of the competition.

Competitive intelligence—Data you collect about your competitors.

Competitive matrix—Grid used to compare characteristics of your business with those of your direct competitors.

Compounding—Way in which invested money grows by earning interest on the interest.

Compromise—An agreement arrived at when all sides have made concessions.

Computer virus—Software program that can cause damage to the data on your computer by erasing files, creating new ones, changing files, or moving them. It can easily spread from computer to computer.

Concession—Something you are willing to give up.

Conditions—Events or circumstances that must occur for the contract to be binding.

Conference call—Three or more parties in different locations speaking to each other over the same phone line.

Confidentiality agreement—Agreement that binds parties to secrecy and usually concerns employees, investors, and others with whom a business owner needs to share a trade secret or other sensitive information. Also called nondisclosure agreement.

Conflict of interest—Situation in which personal considerations and professional obligations interfere with each other.

Consideration—Benefit that each party in a contract provides for the other.

Consumers—Another word for customer; in economics, they decide how much they are willing to pay for a given good or service.

Consumer credit—Extended payment time given by a business to consumers for purchased goods or services.

Contact information—Information about potential customers, such as name, address, phone number, and e-mail address.

Content Management System (CMS)—System that provides the software or programs needed to put content onto a site.

Contract—Agreement between competent parties in which each party promises to take or avoid a specified action.

Contribution margin—Amount per unit that a product contributes toward the company's profitability before the fixed expenses are subtracted.

Controlling—Ongoing process of setting performance standards, measuring actual performance, comparing actual performance to the standards, and taking corrective action if actual performance does not meet the performance standards.

Convenience—An approach to communicating value to customers through designing or redesigning products to be easier to use or simply more useful.

Conversion rate—Percentage of Web traffic that translates into sales. It is a measure of how many potential customers actually buy.

Cookies—Short messages that are given to a Web browser (such as Internet Explorer) by a Web server when you visit that site.

Cooperative—Business owned, controlled, and operated for the mutual benefit of its members—people who use its services, buy its goods, or are employed by it.

Cooperative advertising—When two companies share the cost of advertising.

Copyright—Exclusive right to perform, display, copy, or distribute an artistic work.

Core business—Most important focus of the business.

Corporate social responsibility—Acting in ways that balance a business's profits and growth with the good of society.

Corporation—Legally defined type of business ownership in which the business is considered a "person" ("entity") under the law, and limited liability is granted to the business owner(s).

Cost of Goods Sold (COGS)—Variable expense that is associated with each unit of sale, including the cost of materials and labor used to make the product.

Cost of Services Sold (COSS)—Variable expense that is associated with each unit of sale, including the cost of materials and labor used to provide the service.

Cost-based pricing—Pricing method that sets a product's price based on what it costs the business to provide it.

Cost-per-sale—In affiliate marketing, commission that the merchant pays the affiliate when a customer actually buys an item. Also known as pay-per-sale or revenue sharing.

Cost-per-thousand (CPM)—Amount it will cost to reach potential customers with a particular advertising type and time slot.

Cost/benefit analysis—Process of adding up all the expected benefits of an opportunity and subtracting all the expected costs.

Cost structure—A business design that ensures the business will be profitable with each sale after expenses.

Coverage—Protection provided by the policy.

Creative thinking—Thought process that involves looking at a situation or object in new ways; also called lateral thinking.

Creativity—A characteristic of the Entrepreneurial Mindset that includes the process of developing original ideas.

Credibility—Quality of being believable and trustworthy, and keeping one's promises.

Credit—Granting of extended time to pay off a debt.

Credit bureau—Business that collects and maintains credit history records and sells the information under certain circumstances.

Credit history—Record of credit transactions that includes information about whether or not they were repaid in accordance with the credit terms set by the creditor.

Credit terms—Particular conditions set by creditors when they grant credit.

Credit union—Nonprofit cooperative organization that offers low-interest loans to members.

Creditor—Person or business that grants credit.

Critical thinking—Logical thought process that involves analyzing and evaluating a situation or object; also called vertical thinking.

Crowdfunding—Funding a business by raising monetary contributions from a large number of people online.

Current assets—Short-term assets that can be converted into cash within one year.

Current liabilities—Short-term debts that must be repaid within one year.

Current ratio—Current assets divided by current liabilities.

Customer financing—Type of financing in which the customer provides either debt or equity financing for your business.

Customer profile—Detailed description of your target market's characteristics.

Customer service operation—Part of a business that provides a way for the customer to get help, whether it's for placing an order, getting information, or making a complaint.

Customization—An approach to communicating value to customers through personalizing products and services for the specific needs of customers.

Cyberspace—Virtual world of computers.

Cyclical—Refers to cash flow that varies according to the time of year.

D

Damages—Payment to reimburse an injured party for loss.

Data mining—Using a computer program to search large collections of electronic information and look for patterns or trends.

Debt capital—Money obtained by a business through a loan.

Debt financing—Obtaining money by borrowing it, thereby increasing your company's debt.

Debt ratio—Ratio of a business's total debt divided by its total assets.

Debt-to-equity ratio—Ratio of the total debts (liabilities) of a business divided by its owner's equity.

Dedicated server—Server that gives a website its own space.

Deductible—Amount the insured must first pay before the insurance company is required to chip in.

Deduction—Item or expense subtracted from gross income in a tax return, with the effect of reducing one's taxes.

Delegating leadership style—Practiced when a leader gives employees complete freedom to decide what tasks need to be done and how to do them.

Demand curve—Curve on a graph that shows the quantity of a product or service consumers are willing to buy across a range of prices over a specific period of time.

Demand forecasting—Predicting future sales based on past sales data or other available information and expected market conditions in the future. Also referred to as sales forecasting.

Demand—Quantity of goods and services consumers are willing to buy at a specific price and a specific time.

Demand-based pricing—Pricing method that focuses on customer demand. How much customers are willing to pay for a product.

Democratic leadership style—Practiced when a leader seeks input from employees about what tasks need to be done and how to do them, but ultimately makes the final decisions.

Demographics—Objective social and economic facts about people.

Depreciation—Accounting method of spreading the total cost of the equipment a business buys over the amount of years it will be used.

Depreciation expense—Amount of depreciation calculated per year.

Derivative—Artistic work based on one or more existing works, such as a movie sequel or a translation in another language.

Differentiator—Unique characteristic that distinguishes your business from other businesses.

Direct channel—Distribution pathway in which a product goes from the producer straight to the consumer.

Direct competitor—Business in your market that sells a product or service similar to yours.

Direct mail—Form of print advertising that uses one-to-one communication.

Direct sales force—Salespeople who work directly for you as full-time employees; also called internal salespeople.

Directing—Ongoing process of leading, influencing, and motivating employees so they will work together to achieve specific goals.

Disposal value—Amount for which equipment can be sold at the end of its business life. Also called salvage value.

Distribution chain—Series of steps through which products flow into or out of a business. Also referred to as a distribution channel.

Distribution channel—Way in which a product can reach the consumer; series of steps through which products flow into or out of a business. Also referred to as a distribution chain.

Distribution management—Management of materials and processes associated with incoming and outgoing products.

Diversification—Spreading money over different types of investments as a protection against volatility.

Diversification growth strategy—Growth strategy in which a business grows by offering goods and services that are different from its core business.

Diversified market segment—An approach to targeting customers where a business will serve two segments with different needs and wants with the same product or service.

Dividend—Payment corporations make to their shareholders, being a portion of the corporation's profit.

Domain name—Primary part of a website's address (as in www.name.com), which may be the name of the website itself.

Domain name registration—Way to reserve a Web address.

Domain registrar—Site that manages domain names.

Domain suffix—Part of a website's address (such as .com) that refers to the largest groupings of domains. Also called the website's top-level domain (TLD).

Dot-com company—A business run entirely on the Internet. Typically, these companies use an electronic address that ends in ".com."

Double-entry accounting—Accounting system where every business transaction affects at least two accounts.

Drop-down menu—Menu at the top of a Web page that allows users to navigate through the site.

Duality—Key accounting concept. In a single-column method, duality means that for any transaction, all changes on the asset side minus all changes on the liability/owner's equity side must equal zero. In the double-column method, duality means that for any transaction posted to the general journal (and any special journals), all debits must equal all credits.

E

E-commerce—Process of buying and selling goods online.

E-procurement—Purchasing conducted through electronic means, such as Internet websites.

Economic—Social science concerned with how people satisfy their demands for goods and services, when the supply of those goods and services are limited.

Economic system—Method used by a society to allocate goods and services among its people, and to cope with scarcity. Also referred to as an economy.

Economics of one unit—Calculation of the profit (or loss) for each unit of sale made by a business.

Economy—Method used by a society to allocate goods and services among its people and to cope with scarcity. Also referred to as an economic system.

Economy of scale—Cost reduction made possible by spreading costs over a larger volume.

Elevator pitch—A business pitch succinct enough to be completed in an elevator ride; the entrepreneur must communicate in fewer than thirty seconds what the product does and how the consumer will benefit. See also business pitch.

Embedding—Process of incorporating audio and video content into a website by using HTML.

Embezzlement—Crime of stealing money from an employer.

Emergency fund—Amount of money a business should have available in the first three to six months for the emergencies that often arise when a company is just beginning; cash saved to cover personal expenses for at least three months.

Emoticon—Symbol or combined punctuation marks used to convey an emotion.

Employee—Person who works in a business owned by someone else.

Employee stock ownership plan (ESOP)—Fund established when a business owner sells his or her ownership shares to a retirement fund for the employees.

Enterprise—Another name for business.

Enterprise zone—Geographic area in which businesses receive economic incentives to encourage development there.

Entrepreneur (on-tra-prih-NER)—Someone who creates and runs their own business.

Entrepreneurial (on-tra-prih-NER-ee-uhl)—To think or act like an entrepreneur.

Entrepreneurial mindset—A blend of characteristics, attitudes, and skills that describe how successful entrepreneurs think and act; it can be useful for everyone to develop an entrepreneurial mindset for their own lives and careers.

Entrepreneurship (on-tra-prih-NER-ship)—Process of being an entrepreneur.

Equilibrium point—Point at which the supply curve and the demand curve intersect. It is the point at which supply and demand are balanced.

Equilibrium price—Price at which supply equals demand.

Equilibrium quantity—Quantity at which the supply equals the demand.

Equity capital—Money obtained by a business from an investor in exchange for a share of ownership (equity) in the business.

Equity financing—Method of financing a startup business by selling shares of ownership in the business.

Ergonomics—Study of designing environments to fit the people who use them.

Ethical sourcing—Buying from suppliers who provide safe working conditions and respect workers' rights.

Ethics—Set of moral principles that govern decisions and actions.

Excise tax—Tax on a specific product or commercial activity.

Exclusive distribution—Type of distribution that gives a specific retailer, or authorized dealer, the sole right to sell a product in a particular geographical area.

Executive summary—One- or two-page summary of the business plan's highlights and the key selling points of the investment opportunity.

Expense—Things you have to buy to keep the business running.

Exporting—Business activity in which goods and services are sent from a country and sold to foreign consumers.

Express contract—Contract in which the terms are explicitly stated, either verbally or in writing.

External sales—Sales obtained by hiring another company, or an outside individual, to do the selling for you.

F

Facilitated giving—Type of cause-related marketing in which a business makes it easier for customers to contribute to a cause.

Fair Labor Standards Act—Federal law that guarantees most hourly workers a minimum hourly wage, a maximum number of hours worked, and extra pay for working overtime.

Fair trade—Policy encouraged by private organizations with the goal of ensuring that small producers in developing nations earn sufficient profit on their exported goods to improve their working, environmental, and social conditions.

Fair use—Doctrine that provides for the limited quotation of a copyrighted work without permission from or payment to the copyright holder.

Fax (facsimile) (fak-SIM-uh-lee)—Exact copy of something.

Feasibility—How possible or worthwhile it is to pursue an idea, to see if it is actually a realistic opportunity.

Features—What a product does and how it appears to the senses (sight, sound, taste, smell, and touch).

Federal Deposit Insurance Corporation (FDIC)—Independent agency of the federal government that insures savings, checking, and other types of deposit accounts.

Federal Trade Commission (FTC)—U.S. government agency that administers consumer protection laws and regulates certain business practices.

FICA—Acronym for Federal Insurance Contributions Act, the law that requires employers and employees to share the cost of the federal government's insurance and retirement program through deductions from wages and income.

File sharing—Ability of computers to share files so everyone involved can look at the same documents without having to store copies on their individual computers.

Financial—Resource money that the business uses in daily operations (for example, money to pay for deliveries), or money the business has in savings.

Financial ratio—Relationship between important financial data that is expressed as a fraction or percentage.

Financing—Raising money for a business.

Financing activities—In relation to the statement of cash flows, these primarily consist of debt and equity financing.

Firewall—Software program or hardware device designed to prevent unauthorized electronic access to a networked computer system.

Fiscal year—Any month period you choose to treat as a year for accounting purposes.

Fixed expense—Expense that isn't affected by the number of items a business produces.

Flash animation—Software program used to create animated graphics.

Flextime—Flexible work schedules.

Floating ad—Ad that floats or flies over the Web page for a few seconds.

Focus group—Small number of people who are brought together to discuss a particular problem, product, or service.

Fonts—Styles of typefaces.

Foreign exchange rate—Value of one currency unit in relation to another.

Franchise—Business arrangement in which an established company sells the right for others to use the company's name and operating plan to sell products or services.

Franchise agreement—Legally binding contract between a franchisor and franchisee that lists the rights and responsibilities of each party.

Franchise disclosure document—Legal document that provides detailed information to potential franchisees about the franchisor.

Franchise fee—Upfront charge that is usually sizeable (from many thousands of dollars to more than a million) and allows the franchisee to join the franchisor's system.

Franchise operations manual—Manual produced by a franchisor that gives detailed instructions to a franchisee about how to operate, staff, and manage a franchise unit.

Franchise royalty—Regular, ongoing payment paid by the franchisee to the franchisor. It is typically a percentage of the sales the franchisee earns.

Franchisee—Franchise buyer.

Franchisor—Franchise seller.

Free enterprise system—Another name for the market economy, also known as capitalism, where people are free to become entrepreneurs and own and operate an enterprise (business).

Free on board—Delivery term that is followed by a word or group of words that identify a specified location at which the ownership responsibility for the shipment switches from the seller to the buyer.

Free Web host—Opportunities that allow you to set up a website for free.

Freemium—A cost structure model where customers can get a free version with limited features and/or advertisements, or pay for a version with all features and/or no advertisements.

Future value of money—Amount to which a given sum will increase over time through investment.

G

Gantt chart—Bar chart that shows schedule goals for a list of tasks and the duration (length of time) of each task and the progress made at achieving each task.

General journal—Accounting record that shows all the transactions of the business.

General partnership—Partnership in which all partners have unlimited liability.

Geographics—Market segments based on where consumers live or where businesses are located.

Global economy—Flow of goods and services around the whole world.

Goodwill—Business term that encompasses the intangible positive aspects of a business, such as location, employee knowledge and skills, brand awareness, intellectual property, relationships with suppliers and customers, and reputation in the community and the industry.

Green company—Company that adopts business practices aimed at protecting or improving the environment.

Green procurement—Act of purchasing goods and services that are environmentally favorable in some way.

Greenwashing—Trying to appear environmentally responsible by overstating one's commitment.

H

Hackers—People who write and often use programs that enable access to computers and networks by unauthorized users.

Harvesting—Exiting a business and gaining the value of the business in cash as one leaves.

Headers—Lines of text that appear at the beginning of paragraphs or at the head of sections of your website copy.

Home page—Website's main page.

Horizontal diversification—Growth strategy in which a business adds new products or services that are not related to its existing products or services, but appeal to its existing target market.

Horizontal integration strategy—Intensive growth strategy in which one business acquires another business at the same supply chain level as itself.

HTML—Stands for Hypertext Markup Language. It is the language that programmers use to identify how text is used on the Web page. It also controls the appearance of a Web page.

Hubs—Devices that connect computers both to each other and to the Internet.

Human resource—People that help make the business run; can include people hired for a specific skill that not many others have.

Hyperlinks—Another term for links that take you to other pages on the website.

I

Idea generation—Part of the entrepreneurial process that includes coming up with many business ideas.

Idea map—Idea generation tool that allows one to come up with numerous potential business ideas at once by linking ideas together in a visual aid.

Ideation—Process of forming ideas; in entrepreneurship, the first phase of the entrepreneurial process.

Implied contract—Contract made when the parties' actions demonstrate their agreement.

Importing—Business activity in which goods and services are brought into a country from foreign suppliers.

In-kind donation—Donation of a good or service.

Income statement—Financial document that summarizes a business's income and expenses over a given time period and shows whether the business made a profit or took a loss. Also called a profit and loss statement.

Incorporate—Set up a corporation in accordance with the laws of the particular state where the business is located.

Indemnification (in-dim-nih-fuh-KAY-shun)—Protection from legal action, fines, or other damages.

Indirect channel—Distribution pathway in which the product goes from the producer to one or more intermediaries before it reaches the consumer.

Indirect competitor—Business that sells a different product or service from yours but fills the same customer need or want.

Individual Retirement Account (IRA)—Type of investment on which you won't have to pay taxes until you withdraw the money in the account.

Industry—The production of goods or services within an economy; can include anything from farming, to furniture making, to health care services.

Infomercial—Product demonstration, usually produced as a cable television show, that typically lasts from thirty minutes to an hour in length.

Information technology (IT)—Study, design, development, implementation, support, and management of computer-based information systems.

Infrastructure—System of physical structures and services that a society needs to function and be productive.

Infringement—Violating a copyright or patent holder's rights; violating the rights provided by a copyright or patent.

Initial public offering (IPO)—First sale of shares of stock to the general public by a privately held company.

Injunctive relief—Order for the violator of a contract to stop the illegal activity.

Innovation—The act or process of introducing new ideas, devices, or methods.

Instant messaging (IM)—Immediate communication using typed text over the Internet. Also called texting.

Intangible—Nonmaterial.

Intangibles—Things that have value but are not material goods.

Integrative growth strategy—Growth strategy that emphasizes blending businesses together through acquisitions and mergers.

Intellectual property—Artistic and industrial creations of the mind.

Intellectual resource—Unique inventions or processes that the business created that other businesses do not have access to; also see intellectual property.

Intensive distribution—Type of distribution that makes a product available at as many sales outlets as possible.

Intensive growth strategy—Growth strategy that focuses on cultivating new products or new markets, and sometimes both.

Intermediary—Bridge between a producer and a consumer; may include agents, brokers, wholesalers, distributors, and retailers.

Internal audit—Audit performed by an accountant hired by a company to check their books.

Internal resource—Supply of possessions managed by the business in order to function effectively; can include physical, financial, human, or intellectual resources.

Internal sales—Sales obtained by you or your employees who sell your products/services exclusively.

Internet—Global system of interconnected networks.

Internet protocol (IP) address—Unique string of numbers that identify the domain.

Internship—Work program that provides practical, on-the-job training in a business setting. See also apprenticeship.

Interpersonal skills—Skills used by people as they interact with others, particularly in a one-on-one setting.

Interstitial ad—Ad that appears in its own window before a Web page loads.

Intrapreneurship (in-tra-prih-NER-ship)—Practice of giving employees opportunities to be creative and try out new ideas within a company.

Intrastate sales—Sales made within the state where the company is physically located.

Inventory investment—Money paid for inventory.

Inventory level—Quantity of merchandise.

Inventory management—Process of keeping track of the items for sale, storing them, and shipping orders.

Inventory shrinkage—Any loss of inventory that occurs between the time the inventory is purchased and the time it is sold or otherwise removed from the shelves.

Inventory system—Process for counting and tracking inventory so inventory value can be calculated.

Inventory turnover—Number of times during a given time period that inventory is completely sold out (and therefore replaced), or the number of times during a given period that the average inventory investment is recouped (earned back). Also referred to as inventory turns.

Inventory turns—Number of times during a given time period that inventory is completely sold out (and therefore replaced), or the number of times during a given period that the average inventory investment is recouped (earned back). Also referred to as inventory turnover.

Inventory value—Monetary value of merchandise.

Investing activities—In relation to the statement of cash flows, these involve buying assets that will last more than one year.

J

Job description—Explanation of a position's purpose, tasks, and responsibilities and the qualifications needed to perform it.

Job enlargement—Adding responsibilities to a position.

Job enrichment—Increasing the depth or involvement of a job.

Job shadowing—Process of learning a job by watching an employee perform the job over a period of time.

Just-in-time (JIT) inventory system—System in which the goal is to maintain just enough inventory to keep the business operating, with virtually no inventory kept in storage.

K

Keyloggers—Programs used for surveillance by companies to make sure their employees are only using their computers for business. Keyloggers are also used to spy on unsuspecting users by recording the letters and numbers (keystrokes) made on a keyboard.

Keywords—Words or phrases that represent a Web page's content.

L

Labor—The amount of money being paid in return for someone's time, usually in the form of full-time or part-time employees.

Landing page—Page that appears when the visitors click on an advertisement or search engine link.

Lateral thinking—Thought process that involves looking at a situation or object in new ways; also called creative thinking.

Law of large numbers—Theory that says if you want to predict how likely an event is to occur, you will get the most accurate answer by looking at the largest number of cases where it might.

Layout—Physical arrangement of objects and spaces.

Lead generation—Process of obtaining leads.

Lead lists—Contact information for potential customers that is sold by lead-generation services to website owners.

Lead time—Time period between starting an activity and realizing its result—for example, the time between order placement and receipt of shipment.

Lean startup methodologies—Starting a business as soon as possible with very limited resources and using ongoing research to fine tune the business.

Lease—Written contract in which a property owner gives temporary use of that property to another party.

Liability—Legal obligation of a business owner to use personal money and possessions to pay the debts of the business; any outstanding bill or loan that must be repaid.

Liability insurance—Provides protection when a business's actions or lack of action injures another party.

License—Providing rights to use intellectual property; legal document issued by the government that allows a business to provide a regulated product or service.

Limited liability—Business owner cannot be legally forced to use personal money and possessions to pay business debt.

Limited liability company—Legally defined type of business ownership similar to a C corporation but with simpler operating requirements and tax procedures, and greater liability protection for the business owners (who are called members).

Limited partnership—Partnership in which at least one partner has limited liability for the debts of the business.

Line organization—Direct chain of command through levels of personnel who are directly involved in a business's main occupation.

Line-and-staff organization—Expanded version of a line organization.

Link—Method used to connect to a related Web page or another website. Also called a hyperlink.

Link trades—Site owners agreeing to link to each other's sites.

Liquidation—Process in which the tangible assets of a business are sold.

Liquidity—Ability to convert assets into cash; ease of converting a non-cash asset (such as a business) into cash.

List-rental company—Company that provides names and contact information for specific groups of consumers or businesses.

Local area network (LAN)—Network used in a limited area such as an office, school, or other building.

Local economy—Economy that covers a limited area, such as a community or town.

Logistics (lo-GIS-tix)—Handling and organizing of materials, equipment, goods, and workers.

Long-term assets—Assets that usually take longer than one year to turn into cash.

Long-term liabilities—Debts that usually take longer than one year to repay.

M

Main domain—Home page of a website.

Maintenance—Upkeep and routine care of equipment to keep it in good working order.

Malware—Various types of malicious software, including computer viruses, Trojan horses, and spyware.

Management—Skillful use and coordination of all the business's resources (money, facilities, equipment, technologies, materials, employees) in a systematic and effective way to achieve particular goals.

Management buyout—Exit strategy in which a business owner sells his or her ownership shares to the business's managers.

Manufacturer—Business that converts materials into goods suitable for use and sells those goods to others. Also referred to as a manufacturing business.

Manufacturing business—Business that converts materials into goods suitable for use, and sells those goods to others. Also referred to as a manufacturer.

Markdown price—Price created when a retailer wants to reduce the price of an overstocked product.

Market—Group of potential customers (people or businesses) who are willing and able to purchase a particular product or service.

Market development—Intensive growth strategy that focuses on reaching new target markets, such as customers in another geographic area or customers who have different demographics from current customers.

Market economy—System in which suppliers and consumers control the production, allocation, and prices of goods and services.

Market penetration—Intensive growth strategy that emphasizes more intensive marketing of existing products.

Market research—Organized way to gather and analyze information needed to make business decisions.

Market segment—Small group of consumers or businesses within a particular market that has one or more things in common.

Market share—Percentage of a given market population that is buying a product or service from a particular business; percentage of the total sales captured by a product or a business in a particular market.

Marketable securities—Investments, such as stocks or bonds, that can be converted to cash quickly.

Marketing—Way of presenting your business to your customers that clearly communicates the value of your product or service.

Marketing mix—"Recipe" for reaching and keeping customers that combines five marketing elements called the Five P's: people, product, place, price, and promotion.

Marketing plan—Detailed guide with two primary parts: marketing goals and strategies for reaching those goals.

Markup—Price increase imposed by each link in a distribution chain or channel.

Markup price—Price created when a retailer adds an additional amount to the cost of a wholesale product to make a profit.

Mass market—Market that includes as many customers as possible.

Media—Communication channels.

Memo—Brief note that informs employees about a business-related matter (short for memorandum).

Mentor—Person who provides free guidance, tutoring, and suggestions for achieving your goals.

Message thread—Series in an e-mail that shows every previous message.

Metatags—HTML tags that provide information about a Web page.

Microloan—A small loan; ideal for a small startup company that doesn't need much capital and has a limited credit history.

Micromanager—Individual who interferes too much in the decisions and tasks of associates or employees.

Milestone—Significant point of progress in a process or timeline.

Milliseconds—Thousandths of a second, which is the unit of measurement used to determine the time it takes to access information on a hard drive.

Mind share—Awareness or popularity a certain product has with consumers.

Minimum viable product—A prototype or first attempt at an idea built quickly and cheaply that the entrepreneur tries to sell to get feedback from potential customers.

Mission statement—Describes why a company exists and guides a company's organization, work, and actions.

Mixed economy—Economic system that blends elements of the command economy and the market economy.

Monopoly—Single supplier who is a market's only provider of a certain product.

Multi-sided market segment—An approach to targeting a market that focuses on multiple interdependent segments; websites or blogs are good examples for multi-sided market segments because websites charge advertisers for space on their websites, which are "free" to the public.

Multi-user license—Legal document allowing multiple users to use software in a networked hardware environment.

Multiple of earnings method—Method of valuing a business in which the amount of business earnings over a specific time period (usually one year) is multiplied by a number (typically 3 to 5) to determine a reasonable sales price for the overall business.

N

Nanoseconds—Billionths of a second, which is the unit of measurement used to determine the time it takes to access information in primary storage.

Need—Something that people must have to survive, such as water, food, clothing, or shelter.

Negotiation—Process in which two or more parties reach an agreement or solve a problem through communication.

Net worth—Accounting term that refers to total assets minus total liabilities according to a company's balance sheet. Also referred to as book value or owner's equity.

Network server—Computer that stores files used by the networked computers. It may also store programs.

Networking—Process of meeting new people though current friends and business contacts.

Newsgroup—Online message board where people post information about a particular topic.

Niche market segment—Narrow group of potential customers who share specific characteristics.

Nondisclosure agreement—Legal document in which a person or group agrees to keep certain information confidential; agreement that binds parties to secrecy and usually concerns employees, investors, and others with whom a business owner needs to share a trade secret or other sensitive information. Also called confidentiality agreement.

Nonperiodic reordering—Ordering items at irregular intervals.

Nonprofit corporation—Legally defined type of business ownership in which the company operates not to provide profit for its shareholders but to serve the good of society.

Nonprofit organization—Organization that operates solely to serve the good of society.

North American Industry Classification System (NAICS)—Classification system that assigns a numerical code to every industry in North America based on its primary business function.

O

Objections—Reasons why a customer may be reluctant or cautious about buying.

Objective—Thinking and acting fairly, without emotion or prejudice. Not being objective would be looking at information subjectively.

Obsolescence (ahb-suh-LESS-ence)—Process of becoming obsolete, which means no longer useful or desired.

Occupational Safety and Health Administration (OSHA)—The federal agency responsible for setting and enforcing standards of safety in the workplace.

Offshoring—Outsourcing and giving the project to a company or individual in another country.

One-user license—Legal document giving one user the right to use the program, which is sold with the stand-alone version of the software.

Operating activities—In relation to the statement of cash flows, these are the day-to-day activities. Most cash changes fall into this category.

Operating expense—Expenses involved with running the business; also called overhead.

Operating ratio—Percentage of each dollar of revenue, or sales, needed to cover expenses.

Operational plan—Details the everyday activities that will achieve the goal of the tactical plan (and ultimately, the strategic plan).

Operations—Everyday activities that keep a business running.

Operations management—Management of the everyday activities that keep a business running.

Opportunity cost—Value of what you will give up to get something.

Opt-out—Option to deny permission for a business to make contact via the Web.

Order getting—Sales role in which the primary responsibilities are finding prospects, presenting the product/service, and helping to "close" sales.

Order taking—Sales role in which the primary responsibility is recording and processing orders from customers who seek out your product/service.

Organic growth—Growth achieved by expanding a business internally, such as adding new products or services for sale.

Organizational structure—System for dividing work, authority, and responsibility within a company.

Organizing—Ongoing process of arranging and coordinating resources and tasks to achieve specific goals.

Orientation—Process of gradually integrating an employee into a workplace.

Outsourcing—Hiring another company or individual to handle part of a business's everyday operations or to do special projects.

Overhead—expenses involved with running the business; also called operating expenses.

Owner's equity—Value of the business on a specific date if all the assets were sold and all the liabilities were paid; accounting term that means total assets minus total liabilities according to a company's balance sheet. Also referred to as net worth or book value.

P

Pacioli check column—Column in an accounting worksheet that ensures that the accounting equation always balances after each transaction.

Packing slip—List of all items in a shipment.

Parked domain—Web address that has been bought but remains unused.

Partial inventory system—Combines elements of the perpetual inventory system and the periodic inventory system.

Partnership—Legally defined type of business organization in which at least two individuals share the management, profit, and liability.

Partnership agreement—Legal document that clearly defines how the work, responsibilities, rewards, and liabilities of a partnership will be shared by the partners.

Pass-through business—Business in which the business owner is taxed in the same way as income earned as an employee since the business's income is the owner's personal income as well.

Patent—Exclusive right to make, use, or sell a device or process.

Pathway—Helps job seekers and individuals interested in specific careers to identify professions that best suit their interests and abilities within career clusters.

Pay-per-click—In affiliate marketing, commission the affiliate receives when visitors on the affiliate's site click on the link to get to the merchant's site.

Pay-per-lead—In affiliate marketing, commission the affiliate receives when the visitor registers or fills out a form on the merchant's site.

Pay-per-sale—In affiliate marketing, commission that the merchant pays the affiliate when a customer actually buys an item. Also known as cost-per-sale or revenue sharing.

Payback—Amount of time, measured in months, that it takes a business to earn enough in profit to cover the start-up investment.

Payee—Person to whom a check is written.

Periodic inventory system—System that calculates inventory value for accounting purposes at periodic times (for example, at the end of the month or end of the year) when a physical inventory count is performed.

Periodic reordering—Ordering items at regular time intervals.

Permanent cookie—Cookie that is stored on the hard drive. Also called persistent cookie.

Permit—Legal document that allows a business to take a specific action.

Perpetual inventory system—System that tracks inventory on a continual basis and calculates the inventory value, for accounting purposes, after each inflow or outflow occurs.

Perpetual life cycle—Product life cycle in which a product never undergoes a final decline, because it remains in the maturity stage forever.

Persistent cookie—Cookie that is stored on the hard drive. Also called permanent cookie.

Personal selling—Direct (person-to-person) effort made by a company's sales representatives to get sales and build customer relationships.

Philanthropy—Donating money and other resources for a socially beneficial cause.

Phishing—Spam scam in which you receive an e-mail that appears to be from a legitimate business, such as your bank, requesting that you click on a hyperlink to verify certain information, such as your social security number or bank account number.

Physical resource—Any tangible asset that the business owns; can include a store location, warehouse, or equipment used to make products.

Pilfering (PILL-fur-ring)—Stealing, particularly of small amounts over time.

Pitch letter—Cover letter that's often sent with a press release to introduce it.

Pivot—An ongoing process of returning to a business idea and changing and revising your initial idea until you get a better opportunity.

Planning—Ongoing process of setting goals, deciding when and how to accomplish them, and determining how best to accomplish them.

Policy—Written contract between the insurer and the policyholder; procedure or set of guidelines that specifies exactly how something should be done or handled.

Pop-up ad—Ad that appears, or "pops up," in its own window on top of a Web page.

Posted—Act of writing a transaction in the accounting worksheet.

Premium—"Give-away" item or free gift that usually has the company's name, address, and telephone number printed on it; amount of money the policyholder pays for coverage.

Press release—Written statement, typically consisting of several paragraphs of factual information, that's sent to the news media about a product or business.

Price discrimination—Charging competing buyers different prices for the same product.

Price fixing—Competitors agreeing to set the price of goods or services, or the terms of business deals.

Primary data—New information that is collected for a particular purpose. It is obtained directly from potential customers.

Primary storage—One of two types of storage used by the computer. It is contained in the computer and is directly accessed by the central processing unit (CPU). The data stored in primary storage is wiped clean when you turn off your computer. Also known as random access memory (RAM).

Privacy policy—Policy that a website has saying it won't give, sell, or rent your e-mail address to other companies or people.

Procurement—Act of purchasing.

Product—A physical, tangible item that a business sells to a customer.

Product development—Intensive growth strategy in which businesses develop new products or enhance their existing products.

Product life cycle—Series of stages (introduction, growth, maturity, and decline) that a product may pass through while it is on the market.

Product mix—Combination of products that a business sells.

Product placement—When a company pays a fee to have a product displayed during a movie or television show.

Product positioning—Process of creating a strong image for your product; a way of influencing customers to distinguish your brand's characteristics from those of the competition.

Product specification—Written detailed description of the characteristics (size, shape, capabilities, etc.) of a product.

Production management—Management of the processes that produce goods and services.

Productivity—Measure of business output compared to business input. For example, the number of items produced per employee or the number of customers served per day.

Profile—A user's own Web page placed on a social or business networking site.

Profit and loss statement—Another name for an income statement.

Profit motive—Incentive that encourages entrepreneurs to take business risks in the hope of making a profit.

Program Evaluation and Review Technique (PERT) chart—Scheduling diagram that shows tasks as a sequence of steps and illustrates how steps are dependent on each other.

Project organization—Employees from more than one department working together as a team on a specific goal.

Promotion—Process used to make potential customers aware of your product/service and to influence them to buy it.

Promotional campaign—Group of specific promotional activities built around a particular theme or goal.

Promotional mix—Combination of promotional elements that a business chooses (advertising, visual merchandising, public relations, publicity, personal selling, and sales promotions).

Property insurance—Protects a business's possessions in the event of fire, theft, and damage from the weather.

Prospect—Person or company with many of the characteristics of the target market, including some key characteristics.

Protégé—Person who receives guidance in a mentoring relationship.

Prototype—Model on which future reproductions of an invention are based.

Psychographics—Psychological characteristics of consumers, such as attitudes, opinions, beliefs, interests, personality, lifestyle, political affiliation, and personal preferences.

Public domain—Status of creative works for which the copyright or patent has expired.

Public relations (PR)—Activities aimed at creating good will toward a product or company.

Publicity—Form of promotion for which a company does not pay; sometimes referred to as "free advertising."

Purchase order—Detailed, written record of a business's request for supplies or inventory, often referred to as a PO; document issued by a buyer to a vendor that lists the items to be purchased, their quantities and prices, and other relevant information, such as delivery of payment terms.

Purchase-triggered donation—Practice in which a business contributes a certain amount of money or a certain percentage of an item's purchase price.

Purchasing—Buying materials, products, and services for business purposes.

Pure risk—Chance of loss with no chance of gain.

Q

Quality circle—Group of employees who provide input and suggestions about ways to improve the quality of the goods or services that they produce.

Quality control program—Program used by a business to ensure that its products or services meet specific quality standards.

Quantity discount—Discount given to buyers for purchasing a large quantity of a product or service from a vendor.

Query—Question or phrase that you type into a search engine when looking for information.

Quick ratio—Comparison of cash to debt, based on the concept that a business should have at least enough money on hand to pay its current debts.

Quota—Limit on the quantity of a product that can be imported into a country.

R

Random access memory (RAM)—Another name for primary storage.

Rapport (ra-POR)—Emotional connection between people based on feelings of mutual trust and respect.

Recall—Notice for customers to return a product that poses a risk of injury or illness.

Receipt—Detailed written proof of a purchase.

Recruit—To find and hire qualified candidates for a job.

Referral—One person providing contact information for another who may be interested in your product/service.

Repeat customers—Customers who come back again and again.

Replacement cost—Cost of replacing property at current prices.

Request for proposal (RFP)—Formal way of asking a company to make a bid for a sale; includes details about what the prospect wants.

Research cycle—A six-step process that entrepreneurs use to answer a question about their business by gathering and analyzing data.

Research objective—A question about a prospective business opportunity that provides guidance to market research done for the business.

Reseller's permit—Special permit, required by most states, that retailers must have to purchase goods tax-free from wholesalers and collect sales tax from end buyers.

Reserve for fixed expenses—Money that a business should have set aside to cover their fixed expenses for at least three months.

Reserve price—Minimum price the seller will take for an item.

Resume—Written summary of work experience, education, and skills.

Retailer—Business that buys goods, often from wholesalers, and resells the goods in small quantities directly to consumers. Also referred to as a retailing business.

Retailing business—Business that buys goods, often from wholesalers, and resells the goods in small quantities directly to consumers. Also referred to as a retailer.

Return on investment (ROI)—Profit on an investment expressed as a percentage of the total invested.

Return on sales (ROS)—Financial ratio calculated dividing net profit by sales.

Revenue—Amount of money a business receives during a specific time period before expenses.

Revenue sharing—In affiliate marketing, commission that the merchant pays the affiliate when a customer actually buys an item. Also known as cost-per-sale or pay-per-sale.

Revenue stream—Individual methods by which money comes into a company.

Reward—What entrepreneurs get in exchange for starting a business; can include money, personal satisfaction, or independence.

Rework—Manufacturing term meaning the work performed to correct defects in a product.

Rider—Amendment to policy that changes the benefits or conditions of coverage.

Risk—The chance of losing something. An entrepreneur risks losing of money, time, and energy in the hope of getting greater rewards, or benefits.

Risk transfer—Shifting risk to another party.

Royalty fee—Regular, ongoing payment to a franchisor based on a percentage of the sales a franchisee earns.

Rule of 72—Quick way to figure how long it will take to double your money at a given rate of return.

S

Safety stock—Minimum amount of inventory kept to protect against a stock-out due to unusually high demand or unusually long lead times on delivery.

Salary—Fixed amount of money that an employee is paid on a regular basis, such as weekly, biweekly, bimonthly, or monthly; weekly, bi-monthly, or monthly payment to employees for jobs where the hours and schedule vary.

Sales account—Established customer.

Sales call—Contacting a sales lead, prospect, or established customer by telephone or in person.

Sales contract—Agreement that includes the items sold, the selling price and how it will be paid, and the date and location of the transaction. Also describes each party's right and obligations.

Sales force—Employees in a company who are directly involved in the process of selling; another term for salespeople or sales representatives.

Sales forecast—Prediction of the amount of future sales your company expects to achieve over a certain period of time.

Sales forecasting—Predicting future sales based on past sales data or other available information and expected market conditions in the future. Also referred to as demand forecasting.

Sales invoice—Itemized list of goods delivered or services rendered and the amount due.

Sales lead—Person or company with some characteristics of your target market.

Sales promotion—Short-term activity or buying incentive, such as providing coupons or free samples or conducting product demonstrations.

Sales quota—Target amount of sales per month or quarter that a salesperson is expected to achieve.

Sales support—Positions that mostly involve assisting others with selling activities.

Sales tax—The most common consumption tax required by some local and state governments on goods that are used, or consumed.

Sales territory—Specified geographical area for which a salesperson is responsible, such as a city, county, state, or region.

Salutation—"Greeting" that begins a letter.

Salvage value—Amount for which equipment can be sold at the end of its business life. Also called disposal value.

Same-size analysis—Comparison of total revenue or other financial data against that same data converted into percentages of sales.

Savings account—Bank account in which money is deposited and on which the bank pays interest to the depositor.

Scarcity—State when there are not enough goods or services to meet the demand.

Screen recorder—Type of spyware that takes a picture of your computer screen.

Search engine optimization (SEO)—Variety of techniques that improve a site's ranking.

Search engine ranking—Order of specific words or groups of words in a particular search engine. An e-business owner's goal is to be on the first page of search results.

Secondary data—Existing information that was previously gathered for a purpose other than the study at hand.

Secondary storage—One of two types of storage used by the computer. It is a more permanent type of storage, not directly accessed by the central processing unit (CPU), and does not lose data when the computer is turned off. The most common type of secondary storage is a computer's hard drive.

Secure sockets layer (SSL)—Security measure that "locks" the site, making it secure so it cannot be read by outsiders. It is important for online credit card processing.

Seed money—Another term for start-up capital or start-up investment.

Segmented market segment—A larger target market that is divided up into even smaller segments based on customer needs and wants.

Selective distribution—Type of distribution that allows a product to be sold at a moderate number of sales outlets, but not all, in a particular geographical area.

Self-assessment—Evaluating your strengths and weaknesses.

Self-financing—Obtaining the funds for growth from existing operations, for example, by reinvesting cash reserves (profits).

Serial entrepreneur—People who take what they learn when starting a business to start many more.

Server—Computer that contains all the information you see on the website.

Service—Something that a business does for a customer in exchange for money.

Service business—Business that provides and sells services to customers for a fee.

Service contract—Agreement that includes the service provided, the price and how it will be paid, and the date and location of the transaction. Also describes each party's right and obligations.

Service mark—Word, phrase, or symbol a service provider uses to identify its services.

Session cookie—Cookie that is erased when you close the browser.

Severance pay—Amount of money given to employees when they are terminated for reasons other than performance.

Share of stock—Unit of ownership in a corporation.

Shared Web hosting—Process of sharing server space with other websites.

Shareholders—Owners of a corporation. Also referred to as stockholders.

Shopping cart—A type of payment system used by e-commerce sites to process orders. Shoppers place selected items in their "cart" and pay for them when they finish shopping.

Shortage—In economics, when the quantity supplied can't meet the demand.

Sidebar ad—Ad that appears in a vertical format at the side of a Web page.

Sidebar—Area on the left or right side of a Web page where there are links to pages within the site or to other websites.

Signature—In an e-mail program, text that is added to a letter along with your name.

Site registration—Signing up to a site by providing an e-mail address.

Site traffic—Number of visits a website gets over a specified period.

Site traffic analyzer—Tool that shows the number of visitors who came to the site on a hourly, daily, and monthly basis, as well as a visitor's location and type of browser.

Site-ranking portal—Web company that lists top-ranking websites.

Skill—Ability that's learned through training and practice.

Social media—Interactive electronic forms of communication.

Social networking sites—Sites where people can share information.

Sole proprietorship (pruh-PRY-uh-tur-ship)—Legally defined type of business ownership in which a single individual owns the business, collects all profit from it, and has unlimited liability for its debt.

Source document—Original record (source) of a transaction, including receipts, cancelled checks, invoices, bank deposit slips, and other records.

Sourcing—Choosing appropriate vendors to supply desired business goods or services.

Spam—Junk e-mail; unsolicited bulk e-mail; e-mail that's usually advertising a product and sent to hundreds of thousands of recipients.

Spam blocker—Program that stops spam from going into your e-mail inbox. Also called a spam filter.

Spam bots—Programs that crawl the Internet to collect e-mail addresses.

Spam filter—Program that stops spam from going into your e-mail inbox. Also called a spam blocker.

Spam folder—Separate folder in which spam e-mails accumulate.

Spammer—Person who sends out spam.

Speculative risk—Risk that holds the possibility of either gain or loss.

Spiders (search engine robots)—Computer robots that scan individual Web pages.

Sponsorship—Sponsoring a community event or service in exchange for advertising.

Spoofing—Hiding the origin of an e-mail message, the information in the "from" field.

Spyware—Software that lets computer users spy on other users.

Start-up capital—Another term for seed money or start-up investment.

Start-up expenditures—One-time purchases you have to make in order to get your business running.

Start-up investment—One-time sum required to start a business and cover start-up costs. Also called seed money or start-up capital.

Static content—Web content that stays the same over time.

Stationery—Pre-set selection of fonts, font color, background color, and graphics that resemble printed stationery and make your e-mails look more finished and attractive.

Stock-out—Item in inventory is completely gone.

Stockholders—Owners of a corporation. Also referred to as shareholders.

Storefront creation—Designing a website that can list products, prices, payment terms, and shipping costs, as well as process orders.

Straight-line method of depreciation—Method used to calculate the depreciation of equipment based on how long the equipment will last.

Strategic plan—Lays out a broad course of action to achieve a long-term goal, typically three to five years in the future.

Strong direct competitor—Business in your market that whose main product or service is similar to yours.

Subchapter S corporation—Corporation that differs from a C corporation in how it is taxed. Its income or loss is applied to each shareholder and appears on their tax return.

Subdomain—Domain within a website, such as an individual product page.

Subjective—Thinking and acting while affected by existing opinions, feelings and beliefs. Not being subjective would be looking at information objectively.

Subscription—An ongoing fee for access to a service (e.g., a gym membership, computer games with online access).

Subsidy—Financial aid from the government to support an industry or public service.

Supply—Quantity of goods and services a business is willing to sell at a specific price and a specific time.

Supply-and-demand curve—Graph that includes both a supply curve and a demand curve. It shows the relationship between prices and the quantities of a product or service that is supplied and demanded.

Supply curve—Curve on a graph that shows the quantity of a product or service a supplier is willing to sell across a range of prices over a specific period of time.

Surplus—In economics, when the quantity supplied is greater than the demand.

Sustainability—Another term for sustainable economic development.

Sustainable—Meeting the planet's current needs while preserving resources for future generations.

Sustainable economic development—Economic development that does not harm society or the environment. It ensures that human and natural resources are maintained for future generations.

SWOT analysis—Business evaluation method that draws its name from the four areas it evaluates: Strengths, Weaknesses, Opportunities, and Threats.

Syndication—Allowing others to use your creative works at a cost (more frequent in TV and radio).

Synergistic diversification—Growth strategy in which a business adds new products or services that are related to its existing products or services.

T

T-account—Double-sided presentation that shows credits and debits.

Tactical plan—Outlines specific major steps for carrying out the strategic plan.

Target market—Limited number of customers who are most likely to buy a specific product or service.

Tariff—Fee, similar to a tax, that importers must pay on the goods they import.

Tax avoidance—Using legal strategies to reduce one's tax liability.

Tax credit—Dollar-for-dollar reduction in taxes owed.

Tax evasion—Trying to avoid paying taxes through illegal or deceptive means.

Tax-increment financing (TIF)—Strategy of spending taxpayer money to encourage businesses to locate in an area or improve their property there, with the goal of starting a cycle of growth and prosperity.

Taxes—Money required by the government to support its various functions.

Team building—Motivating individuals in a group to work together to achieve a shared goal.

Telecommuting—Working from a location other than the business site, linked by telecommunication technology.

Telemarketing—Promoting or selling products/services one-to-one over the telephone.

Texting—Another name for instant messaging.

Third-party transaction—Occurs when a third party collects the money from the buyer and then pays the seller.

Third-party providers—Professionals or companies to which jobs are outsourced.

Top-level domain (TLD)—For a website, this is identified by the domain suffix (such as .com).

Trade barrier—Governmental restriction on international trade.

Trade business—Term used to refer to a wholesale business or a retail business.

Trade credit—Extended payment time given by one business to another business for purchased goods or services.

Trade discount—Discount given to resellers who are in the same trade, industry, or distribution chain as a vendor.

Trademark—Symbol that indicates that the use of a brand or brand name is legally protected and cannot be used by other businesses. It is a type of intellectual property.

Trade-out—As a promotion strategy, a bartering practice whereby you trade your company's products or services for free air time on a radio station.

Trade secret—Any information that a business or individual keeps confidential to gain advantage over competitors.

Trade show—Convention where related businesses come to promote their products or services.

Traffic log—Record of the raw traffic data that a server collects.

Transaction—Any payment or income received.

Transaction fee—Fee for using the business's services (e.g., ATM fees).

Transparency—Openness and accountability in business decisions and actions.

Trojan horse—Software program that takes control of your computer without your knowledge.

Typeface—Design of a printed character (font).

U

Unicast ad—TV/Web commercial that appears in its own window.

Unit of sale—What a customer actually buys from you. It's the amount of product (or service) that you use to figure your operations and profit.

Universal values—Values shared by all cultures throughout history.

Unlimited liability—Business owner can be legally forced to use personal money and possessions to pay the debts of the business.

Uptime—Amount of time that a website is online.

User Experience Testing (UE Testing)—Research technique often used in the tech space, researchers will ask customers to interact with the product and observe the experience.

V

Value—The relative worth of something, such as money, a product, or an idea; can be tangible like price or size, or intangible, like customer service.

Value analysis—Process for assessing the performance of a good or service relative to its cost.

Value proposition—Short statement that summarizes all the benefits a company gives to its customers.

Variable expense—Expense that changes based on the amount of product or service a business sells.

Vendors—Businesses that sell products to other businesses.

Venture capital—Money invested in a potentially profitable business by a specialized company whose purpose is to invest in startups.

Vertical integration strategy—Intensive growth strategy in which one business acquires another business in its own supply chain, but not at the same supply chain level.

Vertical thinking—Logical thought process that involves analyzing and evaluating a situation or object; also critical thinking.

Videoconference—Meeting in which participants in different locations see and hear each other through monitors, cameras, microphones, and speakers.

Viral marketing—Word-of-mouth promotion on the Internet.

Vision—"Picture" of what you want the future to be.

Vision statement—An ultimate goal of the business that keeps the business open working towards accomplishing the vision; is usually related to the mission statement on a grander scale.

Visual inventory system—Physically counting inventory items.

Visual merchandising—Use of artistic displays to attract customers into a store and visually promote products inside a store.

Volatile—Changing frequently and unpredictably. Stock prices that change in reaction to information are volatile.

Volume buying—Purchasing a large quantity from a vendor, typically to take advantage of a quantity discount. Also referred to as buying in bulk.

Volume discount—Discount for buying greater quantities.

Voluntary exchange—Transaction in which both suppliers and consumers believe they benefit.

W

Wage—Payment to employees per hour worked or piece of work completed.

Want—Product or service that people desire.

Warranty—Statement from a seller, usually in writing, that promises that purchased goods or services meet certain standards and describes the conditions under which particular problems will be taken care of by the seller at no cost to the buyer.

Weak direct competitor—Business in your market that offers a similar product or service as their secondary focus.

Web 2.0—For the first time, allowed interaction between websites and Web surfers on the Internet, opening the door to commerce.

Web analytics software—Various programs that measure and monitor the traffic to a website.

Web analytics tool—Tool used by e-commerce website owners to track daily traffic, length of stay on the site, sales, and conversion rates.

Web banner—Electronic advertisement that you pay other companies or organizations to embed on their websites.

Web browser—Software that enables you to navigate the Web.

Web designer—Professional who designs websites that will stand out from other websites.

Web domain—Primary part of a website's address (e.g., www.domain.com).

Web hits—Number of visitors to a site, tabulated by the Web host.

Web host—Business that stores all the information for a website on its servers.

Web page—Document on a website.

Web search engine—Way of finding information online.

Web surfing—Process of visiting one website after another.

Web template—Pre-made website that includes already-created graphics and an established layout.

Web traffic—Number of visitors a site gets over a specific time period.

Webcasts—Web presentations where there is no interaction.

Webinars—Short for Web-based seminars or lectures.

Webmaster—Person who manages a website.

Website—Collection of Web pages.

Website slogan—Short phrase that describes what the company does.

Whistle-blower—One who reports illegal or unethical conduct to superiors or to the public.

Wholesaler—Business that buys goods in large quantities, typically from manufacturers, and resells them in smaller batches to retailers. Also referred to as a wholesaling business.

Wholesaling business—Business that buys goods in large quantities, typically from manufacturers, and resells them in smaller batches to retailers. Also referred to as a wholesaler.

Wide area network (WAN)—Network that connects large geographic areas such as one city to another or one country to another, through the Internet.

Wikis—Collaborative websites where anyone can edit, delete, or modify content.

Window of opportunity—Period of time in which you have to act before a business opportunity is lost.

Wireless network—Network that operates on a radio frequency, in much the same way that cell phones work.

Word of mouth—Verbal communications or publicity.

Workers' compensation insurance—Covers losses to employees due to job-related injury or illness.

Workplace climate—General feeling in a business shaped by the psychological state and attitudes of the people who work there.

World Wide Web—Important part of the Internet; huge set of documents, pictures, and other elements that are linked together.

Z

Zoning laws—Local laws that specify the types of development and activities (residential, commercial, industrial, or recreational) that can take place on particular pieces of property.

INDEX

Cuban, Mark, 347–348
cultural sensitivity, 240–241, 321, 322
curiosity, 23
currency, 243
current assets
    on balance sheet, 568
    comparative balance sheet, 570
    current ratio, 577
    defined, 567
current conditions, in sales forecast, 525
current liabilities
    on balance sheet, 568
    comparative balance sheet, 570–571
    current ratio, 577
    defined, 567
    quick ratio, 577
current ratio, 577
customer financing, 555–556
customer profiles, 289, 293, 318
customer service, 346, 420–421
customers. *See also* communicating value to customers;
        marketing; promotion; target market
    building awareness, 345
    in business plan, 98
    creating value, 305–307
    credit policy for, 416
    delivering value to, 101, 371–373
    difficult, dealing with, 354–355
    versus distance, in sales forecast, 526
    franchise, as reason for success, 144
    government regulations protecting, 622–626
    helping, as value proposition, 308
    importance of business ethics to, 86
    including in pitches, 339
    in market research, 167
    market segments, 292–293, 295–297
    niche markets, 295
    posing as to gather competitive intelligence, 263
    as primary data source, 174–175, 176–177
    prospects, 335
    repeat, 420
    responsibility to, 65–66
    retaining, 345–346
    sales accounts, 337
    solving problems of, in persuasive messages, 267
    types of, 289–290
    value propositions, 308–309

customization, as creating value, 306
cyclical cash flow, 514

D

Dallas Mavericks, 347–348
Dashiell, Andrea, 223–225
data, supporting persuasive messages with, 267
data breach, at Target, 432
data mining, sales leads from, 335
data sources, market research, 171–175. *See also* market
        research; primary data; secondary data
data storage, 112
database applications, 175–176
database approach, accounting, 640, 641, 643, 652
Date column, accounting worksheet, 653
Davidson, Arthur, 12
daydreaming, as creative thinking technique, 127
DBA (doing business as) names, 454
de Mare, Anne, 603–604
debit, in banking, 492
debit cards, 634
debits, in double-column accounting, 641–643
debt capital, 720
debt collection businesses, 553
debt financing
    banks, 547–548
    credit cards, 550
    credit unions, 549
    defined, 546
    microloans, 549
    overview of sources of, 546
    payback, 550–551
    personal savings, 546–547
    relatives and friends, 549–550
debt ratio, 547–548, 576
debts. *See* liabilities
debt-to-equity ratio, 547, 576–577
decision making, 24, 774–776
decline stage, product life cycle, 710
dedicated servers, 700
deductibles, insurance, 444
deductions, tax, 687–688
Def Jam Records, 212
defense, as funded by taxes, 677
delegating leadership style, 601
delegating responsibility to employees, 759–760
delivery policies, 417

defined, 279
registration, 369
domain registrar, 279
domain suffixes, 279
donations, 77
dot-com companies, 13
double-column approach, accounting, 641–643
double-entry accounting
basic process, 643
chart of accounts, 640–641
defined, 640
double-column approach, 641–643
duality, 643
single-column, database approach, 641
drawings, for patent applications, 401
drop-down menus, 202
drug safety regulations, 622
duality, in accounting, 643
Ducey, Doug, 726
Ducky website, 124
Dunkin' Donuts, 262
Dyson vacuum cleaners, 302

E

E*Trade, 137
Early Development of Global Education (EDGE)
Charitable Foundation, 620–621
e-business/e-commerce, 254, 378, 476–477, 590–591
economic climate, and growth, 709
economic systems
command economy, 213–214
defined, 211
global, 241–244
market economy, 214–215
types of, 213
economics. *See also* competition
defined, 210
equilibrium point, 225–226
fundamental questions of, 211
overview, 210–211
role of entrepreneurs in, 216–218
supply and demand, 222–223
types of economic systems, 213–215
visualizing supply and demand, 227–229
economics of one unit of sale. *See* EOU
economy of scale, 490–491
e-Council, NFTE, 224–225

EDGE (Early Development of Global Education)
Charitable Foundation, 620–621
The EDGE Curriculum, 621
Edison, Thomas, 11–12, 122
education, 25
Education & Training career cluster, 43
EEOC (Equal Employment Opportunity
Commission), 619, 628
EGI (Equity Group Investments), 637–639
Ehow.com, 369
EIN (Employer Identification Number), 407, 454
Ekeagwu, Onyekachi C., 679–680
electronic business, as helping environment, 72
electronic spreadsheets. *See* spreadsheet software
Elementbars.com, 504
elevator pitches, 339, 340
Eli's Cheesecake Company, 484
Eli's Coffee Shop, 62
Elite Basketball Academy, 787–788
e-mail, 216, 608–609
embezzlement, 647, 661
emergency fund, 542–543, 795
empathy, 23
employee compensation
determining, 746–747
as tax deduction, 687
employee handbook, 407
employee stock ownership plan (ESOP), 790
employee turnover, 598
employees. *See also* hiring employees; human resources
advantages of having, 406–407
as assets in security, 438
bonding, 447
defined, 4
disadvantages of hiring, 407–408
dismissing, 763–764
effect of business ethics on, 87
versus entrepreneurs, 5
evaluating, 761–764
government regulations protecting, 617–620
guarding information shared among, 439
job shadowing, 753
knowledgeable, in customer service policies, 421
motivating, 757–761
orientation, 753
practical challenges of growth, 720
promoting, 762–763

quality circles, 734
responsibility to, 64–65
sole proprietorship, 454
thinking like entrepreneurs, 34–36, 37
training and development, 752–755
variable expenses related to labor, 486–487
employer expectations, 10–11
Employer Identification Number (EIN), 407, 454
employment practices liability insurance, 446
encryption, 661
Encyclopedia of Associations, 172
Endangered Species Act, 626
endorsements
paycheck, 685
promotion strategies, 358
endowment funds, 77
energy, alternative, 70
Energy Star® label, 72
energy-efficient workplaces, 72–73
enforceable contracts, 460–461
engagement, generating in pitches, 340
enlargement, job, 759–760
enrichment, job, 759–760
Enron Corporation, 652
enterprise, defined, 215
enterprise zones, 677–678
enthusiasm, 23
Entrepreneur Board of Venture for America, 383
Entrepreneur.com, 98
entrepreneurial discovery, 99–102
entrepreneurial mindset
in career exploration, 56–58
case study, 114–116
ideation phase, 102
NFTE, 27–29
entrepreneurial thinking, 34–36, 37, 57
entrepreneurs/entrepreneurship. *See also* case studies;
social entrepreneurship; *specific entrepreneurs
by name*
backgrounds, diversity of, 18–19
big business versus small business, 6
characteristics for success, 21–23
in China, 210
creative thinking and, 120–125
defined, 4, 11
versus employees, 5
history of, 11–14
international trade and, 242–244

NFTE entrepreneurial mindset, 27–29
overview, 4
present day, 13–14
reasons to study, 34–36
rewards of, 8–9
risks of, 9–10
role in economy, 216–218
serial entrepreneurship, 14
skills needed, 24–27
thinking like entrepreneurs, 34–36, 37, 57
volunteer work, 77–78
environment, business. *See* business environment
Environmental Protection Agency (EPA), 626
environmental responsibility
case study, 68
energy-efficient workplaces, 72–73
entrepreneurial ventures in, 70–71
government regulations, 626
overview, 69
"people, planet, profit" approach, 253
of Styles by Ambar, 251
EOU (economics of one unit of sale)
in business model validation, 101
business planning, 500
for business selling more than one product,
495–497
competition and, 255–257
for manufacturing business, 493–494
overview, 490, 500
for retail business, 495
revenue streams and, 521, 522
for service business, 497–498
for tech-based businesses, 499
for wholesale business, 494–495
EPA (Environmental Protection Agency), 626
e-procurement, 739
Equal Employment Opportunity Commission
(EEOC), 619, 628
equilibrium point, 225–226, 228, 229
equilibrium price, 226
equilibrium quantity, 226
equipment
comparative balance sheet, 570
depreciation of, 506
leasing, 516
as long-term asset, 568
maintenance of, 733
purchasing for growing businesses, 720

indemnification, 778

independent business, buying, 142–143

independent insurance agents, 441

indirect channels, 384

indirect competition
  analyzing, 268
  in business model validation, 100
  business planning, 244
  defined, 235

Individual Retirement Account (IRA), 528, 793

individuals, responsibility to, 64–67

industrial goods, 379

industrialization, 617

industry
  in business model validation, 100
  in business planning, 218
  defined, 216–217
  role of entrepreneurs in, 216–217

industry cycles, 526

industry standards, 525

inflows, cash, 512–513, 515

infomercials, 350

information, safeguarding, 439

Information Technology career cluster, 49

information technology (IT)
  competing online, 590–591
  e-commerce, 476–477
  general discussion, 112–113
  Internet promotion, 809–810
  practical challenges of growth, 720
  Web design, 202–203
  Web domains, 279–280
  Web hosts, 700–701
  website branding, 369–370

informational interviews, 56

informational messages, writing, 608–609

infrastructure, 675

infringement, 93, 94

in-home business policies, 442

in-house training and development programs, 753–754

initial public offering (IPO), 790

initiative
  case study, 264–265, 456–457, 679–680, 729–730
  importance of, 20–21
  NFTE entrepreneurial mindset, 28

InkHead Promotional Products, 357

innovation. *See also* creative thinking
  by Apple, 120

case study, 123–125, 347–348, 396–398, 507–508, 712–713

competition between suppliers and, 249

defined, 121

intellectual property law and, 395–396

market saturation and, 780

NFTE entrepreneurial mindset, 28

by Quirky, 487–488

Instagram, 84

installment buying, 718

instant messaging, 216

insurance
  case study, 436–437, 594
  as fixed expense, 505
  liability, 445–447
  "no-fault," 447
  obtaining coverage, 441–442
  overview, 443, 448
  property, 444–445
  as risk management, 443–444
  special types of, 442
  as tax deduction, 687
  workers' compensation, 447

insurance agents, 44, 441, 443

insurance policies, 441–442, 444

insurance premiums, 440, 444

intangibles, 156, 395

integrative growth strategy, 716

intellectual property
  benefits of laws protecting, 395–396
  copyright, 93, 94, 398–399
  defined, 93
  patents, 93, 145, 400–402
  protecting, 398–403
  risk management, 92–94
  trade secrets, 403
  trademarks and service marks, 402–403

intellectual resources, 395. *See also* internal resources

intensive distribution, 320

intensive growth strategy, 714–715

interest
  in AIDA model, 345
  in banking, 492
  credit card rates, 550
  as fixed expense, 506
  on savings accounts, 528

interests, personal
  combining with skills, 508

PHOTO CREDITS

Chapter 1: p. 2 Vico Collective/Alin Dragulin; p. 5 bikeriderlondon/Shutterstock; p. 9 AVAVA/Shutterstock; p. 10 Syda Productions/Shutterstock; p. 12 PhotoHouse/Shutterstock; p. 13 123rf.com

Chapter 2: p. 16 123rf.com; p. 19 mangostock/Shutterstock; p.23 123rf.com; p. 25 Monkey Business Images/Shutterstock; p. 27 mangostock/Shutterstock

Chapter 3: p. 32 michaeljung/Shutterstock; p. 35 mangostock/ Shutterstock; p. 39 José 16/Fotolia; p.40 ndoeljindoel/Fotolia; p. 41 Dirima; p. 42 FotolEdhar/Fotolia; p. 43 Rido/Fotolia; p. 44 michaeljung/Fotolia; p. 45 auremar/Fotolia; p. 46 wong yu liang/Fotolia; p. 47 TessarTheTegu/Fotolia; p. 48 Monkey Business/Fotolia; p. 49 dmitrimaruta/Fotolia; p. 50 aijohn784/Fotolia; p. 51 ndoeljindoel/Fotolia; p. 52 Ariwasabi/Fotolia; p. 53 Semen Barkovskiy/Fotolia; p. 54 CandyBox Images/Fotolia; p. 57 Goodluz/ Shutterstock

Chapter 4: p. 60 Goodluz/Shutterstock; p. 64 Rawpixel/Shutterstock; p. 66 Marcin Balcerzak/Shutterstock; p. 70 123rf.com; p. 71 123rf.com; p. 71 Provasilich/Shutterstock; p. 73 Greywind/Shutterstock; p. 75 Monkey Business Images/Shutterstock; p. 76 Monkey Business Images/Shutterstock

Chapter 5: p. 82 123rf.com; p. 85 rSnapshotPhotos/Shutterstock; p. 87 123rf.com; p. 88 T.B. Harry S. Trumamn Presidential Library; p. 89 Golden Pixels LLC/Shutterstock; p. 93 Elnur/Shutterstock; p. 95 Ekkapon Sriharun/123rf.com; p. 98 123rf.com

Chapter 6: p. 118 123rf.com; p. 121 racorn/Shutterstock; p. 122 vCREATISTA/ Shutterstock; p. 123 Marc Dietrich/Shutterstock; p. 123 ThomasLENNE/Shutterstock; p. 123 Andrii Gorulko/Shutterstock; p. 123 Alexey Boldin/Shutterstock; p. 125 Blend Images/Shutterstock; p. 126 wavebreakmedia/ Shutterstock; p. 129 lunamarina/Fotolia

Chapter 7: p. 132 Diego Cervo/Shutterstock; p. 140 Maxim Blinkov/Shutterstock; p. 143 michelaubryphoto/Shutterstock; p. 145 Ditty_about_summer/Shutterstock

Chapter 8: p. 150 Goodluz/Shutterstock; p. 156 123rf.com; p. 158 Mila Supinskaya/Shutterstock; p. 158 hurricanehank/Shutterstock

Chapter 9: p. 164 jannoon028/Shutterstock; p. 167 Estelle; p. 169 Stephen Coburn/Shutterstock; p. 172 123rf.com; p. 173 Census Bureau; p. 175 Pixsooz/Shutterstock; p. 177 Eviled/ Shutterstock

Chapter 10: p. 180 123rf.com; p. 183 Robert Kneschke/Shutterstock; p. 187 Monkey Business Images/Shutterstock; p. 187 Jim Barber/Shutterstock; p. 190 123rf.com

Chapter 11: p. 208 Klaus Tiedge/Getty Images; p. 214 bikeriderlondon/Shutterstock; p. 217 mangostock/Shutterstock

Chapter 12: p. 220 Blaj Gabriel/Shutterstock; p. 223 123rf.com

Chapter 13: p. 232 Pressmaster/Shutterstock; p. 235 xy/Fotolia; p. 239 Tijana/Fotolia; p. 241 Getty Images/Digital Vision; p. 242 PaulPaladin/Shutterstock

Chapter 14: p. 246 123rf.com; p. 249 xy/Fotolia; p. 253 Mike Flippo/Shutterstock; p. 253 worker/Shutterstock; p. 253 xy/Fotolia

Chapter 15: p. 260 mangostock/Shutterstock; p. 263 Andresr/ Shutterstock; p. 266 Sergey Karpov

Chapter 16: p. 286 auremar/Shutterstock; p. 289 Tyler Olson/Shutterstock; p. 290 123rf.com; p. 293 Andy Dean Photography/Shutterstock; p. 296 Monkey Business Images/Shutterstock

Chapter 17: p. 300 Olesya Feketa/Shutterstock; p. 303 Ministr-84/Shutterstock; p. 306 123rf.com; p. 308 Jules Selmes/Pearson Education Ltd

Chapter 18: p.315 Vaju Ariel/Shutterstock; p. 319 Kzenon/ Shutterstock; p. 322 JohnKwan/Shutterstock; p. 325 123rf. com

Chapter 19: p. 328 bikeriderlondon/Shutterstock; p. 332 HONGQI ZHANG/123rf.com; p. 336 Goodluz/ Shutterstock; p. 340 bikeriderlondon/Shutterstock

Chapter 20: p. 342 Monkey Business Images/Shutterstock; p. 345 hxdbzxy/Shutterstock; p. 350 My Life Graphic/ Shutterstock; p. 358 123rf.com

Chapter 21: p. 375 Monkey Business Images/Shutterstock; p. 380 wavebreakmedia/Shutterstock; p. 388 Ifong; p. 389 Kuzma

Chapter 22: p. 393 michaeljung/Shutterstock; p. 395 James Steidl; p. 399 Arieliona/Shutterstock; p. 401 ExaMedia Photography; p. 403 Alexey Boldin/ Shutterstock; p. 406 kurhan/Shutterstock; p. 408 AR Images/Shutterstock

Chapter 23: p. 412 HBSS/Image Source; p. 415 Samantha Grandy; p. 416 Kzenon/Shutterstock; p. 417 Peter Hansen; p. 420 arek_malang/Shutterstock; p. 424 Don Bayley; p. 427 billdayone/Shutterstock

Chapter 24: p. 430 Pressmaster/Shutterstock; p. 434 Aleph Studio/Shutterstock;   p. 438 Zimmytws; p. 439 Prykhodov/Shutterstock; p. 440 Anthony Hall; p. 440 iStockphoto.com; p. 442 Pablo77/Shutterstock; p. 445 123rf.com; p. 446 Laura Clay Ballard; p. 447 bikeriderlondon/Shutterstock

Chapter 25: p. 450 Monkey Business Images/Shutterstock; p. 454 Image Source; p. 458 ben bryant/Shutterstock; p. 459 Corbis; p. 462 baranq/Shutterstock

Chapter 26: p. 482 123rf.com; p. 485 AlexRoz/ Shutterstock; p. 489 vipman/Shutterstock; p. 496 aodaodaodaod/Shutterstock; p. 498 Scorpp/Shutterstock

Chapter 27: p. 502 OtnaYdur/Shutterstock; p. 509 Miroslav Tolimir

Chapter 28: p. 518 Klaus Tiedge/Getty Images; p. 521 starush/Fotolia; p. 529 123rf.com

Chapter 29: p. 538 KlausTiedge/Getty Images; p. 541 Scott Griessel/Fotolia; p. 546 Donald R. Swartz; p. 548 Goodluz/ Shutterstock; p. 554 HONGQI ZHANG/123rf.com; p. 556 Marcel Jancovic/Shutterstock

Chapter 30: p. 558 Pressmaster/Shutterstock; p. 564 PhotoBarmaley; p. 556 Sebastian Kaulitski

Chapter 31: p. 596 Stephen Coburn/Shutterstock images LLC; p. 602 wavebreakmedia/Shutterstock

Chapter 32: p. 614 Goodluz/Shutterstock; p 617 Erica Guilane-Nachez/Fotolia; p. 619 Tyler Olson/Shutterstock; p. 623 Monkey Business/Fotolia; p. 625 Michael Shake/ Shutterstock

Chapter 33: p. 630 Alex Staroseltsev/Shutterstock; p. 634 sanjagrujic/Shutterstock

Chapter 34: p. 650 Lisa S./Shutterstock

Chapter 35: p.672 Plush Studios/DH Kong/Blend Images/ Getty Images; p. 675 Blue Moon/Fotolia; p. 675 Zhu Difeng; p. 677 Straight 8 Photography/Shutterstock; p. 678 Arkady Mazor; p. 682 Charles Taylor; p. 684 mikeledray/ Shutterstock; p. 687 Deklofenak/Shutterstock

Chapter 36: p. 706 DreamPictures/Blend Images/Getty Images; p. 709 Andy Dean Photography/Shutterstock; p. 711 123rf.com; p. 714 danr13/Fotolia; p. 717 gpointstudio/Shutterstock; p. 719 123rf.com; p. 720 Caruntu

Chapter 37: p. 724 Elena Elisseeva/Shutterstock; p. 728 Michael Shake/Shutterstock; p. 733 Blaz Kure; p. 739 Photographee.eu/Shutterstock

Chapter 38: p. 742 123rf.com; p. 747 Wendy Farrington; p. 748 FotolEdhar/Fotolia; p. 752 Max Blain; p. 754 SergeBertasiusPhotography/Shutterstock; p. 755 Rawpixel/ Shutterstock; p. 758 Alaettin YILDIRIM/Shutterstock; p. 759 Monkey Business/Fotolia; p. 760 aleksandar kamasi/ Fotolia; p. 763 iofoto/ Shutterstock

Chapter 39: p. 766 Yuri Arcurs/Shutterstock Images LLC.; p. 769 jovannig/Fotolia; p. 771 VadimGuzhva/Fotolia; p. 773 cook_inspire/Fotolia; p. 777 cunico/Fotolia

Chapter 40: p. 782 Monkey Business Images/Shutterstock; p. 785 Sozaijiten; p. 786 Ken Brown; p. 789 Kash76